Jeanne Hayden Brinkley is a former Teacher Educator at the School of Home Economics, the Florida State University, Tallahassee, Florida. Mrs. Brinkley's professional experiences also include those of Occupational Consultant for High School Home Economics, State of Florida; Acting Assistant Director, Home Economics, State of Florida; home economics teacher on junior high school and adult levels in Orlando, Florida; and County Supervisor of Home Economics Education, including Continuing Education for Adults, for Orange County, Florida. Mrs. Brinkley has served as a member or chairwoman of numerous state curriculum and vocational workshops and textbook criteria and accreditation committees.

Valerie M. Chamberlain, Ph.D., is an Associate Professor, College of Home Economics, Texas Tech University, Lubbock, Texas. Her professional experiences include graduate faculty positions at the University of Hawaii, Honolulu, and the Florida State University, Tallahassee; home economics teacher, Milton High School, Milton, Vermont, and Clearwater High School, Clearwater, Florida. She has served as consultant to the Pennsylvania Department of Education, Western Region; the Department of Education, State of Hawaii; and the Division of Continuing Education, the Florida State University. Dr. Chamberlain is coauthor of CREATIVE HOME ECONOMICS INSTRUCTION, a professional book published by McGraw-Hill.

Fourth Edition

Teen Guide to Homemaking

Jeanne Hayden Brinkley,
formerly Teacher Educator, School of Home Economics,
The Florida State University, Tallahassee, Florida

Valerie M. Chamberlain,
Ph.D., Associate Professor, College of Home Economics,
Texas Tech University, Lubbock, Texas

Frances Champion,
formerly Director, Home Economics, Department of
Education, State of Florida, Tallahassee

Webster Division, McGraw-Hill Book Company

New York   St. Louis   San Francisco   Dallas   Atlanta   London   Montreal
Sydney   Toronto

Editors   Patricia M. Channon, John Aliano, Marian Hugus, Sally Pacheco
Designer   Peter Bender
Editing Supervisor   Faye Allen
Production Supervisor   Renee Guilmette

Library of Congress Cataloging in Publication Data
Brinkley, Jeanne Hayden
  Teen guide to homemaking.

  Third ed., 1971 by M. S. Barclay, et al.
  Includes index.
  SUMMARY: A textbook planned to assist teenage boys
and girls in assuming responsibilities in the home.
Provides guidelines for family living, making decisions,
clarifying values, budgeting, personal grooming, and
cooking.
  1. Home economics. [1. Home economics] I. Chamberlain,
Valerie M., joint author. II. Champion, Frances,
(date), joint author. III. Title.
TX167.B34 1977 640 76-5804

ISBN 0-07-007840-8

Preface

In today's world, teenagers tend toward being genuinely interested in other people. They want to look beyond the surface of their fellow human beings to gain an insight into the thoughts and actions of others. Their concern also leads them to be interested in their environment. They understand that only if resources are used intelligently will these same resources continue to be available for future generations.

Today's teenagers are capable of learning that an upheaval has occurred on the surface of the earth or in the world's political structure. But to them, a fact is only a starting point. They want to know what caused the upheaval, the eventual results they can expect, and the likelihood of its recurrence. This generation of teenagers can assimilate facts, as could their predecessors, but they seem unique in their ability to develop patterns of logical reasoning through serious questioning of existing systems. Their constant exposure to worldwide news events through television and radio allows them to relate to the world as it exists while they idealistically search for ways to improve it.

Young people understand that much remains to be done in areas of interpersonal relationships and environment. However, more than any previous group, they have been able to effectively combine idealism with realism. They understand that whether they live in one of the great inner-city areas, in the suburbs, or in relatively rural regions of the country, successful living depends on their building successful interpersonal relationships in a socially and ecologically sound environment.

TEEN GUIDE TO HOMEMAKING provides a wide range of information while recognizing the modern teenagers' unique interests, concerns, and experiences. This new edition has been extensively revised to meet the challenge of a rapidly changing society.

Behavioral objectives at the beginning of each chapter introduce the basic concepts covered within the chapters.

The metric system of weights and measures is used throughout to prepare students for the inevitable change. Dual dimensions are used; customary units are followed by their metric equivalents. This format both encourages familiarity with this new system and eliminates the need and inconvenience of consulting other conversion sources.

In *acknowledgment of the changing and broadening roles* of men and women, text material has been revised and updated and photos selected to appeal to boys and girls alike. The book can be used successfully with all-boy, all-girl, or co-ed groups.

This edition of TEEN GUIDE TO HOMEMAKING concerns itself with the development of the total individual. An effort has been made to approach the broad concepts involved in successful family living from the viewpoint of concerned teenagers who have become involved in the problems of the world around them. In order to cover a many faceted subject, basic areas are presented in units. Unit 1, YOUR RELATIONSHIPS, deals with the area of *human development and the family;* Unit 2, YOUR HOME AND FAMILY, and Unit 3, YOUR RESOURCES, when coupled, cover at appropriate levels the areas of *personal, family, and environmental management and consumer education* and also *housing;* Unit 4, YOUR CLOTHES, introduces the information necessary for making decisions in the area of *textiles and clothing;* Unit 5, YOUR FOODS, deals with the results of decisions made in the area of *foods and nutrition;* and Unit 6, YOUR RECIPES, includes recipes to demonstrate *basic cooking principles.* The recipes include spe-

cial home-prepared mixes which combine the speed of convenience foods with the economy of foods prepared at home. Cost and availability of ingredients have been planned to fit the school food budget. Some ethnic foods have been suggested as a means of adding interest and universal appeal. Emphasis on nutrition has brought about the inclusion of several pages of charts giving the caloric and nutritional values of many different foods.

As independent of each other as the units are, there are some elements that are common to all.

Consumerism is presented from the viewpoint of buying wisely, emphasizing *decision making and value clarification,* considering needs before wants. Special areas where teenagers are likely to spend money are discussed. Clothes, food, general school expenses, and expenses involved with the teenager's social life are given special consideration. Laws protecting the consumer and the consumer's rights and responsibilities are also discussed.

Vocational information is introduced by a wide range of professions at various educational levels. Jobs and careers are described so students can have brief glimpses of many types of work. The insignia ⬛ calls attention to job descriptions so they are easily recognized as they appear throughout the book. These descriptions introduce job and career opportunities to the students and will spark an awareness for further investigation to determine whether they have a real interest in, or aptitude for, a given occupation.

The *side columns* have been designed for *student involvement.* The activities are presented in a manner which will encourage student participation. In general, side columns that carry the insignia ⬛ lead students to want to participate in classroom or home-centered *activities.* Columns which are marked ⬛ can be considered *enrichment* materials which add to the information provided by the text itself. Columns marked ☑ deal largely with *attitudes*. Debates, discussions, and thought-provoking situations to which students can react emotionally are often included.

The side-column activities cover a broad range of interest- and ability-centered learning experiences. This variety provides each student with several activities which may be of particular interest.

Bulletin board ideas have been provided in each chapter. Simple and educational in content, the directions are worded so students can prepare them with little or no help from the teacher.

The *testing program* incorporated in the third edition of TEEN GUIDE TO HOMEMAKING is also included in this edition. An introductory test precedes each chapter. It is designed to increase students' interest in learning and to give them a basic idea of how much they know about the subject. A more comprehensive test follows each chapter. By taking both the pretest and posttest, students can determine their own progress.

TEEN GUIDE TO HOMEMAKING provides for comprehensive learning in home economics whether units are studied sequentially or in random order to suit individual preferences. The use and application of the pre- and posttesting program and the involvement-oriented side-column activities, combined with the text, allow the students to learn at their own rate. Thus they can grasp at their individual levels the concepts through which successful family living can become a matter of decision. It is understood that each person now lives and will continue to live in some type of family group. The decisions made within the home will lead toward happiness or dissension. *For teenagers to learn to understand and accept the results of their own decisions* is the underlying theme of the book.

The authors wish to acknowledge the counsel and help of the following individuals:

Mrs. Louise Baxley, Teacher, Union Park Junior High School, Orlando, Florida

Dr. Harold I. Coe, Dentist, Orlando, Florida

Mr. Robert Cook, Cosmetologist, Winter Park, Florida

Mrs. Carol Fisher and Mrs. Myvette Gaines, Home Economics Teachers, Winter Park Junior High School, Winter Park, Florida

Mrs. Jane Keeley, Director, Appliance and Home Care, *Good Housekeeping Magazine*, New York City; and member of Metric Committee, American Home Economics Association

Mrs. Clara McPherson, Associate Professor, Department of Food and Nutrition, Texas Tech University, Lubbock, Texas

Miss Gail Trapnell, Specialist for Program Planning and Budgeting, Distributive Education, Florida State Department of Education

Dr. Lawrence T. Wagers, Dermatologist, Winter Park, Florida

Dr. Edward K. Walker, Optometrist, Tallahassee, Florida

Miss Barbara Wilkie, Curriculum Instruction Specialist and coauthor of FUN THINGS FOR LEARNING IN HOME ECONOMICS

Jeanne Hayden Brinkley
Valerie M. Chamberlain

Contents

Unit 1

Your Relationships

1 Chapter
Pretest

Number from 1 to 31. Beside each number indicate whether the corresponding statement is true or false. *Do not* write in this book.

1 Available knowledge has doubled in the past five years.
2 Events in other countries can immediately affect people in many parts of the world.
3 Your environment is limited to your family and your home.
4 TV and radio have made it possible for events around the world to be reported immediately in individual homes.
5 A teenager's life is simpler today than it was in earlier times.
6 The world supply of some natural resources is being used up.
7 Communities differ in the opportunities they offer teenagers for their growth and development.
8 Citizenship includes responsibilities as well as privileges.
9 A nation's human resources include its industries and machines.
10 Ideally individuals are concerned about the personal growth and development of others in their families.
11 How well adults assume mature roles depends largely on how they adjusted to their environment as teenagers.
12 Having friends gives a teenager the opportunity to learn to get along with others.
13 When people have the privilege of religious freedom they also have the responsibility to be tolerant of religious beliefs different from their own.
14 Men's and women's roles are more clearly defined than in the past.
15 Worthwhile goals and values usually include concern for family members and friends.
16 Taking part in community activities provides a person with the opportunity to grow socially, emotionally, and mentally.
17 Boys usually mature physically at an earlier age than girls.
18 More boys than girls die at birth and during the first year of life.
19 Women have a shorter life expectancy than men.
20 What you learn at school is limited to what you read and study.
21 Families today are more dependent upon others than in the past.
22 The social pressures on youth today are less than they were on the young people of previous generations.
23 Examples of community resources are libraries, schools, recreation centers, hospitals, and parks.
24 The waste of resources in one nation of the world can have an effect on people in other countries.
25 Citizenship begins when a person reaches eighteen years of age.
26 Ideas influencing our values and goals are picked up from all over the world.
27 As population increases, social pressures, tension, and frustration are lessened.
28 Teenagers assume many and varied roles.
29 All families have the same goals.
30 One of the greatest challenges presented to teenagers of today is to prove they can live together peacefully.
31 Females can develop the strength and stamina comparable to males when given the opportunity.

Give the following information on a separate sheet of paper.

1 Give three examples to show that the geographic area in which people grow up can affect their lives.
2 List three ways in which a student can show good citizenship.
3 Give two examples of services which are available to the consumer today that were unavailable five years ago.
4 List three goods available to consumers today that were not available five years ago.
5 Give three reasons why more women are employed outside the home today than were employed ten years ago.

Chapter 1

Teenagers in Today's World

After reading this chapter, you should be able to:

1 Define *environment*.
2 List factors that could change a person's life very quickly.
3 Give examples of ways the environment influences peoples' lives.
4 Describe challenges teenagers face today.
5 Explain how changing roles of men and women relate to your present and future life.
6 Accept responsibilities as a student, friend, and citizen as evidenced by your behavior.
7 Outline ways life is different for teenagers today than it was for teenagers of previous generations.
8 Point out environmental factors affecting teenagers' roles.
9 Develop and carry out a plan for showing responsible behavior as a family member, student, friend, or community citizen.

At one time our world was limited to our homes, our families, and our neighborhoods. The world beyond was off limits. Events moved at a slow pace. There seemed to be lots of time to do the things we enjoyed. There was time to think, to try and fail, and to try again. There was time to dream.

Now the world is changed. Available information doubles every few years. In order to survive in this fast-moving world of change, we have been forced to step up our pace of living. We have, of necessity, become fast-moving individuals. We are successful to the degree that we are able to adapt to the world around us.

THE WORLD YOU LIVE IN

Today, you may listen to a transistor radio made in Japan. You may walk in shoes made in Spain, Italy,

Give examples to illustrate the statement, *Knowledge doubles every five years.* Answer:

1 What do scientists know today that they did not know five years ago?
2 What technological improvements have been made in the past five years?
3 What advances have been made in the medical field during this period?
4 How has homemaking and family life changed?
5 What goods and services are available to you today that were not available five years ago?

Make up captions for pictures of teenagers found in magazines. What do your captions reveal about the world in which teenagers live? What do the captions reveal about your own environment?

Tell how the daily lives of people of various religions are affected by their beliefs. Mention dress, grooming, dietary habits, or patterns of family living.

Explain the meaning of the expression, *No man is an island.* In what ways are you dependent on others? How are others dependent on you?

or Brazil. You may wear a shirt or blouse made in the Republic of China, Taiwan, or Mexico. You may listen to English, Russian, French, or German records.

TV, movies, and books bring you people, places, and ideas from every corner of the globe and the space beyond. At no earlier time in history has the world been so complex or so exciting as now.

You pick up ideas from all over the world. While building your own set of values and determining your own goals, you must somehow manage to fit into a world as well as into a neighborhood.

A World of Happenings

News travels fast. A political event or economic change taking place in Europe, the Middle East, or Asia today can make a change in your life tomorrow. A war declared in any part of the world may affect the politics and economies of many other countries. A failure of a food crop in another nation may affect the price you pay for food. The indifference of a single government to the sale of dangerous drugs can have tragic consequences for many people in a number of countries. Carelessness in the use of natural resources of the land or sea affects the quality of life for people all over the earth.

A World of Opportunity

There is work to be done in today's world. There are people to house,

to feed, and to clothe. There is a natural environment to protect. The vast resources of our planet can no longer be taken for granted. Many are being used up. Others are being wasted or destroyed. As the population increases, social pressures, tension, and frustration mount. In the struggle for a better environment for all, you will share an ever-increasing number of human problems with an ever-rising number of people. Perhaps the greatest opportunity presented to today's teenagers is the chance to prove that they can live and work peacefully together.

A World of Challenge

Today's teenagers know that important events happen daily. You and other teens are a part of the *real* world. You know problems exist. You want to join others who share your feelings, interests, and enthusiasm in working for world improvements.

As a group, teenagers are conspicuous. They have a life-style of their own. They have their own fads. They have their own language, tastes, and heroes. Events involving people in their teens appear regularly in the daily news reports. As a teenager, you may be annoyed when the news seems to emphasize only the bad things teenagers do. In common with most teens, you have probably developed worthwhile goals and values which include the welfare of others.

Public recreation facilities give us an opportunity to experience, with others, the total environment of nature, people, and technology.   *Girl Scouts of the U.S.A.*

Home and neighborhood surroundings also provide opportunities for outdoor recreation.
Henry Monroe/McGraw-Hill

YOUR TEENAGE ENVIRONMENT

Your environment is all the people, things, and events surrounding you. There is a natural environment of plants, animals, and weather. There is a human environment of people. And there is a technical environment of chemicals, industry, and machines. Each of these — nature, people, and technology — fits into the total environment necessary for modern living.

Write the word ENVIRONMENT on a chalkboard by arranging the letters in a vertical line. Beside each letter, list several things affecting your total environment. For example . . .

E Events, experiences
N Neighborhoods (and neigh-
  bors), natural resources
V Values, vapors, vehicles
I
R
O
N
M
E
N
T

Collect articles from newspapers and magazines about events in distant places which may have an effect on you as an individual. Give examples to show how these events could directly or indirectly change your life.

Research and report on the story of Romulus and Remus who were said to be reared by wolves. Discuss the effects of their environment on their development.

Pretend you are an Eskimo. Describe how you think you would feel if you moved to the southeastern or southwestern United States.

Tell the class about a special or unusual custom in your family. Find out when, why, and how this custom began. Do you plan to continue this in your own family some day? Why or why not?

Using different time periods, discuss the effect of those times (war, peace, depression, inflation, high interest rates) on teenagers' lives.

Study classified ads for housing. What points about a neighborhood are mentioned to make it sound appealing?

Describe resources in your community which are available for recreation during different seasons of the year.

Discuss community goods and services that families could use which are available without spending money. Include the services offered by health, welfare, and recreational agencies.

List local opportunities for people your age to become involved in community service. Tell about some of the types of community service in which you or some of your friends have participated. In what ways did this work give satisfaction or a feeling of accomplishment?

Your environment, while fast-moving, remains basically one of home and family, school and friends. You are a member of a community. People in a community have much in common. You may already be involved in some form of community service. You are also a citizen of your country and a member of the world community. As a citizen, you are protected by the law. You have a responsibility to learn which rules and regulations apply to you and the reasons behind them. Each community — local, national, or worldwide — is strong in relation to the strength of its individual citizens.

Your Family

Perhaps you are becoming more aware of the relationships within your family and the relationships of your family within the community. You know a family is more than a group of people living together under the same roof. Ideally, it is a group, usually related by blood or marriage, who work together for an environment in which each can experience personal growth.

No two families look, act, or feel exactly alike. In some families there are strong family ties. Family members enjoy each other's company and enjoy doing things together. The people who live in such families share warm feelings of love and loyalty. Other families with equally warm feelings show their love by allowing each member to be independent in finding meaningful activities. In still other families there may seem to be little closeness between family members. Many families are a combination of all these types at different times and occasions. No matter what type your family is, you have something to give to and something to gain from others in your family.

Your Religious Group

If you are a member of a religious group, you have certain responsibilities to those with whom you worship. You probably know many people who gain inner strength from their religion. It can be a steadying force in times of trouble.

In Canada and the United States, as in most countries of the Western world, religious freedom includes religious tolerance. This tolerance includes the understanding of the religious practices of others — from extreme active participation on the part of some to no religious participation at all by others.

Your Community

The country in which you are born, the section of the country, the state, and even the town or city in which you live affect your thinking. Your speech, your ideas, your dress, and your social attitudes are all affected by your community.

Communities differ. Some are urban. Some are suburban. Others remain rural. They differ in how much opportunity they offer their people for various types of growth. In some places, schools and colleges are the centers of community life. Some towns and cities have activity centers or other recreational facilities especially for young people. Some communities are sports towns where home teams are enthusiastically supported. Others heavily support musical events, art museums, and libraries where people can learn to appreciate the world's culture.

The opportunities for education, for work, for social growth, for health, and for recreation are among the most important community resources.

Your Nation

As a citizen, you have certain responsibilities. Each citizen is expected to obey the law. In a system allowing for differences of opinion, your right to express your opinion brings the responsibility to respect the rights of others as they express theirs.

An interested citizen generally wants to learn about government at every level. You can participate in government through volunteer work with a political party. You can write letters expressing your opinions of local, state, and federal matters to legislators. Being a citizen of a country, however, includes more than being active in politics. Through participation in groups working to improve your environment, the safety of your neighbor-

hood, or the spirit of your school, you are practicing sound national citizenship.

Your World

As you move toward independence as an adult, you will begin to see how interdependent people are; that is, how they must lean on one another. The earth, air, sky, and water are all shared, even though nations set up boundaries between themselves. As problems are compounded by an increasing world population, you will be expected to make increased contributions toward world improvement. Consider what some of these contributions might be.

Discuss specific examples which illustrate how the section of the country in which people are reared may influence their lives. Tell about differences you have observed in the dress, speech, and activities of people from different areas.

Tell about ways in which your environment has influenced your behavior and manners.

Teenagers frequently find their lifetime occupations while working on projects supported by their local communities. *James H. Karales/Peter Arnold Photo Archives*

List occupations in which men are more frequently employed than women. List occupations in which women are more numerous than men. Give reasons why these differences exist. Which reasons are most valid and why?

Tell about a woman who is employed in a *man's job*. Tell about a man who is employed in an occupation which is usually held by women. What was your reaction when you found this person doing that work? Why did you react in that way? What problems may people face in working in jobs traditionally thought to be unusual to their sex roles? How can such problems be overcome?

Interview a family with a mother who has recently taken a job outside the home. Ask what changes her new work has made in their homemaking practices. Ask how their lives have changed because the mother is working. Share your findings with your classmates.

TEENAGE ROLES

In everything you do, you take on a *role*, a way of acting that seems to you to fit the situation. Your ability to fit into society will be determined by how you play your various roles. The roles you play well as a teenager are an indication of the types of roles you can fill successfully as an adult.

As a Member of Your Sex Group

From the moment the attending doctor or midwife announces, "It's a boy" or "It's a girl," a human being is treated as a member of that sex. This one factor has lifelong impact on everyone. From the moment you can first remember, you thought of yourself as son or daughter, brother or sister, nephew or niece, grandson or granddaughter. At one time it was popular to speak of women as the weaker sex. Research has shown, however, that more boys than girls die at birth and in the first year of life; girls mature a year or two ahead of boys, and given the opportunity, females can develop strength and stamina comparable to males. Further, women, as a group, live longer than men. Consider how being a boy or a girl has influenced the way you think about yourself.

In the past, certain work was *man's work* while other tasks were

As boys and girls mature, they find joy in fulfilling their roles as adults. *James H. Karales/ Peter Arnold Photo Archives*

Within their own families, teenagers often find themselves between the easy-going world of childhood and the adult world of serious decision making. *Henry Monroe/McGraw-Hill*

Discuss the advantages of belonging to one or two organizations and being an active member of each. Compare these to the advantages of belonging to a larger number of organizations while being relatively inactive in each.

Do some research on a school club you think you would like to join. Talk to the sponsor and some of the members. Ask about the cost of the club in time, effort, and money. What would be expected of you as a member? What could you expect to gain by joining?

Discuss the qualities needed by a person if he or she is to be a good club member.

List responsibilities and privileges of a citizen at home, at school, and in the community.

Compare effective school citizenship for students with good citizenship for adults.

List the ways in which you could help as a club member. Consider any special interests or talents you have.

Discuss the results of the attitude *Let George do it*.

Distinguish between natural, human, and technical resources.

called *woman's work*. Since much housework has become a matter of time- and energy-saving push buttons, chemicals, and equipment, ideas of home and work roles have become less rigid. Many women now have the time for work and other activities outside the home. Many men now find it enjoyable to share child care and other home-making responsibilities. Most men and women work to support their families, for the sense of satisfaction they get from their jobs, and for social and cultural opportunities outside the home.

Legislation doing away with job discrimination on the basis of sex has opened new doors to everyone. It is no longer true that only men can be miners or telephone installers or managers while only women can be telephone operators, nurses, or secretaries. The satisfaction people get from their jobs and the happiness of a family are recognized as more important than the type of work performed.

As a Family Member

We all have a role to perform within our own families. You can be aided in this role by learning more about your own feelings and the feelings of other family members. You can then better enjoy the relationships

21

Plan a *K and C* week (kindness and consideration). Draw a classmate's name from a grab bag. Do not tell anyone whose name you draw. For one week try to show this person considerations and acts of kindness. At the end of the week, try to name your secret K and C partners. Give reasons for your selection by telling the kindnesses and courtesies shown you.

Brainstorm for ideas of things to be done to improve conditions in your school and community. Develop one of these ideas into a plan of action. This school or community improvement project may be part of a school or club program for the year.

Bulletin board IDEA
Title: *Are You on the Beam?*
Directions: Place a silhouette of a pole lamp on one side of the bulletin board. Label the light beams with qualities of a good school citizen as suggested by class members.

within the family, or, if necessary, you can work to improve them. Each family tends to offer privileges to its members along with responsibilities. Both privileges and responsibilities increase as we mature. What responsibilities do you accept at home? What privileges can you enjoy while fulfilling your present role as a member of the family?

As a Student

Your major role in school is that of student. You learn to follow regulations as you grow both socially and mentally. As you enjoy such student activities as school publications, athletic events, and student government, you are learning to live in the larger world beyond the school.

As you follow the school regulations concerning attendance, safety, and the use of such study aids as the library, you learn to cooperate within the community. As you study, you are finding areas of special interest which may help you choose meaningful work in the future.

To a certain degree, you close some doors as you open others. For instance, people may have both musical and athletic abilities, but they may not be able to pursue both activities at once. In such a case a young trumpet player may join the school band and so need to forget the basketball team. Perhaps this is wise. However, by continuing to be interested in all types of activities, at least as a spectator,

Friendships offer opportunities for teenagers to understand one another on a one-to-one basis.
Erika/Peter Arnold Photo Archives

many doors can be left partially open for later roles which a person may play.

In what ways do *your* school roles open doors to the worlds of challenge and opportunity which lie beyond the school? How do your school roles help you prepare for activities in the world of work which becomes increasingly important as you continue to grow?

As a Friend

The teen years are usually thought of as a friendly time. Many activities, combined with your growing ability to do things on your own, offer special opportunities for forming lasting friendships. The role of friend can give you a chance to grow in your understanding of other people. As a friend, you can test your attitudes and ideas on others. Friendship can help you understand the kind of person you are. You can learn to see yourself as others do. Friendship also gives you confidence in yourself and in your ability to get along with others.

What are your responsibilities in your role as a teenage friend? In what ways can friendship help you learn from others?

As a Citizen

What are the responsibilities of the teenage citizen? This question confuses some young people, because they think citizenship begins when a person is old enough to vote. This is not true. Instead, citizenship be-

gins the day a person is born. A citizen can begin early to make useful contributions to the home, the community, the nation, or the world. What contributions are you ready to make today? What contributions will you be ready to make next year, or when you are an adult?

As a teenager, you fill many roles. These roles help you to grow as a member of your own sex group, your family, your school, and the world beyond. The effort you put forth to play each of these roles will largely determine the contributions you make to the world in which you live.

Sometimes acting in fun and sometimes working seriously, teenagers show awareness of their responsibilities as citizens.   *Yoram Kahana/Peter Arnold Photo Archives*

23

1 Chapter Posttest

Fill in the blank in each sentence with the *best* word to complete the statement. *Do not* write in this book.

1 In the past, men's and women's __(1)__ were more clearly defined than today.
2 Part of the process of growing up includes learning to spend money wisely for goods and __(2)__ which are available to you as a consumer.
3 Worldwide careless use of natural __(3)__ can affect your daily life.
4 Some of the greatest worldwide concerns facing people today are the problems of the continually increasing world population, unemployment, pollution, and __(4)__ .
5 All the people, events, and things that surround you make up your __(5)__ .
6 People can be successful and happy if they are able to __(6)__ to the people and events of the world around them.
7 It is generally evident between the ages of twelve and fourteen that girls __(7)__ physically at an earlier age than boys.
8 In recent years men's and women's __(8)__ choices have become less influenced by tradition than in the past.
9 As teenagers grow up and gain privileges, they are also expected to assume __(9)__ .

10 Regardless of their ages, people who are making worthwhile contributions to their homes and communities are practicing good __(10)__ .

Give the following information on a separate sheet of paper.

1 List three recent political events or economic changes in other parts of the world that have had an effect on people who live in your community.
2 Give three examples to illustrate that world news travels quickly.
3 Describe five characteristics of students who are good citizens.
4 Give two examples to illustrate that many women assume responsibilities today which were considered *men's work* in the past.
5 Point out five ways in which the behavior of boys and girls usually differs.
6 Point out three ways in which men may assume responsibilities today which were considered *women's work* in the past. Discuss environmental factors which have influenced these changes.
7 Point out five ways in which teenagers' lives have changed in your community in the past five years.

2 Chapter Pretest

Fill in the blank in each sentence with the *best* word or words to complete the statement. *Do not* use a word which already appears in the sentence. *Do not* write in this book.

1 Parents and children living together are a(an) __(1)__ family.
2 A large household of people with several generations living together is a(an) __(2)__ family.
3 An authoritarian family in which the father makes decisions, controls money, and establishes rules is a(an) __(3)__ family.
4 The ideals which influence the decisions you make and the goals you set are called your __(4)__ .
5 People who are closely related by blood or marriage pass through various stages of the __(5)__ .
6 In the United States at least one out of every __(6)__ families moves every year.
7 Listening is an important part of __(7)__ which contributes to a healthy family atmosphere.
8 When family members share the work to be done and respect the rights of others, there is a spirit of __(8)__ .
9 If you are truthful, honest, and dependable, others will trust you and have __(9)__ in you.
10 Being concerned and thoughtful about the rights and feelings of other family members shows that you are a(an) __(10)__ person.

Chapter 2

Relationships in Today's Families

After reading this chapter you should be able to:
1 Define the term *core (nuclear) family*.
2 List factors that cause changes in families.
3 Explain the term *extended family*.
4 Describe ways families differ.
5 Give examples of authoritarian, permissive, and democratic families.
6 Analyze factors that make families different.
7 Show concern for families different from your own by doing extra reading, making a report, or analyzing given situations.
8 Outline stages in the family life cycle.
9 Point out your family's stage in the family life cycle.
10 Plan and carry out a specific course of action to improve your Seven C's of family living.
11 Judge why each of the Seven C's of family living is important.

Suppose you were given the assignment of describing a typical family to be found anywhere in the world. What would you say? Would you include a mother and a father, two or three children, maybe a dog or a cat? You need only look around your own neighborhood to see that this is just one version of a family.

If you look far enough to include all of the world's families, you notice the family is the basic social unit. Most families do indeed have a core of parents and children. However, sometimes a family may consist of only two people. Other times, many relatives cluster around the *core family*. Aunts, uncles, and grandparents may all live as a group with the parents and their children. In some cultures, there are several wives. In others, everyone in the community is

Pretend you are moving to another planet tomorrow and will not return. Make a list of things you would do during your last twenty-four hours on Earth. What does this show about the things that are most important to you?

Pinpoint on a map the birthplaces of the grandparents of your classmates. Discuss how differences in place of birth can affect an individual.

Interview a person in your community who has lived in another country. Find out what customs are practiced in that country that we do not have. Tell the class what you learned from this interview. If possible, invite someone from a foreign country to class to tell about family life there.

Bulletin board IDEA

Title: *Steps Toward Making Happy Homes*

Directions: Mount a picture of a pleasant, warm, and friendly-looking family or home. Place cutouts of footprints or stepping-stones leading to the picture. On each footstep or stone write words such as *love, security, understanding,* and *common goals.* Use as many "steps" as you think necessary.

The core family includes parents and their children.   *Peter Arnold*

considered a relative and is treated as a sister or a brother.

Not long ago, it was common in this country to find several generations living together in a single household. Each person had a special role to play in the family, and each was necessary to the welfare of the whole group. This large household of people is called an *extended family.* Although the extended family is still found in many parts of the world and in some parts of our country, the *core, or nuclear, family* is most common in modern America. In fact, houses are much smaller today than a century ago because the families which occupy them are smaller.

HOW FAMILIES DIFFER

Think for a moment about the many different families in your community. Do you know a widower and teenage son who live alone? Or a divorced mother and two children? Or a mother and stepfather and daughter? Or a fatherless family with eight children? None of these examples fits the common idea of the traditional American family. Yet they are families. You may have become so used to the idea of both parents and their children living together that you overlook the countless other combinations of people who live together sharing common resources, customs, goals, and values. Each in its own way is functioning as a family, the basic social unit in our society.

Families are as different as the people in them. As you think about *who* lives together in a family, think also about *what* it is that draws a family together. Do resources, customs, goals, and values set your family apart from the one next door, or across the country, or around the world?

Resources

Families have different resources. For example, their incomes vary. The family with a seven-thousand-dollar annual income lives quite differently from the one with a thirty-thousand-dollar annual income. Family possessions are different, too. Perhaps one family has a great deal of furniture or tableware. Another family may prefer to have sports equipment or other recreational possessions. Another may care to own books or artwork. Still another may not care for many possessions at all.

Families also differ in the talents and skills their members possess. Perhaps one family has members who can contribute art or homemade clothing to the family's wellbeing. Another family may be capable of earning money with which to buy similar articles. As you can see, resources differ from family to family, and energy, skills, talents, and attitudes can contribute as much to family life as the dollars family members can earn.

Customs and Traditions

As long as people have maintained a home life, they have established certain traditions and customs which have helped to bind the family together and to give it special meaning. For example, in pioneer western America, a passing stranger was often greeted with a warm invitation to stay for dinner. On special occasions in Russia, guests are greeted at the door with a loaf of bread and a mound of salt. The hostess offers the guests pieces of the bread, which they then dip into the salt. Her greeting is, *"Dobro pojalorat,"* which means, "Welcome with good will."

While some customs vary according to country, others depend upon the family's religious beliefs. Religion often determines such customs as the blessing said before meals, the food eaten, and the family's activities.

Then there are customs which are special to the individual family, such as the ways birthdays and holidays are celebrated. Such customs might seem pointless or very

 Tell about special events you have enjoyed with your family. Analyze the reasons why these were happy experiences.

Tell about customs and traditions in other countries about which you have read or heard. What customs and traditions do we have in some parts of the United States that may seem unusual to people living in other areas? Report on traditional customs observed by various ethnic groups within this country.

Finish the following sentences:

When mothers work outside the home, their children usually . . .
Some women work outside the home because . . .
Whether a married woman works or not, her family has the right to expect . . .
Whether a woman works or not, she has the right to expect her family to . . .
When a mother goes to work, family members may have to . . .

Analyze how your own values and goals influenced the way you completed each sentence.

Explain the statement, *The smallest unit of society is the family.*

List some of your family's goals. Describe how your family's values have influenced its goals.

Tell how a certain person, experience, or event has influenced your values and goals.

Identify short passages from books, plays, or songs that illustrate values held by the characters. List some of the values expressed. Try to determine if each value was influenced primarily by the home, friends, school, religion, or community. Defend your selections.

Collect pictures of families in a variety of situations and circumstances. Suggest some of the values which seem to be important to each of the families. Identify the clues which helped you determine their values.

serious. Perhaps you take some customs you do follow so much for granted in your everyday life that you cannot easily call them to mind. Can you, for example, think of five customs your family has? Compare your list with those of others in the class. Are your customs a result of your nationality, the area where you live, or your religion? Are they special to your family alone? Whatever your customs may be, they help to form a bond between family members.

Goals and Values

Most families have family goals. Your family may be planning to paint several rooms of your home or to buy trundle beds so you can share your bedroom with a certain degree of privacy. Or you may all be concerned about seeing to it that each one gets a good education. The goals which your entire family share may or may not be far-reaching enough to affect others. For example, a home improvement project may affect the comfort and happiness of your family and close friends. But your family's plans to give you an education to become a teacher, nurse, or mechanic will probably be an asset to the whole community.

No two families have exactly the same goals. There may be four families in your neighborhood with the same amount of income. Yet they will probably spend their money differently. One family might plan to spend some of their money on a summer vacation. Another might decide to buy a new car. A third family might be planning for a new baby. And the fourth might be saving for retirement. What makes families and individuals use money for such different purposes? How do goals give directions to a family's plans?

If you think of your goals as *where* you are going, then your values are *why* you are going that way. Values are your ideals, what you consider most important in life. By the time you started school, you had already developed a sense of right and wrong behavior by following the examples set by your family. In school and among friends, you have been exposed to many other values. You may have begun to doubt some of the things you had accepted all along. You are now faced with some important decisions. You are beginning to set about the serious task of choosing the values which will help you make decisions and set goals throughout your life. Most of your values — for example, ideas about honesty, love, privacy, respect, patriotism, and responsibility — are affected by your family. But your friends, teachers, movies, television, magazines, books, and various organizations also influence your thinking. It is the blending of your values with those of other family members which finally determines your family's set of values.

Personal development is often achieved through activities that you enjoy doing. *Paul Fusco/ Magnum*

Act out situations showing authoritarian, permissive, and democratic families. Discuss the strengths and weaknesses of each type of family as seen in the dramas.

Find or sketch cartoons or collect pictures suggesting authoritarian, permissive, and democratic families. Explain what influenced you to classify the families as you did.

Bulletin board IDEA
Title: *Bill of Rights for the Democratic Family*
Directions: Use appropriate pictures with the following captions:
Respect for Individuality (Illustration might show a teenager wearing a current fad or bedrooms decorated to suit each family member.)
Financial Independence (Illustration might show a teenager baby-sitting or doing other work.)
Mutual Cooperation (Illustration might show family members working together or having a discussion.)
Freedom of Choice (Illustration might show a teenager shopping for clothes or personal items, or family members enjoying different kinds of music or other entertainment.)

Family Patterns

Families differ in their ideas of how to bring up children. At one time, family patterns were fairly clear-cut. With changing times and changing roles of men and women, family patterns have changed, too. They reflect the changes in relationships between husbands and wives and between parents and children. Families are often classified according to the source of family authority. There are families where the father is clearly the head of the home. In others, the mother heads the home. In many societies, one or the other is the customary head of family life. In modern America, permissive and democratic families have developed. Many families fall clearly into the categories described below. However, a family may be a combination of each type at different times or may change over the years from one type to another.

The authoritarian family

Have you seen pictures of the old-time *patriarchal*, or father-ruled, family? The father is sitting. His wife and children stand. If there are very young children, the mother may be sitting as she holds a young child

Match the *descriptions* given in List A with the *types of families* given in List B. Use a family type from List B only once. *Do not* write in this book.

List A: Descriptions

A A large household of people with several generations living together.

B Nucleus of parents and children.

C Opposite of the authoritarian family because almost anything is allowed and there are few rules.

D The mother rules and makes the major family decisions.

E The father rules and is the final authority.

F Family members cooperate in making decisions, and individual family members are expected to be responsible for their actions.

List B: Types of families

1 Core
2 Democratic
3 Extended
4 Matriarchal
5 Patriarchal
6 Permissive

Debate, pro and con: *Families are becoming outdated.*

The democratic family searches for outlets through which each member may develop personal talents or skills. *Barbara Pfeffer/Peter Arnold Photo Archives*

for the picture. The picture leaves no doubt about who is boss. The father in this type of family makes all the family decisions. He controls the money. He, and he alone, has the last word in family affairs. Although the patriarchal family is not as common as in earlier centuries, some modern families work well on this principle.

Another form of authoritarian family also exists. The *matriarchal*, or mother-ruled, family may seem to be different from the family just described. In general, however, the family pattern is the same except that the powers of the mother and father are reversed. It is the mother who makes the final family decision.

The permissive family

In some families, there appears to be a policy of *anything goes.* Each family member does whatever he or she wishes. These are called *permissive* families. Such families are often an outgrowth of the desire to let family members be free to make their own decisions. Studies show that in some such families with no rules at all, children have a hard time growing up with a positive self-concept.

The democratic family

A family often mirrors the larger society around it. Our democratic form of civil government reflects itself in a democratic form of family government. In such families, young members are taught how to take responsibility for their actions. To reach family goals, each member may offer a different talent, skill, or resource. Cooperative efforts tend to yield the desired results. When a set of realistic rules is developed and followed, such families can be happy ones.

HOW FAMILIES CHANGE

Once formed, a family does not always remain the same. Some changes happen in the family itself. The membership changes through birth, growth, marriage, illness, death, or divorce. Most changes come about as part of a series of natural events called the *family life cycle*. These changes can be expected. Understanding something about the family life cycle can help a family plan for future needs.

Family changes occur through forces outside the family. For example, the economy of the country has helped to bring about a change in the roles played by different family members.

The Family Life Cycle

You may already have shared in certain important family events, such as a wedding, a baptism, a confirmation, or a bar mitzvah. A silver or golden wedding anniversary may have taken place. Such events can be expected to occur as families pass through certain stages of the *family life cycle*. These stages can be described as the *Young Married Stage*, the *Founding Family Stage*, the *Growing Family Stage*, the *Teenage Stage*, the *Launching Stage*, and the *Empty-Nest Stage*.

Families in each stage share certain problems. As young marrieds, a couple sets up a new home. At this stage a husband and wife usually acquire the basic household furnishings and equipment they need to start a home. During this stage, both husband and wife may work. When they have their first baby, they enter the Founding Family Stage. New investments in baby clothing, equipment, and furniture are needed. With a new baby, the mother may not want to hold a job outside the home. If more children are born, the family enters the Growing Family Stage. This stage tends to keep both parents extremely busy. When children start school, the household schedule may take on an even more hectic pattern. When children enter the teens, the family enters the Teenage Stage. Your family is probably in that stage now. In the Teenage Stage, children develop varied interests outside the home. Once children leave their parents' home to work, to study, or to start families of their own, the Launching

Collect pictures of families in different stages of the family life cycle. Identify the stages of the cycle for these families. Give reasons for your selections.

Describe a fictional family from a TV series or from a book you have read. Place this family in one of the stages in the life cycle. Explain what influenced you to classify the family as you did.

Discuss why one-parent families are often featured in TV family series shows.

Divide into teams to play this game. Have one person on each team draw stick figure cartoons to show a stage of the family life cycle. The rest of the team figures out which stage was drawn. The team with the most right answers is the winner.

Explain how stages in the family life cycle may overlap in some families. Give examples of situations which are typical of different stages.

Make a flannel board or tack board display showing how housing needs differ for families at various stages of the life cycle. Use the title: *Mr. Blueprint, Consider Our Needs*.

Find newspaper and magazine articles to support the following facts about family life.

1 More mothers are employed outside the home.
2 Families are becoming smaller.
3 Families move more than in the past.
4 The number of one-parent families is increasing.
5 More men are given custody of their children after divorce than in the past.
6 The amount of time available for family recreation is increasing.
7 The number of people treated for mental illnesses is increasing.
8 Machines have eliminated some jobs and created others.
9 Energy must be conserved.
10 Individuals can expect to live longer than in the past.

Your career
Sociologist

You would study people to see how they live and work together as a group. The group might be as small as one family or as large as a city. You might work for colleges and universities, government agencies, businesses, and institutions such as hospitals and prisons.

Stage has been reached. When all children have left home, the parents are left with an Empty Nest. The children are no longer the center of family attention. New concerns and interests develop as parents plan to retire.

Each person who marries will share a part in at least two cycles: that of the family he or she grows up in and that of the family started when he or she marries. In each stage, the family must make new adjustments. It will face new problems. It will have new standards to meet. It will set new goals. New decisions will have to be made.

Although all families pass through similar stages of the family cycle, no two go through the same stages in the same way. Some families may skip a stage, or backtrack, or even overlap stages. A childless couple, for example, will go through fewer stages than a family with children. If a couple with grown children ready to be launched has a new baby, that couple will repeat several stages. If one parent dies and the other remarries, there will be overlapping and perhaps some backtracking in the cycle. The same is true if parents divorce and remarry.

What stage in the family life cycle has your family reached? How is life in the family different now than in the previous stage? What new needs does your family have? What adjustments have to be made?

As the family goes through various life cycles, its members often take on new and different responsibilities. *Sybil Shackman/Monkmeyer*

Changing Roles

To do the work of a family, parents and children form a team. Each member of the family team has a different role to perform. How these roles are defined will vary from family to family. However, with changing life-styles today, more and more men and women find they must share the tasks of financial support, homemaking, and child care to keep their homes running smoothly.

As a family reaches the Teenage Stage, many of the tasks earlier performed by parents are taken over by teenagers. Can you sense change in your family? What tasks can you now assume that were previously more than you could manage?

The Industrial Revolution brought about profound changes in family life. Before the Industrial Revolution, more families lived on farms than in cities. A family could produce almost all of what it needed in the way of food, clothing, and shelter. In addition, families were largely responsible for educating their children. Daughters learned the role of mother-homemaker, and sons learned the role of father-provider in the home setting. Each family member, including many other relatives in the household, was important. Each had definite duties. Children were assets because they could be put to work. In a large family there were more hands to pitch in and help.

Few families today fit this description. After the Industrial Revolution, many families left farms in search of work in towns and cities. As a result, individual families produced less for themselves. They began to depend more on outsiders to produce food, housing, and clothing. They looked to the community to provide jobs, education, and entertainment. This was the beginning of the *family consumer group.* No longer were children seen merely as extensions of the family. Children became accepted as individuals in their own right. Children no longer followed in their parents' footsteps as a matter of course. They began to select their mates for personal rather than family reasons. They began to select careers in line with their own abilities and interests.

Outside Forces in Change

There are many outside forces that make modern families entirely different from those of other times. These changes occur at all stages of the family life cycle. Families are affected by political, economic, and social events. At best, families have only a limited control over these happenings. An international pact, a strike, a company move, or changed social standards all influence the quality of family life. What current events are affecting

Explain each of the following statements in your own words. Give an example to illustrate your understanding of each statement.

1 In this century, the family has changed from a *producing* to a *consuming unit.*
2 Individuals and families are more mobile than in the past.
3 Male and female roles are changing and becoming more flexible.
4 TV has a great influence on individuals as well as on families.
5 The family has shifted from a rather self-sufficient unit to one which is dependent on outside resources.

Bulletin board IDEA
Title: *Focus on Families*
Directions: Use a cutout of a camera and pictures, sketches, or cartoons of families mounted to look as if they are framed. Include illustrations which suggest core, extended, authoritarian, permissive, and democratic families.

Interview people who have moved within the past five years. Find out how far and why they moved. Summarize your findings.

Make a booklet or leaflet similar to those given by moving companies to their customers. Give suggestions for making a move as smooth as possible. The following examples may be of some help.

1 If the move is some distance, read about the new area ahead of time.
2 Obtain pictures, perhaps postcards, of the new community.
3 If possible, get a picture and floor plan of the new home.
4 Do as much packing as possible ahead of the actual moving day.

Justify your list of suggestions as well as those above.

Bulletin board IDEA
Title: *The Core of Family Living*
Directions: Use a cutout of a very large apple. Make it look as if a bite had been taken from it. In this part, shaped like a C, write the Seven C's of family living.

Moving to a new community often means transferring to a different school. Sometimes extra help at home helps the student adjust to the new environment. *Sybil Shackman/Monkmeyer*

your family? Do you consider the changes minor or major?

Mobility

Each year one family out of every five moves. Often this means adapting to a new community and a whole new way of life. Reasons for such moves include new job opportunities, the lure of faraway places, a desire to get a new start, and climate and health factors. Since these moves usually mean leaving relatives behind, parents and children are more dependent upon one another for companionship and security and less dependent upon a large group of relatives. There may be more conflict between parents and children in a mobile core family than in extended families, in which children answer to several relatives. Knowing the tendency toward conflict in a small family unit, it is important for both parents and children to develop bonds of closeness. The wise transplanted family learns to talk easily together. Often they find substitute grandparents, aunts, and cousins.

THE SEVEN C'S OF FAMILY LIVING

Do you know a family with members that really enjoy each other? What makes their relationship so special? Family relations are improved by the Seven C's of family living: cooperation, communication, confidence, concern, commitment, companionship, and consideration. The Seven C's are a good key to getting along with other people, too.

Relatives who live some distance from one another might only get together for special occasions. *Mazola Corn Oil*

Cooperation

In family living, cooperation means that every person has a position and fulfills the duties it implies. At the same time, each respects other members of the family. Family cooperation is a two-way deal: You give a little; you take a little. Everybody benefits. You show cooperation when you arrive at meals on time, when you do your share of home duties without being reminded, and when you take other people's wants and needs as seriously as your own. To show a spirit of cooperation, you can pitch in on some of your parents' projects. Perhaps you can share in do-it-yourself home improvements or neighborhood charity drives. You can volunteer to help your brother or sister with homework or a broken toy. You can stay out of the way when older brothers and sisters entertain. You can give in without sulking when you are overruled in a family decision. If you are willing to cooperate with other family members, you can expect to find them cooperating more with you.

Communication

In a healthy family atmosphere, the channels of communications are always open. Two-way communication helps a family avoid misunderstandings and hurt feelings. Instead of tuning out your parents when they discuss a subject you would

Family cooperation implies that each member will pull his or her share of the load in projects planned by the family, as well as in everyday chores. *Mimi Forsyth/Monkmeyer*

Discuss *I didn't ask to be born* as an attitude affecting family relations.

Divide a sheet of paper in half lengthwise. On one side, list all the things your parents do for you. On the other side, list all the things you do for your parents. Which list is longer? Why?

Make a list of basic rules you feel would be reasonable for your parents to set for you. Discuss the reasons why rules for teenagers are different in different homes. Discuss mature ways in which you may try to change rules you think are unfair.

Write *A Bill of Rights for Parents* and *A Bill of Rights for Teenagers*.

Place two chairs next to each other, back to back. Sit in one chair and carry on a conversation with a person sitting in the other chair. After a short time, move the chairs several feet apart, still back to back. Continue talking. Again, after a few minutes, move the chairs still farther away from each other. Keep on talking. Why was it more difficult to talk as the chairs were moved farther apart? What does this tell you about communicating effectively with others?

Complete the crossword puzzle using the Seven C's of family living.

ACROSS

1 Being able to keep a secret so people trust you.
6 Your interest in and care for others.

DOWN

1 Listening and getting problems out in the open.
2 The lifetime acceptance of family members during periods of joy and sorrow.
3 The enjoyment which comes from the company of other family members.
4 Give-and-take and doing your share of work.
5 Being thoughtful of the rights and feelings of others.

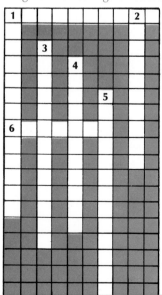

prefer they ignore, be fair-minded and listen. You may not always agree, but communications fail unless everyone, parents and children, have the right to be heard. If you ask for help when you need it, your family may be more likely to save words of advice for those times.

Some families keep communication lines open by setting aside a special time when everyone can get together to exchange ideas and contribute to decision-making. Other families get together casually as problems come up. However they go about it, a family needs to get problems out in the open. When a decision affects the whole family, a democratic family tries to find ways to consider each member's needs. Can you remember a time when you found yourself willing to go along with a decision simply because you had a part in making it?

Confidence

The confidence other members of the family have in you grows as you show that you are honest, trustworthy, and dependable. Be truthful. Actually, telling the truth is easier than lying since one lie often starts a chain reaction. It may be hard to remember a lie or to make a group of lies consistent and logical. Once you are caught in a lie, part of

Communication is easy when family members share interests. *Poinciana*

Concern for other family members can be learned very early in life. *Cosco Household Products, Inc.*

the confidence others have in you is lost.

Learn to keep family secrets. You show maturity when you respect family privacy. Learn to distinguish between what is and what is not private family business. Perhaps you have laughed at the embarrassing stories young children tell about their families. But part of growing up is realizing what is better left unsaid to people outside the family. An outsider may remember an embarrassing family problem long after the family has solved and forgotten it. Why tell family problems to friends when this practice causes hurt feelings that are hard to heal? When you need to confide

in someone outside your family, turn to a professionally trained counselor. The counselor may be a minister, social worker, school counselor, or youth-group leader. Such a person can be trusted to treat your family problems confidentially.

Concern

The concern which family members show for one another is an indication of the strength of a family. Often there isn't much you can do in a physical way to help when troubles arise within the family group. But the way you show your willingness to understand when the going gets rough for any family member is a mark of your value as a family member.

Perhaps there is a bully on the street who has convinced your five-year-old brother that a step outside the front door means real trouble. Perhaps your older sister has broken an engagement after wedding gifts have arrived. Perhaps your mother finds her new boss is almost impossible to work for, or your father is grieving over the loss of a parent. Maybe your brother can't find work or failed to pass his exam for a driver's license. Any member of a family may from time to time find his or her load too heavy to bear alone. At such times it is the loving concern shown by other family members which makes each one feel a worthwhile part of the family.

 List three things that are worrying you a lot today. Put the list away. A month from now get out the list. Are the same things still worrying you? What does this tell you about worrying? Make suggestions for lessening the causes of worry.

Suggest some of the reasons why parents worry about their teenage children. Suggest ways in which teenagers can help their parents overcome these worries.

Suggest ways in which you can show your parents and your brothers and sisters that you care about them. Discuss the ways in which parents express affection toward their children. Discuss the reasons for the many differences in the ways people show they care about others.

Describe a family in a book you have read or a TV program you have seen. Tell whether you would like to be a member of this family. Give reasons to support your decision.

List five things which give you the greatest happiness in your home. Do not sign your list. Combine the lists of all the class members. Discuss the most frequently mentioned items.

Select one of the following ideas for getting along well with your family. Make a specific plan for improvement. Report progress.

Show you are dependable and can be trusted.

Put yourself in the place of your parents and try to understand their point of view in home situations.

Express affection for your parents, and let them see that you mean it.

Show pride in your parents in front of your friends. Do your share of work around the home.

Do your best with the educational opportunities your parents give you.

Be loyal and honest in family matters.

Tell your parents about your experiences in school or social life, and show interest in their hobbies and activities.

Ask your parents to join you in some of your activities.

Extend to your parents the same courtesies you would to people outside the family.

Ask your parents to let you share in decisions on such matters as the hours you keep and how you spend your time and money. Follow the decisions and tell your parents what your plans are.

Commitment

Commitment is the acceptance of a charge, or trust. In family life this means the acceptance of lifetime concern for other family members. It means acceptance of all the burdens and joys which come to the family.

Parents generally understand that commitment is necessary for happy family living. Perhaps some parents are at fault when, in their efforts to make life happy for their children, they try to hide the difficult periods through which the family must pass. In general, all children, and particularly teenagers, want to know the facts when problems affect their family. If money is short, if there is a possible move to a distant city, if one of their parents is seriously ill, or if there is an unexpected financial setback, they deserve to know. Most teenagers are understanding and want to help in such times.

Everybody likes to feel independent to an extent. But in family groups which are committed to the well-being of the family, everyone pulls together during life's difficult times.

Companionship

Frequently teenagers think of companionship as the pairing off of two people into a friendship arrangement. They see their parents as companions and feel they must look beyond the family circle for companionship. Of course, in one way this is right. Teenagers often must look beyond home base for teenage friends. Certainly in the search for companionship, many friendships outside the home are usually desirable.

There is a companionship within the home, however, which members of families experience. Can you remember a confidential talk you had with your mother as the two of you worked to get the evening meal on the table? Do you remember a conversation one night, long after your parents were asleep, when your older sister explained to you some of the facts of teenage growth which were bothering you? Do you remember comforting your father simply by being there and understanding while your mother was very ill? Perhaps you remember quietly listening while your divorced mother told you some of the background of your parents' problems. Do you remember teaming with your little brother and promising to plead for a puppy he wanted very badly?

Certainly there is companionship in family life. And the family which shares with each other this form of companionship knows a great deal of the happiness family life can bring.

Consideration

Consideration, as applied to family living, simply means that family members are thoughtful of the rights and feelings of others. Perhaps if there is one place where children as a group fall down in their contribution to family living, it is in consideration. And probably this failing is caused by thoughtlessness. Most children do not intend to be inconsiderate.

Have you ever behaved in any of the following ways? Your parents have been planning a big night for months, and you have agreed to stay at home with a young brother or sister. At the last moment you get a chance to go to a very special event. You do stay at home as agreed, but you are so disagreeable that your parents' evening is spoiled.

Perhaps this has happened to you: You get a chance to be cheerleader and find the cost of a uniform and transportation to the games may be more than your family can easily afford. You find yourself making your parents miserable by crying far into the night over your personal disappointment, never thinking they may feel as badly as you.

Has this ever happened to you? Your brother refuses to hear alarm clocks. He oversleeps and misses his bus to school or to work. He gets in trouble, and you tease and tell him that it serves him right.

Consideration can be shown through frequent correspondence when you are away from home. *Bob Cook*

Do you see yourself in any of these situations? Not if you are doing your part to help make yours a happy family. You are considerate when you are able to sympathize with others who are in trouble. When your concern is even deeper than sympathy, you have *empathy*. This means that you can understand how other family members feel. Such consideration, when practiced, contributes to family happiness now. Too, it gives each child a good springboard from which to bound successfully into the uneven stream of life.

Act out some problem situations teenagers may have in getting along with their families. Suggest solutions to the problems. Situations such as these may be used:

1 Bob and John share a bedroom. They each say the other is messy. They argue about who should clean the room.
2 Gene gets up from the dinner table quickly. He says he is going out and leaves. His parents are upset.
3 There are five people in the Green family. There is one bathroom. Everyone seems to need the bathroom at the same time in the morning.
4 Grandmother criticizes her granddaughter's makeup and clothing.
5 Grandfather complains about the noise his teenage grandchildren make.

Make plans for showing special considerations to an elderly person you know. How can you show this person that he or she is wanted and needed? Report your progress.

Find out about the opportunities your community offers older people for recreation. Report to the class. Make a list of all the facilities and opportunities found. Circulate this list to community members.

Match the *events and situations* in List A with the *stages of the family life cycle* in List B. Use a choice from List B only once. *Do not* write in this book.

List A: Typical events or situations

A Children approximately thirteen to eighteen years old with interests outside the home.

B Couple usually acquires basic household furnishings and equipment. The wife often works outside the home.

C Children leave home for college, work, or marriage.

D First baby is born. Couple invests in clothing, furnishings, and equipment needed by the baby.

E Additional children may be born and the oldest child may start to school. Very busy years for parents.

F Couple prepares for retirement.

List B: Stages in the family life cycle
  1 Young married
  2 Founding family
  3 Growing family
  4 Teenage
  5 Launching
  6 Empty nest

Define these types of families:

Core	Permissive
Extended	Democratic
Authoritarian	

Unscramble the Seven C's of family living, one letter to each square. Tell in your own words what each means and why it is important. *Do not* write in this book.

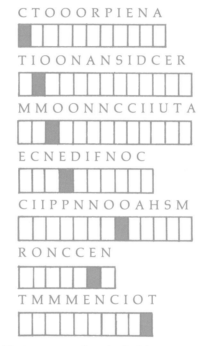

Now arrange the shaded letters to form another word which begins with C. This word tells of something you and your family have if you have the other Seven C's.

Explain in your own words the meaning of the following:

Resources	Mobility
Goals	Empathy
Values	

Fill in the blank in each sentence with the *best* word to complete the statement. *Do not* use a word which already appears in the sentence. *Do not* write in this book.

 1 The way in which you view yourself is called your (1) .
 2 The period during which a child matures into an adult, normally occurring during the teen years, is called (2) .
 3 Basic human needs are divided into physical, emotional, mental, and (3) needs.
 4 As people mature and grow away from the family circle, they are gaining (4) .
 5 Your accent, manner, and behavior are examples of (5) characteristics.
 6 People who are able to adjust and adapt to their environment as it actually exists, rather than as they wish it would be, are (6) .
 7 The three basic emotions are fear, anger, and (7) .
 8 Inborn abilities in mechanics, mathematics, or foreign languages are called (8) .
 9 An inborn ability which is highly developed through training and practice is a (an) (9) .
10 When people are frustrated in their need for love and acceptance and are angry with everyone, everything, and especially with themselves, they are (10) .

Chapter 3

Your
Self-Concept

Each person sees himself in his own way. Your view of yourself is called your *self-concept*. This self-concept has developed from the time you were born. It is at the center of your personality. It influences everything you think and say and do. All of your traits are, in a sense, screened through your self-concept before other people see them. Your attitude toward yourself is reflected by it. A strong self-concept shows confidence in yourself and your abilities. A weak self-concept makes it hard to become the best person you can become. When you understand this, you can take steps to strengthen your personality.

An ideal home is one where all members are accepted *as* they are and for *what* they are. A feeling of acceptance is important in the building of a healthy self-concept. When people feel rejected, they are likely to feel uneasy and unhappy. If they

Describe someone you know who seems to have a strong self-concept without being conceited. Keeping the name a secret, list the personality traits this person possesses. Describe someone who seems to have a weak self-concept. List the personality traits this person possesses. Compare the traits in these two lists.

do not receive emotional support at home, they must look elsewhere for help and guidance. Often they can find this help in school or club activities. Adults and students involved in providing these activities are interested in helping others become secure and self-accepting.

WHAT IS A TEENAGER?

The Industrial Revolution ushered in the age of machines and changed the way people lived. Prior to this time, no emphasis was placed on the teen years. Young people went from childhood to adulthood with very little fuss. They simply went to work. Children as young as six years old frequently labored long hours on farms or in factories.

Cruel child-labor practices were among the first abuses of children to be corrected by law. Increased production with machinery made it possible for goods to be produced by a smaller number of workers. As a result, laws were enacted which gave children time to develop into healthy adults. This growing time allowed a group to develop who are known as *teenagers*. This group of people are also called *adolescents*. Adolescence is defined as the period of life during which a child matures into an adult.

BASIC HUMAN NEEDS

As a human being, you share certain basic needs with other people. These include needs which are physical, emotional, mental, and social by nature. The things people need are provided by their *environment*. Since your environment consists of all the people, places, things, and events around you, it is these surroundings which must provide your needs.

Physical Needs

To stay alive, you need a steady supply of air and water. For life to continue, you need food, shelter, sleep and rest, and space in which to move. The better these needs are met, the more easily the *real* you, the person within your body, can

In a social situation, teenagers are offered opportunities for recreation while learning how to get along with one another. *Hanna W. Schreiber/Photo Researchers*

42

develop the special qualities of an individual person.

In a simpler time, people could perhaps turn to nature's abundance and survive. Today we must plan, work, and cooperate with others to get from our environment the things we need in order to live.

Emotional, Mental, and Social Needs

Have you heard the saying that man cannot live by bread alone? This means that, for people to find life rewarding, their whole being must be fed, as well as their stomachs. Needs are similar in all human beings. They can be met, however, in different ways. If peoples' basic needs are not met to some degree, their lives may seem hardly worth living. For example, babies who are cared for physically, but who receive no love (emotional care), are slow to develop. They have very little desire to learn. Their will to live is related to how well their emotional needs are met. Mental and social growth also depend on the attention a person receives.

We have many needs. Some are simply physical. Most needs, however, are combined ones. When met, they help us grow emotionally, mentally, and socially into complete people.

Love

Much has been said about the need for love. Yet love means different things to different people at different times in each of their lives. With proper care and guidance, we grow in our ability to love in much the same way we grow in size and weight. To helpless babies, love means prompt attention to their needs. Love is shown in the way they are held and cared for. Even small babies know when they are wanted. Through love, they develop a sense of trust. Kind attention tells them that they are worthwhile. It helps prepare them for social growth and learning. Without love, they cannot form the framework into which the pieces of their personalities must fit.

Young children need love, too. So do teenagers. And how about parents? Do people ever outgrow their need for love?

Acceptance

To know someone accepts you as you are is necessary for your good

Draw stick figures, sketch cartoons, or make a chart showing the types of love people may experience in a lifetime. Begin with the self-love of the infant which grows into love for parents. Show how love may grow to include brothers and sisters, friends, a marriage partner, one's children, humanity in general, and a nation.

Explain the following statement: *Love is when another's wishes and desires are more important to you than your own.*

Look up 'love' in the dictionary to find its many meanings. What other meanings can you give to *love?*

Social growth is evident when teenagers can enjoy working together toward a worthwhile goal. *Bettina Cirone*

emotional health. Some people are hard to love. But we can accept them for what they are. They may be different and their ideas may seem strange. Even so, they need friends and associates who accept them as people. We all need to feel we are members of the human race.

Appreciation
We each need to feel that we have done something on our own. We need to feel what we have done is appreciated. Unless we feel our efforts bring some rewards, we will soon give up trying. Rewards can come in such forms as money, praise, good grades, and prizes. In whatever form, rewards strengthen our personalities and stimulate our will to try.

Security
To make the most of ourselves, we must feel safe and secure. We need to feel that the things and people important to us will be there when we need them. If they are not, we will feel afraid. Fear that causes us to stop trying will make it hard for us to grow into healthy, well-adjusted people.

Variety
As human beings, we are naturally curious. We are quickly bored. We need to experience variety, or change. This need can be met through creative work. It can also be met through the imaginative use of leisure time. Variety can be ex-

pressed in our choice of food, clothing, and housing.

Independence
To become truly grown up, a person must gain a degree of independence. Achieving independence is a gradual process of separating what is *you* from what is *your family*. You gain independence from your family little by little. From childhood on, you have been allowed to do certain things on your own, to go places without your family, and to make some of your own decisions. As you enter your teens, you are even more concerned about becoming independent.

Independent people can provide for themselves the things others once provided for them. To achieve independence, we must recognize our basic needs and find socially acceptable ways to meet them. Among the things we must acquire are food, clothing, and shelter. These basic necessities are not free. Work must be performed. Someone has had to work to provide these necessities in the past. As you take over work which was earlier done by others, you move another step toward independence.

Do you want total independence? Since we all must depend on the environment for survival, we can never be completely independent. Nor is total independence desirable. Perhaps the goal of teenagers should be eventual economic independence. Since we never outgrow

A degree of independence can be gained by those who develop salable job skills.

our need for love, total emotional independence may never come.

Meaningful communication

As people mature, they ask themselves questions about life and its various meanings. They need to feel there is more to life than mere existence. They feel a need to share their thoughts with others and learn what others think. This sharing of thoughts and accepting of new ideas is a part of growing toward maturity.

INDIVIDUAL DIFFERENCES

In 1830 there were 1 billion people in the whole world. By 1930 there were 2 billion. By 1960 there were 3 billion. During 1970 the world's population grew to some 3½ billion persons. At this rate, by around the year 2000, there will be 7 billion people in the world. Yet with billions of people on the earth, there is something special about each person. Of the 3½ billion people in the world today, the over 200 million in the United States, and the millions or thousands of people in your state or city, there is only one *you*. You are one of many in your school. You are one of perhaps twenty or thirty in your classroom. You are one of several people in your family. Out of all these people, you are an individual, one of a kind.

Suggest ways, in addition to those given below, in which you can show your parents that you can assume responsibility.

1 Clean up your home after you and your friends have had fun. Your parents will be more willing to have your friends visit again.
2 Return home when your parents expect you. If the time you are expected home seems unreasonably early, talk things over with your parents. Perhaps a compromise can be made, but once a curfew is set, meet it.
3 Have a good time with your friends at home without making too much noise.

Tell about an incident where you know you did not act your age.

Present short skits to show childish behavior in teenagers.

Discuss the following questions:
1 What TV programs (books, movies, music) do you now enjoy that you did not enjoy when you were younger? Why?
2 Which TV programs (books, movies, music) do you no longer enjoy that you did at one time? Why?

List ways in which teenagers most frequently express their individuality.

Leslie Holzer
Lee Battaglia/Photo Researchers

Owen Franken/Stock, Boston

Individuality

Owen Franken/Stock, Boston

John H. King

Iris Kleinman   Bob Cook   Leslie Holzer

Discuss the relationship between a teenager's growing independence from family and responsibility toward the family. Divide a sheet of paper into two columns. In the left-hand column list the kinds of independence you would like to have. In the right-hand column list the responsibilities you should assume for each type of independence gained. For example . . .

Choose my own clothes.

Keep clothing costs within the family budget.
Buy clothes which can be used with others already in my wardrobe.
Consider quality and care when buying.

Suggest ways you could benefit your family by being more independent. Suggest ways you could assume greater responsibility to show you are growing in maturity.

Choose sides, pro or con, and debate: *There are more advantages to growing up in a large family than in a small one.*

Name organizations and recreational facilities in your area that have affected your development.

Your personality and self-concept grow as you learn to communicate with and understand others. *Coca-Cola Company*

The sum of all the things that make you an individual is called your personality. Such things as your sense of humor, your shyness or lack of shyness, your ability to learn, the color of your eyes and hair, or your height, are called *characteristics*. Many of the characteristics you possess were inherited from your parents. They were passed along to you at birth. They are called *inherited characteristics*. You developed others as you grew up. They are called *acquired characteristics*. You can acquire new characteristics as long as you live. You should try to acquire those characteristics which will make you a happier, more useful person.

People have much in common, but it is their differences that cause them to be individuals. Even identical twins do not have the same acquired characteristics. Knowing how people differ from one another will help you to understand them better.

Physical Makeup

Every boy and girl inherits certain traits from parents, grandparents, and even more distant ancestors. Carried in the sex cells, these characteristics set down certain lines of development for each person. While these traits may be influenced by the environment, they can never be completely changed. From babyhood on, however, a person's development depends on the food, housing, and care received. Thus, environment and heredity combine to create an individual with special characteristics. For example, heredity determines that your body can grow only so tall. But you need proper food, rest, and exercise if you are to reach that height.

Body build and muscle shapes

Your body shape — height and breadth — is determined by both your bone structure and your muscular development. Barring illness, accident, or injury, you will grow according to a pattern set by heredity.

Heredity controls the growth and shape of your bones and muscles. It also determines where fat will be deposited. This is why certain body types seem to run in families. Proper nutrition can influence weight. Exercise can change appearance by providing muscle tone and by trimming excess fat. Even though all these conditions affect it, your body is still shaped by inherited traits. You will only grow to the height determined by heredity. Your bone shapes were determined before your birth.

Strength and endurance

Strength depends on the development and coordination of muscles. In the teens, coordination may be hard to establish for a time because of different rates of growth for different parts of the body. Some people who develop good coordination of the large muscles may make good athletes. Other people are able to develop good coordination of their small muscles. They may become skilled at working with tools or at playing some musical instrument.

Display photos of class members when they were younger and pictures of their parents. Try to match children and parents. What caused you to make certain pairs? What does this tell you about inherited characteristics?

Discuss the ways height, weight, body build, or particular physical characteristics might affect a person's happiness or success in life.

Name movie or TV personalities who have capitalized on a physical characteristic which could have been considered a handicap.

Make a report on individuals who have made great achievements in spite of physical limitations. Franklin Roosevelt, Beethoven, and Helen Keller are a few examples. Why were these people able to overcome their limitations?

Bulletin board IDEA
Title: *Are You like This?*
Directions: Use silhouettes of the following labeled with similar captions:
Balloon — Full of hot air?
Basketball — Have your ups-and-downs?
Kite — Gone with the wind?
Use other items and captions suggested by class members.

People of varied body builds can acquire physical strength and endurance through exercise.
Abigail Heyman/Magnum

Classify the following characteristics as being *primarily* inherited or *primarily* acquired:

Values
Sex
Physical resemblance to ancestors
Fears and anxieties
Manner of speech
Eye color
Eating habits
Ability to get along with others
Color blindness or lack of it
Athletic ability
Mental capacity
Potential height

List inherited characteristics and tell how they are affected by a person's environment.

Write the word ACQUIRED vertically on the chalkboard. After each letter, list characteristics primarily *acquired* from one's environment. For example . . .

A Attitudes, appreciations, acceptance
C Cooperation, courtesy, conscientiousness
Q Quietness, quaintness, quarrelsomeness
U
I
R
E
D

Endurance, as thought of in relation to good health, is the ability to work or play without getting tired easily. If good health continues, this quality improves with practice. Physical endurance is particularly important during the teens.

Even though teenagers seem to have boundless energy, they are subject to considerable physical stress. A schedule which includes school, recreation, sports, and sometimes work is a heavy one. Most teenagers like to keep busy. However, when young people participate in so many activities, they need to take certain precautions to prevent physical stress. Energy must be continually renewed through good food, exercise, and sleep and rest.

Allergies
The body of each human being is made up of a cell combination unlike that of any other person. Because of this difference, each person reacts differently to the environment. The person who is extremely sensitive to substances in the environment is said to be *allergic* to them.

Although any person may be allergic to a specific substance, allergies tend to run in families. They are still another of your possible inherited traits. Certain substances may cause sneezing, hives, stomach upsets, watery eyes, or other signs of discomfort when you come in contact with them.

Allergies are among the most difficult to identify of all personal discomforts. It may take a long series of tests by a doctor to find the cause of these symptoms. Often a person can make a correct guess at what causes allergic reactions just by observation. Such guesses may be checked by medical tests. Awareness and avoidance of the causes of allergy can cut down unnecessary discomfort.

Inherited and contracted diseases
Most people have some physical flaws, or handicaps. The seriousness of such flaws depends to some degree upon the individual's attitude toward them. Minor handicaps are generally handicaps only to the extent that a person allows them to be. Of course, there are cases where babies are born with defects such as congenital heart disease or cleft palate, which require immediate attention. Such children may be hampered in living happy, productive lives.

For the most part, with the help of modern science, people can learn to live with diseases. This is true of both inherited and contracted (germ-caused) diseases. For example, there is medicine to control diabetes, for which some people inherit a tendency. There is medicine to control tuberculosis, a contracted disease. Many childhood diseases can be avoided or lessened with preventive medicine and inoculations.

Appearance

A person's general appearance is a combination of inherited and acquired characteristics. Facial features and the color of skin, hair, and eyes are all controlled by inheritance. However, the overall attractiveness of a person's appearance is controlled through acquired habits of health, and grooming, and personality.

Mental Makeup

The human brain is a mass of nerve cells. Its complexity may never be fully understood. It is known, however, that the brain is the center of human thought. The brain makes it possible to learn from experience. Your mental capacity contributes much to determining the kind of person you are. Learning ability, talents, skills, and attitudes are all the product of the brain. Some mental qualities are inherited. Others are learned. The goal of the wise person is to combine his or her inherited and acquired mental powers for favorable mental growth and development.

Intelligence

The ability to learn is called *intelligence*. Each person is different from others in mental ability. However, no one develops complete brain capacity. In almost any person you might think of, there is still room for mental growth.

There are different learning areas. Not everyone is good in math.

People develop healthy self-concepts and good personalities by developing skills and aptitudes to their fullest potential.   *Sepp Seitz/ Magnum*

Not everyone has a good memory. Not everyone can see space relations in the same way. People vary in the learning areas in which they are strongest and weakest. That is why each person's ability to learn is special. The quality of your brain power is inherited. But how much brain power you will develop is up to you. In what areas can you develop more effectively?

Aptitudes and talents

An inborn ability is called an *aptitude*. People have different aptitudes. Some people have mechanical aptitudes. They work well with engines and machines. Some are

Give examples to illustrate ways in which the following qualities might be learned from one's family.

Loyalty   Promptness
Honesty   Friendliness
Self-respect   Tactfulness
Sportsmanship
Tolerance
Orderliness
Dependability
Courtesy
Unselfishness
Cheerfulness
Consideration
   for others

Choose one of the above traits and list all the possible ways you can think of to develop it. Through a class discussion, add your ideas to those of your classmates.

List attitudes, biases, and prejudices which may be *learned* in one's family. Give examples of *how* each may be learned.

Give examples of expressions used in certain areas of the country. Examples may include . . .
Ya' all   Fixin' to
Downstreet   Wait up
Might-could   Take care

How does the location in which you grow up affect the way you talk?

Sit in a large circle. Underline your name at the bottom of a piece of paper to show clearly that it is yours. Pass papers to the right, one at a time. As each classmate's paper comes to you, write at least one thing about that person that you like. Do *not* make any negative comments. Fold the paper over so your comments, and those written by others before you, will not be seen by the next person. Continue until your own paper comes back to you. Identify the positive characteristics mentioned about you most frequently.

Choose five students in your class and determine one special ability or talent of each. Discuss ways in which these abilities or talents might be used for class, school, home, or community projects.

Bulletin board IDEA

Title: *Good times are like flowers—you can't have too many!*

Directions: Use pictures of teenagers enjoying activities alone, together, and with family members. Mount them on construction paper cut in the shapes of flowers.

able to solve math problems easily. They have a mathematical aptitude. Some people have a way with words or languages. They are said to have a verbal aptitude.

There are tests to help identify aptitudes. If you learn what you can expect to do well, you will be better able to make sound decisions in your choice of education or job.

A strong aptitude is called a *talent*. Some people have an ear for music or an eye for color. They are fortunate to have been born with this special talent.

Most talents are developed through training and practice. It is important to identify your talents early so that they can be developed while you have time for learning.

Skills

Modern living involves learning many skills. A *skill* is the ability to do something well. Cooking, mechanics, painting, sewing, and woodworking are all skills. Skills are perfected by practice. People can develop skill even when they have neither an aptitude nor a talent. It may take a great deal of effort, but a skill can be developed. Learning a salable skill in the teens can help prepare for economic independence. Combining a talent and a skill can result in outstanding achievements. A talent for understanding how things work, plus the skill of fixing them, can lead to a successful career in mechanics.

Emotional Makeup

Notice the many types of people among your friends and schoolmates. Some are happy-go-lucky. Some always seem to be worried. Some are kind and generous. Some are critical and hard to please. These people are different in their emotional makeup. How did they get this way?

A number of causes and effects build any given personality. People are born different. Too, the basic needs for physical, mental, and emotional attention have been well met for some people, while others are less fortunate. Emotional makeup is caused by the interaction of heredity and environment, and a stable emotional makeup is caused by a good mixture of the two.

An *attitude* is a learned way of looking at things, people, and actions. You have a special set of attitudes toward yourself, people, customs, and events. Your likes and dislikes reveal your attitudes. You learn these attitudes from your family and friends.

Most of your actions are based on your attitudes. Positive attitudes which show self-confidence will be a great help when you are trying to make decisions. On the other hand, negative attitudes often reflect fear, or insecurity. The fear of failure brought on by negative attitudes may make it hard for you to make good decisions or to get along well with other people.

A positive attitude toward studying can give you the self-confidence necessary to do well on an exam. *Bob Cook*

Explain in your own words steps toward achieving emotional and social maturity. Describe ways in which you see others growing toward emotional and social maturity. Make up a description of someone who is not growing up emotionally. What does this person do that shows emotional immaturity?

Answer these questions to determine your own mental, emotional, and social growth:

1 Are you working in school to the best of your ability?
2 Are you able to control your emotions?
3 Do you work well with other people?

Compare the recreational opportunities in your community with those of other communities. Ask class members who have lived in other places to tell about the recreational opportunities there.

Bulletin board IDEA
Title: *Little Things Can Mean So Much*
Directions: Mount pictures which depict the tenderness parents show their baby, the affection family members feel for each other, the gift a child has made, or any other appropriate ideas.

Most feelings can be regarded as some form or some combination of the three basic emotions: love, anger, and fear. Each basic emotion has its place in human life. Love can make you tolerant and understanding. Anger can make you go out and strive to overcome obstacles. Fear can help you avoid danger. No one needs to be ashamed of feelings. But we are each responsible to ourselves and to others for how we express our feelings. During the teens, you will need to increase your ability to deal with your emotions in socially acceptable ways.

When people are frustrated in their basic need for love and ac-

ceptance, they may feel angry at everyone and everything. This kind of anger is called *hostility*. They are angry at others because they are angry with themselves. When they strengthen themselves through their own efforts, these feelings are usually reduced. Often doing something well makes a person feel less hostile, or even happy. Can you think of some possible accomplishments or achievements which would improve a teenager's self-concept?

People who are afraid they are not getting the love they need experience *jealousy*. Jealousy is a hard emotion to deal with. It is fre-

Give an example to show your understanding of each of the following types of maturity:

Chronological: *how old a person is in months and years.*
Physical: *how developed a person's body is.*
Intellectual: *how grown-up a person's thinking is.*
Emotional: *how grown-up a person is in expressing feelings.*
Social: *how well a person gets along with others.*

List characteristics for each type of maturity listed above.

Write or act out several discussions which might take place in the following situation:

Tom is thirteen and his brother, Jerry, is almost ten. Tom resents Jerry's tagging along with him. Tom is trying to express his feelings to Jerry. Jerry is trying to tell Tom why he wants to go places and do things with the older boys.

Which discussion is most likely to lead to a satisfactory solution to the problem? Why? Which discussion is least likely to lead to a satisfactory solution? Why? How did each boy show maturity and immaturity?

quently found between brothers and sisters within a family. Jealous people are their own worst enemies. They must keep convincing themselves that they are worthwhile people.

Teenagers experience many new emotions foreign to childhood. Moods of loneliness or sadness, followed by periods of extreme happiness, are all a part of growing up. But it is sometimes difficult to cope with the ups-and-downs of adolescence. This is especially so if one can remember the long smooth-running years of a happy childhood.

Teenage independence can cause a good deal of emotional stress. For example, you may feel extremely happy with the independence gained from money earned by working. But the lost security of leaning on your parents for the money needed may tug at you, removing much of the joy independence brings. Your wish to make many friends may conflict with your desire for a steady date. Your desire for good grades may conflict with your attitude toward studying.

When emotional stresses occur, you may need someone with whom to talk over your problems. There are many people who may be able to help you cope with emotional stress. In addition to your parents and family, it is often wise to talk with another trusted adult, such as a clergyman, teacher, social worker, or guidance counselor.

STEPS TOWARD ACHIEVING MATURITY

Becoming a mature person takes time and effort. Maturity is achieved gradually, over a long period of time. People share basic needs, but they want different things. We also differ in how soon and how well our wants and needs can be met. We must learn to make good choices, choices which will satisfy our needs and wants in socially acceptable ways.

Making Decisions

Sooner than you may believe, you and others like you will be making some of the world's major decisions. The know-how you gain in making simple decisions will help you to make those bigger decisions wisely. For example, at this time you can make some decisions about friends, food, clothing, school, money, and behavior. These decisions will all have a bearing on your life and also on the lives of other people. To make the most of your teen years, you will want to better understand yourself and others. Understanding is a first and an important step to making wise decisions.

Separating Wants from Needs

You understand that each person has basic *needs*. But you know that people want certain things, too. Perhaps the wanted object is a car, a record, or a piece of clothing.

When faced with choices, most teenagers are able to translate the facts they understand into wise decisions. *St. Louis District Dairy Council*

Many wants are created by advertising and by pressure from other people. Because we cannot always have everything we want, we must learn how to separate these wants from our *real needs*.

Identifying Your Values

The things near and dear to you are the things you value. Some people value success, while others value popularity, loyalty, sincerity, or generosity. Many value independence and freedom. No one is born with a set of values. Values are learned from parents, family, religious group, friends, and teachers. Values may also be learned from movies, TV, magazines, and books.

They help you decide just how important something is to you. A sound set of values is a great help in guiding your life. Your values can change as you gain in experience and wisdom. It is probable, however, that some of the values you learned early in life will be with you always. What values are guiding your life today? What values would you expect to guide you in the future?

Choosing Your Goals

A *goal* is something in the future toward which you are willing to work. Goals give your life direction by making you act. When you reach one goal, you can strive for another. Reaching goals is one way to meet your need for achievement and independence. Which goals have you achieved thus far in your life? Which goals have you set that will help you achieve independence?

Postponing Gratification

Wants and needs cannot always be met promptly. In fact, there are many wants and needs that cannot be met without long-range planning. There are few instant solutions to problems. Some things are worth waiting for and working for. You can't be an instant athlete or concert pianist.

Real satisfaction in living comes through effort and a willingness to plan. For example, you may have a friend who feels he or she must have a certain sweater. Your friend

 Read the following incidents and decide what you would do in each situation. Discuss the values influencing your decisions.

You are a student assistant in the school office. The secretary has given you a final exam to proofread and duplicate. It is your homemaking test. The secretary does not know that it is a test for one of your classes.

Your parents have gone away for the weekend and have left you at home with your older sister. They have asked you not to have any one over while they are away. Two friends come over to the house on Saturday night while your sister is out. They say they only want to come in for a little while to play records and talk.

Two teenage girls, Susan and Patty, have just returned from a party at which some of their friends got drunk. Susan didn't drink at all and Patty has accused her of being afraid to try it.

Pretend you are stranded on an isolated island. What are the things you wish you had done before this happened? What do your thoughts tell you about your values and goals?

Assume that you are a newborn baby. What do you want? Why do you want that? Ask these same questions for various ages and stages during the family life cycle. For example, what does an eighty-year-old grandmother want and why? How are age and maturity related to one's values and goals?

Pretend you can plan your reincarnation. How would you come back? What does this tell about your values and goals?

Determine one of your best characteristics which makes you a unique individual. Make a sketch, drawing, or cartoon illustrating this point about yourself.

Bulletin board IDEA
Title: *Put Some Swing in Your Personality*
Directions: Cut a baseball bat out of construction paper or use a toy bat. Around it place circles of paper made to look like baseballs. Label with appropriate words such as:

Friendly	Considerate
Cheerful	Thoughtful
Dependable	Loyal

Achieving planned goals usually guides the way toward accepting responsibility and independence. *Owen Franken/Stock, Boston*

has five dollars, but the sweater costs ten dollars. What can your friend do? There are a number of choices. It is possible to leave a five-dollar deposit, ask the clerk to lay away the sweater, and then set about getting the other five dollars. Your friend may decide to gratify this need instantly by borrowing the money or may even be tempted to shoplift. What would you do?

Making Adjustments

You can't have your own way all the time. There are some things in life that can't be changed. Circumstances require people to adjust and often to compromise. You can waste a lot of time and energy if you don't face this fact. Adjustment does not always mean doing things the other person's way. It often means changing your way of doing things in order to reach sound goals. Sometimes you may have to substitute one goal for another.

Accepting Responsibility

When you were a child, many things were decided for you. Now you are expected to make choices and decisions to solve problems.

You have grown to a point where you want to stand on your own two feet. Right now you know what you *do not* want: too much advice, early curfews, and a long list of rules. But do you know what you *do* want? Are you ready to take full responsibility for your behavior? Is it still more comfortable to let your family make some of the decisions for you? Rebellion, to a certain extent, is a part of teenage growth, but independence is not simply a rejection of all adult values and authority. Rather, mature independence is the ability to make decisions based on your own values and to follow them.

Do you think independence is achieved just by moving out of your family home? Unless you are prepared to meet basic needs, you will soon learn the difference between independence and self-deception. There are many teenagers who are independent while living at home. There are others who may be hundreds of miles away at college, working, or married who are still emotionally dependent and homesick.

On the basis of all your experiences and knowledge collected through childhood and in the teen years, you can begin to set your own standards. You can begin to develop your own values, set your own goals, make your own decisions, and accept responsibility for your actions.

Learning from Failures and Successes

Everyone is bound to encounter failure and defeat at times. Such experiences are a part of life. It is what you learn from these experiences that is really important. Many people have even turned one kind of failure into a success of another kind. Some teenagers have difficulty in adjusting to their new, more adult roles. They may get into trouble of various kinds. But a failure can be the beginning of a success if it is handled correctly.

Have you heard the adage, *Nothing succeeds like success?* It is also true that what appears to be *overnight success* is usually the result of years of hard work. The satisfaction gained from success is a spur to further achievement. Learn from your failures. Build on your successes. No one is a *born loser.* Losers, like winners, are self-made.

Understanding Yourself

There are many parts to your total self-concept. Body, mind, and spirit blend together to make the one and only *you.* Is it any wonder that some people call their personality a puzzle? And like a puzzle, the personality is understood when all the parts are fitted together and you see the whole picture, your own self-concept. This understanding of yourself will allow you to make wise decisions as you fit together your values, standards, and goals to build a sound philosophy of life.

 Finish this story to show how Ann is able to assume responsibility. Compare the ending of your story with that of other students. What evidences are there in your stories that Ann is a good citizen?

Ann is thirteen years old and goes to your school. She lives on Main Street in a small, neatly kept house. Ann's mother, Mrs. Smith, is a nurse's aide at the hospital. Mr. Smith works for the county. Billy and Joe are in elementary school, and Grandmother stays home with the baby. With her mother and father working all day and with Grandmother taking care of the baby, Ann, being the oldest child in the family, finds that she has many privileges as well as many responsibilities. Ann was walking to school one day when suddenly . . .

Give an example to show how one small success for an individual can lead to other achievements. Also give an example, from real life or fiction, to illustrate how one failure may lead to a series of failures. Discuss the reasons why people react to failures differently. Show how a failure actually can be a *blessing in disguise* depending on how the person reacts to it.

57

Fill in the blank in each sentence with the *best* word to complete the statement. *Do not* write in this book.

1 Your self-concept begins to develop when you are __(1)__ .
2 A strong self-concept indicates you have confidence and faith in __(2)__ .
3 The period between childhood and adulthood occurring during the teen years is __(3)__ .
4 Food, shelter, and clothing are examples of your __(4)__ needs.
5 Your school may have a lot to do with how well your social, emotional, and __(5)__ needs are met.
6 A southern or midwestern accent is an example of a(an) __(6)__ characteristic.
7 People are all individuals because of the combined effects of their heredity and __(7)__ .
8 Your ability to learn is called your __(8)__ .
9 Your appearance is determined by both your acquired and your __(9)__ characteristics.
10 A strong aptitude such as musical ability is called a(an) __(10)__ .
11 People who feel they are not getting enough attention may feel unhappy, frustrated, and __(11)__ about others' successes.
12 The way you look at your surroundings, your actions, and your self-concept reflect a positive or negative __(12)__ toward life.
13 The future things for which you are willing to postpone your desires are your __(13)__ .
14 The things which are important to you and that guide your life are your __(14)__ .
15 As people grow toward maturity they are expected to accept __(15)__ for their actions.

Complete the crossword puzzle below using the five types of maturity. On a sheet of paper write the words for 1 to 4 DOWN and 5 ACROSS. *Do not* write in this book.

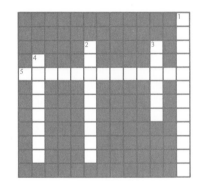

DOWN
1 How grown-up your thinking and reasoning are.
2 How well you control your feelings.
3 How mature your relationships with other people are.
4 How mature your body is.

ACROSS
5 How many birthdays you have had.

Fill in the blank in each sentence with the *best* word to complete the statement. *Do not* write in this book.

1 People who think well of themselves usually present a positive __(1)__ .
2 Posture, facial expressions, and gestures are forms of body language or __(2)__ communication.
3 Biting nails, twisting hair, and chewing on pencils are annoying mannerisms, or __(3)__ , which may suggest a lack of self-confidence.
4 Your posture affects the way you sit, stand, and __(4)__ .
5 Good health and attractive personal appearance depend on posture, cleanliness, what you eat, sleep and rest, medical care, and __(5)__ .
6 A product used to stop body odors by reducing the normal flow of perspiration is a(an) __(6)__ .
7 An ophthalmologist specializes in the care and treatment of __(7)__ .
8 Pimples and blackheads are caused by __(8)__ which has not been removed from the openings of the glands.
9 Brittle or splitting nails are usually the result of poor __(9)__ .
10 A poor complexion may be related to __(10)__ stress.

Chapter 4

Your Image

After reading this chapter, you should be able to:

1. List ways people communicate with others.
2. Describe barriers to effective communication.
3. Explain the importance of verbal and nonverbal communication.
4. Explain how a person can present a positive self-image.
5. Give examples of health practices contributing to personal attractiveness.
6. Show interest in self-improvement by planning a project related to improving your image.
7. Determine specific ways to improve your image.
8. Develop and carry out a specific plan or project for improving your image.
9. Evaluate the results and success of your self-improvement project.

Most people care a great deal about how other people react toward them, but many do not understand the reasons behind some of these reactions. Such people do not realize that their own looks and actions are the cause of most of the reactions of others toward them. In general, people like other people who present a *positive image*. If you think well of yourself, you can present such an image without seeming overbearing or conceited.

A positive image can also be presented by displaying thoughtfulness toward others. People who think well of themselves can easily be kind to others. On the other hand, those who are curt, rude, or surly may reflect a lack of self-confidence and self-esteem. Impolite people often do not

59

Unscramble the italicized letters in the following sentences:

1 The way in which you spend your time reflects your *sstteenri*.
2 How grown-up you act reflects your *tuitarmy*.
3 The things you do are your *seitivitca*.
4 Those things you are working for in the future are your *laogs*.
5 No other person has had exactly the same *cpexseenier* as you.

Take the first letter of each unscrambled word to find the secret word. Discuss how each unscrambled word relates to the secret word.

Bulletin board IDEA
Title: *Is This Your Hang-Up?*
Directions: Around the silhouette of a telephone write suggestions for good telephone manners. Outline these suggestions in clouds like the dialogue of cartoon characters is outlined.

like themselves. Their negative self-concepts result in images others do not like. Your relationships with other people can be good or bad, depending on the image you present.

Can you improve your image if you feel you need to? Certainly, you can. A person can learn to communicate easily and develop a happy disposition. If you are also careful with your personal habits and appearance, you will present a positive image. This positive image will serve to encourage lasting friendships.

THE IMPORTANCE OF COMMUNICATION

Of all the skills you develop during your teen years, the skill of communication is one of the most effective in presenting your image to others. Communication is a two-way arrangement between a sender and a receiver. That means you need to listen as well as to talk. There are many forms of communication. Speaking, or verbal communication, is only one. Writing is another. How well you communicate depends on your skill with writing, the spoken language, gestures, facial expressions, and voice tones. Such things as shyness, fear, poor vocabulary and not really listening to others make communication difficult. Being aware of these barriers will help you overcome them.

When you are not seen by the person with whom you are speaking, your voice is a key factor in revealing your emotions and attitudes. *Bob Combs/Photo Researchers*

Verbal

Teenagers often have a vocabulary of their own. This private language sets them apart from adults. Each generation of teenagers seems to develop its own version of the spoken language. Slang is usually short-lived. It is constantly changing. It serves one important purpose, however. It unifies the teenage group.

To many teenagers, the most important people in the world are other teenagers. But since young people must talk with adults as well as each other, they usually develop two kinds of conversation, one for adults and another for their own group.

Using the telephone

Given the opportunity, you may spend a great deal of time talking on the telephone. Your parents may wonder how you can find so much to talk about. One explanation may be the way the telephone answers the need for closeness in communication without close physical contact. Since many people find communications of a personal nature too difficult to handle along with eye-to-eye contact, the telephone becomes for them an easier way.

The telephone is a family resource, however, and everyone should have a fair chance to use it. People who use the phone too much may be holding up important calls to other members of their families. You show maturity when you limit the length of your conversations. You might also time your calls so they do not interfere with the telephone needs of other family members. You should be doubly careful if your family's phone is a party line. When several families are involved, considerate individuals limit telephone calls to short periods.

Nonverbal

Body language is a term sometimes used to refer to nonverbal communication. People communicate in nonverbal ways through touch and facial expressions. A pat on the shoulder or a sincere look of sympathy may communicate more to a person in trouble than any words could. But just as nonverbal communication can express kindness, it can also express negative feelings. A frown or a look of disapproval are nonverbal communications you have experienced. Turning your back or refusing to shake hands are also negative forms of communication. What other nonverbal forms can you think of? When you realize that your actions often express your thoughts, you may see new importance in controlling them.

Written

With the telephone so handy, many people rarely write social notes. But the written word remains an important form of communication. Out of courtesy to the sender, social correspondence should be answered. No matter how pleasant your note may be, if you wait too long to send it, the delay may seem like a lack of appreciation. A few well-chosen words mailed promptly can show appreciation for gifts or other kindnesses. A brief card or note sent to a shut-in can help brighten days that seem endless. Letters to pen pals, relatives, or friends can strengthen ties you wish to keep strong.

Barriers to Communication

Unfortunately, communication is not always easy. It can be made difficult by a number of things.

 Write a thank you note to someone who has done something for you, your class, or your school. Describe what the note means to you and what you hope it will mean to the receiver.

Demonstrate nonverbal characteristics that give the impression a person has a poor self-image. Discuss ways in which a person can nonverbally communicate feelings of security and poise.

Convey the following messages without using any words:
1 Come here, sit down *now*.
2 How nice to see you. Please sit down.
3 Don't do that.
4 I do *not* agree with you.
5 I'm pleased to meet you.
6 I disapprove of what you're doing.

View part of a movie with the sound turned off. Discuss what you think was happening. What led you to make these conclusions? Replay that part of the movie with the sound turned on to see how the actors communicated without verbal language.

Say one word or phrase in a variety of ways to give it different meanings. For example, say *no* so that it means *no, maybe,* and *yes*. Discuss the importance of voice in communicating what you really mean.

Discuss how speech impediments, accents, and physical and mental limitations may make it difficult to communicate with others. Suggest ways in which you can help people feel more at ease in their efforts to communicate with you.

Explain the meaning of these expressions:

Half of being an effective conversationalist is listening.

A street angel and a home devil.

The most important thing you wear is your expression.

Often emotions interfere. For instance, a person who has grown up in a family where children are not allowed to express themselves freely may speak and listen only with great difficulty. Too, a person who has been made to feel foolish for things he has said may remain quiet in self-defense. If no one has listened during childhood, a person may have lost the desire to listen to others.

Sometimes there are physical bars to communication. A person who is hard of hearing or who has a speech difficulty needs patience and consideration from others. Educational differences may make it hard for people to speak easily together. In these situations good will on both sides is needed to establish lasting lines of communication.

In this nation and throughout the world, there are many cultures. Cultures vary from country to country and from group to group within a country. Each culture has desirable and undesirable characteristics. Just because cultures differ does not mean one is superior to another. It only means certain traditions have been adopted by people because of their way of life and past experiences. For example, Eastern and Western civilizations have different ways of looking at problems and different ways of expressing thoughts and feelings. Problems arise when these cultural differences bring communication to a dead end. If it is to start again, both sides must be willing to try. It is helpful to be aware of cultural differences. Respect for another person's point of view, no matter how different from your own, is necessary if communication is to be successful.

Manners and mannerisms

Your manners and mannerisms tell others many things about you. Do you fidget? Do you speak harshly before you take time to think? Do you burst out in giggles for no reason? Do you say, "you know" with every sentence? Most people develop mannerisms they may not be aware of. Many of these are the result of nervousness or uncer-

Children who grow up in emotionally healthy homes tend to find relatively few communication barriers in the outside world. *American Gas Association, Inc.*

Make an effort to choose a suitable time and place for joyful, noisy activities.   *Margot Gran-itsas/Photo Researchers*

tainty. Such personal mannerisms as a broad smile, a firm handshake, or a friendly wave attract people. Other mannerisms may turn them away.

Public Conduct

The words *please* and *thank you* are chain-reaction words. People usually react positively to them. Your awareness of the feelings of others is an indication of your maturity.

Young people, being full of energy and good humor, are often noisy. Most understanding adults would not want them to be different. However, when the public behavior of some interferes with the rights and comfort of others, there may be good reason to be annoyed.

In most public places, the noise and confusion levels are generally quite high. Consideration for others can help reduce such noise levels. You and your friends can avoid shouting, screaming, shoving, or playing music loudly in public areas. Such activities may be accepted in the right time and place but not just anywhere a group gets together.

Courtesies to salesclerks, service employees, and older people are

In addition to *please, thank you,* and *I'm sorry,* list other chain-reaction words which show a person's concern and regard for others.

Demonstrate and discuss mannerisms and personal habits indicating both strong and weak self-concepts.

Find pictures of people's hands. Describe the people whose hands are pictured. What does this tell you about the importance of your hands in creating an image?

Suggest ways to overcome nail biting. Tell about a method successful for you, a friend, or a member of your family. Discuss the reasons why some people bite their nails.

Discuss reasons why some teenagers smoke, drink alcoholic beverages, or use drugs. Discuss the harmful effects of these practices. Draw conclusions about the personalities and images of teenagers who do these things and the effects these practices have on their acceptance by others. Why do adults sometimes do these same things?

Make a collage of pictures showing grooming aids and health practices contributing to attractive personal appearance.

Plan a good-grooming kit. Discuss the advantages and disadvantages of the items in it. Decide which items are essential and which might be considered luxuries. Suggest substitutes for the more expensive items in the kit.

Display various types and brands of deodorants and anti-perspirants. Compare them for cost per fluid ounce, advantages and disadvantages.

Make your own deodorant by mixing and blending equal amounts of talcum powder and baking soda. Compare it to ready-made deodorants.

Collect newspaper and magazine advertisements for grooming aids. Discuss the ads. What appeals are made to the consumer? Are the appeals mainly factual or emotional? Why?

List daily and weekly routines for good grooming. Ask your classmates to do the same. Use the ideas to develop a chart or check list. Have it duplicated. Check yourself while other students rate themselves. Continue about two weeks.

further signs of continuing growth toward maturity. Your understanding of the difficulties others face shows that you are considerate.

Facial Expressions

One of the first things people notice about you as an individual is your facial expression. It can reveal many of your attitudes. Are you smiling? Are you frowning? Are you relaxed? Are you tense? Try to expect good things to happen. This kind of thinking will show itself in your facial expression. Remember, a smile is as catching as a cold is.

Personal Mannerisms

Even the most attractive person can ruin the effect of a good appearance by developing unpleasant mannerisms. Such habits as tugging at clothes, constant hair combing, fussing with accessories, or frequent peeks into the nearest mirror all suggest a lack of self-confidence. Biting nails or snapping gum annoy people and may lead them to avoid your company.

Personal Problems

Some young people, because of boredom, a negative self-concept, or pressure from others have turned to the use of cigarettes, alcohol, or drugs. All three products introduce harmful chemicals into the body that affect body functions. While tobacco appears to damage only the physical body,

alcohol and drugs affect mental processes as well.

People, young and old, offer different reasons for experimenting in these dangerous areas. However, young people who use them seem to have three characteristics in common. They want to feel accepted, they want to feel important, and they want to feel grown-up. They fail to realize that maturity is the result of personal growth. Substitute routes to maturity are bound to fail. Once established, such habits are damaging to physical and mental health. Their effects may be long-lasting. All young people owe it to themselves to learn the facts about tobacco, alcohol, and drug abuse. At the same time, they should search for successful ways to become secure and confident adults.

AIDS TO PERSONAL ATTRACTIVENESS

If you, like most teenagers, are interested in improving your attractiveness, check your general health habits. Posture, exercise, diet, rest, and personal care are all important aids to appearance. Cosmetics and attractive clothes become effective only after good health habits are established.

Posture

Have you ever carefully observed an actor or actress on TV? Notice how they indicate the character they are playing by the way they stand or walk. A glamorous leading lady has her head high, her shoulders erect, her back straight, and her hips tucked in. When she walks, her legs swing forward from the hips rather than from the knees. With knees flexed and toes pointed straight ahead, she moves forward with an easy motion. She avoids coming down hard on her heels, but rather touches her heel to the ground lightly and shifts her weight forward smoothly on the ball of her foot. As she walks, she keeps her knees close together. A handsome hero type also holds his head high, his shoulders erect, his back straight, and his hips tucked in. When he walks, he too moves forward with a smooth, easy motion. He avoids shuffling or bouncing.

If actors or actresses are playing characters who are unhappy, unsure, or old, the walk is very different. The body is allowed to slump. The toes may point out or in. The legs are thrown awkwardly. The shoulders are rounded in a slouch.

Posture is a chain reaction. If the shoulders slump, the stomach and the hips are thrust forward. Then a person's clothes hang wrong, and it is impossible to walk gracefully.

Perhaps the easiest way to get your body aligned properly is to imagine you are suspended in air, with your feet barely touching the floor. To achieve good posture while standing, take hold of your hair directly above the ears and pull up. Straighten yourself up in the direction you are pulling your hair. Now relax your knees so they rock easily and are not locked into place. Pull. Can you feel your head assuming an upright position? Now return your arms to your sides and look at yourself in a mirror. Study both your front and side views to see if you look better. Do you feel better? Do you feel your shoulders straighten? Is your rib cage lifted out of your waistline? Are your hips tucked under? Do you feel taller?

Your posture when you bend or stoop to pick up something from a low position can be either awkward or graceful. Avoid bending from the waist to reach the floor unless you are doing exercises. Rather, bend your knees and keep your back as straight as possible. Then as you lift or stand, the strain is on your strong leg muscles rather than on your back. This motion is not only more graceful but also helps protect your back from injuries.

Your sitting posture is as important as your walking posture. To protect your spine and to give your internal organs room to work properly, it is necessary to sit up straight. Keep the base of your spine placed firmly against the back of your chair. The chair will help support your weight so you can keep your spine straight. This position is not only better for your health and appearance, it is more

Play *Posture Raid.* Each day while you are studying this unit, three students may call out *Posture Raid* any time during one class period. When this happens, all students must freeze without changing their positions at all. Several may be called upon to analyze their posture. Students with good posture may be called on too.

Demonstrate and practice exercises for improving posture.

Bulletin board IDEA
Title: *How Charming are YOU?*
Directions: Make a looped chain from circles of foil. Drape this across the bulletin board. From the chain hang foil cut in the shape of bracelet charms. On the charms mount pictures of well-groomed and attractive teenagers, or aids for good grooming.

Rate your posture. Stand against a door frame or wall and note if your head, shoulder blades, hip bones, and knees are centered in a straight line.

Demonstrate and practice correct posture and easy movement when doing such things as . . .
Sitting down and getting up from a low chair.
Picking a heavy object up from the floor.
Getting into a car.
Putting on a coat without help from another person.
Modeling a garment.
Walking up stairs.

Make a notebook or tack board display of pictures and articles concerning posture and exercises.

Exercise is important for maintaining the stamina necessary for the rapid pace of teenage living.
Holland Evening Sentinel

comfortable. Try it and see if you don't look and feel better. Notice your friends as they sit in the classroom. Do they look alert yet comfortable or lazy and slouched?

Exercise

Exercise is a desirable health practice. Taken regularly and correctly it adds to your overall attractiveness. Exercise develops body muscles. It stimulates the appetite and aids the processes of digestion and elimination. Exercise in clean air helps you fill your lungs with the oxygen you need for good health.

There are many ways to get the exercise you need. Walking is a good exercise for most people, young or old. Teenage boys and girls can exercise regularly by taking part in sports and various kinds of dances. If your health is good, jogging and gymnastics help to maintain muscle tone and to trim excess weight.

Most teenagers are in a period of rapid growth. Sometimes their bones grow faster than their muscles do. For this reason, they should have a doctor's permission before engaging in interschool competitive sports such as basketball or football. Don't overlook your everyday activities as useful forms of exercise. The errands you run, the household tasks you perform, and the special chores you carry out provide useful forms of exercise.

Cleanliness

Body cleanliness is a *must* for good health and good looks. For clean-

Frequent baths or showers are important for active teenagers. *Winthrop Laboratories*

liness, lather the entire body with mild soap and water. Follow a sudsy bath with some kind of clear-water rinse. Dry the body quickly and completely by rubbing briskly with a clean bath towel. The pores of the skin are cleaned by a daily bath, sponge bath, or shower. Bathing removes perspiration and helps prevent body odor. If your skin tends to be dry, try putting some baby oil in your bath water.

Deodorants and antiperspirants

Because the body perspires constantly and perspiration contains waste material, body odor can be a problem even when a daily bath is taken. Many people use deodorants and antiperspirants to help solve body odor problems.

Deodorants stop odors while allowing perspiration to flow normally. In order for them to be effective against odor-producing bacteria, they must be applied to clean skin. Deodorants cannot be expected to be effective if applied to an unbathed body.

Deodorants are available in many forms. Read the label carefully, and follow the directions for using the form of deodorant you have chosen. You may wish to try different kinds of deodorants to find the best one for you. Because the body sometimes builds up a resistance to a particular deodorant, try changing brands occasionally.

Usually deodorants are used on the underarm area. However, since

Discuss the following list of aids for getting a good night's sleep. Why does each help?

1 Follow a schedule of going to bed at approximately the same time every night.
2 Get some exercise every day.
3 Avoid excitement just before bedtime.
4 Try to forget your troubles when you go to bed.
5 Refrain from eating foods which are difficult to digest just before going to bed. If a snack is desired, eat something light and nutritious.
6 Have enough, but not too much, covering. Very heavy coverings can make you feel tired when you get up.
7 Wear a loose-fitting and comfortable sleeping garment.
8 Arrange for good ventilation in the room.
9 Darken the room and shut out as much noise as possible.

Bulletin board IDEA
Title: *There are Some Things You Can't Fake*
Directions: Display makeup containers, false eyelashes, diet food packages, and body-building advertisements. Around these write *clean skin, sleep and rest, sensible food, exercise.*

List habits of good eye care. The following items will help you start your list.

1 Tilt material you are reading at approximately the same angle you tilt your head. Have an equal amount of light on all areas.
2 Glance at a distant object occasionally to rest your eyes when reading.
3 Do not look directly into sunlight or bright lights.
4 Sit at least seven feet away from a TV set and have a light on in the room when watching.
5 Have your eyes examined regularly and wear glasses if they have been prescribed.

Brush your teeth correctly following these practices:
1 Place the bristles of your toothbrush against the gums at the start of each stroke. Brush down on the upper teeth. Brush up on the lower teeth.
2 Brush flat across the chewing surfaces of the teeth. Do not brush across the sides of the teeth.
3 Use dental floss to clean between the teeth.
4 Massage the gums for at least one minute each day. Use the rubber tip of the toothbrush, your fingers, or a clean cloth.

one's foot odors can also be very unpleasant, particularly when participating in sports, preparations can be used to prevent foot odors. The insides of shoes can be swabbed with rubbing alcohol after wearing to further reduce foot odors.

Antiperspirants are used to reduce the flow of perspiration as well as to prevent odors. Since many people are bothered by a heavy flow of perspiration during periods of tension, antiperspirants are very helpful. They help avoid the embarrassment and damage caused when heavy underarm circles show on clothing. Antiperspirants should be used only according to the directions given on the label to avoid irritating the skin or damaging clothing.

It is often difficult to know if one has an offensive odor. It is wise to bathe or shower often and use deodorants or antiperspirants when necessary. This is especially important during periods of physical or emotional stress.

Nutrition

Lack of pep, a blotchy complexion, dull-looking hair, and extra pounds can be the results of poor eating habits. This is not a promising start for anyone who wants to be attractive. Changes in food habits can improve appearance. Include at least two servings of meat and four servings each of milk, breads and cereals, and fruits and vegetables in your daily diet.

Good nutrition is basic to good looks and good health. *Tang Instant Breakfast Drink*

Elimination

An important health practice is the establishment of regular habits for body elimination. A bowel movement at regular intervals is part of a good health routine.

Sleep and Rest

Your body requires daily rest, relaxation, and sleep if it is to grow as it should. Sleep and rest also help you to be alert, lively, and agreeable. When you sleep, your whole body is at rest. The heart beats more slowly, and all body processes are slowed. After proper sleep and rest, you are refreshed and ready for activity.

Care of the Eyes

Attractive eyes are clear and sparkling. Healthful living habits add to their beauty. Since eyes are used for seeing, your chief concern is to keep them in good working order. Unfortunately, people often do not realize the priceless value of their eyes until they have allowed them to become damaged.

Approximately one-fourth of the American teenage population has defective vision which needs attention. Nearsightedness is the most common teenage eye defect. While not an actual disease, nearsightedness makes it difficult or impossible to read a chalkboard from any distance. In order to see, nearsighted people often squint and develop a worried, unattractive frown. Certainly if you need glasses or contact lenses for nearsightedness or any other reason, you should make arrangements to get and wear them. If you suspect any kind of eye defect, consult a competent eye doctor, called an ophthalmologist. Other specialists who make eye examinations and fit glasses are called optometrists. Opticians grind lenses and make glasses.

Care of the Teeth

In a way, your teeth are much like your eyes. While noticed for the way they add to or detract from your looks, they make a definite contribution to your health. Oral hygiene helps reduce decay of the teeth, unpleasant breath, and possible diseases of the mouth and gums. Sound teeth, free of decay are due primarily to a good diet, regular and effective tooth care and periodic dental checkups.

During the formation and growth of teeth, which ends at about eighteen years of age, the food you eat affects the strength of your teeth. For the maintenance of healthy teeth, good food continues to be necessary. Daily care is also essential. Since tooth decay frequently occurs when food clings and ferments between the teeth, you should form the habit of brushing them as soon as possible after eating. When this is impossible, rinse your mouth with water. Dentists recommend using dental floss at least once every day to remove decayed food particles, bacteria, and saliva. This material, called *plaque*, collects constantly between teeth and along the gums and is the main cause of tooth decay. Water jet spray cleaners also help remove food particles.

Teeth should be carefully brushed with a brush soft enough to prevent damage to the gums. Choose a dentifrice, or toothpaste, containing fluoride as it will definitely help prevent cavities. If your community water supply does not contain fluoride, your dentist may recommend fluoride treatments or prescribe a vitamin preparation with fluoride.

 Demonstrate how to wash hair. Explain the purpose of each step.

1 Brush and comb your hair.
2 Wet your hair with warm water.
3 Lather your hair with a commercial shampoo or use a soap jelly made by dissolving pieces of mild soap in warm water. (Avoid rubbing bar soap directly on your hair. This causes a soap film which makes your hair look dull and lifeless.)
4 Massage the lather thoroughly into hair and scalp. Use your fingertips rather than your fingernails.
5 Rinse with running water.
6 Repeat steps 3 through 5. (Omit if your hair is dry.)
7 Be sure the final rinse is thorough. Thoroughly rinsed hair will "squeak" when pulled through the fingers.
8 Use a clean towel to blot excess water.

Wash your comb and brush using this procedure:
1 Place in enough water to cover.
2 Add a teaspoon of household ammonia.
3 Let stand for a few minutes.
4 Rinse in clear water.
5 Shake out excess water.
6 Dry with the bristles up, preferably in a sunny place.

Make a transparency by drawing various face shapes on acetate. On separate sheets, draw different hair styles. Try the hair styles on the different face shapes. Decide which are the most and which are the least becoming. Tell why a particular hair style is flattering to a particular face shape. Discuss factors such as height, texture of the hair, length of the neck, and current fashions in relation to hair styles.

Your career
Cosmetics and toiletries salesperson

You would sell cosmetics and toiletries such as skin creams, scents, hair care products, and makeup. You might also demonstrate methods of application and explain beneficial properties of products to the customer. You could specialize in one brand of products or have a basic knowledge of many. You might also be responsible for inventory and sale displays of products. You could work for department stores, specialty shops, and beauty shops. You might also sell products in your home or visit customers in their homes.

Care of the Hair

Hair is most attractive when it is kept clean, shiny, and shaped to fit the individual face and head. A large part of the millions of dollars spent in the United States each year on beauty aids is spent for hair styling and care. Most simple hair styles which look best on teenagers can be cared for at home economically and effectively.

Daily care

Shiny hair is healthy hair. Healthy hair also depends upon the overall general health of the body. Hair is nourished at the roots by your blood. Good health habits help your blood supply all the nutrients your hair needs. Massaging the scalp with the fingertips encourages good blood circulation to the roots of the hair. Brushing the hair stimulates circulation and helps distribute oil along the length of each strand from the oil gland at the base of each hair. Normal hair can benefit from daily brushing with a stiff-bristled brush. However, oily hair may become even more oily if brushed too often. Also, bleached, dyed, or damaged hair may split or break if brushed too hard.

Bleaching, dyeing, or rinsing the hair with color is popular with both sexes and at all ages. Properly applied hair-coloring agents do not seriously damage the hair and may make you look and feel more attractive. However, improper hair color-

ing can be dangerous. It is best to get the advice of a professional hairdresser before changing the color of your hair. If you plan to color your hair at home, be sure to carefully follow the directions given for the preparation you are using.

Shampooing

Hair should be shampooed as often as is necessary to keep it sweet-smelling, clean, and shiny. The need for a shampoo depends upon your surroundings, your activities, and the amount of oil in your hair. It does not harm the hair to shampoo it frequently if a neutral shampoo — one that is neither acid nor alkaline — is used and hair is rinsed thoroughly. People with skin problems often wash their hair every day. Daily washing helps remove oil and dirt which irritate the skin as the hair brushes against it.

After rinsing your hair, blot it with a towel. When it is almost dry, style or set it, and allow it to dry before going out. There are many new blower-type combs, electric rollers, and home dryers for hair styling. There are also dry shampoos that remove excess oil and add shine to your hair between regular washings. It should not be necessary to appear in public with dirty or wet hair or hair set in curlers.

It is important to clean your brush and comb frequently, at least as often as you wash your hair. Your hairbrush and comb should not be used by other people, nor should

Shampoo your hair as often as is necessary to remove excess oil. *American Gas Association, Inc.*

Hair problems

Typical hair problems include hair which is too oily, too dry, too thin, too thick, too fine, too coarse, dull-looking, or lifeless. No matter what the exact problem, a balanced diet, and regular brushing and washing tend to improve the condition. Hair which is too thick can be thinned during cutting, while thin hair tends to look thicker if cut short or treated with a body permanent.

Care of the Face

In addition to a daily bath to cleanse the entire body, the face requires special attention. Whether your facial skin is oily, dry, or normal, it needs care.

Teenage skin problems

A clear, smooth complexion is a part of good looks. Unfortunately, many teenagers have difficulty in keeping their skin free from blackheads and pimples. While skin blemishes can cause embarrassment, they are not necessarily a sign of a lack of cleanliness. In the early teen years there are many physical and psychological changes taking place. The glands which control the supply of oil to the skin, especially of the face, back, and shoulders, become very active. The extra amounts of oil, if not removed from the openings of the glands, can cause blackheads. If the oil accumulates below the surface of the skin, whiteheads will form. These oil-plugged gland openings

Demonstrate the proper way to wash your face. Explain each of the steps.

1 Wash your face and neck with a lather made from warm water and a mild soap. Apply the lather with your freshly washed hands or a soft, clean washcloth.
2 Apply the lather gently, using an upward and circular motion. Reach the creases in the skin around the nose, corners of the eyes, and ears. Clean to the hairline around the forehead, ears, and back of the neck.
3 Rinse away the soap thoroughly.
4 Pat your face dry with a clean, soft towel.

Determine the shape of your face. This may be done by pulling your hair completely back and outlining your face on a mirror with soap. (Be sure to clean the mirror afterward.) Divide the class into groups —those with round-shaped faces together, those with long-shaped faces together, etc. Decide which types of hair styles and necklines are most becoming to each face shape. Select one student in each group to show the class a flattering neckline and hairdo the next day.

you use theirs. Diseases of the scalp and the eggs of lice or other insects can be carried from person to person by using a common comb or brush.

Styling

Both boys and girls are interested in finding a hair style suited to them. The shape of the face and features determine what arrangement is most becoming. No matter what style you choose, it will look better if your hair is clean, well brushed, and generally well cared for.

Discuss proper shoe care in relation to the prevention of foot problems. Include such procedures as the use of a shoehorn when putting on shoes, proper shoe storage, proper methods of cleaning various types of shoes, the care to be given to wet shoes and boots, and the importance of shoe repair. Explain how each will help prevent problems.

Make your own hand lotion: Mix together 1 teaspoon (5 milliliters) powdered gum tragacanth (available in a pharmacy), 4 tablespoons (60 milliliters) glycerine, and 1 cup (0.24 liters) of water. Let the mixture stand 12 hours. Add another cup of water and shake.

Your career
Cosmetologist

You would provide beauty services for customers, suggesting makeup and hair styles according to their physical features and current fashion trends. Special training and a license to perform these services are necessary in most states. You might work in department stores, specialty shops, beauty shops, or you could be self-employed.

Most teenage facial skin problems can be helped by regular and thorough cleaning of the face.   *Winthrop Laboratories*

can become inflamed and cause troublesome pimples.

Daily skin care

To help prevent skin blemishes, teenagers must give special attention to skin cleanliness. Thorough cleansing with warm suds, an abrasive-type scrub cream, or cleansing grains will help remove surface oil. This should be followed by very careful rinsing to be sure all the soap has been removed. If the skin is very oily, it may be helpful to wipe it with a cotton ball dampened with a solution of rubbing alcohol. Be sure to rinse again thoroughly to remove the alcohol. Makeup, including oil-free makeup, may aggravate skin problems and should be avoided on all oily areas of the skin. Eye makeup and lipstick may be used as there is less oil around the eyes and mouth areas.

The young person with facial skin problems needs to be especially careful of daily living habits. Plenty of sleep, adequate exercise, and a well-balanced diet with plenty of fluids — six to eight glasses a day — are all recommended by doctors. Doctors now feel many skin problems are caused mainly by emotional stress. Exercise, rest, and proper nourishment all help reduce nervousness.

Picking the face irritates the skin and makes blemishes worse. Keep fingers, soiled handkerchiefs, and dirty powder puffs or makeup brushes away from your face. If skin trouble persists in spite of your best efforts, see a doctor. Depending on the nature of the trouble, you may be referred to a dermatologist, a doctor who specializes in the treatment of skin problems.

Cosmetics

If makeup is used, it should be applied to a clean skin and, even then, lightly. Fashions in makeup tend to change rapidly. Many teenagers prefer to use very little or no makeup at all, while others choose the other extreme. Excessive makeup is unattractive for daytime wear.

In selecting any preparation for skin, hair, or eyes, make a careful choice of brands. To find out which ones are best for you, try out several brands. Information found on labels or given by consumer reports should be considered. Regardless of the brand, choose colors to blend with your personal skin tone.

Your eyebrows frame your eyes. The most attractive eyebrows are smooth and natural-looking. If necessary, you may want to smooth the shape by plucking hairs from the lower edge of the brows. An eyebrow pencil may be used with light, short strokes to make thin brows look heavier.

Teenagers who show a special talent for hairstyling and enjoy teaching styling techniques to their friends may consider hairdressing as a career possibility. *Bob Cook*

Care of Hands and Fingernails

Your hands are in sight most of the time. To be attractive, they must be clean. Fingernails and cuticles require daily attention as well as a weekly manicure.

Daily care

Wash your hands frequently, many, many times a day: before and after meals; after working, playing, or handling anything dirty; before working in the kitchen or starting to sew; and after going to the bathroom. Use a mild soap and water. Rinse and dry your hands completely so they will remain smooth and soft. A hand lotion, baby oil, or petroleum jelly rubbed or patted into the skin will help prevent dryness and chapping.

Well-kept fingernails are an essential part of well cared for hands. Nails can be attractive if treated with care. Do not bite them or use them as tools to dig, scrape, or pry. Keep them clean by scrubbing them with a soft brush. Your cuticles will stay soft if you push them into place with the towel each time you wash your hands. You can also use an oil or cuticle cream at night.

Manicuring the fingernails

The complete care of your nails includes a weekly manicure. Necessary equipment includes an emery board, perhaps a nail file, a soft orangewood stick, and warm, soapy water. Girls may wish to use

Care for your nails by:
1 Filing your nails only when your hands are dry, not after soaking them.
2 Pushing the cuticle back around each nail after washing your hands. Use a washcloth or towel.
3 Using an orangewood stick, not a metal instrument, to clean under the nails and around the cuticle.
4 Eating a balanced diet as recommended in the Daily Food Guide.

Demonstrate the correct way to give a manicure.
1 Remove old nail polish using absorbent cotton and polish remover.
2 Clean under the nails with an orangewood stick wrapped in cotton that has been moistened with soapy water.
3 Shape the ends of the nails with an emery board. Use short strokes going toward the center of the nail. Shape the nails to conform to the shape of your fingers.
4 Push back the skin at the base of the nails with an orangewood stick wrapped in cotton that has been moistened with soapy water or cuticle oil.
5 Wash and dry the hands and nails thoroughly.

List background factors (family and environmental) that usually contribute to a positive self-image. Identify self-improvement projects that can contribute to a more positive self-concept. Examples may include losing weight, improving posture, selecting a more becoming hair style.

Select anonymously one person who seems to have a weak self-concept. Plan ways you can help improve this person's self-image. After a set time, report progress.

Act out scenes in which an individual's behavior may have negative effects on another person's self-concept. Discuss how the situations could have been handled differently. Have an *instant replay* using some of the ideas suggested.

Discuss the meaning of the statement: *Your self-image determines your behavior.*

Bulletin board IDEA
Title: *Are You a Good Egg?*
Directions: Cut construction paper in the shape of large eggs. Place these around a basket or nest. On the eggs write words such as . . .

Friendly	Courteous
Cheerful	Thoughtful
Polite	Prompt

cuticle oil and nail polish. Work on a well-protected, flat surface. To avoid accidents, never work in your lap.

If nail polish is used, it should be removed or repaired as soon as it begins to chip. Both boys and girls should keep their nails clean and well shaped at all times.

Fingernail problems
Have you ever asked yourself what to do about the habit of nail biting? Keeping nails in good condition, filing rough edges, and softening the cuticle are positive ways to combat the nail-biting habit. Hangnails can be prevented by caring for the cuticles. Brittle or split nails may be a sign of poor nutrition and should be discussed with a doctor.

Care of the Feet and Toenails

People frequently mention being exhausted when only their feet are tired. Since they must support the entire weight of the body while a person is standing or walking, feet should receive constant care. Care includes cleansing and checking for fungus growth and toenail problems. It also includes the general attention given to properly fitted shoes and hose.

Daily care
Because perspiration is trapped in shoes and stockings, feet need to be washed daily with mild soap and warm water and dried well, especially between the toes. Occasion-

ally the feet should be massaged with a cream or oil to prevent dryness or chapping. A deodorant foot powder applied to the feet will help prevent offensive odor.

Check for fungus growth between the toes. Infections such as athlete's foot usually can be controlled by using drugstore preparations. Stubborn infection should be called to the attention of a doctor.

Toenail and foot problems
Toenails should receive regular care to prevent serious foot problems. Frequently file or cut the nails straight across the top, and push back the cuticles gently.

Ingrown toenails are usually caused by wearing shoes, socks, or stockings that are too short or shoes that are too narrow. Ingrown toenails are painful and may cause serious infection. An obvious remedy is to wear the right sizes in shoes and stockings. Soaking the foot in hot water and placing a bit of absorbent cotton under the corner of the infected nail will give immediate relief. If pain continues, consult a doctor.

Other foot troubles, such as corns, calluses, and blisters, are caused by poorly fitting shoes. When you choose your shoes, be sure they allow ventilation for the feet as well as support for walking and standing. It is a mistake to choose shoes only for style.

Fashion sometimes calls for such extreme styles as high heels, plat-

74

form soles, or pointed toes. Cramming your feet into uncomfortable shoes can cause long-lasting damage. Think of comfort and support first. Then choose a becoming style. If the shoes fit when they are purchased, they will wear evenly and keep their shape.

Stockings, pantyhose, and socks should be long enough and wide enough so the feet are not cramped. Poorly fitting hose can cause such foot troubles as bunions and ingrown toenails. The length of your foot determines the sock size to buy. Most packages and labels tell you the correct sock or stocking size for your shoe size. Your height, weight, and body build should also be considered when purchasing pantyhose.

THE IMPACT OF IMAGE

Many people fight accepting the importance of their image. To them it seems their friends know what they really are like. Friends, they feel, will understand if they have poor habits of speech or dress. Friends will overlook annoying manners or mannerisms. Friends will look beneath their personal appearance to the real person inside. Are such people reasoning correctly, or are they deceiving themselves?

Happy people live in the world as it exists. While they strive for improvements, they understand that people are accepted or re-

jected, at least to a degree, at face value.

Are you satisfied with your image? Are you accepted? What is acceptance worth to you? Can an image be changed overnight? What changes can come quickly? Which changes will take some time? What is the price? Are you willing to pay it?

In every aspect of life, decisions must be made. Goals must be set. The carry-through tasks must be begun. Evaluation is necessary from time to time. Long practice periods are quickly forgotten when worthwhile goals are reached.

Bulletin board IDEA
Title: *Cash in on Good Grooming*
Directions: Use a large line drawing of a cash register with the drawer open. Mount green cutouts made to look like dollar bills. On them write the words *posture, exercise, cleanliness, nutrition, sleep and rest,* and any other aids to good grooming.

Your image is a combination of your physical appearance, dress, manners, mannerisms, and habits. *Erika/Peter Arnold Photo Archives*

Fill in the blank in each sentence with the *best* word to complete the statement. *Do not* write in this book.

1 People are accepted or rejected, at least to a degree, at face (1).
2 Communication with others is primarily through talking, body language, and (2).
3 The way you sit, stand, and walk is affected by your (3).
4 Regular and correct (4) adds to overall attractiveness, develops muscles, stimulates appetite, and aids body processes.
5 Brittle or splitting nails can be the result of poor (5).
6 A product used to reduce body odors while allowing perspiration to flow normally is a(an) (6).
7 Posture, personal care or grooming, exercise, wise clothing selection, sleep, and a sensible (7) are necessary for attractive personal appearance.
8 A person who makes eye glasses and contact lenses is a(an) (8).
9 In the daily care of your teeth, it is the (9) that is vital in cleaning them.
10 A chemical added to some brands of toothpaste to help prevent tooth decay is (10).
11 The first step in washing your hair should be to (11) it.
12 As one grows older the supply of (12) to the hair and skin decreases.

13 The most important consideration in preventing and lessening blackheads and other skin blemishes is (13).
14 A doctor who specializes in the care and treatment of the skin is a(an) (14).
15 Effective communication and an attractive personal appearance are important factors in developing a pleasing personality, creating a favorable impression, and presenting a positive (15).

Give the following information on a separate sheet of paper.

1 List five forms of nonverbal communication.
2 Name three barriers to effective communication.
3 Identify five mannerisms or habits which suggest a lack of self-confidence.
4 Give examples of three chain-reaction words which have a positive effect on other people.
5 Give four general rules to follow for an attractive complexion which are also guidelines for overall good health.
6 List five characteristics which contribute toward making a positive impression on others.

Fill in the blank in each sentence with the *best* word to complete the statement. *Do not* use a word which already appears in the sentence. *Do not* write in this book.

1 A person who has tact, can make introductions smoothly, and is able to communicate easily with others has acquired (1) skills which are helpful throughout life.
2 Friends help you fulfill your basic needs for love, appreciation, security, variety, independence, and (2).
3 Manners, or guidelines for behavior in social situations, are referred to as (3).
4 A closed circle of people who limit their friendships outside the group is a(an) (4).
5 Teenagers sometimes go steady because it gives them a feeling of (5).
6 If you can listen and are able to get your date to talk about his or her interests, you are considered a good (6).
7 Your progress toward selecting a satisfying lifetime job, occupation, profession, or trade refers to your (7) growth.
8 The purpose of a job is to produce goods or (8).
9 Generally, the level of peoples' education is related to their overall lifetime (9).

Chapter 5

Your Future

After reading this chapter, you should be able to:

1. List salable job skills.
2. Name social, vocational, and educational opportunities available in your community.
3. Identify sources available to help young people make important decisions.
4. Give examples of decisions made now that may affect your future.
5. Summarize the values of having a wide circle of friends.
6. Explain how dating may contribute to social growth and maturity.
7. Assume responsibility for finding out about careers that interest you by having interviews or doing additional reading or research.
8. Point out the strengths and weaknesses you have for careers that interest you.
9. Judge your salable work habits.

One thing certain about the teen years is that each person must do his or her own job of growing up. You are on your own when it comes to making the most of yourself and your opportunities. When you were a child, other people carried the main responsibility for your welfare. Now, and as you grow older, you will be taking an increasingly greater share of the responsibility.

Now is the time to begin developing skills you can use to earn a living, raise a family, or even make friends. Some of these skills are called salable job skills, as you can expect to receive pay for performing them. Some are social skills to help you get along with other people. It is likely that many people — family, friends, teachers, employers — will be able and willing to help you. Yet, even with help, you must be ready to develop these skills for yourself.

Give an example to show how planning for the future helped someone you know reach a career goal. Give an example to show how a goal was met only after several attempts to achieve it.

Ask students who are employed to describe their work. Ask what they like and dislike about it. What skills are needed for these jobs?

List personal characteristics that would be helpful in all occupations. List traits that would be handicaps in work situations.

Visit a vocational-technical school to see the programs in action. Ask about expenses and how to enroll. Tell the class about your visit.

Make a scrapbook containing information, pamphlets, leaflets, and newspaper and magazine articles about occupations that interest you.

Point out occupations requiring:
Mechanical aptitude
Mathematical aptitude
Musical talent
Sewing skill
Typing skill
Add other aptitudes, talents, and skills to the list.

YOUR OPPORTUNITIES

The teen years are social years. Teenagers enjoy parties, sports events, and other forms of entertainment. Maturity for most teenagers also brings an interest in job opportunities. They begin to grow interested in working for money. The two interests seem to go hand in hand. Work provides money which may be used in part to pay for interesting hobbies or forms of social entertainment.

Social Opportunities

The teenage practice of frequently getting together with others leads to social growth. Parties, dates, and group activities are important aspects of the social scene. Some teens envy their friends who seem to have a natural ability to be at ease as guests or as hosts or hostesses, to make introductions smoothly, or to carry on meaningful conversations. Actually, basic social skills such as these do not require a special natural talent. They can be learned by the teenager who makes the effort to practice them.

If you have both boys and girls among your friends during your teen years, you will have many chances to develop a more interesting personality. For example, you can learn to talk about the hobbies

Boy-girl friendships offer teenagers a chance to understand and appreciate each other. *Mahon/Monkmeyer*

Combining artistic talent and business ability at this early age shows real initiative and potential for a successful career. *Jan Lukas/Photo Researchers*

 Write your own recipe for success. An example follows:

Ingredients

   1 T. friendliness
   1 T. poise
   2 T. tact
   3 c. loyalty
   1 sense of humor
   2 c. patience
   2 c. sincerity
   1 willing spirit
   2 willing hands and feet
  ½ c. of thoughtful deeds
1½ c. of concern for others
   1 c. of cooperation
   1 large understanding heart
   1 warm smile

Directions

1 Blend together the friendliness, poise, and tact.
2 Add the loyalty, humor, patience, and sincerity. Stir until well mixed.
3 Gently combine the willing spirit, hands, and feet.
4 Carefully blend the above mixtures together.
5 Fold in the thoughtful deeds and the concern for others.
6 Blend in the cooperation until no more can be absorbed.
7 Mold the mixture into a human form, placing the understanding heart in the center.
8 Garnish with the warm smile.

For best results, make enough to cover the earth.

List resources available in your school and community for personal and vocational guidance and counseling.

Name school and community organizations which provide experiences and opportunities which could influence your choice of an occupation.

Investigate scholarships and financial aid programs available to high school students to help them further their education. Find out how one can qualify and apply for such assistance.

Discuss ways people can increase their understanding of the world and the opportunities it offers. What provisions does society make for individuals to broaden their experiences by taking advantage of these opportunities?

Bulletin board IDEA
Title: *Clues to Career Choices*
Directions: Use a detective cartoon character and a magnifying glass. On cutouts of three large footprints, write *social skills, vocational guidance,* and *educational opportunities.*

and interests others enjoy. In order to talk easily, you will probably need to learn something about the things that interest your friends, such as fishing and other outdoor sports and games, cooking, model making, ham radio operation, record collections, car repairs, and musical instruments or groups.

Young friendships help you to appreciate the friendships adulthood will bring. They also give you a chance to compare and understand other people. Young boy-girl friendships can help prepare you for the selection of a mate if and when you decide you are ready for marriage.

Vocational Opportunities

With many new interests, young people may begin to earn some of their own money. Laws tend to limit the hours and conditions under which teenagers can work. But the teen who wants a summer job or after-school work will usually find job openings in restaurants, supermarkets, stores, and many other businesses. Sitting with children, working in yards, shoveling snow, running errands, and delivering newspapers are jobs available to young teens.

Some young students are eligible for special learn-while-you-earn, or work-study, programs. These programs allow them to earn varying amounts of money while they complete their vocational and general educations.

Sources of Assistance

Today you will find many people are ready to help you along the road to a satisfying life. Once, young people had only their families to rely on. They turned to grandparents, uncles, cousins, and distant relatives when they needed help or advice. With the decline of the extended family, it has become necessary to combine family and community resources so teenagers may be given assistance in finding available opportunities.

Parents and other family members

As in years past, ties remain strong in many families. In such families, young people turn to their parents when they need advice. You are fortunate if you have family members who can offer good advice and help concerning your future.

Once there were family businesses and family trades. Young people were employed by the family as a matter of course. Today, a carpenter's son may become an astronaut, and a restaurant owner's daughter may prefer to work in a garage. Some families find it hard to accept such changes from family traditions. But more and more people are recognizing that each person needs a job which is personally satisfying rather than only pleasing to his elders.

Friends

Some of your friends may know you almost as well as your family does.

Schools and community centers often help students find part-time jobs by posting available positions. *New York University Creative Services*

Good friends can talk about their plans and problems as they work together. *What's New in Home Economics*

 As a class, list on the chalkboard the qualities desired in a friend. Develop them into a check list entitled *How good a friend am I?* Using a scale such as 1 = poor, 2 = fair, 3 = good, 4 = very good, and 5 = excellent, rate yourself. For the three friendship qualities on which you rate the lowest, make a definite plan for improvement. Report your progress toward strengthening these points. Your friendship check list might include points such as:

Dependability — I can be
  depended upon to do what is
  expected of me.
Loyalty — I am loyal to my
  friends and do not talk behind
  their backs.
Tact — I say things without
  hurting others' feelings.

Bulletin board IDEA
Title: *A Friend Is a Present You
    Give Yourself*
Directions: Cover the bulletin board with gift-wrapping paper. Attach a bow or ribbon to make the board look like a gift package. You may also use old greeting cards with short sayings or poems about friendship.

Divide a sheet of paper into two vertical columns. In the left-hand column list traits you like your friends to have. In the right-hand column list traits you would want an employee to possess if you were in the position of hiring workers. Compare the lists. Draw conclusions concerning the relationship of the two lists.

Discuss the merits of this statement, *If I have ten real friends by the time I'm eighty years old, I'll be a rich person.*

Pretend that you are going to the moon for six months. You may take two friends with you. Who would they be? Why?

Describe a friend everyone would like to have.

Divide into groups of three or four and have each group present a skit showing how to be a good friend. In the skits illustrate some of the responsibilities of good friendship.

Bulletin board IDEA
Title: *Don't Get Scared*
Directions: Arrange Halloween-type characters such as skeletons, ghosts, witches, or owls. Attach signs to each goblin with phrases such as *study now, stay in school, seek help.*

You can try out new ideas on them. You can share your thoughts and feelings, too. You can be very honest with a good friend. While friends your own age may not have had enough experience to offer good advice for your future, they can provide real encouragement. This can be especially helpful when you have a problem. Both encouragement and guidance may be offered by older friends. Friends, too, can share their experiences with you, or show kindness and understanding about situations or problems they have already lived through. Perhaps an older neighbor or a family friend can make helpful suggestions concerning a social or vocational problem and advise you on alternatives to a situation.

Teachers
People usually become teachers because they want to share their knowledge and because they want to help young people. If you find a teacher who seems to understand you particularly well, talk with him or her. Teachers may be easiest to approach in such informal situations as physical education classes or laboratories in science, home economics, and industrial arts. Most teachers are more than willing to give assistance. Although teachers are hired to teach certain subject matter, they are interested in your social and vocational growth as well. Call on them when you need advice or assistance.

Counselors
There are many kinds of counselors who can help you plan for your future. There is your school guidance counselor. Your counselor can help you review your school record and arrange for tests to help you find your talents and skills. Leaders of youth groups have wide experience with young people. If you have been a 4-H-er, Scout, Future Farmer, Future Homemaker, Future Teacher, or a member of a similar group, you know leaders to whom you can turn with confidence. Let them know if you need help.

Social service workers and community aides are trained to help you in many areas. Whether your problems are concerned with physical, mental, or social growth, feel free to ask for help when it is needed.

Other professional leaders
Doctors, dentists, and nurses can help with personal problems as well as with health problems. Many personal worries can be helped by better nutrition, better health care, and counseling. Such conditions as underweight, overweight, and skin infections are problems you need not try to handle alone. Consult a doctor or your school nurse about these conditions as well as any long-lasting sign of ill health such as sleeplessness, poor appetite, stomach upsets, or lasting feelings of depression. As these problems are faced and dealt with in construc-

Activity sponsors are generally people with whom you can work easily. *Future Homemakers of America*

Tape-record conversations with several students who are considered leaders in school. Ask the boys to comment on the qualities they like and dislike in girls. Ask the girls the same questions about boys. Replay the tapes so the class may discuss the points made. If a tape recorder is not available, take notes on each interview and report to the class.

Bring to class articles from the school paper, magazines, or newspapers which might be a basis for conversation. Practice conversing in groups, using these articles as topics of conversation. Why did some people participate less than others?

tive ways, you will find yourself gaining in assurance, wisdom, and maturity.

SETTING FUTURE GOALS

When you understand yourself, your opportunities, and your available sources of help, you can begin to move in the direction you want to go. The courses you elect in school, the books you read, the friends you make, the activities and clubs you participate in, and the after-school employment you seek can each lead toward the life-style and job choices you make for yourself.

Personal Goals

What kind of a person do you want to be? Confident? Competent? Considerate? Interesting? Well-liked? Responsible? These are goals worth working for. Much of the personal shaping you give to your life takes place between your twelfth and twentieth birthdays. Both your social activities and the things you learn in school aid in this development. Do you want a good education, successful career, happy marriage, close friends, or other worthwhile accomplishments and achievements?

Bulletin board IDEA
Title: *What Do You See in Your Future?*
Directions: Mount a cutout of a telescope. Around it write or use pictures to illustrate college, technical school, military service, on-the-job training, and full-time homemaking situations.

Study the charts here and on the next page. What do they tell you about the average differences in the physical maturity of boys and girls?

APPROXIMATE HEIGHT IN INCHES (CENTIMETERS)

Age		Boys	Girls	
2		35 (87.5)	35 (87.5)	
3		37 (92.5)	37 (92.5)	
4		40 (100)	39 (97.5)	
5	Childhood	42 (105)	43 (107.5)	Childhood
6		45 (112.5)	46 (115)	
7		48 (120)	47 (117.5)	
8		51 (127.5)	49 (122.5)	
9		54 (135)	51 (127.5)	
10		55 (137.5)	53 (132.5)	
11		57 (142.5)	55 (137.5)	Pub.
12	Pub.	57 (142.5)	58 (145)	
13		60 (150)	63 (157.5)	
14		63 (157.5)	64 (160)	
15	Adol.	67 (167.5)	65 (162.5)	Adol.
16		69 (172.5)	66 (165)	
17		70 (175)	67 (167.5)	
18		71 (177.5)	67 (167.5)	

Discuss the reasons why there are great differences in individual height-weight growth patterns.

Discuss why it is normal for some individuals to vary greatly from the height-weight patterns. To what can these individual differences be attributed?

The personal goal of becoming a skilled musician requires self-discipline and many hours of practice. Being rewarded with a lifetime of pleasure often makes it all worthwhile. *Herb Levart/Photo Researchers*

Occupational Goals

What job would you choose for a lifetime occupation? Would you rather work with ideas, people, or things? All work has value, both to the person who does it and to the society that benefits from it. Since work is a part of purposeful living, everyone needs some kind of job.

A lifetime occupation is a serious matter. Many new jobs have developed during your lifetime. There are also thousands of time-honored jobs from which to choose. One of these occupations is the right one for you. Choose a job you like and can do well.

Avoid choosing your lifetime occupation by accident. Your future happiness or misery may depend on the satisfaction you find in working.

YOUR WIDENING CIRCLE OF FRIENDS

As you grow up, you need to establish relationships outside the home. You will continue to love your family and want to be with them. You also will want friends of your own with whom to share some of your hopes, problems, experiences, and secrets. With friends you can develop common interests,

APPROXIMATE WEIGHT IN POUNDS (KILOGRAMS)		
Age	Boys	Girls
2	29 (13.05)	27 (12.60)
3	30 (13.50)	28 (15.75)
4	40 (16.00)	35 (19.35)
5	48 (21.60)	43
6	51 (22.95)	48 (21.60)
7	55 (24.75)	52 (23.40)
8	62 (27.90)	58 (26.10)
9	70 (31.50)	64 (28.80)
10	78 (35.10)	78 (35.10)
11	84 (37.80)	90 (40.50)
12	92 (41.40)	100 (45.00)
13	110 (49.50)	118 (53.10)
14	140 (63.00)	130 (58.50)
15	147 (66.15)	134 (60.30)
16	151 (67.95)	136 (61.20)
17	157 (70.65)	138 (62.10)
18	161 (72.45)	140 (63.00)

(Boys column markers: Childhood, Pub., Adol. — Girls column markers: Childhood, Pub., Adol.)

Volunteering your time and services in an area that interests you can help you later with the decisions you will make concerning a career. *Bob S. Smith/Photo Researchers*

Your career
Dietitian for nursery school

You would plan, prepare, and serve meals or snacks for small children. You should have a knowledge of the nutritional value of foods and general food preferences of children of various ages and backgrounds. You might find employment with day-care centers, nursery schools, churches, or large department stores, shopping centers, or malls.

Write the word FRIENDSHIP on the chalkboard by arranging the letters in a vertical line. Beside each letter write words which describe the kinds of friends you like to have. For example:

F Friendly, forgiving, frank
R Reliable, reassuring
I Interesting
E
N
D
S
H
I
P

Redo the graph, substituting words which describe people you do *not* want as your friends. For example:

F Fretful, flighty, forgetful
R Rude, rebellious
I Impolite
E
N
D
S
H
I
P

Read newspaper advice column letters concerning friendships. Do not read the columnist's response. Write a reply as if you were the columnist. Compare your answer to the one published.

gain new experiences, and enjoy old and new hobbies.

Has it occurred to you that others just like you are looking for true and lasting friendships? Just as you are looking at others, so, too, are others deciding whether they want you for a friend.

Making and Keeping Friends

Most people agree that friendships are important, but some people don't seem to know how to make friends. Friendship is earned and must be deserved. Most people agree that good friends have certain traits in common. What do you look for in a friend? Loyalty? Dependability? Truthfulness? Sincerity? Tolerance?

Friends are people who enjoy being together. They help each other when there is trouble. Do you possess the following set of traits? Can you improve with effort?

1 I can be depended upon to finish those jobs I agree to do.
2 I only make promises I can keep.
3 I am sincere and have a genuine interest in others.
4 I am tactful and considerate of the feelings of others.
5 I look for things to praise rather than to criticize.
6 I am honest and loyal and do not reveal secrets or confidences.
7 I respect others' belongings. I seldom borrow, I take good care of borrowed items, and I return them.

Friendships are likely to begin in the neighborhood or at school. If you are friendly and relaxed and treat all people in a considerate way, you will attract friends. Friendship cannot be bought. A person who tries to impress others with possessions will not attract sincere friendships.

It takes time to make a real friend. If you are new in a neighborhood and feel unaccepted, be patient. Friendships worth having are worth waiting for and working toward. Enter into activities which interest you. It is natural for people to select their friends from among those who enjoy the same kinds of activities they themselves like. Similar values also attract people to one another. You may need to study a new friend's actions before deciding whether to continue a friendly association.

Friendships need not end when people move. You can keep in touch through letters, cards, visits, or telephone calls.

Values of Friendships

Friendships enrich our lives by what we give as well as by what we get. Friends make each other feel like worthwhile people. They accept each other. In so doing, they fulfill each other's basic need for acceptance. A wide variety of friends usually helps to make a person more interesting. In many communities there are students who have lived in other states and

Friends share interests, good times, and mutual respect for one another. *Erika/Peter Arnold Photo Archives*

Present miniskits showing correct and incorrect ways for a boy or girl to ask a date to a party. Plan skits which show correct and incorrect ways to refuse the invitation.

Act out situations in which a date comes to a girl's home to pick her up. Include the girl's family in the scene. Discuss ways the situation was handled well. If appropriate, make suggestions for improving the situation.

Practice mock situations in which a couple on a date order refreshments. Show the difficulties girls face when boys do not give them hints concerning the cost of food to order. Discuss the problems of spending too much on a date.

Bulletin board IDEA
Title: *Fishing for a Date?*
Better Check Your Bait!
Directions: Use a large figure holding a stick that looks like a fishing pole. Dangle string from the pole. On cutouts of fish at the bottom of the board, write traits of a good date such as *good conversationalist, sense of humor, considerate, good manners.*

countries. Friendships with such people can broaden your understanding of your country and the world.

It is important to have friends of both sexes and many different backgrounds. You can learn something from everyone. Friendship with a member of another race or ethnic group can help you learn to appreciate how much alike all people are. Such friendships also help you see how silly, unfounded, and wasteful prejudice can be.

Practice making introductions. Include examples which illustrate introducing:

A friend from school and your mother

A teacher and your grandmother

A man and a woman

Two of your friends, one a boy and one a girl

Your career
Resident manager

You would act as manager, advisor, and counselor to a group of people living in a single residence. You might order household supplies, plan menus, and determine need for maintenance, repairs, and furnishings. You might also assist in planning recreational activities, and supervise work and study programs. Attending group-sponsored trips and social functions as a chaperon might also be a part of your job. You might find employment with boarding schools, colleges, children's homes, and halfway houses or rehabilitation homes.

It is equally important to be aware of the problems involved with being a member of a gang or *clique*, a closed circle, within your school. A clique usually bands together for security or status reasons. The general student body may consider members of cliques to be unfriendly. As a result, young people in the closed circle lose opportunities to form friendships among interesting students outside the group.

YOUR SOCIAL GROWTH

Social growth pertains to growth in the area of human relationships. Whether you are learning to live with your family, schoolmates, or casual acquaintances, you are experiencing social growth. Boy-girl relationships often become the area of social growth in which teenagers are most keenly interested.

The difference in the rate of social maturity between boys and girls is rather clearly pronounced by the time they become teenagers. The fact that girls become interested in dating before boys of the same age frequently causes problems. At certain stages of social development, boys who can work happily in mixed groups to complete class projects tend to prefer the company of boys for social occasions. This can make girls feel rejected.

Wise teenagers understand there is a real difference in dating readiness between boys and girls during the early teens. Group functions and group activities allow for normal social growth of both boys and girls.

Certain customs have grown up around the dating involved with social growth. Local customs differ, but in general a few common practices apply. In the beginning, girls and boys simply attend the same social events. Adults are often responsible for safe transportation to and from such occasions.

As teenagers begin to take a special interest in one another, the approach changes. Boys and girls begin inviting each other to special functions. The invited one must then accept or reject the invitation. Whether the answer is *yes* or *no*, courtesy is required. Both boys and girls should have an understanding with their parents about the time they will be home after a date, and there should be an arrangement to inform both families of any changes in these plans.

Group Dating

Group dating is usually the first sign of boy-girl social interest. A group of boys and girls may plan an outing. This may include swimming, bowling, skating, or hiking. The number of boys and girls may or may not be equal. In such a group, everyone can have a good time. School events and those sponsored by other organizations provide opportunities for young teens to learn how to get along easily with members of the opposite sex. When group activities are planned, each individual usually pays his own way. However, when a group goes to a park or a beach to cook dinner and spend the evening, the food may be furnished by some and the transportation by others. Music from a portable radio or record player may be their entertainment.

Double Dating

After a certain amount of experience in group dating, two girls and two boys may plan a double date. A double date is most enjoyable when both couples are about the same age and share the same interests. Activities enjoyed by larger groups

Two people are able to learn more about each other as they spend time together. *Chester Higgins, Jr./Photo Researchers*

are also suitable for double dates. Each boy may assume the financial obligation of one girl or a pay-your-own-way arrangement may be the local custom. When expenses are to be shared on a date, it should be made clear in advance.

Sometimes double-daters will join a larger group to share the fun of a local party. The presence of others helps beginning daters to feel more at ease.

Single Dating

As teenagers mature, they may go on single dates, social occasions which include only two people. At other times they may prefer to join another couple or a group. In many places, single dating is not practiced by young teenagers. Since so much of the fun of dating is the sharing of activities, many young people prefer to date in groups.

Going Steady

A *steady* arrangement, where one boy and one girl date each other exclusively, sometimes follows single dating. To some teenagers, this dating arrangement gives the assurance of a dating partner. It does cut down, however, on opportunities to meet others.

Going steady also has the disadvantage that, if one member tires of the arrangement, the other may be very hurt and confused.

The attitudes of families toward steady dating arrangements vary. Some families approve heartily of

Suggest places to go and things to do in your community for group, double, and single dates. Include activities which cost little or no money.

Give advantages and disadvantages of group, double, and single dates. Discuss reasons why many teenagers prefer to begin dating in groups.

Discuss the advantages and disadvantages of going steady. Describe how going steady can mean different things to different people. Give examples to illustrate how going steady has different meanings for different people and in different communities.

Divide into discussion groups to read a letter about a dating problem appearing in an advice column of a daily newspaper. Discuss possible solutions to the problem. Decide, as a group, on your best ideas for answering the letter. Share them with the class. Ask other class members for solutions to the problem. Discuss all the suggestions and compare them to the columnist's reply.

Divide the chalkboard into three vertical columns. Label the left-hand column *friend*, the middle column *date*, and the right-hand column *mate*. Brainstorm to list the qualities desired in each kind of companion. Discuss the reasons for the similarities and differences in the lists.

Tell about an experience when a person was dressed inappropriately for a particular occasion. Discuss the ways in which this situation could have been avoided.

Use a tape recorder to hear how your voice sounds to others. Make suggestions for improving your voice and enunciation.

Let students in the class who have a flair for the dramatic, each present a monologue in which they are trying to carry on a conversation with a shy member of the opposite sex. Afterwards, suggest questions this person might have asked to stimulate the conversation and to draw out the untalkative person. Give examples of the types of questions which should be avoided such as those which are too personal, too difficult, or require only a yes or no answer.

teenagers going with only one person. They feel they can trust their judgment in choosing places to go and in getting home safely. Other families definitely disapprove of the idea of steady dating. They fear teenagers are likely to become emotionally involved with each other long before serious ideas of marriage can be considered.

Wise teenagers go along with their parents' wishes concerning dating activities and the time to return home. When they prove their parents can trust them, rules are usually loosened to the point that dating and social activities can be of their own choosing.

Dating Etiquette

Successful dating takes at least two thoughtful people. They are careful as they ask for and accept dates. They are careful to keep their parents informed of their plans. They are thoughtful enough to dress in an acceptable manner and to help their dating partner have a good time.

Planning entertainment
Often good times happen almost on the spur of the moment. However, it is usually safer to make plans in advance. That way, both daters are dressed appropriately for the planned event. Can you think of anything more likely to get a date started wrong than to have the girl show up in jeans when the boy is wearing his new suit?

A boy and girl can have fun on a blind date if the plans have been made by friends who know both of them. For instance, a cousin or friend may arrive at your home unexpectedly. If you have already made dating plans, it is all right to consult your date about finding someone to make up a foursome. Plans for this type of date might include a movie and a snack. Such a plan allows you to help a friend entertain your guest who is a stranger to him or her.

Shared interests often make the best basis for a successful date. For example, couples who enjoy ice skating may have fun on a skating date. The date could be rather disappointing, however, if only one of them can skate. Sometimes at the close of an enjoyable occasion, arrangements may be made for a future date.

Asking for a date
When asking someone for a date, you both should be clear about the plans. Asking only, "Are you doing anything Friday night?," can be an embarrassing question for both parties. A far better approach would be, "Can you go with me to the basketball game Friday night?" The invitation can easily be accepted or rejected without hurting or embarrassing either person.

A date can be arranged in person or by a telephone call. If friends live far apart, plans can be made by letter.

Accepting a date

You have an obligation to make a prompt decision concerning an invitation. It is unfair to keep a person dangling in hopes that something better may turn up. If you must check with your parents before accepting an invitation, you should say so rather than hedge. Others understand that many teens have family regulations. They can appreciate the family concern. If you cannot or do not care to accept an invitation, be considerate of the other person's feelings. Refuse politely.

Dressing for a date

Because parties, ball games, movies, and other teenage functions are run on a time schedule, courtesy requires you to be dressed and ready when a date calls for you. This includes being dressed appropriately for the occasion.

Acceptable clothing for dates varies from one area to another and from year to year. If you do not know what to wear, your friends can give you suggestions. Knowing you will be dressed in the same manner as others in the group will help give you self-confidence.

There is a difference between being casual and being sloppy in your dress. Even a fancy party dress, suit, or sport coat can be sloppy if it is soiled or ill-fitting, while jeans and a knitted shirt can be clean and neat. It isn't *what* you wear as much as *how* you wear it that counts.

We should all avoid appearing in public in conspicuous clothing. Clothing not suited to the wearer or appropriate to the occasion can make the wearer and others feel ill at ease. A see-through shirt or beachwear in a restaurant or formal clothing at a casual dance can all cause embarrassment.

Gaining family approval

Parents are responsible for their children until the children are launched into lives of their own. When families ask about dating

A moment spent informing parents of changed plans is a courtesy which encourages parent-teenager understandings. *Bob Cook*

List occupations which exist today which were unheard of in your grandparents' day. Name occupations which were important in the past for which there is no longer any demand. What caused these changes?

Suggest possible part-time job opportunities for teenagers in various types of seasonal work associated with holidays, harvest times, tourist seasons, sports events, and special festivals or local celebrations.

Name occupations for which there is on-the-job training. How do businesses provide ways to keep employees up-to-date on new methods, trends, and advances? How do self-employed people keep up with new developments?

Present a fashion show of outfits that might be worn in a variety of job situations. Try to determine the work of each model by the clothes worn.

Analyze your personality, aptitudes, and interests. Then select several occupations for which you might be suited. For each of these, find out about the demand, the amount of education or training required, chances for advancement, beginning and potential salaries, advantages, and disadvantages.

Answer this letter as if you were Pat's long-time friend and advisor:

Dear Fran,

I wish I could see you and talk over something very important. You always have a level head and give good advice. I could use some now. Here's the situation — I have been offered a job. It is a good job, $2.50 an hour, down at the Center Cafeteria. They need someone immediately and tell me that they don't care whether I have a high school diploma or not since they are so short-handed. They tell me I can learn food service while I am working. Just think, I can earn about $100 a week. What I couldn't do with that! That's the score. Should I stick with school or grab this opportunity? I must decide soon or the job will be gone. Please answer right away.

As ever,
Pat

List opportunities in your community for boys and girls your age to make money.

plans, they are usually showing responsible interest and concern, rather than trying to interfere. Thoughtful teenagers respond to this interest by telling their families where they are going, how they will get there, and when they plan to return home.

A considerate boy arrives at the girl's home at the time set for the date. He always calls for her at the door. If he has not met her parents, she will invite him in and introduce them. In using the commonly accepted form of introduction, the girl presents the boy to her parents, saying, "Mom and Dad, this is . . . ." She may mention her parents' last name if it is different from her own. Sometimes the girl's parents will mention what time they expect their daughter to return home. The girl and boy should respect her parent's wishes in this matter.

With her parents' permission, a girl may invite her date in for a snack after he brings her home. An at-home snack is one of the ways a girl can help balance out a boy's dating expenses.

It is unwise to invite a date into the house if a parent or other adult is not at home.

Dating behavior

On a date for which a boy has extended the invitation, he usually takes care of the expenses involved. Since the boy's finances may be limited, the girl should be considerate in her suggestions for entertain-

ment and food. If two people get along well together, such inexpensive events as school activities and neighborhood gatherings can be enjoyable. Overspending seldom adds to the success of a date.

Having arranged a date, both people are responsible for making the event enjoyable. If they join another couple or group, each should be sure the other is having a good time. Activities should be continual so embarrassing silences do not occur. Keeping the conversation going is the responsibility of both parties. Conversation is not a monologue, with one person doing all the talking, but a dialogue in which two people take part.

Some girls feel they do not know what to talk about when they are with boys. And some boys feel the same way with girls. Here is where a little knowledge of many things and the development of many interests can be important. Ask questions to find the interests of your date. At the same time, be willing to answer your date's questions in a pleasant manner. If you help your partner talk about his or her interests, you are sure to be considered a good conversationalist.

Avoid the mistake of talking only about yourself, especially on dates. That sort of conversation can be very tiresome. Equally boring and in poor taste are descriptions of other occasions or other dates.

It is your responsibility to keep track of the time and to get home on time. This may not be easy, especially when a group is having fun, because the hours have a way of slipping by.

Your ability to be a good date depends on how well you get along with others and how pleasantly you adjust to group decisions. Being a good date, however, does not mean you must disregard your own values or your own code of behavior. The decisions of another person or the crowd are not always best for you. *You* have to decide when to go along with a plan and when to use your own judgment as to your actions.

If it is necessary, as it may be, for one party to break a date, he or she must be honest and tell the other the reason, expressing regret. One date should not be broken to accept another date. Dates should be broken only when absolutely necessary. Keep in mind how you would feel if someone broke a date with you to go out with another person. Making and breaking dates carelessly is a sign of immaturity and selfishness.

YOUR VOCATIONAL GROWTH

Growth, as most people view it, means getting taller, or heavier, or bigger in some way. From a vocational point of view, growth doesn't come about in this manner. Vocational growth is measured in the education, attitudes, and skills you are acquiring.

In a social situation, activities are centered around people. Your ability to get along well with people is also important in work situations. However, the emphasis is changed. The purpose of a job is to produce goods or services. Your ability to adjust your thinking away from yourself and to the job at hand determines your readiness for vocational undertakings.

The Economics of Your Job Choice

Most jobs require some education or skill. As the world of work continues to become more technical, special training is necessary for most any job. Of course, there is a relationship between education and earning power. However, with the push in our society for a good education for every child, many people have been educated in the wrong direction. It is possible that too many people are being educated for *professional* work and too few are training to become *skilled* workers.

You are facing vocational choices at a time when there is a change in the total thinking affecting the world of work. Today may be the time when people can choose and train for jobs they like. Income may be based on the *quality* of work rather than *choice of occupation*. What kind of work would you like?

Possible Job Choices

You have something of value to offer to society. It is time to think

 Invite a school counselor to come to class to discuss occupational opportunities in your local area and in the state. Ask about the type of education and training required to fill one of these positions. You may also ask about the costs involved in attending a junior college, private or state college or university, business school, or a vocational-technical school.

Invite a person from the local state employment office to come to class to discuss the employment situation in your community. Discuss the effects of the local employment situation on teenagers and their families.

Bulletin board IDEA
Title: *Graze in the Fields of Career Opportunities*
Directions: Mount a large drawing or cutout of a cow, giraffe, horse, or other grazing animal on the bulletin board. Or use a stuffed animal toy or pillow. On cutouts of leaves, write the names of careers in which students have expressed interest.

CAREERS IN HOME ECONOMICS

Child Care   *Grand Valley State College*

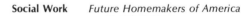

Interior Design   *Lubbock Avalanche-Journal*

Textile Research   *Celanese Fibers Marketing Company*

Social Work   *Future Homemakers of America*

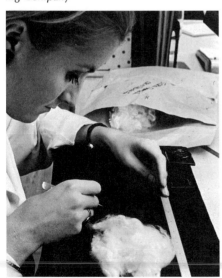

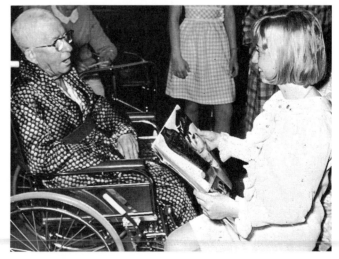

seriously about the things you can offer as well as the opportunities available. It may be too early for setting your final vocational goal, but it is wise to begin thinking of things you would like to do. Consider your talents and abilities as you think of possible job choices. Try to be sensible in choosing a job you can do successfully.

By now you have noticed occupations briefly presented in the illustrations and side columns of this book. When you read about an occupation which particularly interests you, search in your school library for facts concerning that occupation. Ask your teacher or counselor for information or help as you begin to think about your future in the world of work.

Check yourself

As you consider your occupation of the future, think of the work habits and attitudes you are developing to help you make a success of your life's work. Check the statements listed on the following chart (page 96). Your ability to honestly say *yes* in relation to the job of your choice indicates your growth toward vocational success.

Tying Present to Future

As you continue to study home economics, you will become aware of many job opportunities in this field. As a young teenager, you may make a general study of the various areas within home economics. In advanced courses you may study a single area in greater detail.

Home economics is divided into seven large areas. They include:

- Family relations
- Child development
- Housing and home furnishing
- Consumer education
- Home management
- Clothing and textiles
- Food and nutrition

In each of these seven areas there are a number of jobs requiring various amounts of formal education. You might enjoy working with families. Perhaps your interests are in working with small children. Perhaps you would like to work in a hospital kitchen or in a restaurant or school cafeteria. Perhaps your interests lie in the fields of foods or textile research. Perhaps you would prefer to design clothing or to work in the field of merchandising. Perhaps you would like to work with architects to build efficient housing. Or perhaps you would like to work with furniture, colors, and fabrics in the field of interior decoration. Whatever your choice, there are opportunities at many levels in every field.

These are only a few of the opportunities open to both men and women. The occupation you choose may determine whether you will work while finishing high school or whether you will continue your education at a technical school, a community college, or a

Divide the class into seven discussion groups. Let each group take one of the following areas of home economics and brainstorm for occupational opportunities in that field:

Child Development
Consumer Education
Home Management
Family Relations
Foods and Nutrition
Textiles and Clothing
Housing and Interior Design

List for the class the occupations mentioned in each area. Ask the class as a whole to suggest additional opportunities in each of these fields.

Interview people employed in occupations relating to the seven areas of home economics. Find out what they like about their work. Develop a list of qualifications for people engaged in each of these occupations. Tell the class about your interviews.

Your career
Visiting homemaker

You would visit homes to assume the responsibilities of the homemaker. This might be a temporary or long-range position in homes where illness or death have deprived the family of the homemaker's services. You might also visit the homes of elderly or ill adults to aid them in homemaking chores. You might find employment through government or private agencies or community services.

Bulletin board IDEA
Title: *Fly the Flag of Home Economics . . .*
Directions: Use poster board or construction paper to make flags shaped as if the wind were blowing through them. On the flags write *Food and Nutrition, Child Development, Home Management, Housing, Clothing and Textiles,* and the names of other areas in home economics. Underneath write . . . *That Interests You Most*

Check your salable work habits

1 I have a real desire to learn new skills and new ways of doing things.
2 I am neat in my personal appearance and my personal work habits.
3 I am punctual.
4 I can apply myself to a job without being easily bored or distracted.
5 I can work under pressure, when necessary, without becoming nervous or upset.
6 I can adapt to new or unexpected situations.
7 I have confidence in my own abilities.
8 I have a sense of duty and responsibility.
9 I can cooperate with other workers.
10 I can gain the friendship and respect of other workers.
11 I can cooperate with supervision and management.
12 I respect authority and can follow directions willingly and without argument.
13 I can understand instructions and carry them out accurately.
14 I can accept criticism without feeling hurt.
15 I can work without constant supervision.
16 I ask questions about things I don't understand.
17 I can complete a job once I start it.
18 I am a pleasant person to work with.
19 I like people.

How did you do? If you answered yes to most of the statements, you will probably be a good employee.

---

university. Be fair to yourself; try to get the best education common sense will allow you to obtain. Each person's educational goals are affected by his family's financial situation and his own ability to learn. Yet, there is some form of education or training suitable for every person who wants it. Education is very often related to earnings over a lifetime.

As early as possible, decide what you would like to do. Learn the requirements necessary for work in that field. Your day-to-day actions can easily determine the degree of success you will have in your chosen occupation.

Match the *descriptions* in List A with the *terms* in List B. Use each term from List B only once.

List A: Descriptions

A Good education, successful marriage, useful and satisfying occupation.

B Sincerity, honesty, loyalty, reliability.

C Actions and behavior.

D A circle of friends which tends to exclude others.

E Employment skills.

List B: Terms

1 Clique
2 Personal goals
3 Standards of conduct
4 Values
5 Vocation

Number from 1 to 20. Beside each number indicate if the corresponding statement is true or false. *Do not* write in this book.

1 The satisfactions people find in their occupations have an effect on their overall happiness in life.

2 Some people try to buy friendship with material possessions.

3 It is unreasonable for parents of teenagers to expect their children to be home from a party at a predetermined time.

4 Double dating has some advantages that single dating does not have.

5 When two boys and two girls pair off and go out together, it is called a double date.

6 A good way to ask for a date is to inquire, "Are you busy Saturday night?"

7 When a boy asks a girl for a date, he should tell her where they will be going.

8 It is socially acceptable to break a date with one person to accept a date with another.

9 It is poor manners to remain in the car and blow the horn to indicate to your date that you are there.

10 After a date arrives at your house, you should take five to ten minutes to finish getting ready so that you will not appear too eager.

11 Good grooming indicates respect for your date as well as self-respect.

12 The best way for you to introduce a friend to your parents is to say, "Leslie, I'd like you to meet my mother and father."

13 On a date, it is poor manners to talk about dates you have had with other people.

14 On a date, it is your responsibility to keep track of the time and to say when it is time to go home.

15 A blind date is arranged by others without the two people involved knowing anything about the situation.

16 Dating contributes to preparation for marriage.

17 Vocational growth is achieved only through education.

18 Careers in the fields of home economics are for women only.

19 Social skills are an asset in any occupation.

20 Because there will be new and different career opportunities when you are out of school, there is no need to plan for the world of work now.

Give the following information on a separate sheet of paper.

1 Name four sources of vocational guidance.

2 Describe eight salable work habits which would be assets in any occupation.

3 Give three disadvantages to going steady in the early teens.

4 List five courtesies, or rules of etiquette, to be followed in accepting or rejecting an invitation.

98

Unit 2

Your Home and Family

Number from 1 to 15 on a piece of paper. Beside each number write the letter which corresponds to the *best* answer for that question. *Do not write in this book.*

1 Which is a basic *physical* need?
  a Acceptance
  b Security
  c Independence
  d Shelter

2 Which is the most important *emotional* need provided by a family?
  a Money
  b Food
  c Clothing
  d Security

3 Which has the greatest influence on men's and women's roles?
  a Number of children in the family
  b Family cultural background
  c Total family income
  d Place of residence

4 Which child in a family is most likely to be self-reliant?
  a An only child
  b The youngest child
  c A middle child
  d The oldest child

5 Which child in a family is most likely to be *dependent* on parents?
  a An only child
  b The youngest child
  c A middle child
  d The oldest child

6 Which child in a family is most likely to experience feelings of jealousy?
  a The youngest child
  b A middle child
  c The oldest child
  d A twin

7 Which is most likely to cause quarrels among brothers and sisters?
  a Use of allowance
  b Use of leisure time at home
  c School work
  d Household chores

8 Which family member usually makes the greatest number of consumer decisions?
  a Mother
  b Father
  c Sister
  d Brother

9 Which is another name for a family spending plan?
  a Expense account
  b Budget
  c Cost of living
  d Mortgage

10 Which is the most important consideration in selecting a gift for one of your friends?
  a It is something you would like to have.
  b It can be wrapped easily.
  c It is something your friend would like to have.
  d It looks as if it cost more than it did.

11 Which is *least* likely to change if a mother goes to work?
  a Total family income
  b Children's choice of friends
  c Mother's role
  d Father's role

12 Which has had the *least* influence on changes in men's and women's roles?
  a The rising cost of living
  b Higher education for women
  c Modern household equipment and appliances
  d Commercially made clothes

13 Which of the following is *not* a true statement?
  a People live longer today than they did in past generations.
  b Loneliness may accompany old age.
  c Physical changes are evident during a person's later years.
  d A three-generation family is bound to be an unhappy one.

14 Which is *not* a material possession?
  a Money
  b Car
  c Skill
  d TV set

15 Which is *not* a family resource?
  a Material possessions
  b Talent of a family member
  c Services of a family member
  d Poor health of a family member

Chapter 6

Enjoying Your Home for Family Living

A home is more than a house. It is the combination of all the materials, talents, skills, activities, feelings, and hopes which a group of people draws upon to build itself into a family. Think of what a home can offer: physical protection; mental, social, emotional, and moral guidance; love, security, and a sense of belonging. These provide a background against which a family helps its young members prepare for adulthood and older members for satisfying lives. In fact, it is this kind of background which makes a happy, meaningful home for anyone who lives there.

MEETING PHYSICAL NEEDS

Food, clothing, and shelter are basic and necessary for normal development. But if a child is to grow into a well-rounded adult, basics are not

Decide which of the following you consider essential for happy family life. Discuss your decisions in class. *Do not* write in this book.

1 The parents provide the children with plenty of spending money.
2 The parents encourage the children to share and to be cooperative.
3 All family members speak English.
4 The parents require that the children be good athletes, good musicians, and good students.
5 Plans are made which allow for all family members, including very young ones, to have some experiences away from home.
6 The home is located in the best section of town.
7 The mother does most of the work, and the children have no home responsibilities.
8 Rest and relaxation are planned for all family members.
9 Family members are encouraged to have friends their own age.
10 The family is interested in helping each member do at least one worthwhile thing well.
11 Each child has his or her own room.

enough. Quality enters in. Within the home, each child needs to receive *nourishing* food, *appropriate* clothing, and *clean, dry* shelter from the elements. The home which meets each of these needs adds further meaning to life if it does so in a spirit of love. How does your home add meaning to your life?

MEETING MENTAL AND EMOTIONAL NEEDS

The family providing love and security offers its members the opportunity to grow mentally and emotionally. Being able to talk to others at home and having them listen contributes to emotional development. Mental and emotional needs are also met in the environment of the neighborhood and school and through social activities. Through activities at home or those approved by the family, young people grow at a more rapid pace than if neglected by older family members.

Security is one of the most important things a home can offer its members. When family members are accepted for what they are, they are better able to develop as secure members of the family group. In modern society, many young people are accepted into a home other than their natural one. If they are

Most parents attach great importance to the security and the social and physical development of their children. *Erich Hartmann/Magnum*

accepted for what they are, generally there soon develops a close family relationship between all of those who live together.

The security a home gives is not just financial or material in nature. It also includes the assurance you feel when there is a special spot only you can fill. Perhaps only people who have lived alone for a long time can appreciate fully the security of a home. They know what is missing in a life where there is no family to turn to for advice, comfort, appreciation, or understanding.

You may take your home for granted now, not realizing its true value. You may feel your family doesn't understand you very well. But even when there is some quarreling and bickering at home, the family circle is the place where most young people feel more secure, comfortable, and loved than in any other group. For them, the home offers stability they may never again find until they have homes of their own.

GETTING ALONG WITH PARENTS

Have you ever considered the many roles your parents play as parents? In a world that is changing as rapidly as ours, their responsibilities are many and sometimes heavy. Financial pressures, the day-to-day grind of a job, illness, or personal problems may make them worried and tense at times. Often they are tired.

Still, they must go on with the job of being a parent and continue with their other activities as well.

Many of their responsibilities are rewarding. Parents are happy to see the growth and development of their children. Most of them enjoy their family's achievements and find pleasure in being with their children. By showing pride in your parents' achievements at work or at home, you can make life seem more rewarding to them.

Being a Parent

The job of parenthood is, in a sense, the most responsible job a person ever accepts. With parenthood comes the responsibility for the growth and well-being of a child, whether natural or adopted. The outcome of a life rests to a large degree in the hands of parents. Imagine what your life would be like if your parents were not on the job every day. Then consider the many ways in which you are dependent upon them and the many responsibilities they have.

Providing for the family

Most families try to provide for their children's physical needs, as well as to give the protection, guidance, love, and security their children require. Parents, or parent substitutes, need to be on hand so children can talk over problems with them in the hope of making wise decisions. At the same time they can make an effort to steer the

12 The family generally enjoys doing things together.

13 The family provides opportunities for the children to make money by helping around the house.

14 The father earns a big salary.

15 The children's clothes are always new and store-bought.

16 The parents express their love for their children through their actions.

17 The family always eats in a dining room.

18 The family's food is nutritious.

19 All foods served are made from scratch.

20 The house is up-to-date and modern with the newest types of equipment.

21 The father is employed in a professional occupation.

22 The house is warm, dry, and comfortable.

23 The family goes regularly to a doctor or to a clinic.

24 The mother has a career outside the home.

25 The family members are proud of each others' accomplishments.

Why are there no right and wrong answers to some of these questions?

Why do the class members consider different factors essential for happy family living?

Relate human growth and development in a family to the story of a tree below.

A seed was once planted in a garden. It sprouted to be handled with tender loving care and knowledge by the gardeners. Mistakes were made, but none of them permanently scarred the tree. As the tree grew older, it began to show its independence and self-sufficiency. The tree was still loved, but the gardeners knew that the same amount of care and attention given the tree as a tiny twig would only smother and suffocate it as it was growing now. The gardeners stood by the tree, though, ready to help in times of disease, drought, or wintry storm.

Discuss factors which have contributed to famous personalities' character development. Include people such as Abraham Lincoln, Martin Luther King, Rose Kennedy, or Nelson Rockefeller. How did early guidance and experiences in these people's lives contribute to their view of the world and their attitudes toward life?

List the concerns, responsibilities, problems, and worries your parents have. List your own concerns, responsibilities, problems, and worries. Compare the lists. Draw conclusions from this comparison.

A parent frequently fills the roles of both companion and teacher in today's society. *Paul Fusco/Magnum*

family along a smooth course, hopefully preventing small irritations from becoming major problems. They also must handle day-to-day tasks as they plan ahead for the family's future.

Understanding parents' problems

Parents are expected to set a good example. Often, however, this is difficult because adults have problems as serious as those of their children. Sometimes teenagers forget that their parents have many of the same difficulties they have and also many of the same desires. Parents may be facing problems such as getting along with each other, helping their own aging parents or other relatives, and handling heavy job responsibilities. They may have worries about unemployment, the cost of living, personal appearance, health, or other things they never mention. As young people begin to understand that other people have problems important to them, the tensions within their homes tend to ease.

In families where parents do not get along well with each other, young people need to be especially cooperative and understanding. The teenager's cooperation is even more important in situations where parents are separated. Parents may be divorced, and children may live with one parent or with their mother and stepfather or with their father and stepmother. Such situations may call for more understanding than teenagers can give unless they get the help of a trusted outside person.

In your relations with your parents, it is essential you try to understand their side of any matter. Also, try to explain your side so they can understand your way of thinking. A certain amount of give-and-take is necessary in happy parent-child relationships.

Changing Family Roles

When this country began, men's and women's roles were much more clearly defined than they are today. Men were expected to be the breadwinners, to make the laws, and to run the government. Men were the leaders in society. Women were expected to serve men's needs. Women were responsible for baking and cooking, cleaning the house, rearing the children, and caring for the sick. Traditionally, women were expected to stay at home and take care of the homemaking tasks.

People's cultural backgrounds influence what tasks they expect men and women to do. There are no *good* or *bad* cultural patterns, but there are different cultural patterns with different expectations for men and women. These depend largely upon family background.

Technological advances, scientific discoveries, social changes, and economic conditions have affected family life. In many homes there are no longer *men's jobs* and *women's jobs*. Responsibilities are more likely to be shared.

Many men work shorter and more regular hours than in the past. This leaves time for child care and homemaking tasks. Modern home appliances and equipment may have made homemaking more appealing to some men. It is not at all unusual to see a father and his children buying the groceries or doing the family laundry at the local laundromat.

Family members frequently perform tasks formerly considered to be only a mother's responsibility, while she does things that traditionally were not part of her role.
Mimi Forsyth/Monkmeyer

Classify each of the following tasks as traditionally being men's or women's work around the house.

Taking out the garbage
Changing baby's diaper
Preparing dinner
Washing the car
Mowing the lawn
Mending torn clothes

Add other chores to the list. How have roles changed so these jobs are no longer necessarily men's or women's work? How have changes in society influenced changes in ideas about traditional roles?

Identify families in books, TV programs, and movies in which individual family members portray traditional roles.

Write and present skits showing how men and women may share homemaking tasks when both are employed.

Give examples of technological advances and new household equipment and appliances that have made homemaking less time-consuming than in the past.

Listen to an appropriate short dramatic reading or tape recording from *God's Little Acre* or *The Grapes of Wrath*. Discuss the effects of environment on the interpersonal relationships of the people characterized.

Your career
Homemaker's aide

You would assist busy home-makers with routine cleaning, laundry, meal preparation, and child-care responsibilities. You might help with planning parties and serving guests. You would work in homes where your services were needed on a full-time or part-time basis. A government or private agency might help you find work.

Bulletin board IDEA
Title: *Making a House a Home*
Directions: Use a picture or sketch of a house or apartment building in the center. Around it mount pictures showing activities such as a family enjoying a meal together, a parent giving a child tender loving care, a family entertaining friends and relatives at a cookout, or children's artwork hanging on the wall.

As a break from hectic routine schedules, parents need to spend some relaxed time together.
Robert Capece

In many homes, both parents work. One may work during the day, and the other may work at night. The parent who is at home often takes care of the children. In some families, traditional roles have even been completely reversed. The mother may work full time, and the father may be a full-time homemaker. Men and women are increasingly becoming the heads of one-parent families. Laws have been revised in many states to allow single people to adopt children.

When the parent responsible for the smooth running of the home is also working outside the home, help, cooperation, and understanding of other family members is required. Responsibilities should be shared so that family members have a reasonable amount of leisure time to be enjoyed together or in pursuit of personal interests and hobbies.

UNDERSTANDING BROTHERS AND SISTERS

There are advantages and disadvantages in being one of several children. Each child plays a role in the family. The roles may vary, depending on the age of the child, the position of the child in the family, and on the size of the family. If you are a member of a large family, there may be times when you depend on the

106

Children within a family generally learn to adapt to a family situation, whether they are an only child or one of several. *Evelyn Appel*

warmth of your relationship with your brothers or sisters. Then there may be times when you get tired of having brothers and sisters and wish you could be completely free of them. You may feel guilty if you are annoyed to this point. It is not unusual to feel annoyed with those with whom you must associate. Even your best friend would probably irritate you if you lived and worked together in the same home day after day.

Accepting That Children in a Family Are Different

Within a family, children frequently have very different traits, values, goals, and personalities. The only child in a family may take an entirely different outlook on life from that of children in larger families. Twins, while often different from each other, share a companionship unlike that held between any other family members. In large families, children soon learn to share with others.

There are likely to be some differences in the way children are affected by their positions in the family. That is, whether you are the oldest child, a middle child, the youngest child, or an only child can influence your personality, responsibilities, and reactions to family situations.

Oldest children

The oldest child was an only child until a younger brother or sister was

Divide into four groups: those students who are the oldest in their families in one group, those who are the youngest in another group, those who are middle children in another group, and those who are only children in another. In these groups, discuss the advantages and disadvantages of that particular position in a family. Report the results of these discussions to the entire class. What general conclusions can be made?

Discuss the reasons why *identical* twins may develop different personalities although their hereditary backgrounds are more alike than those of any other two individuals.

Discuss the advantages and disadvantages of being the only boy in a family of all girls or the only girl in a family of all boys.

Suggest ways in which an expectant mother can prepare an older child for the arrival of a new baby. Suggest things the parents and other family members can do after the new baby has come home which will give older children a sense of security.

Suggest ways to control jealousy and anger in yourself and in others. Be specific.

Act out situations showing possible sources of conflict because children of varying ages in the family have different activities, interests, and friends. Situations may involve:

Family chores and responsibilities
Use of the telephone
Use of others' possessions
Freedom to choose own clothes
Use of makeup
Age to begin dating

Plan a home experience project for improving yourself as a family member. Carry out your plan for one month. Report the results to your class or teacher.

Write *Golden Rules for Getting Along with* _____. Choose someone in your family with whom you would like to improve your relationship.

Tell the class about incidents you have observed, read about, or seen on TV in which a family cooperated to work out a conflict.

Bulletin board IDEA
Title: *The Lid Is Off*
Directions: Use a simple line drawing of a jack-in-the-box. Mount cartoons relating to quarrels among family members. Discuss the humor in the situations pictured. Suggest possible reasons and solutions for the problem situations.

By taking an active part in the care of a new brother or sister, the oldest child gains a sense of love and responsibility. *Burke Uzzle/Magnum*

born. An only child enjoyed the undivided attention of parents until younger brothers and sisters joined the family. Sometimes improperly handled oldest children never fully accept their brothers and sisters. They resent the fact that their parents' attention must be shared with others. As a rule, however, they outgrow this resentment. They are happy in helping with the younger children and may assume many more responsibilities than the younger children do. As a result, they may become quite self-reliant. At the same time, they may tend to be bossy toward younger brothers and sisters. Of course, because they are older, it is also likely that they will have some special privileges along with special responsibilities.

Middle children
Sometimes it seems that middle children have a difficult place in the family. They may envy or try to do things done by the oldest child in the family. At the same time they may seek the kind of attention being given a younger brother or sister. There are advantages in the middle family position, however. Middle children may be spared some of the mistakes made by parents in working with the first child in the family. Too, they are likely to grow out of babyhood sooner than if they were the youngest child.

Youngest children

Sometimes youngest children may have too much done for them. Their parents often do not expect as much of them as was expected of their older brothers and sisters at the same ages. Brothers and sisters tend to help younger children out of difficult situations. They may think of them as babies, even when they are old enough to do many things for themselves. On the other hand, youngest children have brothers and sisters to act as playmates and to show them how to do things. Generally, they grow up feeling accepted as an important member of the family group. Nevertheless, they need to be aware, as they move into circles beyond the home, that they may have to carry a larger share of responsibilities.

Only children

Although only children do not have brother-sister problems, they may have other, more serious difficulties. Their parents are more likely to continue to consider them their babies. Only children may find it difficult to become independent as they grow up. They may lack companions of their own age. They may be lonely and desire the companionship of brothers and sisters which their friends enjoy.

Of course, there are also a number of advantages in being only children. Parents are able to give them individual attention and, if they need it, a larger share of the family dollar. They do not need to compete with brothers and sisters for recognition by others. They may be able to spend more time with parents and other adults.

Twins

Some twins look so much alike that it may be difficult to tell them apart. Others may look entirely different. Twins may seem to enjoy having everything alike — their toys, their clothes, and their daily routine. As they grow older, though, they may wish to be treated as individuals and may develop very different personalities just as anyone else.

As young children, twins may not seem to need as much attention from brothers, sisters, and parents as other children do. They have each other for companionship. However, as they build their own personalities, they tend to separate into two individuals, requiring that their own physical, mental, social, and emotional needs be met.

Understanding Quarrels among Brothers and Sisters

Research has shown that some quarreling among brothers and sisters is normal. In fact, the family without some conflict is unusual. The causes of brother-sister quarrels include the following: (1) household chores and responsibilities; (2) favors by parents to one or another of the children in the family; (3) invasion of privacy; (4) personal possessions being bor-

Collect newspaper and magazine columns containing letters about teenage-family relationships. Divide into groups of three or four students. Each group should read and discuss one letter without looking at the published reply and then write an appropriate reply. Read the published letters and your group's response to the rest of the class. Discuss these and then compare them with the columnists' answers.

Write a skit illustrating two or more people having a destructive argument. Replay the scene showing how the same type of argument could be constructive for the individuals involved.

Your career
Family therapist

You would be trained to work with families to try to help them solve the many varied problems they may have. These may include conflicts between teenagers and parents, or between parents, that may be disturbing to children. Studies in social work, psychology, family relations, or psychiatry are required. You might work in hospitals, clinics, or social service agencies.

List household jobs you think it is fair and right for parents to expect teenagers to do. Discuss why class members' lists are different.

Give examples of situations that reflect traditional ideas about male and female roles. Examples might include situations like these:

A parent says, "Big boys don't cry."

A father gives his two-year-old son a football helmet for a special occasion.

A grandfather exclaims, "Boys don't play with dolls."

A young girl is told to "act like a lady."

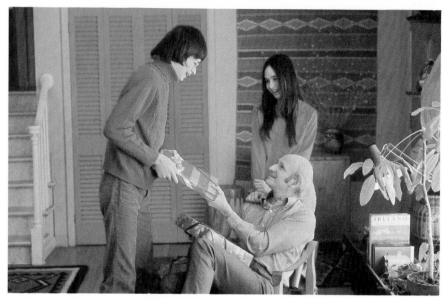

Thinking of others on their special days is a way to express your love for them.   *Sybil Shackman/Monkmeyer*

Bulletin board IDEA

Title: *Don't Give YOUR Family Static*

Directions: Use strips of bright colored paper to make bold zigzag lines. Mount pictures of teenagers doing things with their families and helping with homemaking tasks. Examples might include pictures of young people washing dishes or mowing the lawn, playing with younger children, or caring for an ailing parent or grandparent.

rowed or lent; and (5) care of younger children in the family.

As in all relationships, it usually isn't the obvious thing that causes a quarrel. A deeper problem may be triggered by something as simple as a friendly "hello" your younger sister gives your best friend. Deeper problems may be caused by resentment, insecurity, envy, or anger with self. There is very often some jealousy between brothers and sisters. One of the children may be better looking, more popular, earn better grades, or be better at sports. Most jealousy will be outgrown in time. In any case, one way to play down hostile feelings toward brothers and sisters

is to be proud of them. Try to feel and act happy when your brother has been chosen to be in the band or your sister has made the basketball team. Generally, as your brothers and sisters react to your interest in them, quarrels tend to be less frequent.

Understanding Older Family Members

Grandparents frequently play an active role in the total family situation. They may be comparatively young, vigorous people who have full-time jobs which will keep them busy for a number of years. They may have their own homes with teenagers or young adult children of their own. Often, also, they may assume the care of a grandchild or grandchildren whose mother works. Some do part-time work or take part in community activities after retirement. If they are in good health, they may prefer to be independent, living alone and visiting only for short periods with their children's families.

When grandparents or other elderly relatives live with the family, their presence may be a source of joy or irritation. Young people should try to understand the needs and problems that many older people experience. Unless they do, difficulties may develop.

Accepting Changes of Old Age

Men and women reaching retirement age today can expect to live longer than if they had lived a generation ago. This general lengthening of the life span causes them to be faced with many changes that go along with what is sometimes called the *golden years*.

People are always changing physically, and this change is very pronounced during old age. Hearing and vision may be affected. It may not be as easy for older people to move around as it once was. There may be frequent aches and pains. There may even be imagined pains, pains that cannot be relieved.

Visit a home for elderly people. Prepare refreshments to take and plan some form of entertainment. Perhaps some students would like to return to the home later to visit with, read to, or write letters for the residents. This may be done as a class or club activity.

Invite grandparents who get along well in three-generation families to come to class. Ask them to discuss the adjustments which were necessary for happy family living in their particular situations.

Suggest ways in which older people can be made to feel wanted and useful by contributing to the family's well-being.

Discuss and demonstrate the courtesies which younger people are expected to show to older people.

Visit a Golden Age Club in your community to demonstrate some special skill which would be of interest to the members. This may involve doing some kind of handicraft, making seasonal decorations, or demonstrating how to make inexpensive gifts and novelties.

Loneliness that accompanies old age is lessened when grandparents can exchange feelings of affection with their grandchildren. *Hunt-Wesson Foods, Inc.*

Discuss the differences there might be in the amount of money you are allowed from the family income in each of the following situations:

1. Both of your parents are employed.
2. You have several brothers and sisters of preschool age.
3. You have a brother or a sister in college.
4. You are an only child.
5. You are a twin.

Examine the expenditures made by several families over the same period of time. Determine each family's stage in the family life cycle. List some of the values and goals held by each of the families. Identify the expenditures which influenced you in drawing your conclusions.

Justify this statement: *The difference between a happy and an unhappy family may not be the amount of money it has to spend, but rather how it spends the money it does have.*

Older people often need food that is easily chewed and digested. Sometimes they must be urged to drink milk and to eat fruits and vegetables. They may eat heavy breakfasts but prefer light lunches and early dinners. They often go to bed earlier and get up earlier than other family members.

A feeling of loneliness is frequently a part of old age. As people grow older, they find that many of their loved ones and old friends are gone. Younger people, with different interests and little free time, may seldom stop to visit with them. As they become less active and as their hearing and eyesight become less keen, some older people may begin to lose contact with the world around them. They may begin to feel helpless, or worse yet, useless. All of these aspects of old age may tend to complicate life in a home where three or more generations live together. However, understanding older people's needs and having patience with them contributes to positive relationships.

Welcoming Older Family Members

Often young people can do more than anyone else to make the three-generation family a happy one. While rebellion at the thought of older folks about the house is very common among teenagers, an acceptance of aged grandparents is a necessity.

Teenagers who are mature enough to accept grandparents, sometimes even sharing a room with them, frequently find themselves admired by their own friends. Often friends will join them and their grandparents in playing games, telling stories, or in special activities such as gardening, knitting, or playing a musical instrument.

Many things can be done to make the three-generation family a happy one. Besides taking care of grandparents' physical needs, teenagers can give them companionship, consideration, and respect.

Older people may enjoy having you read to them or talk about things that happened during the day. Frequently all they need is someone who will listen. As you mature, you may find a new, more adult relationship with your grandparents. By sharing their views and experiences, grandparents can be friends and companions as well as relatives. As you grow older, you will treasure firsthand stories of a childhood lived long ago, whether in this country or another. You may have read great novels by writers who, as children, enjoyed listening to adventure tales told by their elders.

Older people may enjoy being included in family games. Some grandparents enjoy gardening, woodworking, painting with oils or watercolors, hooking rugs, quilting, or doing needlework. These activities may be even more meaningful for grandparents if, while working at such hobbies, they feel they are teaching interesting skills to their grandchildren.

A feeling of usefulness and acceptance is just as necessary to older people as it is to any other age group. Older people can often help with homemaking tasks. However, suggestions for ways they can help should be made with their age or any physical limitations in mind.

Older people may enjoy an occasional opportunity to baby-sit with young children. On the other hand, if the older person is not strong and the children are boisterous, other arrangements will be necessary. Older people's services are not to be used as a convenience. Through their years of service, they have earned a lifetime right to the family's affection and respect.

SHARING IN A FAMILY

Most families first learn to share by sharing family activities. They also share resources such as money and possessions. Too, a family can share fun, friends, and special occasions. Of course, family responsibilities must also be shared by family members. Although each member need not share in every single family function, the successful family is generally bound together because it shares a *singleness of purpose*.

Sharing home duties offers an opportunity for sharing thoughts, ideas, and problems. For instance, working with a parent in preparing meals gives a teenager a chance to talk about pleasant happenings at school, to tell about a perplexing situation with a friend, or to discuss future plans. Cleaning up after meals presents a similar opportunity for those involved to share confidences or experiences.

As children become teenagers, it becomes more difficult for the family to share time together. Family members' interests tend to pull them from the family group. However, with effort, all members may operate in their own circles of interest while the family remains close in spirit.

Usually the members of a family are proud of the part any one of them takes in community activities or any talent displayed in athletics, art, music, or dramatics. But with many outside interests, most families have to make a real effort to find time for family activities.

Knowing their true and lasting value, many families make a strong effort to have family-centered activities. Often it is the quality of the shared experiences rather than the number of occasions shared which gives a family a sense of unity. Whether time spent together is used for hobbies, conversation, or community service, it is common interests shared together which weld a family into a strong unit.

Sharing Family Resources

A family's resources are made up of its material possessions as well as its

 Plan a *Family Fun* activity which you can organize and manage. This might be a surprise for your family and something which would be enjoyed by all. For example, it might be preparing and serving Sunday breakfast, organizing a skating party, or baking a cake to celebrate a special occasion. Make your plans carefully and let your teacher check them. Tell when you plan to carry out your *Family Fun* project. Try not to tell your family that you are doing this for a school assignment.

After carrying out your project, make a brief report answering the following questions:

1 Were you able to carry out your original plan? If not, why not? What did you do instead?

2 Was your planned activity really fun? Why, or why not?

3 Would you enjoy doing this again? Why, or why not?

4 Did you tell your family that this was a school assignment? If yes, did you have to tell and why? If no, explain if this made it a more enjoyable experience for you and the rest of your family.

Make complete plans for celebrating a special family occasion such as a birthday, anniversary, graduation, holiday, or special achievement. Discuss the values which are gained from celebrations such as these. If possible, carry out your plans at home and tell the class about your celebration.

List indoor activities which can be fun for the entire family. List places to go in your community and activities that a family could enjoy as a group.

Divide into discussion groups of four or five students. In groups, select appropriate games, ideas for entertainment, refreshments, and decorations for one of the following:
Birthday party for a friend
End-of-the-school-year party
Club Christmas party
After-the-game party
Anniversay party for grandparents
Get-acquainted party for a new
 family in the neighborhood

Demonstrate ways to prepare in advance foods such as sandwiches, cookies, and cakes suitable for parties.

List foods your family would like to have on an emergency shelf and, if possible, purchase these foods. Plan and prepare meals from the emergency shelf.

talents, skills, attitudes, and health. Together they make it possible for people to live together as a family. While money is a necessary resource, another equally important one is the labor given by family members in producing necessary articles or in making the home run smoothly.

The family money
Money usually comes to the family as wages or salary earned by family members. The way in which the family spends its money often makes the difference between a successful family and one which flounders. In successful families, income is used for necessities before frill items are purchased.

A family's spending plan, or *budget*, helps the family spend its money wisely. A financial plan includes provision for the needs of the family. The usual items included are food, shelter, operating expenses, clothing, education and training for advancement, recreation, and savings. Most spending plans leave some money for things the family wants beyond everyday necessities.

For any spending plan to be successful, family cooperation is necessary. If expenses are greater than it seems they should be, everyone needs to try and find ways to cut down on spending. If the whole family has a fairly good idea of what the problem is, it is easier to share in the solution. Talking over the

situation in an informal family discussion works in many homes. When family members truly understand how and why money is spent as it is, cooperation is possible. It is useless, however, to expect family members to avoid spending if they do not know a financial problem exists.

Sometimes family members can stretch their money by doing work themselves, rather than buying the services of others. Each family must make a decision as to how much of the work of maintaining the home is to be done or can be done by the members themselves. Too, they must decide how much they must have done or can afford to have done by others.

Many times a family starts on a cooperative labor plan, only to find that one or more members are unwilling or unable to carry their agreed upon share of the load. Often in such cases it is better to back up and start over, hiring help for certain tasks if necessary. Sacrifices in other areas are then necessary. But when the choice is between material things and family happiness, successful families put family happiness first.

Family possessions
In a home where the rights of each person are respected and where no person behaves too selfishly, young people usually realize that they must take turns in using and caring for family property.

Outings which family members share together can be remembered and treasured for a lifetime.
Bettina Cirone

 Discuss your responsibilities when your parents have guests and your parents' responsibilities when you have guests.

Decide which of the following activities are essential parts of being a good party host or hostess and explain why each is important.

Decide on the date, place, and kind of party.

Make advance arrangements for the place where the party will be given.

Plan the guest list very carefully.

Plan the refreshments and entertainment.

Purchase the supplies for the refreshments, favors, and decorations.

Send out or extend the invitations.

Prepare or make arrangements for the refreshments and decorations.

Greet guests and make them feel welcome.

See that the guests are introduced to each other.

Tell something about the guests as you introduce them, to help get the conversation started.

Show an interest in all the guests and try to see that everyone has a good time.

See that everything is left in order at the end of the party.

115

Check the following list of safety precautions to follow when entertaining. Add other safety precautions which seem important to you.

1 Remove fragile articles from the party area.
2 Be sure that rugs are placed so that guests will not trip over them.
3 Be sure that none of the decorations or costumes used are flammable.
4 When entertaining a large number of people, be sure that the rooms are not so full of furniture that exits are blocked.
5 Exercise the utmost caution when cooking outdoors. Use lighter fluids only before the fire is lighted.
6 Be sure to have all walkways well lighted.

Discuss what to do if you are a guest and the following should happen:

1 You accidentally knock over a vase, breaking it and spilling the contents.
2 You do not like the food served.
3 You are late for dinner because a tire on the car or your bike became flat while you were on the way to your friend's house.

With older brothers and sisters, disagreements may center around use of the bathroom, the telephone, clothing, or the family car. With younger ones, sharing may involve such things as a bicycle, favorite books or games, or the TV set. It helps if the persons concerned are agreeable and reasonable in making arrangements in advance and in abiding by the schedules later. When there is a sincere effort to work out plans for sharing family possessions, bickering and quarreling are lessened.

Sharing Family Work

Consider the number of tasks that have to be done in any twenty-four-hour period to keep a family comfortable, well fed, and adequately clothed. The house has to be straightened and kept at a comfortable temperature. Food must be available, meals prepared and served, the table cleared, and the dishes washed. Proper clothing for each member has to be in readiness — that is, clean, in repair, and adequate for the weather and the family members' activities.

Household tasks

As young people mature, they begin to realize that providing clean clothes, nutritious, appetizing meals, and a neat home takes a great deal of effort. The sooner young people learn to share in household duties, the sooner the household runs smoothly.

Care of younger children

Looking after younger children is a family responsibility and one which may be accepted on a part-time basis by teenagers in the family. Caring for younger brothers and sisters may mean that some of your free time is spent with them. You may be asked to feed them, put them to bed, or play with them. Sometimes more than one of the older children take turns with younger ones. Here is an opportunity for cooperation and even compromise. Usually child care can be fun rather than a chore if you develop a good attitude toward it.

Sharing Family Fun

Family members can have fun together. In a family that works and plays together, parents and children learn to share and care.

Planning good times in the family

Even in the busiest of modern families, plans can be made for celebrations, holidays, and special events which enrich and strengthen relationships in the family. Even family members who are not particularly fond of a majority decision in such matters can enjoy the activity or occasion. Perhaps part of their pleasure is derived by knowing that they are being cooperative family members.

The family's interests usually determine the activities planned for family fun. A sports-loving group might enjoy fishing or bowling together. Another family might get more pleasure out of indoor games, a picnic, or a cookout. If both the parents and children play musical instruments, such a family would doubtless enjoy playing or listening to music.

The equipment for family fun need not be expensive. The activities chosen should be those for which space and equipment are available or easily secured. It isn't the equipment that makes the fun but the people who are involved. Outdoor cooking and eating, for instance, may be as simple as a hot-dog roast in a park. Fishing off a bridge or pier with simple equipment can be as much fun and as satisfying as an expensive deep-sea fishing trip. A family can have just as much fun with simple equipment as with the most expensive kind.

Variety can add interest to family activities. Most people like to do something new and different occasionally. A new game or a picnic in a new spot may provide a change the whole family enjoys. If you generally have family fun outdoors, you might like to try something indoors. If you are used to staying indoors, you might enjoy going to a ball game together. Suggest that family members think of new activities they would like the family to try. From these you can decide on something which is fun for everyone.

Fun at home can be shared by all family members. They may choose to listen to records or tapes, play games, or watch TV. Occasionally they may enjoy talking about something that interests all of them. In fact, some students who at school appear to be well informed on a current subject may have formed their opinions while discussing the matter at home.

Children and parents may, with little or no forethought, find themselves working on a yard or home improvement project, harmonizing in group singing, or playing games together. A teenager might demonstrate a new dance step and offer instruction to parents or younger family members during such an evening. Parents may offer advice or assistance with new hobbies or crafts.

Fun away from home offers many possibilities for family activities. Making homemade ice cream, eating pizza together, or going to a museum or art gallery may be of special interest to some. Others may prefer a movie, a play, or a swim at a nearby lake. Any activity which gives parents and children a chance to enjoy being together is usually worthwhile.

Family outings such as picnics, school carnivals, and beach parties remembered a lifetime usually last only a few hours at the time. Longer outings may be planned which involve a weekend sight-seeing trip, a camp-out in a state park, or a visit with family friends or relatives in another area. A vacation trip usually

 Follow these guidelines when spending the night at a friend's home or when you are the house guest of another family.

Try not to make extra work.

Make a decision when given a choice of food or activity.

Be on time for meals and other activities.

Eat what is served and express appreciation for it.

Offer to help with household tasks.

Make your bed.

Be careful of furniture, personal items, and equipment belonging to the family.

Replace anything that may be broken.

Pay for any long-distance telephone calls made.

Take care of your own personal belongings, keeping them together and not scattering them around the house.

Pack carefully when leaving so that nothing is forgotten.

Show appreciation for the hospitality by promptly sending a thank-you note and perhaps a gift.

Pretend you have spent a week visiting with a friend. Write a note of thanks to your friend's parents expressing appreciation for their hospitallity.

Write and present short skits showing the possible effects of situations such as:

1 You are a weekend guest at a friend's home. You are having such a good time that you have decided to stay longer. You have not asked your friend's parents if this is all right.
2 You did not write *RSVP* on party invitations you mailed.
3 You forgot the time of an invitation and realize you have arrived one half hour early.

List points which should be included in any invitation to a party. Write some invitations and include all the points.

Make and display some appropriate gifts for a hostess.

Demonstrate to the class how to make a gift item or seasonal decoration of your choice. Be well prepared and organized, perhaps having some steps already completed. The demonstration should be so clear that another student could make the item at home without written directions.

Make a coupon book as a gift for someone in your family. Items such as these may be included:

1 car wash by *(your name)*
1 vacuuming of the house by *(your name)*
1 homemade dinner prepared and served by *(your name)*

requires careful planning. Often the planning and fond remembrances are as much fun as the trip itself.

Sharing Family Friends

Hospitality offers another way of having family fun. In a home where guests are made welcome, all family members feel free to invite their friends. Your brother may bring friends in to watch TV. Your sister may ask her friends over to talk. Your father may invite someone from work home for the evening. Remember to consult your parents in the planning, so everyone does not bring a guest at the same time.

In some homes it is the practice to have a special evening meal once a week. At this meal, family members may invite guests by taking turns. Everyone makes a special effort to make the visitors feel welcome so they feel they are guests of the entire family.

Welcoming guests

Certainly you will want to share in making guests feel comfortable. You may assist in the duties of the host or the hostess if your help is needed. If the guests are friends of your parents, try to take a minor role in the conversation. It is usually good manners to sit down and chat with them for a few minutes. However, if you see that you are interrupting a conversation, it is better to sit quietly. Perhaps you can add more to the hospitality of

the hour by making coffee, preparing snacks, or quietly serving other needs of the guests.

If a friend of your parents arrives at the door when they are absent, explain that your parents are not at home and that you know they will regret having missed the visitor. If your parents have already told you to invite their friends in when they are away from home, you may do so. Ordinarily the friends will not accept, but if they do come in, ask them to make themselves comfortable with a book, magazine, or TV until your parents return.

Providing instant hospitality

When friends of the family drop in unexpectedly, the welcome you give them should be as sincere as if you had invited them for that particular day and hour.

If company interrupts an activity, the situation can be handled smoothly in a number of ways. You may stop what you are doing and entertain the guests, or, if another family member can take over, you may excuse yourself and continue your own activity. Probably most guests would enjoy chatting while you finish some small job you are in the midst of completing.

Food for the unexpected guest is always available if a special hospitality food supply is kept on hand. Here convenience foods come into their own. Many families have pre-planned menus for instant entertaining. Soups are often included

Family members often enjoy working together to prepare for such special events as baby or bridal showers. *Kraft Kitchens*

among foods kept for such times. They can be served as soup or as sauces on other foods. A variety of canned and frozen meats and vegetables can be kept for casserole dishes. Eggs from the refrigerator might be used in a main dish such as an omelet or a soufflé. Packaged and homemade mixes can be used for biscuits, muffins, cakes, or other additions to an emergency meal. Ice cream is certainly a convenient dessert to have on hand for unexpected guests.

Spur-of-the-moment entertaining is often more fun than any other form of entertainment. Even if school books must be removed be-fore a guest can sit down, everyone is more at ease because the occasion is unplanned. It helps if materials for entertaining are close at hand. One advantage of unplanned entertaining is that no one is over-tired because of long and tedious preparation.

You may be uncertain as to your responsibilities when guests drop by. If they are your guests, they are your responsibility. If they are family friends, the family as a unit shares in entertaining.

Sharing Special Family Occasions

The special days that are celebrated together by family members are often those remembered longest. Many people recall happily the good times they had when birthdays, anniversaries, and holidays were occasions for family gatherings.

It is important to children that older family members share in the fun of these special good times. Whether they are trimming a Christmas tree or having a Fourth of July picnic, the event means more to children when others enjoy it, too.

Celebrating special occasions
Families may be quite different in the ways they choose to observe special occasions. In some families, members are permitted to select just how their own birthdays will be celebrated. One teenager may prefer a party, while another chooses to eat at a special restaurant.

Follow these guidelines when wrapping gifts and other packages:

1. Cut the wrapping paper to fit the box. The paper should be large enough to lap over at the center about 1 inch (2.54 cm). At the ends, the paper should extend to cover the depth of the box.
2. Place the box face down on the paper so the joining seam will be on the bottom and the top surface will be smooth.
3. Bring the paper around the box. Fasten it with transparent tape or seals.
4. Fold the paper at the ends so the corners are mitered and the ends are neat and smooth. Fasten as you did the center seam.
5. Add ribbon or other decorations appropriate for the gift or the occasion.
6. Do not use crushable decorations on packages to be mailed.

Demonstrate wrapping gifts attractively and creatively by using materials that would not have to be bought, such as old greeting cards, shelf paper, newspaper, berries, greenery, or leaves.

Demonstrate wrapping a package for mailing.

Prepare a booklet of games to use in entertaining your friends or family at a party or social gathering. Get suggestions from the class. If you want to, you could make your booklet part of the home economics department's file.

List the responsibilities of a guest such as:
Acknowledges the invitation
Arrives on time
Leaves at the time suggested by the host or hostess
Mingles with other guests
Joins in the spirit of the party
Makes no unnecessary work or trouble
Offers to help the hostess
Thanks the host or hostess for the hospitality

Prepare attractively wrapped foods for holiday gifts such as plum puddings, fruit cakes, fancy cookies, candies, jellies, dried fruits, and fancy breads.

Preparing decorations for holidays or get-togethers can be fun for family members of all ages. *What's New in Home Economics*

Family parties can also celebrate special family honors. Perhaps a daughter has been chosen class representative to the student council. Perhaps a son makes the honor roll. Perhaps a father is promoted or gets a new job. Perhaps the baby begins to walk. Any of these are occasions worthy of celebration in many families. Youngsters who grow up in such an atmosphere generally enjoy sharing their achievements with other family members.

In many families where the grandmother and grandfather are still living, the family has some special kind of observance of their wedding anniversary. Their children and grandchildren often plan to gather for an afternoon of visiting and invite old friends to share the happy time.

Decorating for special occasions

Although party decorations are not necessary, they can make an occasion more festive. The trend is toward selecting decorations that are simple and inexpensive. Appropriateness and originality are also important considerations. Homemade decorations can be more original than the kind found in stores. They are usually less expensive, too. Fresh flowers are always in good taste when used for adding color to a room or table.

Giving on special occasions

A gift is an expression of the warm feelings of the giver. Presented within the family in a spirit of appreciation and affection, it is of value, not for what it costs, but rather because it is an expression of loving kindness from one family member to another.

In choosing a gift, try to pick something that will be enjoyed by the person receiving it. Any mother's heart is touched when a tiny son gives her a baseball or a toy truck for her birthday. She knows he is giving her the best gift he can think of. However, as you mature, your gifts will represent less what you would want to have.

They will be chosen to please the person receiving them.

It is not necessary, and often not a good idea, to buy costly gifts. Such gifts may cause embarrassment if the receiver cannot or does not want to feel obligated. Most people will especially enjoy an article that you have made yourself.

When the family knows that the person who is to receive their gifts wants a single large, expensive article, the members may pool their funds and get one gift.

Wrapping gifts in interesting and unusual ways can add to the fun of gift giving and receiving. The many unusual wrappings on the market make it easy to create attractive, personalized packages. Sometimes original wrappings and decorations can be made inexpensively at home. Leftover wallpaper, newspapers, store bags, foil or other similar materials can all be used to wrap packages. Scraps of fabric, yarn and string, or simple artwork add a decorative touch.

In deciding how to wrap a gift, there are two considerations: what the gift is, and who is to receive it. Keep in mind the personality and interests of the person for whom the gift is intended. Wrappings may be very simple or quite fancy. Gifts such as flowers, fruits, and cakes need no wrapping, although they may be specially packaged.

Delivering gifts in good condition requires careful wrapping. If you are wrapping a present to be

Warm feelings can be expressed through gift wrappings as well as through the gift itself. *Better Homes and Gardens,* © *Meredith Corporation*

mailed, it will be necessary to put it in a sturdy box. Use flat bows and decorations. Use heavy wrapping paper for the outer covering. Gifts delivered in person may be wrapped with large bows, flower sprays, berries, or various other perishable decorations.

If you receive a gift, except within the immediate household, you are expected to send a thank-you note. Since a gift is more an *expression of feelings* than a *thing,* it is not worth hurting others' feelings by neglecting to acknowledge it.

Your career
Family recreation counselor

You would plan and organize special interest activities and outings for an individual family or a group of families. You might find employment in hotels, resorts, campgrounds, and community centers.

Number from 1 to 22. Beside each number indicate if the corresponding statement is true or false. *Do not* write in this book.

1 One of the most important needs that can be met in a family is the need for security.

2 People in a family can be related only by blood or marriage.

3 People's responsibilities increase when they marry.

4 When a mother goes to work outside the home, there is no need for a change in home responsibilities carried by other family members.

5 In most families, the father makes the greatest number of consumer decisions.

6 More men are heads of one-parent families today than in the past.

7 Family background affects the roles young people assume as adults.

8 Being the middle child in a family with three children has no disadvantages.

9 An only child is more likely to be dependent on parents than is a child who has younger brothers and sisters.

10 Identical twins have identical personalities.

11 Some arguing and quarreling among teenage brothers and sisters is normal.

12 A feeling of uselessness may accompany old age.

13 Listening may be the most valuable contribution teenagers can make to the lives of older people.

14 Because teenagers develop many interests outside the home, there is no reason to share in family activities.

15 A family's resources include skills, attitudes, and talents.

16 The way a family spends its money may be more important than the amount of money it has to spend.

17 Most spending plans make provision for buying some things family members want as well as for the items they need.

18 Family disagreements may be lessened by making arrangements in advance for sharing home responsibilities

19 The amount of fun a family has is related to the amount of money spent for recreation.

20 If some of their parents' friends come for a visit unexpectedly, teenagers have no responsibility for making the guests feel welcome.

21 An emergency shelf of convenience foods can be very helpful when entertaining unexpected guests.

22 There are some advantages in entertaining guests on the spur of the moment.

Fill in the blank in each sentence with the *best* word to complete the statement. *Do not* write in this book.

1 A doctor who specializes in the care of children is a(an) (1) .

2 The most rapid period of physical growth occurs during the (2) year of life.

3 The part of the body that is proportionately the largest at birth and grows most slowly is the (3) .

4 Every stage of human growth contains (4) tasks which individuals learn to perform before moving successfully to the next stage.

5 At very early stages of life, physical growth is closely related to (5) growth.

6 Playing peekaboo as a baby is a sign of (6) development.

7 When young children play alongside each other, but not *with* each other, it is called (7) play.

8 Children between the ages of three and six are usually called (8) .

9 The primary purpose of discipline is to establish acceptable (9) .

10 After children are (10) years old they usually eat the same foods as the rest of the family.

11 The stage of development marking the beginning of physical maturity is (11) .

Chapter 7

Guiding the Development of Growing Children

After reading this chapter, you should be able to:

1 State the characteristic patterns of growth.
2 Identify the characteristics of infants and toddlers.
3 Identify the characteristics of preschoolers.
4 Identify the characteristics of elementary-school-age children.
5 Describe the changes that take place during the teen years.
6 Give examples of the physical needs of children.
7 Describe how the mental needs of children can be met.
8 Explain how the social needs of children can be met.
9 Give examples of ways family members can help children to learn emotional control.
10 Assume responsibility for children by baby-sitting or participating in a community service project.

Have you ever said, "When *I* have children, I won't make them do this or that"? Most people *have* said such things from time to time, especially when it seemed very hard to learn a new skill. But as teenagers mature, they often decide their parents were right in their insistence that children learn certain things at certain ages.

Perhaps you have seen a young child run up to a friend to brag about his older brother's or sister's skill in some area. Although they may not show it, teenagers are just as proud as they see their younger brothers and sisters learn to walk and talk or advance in school. Both the young child and the teenager are sharing the family's pleasure in the growth of its members. The interest family members take in one another helps build strong, lasting family ties.

123

Copy the puzzle ladder below on a piece of paper. Fill in the blank spaces with the letters needed to complete the words relating to family living, children, and child development.

A	D		L		S
M	O			E	R
F		T			R
P	A		E		T
I		F		N	T
F	A				Y
N	U		B		R
B		B	I		S
G	R				H
S				A	L
M		T			L
S	C				L
H		A		T	H
H		B		T	S
S		F			Y

A new baby's arrival brings many changes in the operation of a household. Changes in family life begin even before the baby is born. As soon as a woman suspects she might be pregnant, she should make an appointment at a prenatal clinic or with her own doctor. A doctor who specializes in the care of expectant mothers and the delivery of babies is called an *obstetrician*. A woman who follows the doctor's directions during pregnancy gives herself and her baby an added chance for good health all of their lives. The doctor may suggest extra rest for the mother-to-be. Occasionally she may need help with her regular duties before, as well as after, the baby arrives. Since much of the mother's time will be taken up with caring for the baby, other family members may have to take over some of her usual routine duties in the home. They may also be called upon to help with the care of the baby.

The physical, mental, social, and emotional development of the new baby, and of other family members, often depends on how well older family members understand natural growth factors.

PATTERNS OF GROWTH

Although physical growth is uneven and irregular, there are characteristic patterns of growth. Growth is most rapid in the first year of life and in the early adolescent years. In fact, by the time children are one year old, they often have tripled their birth weight. The second spurt of growth in adolescence is longer than the first. It comes at different times for different individuals. This second growth period lasts longer for some people than for others. Between these two periods of most rapid growth, physical development is slower and more even.

At birth, babies appear to be topheavy. Their heads are proportionately much larger than the rest of their bodies. Physical growth moves from the head down and from the center of the body out. When a baby is born the legs, feet, and hands are the least developed. These are the parts of the body that grow the most at first. The head and arms, which are more developed at birth, grow more slowly. It is easy to remember that physical growth is from head to toe and from near to far.

Babies change in appearance very quickly because different parts of their bodies are growing at different rates. Although the pattern of growth is similar for all children, the rate of growth for individuals varies. Physical growth is affected by heredity, diet, rest, exercise, and the extent to which basic needs are met.

DEVELOPMENTAL TASKS

The students in your school have learned to perform certain tasks as

124

The developmental tasks of childhood can be accomplished as children play with their favorite toys. *Playskool Toys*

Outline pictures of children to obtain silhouettes. Include different ages from infancy through early adolescence. Place the silhouettes in order from the one showing the youngest person to that showing the oldest. How did changes in body proportion help you arrange the silhouettes?

Bulletin board IDEA
Title: *How do Children Grow?*
Directions: Use a cutout of a sprinkling can. Write one of these words on each of four paper flowers placed below the sprinkling can:

Physically   Socially
Mentally   Emotionally

Your career
Children's clothes salesperson

You would sell children's clothing and accessory items. You might design or arrange displays, keep inventory of merchandise, and perform stockroom duties. You might also help customers with their selections, giving advice about children's sizes and styles of garments. You might work in a department store, children's specialty shop, or catalog order house.

they developed. For instance, each learned to sit, stand, walk, talk, read, and make friends. These are frequently called *developmental tasks*. A developmental task is an achievement presented at or about a certain time in a person's life. Successful accomplishment leads to happiness and success with later tasks.

Babies accomplish developmental tasks when their muscles and minds are ready for them to learn the new tasks. However, their families can help them learn these tasks. Family members can see that children have the food, exercise, and rest their muscles need to grow strong. Families can also see that children get to practice their skills.

Bulletin board IDEA

Title: *The Wonderful World of Children*

Directions: On a world map, mount pictures of students taken when they were preschoolers. Put them in a circle to look like a globe. Obtain pictures of people in your school when they were children. Try to get children's pictures showing a variety of activities. Identify each child pictured. Tell what led you to make your decisions.

Unless children succeed in learning the appropriate developmental tasks at each stage of growth, they do not have a firm foundation on which to build for the next stage. People can learn some developmental tasks which were skipped earlier, but these are generally harder to learn during a later developmental stage. For example, children who have learned to handle a pencil easily before they learn to write will learn to form letters more easily than children who must learn to hold a pencil at the same time they learn to make letters.

Teenagers who have never learned to control their tempers do not need to go through the rest of their lives acting like toddlers. But it will be much harder for them to learn this control than it would have been at an earlier age.

As you observe different children growing up, you will notice certain common developmental patterns. However, the final results vary. Most children learn to talk, but even within a single family they may not all talk alike. One child may talk all the time, while another prefers to listen. One child may prefer long sentences with many big words, while another speaks very simply.

As people grow, the developmental stages leading to these final results move regularly from the simple to the complex, from similar tasks to very different tasks, and from general tasks to specific ones. As children mature, former developmental tasks become parts of larger, final results. For example, toddlers learn to catch a rolled ball. They enjoy this skill for its own sake. If the child grows up to become a member of a basketball team, this early developmental task has become a forgotten part of all the skills learned which helped earn the team position.

Some of these general patterns of growth are more noticeable in connection with the physical growth of children, but they apply to mental and social growth as well. The family's ability to accept children in whatever stage they have reached will make it much easier to help them grow and develop at their own pace. For example, it is useless to expect children to walk before their leg muscles have grown strong enough. Nor can they be expected to tie shoestrings before their fingers have mastered simple tasks such as building block houses. They will not learn much about talking until the time that their mouth and throat muscles are developed adequately enough for them to make the sounds necessary for saying words correctly.

Children are helped by encouragement. In working with them, try to make them feel good about their accomplishments and secure in your recognition of their personal needs. This may be your most important contribution to their physical, mental, social, and emotional growth.

A yound child's most rapid growth period occurs during the first year of life.   *Bob Cook*

Give reasons why babies cry. If possible, make tapes of babies crying, cooing, and babbling. Are there different cries? Can you identify cries of sleepiness, pain, or hunger? How do cooing and babbling lead to speech development?

Identify some of the first words children usually say. Discuss why these are among their first words.

Invite a parent to bring a young baby to class. Ask the parent to demonstrate effective ways of dressing and undressing the child.

Demonstrate warming various kinds of baby bottles, testing the temperature of the contents, feeding, and bubbling a baby.

Demonstrate giving a baby cereal or other soft food from a spoon.

Collect pictures of furniture and equipment which can be adjusted to meet the needs of growing children. Collect pictures of multipurpose children's furnishings and tell how the items can be used to serve more than one need. Suggest useful substitute baby equipment such as a plastic dishpan for a bathtub or a drawer or clothes basket for a bassinet.

Infants and Toddlers

The first three years of children's lives are full of changes. Helpless newborn infants gain weight, grow in height and strength, and learn many of the basic skills that allow them to take care of themselves.

People generally grow more rapidly during the first year of their lives than at any other time. Usually at the end of six months they weigh twice as much as they did when they were born, and at the end of a year their birth weight may have tripled. They grow taller as well as heavier, gaining about nine inches in height during the first year of life. Boys generally grow a little faster than girls during this period. They are likely to be taller and heavier than girls of the same age.

At the very early stages of people's lives, mental growth is related to physical growth. Thus, it is very hard to separate physical and mental development of infants. For example, newborn babies cannot focus their eyes. By the time they are about four weeks old, their eyes can follow a moving object, although it is not certain how well they can see it. Slightly older babies can turn their heads as their eyes follow an object.

By the time babies are able to creep, and then to walk, their curiosity is very evident. Their mental growth is less obviously related to their physical development than during the first months of life.

By the time toddlers are three, they know a great deal about their families and the contents of their

Discuss advantages of nursery school for children. Describe conditions under which young children would probably profit most from attending nursery school.

Give examples to illustrate this statement: *Three year olds play at the same time as, rather than with, their friends.*

Suggest family activities pre-schoolers particularly enjoy. Follow these instructions:

1 Sit on a very low chair or stool pulled up to a table of regular height.
2 Use a very large serving spoon and a large mixing bowl.
3 Use the hand which you ordinarily do *not* use for eating.
4 Ask someone to tie a large towel around your neck as a bib.
5 Now eat cereal and milk from the bowl.

Compare the frustrations you feel to those of young children as they learn to feed themselves. This experiment should help you understand young children who are learning to do new tasks that are difficult for them.

List the values to be gained by child development.

When a child's physical growth slows down, mental and emotional growth tends to pick up.
Jan Lukas/Photo Researchers

homes. They are also very interested in objects outside their homes. Toddlers will explore the possibilities of an ant, a bee, a dog, or an automobile with equal curiosity. Unfortunately, they are not very alert to the dangers this curiosity may involve. One of the real problems in training older babies and toddlers lies in finding ways to encourage their curiosity, and thereby their mental growth, while protecting them from physical danger.

At first glance infants may seem to lack any evidence of social develop-ment. But their awareness of others begins much earlier than many suppose. Their first smiles may be for anyone who gives them atten-tion. As long as the people around them take care of their physical needs, they remain happy. This happiness leads them to develop trust in others. As babies grow older and are able to distinguish between the people who approach them, they may become shy and timid with strangers. This apparent set-back is a very normal stage of their social development. If they are allowed to become acquainted with strangers at their own pace, they will continue to develop trust in other people.

Toddlers continue to grow in their awareness of other people. And as awareness of others grows, self-concept also develops. This awareness of self leads to other apparent setbacks in social development. As toddlers try to learn what they may and may not do, they appear from time to time to be stubborn, selfish, shy, demanding, babyish, or bold. They need time to

Muscular skills developed by the preschooler frequently demonstrate mental and social growth. *Burk Uzzle/Magnum*

learn how they may and may not behave with other people. It is not fair to judge them according to standards for older people. On the other hand, it is equally unfair to expect them to learn accepted social behavior by themselves. They need specific directions.

Older toddlers enjoy other children. They are not ready to play with others in the same way that older children do. And they are not really ready to share toys. But two toddlers playing side by side with their own trucks seem to have much more fun than if each is playing alone. When children at this age play near each other, but not with each other, it is called *parallel play*. Their ideas of *mine* and *yours* are not very clear. They need to be watched in their play so they do not hurt themselves or each other and so they can be led away from any quarrels that may develop. Fortunately, toddlers' moods do not last very long.

Preschoolers

Children between the ages of three and six are usually called *preschoolers*. The physical changes of preschool children are not so rapid as were those of the infant and toddler. On the other hand, by the time children are six years old, they have gone through several rapidly changing stages of mental and social development.

Preschoolers experience one of the slow-down periods of physical

 Use your left hand if you are right-handed and your right hand if you are left-handed. With a stubby crayon, color a very small and detailed printed picture. What feelings do you experience? How may these feelings be similar to those young children experience? Why were you asked to use the hand which you ordinarily would not use? How did the size of the picture you colored compare to the size of a picture young children might be given to color? What have you learned from doing this that relates to the development of young children?

Make finger paint from soap flakes, liquid starch, and food coloring. Mix the three ingredients until the desired consistency and color are obtained.

Gather inexpensive indoor play materials such as strings of uncooked macaroni for necklaces and graduated sizes of cans for put-together toys. Make inexpensive toys at home and bring them to school to show the class.

Make a toy chest from cardboard cartons or vegetable crates. Cover it with pictures or adhesive material or paint it.

Discuss the occupational opportunities available for working with children in child care facilities, libraries, hospitals, recreation centers, children's sections of department stores, and toy stores.

Survey your community to find the types of available occupations related to child development. Report findings to the class. Make a list of possible employment situations. How could you create your own job in the area of child care and development?

Interview a preschool or kindergarten teacher to find out what type of assistant would be most valuable.

Find out about the education needed for various occupations in child care. Interview people in occupations related to child care. Look in college catalogs and vocational-technical school catalogs. Describe how requirements differ. Summarize the importance of meeting requirements before applying for a job.

growth. Sometimes this natural slowing down upsets preschoolers' families. They anxiously consult the doctor to find out what is wrong. Although preschoolers' bodies do not change size as rapidly as during babyhood, their physical growth shows up in other ways. Their muscles gain in strength, and they develop greater muscle coordination. Preschool children are ready to learn many physical skills which were beyond their earlier abilities. This greater muscular control shows up as they run, play with wheeled toys, or throw a ball. Their muscular control is also shown as they paint, build with blocks, and play house. These types of physical activities are also important to the mental and social growth of preschoolers.

Preschool children are even more curious about the world which surrounds them than are toddlers. Their manner of approach to mental problems is different. While toddlers poke and taste and are generally active in their explorations, preschoolers take time to think about things, to ask questions about them, and to seek out the relationships between them. This questioning and thinking is added to active investigation. It does not replace it. The development of a mental approach to mental problems is slow and uneven.

As children begin to grasp abstract ideas, they may seem to ask the same series of questions

Displaying works of art can give children a feeling of security and a sense of pride.
Ethan Allen American Traditional Interiors

they asked earlier. Whenever preschoolers do this, either they are seeking reassurance that their ideas are indeed correct, or they are looking for new relationships on a more complicated level. Whatever their reasons for asking, they need direct answers to their questions.

Preschoolers' social worlds expand rapidly from that of their families to that of their playmates. At first, like toddlers, they play alongside a friend. By the age of five, they readily engage in highly organized group play. Quarreling at this age is rather frequent, often very noisy and somewhat violent, but also brief. Preschoolers can remember former disagreements, but in general they do not seek to do so. They do not carry grudges. Their disobedience of adults is their own idea rather than a response to a playmate's dare.

Elementary-School-Age Children

From the ages of six through eleven or twelve, people go through an important stage of development that ends with the onset of *puberty*. Puberty is the stage of development that marks the beginning of physical maturity.

During the elementary-school years, the rate of physical growth is quite slow. However, most boys will double in muscular strength during their grade-school years. Increase in strength is generally slower for girls than for boys.

Puberty brings a rapid change in the growth rate for both sexes. The pubertal period, reached earlier by girls than by boys, gives girls a brief lead in growth. Girls of eleven or twelve may be taller than boys of the same age, but a year or two later they may be shorter than these same boys.

The mental growth of elementary-school children is readily seen as they progress through school. But school reports and advancement should not be considered the

Bring to class a favorite book from your childhood days or one belonging to a younger brother or sister. Why is it a good or poor book for children? For what age children is it best suited?

Practice telling young children stories following these suggestions:
Make the story short.
Use simple words easily understood by the children.
Use the children's names in the story and use names of other people well known to them.
Use appropriate and dramatic facial expressions, gestures, and sounds.
Make up motions the children can use at appropriate times in the story.

View children's TV programs. Select programs appropriate for children of different ages. Make a list of suggestions for improving these programs. Discuss your ideas in class. Send your suggestions to the local television station.

Develop a check list for judging TV programs for children of various ages. Watch some children's programs and rate them using the check list. Develop devices for evaluating magazines, books, records, and movies for children.

As children develop socially, they begin to relate to each other on a one-to-one basis.
Robert Capece

Suggest items which can be used for outdoor play equipment that cost little or no money such as:
Large wooden crates for climbing.
Old tires for swinging.
Large cable spools for rolling.

Discuss what is meant by an educational toy. (Remember there are areas of education which are not a part of school.) Discuss how a push-and-pull toy or puzzle could be educational.

Make a check list for evaluating toys for children at various ages. Bring some toys to class and evaluate them for safety, durability, and educational value.

Suggest everyday household items which make good, safe toys. Discuss why a child may not show interest in an expensive and complicated toy, but may enjoy playing with a wooden spoon, cooking pan, or cardboard box.

Tell about a situation when a toy seemed to be bought for a parent instead of the child. What was the child's reaction to the situation?

Make some toys for your brothers and sisters, a children's home, or to distribute to needy families.

only signs of their mental development. Group activities outside of school, family trips, television programs, and library books all contribute to their mental growth. Throughout the elementary-school years, children enthusiastically start a project, work on it for a short time, then turn to something else. At times they may return to the project or start a similar one on a more advanced level. At other times, the single part-project is enough. This type of behavior is a sign of elementary-school children's urge to explore, rather than an indication that they cannot carry through with their own projects.

During the elementary-school years, children become more concerned with their contemporaries than with other people. Family opinion matters, but it loses its importance whenever it conflicts with the opinion of others in the group. Although it may not seem to be so, this reliance on the group is a sign of growing independence.

Elementary-school-age children have learned a great deal about socially acceptable forms of behavior. They are able to adjust these to match a variety of situations, so they may have *company manners, family manners, school manners,* and *playground manners.*

Although the occurrences are not frequent, quarreling is common throughout the elementary-school years. These quarrels generally concern *differing ideas* or *positions of*

importance rather than possessions. Elementary-school children are more apt to remember their grievances and to stay mad than are younger children, but they are capable of forgetting quickly. Although "the gang" and a best friend are very important during these years, there are frequent realignments of such relationships.

Teenagers

The teen years are a period of rapid change. Some changes are caused by the physical development that begins with puberty. Others are caused by teenagers' widening horizons, which bring new knowledge, new responsibilities, and new privileges.

The second growth spurt in people's lives begins with the onset of puberty. Individual differences in development seem to be more noticeable during this time than during most of the earlier growth periods. Part of the concern over individual differences is caused by the fact that teenagers have a strong urge to be just like their friends. Confusion results when individual differences in physical development occur.

Varying rates of growth of different parts of the body are especially apparent during the teens. Arms may be suddenly longer at one time, legs at another. The nose may lengthen to full adult size before the rest of the facial features

Physical growth and social development in the early teen years progress more smoothly when their importance is understood by family members. *Susan Johns/Photo Researchers*

Research and present an oral report on one of the following topics.

1 Developing desirable childhood habits
2 Teaching a child about work and responsibility
3 Influencing character development
4 Getting ready for a new baby
5 Working mothers and child care centers
6 Understanding and working with exceptional children
7 Adopting a child, or the adopted child
8 Baby-sitting procedures
9 Guidance and discipline
10 Play as a means of development

When possible, use pictures to illustrate your report.

mature. Muscles suddenly become stronger and more powerful.

These changes accompany the more obvious signs of physical development which indicate that the young person is becoming a physically mature man or woman. Although signs of this maturing, such as the deepening voice of a boy or the developing breasts of a girl, are eagerly awaited, their actual occurrence may be embarrassing. This is especially true when the changes seem to occur overnight.

Much of teenagers' strength seems to go into growing rapidly physically and into learning how to handle their constantly differing proportions. Changes may occur so quickly that their bodies require extra rest and extra food. If the need for rest and for nourishment to aid growth is not understood, teenagers and their parents may begin to worry about their apparent lack of energy or their desire to eat much more than in the past.

The teenagers' search for independence may be marked by smoothness or intense disagreements with the family. Oddly enough, teenagers are as apt to worry about a smooth adjustment to their growing independence as they are about unhappy adjust-

Your career
Nursery aide

You would entertain children for a limited amount of time in nurseries provided by some establishments as a service to patrons. You might read aloud to the children, organize and participate in games or parties, and give elementary lessons in arts or crafts. You might find employment in family resort areas, department stores, malls, recreational clubs, or universities.

Bring children's clothing items to class. Discuss the features of each garment from the standpoint of:

Ease of putting on and taking off the garment.

Self-help features.

Comfort.

Washability and ease of care.

Durability.

Safety.

Tell how the following practices encourage children to want to dress themselves:

1 Selecting clothes that are liked.

2 Giving encouragement to try and dress without help and showing pleasure when this is accomplished.

3 Choosing tops with wide or stretch necklines that can be slipped over the head, and selecting pants with elastic waists that can be pulled up easily.

4 Selecting clothing that can be fastened and unfastened easily.

5 Providing opportunities to practice buttoning and unbuttoning clothes, lacing and tying shoes, and putting on socks and mittens.

Recycle clothing items for an infant or young child. Make them from usable clothes that are no longer worn.

ments. People cannot be in complete agreement with others and retain their own identities. The smoothness with which these disagreements are handled is often a sign of the growing maturity of teenagers.

SPECIAL NEEDS OF CHILDREN

If children are to develop good self-concepts, someone must see that they have opportunities to develop sound attitudes toward themselves and others. Older brothers and sisters in a home need to realize that they have a natural position in which they can encourage or discourage younger children's development of these attitudes. If all family members practice the following, most youngsters develop a good self-concept.

1 Set a good example.

2 Respect and safeguard the rights of all family members.

3 Assure all family members of love and affection.

4 Understand and control personal behavior while helping younger family members learn this control.

5 Give positive directions.

6 Help younger family members to help themselves.

Children are not miniature adults. Each developmental stage has its special needs as well as its special opportunities for learning. Children who are forced to take too much or too little responsibility for their own welfare are seriously disadvantaged. They may grow up to have children's frustrated feelings in adults' bodies.

Children's physical, mental, social, and emotional needs are very closely linked. Children need an environment that promotes physical growth. They need opportunities to learn. They need to socialize with others. They need opportunities to develop positive feelings about themselves and other people. They need help in learning to control their behavior.

Physical Needs

Children's homes are the places where their early physical needs are met. Their chances to reach their full potential depend on how well their homes meet these basic needs.

Shelter and furnishings

Infants and children through the elementary-school-age years appear to pay little or no attention to shelter. Concerned adults must see that children are given protection from both extreme heat and cold. They must keep children dry when it rains or snows. Older people must, to a degree, shelter them from wind and sunshine.

Young babies spend much of the twenty-four hours of the day sleeping. They need a sleeping place of their own. At first this may be some sort of basket or drawer with a mat-

134

tress in it, replaced later by a crib. Or a crib may be used from the beginning. The mattress should be firm and flat, and it should be covered with a rubber or plastic sheet under the surface sheet. A washable pad is placed on top. Pillows are not usually recommended for babies because they may affect their posture and can cause smothering. All types of lightweight plastic should be *avoided completely* as babies are likely to smother if they pull it over their faces. Bed coverings should be warm, light in weight, and easily laundered. The room should be well ventilated and comfortably warm.

Small children pay more attention to the furniture in their homes than they do to the buildings and rooms. Although they like bright colors, they are not interested in the quality of the furniture. They do notice the *size* of the furniture. If the family budget does not allow for specially sized furniture, a sturdy, lightweight climbing stool will help small children reach full-sized beds, washbasins, and chairs. The same stool may serve as a necessary footrest for children sitting in adult chairs.

Careful families check all home furnishings and materials for safety. Sharp corners, sharp or rough edges, or splintery surfaces can turn young children's minor tumbles into major injuries. Unsteady furniture can increase the chances

for a fall. Small objects may be swallowed. Some paints are poisonous. Since it is almost impossible to keep very young children from chewing any surface they can reach, it is necessary to remove such paint and to recover such surfaces with nonpoisonous paint.

Clothing

Today's clothing for children is made with comfort and activity in mind. As children outgrow the size or need of certain items, other clothing can be chosen which is equally useful.

As babies, children need plenty of diapers. Diapers may be disposable or easy-wash ones, depending on the amount of money and time available for clothing and its care. Children need soft, warm, stretchy, washable cover-ups, or pajamas. Except for special occasions, modern babies wear mainly these two items. Both day and night, diapers are worn to keep the babies dry. Cover-ups are worn only if they are needed for warmth; blankets or snowsuits are used in cold weather; and plastic pants may be used at certain times to provide extra protection against dampness.

Toddlers and young children need clothing which is appropriate to the weather conditions where they live. Their clothing should help them remain cool in warm weather, but be warm enough to prevent them from becoming too chilly in

 Pretend you are in charge of training buyers of children's clothes. How would you emphasize to the buyers that they need to consider all the points below when selecting clothes to sell? Illustrate your points with verbal explanations, drawings, or role playing.

Select clothes that fit comfortably, give children freedom, and permit good posture.
Choose clothes that are simple, well constructed, and durable.
Select clothes that are easily cared for.
Choose clothes suited to the climate.
Select clothes that are light in weight.
Choose bright colors.
Select clothes with durable fasteners located on the front of the garment.

Bulletin board IDEA
Title:

lothing for hildren

Directions: Mount pictures of children wearing clothes with growth and self-help features.

List facts you may have observed about young children's likes and dislikes about food such as:

1 Most children prefer mildly flavored foods.
2 Young children generally prefer foods served lukewarm rather than hot or cold.
3 Young children like to be able to eat with their fingers.

Plan a typical family dinner menu. Vary it to meet the needs of two-year-old children. Include foods which they could eat by themselves. Plan other menus to meet the needs of children at different ages.

Pretend you have a younger brother or sister who does not like to eat breakfast. Plan ways to make this meal more appealing, such as:

Egg in a nest — egg served in a toast cup or cooked in a slice of bread from which the center has been removed
Funny face — banana slices arranged to make a smiling face on a round pancake
Fruit basket — fruit slices served in an orange or grapefruit half cut to look like a basket

Desirable clothing for children should be easy to put on, easy to remove, and easy to wash or clean. *Ken Wittenberg*

other climates or seasons. It should also allow them to enjoy freedom of movement. At the same time, it must not be too large. Floppy pants legs and dangling sleeves are the cause of many childhood accidents, especially burns and falls. Equally important, children's clothing should be chosen for easy care. Little good is derived from telling children over and over, "Don't get your clothes dirty." Children must learn to be neat. But even more, they need to learn how to run and climb. They need to explore and satisfy their curiosity. These activities are likely to get children dirty. Sturdy clothes which launder easily can be kept reasonably neat.

As children progress through grade school, it is important that they be allowed to choose at least part of their own clothes. Since pressure from the gang is so important, they need to have clothes pretty much like those of their schoolmates. If at all possible, wise families find ways to provide clothing to meet children's social and emotional needs. For example, the fifth-grade girl may need a new baseball shirt more than she needs a new dress. And the boy of the same age may need sneakers more than dress shoes.

Food and nutrition

The basis of children's future health is directly related to the food they eat. The foods mothers eat before their babies are born, and even before they are pregnant, and the foods children get during the first months and years of their lives

Self-feeding is quite an experience for a child. Make it a pleasant one by praising the successes and saying little about the spills.
Ken D'Ortona

determine much of their *physical* and *mental* development during their entire lives.

Adults must be careful to buy food for children rather than for their own likes and dislikes. Children's tastes are quite different from those of older people. Generally, children's foods should be only mildly flavored and barely warm. It is best to avoid snack foods and to concentrate instead on good nutrition.

Because of the rapid growth babies experience during their first year of life, nutrition can hardly be overemphasized. A mother's own milk generally agrees with a young infant. It contains the nutrients the baby needs. Many doctors advise mothers to try to nurse their babies at least during early infancy.

There may be reasons, however, why mothers cannot or do not want to breast-feed their babies. In such cases, babies are bottle-fed with a formula recommended by the doctor. Bottle-fed babies should be held in a position similar to the way they would be held if their mothers were nursing them so they may feel securely loved.

For best growth and development, babies must have other foods besides milk shortly after birth. Vitamins A and D are necessary. These and other vitamins are usually supplied as supplements. Since babies enjoy sucking, many are given fruit juice in a regular nursing bottle. Other usual supplements

Discuss the meanings of the following sayings. Try to form a sound opinion concerning each saying.
1 Children are miniadults.
2 Spare the rod and spoil the child.
3 Children should be seen and not heard.
4 As a twig is bent, the tree is inclined.
5 He is a bad boy through and through.
Why do you think each saying is true, partially true, or untrue?

Discuss the effects of older family members' remarks about food on children's eating habits. Use examples such as these:
"What's that? I don't want any."
"You know I don't like that."
"Try it. It won't kill you."
"Clean your plate. Think of the starving children in other parts of the world."
"If you eat everything on your plate you can have some candy later."
Suggest ways of introducing new foods to children so the foods will be accepted well. Examples may include some of these ideas:
Serving only a small portion of the food the first time.
Serving the new food with familiar and well-liked foods.
Making remarks about how much you like the food.

137

Observe preschool children, other than your own brothers or sisters. Report your observations for three of the following situations:

1 At play
2 At mealtime
3 Being dressed or undressed
4 On a trip or other outing
5 Going to bed for a nap or for the night

You may observe children in nursery school, on a playground, in the neighborhood, in a store, or in their own homes. You may use the same child for all three observations or you may use different children. In your report answer these questions:

A How old were the children? If you do not know for sure, how old do you think they were? What were they doing to help you judge their ages?

B How did the children react to the situation? Why did they react this way?

C What provisions were made for letting children do things for themselves? Did they? Why or why not?

List points to look for in judging a nursery school. If possible, visit one and observe the children, teachers, equipment, toys, furnishings, kitchen, bathroom, and precautions taken for the children's safety.

are well-cooked cereals and such fruits and vegetables as applesauce, bananas, sieved peas, carrots, and potatoes. The sieved yolks of hard-cooked eggs and sieved meats are added later. Busy mothers can buy these foods already prepared for their babies, thus saving many hours of time.

By the end of the first year, children are eating many foods besides a daily quart of milk. They usually learn how to drink from a cup and how to bite and chew regular foods. Their efforts to feed themselves should be encouraged. So should their interest in new foods. Children who have learned to eat and like a variety of foods have an early start toward good health.

In their third year, children will enjoy raw vegetables and fruits in addition to the cooked foods they have already learned to like. After they are three, they can eat the foods prepared for the family, provided the foods are not too rich, too hard to handle, or too difficult to chew and swallow. Rich desserts, fried foods, nuts, highly seasoned foods, hot breads, and beverages such as tea and coffee should not be given to young children.

Protection from dangers

Until they have enough experience and judgment to look out for themselves, children need to be protected. They must be kept safe from physical harm and also from the emotional harm that results from too much teasing, ridicule, and sarcasm.

Adults must protect children from illness and diseases. They can best do this by following the advice of the family doctor or a pediatrician who specializes in child care. Such doctors help families establish proper routines of rest and nutrition to meet individual children's needs. They will also schedule preventive shots at the proper times so that childhood diseases can be avoided.

Every effort should be made to teach young children safe behavior. You may do this by setting a good example, as well as by seeing that they play safely in safe areas. Children need to be taught which activities are dangerous and how to avoid them.

Mental Needs

At no time in life will a human being have as much to learn as in early childhood. Children need to have their mental growth stimulated. They need people, books, toys, and other learning materials in their environment.

Self-Care

Young children, if encouraged, usually want to take care of themselves. For example, at an early age, they want to feed themselves. At first they tend to use their fingers. In time, they want to learn how to use regular eating tools. The skills of cutting, spreading, and spooning are difficult to learn. If children, by the age of seven or eight, have learned to feed themselves in a manner somewhat acceptable to adults, they are progressing at a reasonable rate.

When children are interested in dressing themselves, they should be permitted to do as much as they can. When adults lose patience and dress children to save time, they deprive children of a chance to learn. Children will enjoy trying to dress themselves if their clothing is designed for self-help. Desirable features are simple designs, large buttons and buttonholes, and slide fasteners that can be easily reached and managed. Children can learn to put their clothes on hooks or in drawers if storage places are low enough.

Other ways in which children are interested in self-help include combing their hair, brushing their teeth, turning on the water faucet to wash their hands, and going to the toilet alone. They also enjoy opening doors and walking up and down short flights of steps. You can help them become independent if you let them do for themselves as much as they can and will. Too, when routines in such matters can be practiced, it adds to children's personal security.

Toilet training involves many complicated learning processes. Young children need time to master this task. Most children want to try but will seem to lose ground more than once before the habit of control is firmly established.

Far too much toilet training is done simply to get the approval of grandparents or family friends. Children are usually more relaxed and grown-up about the whole experience if allowed to more or less train themselves. Most youngsters are toilet-trained by the time they enter kindergarten. Toilet training varies widely from family to family. For this reason, when you are caring for young children, find out what is expected of them. Follow family rules so the children will not become confused.

Toys and play equipment

Much of children's learning takes place as they play. Through play they develop alert, imaginative minds as well as strong bodies. Young children need toys and play equipment with which they can learn to control and develop their bodies. Playthings also provide them with opportunities to practice the ideas they are developing. As they play house or build a town with blocks, they are trying out some of the relationships they have seen between the people and the things around them.

Children play differently from time to time. Sometimes they enjoy playing quietly; other times they are boisterous. They play with others, and they play alone. They need opportunities and equipment to aid them in all types of play.

 On a separate sheet of paper, copy the crossword puzzle below. Fill in the answers that correspond to the ACROSS and DOWN items. *Do not* write in this book.

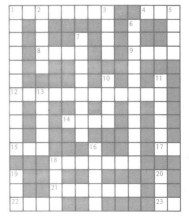

ACROSS

1 Children's growth in height, weight, and muscular coordination refers to their (1) growth.

4 To protect clothing, a young child usually wears a(an) (4) while eating.

8 Most young children enjoy having others (8) to them.

9 It is said that (9) *is the business of children.*

12 A doctor who specializes in caring for pregnant women is a(an) (12) .

14 In the first year of life, girls usually grow more slowly than (14) .

15 Children's clothes need to be made so they will not (15) easily.

17 Many children enjoy programs on (17) designed to meet their interests.

18 Mothers and fathers are called (18) .

21 A two- or three-year-old child is called a(an) (21) .

22 As children grow older their interest in various (22) changes.

23 If young children are frequently told not to do certain things, one of their first words of speech may be (23) .

DOWN

1 A child between three and six years of age may be called a(an) (1) .

2 In parallel play, children do *not* think of toys as *mine* and (2) .

3 All children need affection and (3) .

5 There are many changes in a family when there is a new (5) .

6 Social growth is encouraged by a variety of successful (6) with family and friends.

7 Children may become part of a family by birth or (7) .

10 If you take care of children, it may be helpful to have several baby-sitting (10) for children of different ages.

Tiny babies need little equipment for active play. They play as they kick and pull. As children grow older, they need equipment that will encourage them to use their large muscles. From large blocks, they progress to wheeled toys, such as wagons and tricycles. They also learn to use balancing boards, swings, slides, and climbing equipment. All of these playthings belong in the general environment of children. Families can furnish some of them. Other equipment is available in playgrounds, nurseries, or day-care centers. In one way or another, children should be given opportunities to learn through the use of a wide range of playthings.

Toys and play equipment should be chosen for children's use. For example, small, cuddly dolls that can be dressed and undressed aid in many kinds of learning. On the other hand, large beautifully dressed dolls that must be placed on shelves contribute little to children's development.

Playthings must be safe, but they need not be expensive. An empty box which imagination can turn into a house, a car, an orbiting space ship, or a store can be more fun for children than toys bought for every special purpose. In fact, simple toys are often better than complicated ones because they stimulate the imagination, encouraging children to work out several ideas during a single play period. Playthings must be sturdy enough to survive rough

A child's creative play leads to healthy mental growth.   *David Schaffer*

handling. Older children like to test their strength by moving large objects. They need toys which are strong enough to hold their weight but light enough to move.

Games are enjoyed by very young children. Babies' first *games* may occur when older people help them exercise by pulling them to a sitting position. Babies enjoy not only the muscular exercise but the companionship of older people as well. Later, when they can sit up, babies like games of peekaboo. At about the same age, they enjoy the companionship involved in *retriever,* a game in which they deliberately

11 A child up to one year old is called a(an) (11) .

13 As children grow older, they gradually require less (13) .

16 Children have physical, mental, social, and emotional (16) .

19 Baby sitters usually do not have much time to (19) .

20 Playing with younger brothers and sisters can be (20) for all of you.

Your career
Baby food specialist

You would test the nutritional value, taste, and appearance of baby food and plan menus for infants and small children. You might assist in package design or copywriting for advertisements of the product. You would work for a food manufacturing company or government agency, such as the Food and Drug Administration or the Consumer Protection and Environmental Health Service.

Children discover the real world through their make-believe world of play. As they grow in their awareness, children enjoy imitating adults. *Leonard Freed/Magnum*

drop a toy for the fun of having someone pick it up for them.

True social games do not develop until the late preschool years. Older preschool children enjoy complicated games of make-believe with other children of the same age and with older children and adults. These games can also be fun for older children. The older ones must remember that preschoolers are not ready for formal rules.

Play space should be checked for safety on a regular basis. Children need protection from danger while they satisfy their curiosity. Broken glass, rusty nails, and sharp metal edges can cause serious injuries. Play equipment must be kept in good repair and placed in proper positions.

Indoor play space should be provided for all children. Even very young children can be given safe corners for play. Because their play must be supervised and because their parents will want to be near them as they do their housework, playpens can be a real convenience. Playpens can be moved from room to room so that older babies can go with their parents as they do their daily tasks. Older children may use the living room floor, the kitchen table, or the play area of sleeping quarters for their indoor play space.

Outdoor play is desirable when weather permits. It offers children a chance to move freely to develop endurance, muscular strength, and coordination.

No matter where children play, it is important that they learn to put away their play materials when they are through with them. A box, a drawer, or open shelves should be provided for convenient toy storage. A similar storage space should be provided for larger outdoor equipment. Children will learn to care for their belongings more quickly if storage areas are convenient to play areas.

Language development

Children learn to talk by acquiring words and language patterns from the people around them. They also learn to talk by having experiences which give them something to talk about. They learn to communicate through constant practice.

If older people anticipate the every wish of children, they are denied the opportunity to learn to speak. If people accept children's baby talk without guiding them into correct speech patterns, children are denied a chance for conversational improvement. If people brush off children's attempts to converse by giving them only *yes* or *no* answers or by indifferent listening, children will have little chance to develop language skills.

If children's homes are places where books are treasured and where reading is an accepted family activity, they will very soon acquire the family attitude. Very young children enjoy looking at bright pictures in sturdy books prepared for their age group. As they learn to talk, they take pleasure in pointing to a picture and naming the objects shown. At the same age, they also enjoy having an older person tell them about the pictures as they turn the pages of a book.

In many families a daily period of time is set aside for children to watch television. Wise families help children select programs appropriate to their development. Older people make sure that children's natural interest in television does not interfere with their need for other activities. Young children enjoy programs which are shared with older family members and talked about afterwards.

Young children generally enjoy music. There are many ways in which alert families can encourage this interest. Toddlers can be encouraged to march or drum to a favorite record. They can sing along with others.

Social Needs

Social experiences at a very young age affect people's social behavior as adults. During early childhood, family members provide the environment for most children's social experiences. One of the first signs of social development is when infants smile in response to family members. Another early sign of social behavior occurs when chil-

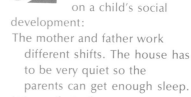

Discuss the possible effects of the following situations on a child's social development:

The mother and father work different shifts. The house has to be very quiet so the parents can get enough sleep.

It is a mile to the nearest playmate's home.

The family does a lot of informal entertaining at home and relatives and friends often stop in unexpectedly.

Many members of the extended family live in the same apartment building.

Give examples of children's possible emotional reactions to some of the following situations:

A child drops an ice cream cone.

A child's pet dies.

A child falls and gets a skinned knee.

A dog barks and jumps up on a child.

A child's new toy breaks.

Discuss why children may have different reactions to similar situations.

Look through toy and play equipment catalogs to find examples of items that help children release emotional energy, such as toys that are pounded, pulled, or ridden. Suggest games that allow children to let off steam.

Being accepted by other children gives a child needed security outside the home. *Owen Franken/Stock, Boston*

Explain the differences between discipline and punishment. Give examples to illustrate your explanation. Find a definition for *preventive discipline*. Give examples to show how discipline problems can often be prevented before they start.

List kinds of punishments you have observed for various types of misbehavior. Discuss the reactions of the children to the punishments used in these situations.

Say the following in different ways to illustrate positive verbal guidance:
"Would you like to put your coat on when we go out? It's very cold outside."
"How about putting your toys away now? It's time for bed."
"Can you get the dog? It's time for us to take the dog for a walk."

Brainstorm for ways to make children feel secure.

Discuss the statement: *Teenagers who have very few responsibilities are disadvantaged.*

dren stop crying when they are picked up. Playing peekaboo, waving good-bye, and crying when left alone are also social reactions. Social behavior varies greatly from one age to another. It also varies from one situation to another.

To get along well with others, children need to be taught basic social skills. They need to be guided so they learn what is expected of them in the world outside their homes. As children grow older, their companions and friends influence their social development. Social development includes learning to behave acceptably, playing by approved rules, and developing positive attitudes toward others. Children need to learn that life is a matter of give-and-take. They can learn that sometimes they must be the givers, and they can learn to enjoy giving. Children need to be taught to consider the feelings and desires of others. This is important because behavior patterns established in childhood tend to remain throughout life. Acceptance by others as a child contributes to satisfying social relationships as a teenager and an adult.

Emotional Needs

In early childhood emotional reactions are often strong and frequent. Common emotions in childhood are fear, worry, anger, anxiety, jealousy, curiosity, joy, and affection. Emotional reactions vary among children and are different from those of adolescents and adults. Even when young children's emotional reactions are very disturbing, they usually last only a short time.

Emotional control is learned. Family members play a vital role in guiding children's emotional development and in helping children to control their emotional outbursts. As their social environments broaden, children gradually learn that biting and hitting are unacceptable behavior. If children learn that temper tantrums will not get them what they want, other behavior will be substituted.

Learning to control emotions early in life is important because it affects the ability to get along well with others. Emotional reactions also affect a person's self-concept as a child and as an adult.

Security

Children need to be regarded seriously as family members. Their security is provided by the people who take care of them. If secure within their family group, they can be taught to cope with familiar situations as well as those that are new and different. When children come to you hurt or bewildered, let them know they can count on you.

Sometimes with the birth of a new brother or sister, children lose their sense of security. They may be helped to overcome their loss by special attention which makes them feel that their parents still love

A child can learn acceptable social behavior while experiencing outings with other children.
Hank Morgan/Photo Researchers

Name famous people in politics, show business, and sports today who have physical limitations. What personal traits have contributed to their success? How may they have compensated for their limitations?

Discuss the following statements:
Children should be accepted for what they are.
Exceptional children should be waited on *hand and foot*.

Give examples of situations when you think it would be best to place an exceptional child in an institution. What factors need to be considered when a family decides to care for an exceptional child at home?

Name local organizations offering services to exceptional children. Consider public school programs, private institutions, specialized schools, health and welfare departments, and civic groups. What services are offered and how much do they cost?

Read an article or guidebook about baby-sitting. Summarize facts dealing with the responsibilities of a baby-sitter. Write and distribute a Code of Ethics for baby-sitters.

them. It is especially helpful if they can be honestly praised for their own achievements. They will also be helped to understand and outgrow this jealousy if allowed to help care for a new baby.

Discipline

Children need to understand that there are real limits in all aspects of daily life. They learn these limits most easily by following the examples set by older family members. Children imitate their older brothers and sisters as well as their parents. This places a great responsibility upon all the older members of a family. Older family members must follow the same rules for health and safety that they expect younger family members to follow.

Firm rules and good reasons are important in establishing acceptable behavior patterns. Little children like to be given specific help in behaving acceptably. When told only what *not* to do, they may be confused and become stubborn and resentful. If you say, "No, that stove is hot. You will hurt yourself," children will begin to see that rules of this type are made to protect them.

Young children must be expected to follow rules. If necessary, they can be picked up and removed from

Describe qualities you would want in a baby-sitter for your own child. Develop these into a check list. Rate yourself as a baby-sitter.

Form a panel composed of parents of young children and student baby-sitters. Ask them to discuss what parents expect of a baby-sitter and what a sitter expects of parents. Discuss pay, transportation, hours of employment, responsibilities to be assumed by the parents and by the sitter, and privileges and restrictions.

Brainstorm to identify factors contributing to good relationships between a baby-sitter and a child's parents, and between a baby-sitter and the child. How may each gain and keep the confidence and respect of the other?

Write a Bill-of-Rights for parents employing baby-sitters and write a Bill of Rights for baby-sitters.

Dramatize making friends with children by acting out good and poor ways to approach children you have just met. After the dramatization, discuss the qualities that children like in baby-sitters and in adults.

danger. Some people think that turning children toward acceptable activities is giving in to them. Instead, this is an effective part of child rearing. Substituting desirable activities for unacceptable ones clearly defines the limits of acceptable behavior. With proper training and practice, children can make desirable substitutions independently as they mature.

Punishment may sometimes be absolutely necessary. In such instances, it should be both positive and instructional. Related to the offense, it should be administered promptly and calmly. There should be no doubt in children's minds as to why they are being punished. Children should be made to feel it is their behavior that is unacceptable, rather than that they are bad children.

Exceptional Children

Exceptional children have physical, mental, social, or emotional abilities different from what is considered normal. Exceptional children may have physical limitations. They may be more intelligent than others, or they may be mentally slower than average. They may have problems getting along with others, or they may have emotional problems. Sometimes exceptional children are affected in several areas of development. An example could be a child with an emotional problem who shows unsociable behavior around others.

Special understanding and guidance may be needed to help exceptional children develop as normally as possible. The adjustment of exceptional children is determined largely by the attitudes of others toward them. Harmonious family relationships that contribute to the development of a good self-concept are especially important when there is an exceptional child in the family.

Many communities have organizations offering special services to families with exceptional children. Such organizations can help family members to better understand their child. They may offer advice on possible problems and how best to help the exceptional child develop fully. Some organizations can also help ease the financial costs that may be involved in meeting the special needs of exceptional children and their families.

TAKING RESPONSIBILITY FOR CHILDREN

You may already have had a chance to care for young children. Taking care of youngsters is a very responsible job. Little children look up to older children. To toddlers, teenagers are grownups. It takes patience and understanding to work with children. As a babysitter, you are in a position of great trust. Before you accept this responsibility, ask yourself whether you are prepared to act in a mature way.

Can you keep calm? Can you be fair? Can you direct children's interests from harmful to constructive play? Can you think clearly in a real crisis and get the kind of help you need?

Being a Baby-Sitter

Your first experience with baby-sitting may have been at home when you were asked to take care of younger brothers and sisters. You know the rules at home. You also know your family's routines and the family standards of child care. Families differ on whether family members are paid for baby-sitting. When you sit for others, you usually do so for pay. In assuming responsibility for other people's children, you need certain very definite preparation for the job. If you are a baby-sitter, you are expected to know what to do in any situation that may arise.

Baby-sitting is a part-time occupation chosen by many mature people as well as by teenagers. It is more than sitting, certainly, and it involves having up-to-date information on child care, guidance, and health. Baby-sitting offers an opportunity for young people to earn money. Valuable, too, is the training obtained in making decisions, meeting emergencies, and learning how to get along with adults as well as children.

Baby-sitting may involve feeding and dressing children, reading

Unscramble the ten words below. Put one letter in each square. Each word relates to child development. *Do not* write in this book.

1. H T A B
2. P I E D A R
3. T O T L E B
4. Y L A P
5. R E S T C U I Y
6. C A N D G U I E
7. T E A S F Y
8. S O R S I E T
9. M A G E S
10. Y I I I O E S S T L R B N P

Now arrange the ten circled letters to form two words. These two words may refer to you. If so, the ten words above are some of your concerns.

A baby-sitter is also responsible for the well being of the children and should keep them away from dangerous activities which might cause them harm. *PPG Industries*

Plan and give a class party for four- and five-year-old children. List all the things that have to be done before, during, and after the party. Divide into committees to assume different responsibilities, such as preparing and serving refreshments, planning and playing appropriate games, and cleaning up. Evaluate the party by telling what was good about it and by discussing how it could have been improved. What did you learn about giving parties for children? What did you learn about four- and five-year-old children?

Give a puppet show at a children's party for elementary students. Why is it important to keep the puppet show short? What affects the length of a child's interest span?

Role play scenes showing a child meeting a child care employee for the first time. Describe the employee's personality characteristics which would probably appeal to all young children.

Select or write stories for children of varying ages. Get permission to read these during a planned story-telling hour at the local library. Or read stories to children in the hospital.

stories to them, playing out-of-doors, putting them to bed, or perhaps keeping a convalescent child quiet and amused. It is wise for younger teenagers to accept only daytime or early evening assignments in homes of people they know.

While a knowledge of the behavior of your own brothers and sisters will be helpful in baby-sitting, the problems presented by other children may be different. Therefore, as a would-be baby-sitter, you need to know what type of behavior to expect from children of different ages. You should also know how to make financial and transportation arrangements, how to dress, and what to do after you arrive at the home.

Caring for Babies

Even though you may not have complete charge of babies very often, it is important for you to know how to take care of them. Babies usually cry because something is wrong. Parents soon learn to tell from the tone of their babies' cries whether they are thirsty, hungry, uncomfortable, sick, or merely seeking attention. When you are caring for a baby, one of the parents will generally tell you the types of crying to expect.

Holding babies

Young babies' muscles are soft and relatively weak. They cannot hold their heads up without help. To support a baby's head and the upper part of the back, slip one hand under the head and place your other hand and arm under the lower part of the back. Then you can safely lift the baby to your shoulder, where the head will be securely supported by your body.

Pick babies up by grasping their entire bodies, rather than their arms. Hold them firmly in your arms, either resting them against your shoulder or cradling them in your arms. This gives babies the support that makes them feel secure. Young babies have an instinctive fear of falling.

Feeding babies

In caring for babies, you may need to feed them. Be sure that a parent has shown you how to hold the baby securely. Be careful not to rush babies through the feeding, and be sure they are well bubbled both during and after their feedings.

You probably will not be asked to prepare the baby's formula. If you are asked to do this, you must be given the directions for sterilizing, measuring the ingredients, mixing the formula, and storing the bottles. You must follow these directions exactly. Usually formula enough for a twenty-four-hour period is prepared at one time.

Bathing and dressing babies

You may be asked to give older babies a bath. A bath should be fun

A baby-sitter's duties include keeping children busy, interested, relaxed, and happy while their parents are away. *Sybil Shackman/Monkmeyer*

Tell how a young child's fascination with melting ice, growing plants, or cloudy skies shows mental development. Why do young children ask so many questions? What questions have young children asked you that were difficult to answer? Give examples to show that a child's interest span or period of concentration increases with age.

Your career
Nursemaid

You would observe and monitor play activities or amuse children by reading to them or playing games with them. You might also prepare and serve meals or formulas, sterilize bottles and other equipment used for feeding infants, dress or help children to dress themselves, bathe or help children bathe, accompany children to and from school or special interest outings. You might be employed by a private or government agency, or you might be self-employed.

for babies. They must be watched constantly while being bathed, since they can slip so easily. Never leave them alone or unsupported for any reason. Even when they are old enough to sit alone, babies are bathed in a comparatively small amount of water.

You may need to dress babies while you are in charge of them. Babies of any age may feel uncomfortable if their clothes become wet and sticky. One of the baby's parents will have shown you where to find changes of clothing. If cloth diapers are used, ask parents to show you how they want the diapers folded and fastened. As a safety precaution in pinning the diaper, place your fingers between the baby's body and the diaper before inserting the pin. Keep pins out of the baby's reach. Learn to dress the baby with as little handling as possible. It disturbs babies to feel tied down as their arms and legs are being clothed or as the clothing is being placed over their heads.

Providing sleep and rest for babies
When it is time for babies to sleep, be sure they are comfortable. Check their clothing to see that it is dry and that they are comfortably

Try to button a garment while wearing bulky gloves. Crawl in a skirt or baggy pants. Hang up clothes in a closet from a kneeling position. Tell how these activities relate to young children's experiences as they are trying to become independent.

Act out emotional situations involving children. Situations might include the following:

A child wants a cookie in the grocery store.
A child wants to take home another child's toy.
A child bites someone.

How did the older people involved handle the situation? How might the situation have been handled better?

Bulletin board IDEA
Title: *Seeds Need Planting*
Directions: Outline the bulletin board with packages of vegetable and fruit seeds. On paper cutouts of different shaped leaves, write words such as *nourishing food, enough sleep, exercise, mental stimulation, social activities,* and *emotional guidance.*

A young child can be allowed to enjoy a bath while an older person watches carefully. *Culligan International Company*

warm. Place them in bed and adjust their covers according to the directions the parents have given you. Be sure that babies are protected from unusually bright lights and loud noises. Then leave them quietly so that they can doze off undisturbed. Be sure to remain within hearing distance so you can go to them immediately if they need you. You may want to check occasionally to see if they are covered and resting comfortably.

Caring for Young Children

Taking care of young children is different in many ways from taking care of babies. Young children need someone to look after their physical needs, but as they grow and develop, they need help in other ways as well. They must be guided in their play, protected from injury, and taught how to live with others. As their world expands, so do the responsibilities of those who direct their development. Many teenagers spend the summer months as effective companions for young children.

Feeding young children

You may be asked to help young children with their meals. If so, prepare their food according to the parent's directions. Be patient with toddlers if they have trouble feeding themselves. Help them if they need help, but allow them to do what they can. Be sure to tell their returning parents just how much they have eaten.

Bathing and dressing young children

If you are asked to bathe young children, make sure they enjoy the experience. Be fair to them by selecting a time when they are between activities and are willing to bathe. They need a chance to splash, to play with soap and toys, and to use the washcloth. Although they enjoy washing themselves, they probably will not do a very good job. Washcloths for each of you will allow you to bathe them while they enjoy their growing ability to take care of themselves.

Young children can drown in only a few inches of water. If they turn on the hot water while they are alone, they can be severely scalded. Your presence is needed both for their safety and for their security.

Help children dress themselves in the clothing provided for them. Remember to be patient. Be ready to help them when they need help, but be careful not to take away their joy in being able to do things for themselves.

It is not necessary for you to keep young children shining clean every moment they are in your care. See that they wash their hands and face before eating, and help them brush their teeth afterward. They will naturally get messy during their activities. Let them enjoy their play. Then clean them up before they go to bed.

Getting young children ready for bed

In getting children ready for bed and for sound, restful sleep, be sure that you do things in a relaxed manner. Toddlers and preschoolers do not drop off to sleep as easily as babies do. Allow children of these ages a chance to unwind. Perhaps a quiet story or song will help them relax. Be sure toddlers have their favorite toy with them if they usually sleep with it. When you are certain young children are comfortable, leave them to rest alone in their usual place. Remain free enough so that you can go to them immediately if they need help.

Make a baby-sitting kit full of surprises. This might include crayons and paper, storybooks, puppets, or any other items which would interest children you baby-sit.

Brainstorm for ideas of thoughtful things baby-sitters can do that are not expected of them. Examples: making young children's beds after their naps; putting soiled clothes in the proper containers; and cleaning up the bathroom after children's baths.

Your career
Sitter services

You would visit homes to entertain children, elderly people, or invalids when other family members are not available. You might also perform simple household services during your visit. You might work for a government or private agency, or you might be self-employed.

Number from 1 to 10 on a piece of paper. Beside each number write the letter corresponding to the answer that *best* completes the sentence. *Do not* write in this book.

1 A doctor who specializes in the care of expectant mothers and delivers babies is a(an):
a general practitioner.
b pediatrician.
c obstetrician.
d podiatrist.

2 The longest period of rapid physical growth is usually during:
a the first year of life.
b the toddler stage.
c the elementary-school years.
d adolescence.

3 Accomplishing physical developmental tasks depends primarily upon:
a emotional control.
b an intellectually stimulating environment.
c social activities.
d muscular growth and coordination.

4 Social development in babies is shown when they:
a sit up alone.
b turn over.
c smile.
d crawl.

5 Most young children prefer foods:
a highly seasoned.
b served hot or cold.
c easily eaten with the fingers.
d strongly flavored.

6 A typical characteristic of preschoolers is:
a emotional control.
b curiosity about the world around them.
c rapid physical growth.
d carrying grudges.

7 Just before young children go to bed it is best to:
a play an active game with them.
b threaten that something bad will happen if they aren't good.
c read a pleasant story to them.
d watch an exciting TV show.

8 The time when the opinion of the gang is most important is usually during:
a the toddler stage.
b the preschool years.
c the elementary-school years.
d the later adolescent years.

9 Helping children learn self-discipline involves:
a setting a good example.
b threatening them.
c saying *no* frequently.
d punishing them by making them stay in a room alone.

10 The beginning of puberty usually occurs:
a at an earlier age for girls than for boys.
b at the same age for all youth.
c when emotional control is fully developed.
d on the twelfth birthday.

Fill in the blank in each sentence with the *best* word or words to complete the statement. *Do not* write in this book.

1 The most important aspect of home management is careful __(1)__.

2 The first step in the problem-solving approach is __(2)__ the problem.

3 The last step in the problem-solving approach is __(3)__.

4 Before moving furniture, it is wise to __(4)__ both the furniture and the place where you are considering placing it.

5 Another term used for the traffic flow in a home is the traffic __(5)__.

6 A TV stand with lower shelves for storing books is an example of a(an) __(6)__ piece of furniture.

7 A pot holder is most efficiently stored near the __(7)__.

8 A flour sifter is most efficiently stored in or near the __(8)__ center in the kitchen.

9 If duplicate cleaning supplies are stored, they are most frequently kept in the kitchen and __(9)__.

10 A common childhood disease for which there is no preventative inoculation is __(10)__.

11 The disease that may cause birth defects if contracted in the early months of pregnancy is __(11)__.

12 People who are ill often lose their __(12)__ for food.

Chapter 8

Making Decisions Related to Everyday Living

The main job of the home manager is to keep the family happy during the continual adjustments which the family must make. Planning is an essential part of management. But values must be determined and decisions made almost minute by minute. Using common sense and knowledge wisely in making-on-the-spot decisions contributes to happy family living.

Home management is involved in every aspect of family living. The abilities of family members to get along together or to adjust to new situations are management concerns. The day-in-day-out concern that family members be fed nutritiously and regularly is also a part of home management. So too is the problem of providing suitable clothing for every family member. When to paint, what

Describe someone you know who seems to get things done quickly and easily. How does the person do this? In what ways is this person a good manager?

Describe a decision your family must make, such as buying a new car, deciding where to go on vacation, changing a job, or moving to a new place. Who is involved in making the decision? Why are some family members involved to a greater degree than others? Who will make the final decision? Why?

equipment to buy, and where to live — these are matters of management. To keep the home warm during the winter, comfortably cool during the summer, and dry throughout the year calls for management. Too, the well-managed home, while neat enough for health and safety, is also planned for comfort, convenience, and privacy for the people who live there.

USING THE PROBLEM-SOLVING APPROACH IN HOME MANAGEMENT

How can you manage a home when that responsibility falls on your shoulders? Every teenager at one time or another considers this question. Eventually, whether they realize it or not, successful home managers learn to use common sense. They learn to apply certain methods of problem solving to any problem, big or small.

There are a number of approaches to problem solving. Some approaches are less detailed than others. Some omit steps which are considered important in others. The following steps represent one approach to problem solving. As you become familiar with this approach, you may wish to change it so that it will better meet a given situation. In general, however, each step of this approach should be considered in the suggested order before a definite decision is made.

Stating the Problem

The first step, clearly stating the problem, is often one of the most difficult steps involved in handling a situation. You cannot reach an intelligent solution to a problem until you know exactly what the problem is. And you cannot know what to do in a situation unless you can relate it to your goals and values. Unfortunately, the first statement of a problem may overlook the real issues. For example, you may ask yourself, "Shall I buy this shirt?" If you are asking this question during a personal shopping trip, your question may mean, "Is the shirt a good buy for my purpose?" On the other hand, you may see the shirt while you are shopping for a gift for someone else. In this case, your question may mean, "Should I skimp on my gift selection in order to have the shirt?"

The following set of circumstances might describe a situation similar to one you have faced. Sandy needs a new winter coat. But so does Dan, a younger brother. The family resources will allow for the purchase of shoes for the entire family, some shirts, jackets, and jeans. But there seems to be no workable way to fit two new winter coats into the overall clothing budget.

Few problems are simple. Most are made up of many related parts. Even the simple question, "What shall we have for dinner tonight?"

involves at least four considerations. There is the need to meet the nutritional requirements of everyone in the family. There is the necessity for selecting food which fits within the family budget. There is the desire to choose food which individual family members like. Also, there must be enough time and energy available for proper preparation of the selected foods.

Collecting the Facts

Once the problem is clearly stated, you can begin to collect the facts which will help you make a wise decision. Sometimes this step can be as easy as organizing facts you already know well. At other times you may need to look up all the facts. If the problem is simple, you may be able to organize the facts in your mind and make an immediate decision. If it is more complicated, you may prefer to write down the facts.

In Sandy's case, the parents might explain that there is only so much money available to buy winter clothes for both children. If Sandy wrote down the facts about their needs and what similar articles had cost recently, there would be definite facts and figures to study.

Sandy could list the number and kind of winter clothing items needed by both children. Then the cost of each item could be estimated. After multiplying the number of each item needed by the cost of each item and adding all the totals, Sandy would have the approximate cost in dollars and cents of the clothing needed by both children. This figure might be more or less than the amount of money available.

You may wish to organize facts into groups. There are facts about a problem itself. Your statement of the problem is the first of these. You may need to consider how the various possible solutions will affect the wants and needs of all the people involved. How do the other people feel about the situation? A judgment as to the importance of the problem can be included with this group of facts.

Another group of facts consists of information relating to costs. Although most people consider the cost in money, they may overlook other costs. Some decisions may cost more time or energy than you can afford. Some decisions may require that someone give up a conflicting goal. Although the costs of inconvenience and dissatisfaction are hard to measure, they too must be considered as you search for a satisfactory solution.

A third group of facts concerns your resources. What is available to you to help meet your goals? Since costs and resources tend to be related, they are frequently thought of together. Thus, when you consider how much time an activity will take, you also consider how much time is available. There are certain resources which are often

Brainstorm to identify things you do by habit or without much thought, such as washing your face, brushing your teeth, combing your hair, and eating. Consider what it would be like if you had to make these decisions consciously. What are the advantages and disadvantages of performing some tasks as a matter of habit?

Observe a member of your family for about fifteen minutes. What decisions did the person appear to make consciously? Unconsciously? How could you tell?

List decisions you have made in the last three days. Classify each decision as major or minor. Consider a decision major if it requires further decisions. For example, the decision to get a job requires other decisions such as what kind of work to do, where to work, and how to get the job.

Brainstorm to identify decisions that may result from a major decision, such as going steady, dropping out of school, or moving to another community.

Apply the problem-solving approach to one of the following situations. (You will have to use your imagination in stating some of the factors which affect the situation.)

1 Rusty may choose one elective course this year. Rusty may take home economics, art, chorus, band, or a foreign language.

2 John wants to buy a secondhand minibike which needs repair. Although he has been saving his money carefully, he is still $25 short of the selling price.

3 Roberta wants to take guitar lessons. She also hopes to join a community basketball team. The team practices at the only time guitar lessons are given.

Bulletin board IDEA

Title: *Don't Fiddle Around Play it Right*

Directions: Use a picture of a guitar, fiddle, violin, or other stringed instrument. Write the steps in the problem-solving approach on pieces of paper mounted around the musical instrument.

Before deciding where to place pattern pieces on the fabric, you might consider the amount of fabric and the number of pattern pieces you have. The pattern guide sheet, common sense, and experience will help you in making the decision. *Bob Cook*

overlooked. For instance, do you have the skills that will help you attain your goals? What substitutions can you make in order to reach a satisfactory decision?

At this point, Sandy might begin to reason out a list of possible solutions. Assume Sandy's figures showed that the winter clothing items needed by both children came to more money than was available. Possible solutions might include any of the following:

1 Mother and Dad can get the money we need. They can cut down on the cost of food we eat. They don't really need to spend money on recreation either. They're grown-up now. Clothing is a real need. Our parents should not donate to charities or other worthy causes right now. *We* are their worthy causes.

2 I can make the two shirts I need for fourteen dollars and save six dollars. But that is only six dollars.

156

Would that help enough to count? Would the time used in sewing take away time needed for earning money?

3 I can use the money I earn for clothes instead of entertainment. But Dan makes money on yard work. Is it fair for me alone to make up the amount needed for our winter clothes while he spends his money as usual?

4 Maybe, when we shop, we'll find good buys and it won't be necessary to spend as much as I figured.

Considering the Alternatives

The processes of clarifying the problem and gathering the necessary facts usually suggest alternative solutions. Name other possible solutions you may have overlooked.

 Answer the following questions about the way you make important decisions. Explain your answers.

1 Do you think of all the possible choices?

2 Do you then determine the advantages and disadvantages of each possible choice?

3 Do you consider carefully all of the alternatives?

4 Do you seek help at this point if you need it?

5 Do you decide whether or not your plan worked well?

6 When a decision is a good one, do you use it in similar situations unless there are new developments?

Present a skit showing a teenager faced with a difficult decision. Do not show the decision itself. Divide into small groups and decide which would be the best choice that person might make. What alternatives are there? What might be the consequences of each decision?

The decision to work during the summer might be based on your need for money as well as your desire to gain experience. *David Krasnor/Photo Researchers*

Name major decisions that will have to be made by you and other teenagers in the next ten years. Examples may include:

1 Deciding on the kind and amount of education to seek.
2 Choosing a career.
3 Selecting a marriage partner.
4 Choosing a life-style.
5 Deciding where to live.

Explain who may be involved in each decision listed. What factors are likely to influence each decision?

Evaluate a decision you have made and carried out recently. To what extent did you reach your goal? What changes might have been made in the original decision or in the way it was carried out? Were your goals reasonable? Why?

Apply the problem-solving approach to one of your personal problems. Evaluate the results by answering the following questions:

1 Which decisions were the best and why?
2 How could the plan have been improved?
3 What did you learn by applying the problem-solving approach in this situation?

Tell about an incident when you or someone you know seemed to learn from making a mistake.

Part-time jobs give young people the opportunity to earn money for personal expenses.
Ginger Chih/Peter Arnold Photo Archives

Sometimes people overlook an obvious solution because they are concentrating too hard on the fact that a problem exists.

There is seldom a single, absolutely perfect solution for a problem. Consider the short-term and long-term results of each possible decision. Consider the advantages and disadvantages of each. You may need to gather additional facts or consult an expert in the field in order to be sure that you know all the advantages and disadvantages involved.

As you consider possible solutions, you may discover that one particular choice seems to be the most attractive. Another choice may seem so distasteful you are ready to drop it immediately. Such likes and dislikes are an important part of the problem-solving process, but it is unwise to make them the *only* basis for choice. It is wiser to treat these feelings as part of the facts to be considered. The solution you like may not be the best solution. Perhaps you like it for only one reason. Would that part of the solution fit in with another solution? Checking the facts beyond your first feelings may help you find a new alternative, better than any of your earlier ones.

Could some of Sandy's possible solutions to the problem be distasteful to other members of the family? For instance, would it be right to ask parents to stop supporting a charity of special importance to them? If the parents are trying to improve their personal relationship by doing something special together each week, would it be asking too much to expect them to give up their recreation? If making the shirts means that a sewing machine must be purchased, is this solving any immediate problems? Perhaps only at this point would Sandy consider talking over the problem with Dan. Maybe, by working together, they could both contribute to buying their school clothing for the year.

Considering the Values Involved

In the previous steps, you have already made some value judgments. The importance of the problem and the list of costs involved in different solutions were probably determined by comparing the alternatives to individual or family values.

At this time a manager is wise to consider values again. A workable solution may be inappropriate to the total situation because it conflicts with a goal which is more valuable. Failure to consider all the values involved may result in choosing an unsatisfactory solution.

In considering values, it is necessary to know what goals and ideals are important to all family members. It is also necessary to know the relative importance of the various items on this list. Finally, it is necessary to know where the family members differ from one another, as to specific items on the list and as to the relative importance of these items. Thus, Sandy's brother might not be willing to contribute to their fall wardrobe. In such a case, should Sandy be forced to contribute the entire amount needed? Or should Dan be expected to get by on less?

Making the Decision

In an ideal situation, the problem would now be solved. The problem was clearly and fully stated. All the facts relating to the situation were gathered. All possible solutions were considered. Values were clearly defined. The one best solution should be obvious.

Unfortunately, the ideal situation seldom exists. In a real situation you may find that you have had to define the problem more than once. You needed additional facts, found new solutions, and needed still more facts. At the end of this process, you are left with two or three workable solutions. The difficulty is likely to be a question of values. The clothing problem discussed above may finally boil down to the fact that clothes are not as important to Dan as they are to Sandy. When each understands the other's values, they can usually make a good decision.

Write the words *home management* on a piece of paper, arranging the letters in a vertical line. Next to each letter list the words relating to *home management* that begin with that letter. These examples can help you get started.

H health, housing
O owe, ownership
M manage, money
E effort, efficiency

M
A
N
A
G
E
M
E
N
T

Tell about an incident when family relationships were affected because the following was *not* true: *A place for everything and everything in its place.*

159

Use an area of the home economics department to set up demonstration study areas that could be used in a bedroom, living room, or kitchen.

Illustrate good and poor lighting arrangements for activities such as studying, sewing, or preparing meals.

Collect pictures of lamps, desks, and study areas.

Evaluate the effects of colored lamp shades on the lighting in a room.

Plan a work area in the foods laboratory, making the best use of the light available.

Use scraps of wallpaper or adhesive-backed material to:
Cover a small address book.
Make a protective cover for a
  book.
Cover small boxes to use on a
  desk or to hold pins or coins
  on a dresser or dressing table.
Cover a bulletin board or
  mirror frame.
Make mats for pictures.
Cover a large commercial carton
  to be used as a wastebasket.
Hang pictures in a group by suspending them on strands of ribbon or macramé.

Decorate a chopping board to hang on a wall in your kitchen or dining area or to give as a gift.

Acting on the Decision

As soon as you have reached a decision, the solution you have selected becomes your plan of action. You should be ready to act on your plan immediately. If you delay, the problem may become more complicated. This does not mean that you must rush out helter-skelter to take action. Take time to think about it. Be sure you haven't forgotten any part of the problem. Have you considered the *what, who, when, where, why,* and *how* of the issue at stake? You may need to make decisions concerning related problems and actions. Once the major decision has been made, smaller decisions tend to fall into place rather easily. Remember your decision. You may be able to use it to solve any future problems that may occur.

Evaluating the Results

Even though many people omit this step, the problem-solving process is not really completed until you have evaluated the results. Review successful decisions to see why they were successful. Check to see whether some part of the plan could be improved. Similar decisions will be easier to make when you have learned the strengths and weaknesses of the previous plans you have made.

If Sandy's plan is to earn part of the money for the clothing, make some of the clothes, and shop for high-quality clothing at low prices, this solution would probably work for the situation. Sandy need not feel guilty if Dan prefers to go without his needed winter coat.

In spite of all efforts, there will be times when you choose the wrong solution. Successful people learn from such mistakes. Rather than hiding your mistakes or making excuses for them, review your unsuccessful plans to find what mistakes were made. As you discover what happened and why it happened, you will be learning how to avoid similar mistakes in the future. Once you understand your mistakes, you are ready to move on to the next decision, to try again, this time more successfully.

MANAGING THE HOME EFFICIENTLY

A comfortable home provides for the physical, mental, social, and emotional needs of each family member. A place is needed where everyone can gather to enjoy group activities. Each person needs a place to be alone when quiet is desired. In today's small homes, it may seem impossible to provide comfort, convenience, and privacy for everyone. How can the children in the family have privacy if they must share the same room? How can the family provide space for quiet study if guests are entertained in the same area?

Most families have more usable space than they realize. Careful arrangement of furnishings and wise use of available storage areas can add to the useful living space in a home. Often a family is able to increase the comfort of the home simply by planning multiple uses for each area of the home. Providing comfort, convenience, and privacy is a management problem. Like other management problems, its solution begins with the recognition of the needs of the specific family. Some needs are common to everyone. Others depend on individual situations.

Each family must provide for the physical needs of family members. Food, shelter, rest, and clothing needs are most important. Health and safety also must be considered as basic needs. The exact way these needs are met will depend on the

family. Providing a space for a hard-working parent to stretch out and relax after work is a real need in many families. Providing space for someone to develop a talent or skill may be an equally important need in other families. Only when you know the requirements of your family can you plan to use your space most efficiently.

Planning Furnishings for Comfort, Convenience, and Privacy

Once you know what needs must be met in your home, you are ready to consider how to arrange your furnishings to meet these needs. Can you plan a second use for one room? Moving just one or two pieces of furniture to another position can sometimes make the whole room more useful.

Your career
Interior designer or decorator

You would plan and furnish interiors of homes, commercial and institutional buildings, hotels, clubs, ships, and theaters. You would need a knowledge of color, texture, proportion, and mood to select and plan the arrangement of furniture, draperies, floor and wall coverings, paint, and additional room accessories. You might work closely with the architect or designer of the house or building. You might have your own business or be employed by a large department store. You might also work for a commercial or industrial institution.

Bulletin board IDEA
Title: *Blueprint, Blueprint, Consider Our Needs*
Directions: Mount a house plan in the center of the board. Around it display pictures representing some of the following:
A newly married couple
A family with many children
An older couple
Several geographic locations
Hobbies and activities of family members

A room shared by several people can be planned to include space for study, hobbies, and sleep. *Armstrong Flooring*

Arrange the furniture in the living area of the home economics department to show good and poor traffic patterns. Discuss each arrangement from the standpoint of safety, convenience, and appearance. Include both desirable and undesirable features in your discussion.

Plan a furniture arrangement for a living room, family room, or den. The room plan should be convenient and have a good traffic pattern. Check the arrangement of the furniture in your home. If possible, rearrange the furniture in one room to improve the traffic pattern.

Make a floor plan for a bedroom to be shared by two sisters or two brothers. Plan for the privacy, convenience, and comfort of each person. You may use room dividers, screens, hangings, or any other items which seem practical.

Find pictures of multipurpose rooms — those that serve more than one purpose. Identify the activities for which each of these rooms seems to have been intended.

Perhaps a dining table can be moved from the center of the room to a wall. The room may then appear larger or the storage space may be more useful. If there is enough room at the table for family meals, the new arrangement may be a very wise one. Perhaps the change will give privacy for visitors, while allowing the table to be used for study or hobby work.

Of course, rearranging the furniture in a room is not always as simple as moving one piece of furniture. Sometimes all the furniture has to be rearranged to improve the comfort and usefulness of the room. Sometimes, too, one change suggests another, and one simple change leads to a complete rearrangement.

Furniture is often heavy and hard to move. It is wise to make careful plans before you actually begin to shift any furniture. To be sure the new arrangement will fit, measure the furniture and the part of the room where it is to be placed. There are other factors to consider also. Will the furniture be easy to use in its new position? Will the new use planned for the room fit in with the present uses of the room? Will the new furniture arrangement interfere with traffic patterns, the way people walk through the room? Does the new arrangement provide for storage needs?

As you plan a new room arrangement, consider the types of furniture and different ways of using them. Perhaps you are planning to use your bedroom for a study and sitting room. Arrange beds so they are easy to reach. Give thought to the ease with which they can be made each day. Be sure that the furniture does not interfere with use of a dresser or closet space. There should be enough room to open dresser drawers and to reach into them easily. You should be able to open closet doors wide. Even the neatest person will be tempted to pile things up or leave them lying around the room if it is difficult to reach the proper storage space.

New uses for a room must not conflict with the basic purposes of the room. For example, if you share a bedroom with a much younger child or other family members, you must consider their needs before you plan to change the room into a bedroom-study-sitting room. It may be wiser to use the room as a play area for a younger child as well as a bedroom for both of you. If your room is shared with a grandparent, the older person may go to bed earlier than you do. In either situation, you may decide to use the kitchen table for studying. However, in using the kitchen table for homework you may have to pick up your things every time a meal is prepared and served. There may be another place in your home that can be used for a study area.

Many plans for furniture arrangement are spoiled because of poor

To be able to play or study in a spot that does not interfere with the activities of those around you requires planning when the room is arranged. *David Haas*

Give three examples to illustrate the following principle: *Store items where they will be used first.*

Identify some of your family's possessions that could be stored in out-of-the-way places. Why is it good management to store some items in hard-to-reach places?

Use furnishings in the home economics department to show arrangements of drawer and closet spaces. Suggest ways of making such storage places attractive without spending much money.

Plan a place for hanging clothes in rooms without closets. Consider using a curtain rod, broom handle, heavy rope, or other materials on hand.

Plan a display of storage items. You might include:
Cabinet shelves that pull or swing out
Corner cabinets that revolve like lazy Susans
Racks for cups, plates, spices, knives, kitchen cooking equipment, and keys
Vertical dividers for trays and cookie sheets
Holders for letters, notes, bills, and memos
Caddies for records, tapes, towels, and clothes

traffic patterns. Clear pathways from area to area are important for safety. They also make family living more comfortable and convenient. Unless the furniture is carefully arranged, the natural pathways of the room can interrupt the activities of the people in the room. Suppose several comfortable chairs are arranged near the TV. The arrangement seems to be attractive and convenient. Several people can enjoy a program together. The chairs are placed so that people can visit together when the TV is not being used. However, the arrangement may be inconvenient if the TV program or the conversation is in-terrupted every time someone goes in or out of the room.

Family relationships can be affected by the way furniture is arranged. Sometimes furniture in-terferes with the natural traffic pat-tern. Sometimes people do not like to walk around the bed every time they go from the closet to the dresser. A coffee table in the path between the front door and the entrance to the next room can cause daily irritation. The dining table may be between the china cabinet and the kitchen. If so, serv-ing meals and returning clean dishes to the china cabinet will be unnecessarily difficult.

Make and carry out a plan for improving the storage in one area of your home. This may be in a dresser, closet, or desk. It may involve arranging for a place to hang your clothes or reorganizing items in the kitchen cabinets. The project should fit your needs or the needs of your family.

Make storage and closet accessory items such as the following:
1 Padded hangers
2 Covers that fit over clothing on hangers to protect the garment
3 Shoe bags or shoe racks
4 Decorated shoe boxes for storing small items
5 Tie or belt racks
6 Coat hooks made from old umbrella handles
7 Shelf dividers for better use of space

Perhaps some of the items can be sold as part of a money-making project.

As you plan or arrange furnishings, remember to include storage furniture. For example, if you are making a study area, you need to consider a shelf or cabinet for books. Storage for records or tapes should be included in a stereo center.

Arranging Storage Areas Efficiently

Well-planned storage areas add a great deal to family comfort. Closets and cabinets built into a home often are inefficient for the storage needs of a particular family. With wise planning, you can usually provide storage for all the items family members use.

For efficient storage, try to plan so that items are stored close to the spot where they will be used. Suppose you plan to sew in your dining area. The storage areas in that room should contain the dishes and other tableware you need for regular meals, as well as your sewing equipment. Such materials as cleaning supplies may be frequently needed in every part of the house. It may be most efficient to keep cleaning supplies together in a portable container that can be moved to the area where they are needed. Another plan for efficient management is to have duplicate sets of cleaning supplies in more than one area of the home, perhaps the kitchen and bathroom.

Once you have decided which items should be stored in each room, examine the available storage space. Consider the closets, cabinets, drawers, shelves, and dressers in each room. How much storage space do you have? How deep or how shallow is each space? How easy is it to reach? Can you adjust the shelves so that some can accommodate tall objects and some shelves can hold flat items? Are there places where extra shelves can be added? Can you keep smaller items together in a tray or box located in a larger storage space? Are you keeping items which are no longer useful?

As you fit family belongings into their storage areas, remember to keep the most frequently used items in the most easily reached places. Things like holiday decorations, which are used only once a year, can be stored in out-of-the-way places, such as an attic, basement or garage shelf, or in the back of a deep closet.

If you still have a few items left over, perhaps you can provide some additional storage space. Maybe you can buy an inexpensive chest of unpainted wood or corrugated paper. Perhaps you can add some shelves. Your new storage space need not be used only for leftover items. Use it in the best way possible.

As you rearrange storage areas, check for any possible harm to stored items. If nearby plumbing should break, would the storage area be flooded? This could ruin many of the stored items. Is the

Well-planned storage areas provide for storage of items near areas where they will be used. They can be part of the room decor and serve their functional purpose as well. *Window Shade Mfrs. Assn.*

Follow these safety precautions when using small electric appliances. Add other safety precautions to the list.

1 Follow the manufacturer's directions in using any electric appliance.
2 Dry your hands thoroughly before connecting or disconnecting electrical equipment.
3 Use only one heating type appliance at a time on a single circuit.
4 Never connect electric appliances when standing on a wet surface.
5 Plug the cord into the appliance first, then into the wall outlet.
6 Always disconnect the cord from the wall outlet before removing it from the appliance — otherwise a *hot* plug will be exposed.
7 Grasp the plug rather than the cord when removing a cord from an outlet or an appliance.
8 Disconnect small appliances when not in use to avoid danger of shock or of accidentally touching the *on* switch.
9 Never let the cord dangle. It may cause the appliance to be pulled off the work area.

heating system close to some storage areas? If so, be sure that heat-sensitive items and flammable items are not stored in these places.

PROVIDING FOR GOOD HEALTH AND SAFETY

Considering the health and safety of all family members is another management problem. If family members are to remain healthy, certain needs must be met. Food and clothing must be provided. Adequate housing is necessary. The housing must provide proper heating and ventilation. It must also provide for proper disposal of wastes. For good health, there must be protection against pests and harmful germs. Finally, there must be provision for the emotional health of the family. Emotionally happy family members usually

10 If it is necessary to scrape batter down while the electric mixer is in operation, use a flexible rubber scraper and hold it away from the beaters.

11 Avoid getting batter or liquid into the mechanism of any electrical appliance.

12 Place a heat-resistant pad under the toaster, waffle baker, or coffee percolator.

13 Keep forks and knives out of the electric toaster.

14 Never turn on a blender until the lid is securely fastened. Never remove the blender lid while the motor is on.

15 Plug appliances into wall sockets made for such use. Wiring for lights is not always made to carry current necessary to operate appliances.

16 Disconnect any appliance with exposed coils before cleaning it.

17 Never put a heating unit, electric motor, or electric cord in water, as this may cause a short circuit. Some electric appliances may be partly or fully immersed in water. Follow the manufacturer's directions when cleaning electric appliances.

18 Allow hot appliances to cool before storing.

19 Never use an electric cord if the plug is loose or a screw or bolt has fallen out.

Children should be taught at an early age that electrical outlets are not toys. Safety in the home is the responsibility of all family members.   *Ray Ellis/Photo Researchers*

enjoy being together whether they are sharing necessary work or leisure time.

Checking the Home for Safety

Health and safety habits are often hard to establish. Most people know when an action is *not* safe. But it is easy to forget a safety practice or to skip one simply to save a little time. Families who develop the habit of comparing long-term costs — financial and physical — with the apparent convenience of

skipping a safety practice will generally avoid dangerous situations. Family members can learn to ask themselves, "Can we afford the cost, in case this is the one time something goes wrong?"

There are two ways to ensure safe conditions around your home. First, check the home regularly to be sure you and your family are continuing good safety habits. Second, recheck safety factors whenever you rearrange furniture, buy a new appliance, or change your pattern of living in other ways which could affect health and safety.

Thinking through the following questions will help any family improve the safety conditions around the home.

1 Does the home meet fire safety regulations? Do family members clear away old papers and rags frequently enough for safety? Does the family store its belongings properly to prevent fires? Are inflammable household items kept safely away from the kitchen range and the heating system? Are curtains and towels too close to the range? Does anyone in the family *ever* leave a fire untended? Do all family members *always* turn off all appliances as soon as they are through using them?

2 Is the electrical system safe? Is the wiring safe or has the insulation become frayed? Are the wires which connect the lamps and appliances plugged into one circuit? Can

the appliances be rearranged to even the load on electric circuits? If not, can the lights and appliances be arranged so that they are used alternately? It may be annoying to unplug one appliance in order to use another, but this is much less annoying than the high cost and danger of a fire.

3 Is the home free from factors which can cause falls? Is the furniture placed for safe movement? Are stairs, hallways, and other paths kept clear? Do all family members return all equipment to its proper place as soon as they are finished using it? Are the floor boards and floor coverings smooth and skid-proof? Is loose flooring repaired? Are there sturdy handrails where they are needed? Do family members wipe up all spills immediately?

4 Are the storage areas safe? Are household poisons kept out of the reach of children? Are medicines stored where there is no possibility of their being picked up and used by mistake? Are cleaning supplies kept separate from food supplies and medicines separate from both? Are all containers put back where they belong as soon as they are used? Are all supplies clearly labeled?

5 Is the home free from other common causes of accidents? Are pans and hot dishes placed on the range or table so the handles will not be bumped or reached by young children? Are all items placed far enough from the edges of shelves, tables, and counter tops so that they will not get knocked off? Are hanging items securely fastened to the wall? Are they hung high and out of the way so they will not be bumped by someone going by? Are doors which open out into traffic lanes kept tightly closed except when in use?

Managing the Home for Good Health

Among the dangers to a family's health are communicable diseases — that is, diseases which are passed from one person to another. For instance, one family member can develop a case of the flu, and soon several family members are also suffering from it. There are certain health practices to help families prevent the spread of communicable diseases.

Most families experience the usual childhood diseases. These diseases often start with one child and pass through an entire family. However, many serious childhood diseases can be prevented by inoculation. There are inoculations to prevent diphtheria, whooping cough (pertussis), tetanus, measles, mumps, smallpox, and polio. There still is no preventive inoculation for chicken pox. However, unless there are complications, chicken pox is not a serious disease in childhood.

If older family members have passed through childhood without contracting measles, mumps, or German measles, they would be

 Develop a rating scale or check list for evaluating the safety of your home. Use the rating scale or list to check your home economics department for safety factors.

Sponsor slogans for a safer school. Use as many words as possible starting with the letter S to write safety slogans. Some of the words you might want to use are:

Samples	Snow
Sane	Solution
Scheme	Someone
Search	Spark
Seek	Special
Seems	Speed
Sensible	Stand
Set	Standards
Shovel	Step
Simple	Stoop
Sink	Stove
Slip	Strategy
Slow	Study
Smart	Suggest
Smoke	Support
Smother	Swim

Bulletin board IDEA
Title: *Better Safe Than Sorry*
Directions: Use a cutout of a teddy bear or a stuffed toy animal. Place a real adhesive bandage on it. Place pictures suggesting possible safety and health hazards around the animal.

Demonstrate how to change a fuse. Tell why fuses blow. Show how to repair an electric cord and plug.

Set up a treasure hunt of safety hazards in a kitchen unit or living area of the home economics department. Rope off the area so a student cannot get hurt. Use items such as these:
A partly open drawer or door
A scatter rug that has a corner turned over
An electric cord plugged into a socket but not into an appliance
Scissors or a knife placed near the edge of a table or counter
A pot handle extending over the edge of the range

Your career
Safety Inspector

You would study the blueprint design of a home or building to be sure it meets the building safety codes recommended for its use. You might also visit construction sites to inspect the materials being used and the quality of the work. You might work for a county, city, state, or federal government agency.

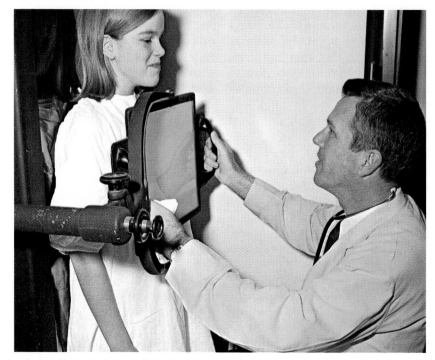

Regular medical checkups and good health habits often prevent the development of serious illnesses. *St. Louis City Medical Society*

wise to get preventive inoculations. These diseases can be very serious when contracted by adults. German measles can cause birth defects if contracted by women during the early months of pregnancy.

Regular visits to a clinic or doctor will ensure family members of getting needed inoculations at the proper time. Regular checkups also allow the specialists to notice and treat health problems which could become serious if allowed to go untended. During regular health checkups, families can also plan ways to improve their general health practices.

Studies show that good health requires adequate sleep and exercise. But even when a family knows these facts, a great deal of planning is needed to see that everyone gets proper rest and exercise.

For example, a family may need to plan a time each day for taking a young child to the park for outdoor exercise. Yet the housework must also be done. This family must plan the day so that other work does not interfere with going to the park.

Some families must plan ways to be sure that TV addicts or bookworms get enough exercise. This may be done by encouraging them to join in community, school, or club activities. A family may have to plan family outings to encourage stay-at-homes to become more active.

Whatever the problem, the family who thinks of health as a management concern will find ways to improve the general family health program.

Housekeeping can also aid in family health programs. For instance, no matter where a family lives, insects and other household pests may be a health problem. All family members can learn to be responsible for habits which help keep such pests out of the home. Toddlers can be taught to close screen doors firmly. Older family members can check to see that screens and screen doors are kept in good repair and fit tightly enough to keep out insects. If all family members learn to wipe up spills quickly, flies and roaches will be less likely to invade the home. Proper storage and removal of waste will further discourage pests. Even young children can be taught to keep waste containers firmly covered.

Health-conscious families know that good grooming habits are also good health habits. Well-brushed hair and well-scrubbed hands and faces encourage good health.

Everyone comes in contact with dangerous diseases frequently throughout life. People who neglect to brush their teeth or to wash and dry themselves carefully may actually allow disease germs and fungus to grow on them. One careless person can spread an infection through an entire family.

Handling Illnesses in the Home

Even with a good general health program, sooner or later each family is likely to experience illness. It is important to be able to recognize the signs of illness. Often quick medical attention will prevent an illness from becoming serious.

Reporting the illness

Illness is often first noticed when a person's facial expression changes. The person may seem to be groggy or may appear anxious. The face may be flushed or pale, dry or very moist. The skin may show a rash. The eyes may seem too bright or dull.

Other easily noticed signs of illness include a discharge from the nose or ears, sneezing, coughing, headache, sore throat, fever, pain, or nausea. The sick person may show a sudden change in appetite or elimination habits. The person may complain of fatigue or general discomfort or may become irritable.

When you suspect a family member is ill, get the person to rest comfortably in bed. Do not give any

Define and give examples of *communicable diseases*. Give examples of *noncommunicable diseases*.

List ways to prevent the spread of communicable diseases.

Make a chart showing the recommended ages for having various childhood inoculations. What immunizations are needed all through life? How often is each needed? What does *DPT* stand for? At what age are DPT inoculations begun? How often are DPT boosters needed?

Your career
Epidemiologist

You would study disease occurrence in human populations. You might investigate the causes and origins of disease breakouts, as well as decide the best use of resources in health care programs for treatment. You might follow the natural course of a disease and report on the effectiveness of treatment. You might also try to predict future epidemics and plan a means of preventing them. You might work in a hospital, government agency, public health department, or community social service agency.

Copy the spiral below onto a separate piece of paper, and fill it in with the *best* word or words to complete the sentences. *Do not write in this book.*

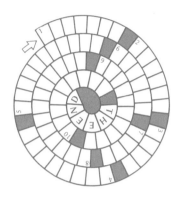

1 A sick person in a hospital is called a(an) _(1)_ .
2 It is important that all family members have regular medical and _(2)_ checkups.
3 In an emergency, if the victim is standing, see that the person _(3)_ down.
4 Do not give a person _(4)_ that has been prescribed for someone else.
5 A sick person's temperature is taken with a clinical _(5)_ .
6 A sick person may be disturbed by loud _(6)_ .
7 The most common communicable disease is a(an) _(7)_ .
8 If a woman contracts _(8)_ during the first 3 months of

medicine, not even aspirin, until you have consulted the clinic or doctor. Giving medicines without consulting a doctor can be very dangerous.

It is usually wise to take the sick person's temperature with a thermometer before calling the doctor. A *clinical* thermometer is used to determine a person's temperature. It is a fragile instrument made of glass which requires careful handling. A thermometer should be stored in its case when not in use. To prevent the spread of disease, disinfect the thermometer thoroughly before and after each use.

When talking to the doctor, describe the conditions which make you suspect that the person is ill. Report the body temperature and the time you recorded it. If the sick person has taken aspirin or other medicine, be sure to tell the doctor. Tell how much medicine was taken and when it was taken.

Caring for the sick
People who are seriously ill are usually cared for in the hospital. But many minor illnesses can be treated at home. Also, a patient may return home from the hospital while recovering from a serious illness or operation. Thus, every family needs to know how to care for the sick.

Even a minor illness will cause changes in regular household routines. Time ordinarily used for other tasks must be used to take care of the patient. Each family must make the adjustments necessary to its own situation. Each family member may have to accept extra duties when someone in the family is ill.

A family may feel tempted to skip some of its regular cleaning during an illness. But cleanliness is more important during an illness than during times of good health. This is especially true in the kitchen, bathroom, laundry, and sickroom, where disease germs can multiply rapidly.

Some tasks can be skipped or simplified. All members of the family must have good food and clean clothes. But simple meals and easy-care garments can be used instead of any special meals or clothing which may have been planned. Cleaning tasks may be lightened in the less used parts of the house.

If the noise of a vacuum cleaner or floor polisher disturbs the patient, perhaps the floors can be cleaned with a carpet sweeper or mop until the patient is stronger.

The sickroom should be kept neat and cheerful at all times. Bright lights and loud noises may be especially disturbing to a feverish person. On the other hand, total dark and complete quiet can also be disturbing. Look for ways to brighten the room with soft lights and soothing sounds.

Medicines and sickroom supplies may be stored neatly on a tray in the sickroom, in a nearby bathroom, or in the kitchen. Be sure that supplies

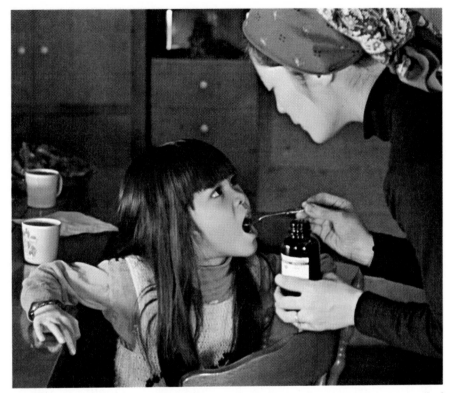

To help the patient recover thoroughly, follow the doctor's instructions for prescribed medicine. *Michal Heron/Monkmeyer*

pregnancy, the baby may be born with a birth defect. (Two words)

9 There is no preventive inoculation for __(9)__ . (Two words)

10 Good health is dependent on adequate sleep and rest, regular exercise, and good __(10)__ .

 Write a dialogue or short skit to show how the following situations might be handled.

1 You find a hair in your food when eating at a friend's house or in a restaurant.

2 A classmate offers you a bite of a partially eaten apple.

3 A friend asks to borrow your brush or comb.

4 You don't feel well and a friend asks to come over to your house to talk about a very personal and important problem.

Bulletin board IDEA
Title: *Treat a Cold*
  Like a Secret —
  Keep It to Yourself!
Directions: Use large pictures of sneezing cartoon characters who are covering their mouths and noses with tissues or handkerchiefs.

for a sick person are kept separate from other household items. Illness can spread to other family members. Giving the patient the wrong medicine can have serious results. It can be equally dangerous for another person to take the patient's medicine.

Patients need special attention given to their meals. Most illnesses lessen the appetite for some time. The doctor will recommend foods appropriate for the sick person. Poorly cooked foods are especially unappetizing when people are ill. Arrange the food to please the eye as well as the taste. Extra attention given to patients shows them how much their families care for them.

As patients begin to feel better, they may become restless. This recovery period is especially hard on young children, but it is difficult for patients of every age. Sometimes patients can be refreshed by being moved to another room for a

Make a first-aid kit appropriate for your home economics department, home, car, or camping knapsack.

Make posters showing what to do in different emergency situations until medical help can be obtained. Use stick-figure cartoons and simple captions on the posters.

Make a scrapbook, joke book, or cartoon collection for a person who will be in the hospital or convalescing for a long period of time.

Suggest ways of showing people who are ill, and whom you cannot visit, that you are thinking of them.

Your career
Emergency Medical Technician

You would accompany an ambulance to the scene of an accident or illness where you would provide the initial supportive and first-aid care to the patient. You might also radio-phone to the hospital for specific instructions and to inform the staff of the patient's condition to ensure their readiness with further medical aid. You would work in a community hospital, health center or clinic.

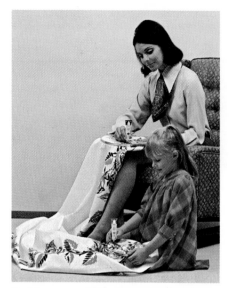
Keeping young children quiet is often one of the most important aids to their recuperation. *Artex Hobby Products, Inc.*

short period each day. If the doctor approves, a friend may be invited to visit. You must take care that such visits do not overtire the patients. Reading aloud can be entertaining for older people as well as pre-schoolers. A new simple game or project can also help patients through the recovery period.

Preparing for Emergencies

Your family will be better prepared to take care of home emergencies if plans have been made before emergencies arise. A well-stocked medicine cabinet will enable you to treat minor cuts and burns that may occur frequently. A knowledge of first aid will help you to know what

to do and when to do it. Such knowledge may prevent minor emergencies from becoming major ones.

Storing medical supplies

Drugs and supplies for emergencies should be stored in a separate place, away from toilet articles or food supplies. Medicines should be kept out of the reach of young children. Stock your medicine chest with the medicines and first-aid supplies recommended by your doctor. The American National Red Cross has prepared a list of supplies that are useful in common emergencies. Medicines that have been prescribed for a specific illness may be stored in the medicine cabinet during the illness. After an illness, it is usually wise to discard leftover medicine.

Check your medicine cabinet about once a month, as well as after any illness. Be sure that you have all the necessary medicines and first-aid supplies. Check to see that all packages are intact, that recommended medicines are still fresh enough to be useful, and that all supplies are clearly labeled and safely stored.

Giving first aid

What *is* first aid? The American National Red Cross defines it as *the immediate and temporary care given the victim of an accident or sudden illness until the services of a physician can be obtained.*

There are many techniques in giving first aid which cannot be described in detail here. You or any member of your family can learn first aid from a reliable source in your community. The Red Cross offers complete courses in first aid. Scouting organizations may be another source of reliable instruction in your community. Some hospitals offer first-aid courses. Schools supply first-aid instruction through home economics, health, and physical education classes and through student organizations.

In an emergency, the immediate treatment given patients generally has an effect on their recovery. It is better to do nothing than to do the wrong thing. On the other hand, if you know what to do, don't be afraid to take necessary action. You may help to save a life or to shorten an illness.

 Suggest ways to maintain a good family health program. Take into consideration such factors as sanitation, adequate rest, and good nutrition.

Discuss what should be done in the following situations:

1 One of the members of your class falls to the floor, losing consciousness.
2 Your little brother cuts his finger. It appears to be a deep cut. You are the only person at home with him.
3 Your mother has fallen in the yard. She appears to have hurt her hip and it is very painful.

Make a record book or information sheet of your own immunizations. Bring this up to date and continue to use it. When might you need to have an accurate immunization record?

Suggest ways of keeping children who are ill relatively quiet and happy. Suggest quiet activities and games for children of various ages.

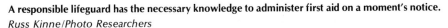

A responsible lifeguard has the necessary knowledge to administer first aid on a moment's notice.
Russ Kinne/Photo Researchers

Number from 1 to 11 on a piece of paper. Beside each number write the letter which corresponds to the *best* answer for that question. *Do not* write in this book.

1 Which is the first step in the problem-solving approach?
a Collecting the facts
b Stating the problem
c Considering the values involved
d Considering the alternatives

2 Which is the step most often left out in using the problem-solving approach?
a Collecting the facts
b Considering values involved
c Acting on the decision
d Evaluating the results

3 Which refers to the direction people walk through a room?
a Landing space
b Traffic pattern
c Dovetailing
d Conversational grouping

4 Which is an example of a multi-purpose piece of furniture?
a Coffee table
b Sofa bed
c Dresser
d TV set

5 Which is the most logical place to store a pancake turner?
a Near the sink
b With the tableware
c Near the range
d Near the pancake mix

6 Which is the *most dangerous* place to store a pressurized can of cleaning fluid?
a Near hot water pipes
b In a linen closet
c Near the washing machine
d In a cabinet at eye level

7 Which disease is communicable?
a Cold
b Cancer
c Multiple sclerosis
d Arthritis

8 For which disease is there no preventive inoculation?
a German measles
b Measles
c Chicken pox
d Pertussis

9 Which disease may cause birth defects if contracted by a pregnant woman?
a Flu
b Mumps
c Diphtheria
d German measles

10 Which is usually the *least* serious medical emergency?
a Severe bleeding
b Poisoning
c Stoppage of breath
d Feeling faint

11 Which should *not* be done in a medical emergency?
a Calling an ambulance
b Making the victim sit up
c Covering the victim with a lightweight blanket
d Talking to the victim

Fill in the blank in each sentence with the one *best* word to complete the statement. *Do not* write in this book.

1 One way to be sure that your room is always neat and clean is to plan a(an) (1) for the tasks to be done.

2 The room needing a thorough cleaning most often is the (2) .

3 Cleaning refrigerator shelves, oven racks, and cabinet doors are tasks that are usually done (3) .

4 Shampooing rugs or carpets is a task that is usually done (4) .

5 Changing bed linens is usually done (5) .

6 The part of a room that should be cleaned last is the (6) .

7 Hardwood floors that are not carpeted are usually (7) to protect their surfaces.

8 Carpeting or rugs for a bathroom or kitchen should be (8) .

9 Because they attract household pests, food wastes need to be removed from the kitchen at least (9) .

10 If household pests cannot be controlled, it may be necessary to get a commercial (10) company to treat the home.

11 The way the outside of your house is kept often gives visitors their first (11) of your home.

Chapter 9

Managing the Household Tasks of Family Living

After reading this chapter, you should be able to:

1. List household tasks that need to be done daily.
2. Give examples of weekly homemaking tasks usually performed in different parts of a home.
3. Describe seasonal household chores that need to be done in most homes.
4. Explain how to care for special storage areas in a home.
5. Practice performing daily, weekly, and seasonal household tasks.
6. Outline a plan for eliminating household pests from a house or apartment.
7. Point out the importance of taking care of the outdoor areas of a home.
8. Develop a schedule to care for some area of the home for a specified period of time.
9. Evaluate your plan to care for one area of the home after following it for the scheduled length of time.

Have you ever seen a dusty furniture display in a shop window? Perhaps the furniture was expensive and well arranged, but the display was unattractive because someone failed to give it the necessary attention. Neglect made it look like nobody cared. When a family neglects its home, the same impression may be given.

A well-kept home is the result of using time, energy, and money wisely. No two families will have exactly the same amount of these basic resources available for household tasks.

Too, each family has its own set of values and goals in housekeeping just as it has in other areas of family living. By considering household chores as home management problems, a family can plan ways to meet its needs. You can learn certain basic skills and facts which will help your family achieve housekeeping goals for family comfort.

Make a survey of the household tasks done regularly by class members. Discuss why there are differences. List the tasks done by the greatest number of students. List tasks in order from those done most to least often. How might your home economics classes help you to learn to perform these tasks more efficiently?

Bulletin board IDEA
Title: *Keys to Good Management*

Directions: Mount cutouts of keys tacked up to look as if they are fastened to a key chain. On each key write one of these words: *time, energy, money.*

ORGANIZING FOR EFFICIENCY

Both cleanliness and neatness are required for the health and safety of all family members. Household equipment and supplies need to be put away. So do toys and clothes. Have you ever been so tired from picking up that you skimped on other cleaning chores?

One way to be sure your home is neat and clean is to plan a schedule for household tasks. Some tasks, such as picking up clutter, are best handled on a daily basis. Other tasks can be done weekly. Still others need to be done only once a month or once or twice a year.

A wise manager tries to plan the work load for proper use of family resources. Job responsibilities can be divided so everyone in the family helps and still has free time for relaxation and recreation.

You may feel that a regular schedule of household tasks will trap you in jobs from which you can never escape. With a well-planned schedule, however, exactly the opposite is true. Certain jobs *must* be done —with or without a plan. With a plan, every family member knows when each task is to be done. There is less danger that the work load will get out of hand. Job responsibilities can be traded to meet special needs.

Good scheduling is not the whole answer to a well cared for home. Family members must look for other ways to make various jobs easier. For instance, some jobs may seem more difficult for your family than for other families you know. If it takes too long to dust or clean, perhaps some of the furniture is too hard to reach. Maybe you can rearrange the room to make cleaning easier. It may be possible to arrange hobby items in a nondust-catching display.

Perhaps you need new equipment to make household tasks easier. It may be something as simple as a new mop or something as expensive as a food mixer. It is easy to make mistakes when you consider buying new equipment. Some people buy so many gadgets to help with housework that it is more difficult to decide which gadget to use than to do the job without a gadget. Everything you buy must be kept somewhere, and housekeeping equipment costs money. You will have to decide if an item really helps you enough to be worth the cost.

PROVIDING DAILY CARE

The list of daily household tasks is so long that some people feel it is impossible for anyone to do even half the work. In every room, small items must be picked up and returned to their proper places. Each room must be straightened. Beds must be made. Meals must be prepared, served, and cleared away. Wastes must be disposed of. Clothing must be cared for. Pets must be tended.

Organizing a room for comfort and convenience is a beginning point for efficient housekeeping.
Michal Heron/Monkmeyer

Name a chore or activity you don't like to do. Find a way to cut down on the time and energy spent doing it. Practice and demonstrate to the class your methods and techniques for increasing efficiency.

Name basic areas of the home. List supplies needed for cleaning each area.

Design a *Karry-all Kleaning Kit* to hold cleaning tools and supplies that can be used in several areas of the home.

Classify cleaning tools from inexpensive supplies to expensive equipment. Examples:
Broom, carpet sweeper, vacuum cleaner
Polishing cloth and *elbow grease*, rented waxer-polisher, purchased waxer-polisher
Scrub board and tub, wringer washer, automatic washer

Show how to use a common piece of household equipment to conserve time, energy, or money.

This does indeed seem like an endless group of chores. Yet many homemakers are employed, do all the daily tasks, take care of small children, and one or two weekly chores each day as well. With only an occasional exception, they still have time and energy for relaxation and family recreation. These homemakers have learned to combine skills and management techniques to simplify housekeeping duties.

Picking Up

A family can divide the pickup tasks so the odds and ends of family living are in place when not being used. This plan helps simplify housekeeping. Each item has a special place where it is kept.

Every room of most homes contains many small items which are frequently used. Often these items are missing when they are needed. Much of the friction of family living is caused by such simple acts as forgetting to put items in their proper places. Time, energy, and good humor are lost simply because some family members fail to use available storage space as planned. Storage needs change from time to

Experiment with inexpensive household products to do cleaning tasks:

Baking soda
To clean tile and glass
To remove coffee stains from china and plastic
Vinegar and water
To clean windows
To soften fabrics when added to the final laundry rinse
To remove hard-water spots from glassware
To brighten aluminum
Ammonia and water
To wash windows and walls
Undiluted ammonia
To loosen grease on oven walls and racks — leave a shallow dish of ammonia in a closed, unheated oven several hours.
What advantages and disadvantages do these household products have? Compare them to other more expensive products made and sold for specific cleaning tasks.

Bulletin board IDEA
Title: *Groom Your Room*
Directions: Mount pictures of teenagers' rooms showing inexpensive accessories, home-built furniture, and innovative storage arrangements.

time. Does your home have a place for everything? Perhaps there could be some improvement.

Actually, putting things away as soon as you are through with them is a matter of habit. It is not too late to acquire this habit. The next time you find yourself dropping an item where you use it, remember how hard it is to search for lost belongings. It is not enough to remember to return the things you use. You must begin by planning to do more than your share.

Once a family has learned to cooperate in keeping small items where they belong, the task of keeping the home neat becomes simple. Many pickup tasks can be performed as family members go about other activities. It only takes a minute to smooth a cushion or straighten a curtain. A sweater or a game can be carried to the place where it is stored each time you go to that part of the house. Such simple acts tend to give a home a cared for look.

Keeping belongings in their proper place is a daily task which involves all of the family and each room that is used. Other tasks involved in keeping rooms straight will depend upon the main uses of each room. As a room is kept straightened each day, a good manager notes the areas which will soon need special attention. In this way, extra cleaning jobs can be scheduled as a part of the regular daily care of the room.

A routine mopping of the kitchen floor keeps it healthily clean. *Sybil Shackman/Monkmeyer*

Caring for the Kitchen and Dining Area

Meals are prepared in the kitchen and served in a dining area which may or may not be in the kitchen. Preparing meals is easier when food and utensils are properly stored. Canned foods, staples, fresh produce, and meats should be put away as soon as they are brought into the house. Only in this way can food keep its nutritive value. Meals can be prepared with a minimum of effort when each pot and pan and

178

each type of food is always stored in a given place.

Bacteria can grow quickly in food. Cleanliness is especially important in the kitchen and dining areas. Spilled food is easier to clean up immediately than at a later time. Sweep or vacuum crumbs from the floor after each meal. Wash the surface of the oven and range top after each use. Wipe up food spills and splashes near the range, refriger-

Effective garbage storage areas provide for easy access and easy removal. *Farley Manning Associates, Inc.*

ator, mixer, can opener, and sink. Wash dishes and cooking utensils or put them in the dishwasher after each meal.

Food wastes must be collected during food preparation and after each meal. They must be disposed of properly. Even with an in-sink garbage disposer, some provision must be made to keep food wrappers from causing odors and attracting pests. Meat wrappers and ice cream cartons often attract such pests as flies and roaches. Rinse these containers before placing them in the kitchen trash container. Unless you have a trash compactor, it will probably be necessary to remove kitchen trash from the home each day.

Caring for the Bathroom

It is easy to keep a bathroom in good order if each person checks its condition and tidies it after each use. Towels and washcloths can be hung up neatly so they air out and dry. Toothbrushes, toothpaste, and other articles can be returned to their proper storage areas. The tub or washbasin can be cleaned after each use. Splashes can be carefully wiped up before you leave the bathroom.

At least once each day someone should check a bathroom for other needs. The toilet bowl may need cleaning. The wastebasket has to be emptied regularly. Paper goods must be replenished. There may be a clothes hamper filled with items

 To make a bed, follow these steps if the bottom sheet is *not* fitted. If it is fitted, put it on the bed going around the bed only once. Then follow steps 5 through 9.

1 Spread the bottom sheet on the bed and center it.
2 Tuck under the same length of sheet at the head as you have allowed for the foot.
3 Make a mitered corner at the head of the bed. Grasp the loose edge of the sheet and lift it to make a triangle which is at a right angle to the mattress.

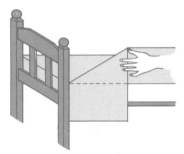

Lay the top part of this triangle on top of the bed. Tuck the base of the triangle under the mattress.

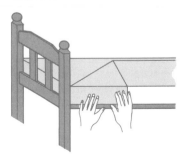

Place your hand near the corner of the mattress while dropping the top part of the triangle that has been on top of the bed.

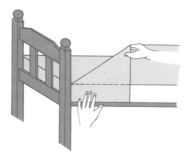

Tuck the top half of the triangle under the mattress, too.

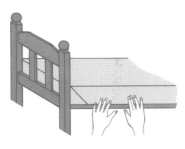

4 Miter the bottom corner of the sheet on the same side of the bed in the same way. Repeat on the other bottom corner and then on the top corner of the other side of the bed.

5 Place the top sheet on the bed with the wrong side of the hem up. Allow enough length at the foot of the bed to tuck the sheet under the mattress. Leave enough

which should be laundered. Fresh towels or a clean bath mat may be needed. The mirror needs to be checked for splashes and cleaned if necessary.

Caring for the Bedrooms

A room looks much neater all day if the bed is made each morning. This task takes only a few minutes. One way to save time and energy is to place the bed, if at all possible, so you can work around it. Start at a top corner of the bed, smoothing the sheets and coverings, and work around to the opposite corner. In this way, you go around the bed only one time. This is an efficient way to save time and energy.

Because there is usually little time in the morning, especially on school days, it is easier to straighten your room *before* going to bed. Clothes that need washing can be put in the hamper or laundry. Other clothes can be hung up or put away. If there is a special place for everything in your room, it will always be easy to find things.

A closet should be arranged so similar items are hung together. For example, all shirts in one section, pants in another, and so on. In this way, it is easy to know where to put things and where to find them. If you share a closet, you will have to divide the available space. If your room does not have a closet, you might use a wardrobe or some other kind of storage for hanging clothes.

Dresser drawers tend to get messy rather easily. You can keep them neat by making a special place for each item. You can make partitions to separate articles by fitting together the tops and bottoms of cardboard boxes. Egg cartons and small and large boxes may be used to hold coins, keys, jewelry, scarves, gloves, mittens, T-shirts, and undergarments.

Caring for the Home Living Areas

The general living areas of the home also need straightening each day. Family activities may cause special cleaning problems in these areas. For example, the floor in a much used entryway may need to be swept or vacuumed each day. Chairs located in front of the family TV set require straightening and floors here may require cleaning more often than those located in other parts of the room.

There may be times when a special project must be left out in an unfinished state. But even if a painting is left on an easel to dry, the rest of the painting materials may be put away. The portable sewing machine may have to be left out. However, the sewing project can be left neatly beside the machine, rather than scattered around the room.

PROVIDING WEEKLY CARE

To have a well cared for home, each room must be cleaned regularly. Just how often is a thorough clean-

A weekly care schedule might include watering plants around the house. *Owen Franken/ Stock, Boston*

sheet at the top to turn it back over the blanket several inches. Miter the two bottom corners of the top sheet.

6 Place the blanket on the bed 8 to 12 inches (20.5 to 30.5 centimeters) from the top of the mattress. Smooth and tuck it under at the foot. Make a half-mitered corner by allowing the top triangle to hang down without tucking it in. It should look like the third illustration.

7 Put the pillowcase on the pillow by holding the pillow against your body and using both hands.

8 Put the bedspread on the bed, smoothing it toward the head of the bed. Fold down enough spread to allow the pillow to be covered with some tuck-in underneath.

9 Check to be sure the finished bed is smooth, the covers hang straight, and no blanket or sheet shows from under the spread.

ing needed in each room? The answer depends on how the room is used, what type of dirt builds up in the room, and how much danger to family health there will be if the room is not cleaned.

Managing Weekly Care in the Kitchen

In most homes every member of the family uses the kitchen each day. Meals and snacks are prepared and may be eaten in the kitchen. Kitchens tend to accumulate stubborn soil such as food splashes, greasy or sticky finger marks, and spills. Because a clean kitchen is essential to good health, the kitchen needs a thorough cleaning more often than any other room of the house.

The floor, cabinets, counter tops, sink, and kitchen appliances such as the range and refrigerator require attention. Fortunately, modern cleaning products and modern equipment can help to ensure clean, healthful kitchens with only a minimum of effort.

Kitchen surfaces

Cabinets, walls, and counter surfaces may need weekly cleaning. An oily film of dirt usually builds up on these surfaces over a period of time. When splashes and finger marks are wiped from kitchen surfaces as part of the daily chores, weekly cleaning may be unnecessary. Stains can often be wiped away in a moment

List responsibilities you think you should and could assume in caring for your room. Make a plan of your time for one week. Include all your room-care activities.

Develop a scorecard for rating the cleanliness and neatness of your room. Include items that should be checked daily and weekly. Rate your room for a period of several weeks. Note the areas you need to improve and make a plan to do so.

Your career
Efficiency expert

You would act as a consultant to different businesses, suggesting ways to do jobs in less time with less effort. You might also suggest ways to increase productivity while decreasing cost and waste. Courses in business or industrial psychology and home management would be helpful. You might work for a large corporation, specialized firm, or as a free lance.

when food is spilled. These same stains may take a lot of effort and special cleaning solutions if allowed to dry and harden.

The most frequently used cabinet surfaces usually require a thorough cleaning about once a week. Other surfaces may be checked weekly and cleaned whenever necessary. The exact cleaning methods used will depend on the type of surface. Paint, enamel, stainless steel, laminated plastic, and wood each require a special cleaning method. Use the method recommended for your type of cabinets.

When necessary check and clean the inside surfaces of cabinet shelves. Drawers and shelves require wiping and straightening as part of the regular cleaning program. It takes little extra time and effort to straighten one storage area each week. By doing a different small storage area each week, all kitchen storage will be clean and fresh at all times.

Kitchen appliances
The type of weekly care necessary to keep a range clean and attractive depends on the quality of daily care it receives. Spills should be wiped up as they occur. Unless the range is equipped with a self-cleaning oven, the racks and oven surfaces may need weekly attention. Microwave ovens have continuous-cleaning action. Surface burners, reflector bowls, and drip trays may also need a general cleaning on a

weekly basis. Gas burners may need to be checked for clogged jets. A weekly inspection will show which parts of the range need to be cleaned. Follow the manufacturer's instructions for the best way to handle such cleaning.

The inside of the refrigerator needs cleaning to keep it free from odor. Here, too, careful daily care will make weekly care less difficult. Many refrigerators have swing-out or pull-out shelves which make it easy to wash the refrigerator wall.

Interior shelves and storage drawers must also be washed regularly. Many families clean the refrigerator storage areas in rotation, doing one shelf or drawer each week. If spills are wiped up as they occur, this plan will keep the refrigerator clean at all times.

During the weekly inspection of the refrigerator, check to see that all food is in good condition. Small storage bowls and covered jars can easily be shoved aside and forgotten. Look for forgotten food at least once a week. Throw out unusable odds and ends. Your refrigerator will work more efficiently and there will be more room for storage.

Many refrigerators are self-defrosting. If yours is not, you will need to check from time to time to see if it will soon need defrosting. This check will allow you to plan ahead. You can schedule the defrosting job for a day when the refrigerator is not full and other

Such convenience appliances as self-cleaning ovens and self-defrosting refrigerators eliminate the need for many weekly cleaning chores. *Westinghouse Electric Corporation*

 Use and care for the kitchen range by following these guidelines:

Use flat-bottomed pans that fit the size of surface units, especially if your range is electric.

Wash and scour drip pans where food and grease have spilled as soon as they are cool enough to handle.

Avoid the use of scouring pads or powders on enamel surfaces of the range. Use soap and water or a nonabrasive cleanser after the range has cooled.

Brush burned food from gas burners and electric units only after the units are completely cooled.

Wash the porcelain interior of the oven with soapy water or household ammonia water. Follow the manufacturer's directions exactly when using a commercial oven cleaner. Be sure the product does not get on the electric heating unit.

Block off the floor in the home economics laboratory into several sections. Try various types of floor waxes and cleaners on each section. Compare and contrast the sections of the floor two and four weeks later.

household chores are light. Care of the freezer section of the refrigerator or of a separate freezer is similar to the care given to the refrigerator itself. Follow the cleaning directions given in your appliance booklet.

Kitchen floors

Kitchen floors are usually covered with a smooth easy-to-clean surface, such as plastic tile or linoleum. With care, these floor surfaces will stay in good condition from week to week. When floors become sticky or dirty, they can be thoroughly washed with a mild cleaning solution. A self-wringing sponge mop, a string mop, or an ordinary sponge may be used.

In some kitchens part or all of the floor is covered with washable carpeting. With this carpeting, spills should be washed up as soon as they occur. A routine sweeping with a vacuum cleaner keeps such carpeting in good condition.

Managing Weekly Care of the Bathroom

Weekly care of the bathroom is similar to the care of the kitchen. Some bathrooms have tile wall surfaces and floors. These surfaces

Write TV commercials for particular household cleaning products or pieces of equipment. Act out the commercials in class. Analyze the commercials by telling the desirable features of the products that were mentioned. What disadvantages of the products were not mentioned in the commercial.

Write a tag or label that you would want to find on a household cleaning product or on a particular piece of household equipment. What information about specific products is the most helpful to you as a consumer?

Your career
Cleaning Service Contractor

You would arrange for cleaning services to be performed in such places as homes, office buildings, hotels and motels, or hospitals. You might contract work for a family or business or be registered with a government or private agency.

may be treated in much the same way as kitchen floors and walls. Check to see if the tiles are made of a material needing special care.

If the tub and washbasin are cleaned after each use, they will need little extra attention. Some families prefer to wash these areas with a disinfectant or special tub cleaner as part of a weekly care program. The toilet bowl requires at least weekly cleaning. Special products are available which help to simplify this job. Be sure the bowl brush, if used, is dried and aired before it is returned to storage. The medicine cabinet and other bathroom storage areas may be inspected and cleaned on a rotation basis in much the same way as that recommended for kitchen storage areas. Fixed bathroom carpets are cleaned the same way as kitchen carpets. Some bathroom carpeting may be removed for washing or cleaning as the need arises.

Managing Weekly Care of Other Rooms

The family recreation room may need to be cleaned as often as the kitchen and bathroom. Less frequently used rooms may need cleaning less often. Floor coverings and storage furniture similar to that in the kitchen can be cleaned in much the same way. Other furnishings in the general living areas must be dusted and perhaps polished. Wax is usually recommended to protect hardwood floors. Carpets in

these rooms may require frequent care. Vacuuming will remove hidden dirt, helping carpets to last longer.

Many vacuum cleaners have attachments to help simplify the weekly cleaning chores. Dusting need not be a difficult job. The upholstery nozzle of the vacuum cleaner can be used to remove dust from the surfaces and corners of upholstered furniture. It can also be used on curtains and draperies. The loosened dust is drawn into the vacuum cleaner instead of being scattered to other parts of the room. The dusting brush can be used to dust tabletops and chairs. It is also helpful for dusting the tops and backs of books in the bookshelves and for removing dust and cobwebs from window blinds, walls, ceilings, and moldings. Special attachments can be used to clean wide areas of floor, as well as carpeting. If rod-type cleaning attachments are available, it is seldom necessary to move all the furniture to clean a room thoroughly.

Some room accessories and furniture may need polishing as well as dusting. Specially treated dustcloths and furniture polishes can be used to clean and polish in one operation. Small objects may have to be picked up for careful dusting. Dust the surface beneath the objects before setting them back in place. Mirrors and picture glass are usually checked in a routine cleaning program. Special glass cleaners can help simplify this cleaning task.

A specially treated dust mop may be useful for cleaning large uncovered wood, tile, or linoleum floors. Such mops apply a protective film to the floor as they remove the dust.

You do not need a large amount of special cleaning equipment or housekeeping aids. Most products have more than one use. Read the labels carefully and select one or two polishes to meet all your needs. Cloths for applying each polish and a clean, soft polishing rag can complete your polishing equipment. Cleaning supplies may be kept together in one container so they can be easily carried from room to room. Some vacuum cleaners hold their attachments within the cleaner case or on the cleaner itself. If the attachments must be kept separately, you may wish to keep them with other cleaning supplies.

Weekly cleaning chores are easier when they are planned to prevent unnecessary work. Even with a vacuum cleaner attachment, some dust from the tops of objects is likely to settle to the floor as you clean. If walls and draperies are cleaned first, then furniture tops and legs, and last the floor, all surfaces will be clean in just three trips through a room.

Bedrooms in regular use require one additional step in weekly cleaning. It is wise to change the bedding before other cleaning is done. Loose lint and dust will settle to the floor. While bedding is removed, use the vacuum cleaner attachments to remove noticeable dust or lint from the mattress and bed.

Fitted or contour sheets are popular because they remain smooth, and edges do not pull out from under the mattress. If the corners on flat sheets and blankets are mitered — folded at right angles — the bed should require only smoothing and straightening between linen changes. In hospitals, beds are made with mitered corners to keep the sheets and blankets comfortably on the patients.

When the bed has been made, the rest of the room may be cleaned in the three-step method — first the walls and window coverings, second the furniture tops and legs, and last the floors.

Most household plants should be watered thoroughly only when the soil feels completely dry — once a week or every five or six days. More frequent watering is harmful to many plants. Flowerpots with holes in the bottom for drainage and those with saucerlike underliners are usually the most satisfactory type. Plants need to be turned every few days so they are evenly exposed to the source of light. Some people occasionally spray plants lightly with a fine mist of water or wipe the leaves gently with a damp, soft cloth.

PROVIDING SEASONAL CARE

Although old-fashioned spring and fall cleaning is no longer necessary,

 List household tasks which are done daily, weekly, monthly, and seasonally. Which list is the longest? Which is the shortest? Why?

Make a schedule for doing the housekeeping tasks necessary in your own room or another room in your home. Plan time for daily, weekly, and monthly tasks. Follow this schedule for a month. What were the strengths and weaknesses of your plan? Consider your family's reactions. What happened to make it necessary to change your schedule? Why does a work schedule need to be somewhat flexible?

Clean the same room twice, allowing a week between cleanings. Follow these two procedures:
1 Clean the floor first, then dust the furniture, and clean the walls and window coverings last.
2 Clean the walls and window coverings first, dust the furniture, and clean the floor last.
Evaluate the cleanliness and appearance of the room following each procedure. Check the room after three days. Which procedure was more effective? Why?

Use newspaper ads and check prices in the stores to find the cost of different household cleaning equipment. Find the cost of renting some of these items. Discuss the factors that might influence a family's final decision to buy or rent this equipment. Include such things as:

Frequency of use
Storage facilities
Amount of money available
Ease of rental
Life of the appliance

Compare and contrast various commercial products and methods of doing the following tasks:
Cleaning windows and mirrors
Dusting and waxing furniture
Cleaning ovens
Cleaning and waxing floors
Shampooing carpets and rugs

Evaluate the products and methods for the following:
Results
Cost
Time needed to do the job
Amount of work involved

Compare and contrast various types of household equipment items such as:
Wet and dry mops
Vacuum cleaners
Rug shampooers
Trash compactors

A garden or yard requires extra care during certain seasons of the year. *Michael Collier/Stock, Boston*

certain tasks are still thought of as seasonal jobs. They may be required as often as once a month or only a few times a year. If jobs of this type are carefully planned, they can be fitted into the regular cleaning routine without creating a heavy work load.

Handling Special Housekeeping Problems

The walls and ceilings of a room gradually build up a film of dirt causing the whole room to look dingy. This dirt is often noticeable around heating outlets and windows. At least once a year, you will want to check each room to see if any special cleaning is necessary.

Sometimes the walls can be cleaned. Most painted walls and some wallpapers can be washed. Wallpaper cleaners can be used to clean papered walls. At other times, the wall covering must be replaced rather than cleaned. Each family must determine its own needs. They must also decide whether they will hire someone to redecorate or whether they can do an adequate job themselves.

Whatever the decision, this is a big job. The room will be upset. Furniture must be moved away from the walls, curtains and draperies taken down. The floors and furniture remaining in the room should be carefully covered.

It may be wise to combine wall cleaning or painting with other special cleaning jobs. In this way you can avoid upsetting the room more than once. If the carpet or the draperies are to be sent out for cleaning, you might consider doing all the cleaning at one time. Furniture repairs may also be considered. The family may be planning to get new slipcovers or new upholstery. Perhaps this should be done now, especially if new paint or paper is being planned.

Of course, the family budget or family members' time may not allow for doing all these special tasks at once. But even if only one part of the job can be done, it is wise to consider all of it before starting. In this way, you will be sure that your plans fit together. The most necessary jobs can be done first. Later the rest of the chores can be done without confusion.

After the walls are cared for, and before the furniture is replaced, it may be wise to wash the windows both inside and out. Hard-to-reach windows may be cleaned more easily when the furniture is moved. Too, paint or paste splatters can be removed while still fresh and painting ladders are available.

You may include windows as part of the general wall cleaning. Or windows may be cleaned as a separate job. Either way, you will want to consider this job at least on a seasonal basis. It is not necessary to clean both sides of the windows at the same time. Some families clean the inside window surfaces whenever necessary as part of the weekly or monthly cleaning. Outside window surfaces may be cleaned only once or twice a year — when screens or storm windows are adjusted or replaced.

Managing Seasonal Floor Care

Although daily and weekly cleaning will keep floors clean, most floors need special attention from time to time. Some vinyl floor covers do not require wax. However, most smooth-surfaced floors look better, stay cleaner, and wear longer if waxed occasionally. How often this is depends on individual family needs. In families with small children, waxing the kitchen floor may be a weekly job. In other homes, it

may be needed only two or three times a year.

A floor needs rewaxing whenever it remains dull after mopping. Many types of floor waxes are available in both liquid and paste forms. Most liquid waxes are self-polishing. Most paste waxes must be applied and then buffed for a good finish. Some types of wax should never be used on certain types of flooring. Read labels carefully. Choose a wax which will give the finish necessary for your floors. Be sure all the old wax is removed before applying new wax. This can usually be done by washing the floor with a strong cleaner and rinsing it thoroughly to remove excess cleaner.

Carpets also require cleaning from time to time. A family may buy or rent special carpet cleaners or a commercial carpet-cleaning firm may be hired. The best choice of cleaning methods depends on the type of carpeting, as well as on the family budget and the amount of time available for such tasks.

Many special pieces of equipment are available for floor care. Some of them are expensive. Before your family decides to invest in a floor polisher or a rug shampooer, take time to consider its true value to the family. Or investigate renting expensive floor-care equipment for special jobs. Rental agencies, hardware stores, and often supermarkets carry equipment such as floor waxers or buffers and the necessary cleaning substances.

 Clean the closet in your bedroom or some other room of your home. Discuss why the following set of guidelines did or did not work well for you.

1 Remove all clothing and other articles.
2 Brush down the walls with a long-handled brush, a covered broom, or an appropriate vacuum-cleaner attachment.
3 Wash woodwork, doors, rods, and floor.
4 Spray the closet with insect spray and close the door for several hours, if necessary. Then air the closet for an hour or more.
5 Sort through the clothing you have taken out of the closet, and dispose of any unwearable articles.
6 Replace wearable articles in the closet.
7 Hang clothes up in this order if possible: clothes which are worn only occasionally in the back, and everyday clothes nearest the door.
8 Store shoes off of the floor on racks, in shoe bags, or in shoe boxes.
9 Store hats in boxes.

Choose projects which might improve the appearance of your room:

1 Redye faded rugs, curtains, or bedspreads to brighten them.
2 Make throw pillows from old party dresses, draperies, or leftover odds and ends of fabric you have at home.
3 Make pillowcases from worn sheets and embroider designs on them.
4 Make book ends from scrap lumber or outdated automobile license plates.
5 Braid an area rug from worn hose or long, thin strips of fabric.
6 Sew together different colored carpet samples to make an area rug.

Your career
Exterminator

You would visit homes or buildings to rid them of insects, rodents, and other pests. Your work would help to improve the health and sanitary conditions of the environment. A public health license might be required in some communities to perform this service. You might be self-employed, or work for private contractors.

Managing Seasonal Care of Appliances

Other seasonal chores are connected with the care of household equipment. Furnaces, water heaters, air conditioners, and similar appliances need special cleaning and servicing. Refrigerators and freezers may need defrosting and thorough cleaning. Follow the manufacturer's instructions or check with utility companies to learn what care is needed to keep each piece of equipment in good working order. Many utility companies employ home economists to help people with problems related to the use and care of household appliances and equipment. These home economists are often able to make home visits when someone needs special help.

Caring for Special Storage Areas

The frequently used storage areas of the home can be kept clean and well organized with regular daily and weekly care. Storage areas for out-of-season items and keepsakes are often overlooked during regular cleaning. These areas can be cleaned at the same time that seasonal items are being removed and replaced.

During this cleaning process, it is wise to examine the contents of storage areas. Some items may have been kept simply because you never thought of throwing them away. Overcrowded storage areas

Special storage boxes and shelves allow for maximum storage in a small amount of closet space. *Sears, Roebuck and Company*

can be dangerous to the health and safety of family members. Too, you may be pleasantly surprised to find how much easier it becomes to make seasonal changes once useless items are discarded.

Many communities have a special collection service to help families get rid of bulky items which are no longer useful. Check to see if such a service is available in your community. If it is, plan the cleaning of basement, attic, garage, and off-season storage areas to coincide with the community cleanup week. Perhaps usable items no longer needed by your family can be given to charity organizations. These organizations sometimes pick up large items at homes or have collection boxes at various locations for your convenience.

CONTROLLING HOUSEHOLD PESTS

Certainly nobody likes flies, roaches, mosquitoes, ants, mice, rats, bedbugs, or other household pests. Pests can carry germs that may make people sick. They can get into food and spoil it. Some may get into closets and ruin clothing. Keeping the whole house clean is very important. Pests need food and they need places to hide.

Be careful that spilled food is not left around the home. Dirty dishes and pans also attract pests. It is wise to get rid of garbage, bits of food, scraps of cloth, and other wastes pests like to eat. Some insects like to hide in beds and bedding. You can avoid such pests by airing bedding and mattresses periodically.

When food shopping, make sure boxes and bags of dry food are sealed and are not broken. Insects often get into the home in shopping bags and boxes used to carry groceries.

It is necessary to close up any holes or places where pests can enter the house. Modeling clay and caulking compounds can be used to seal openings and cracks around sinks, toilet bowls, water pipes, and vents. They can also be used to fill in cracks around baseboards and between floorboards. Tight-fitting screens without any holes help keep out flying insects.

It is sometimes necessary to use special chemical products made to kill insects and pests. These chemicals are usually called *pesticides.* There are different kinds of pest-control products for different kinds of insects and for rodents. Some are sprays. Others are liquids, waxes, powders, and poison baits. When you use these products be sure to read the labels on the containers. Some can poison people and pets or cause other damage.

Keep pest-control products in a safe place, away from children and animals. Read the labels for special storage advice. Be careful not to get a pesticide on food, dishes, or cooking equipment. When using a spray, keep children, birds, fish, and animals out of the room. Follow the manufacturer's instructions carefully. Wash your hands and face thoroughly with soap and water when you are done.

In warm climates where insects are common, many people have an exterminator treat their homes. In warm, humid climates, a professional exterminating service may be the only effective way of controlling household pests.

TAKING CARE OF OUTDOOR AREAS

Some families live in cities, while others live on farms or in suburban or rural areas. Some rent their homes, and some own their homes. Homes are located in large buildings shared by many families and in single-family structures. In some

Copy the puzzle below onto a separate piece of paper and fill in the names of the following household pests. The first letter of each word is given as a clue. *Do not* write in this book.

Ants	Mosquitoes
Bedbugs	Moths
Beetles	Rats
Fleas	Roaches
Flies	Termites
Mice	

Draw stick-figure cartoons showing ways to control household pests in a home. Examples may include emptying kitchen trash containers, sealing holes in house siding, setting a mouse trap, storing insecticides in appropriate places, and covering food tightly.

Describe possible reasons for poorly kept yards. Suggest alternatives for people who lack interest, skill, money, or time to care for yards. Examples: ivy or other vines for ground cover, decorative rocks or cement in place of a lawn.

Discuss ways students can help make the outside of their homes more attractive. Carry out one project to improve the appearance of your own home. Tell the class about your plans. You might pick up litter, plant flowers, make a windowbox, or paint steps or porch furniture.

Plan a project to improve the appearance of your school or community. For example: Collect litter from roadways Landscape a public area

Your career
Landscape contractor

You would work outdoors performing services such as grading terrain, maintaining lawns, and servicing trees and shrubbery. Your work might also include masonry. You might work chiefly on private homes or with grounds-keeping crews for apartment developments or corporations.

homes a custodian is placed in charge of the outside work. In other homes family members take care of these duties themselves. For these reasons, the specific duties involved in caring for the outside of the home vary from family to family. But whatever the situation, the neatness and safety of the approaches to the home are a part of each family's concern.

A clean, well cared for approach to your home is pleasing to friends and neighbors as they come to visit. Too, the outside of your home gives strangers their first impression of your family. Even the young children in the family can learn to keep sidewalks and hallways neat. Stray papers and trash can be picked up whenever they are noticed. Tools and toys can be placed where they belong. Those who pass are quick to recognize places where homes are well kept.

Since a carport is easily seen, its neatness is important to the total outside appearance of a home and neighborhood. A carport or garage with too much clutter could also be a safety hazard. In getting out of a car, it is possible to walk into or fall over items that are in the way. Such items can be dangerous, especially in the dark or in dim light. Keeping a garage door closed makes a home look neater. It also helps to keep the inside area clean. If the garage door is closed when not in use, it helps keep out dust and blowing leaves, papers, and snow.

Neatness outside the home involves more than picking up as you go along. Plants in yards or window boxes require regular care. Plant trimmings, scattered blossoms and leaves, and grass cuttings must be swept or raked up and discarded or stored for mulch and fertilizer. Sidewalks may need to be swept and washed in summer or kept clear of ice and snow in winter.

Windows, doors, shutters, window boxes, railings, fences, and gutters need to be kept clean and neat. They may require frequent attention. Because these areas of the home are exposed to many weather conditions, they may require painting for appearance and protection.

Care of the outside of the home affects family safety, too. Misplaced tools and toys may cause someone to receive a serious injury. Storm windows or screens that are not securely fastened can be hazards. Loose steps and handrails can also be dangerous and lead to serious accidents.

When you know what must be done to keep the outside of your home in good condition, you can organize these chores in much the same way as the indoor chores. Determine which tasks must be done each day, which may be done only once a week, and which may be done on a seasonal basis. With planning, the outside of the home can be pleasant and inviting at all times.

Number from 1 to 30. Beside each number indicate if the corresponding statement is true or false. *Do not write in this book.*

1 Organizing a home for comfort, convenience, and safety is an important step toward efficient home management.
2 By the time a person is a teenager, it is too late to acquire the habit of putting things away when through with them.
3 A cleaning schedule helps you have a well cared for home.
4 The room in the home in which cleanliness is most important is the living room.
5 If any room is cleaned regularly each week, that should be the only cleaning it ever needs.
6 Carpeting for kitchens is usually made of washable fibers.
7 In giving a bedroom a weekly cleaning, it is good management to change the sheets before cleaning the room.
8 The floor should be cleaned before dusting the furniture in a room.
9 Furniture should be dusted before vacuuming the walls and draperies in a room.
10 Furniture can be dusted with a vacuum-cleaner attachment designed for this purpose.
11 Some furniture waxes need to be buffed to obtain a good finish.
12 All uncarpeted floor surfaces should be waxed occasionally.
13 Families with hardwood floors need to own an electric polisher.
14 Remove old wax from floors before applying new wax.
15 In many communities, carpet cleaning equipment can be rented.
16 Learning to put things back in their proper places after using them is good management.
17 All hobby materials and special projects should be completely put away at the end of each day.
18 Seasonal household tasks need to be included in a family cleaning plan or schedule.
19 A thorough and complete spring and fall housecleaning of every room is necessary to ensure that a home is adequately clean.
20 Good management includes having specific places for storing household items.
21 Overcrowded storage areas can create safety hazards.
22 Meals can be prepared with greater efficiency when tools and utensils are stored as near as possible to the place where they will be used first.
23 Once a storage plan has been made it should *not* be altered.
24 It is a poor management technique to clean the inside of a window without cleaning the outside of it also.

25 A family's health and safety may be related to the neatness and cleanliness of its home.
26 Insects sometimes get into a house in cardboard boxes brought in from the outside.
27 Many utility companies employ home economists to help families with problems related to the care and use of gas or electric home appliances.
28 A home that looks neglected on the outside may give others a poor impression of the family living there.
29 For some families, it is better management to pay someone to mow the lawn than to do it themselves.
30 Some outdoor tasks may need to be done more often than weekly.

On a separate sheet of paper, copy the numbers corresponding to the household tasks below. Beside each number indicate if that task is usually done daily (d), weekly (w), or seasonally (s).

1 Change bed linens
2 Use brush to clean toilet bowls
3 Wash window screens
4 Sweep crumbs from kitchen floor
5 Inspect and clean refrigerator
6 Make beds
7 Remove food wastes
8 Shampoo carpets or rugs
9 Hang up clothes
10 Water household plants

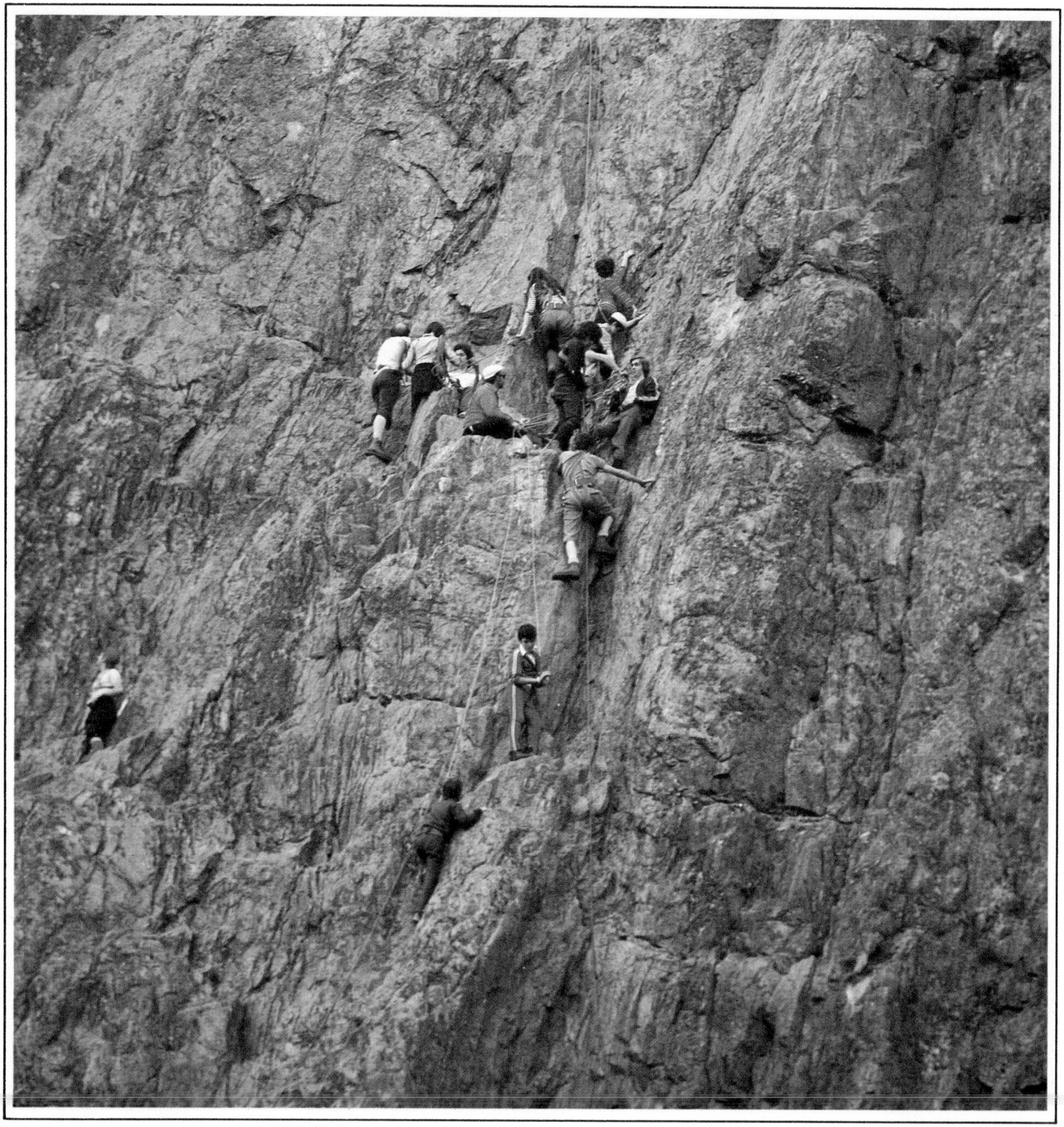

Cary Wolinski/Stock, Boston

Unit 3

Your Resources

Number from 1 to 15 on a piece of paper. Beside each number write the letter corresponding to the *best* answer for that question. *Do not* write in this book.

1 Which is a *natural* resource?
  a Intelligence
  b Clothing
  c Water
  d An aptitude

2 Which is a *material* resource?
  a Housing
  b Minerals
  c A skill
  d Wildlife

3 Which is a *human* resource?
  a Goods
  b Machinery
  c Money
  d Time

4 Which applies to *conserving* natural resources?
  a Using up forests
  b Polluting air
  c Protecting wildlife
  d Allowing soil to erode

5 Which is a threat to the natural environment?
  a Solar energy to heat buildings
  b Industrialization
  c House plants
  d Fabrics made from cotton

6 Which uses the most electricity if each is used for the same length of time?
  a Seventy-five-watt light bulb
  b Surface burner on a range
  c Black and white TV
  d Vacuum cleaner

7 If *time* is very limited, which is probably the best choice?
  a To prepare cookies from basic ingredients
  b To buy and prepare a cookie mix
  c To buy partially prepared cookies that can be sliced and baked
  d To buy ready-made cookies in a store

8 If *money* is very limited, which is probably the best choice?
  a To prepare cookies from basic ingredients
  b To buy and prepare a cookie mix
  c To buy partially prepared cookies that can be sliced and baked
  d To buy ready-made cookies in a store

9 Which is essential if you are to make the best use of your basic resources?
  a Setting realistic goals
  b Having a large income
  c Having the newest equipment
  d Satisfying all your wants

10 Which has probably had the greatest influence on your values?
  a Your school
  b Your community
  c Your family
  d Your friends

11 Which value is held by the largest number of people?
  a Status in the community
  b A new car every year
  c Ability in at least one team sport
  d Personal freedom

12 Which of the following is *not* a true statement about priorities?
  a Needs usually take priority over wants.
  b All teenagers' priorities are the same.
  c Setting priorities may be a difficult task.
  d Some goals take priority over other goals.

13 Which is likely to have the *least* effect on your behavior?
  a Your personal values
  b Your personal goals
  c Your basic resources
  d Your score on a standardized intelligence test

14 Which is *least* likely to affect your energy resources?
  a Daily activities and exercise
  b Food intake and diet
  c Money income
  d General health

15 Which is *most* likely to result from wise management of resources?
  a Independence
  b Dependence
  c Unrealistic goals
  d Low standards

Chapter 10

Achieving Your Goals by Managing Your Resources

After reading this chapter, you should be able to:

1 Name a number of natural, material, and human resources.
2 Give examples of ways you can help conserve natural resources.
3 Describe ways family members can help save generated energy.
4 Explain how basic resources are related to each other.
5 Tell in your own words the difference between a value and a goal.
6 Analyze your goals to determine which seem to be most realistic for you.
7 Analyze situations to determine if material possessions meet needs or wants.
8 Rank your most important values.
9 Point out some of the benefits gained from efficient management of resources.

You probably know people who are considered lucky by their friends. They seem to have a knack for getting the most out of life. They do not seem to be richer or smarter than other people, but they have reached many more of their goals than others have. Actually such people probably are no more or no less lucky than their friends. Their success is usually the result of wise *management* of their resources. You, too, have many resources to help you reach your goals. Some resources are the same for all people. Other resources are different for different people. The important thing is to make the most of the resources you do have.

UNDERSTANDING KINDS OF RESOURCES

Resources are all the things you have to help you reach your goals. There are natural, material, and

Use drawings, cartoons, or pantomime to show ways to save generated energy.

1 Close draperies, shades, and blinds to lower heat loss in winter and to keep out heat in summer.

2 Open draperies, shades, and blinds to let the sun help heat a home in cool weather.

3 Do not block heating and cooling grills with furniture or other items that can stop the flow of air.

4 Close the damper when a fireplace is not in use to keep warm air from going up the chimney.

5 Place aluminum foil behind radiators to reflect heat into a room.

6 Hang clothes outdoors to dry when the weather is warm.

7 Wear layers of clothing, such as vests over shirts, for warmth.

8 Use an afghan or blanket covering while watching TV or reading.

9 Choose garments made of wool or part wool for warmth.

10 Use an electric blanket, if available, for sleeping at night so the heat can be lowered.

human resources. Natural resources include air, sunshine, water, soil, forests, wildlife, and minerals. Goods and equipment and the money which will buy these things are material resources. Human resources include abilities, skills, and personal qualities.

Conserving Natural Resources

Air provides oxygen necessary for life. In recent years people have begun to realize that in some areas the lack of clean, fresh air is a threat to health. Air pollution has become a national concern. Air pollution is an everyday problem for families living in many urban and industrial areas.

Sunshine provides warmth and energy needed to make plants and animals grow. Without sunshine, green plants cannot make the food and nutrients on which all life depends. Heat from the sun, *solar energy*, is being studied as a way to heat homes and other buildings. Pollution, smog, and tall buildings in cities affect the amount of sunshine received.

Water is also necessary for life. Many foods you eat depend on clean, unpolluted water. Water also supplies energy for power plants. In some areas, water has always been in short supply. New sources of water must be found if families are to continue to live, farm, and do other kinds of work in these areas. In other places, water has been polluted by people who have forgotten that supplies of clean water can be used up.

Soil, directly or indirectly, provides most of the food we eat. Some plants are eaten directly. Other plants provide food for the animals we eat.

Forests give us lumber and other products used to build and furnish our homes. Forests also provide places for wildlife to live and grow. Wildlife includes wild plants and animals. Some wild plants such as huckleberries, raspberries, and dandelion greens can be eaten. Some wild animals are hunted for food.

Minerals provide products that add to our everyday living comfort. Coal provides heat and energy. Metals like steel are used to build automobiles and to make household appliances and equipment. Most dishes, cooking utensils, clocks, furniture, and other household items are totally or partially made from minerals.

You can help conserve the world's natural resources in many ways. You can be careful of fire, especially when camping. You can avoid throwing trash on streets and highways. You can buy materials that can be recycled. You can plant trees and shrubs where others have died. You can write letters supporting conservation legislation. Conservation is important to everyone, and everyone can and should take an active part in conserving natural resources.

Solar One is the first experimental house directly converting sunlight into *both* heat and electricity for domestic use.   *University of Delaware and The Institute of Energy Conversion*

Copy the diagram below onto a separate sheet of paper. Unscramble the letters, one letter to each blank, to form nine words. When these words are unscrambled, another word will appear in the vertical column. *Do not write in this book.*

IRA
GERNEY
SAG
LOIS
NNSSUIEH
TAREW
OLAC
MIET
SSTEROF

Your career
Geologist

You would study the composition of the earth, exploring rock formations and soil, to discover fuel, mineral, and water supplies. Much of your time would be spent outdoors in the field. You might make maps and prepare reports of your field findings or do further research of materials in laboratories. You would find employment with the government, utility companies, and large corporations.

Saving generated energy

Much has been said and written in recent years about conserving generated energy, which is the energy supplied to us by converting natural resources. The fuel, electricity, and gas used in homes is only a small part of the generated energy used in this country. Every time we flick a switch, turn a dial, cook on the range or in the oven, use a washing machine, set a thermostat, or go somewhere in a motor vehicle, hard to replace energy is being used. However, most families can do much to lower the use of energy and thus conserve resources.

Electric and gas bills can also be lowered through good management and planning ahead.

In preparing meals there are many ways to save gas or electricity. Whole meals can be cooked in the oven. Large amounts of long-cooking foods can be prepared at once. Then smaller portions can be reheated when needed. If, in the winter, family members wear a few layers of lightweight clothing, the home can be kept at a lower temperature. In the summer, heat can be kept out of the house by closing windows and window coverings on the sunny side of the house. The

Illustrate the following facts with drawings in the form of equations.

1 An iron uses as much electricity as ten 100-watt light bulbs.

2 The average shower takes 10 gallons (38 ℓ) of water while the average bath takes 20 gallons (76 ℓ) of water.

3 An automatic washing machine uses the same electricity for a full load as it uses for a single item.

4 Five regular incandescent light bulbs use the same amount of electricity as one fluorescent light bulb to give the same amount of light.

5 Toasting bread in an oven takes three times as much generated energy as toasting bread in a pop-up toaster.

6 If ceramic or glass utensils are used for oven cooking, 350° F. equals 325° F. (177° C. equals 163° C.).

7 Ninety drops of water per minute from a leaking faucet equal 1,000 gallons (3800 ℓ) of water in a year.

8 It takes two-thirds more time to cook a frozen roast than a thawed one.

9 A color TV set uses 33 percent more electricity than a black and white set.

10 Three lightweight garments keep a person as warm as one very heavy garment.

sun can be used to help heat the home in the winter. Trees and shrubs can be planted to help keep out cold and heat. Using the car to do several errands at one time can save gasoline.

Almost every family can find ways to save energy and lower its utility bills at the same time. You can not only help conserve energy for your country, but you can also help your family. By reducing your energy consumption, the money saved on utility bills is available for other uses.

Using resources for clothing

Our natural environment provides materials for clothing. Some of this clothing is worn to protect us from the environment. When we are through with our clothing we usually throw it away. This can create problems for the environment. Some fabrics made from natural fibers, like cotton and linen, come from plants. Wool and silk, also natural fibers, come from animals. Cloth made entirely from natural fibers eventually decomposes, falls apart. Natural fibers are not a long-term threat to the environment. In fact, some fabrics made from natural fibers can be used to make new and different products, like paper.

However, many of our clothes and household fabrics are made from natural fibers that have been treated with chemicals. Other clothes and goods are made from manufactured fibers, such as nylon,

polyester, rayon, and acetate. Chemically treated natural fibers and synthetic fibers have many advantages, but they can create problems, too. They do not decompose easily. Therefore, it is especially important to think of ways to recycle clothes made from them.

Understanding Material Resources

Material resources may include many natural resources as well as physically useful items such as goods and equipment. Our homes, furnishings, and other useful possessions are among our material resources. Money is also a material resource. Each person within a family and each family has different material resources. One family member may have a bike and another may have a car, but for both individuals these are material resources. One family may have an outdoor clothesline and another family may have an automatic clothes dryer. These are part of each family's material resources.

Understanding Human Resources

Human resources include aptitudes, talents, skills, intelligence, creativity, and personal relationships. Human relationships are important resources because they help people get along with others at home, at school, and at work. Patience, understanding, and tact are some examples of human resources that help to foster good personal relationships.

Save both electricity and hot water by following these guidelines when using an automatic dishwasher.

1 Rinse dishes in cool water before placing them in the dishwasher. Wait until the dishwasher is full before turning it on.
2 Use partial load cycles, rinse-only cycles, midcycle turnoffs, and other special features when available.
3 Load the dishwasher efficiently. (See p. 500.)
4 Turn the dishwasher off after the final rinse and before the drying cycle to let dishes air dry. This can reduce dishwasher energy consumption by one-third.
5 Use the dishwasher during the day in cold weather and at night in hot weather. This can help heat the house or help keep it cool.

Ask a home service advisor to demonstrate how to use and care efficiently for several laborsaving appliances and pieces of equipment.

Natural resources can be used and enjoyed by a great number of people if wilderness areas are handled correctly.   *Bettina Cirone*

Use generated energy efficiently to preserve food in the refrigerator and freezer.

1 Open and close refrigerator and freezer doors as little as possible. Remove several items at one time to reduce the loss of cold air.

2 Defrost the refrigerator before the frost becomes ¼ inch (6 mm) thick so the motor will not be overworked. A self-defrosting refrigerator-freezer uses 36 percent more electricity than a standard model.

3 Cover all liquids stored in the refrigerator. This is especially important in frost-free models. Moisture is drawn into the air from uncovered liquids, causing the motor to work harder.

4 Place foods slightly apart in the refrigerator so air can circulate.

5 Keep the freezer full to prevent heavy icing.

6 Use a thermometer to check refrigerator and freezer temperatures. Settings of 10° F., or −12.2° C., for the freezer and 40° F., or 4.4° C., are usually recommended.

7 Use a chart to show the location of foods in the freezer so items can be found quickly and the door will not be open long.

Human resources also include time given to others or to work and the services performed by people. One of the most important human resources is the physical energy individuals have. Human energy is used to serve others and to make material goods. People use both time and energy to reach their goals.

Human and material resources can be combined to change an unattractive area into a pleasing one. *Mimi Forsyth/Monkmeyer*

MANAGING BASIC RESOURCES AS A TEAM

Your basic resources are your time, physical energy, and money. Basic resources are related to each other. They can be used in combination, or they can be substituted for each other. Sometimes a combination of resources can create a new resource. For example, teenagers who use their time and physical energy to develop the skill of painting can redecorate the family's home for much less money than if a painter were hired to do the job.

The way you use your time, physical energy, and money depends on the amount of each of these basic resources you have available to you. All people have the same amount of time. But people differ from others in the way they *need* to spend their time. They also differ in the ways they *want* to spend it. For example, families with very little money may need to spend a great deal of time cooking to stretch their dollars. On the other hand, high-income families may want to buy quickly prepared meals and eat out frequently to save time for other activities.

People do *not* have the same amount of physical energy to spend during each twenty-four hours. Body makeup determines the maximum amount of energy available to them. Too, general health, daily activities, emotional makeup, and other factors such as emergency situations combine to cause changes in available physical energy resources.

As you plan to use your time, physical energy, and money, you may think of them one at a time, in combination with each other, or in place of each other. In managing these resources, it may be best to think of using them together or as substitutes for each other.

Although time, physical energy, and money are renewable to a certain extent, they can be used up. This is just as true of time and physical energy as it is of money. It is fairly easy to see that you cannot spend the same dollars for a movie and for a new wallet. It is somewhat harder to realize that an hour spent visiting on the telephone cannot be used for homework.

In order to manage your basic resources wisely, you must learn to spend each to best advantage. Suppose you are asked to bring a cake to a party. You can buy a ready-made cake. You can make a cake from a mix. You can prepare a cake from flour, sugar, eggs, etc. No matter which you choose to do, you must spend some time, some physical energy, and some money for the cake. How can you spend two of your basic resources in order to save the third? How much of each basic resource is needed for your best choice? A ready-made cake would probably cost the most money and save the most time and energy. The cake prepared from

basic ingredients would probably require the use of more time and effort, but it might cost the least money. The cake mix would require the use of small amounts of all three resources. If you have a short supply of money, you can make the cake at home. If your supply of time or physical energy is limited, you can buy the cake at a store. If you feel limited in all three resources, you can use a cake mix.

When you sense yourself being held back from making wise decisions because you lack a skill, you may be able to develop the needed skill. For example, if you can't find a bookcase to fit the space you have, you might decide to spend some of your basic resources in making one. As your skill increases, you may be able to make other furnishings while saving time, physical energy, and money for other uses.

Sometimes you will find that you cannot use the basic resources of time, physical energy, and money to best advantage because you don't have a necessary piece of equipment. When this happens, you can choose the second best combination of resources to reach your goal. For example, a family might choose to pay for the use of expensive equipment found in a nearby laundromat. However, they might find that this practice takes one or two of their free evenings each week. A wise manager learns to watch for such situations. They

 Use consumer information materials or conduct experiments to find the following:

1 How much electricity it takes to prepare certain foods in a microwave oven compared to a regular electric oven.
2 How much heat is lost every time the oven door is opened.
3 What kinds of pans retain the most heat so baking can be done at 25° lower temperatures than called for in recipes.
4 How to prepare several foods in the oven at one time when each requires a slightly different cooking temperature.
5 How much time it takes to cook frozen food compared to thawed food.

Bulletin board IDEA
Title: *No Lion, Managing Your Resources Is Important*
Directions: Mount a toy lion or a cutout of a lion. Add pictures to show good management of resources such as a speed limit sign, a watch or clock, play money, or a convenience food. Identify and label the resources illustrated.

Give examples that show when it may be good management to spend extra money to save time and energy. Give examples to show how it might be wise in some situations to spend more time and physical energy to save money.

Complete the following statements.
It is good management for:
• a family to employ someone to do housework if . . .
• a family to use many convenience foods if . . .
• a family member to service the car if . . .
• a son or daughter to make his or her clothes if . . .
• a son or daughter to cut and edge the lawn if . . .

Discuss reasons why students completed these sentences differently. What ideas were expressed most often? Why?

Bulletin board IDEA
Title: *Don't Get Tangled Up*
Directions: Use a string drawing of a spider web. Underneath write: *Plan to Use Your Resources Wisely.*

Physical energy can often be saved if you arrange children's play areas near home work areas. *Frigidaire Division of General Motors*

can be a guide in making long-range plans which might include the purchase of home laundry equipment.

SETTING REALISTIC GOALS

You cannot make wise use of your basic resources unless you know what your goals are. You must also understand your resources in order to select *realistic goals* for yourself. At first, it may seem fairly simple to select a number of lifetime goals.

Perhaps you have planned to be a great leader who will make the world a better place to live. Perhaps you have dreamed of being famous or of owning many beautiful things. Ideals and dreams can spur you on to real achievements, but they are usually not true goals.

It has been said that people can do almost anything they wish if they are willing to make the necessary sacrifices. Sometimes the sacrifices are too great. A person might reach a goal only at the cost of personal and family happiness. Unrealistic goals can lead to lifelong frustration. In order to choose realistic goals, you need to know your resources and to use them wisely. You need to recognize the difference between dreams and possible achievements. Dreams and wishes can provide useful experience as long as reality is kept in mind.

Working for Individual and Group Goals

You are living in a goal-oriented society. Individuals, families, communities, and nations are involved in planning for and reaching goals. Achieving a wisely chosen goal is a sign of progress. What goals is your family working toward? Perhaps you wish to take a special trip or move to a better home. Each person in the family needs to give time, physical energy, or money to make this dream come true. When everyone takes part in the planning, the family works together more easily.

A child begins early in life to develop his or her long-range goal of language development and reading skills. *The New Book of Knowledge*

Reaching Long-Range and Short-Term Goals

Many of your important goals in life will be reached only after years of planning and working. Such long-range goals are usually reached one step at a time. As you consider each of these steps, you are planning short-term goals which fit your overall plan.

There are also short-term goals which are not related to your long-range goals. Both short-term and long-range goals may be equally important. Wise managers learn to judge the value of all their goals.

People are sometimes careless and forget to make such judgments. They may use up their resources to satisfy immediate desires. For instance, the teenager who uses money which could be saved for education to buy lots of clothes may be giving up an important long-range goal in favor of a less important short-term one.

Establishing Priority Goals

A priority is the emphasis you place on a given item or situation. As you make both long-range and short-term plans, you will find that some take priority over others. There will be times when some of your goals conflict with others. In order to use your resources wisely, you must be able to choose the most important of the conflicting goals.

Setting priorities is a difficult task. The first astronauts probably had serious decisions to make when leaving their families to face the unknown dangers of space travel. Difficult decisions must also be made by a family that has to choose between living together in a distant city where the father has a very good job opportunity and remaining at home to be near seriously ill grandparents. To be together or to care for aging parents is a set of priority problems common in our complex society. Which goal would take priority in your family?

Perhaps priorities are not really different now than they were in the past. Some pioneer families were

Divide into small groups. Set a time limit and brainstorm to identify as many ways as possible to save time, physical energy, and money in doing household tasks. The group with the longest list is the winner. Share your ideas with the class. Discuss the ideas in relation to situations when each would be a good course of action.

Make a display or notebook of cartoons, clippings, newspaper and magazine articles, and pictures that show ways to save time, physical energy, and money. Try one or more of these ideas. Tell the class how well it worked.

Write the word RESOURCES by arranging the letters in a vertical line. Beside each letter give examples of different kinds of resources beginning with that letter. For example:

R Relationships
E Energy
S Skills
O
U
R
C
E
S

Keep a record of the purchases you make for a week before, during, and after school. Total the amount spent. Would this total be enough to buy something you have been wanting? How can you manage your spending so your personal needs and some special wants are both satisfied?

Add to the following list other important reasons for learning to manage money effectively.

1 More quantity or higher quality can be bought for a given amount of money.
2 Parent-teenage relationships may improve.
3 Money may be saved for large purchases.
4 Frustrations are lessened.

List, as a class, ten expenditures often made by students your age. Give the approximate cost of each expenditure. Consider the priority each item on the list has for you. Rank the items from 1 to 10. Decide on a cutoff point which separates the things you consider necessary from those you could do without. Compare students' lists and discuss the reasons why they are different.

Learning to play a sport often includes short-term goals of having fun and long-term goals of developing skills. *Rene Burri/Magnum*

faced with setting priorities between living in safe poverty or possible wealth on land with unknown dangers.

Life is full of conflicts. Often you may feel that no matter which way you turn, you end up going in the wrong direction. You need to decide what is most important to you, and set out to reach that goal.

Considering your needs and wants

Your personal goals involve the things you want to be, to do, and to have. These goals differ greatly from person to person. But all may be separated into those which satisfy *needs* and those which satisfy *wants*. For example, clothing is a need. But as people buy for this need, they often fulfill wants as well. A fashionable jacket that can be worn only a few days in a season fulfills a want more than a need.

As times have changed, some goods and services which were once considered wants have become needs. For example, refrigeration is now considered a need for families in the United States. Each situation also determines whether particular goods or services are needs or wants. A car may be a *need* for a family living in a rural area far from town, but a car may be a *want* for a city family living near stores and public transportation. Likewise, a CB (citizens' band) radio may be a *need* for an oil field worker, but it may be a *want* for a person living in a populated area.

Both needs and wants are important to everyone. Wise managers first select goals which will meet their basic physical, mental, social, and emotional needs. Leftover resources can then be used to satisfy their wants.

UNDERSTANDING YOUR VALUES

A value is a belief or feeling that something is important. You probably value certain ideas, people, material possessions, and activities. When you are able to identify your values, you are better able to understand why you act as you do. Every decision you make reflects some of your values.

Most of the values you hold today have been influenced by your family. Your culture, your friends, your community, and your earlier experiences have also affected your values. There are some values that are important to most people. These values include freedom, satisfying family life, good health, and attractive personal appearance. Values such as athletic ability, good grades, and specific material goods are much more important to some people than to others.

Your personal goals will work for you only if they are supported by your values. When your values conflict with your goals, you are likely to experience frustration. Suppose you have dreamed of being a tennis pro someday. You realize that such a goal would satisfy your basic need

Give examples to show how several short-term goals might be part of or contribute to one long-range goal.

Cite examples from books, TV, or real life where people set unrealistic goals for themselves. Discuss why they seemed to be unrealistic goals. If these goals were not reached, what were the reasons and results? In some cases, why were people able to reach goals that seemed to be unrealistic? How can you apply this information to a decision you are now trying to make?

Give examples from books you have read, movies you have seen, or TV programs you have watched that show how individuals and families set priorities today much as they did in the past.

Read or listen to a tape of passages from *Mama's Bank Account, The Glass Menagerie, Life With Father,* or another appropriate story or biography. Discuss values held by family members and some of the goals for which they were striving. What were some of the resources used to achieve these goals?

Give examples to show how *needs* and *wants* change for individuals as they grow older. Give examples to show how some goods and services once considered *wants* are now considered *needs*.

Give an example to show how a *want* for one person may be a *need* for another person. Also give examples to show how *needs* can sometimes satisfy *wants*. Have you ever used a *need* as an excuse for fulfilling a *want*? How?

Bulletin board IDEA
Title: *Weigh Your Resources*
Directions: Use a cutout of a balance scale labeled as follows:

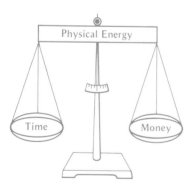

Creativity can be expressed and developed through hobbies and crafts. *Erika/Peter Arnold Photo Archives*

206

 Pretend you have one week of free time to do anything you wish. What would you do with this time?

View pictures of people taking part in various physical activities such as team sports, bicycling, swimming, skating, gardening, cooking, and dancing. Which activity would you enjoy most? Why?

Pretend you have been given twenty-five dollars. What would you do with this money?

Analyze how your choices reflect your values in regard to using your time, physical energy, and money. Why do people's choices differ?

Play records or tapes of songs such as *Bridge Over Troubled Water*, *Joy to the World*, and *Put Your Hand in the Hand*. Analyze the lyrics for the values expressed.

Give examples of peoples' actions that show they value or do not value the following:
  Conservation of resources
  Success in school
  Efficiency
  Material possessions
  Service to others
  Physical activity
  Relationships with others

Name one of your human resources that has been or could be used to benefit your entire family. Tell how this resource has been or could be used to best advantage.

List teenage hobbies and activities which could also contribute to families' resources.

Discuss the following questions:
1 Under what circumstances should teenagers contribute to their family finances?
2 Why is it desirable for teenagers to know about the expenses involved in managing a home?
3 What personal expenses should teenagers be expected to pay with their own money?
4 What expenditures should teenagers expect their families to make?

Compare two people's abilities, talents, skills, basic resources, values, and goals. In what ways does one of these people use basic resources more efficiently than the other person? What effect does management of resources have on reaching short-term and long-range goals?

for recognition. You know you have outstanding athletic ability, stamina, and good health. You know you would need to spend more time and energy practicing than you have in the past. Additional tennis lessons, equipment, and court-playing fees would also cost money. Yet, becoming a professional tennis player may be a realistic goal for you.

For other people, however, such a goal would be unrealistic. Many would not have the self-discipline and drive required to excel in a professional sport.

Some people might value service to others more than they value self-recognition. Teenagers who feel this way might very well choose to spend their time and energy as an assistant Scout leader or as a member of a service club. Such activities would be more in line with their value systems.

These examples picture two sets of values. Neither is right nor wrong. Both help determine individual priorities. Some people are more interested in developing their own abilities, while others are more interested in helping other people develop their skills. People may aspire toward both goals, but their *values* will help them determine which goal takes priority.

The desire to play a musical instrument well is often accompanied by the self-discipline required to practice and develop the talent. *Owen Franken/Stock, Boston*

Considering your interests and abilities

Teenagers usually have a wide range of interests. It is often wise to make plans which include time for developing several interests. Even though other goals may become more important later on, such short-term goals as earning money to buy ice skates, learning to play the guitar, or developing skill in a new game or sport can introduce you to new activities or new friends.

Perhaps you have known people who worked hard to make the team when they were better suited to be on the pep squad. These people selected a goal without considering their abilities. They could be more helpful to their team and their school by being a good pep squad member than by being a poor team member. Perhaps, too, you have known students who wanted to be cheerleaders. But they never realized that successful cheerleaders spend hours practicing before appearing in front of a crowd. They may feel hurt because they were not chosen to be cheerleaders. Successful people recognize their own abilities and that they must practice to develop these abilities fully.

Eventually people must select long-range goals from among their many interests. Most people have more ability in one or two areas than in others. A realistic and worthwhile short-term goal for you would be to recognize and develop your best abilities.

SETTING STANDARDS

You have probably heard the word *standard* used in many ways. You have heard of a standard of living. You have heard of a standard of behavior. You may have heard of a standard of achievement and a standard test. A standard is a means of measuring the outcome of an effort. Without a standard, you have no way of knowing whether you are making wise use of your basic resources. Some standards are personal. Society also sets standards which measure performance, satisfaction, and achievement. Your own standards depend on your values and life goals.

ENJOYING THE RESULTS OF MANAGEMENT

One of the goals most teenagers seek is independence. It can be achieved through the wise management of resources. Typical teenagers begin to want to take charge of their own lives.

You know you are a one-of-a-kind person. Only you can determine what you are capable of achieving.

You must make your own decisions. Good or bad, you must accept the effects of your efforts. The end results are brought about by the use you make of your resources. When you can accept these results, blaming no one for the ups or downs that come with them, you are reaping the rewards of your management abilities.

 List tasks that can be done by family members instead of someone else hired to do the work. Estimate the amount of money that can be saved by doing such tasks as:
1 Shampooing carpets
2 Preserving home-grown foods
3 Doing yard work
4 Changing the car oil
5 Making an item of clothing
Describe circumstances when it might be desirable for family members to do these tasks. Describe situations when it might be desirable to employ someone to do these tasks.

 Your career
Home service adviser

You would discuss with customers effective use of lighting facilities in homes. You might suggest ways to improve room arrangements for best use of space and light. You might also demonstrate how color, decorations, and furnishings can be used to increase lighting, heating, and cooling efficiency. You would work for utility companies, equipment manufacturers, or be self-employed as a consultant.

Fill in the blank in each sentence with the best word to complete the statement. *Do not* write in this book.

1 Air, soil, and forests are (1) resources.
2 Goods, equipment, possessions, and money are classified as (2) resources.
3 Personal qualities, aptitudes, abilities, and skills are (3) resources.
4 The use of your basic resources depends on the amount of each resource available to you and on the (4) you have set for yourself.
5 A nationwide concern in conservation is pollution of air and (5) .
6 To save generated energy when cooking, frozen foods should be (6) in the refrigerator before cooking.
7 The most efficient way to make toast is in a(an) (7) .
8 Fabrics made from synthetic fibers are more of a threat to the environment than those made from (8) fibers.
9 One *basic* resource that all people have in equal amounts is (9) .
10 The wise use of basic resources is the result of intelligent planning and efficient (10) .
11 The amount of sleep and exercise you get, your diet, and your health all affect your (11) level.

12 Using basic ingredients to make a wide variety of food products usually saves (12) .
13 If you use convenience foods to prepare a meal, you are saving energy and (13) .
14 The importance or emphasis you give to a particular goal is the (14) that you give to that goal.
15 To avoid frustration, it is important that your goals be (15) for you in relation to your aptitudes, abilities, skills, and personal qualities.
16 A person's most important goals in life, those reached one step at a time through a period of planning and work, are called (16) goals.
17 All goals can be separated into those that meet needs and those that satisfy (17) .
18 Your values probably have been influenced the most by your (18) .
19 The basis, or rule, by which something is judged is called a(an) (19) .
20 When teenagers begin to take charge of their lives, it shows they are growing in maturity while gaining (20) .

Fill in the blank in each sentence with the *best* word or words to complete the statement. *Do not* write in this book.

1 In making a time schedule, it is wise to separate things you want to do from those things that you (1) to do.
2 The first step in planning a time schedule is to list all your (2) .
3 When you waste another person's time, you are using a(an) (3) that is not your own.
4 Time free from assigned tasks or duties may be thought of as free, unplanned, or (4) time.
5 Physical, emotional, and (5) factors may affect a person's energy level.
6 People who have planned a good (6) program can use money to earn additional money.
7 Unplanned spending usually provides less money for reaching goals than does a(an) (7) .
8 The amount of money children may receive from their parents on a regular schedule is usually called a(an) (8) .
9 Priority spending should be for those things which are real and basic (9) .
10 Expenses which you cannot control are called (10) expenses.
11 Savings should be included in a spending plan so extra money is available if needed for a(an) (11) situation.

Chapter 11

Using Your Time, Energy, and Money

After reading this chapter, you should be able to:
1 List the steps in planning a time schedule.
2 Give reasons for making a time schedule and following it as planned.
3 Summarize ways in which time may be used efficiently and inefficiently.
4 Describe how individual people's physical energy patterns differ.
5 Explain how mental and emotional factors may affect a person's physical energy.
6 Improve your efficiency by scheduling activities whenever possible to correspond with your personal energy-fatigue pattern.
7 Develop a personal spending plan based on your income and expenses.
8 Point out reasons for including savings in a spending plan.
9 Evaluate your spending plan.

Any large school system is likely to represent a wide cross section of society. The variation in its students' resources usually covers a considerable range. For instance, the incomes of families in a community vary. Their amounts of free time and physical energy also differ. Many teenagers do not fully understand that their own time and energy are resources. Yet they are very much aware of the amount of money their friends have to spend. No matter what their resources are, teenagers can be flexible. They are usually successful in forming groups and in playing and working in groups. Although some teenagers may not consider their own time and energy as resources, they know that there are resources besides money. They understand that while one family may have a great deal of money, all families also have other resources which may be equally important.

Use the telephone dial below to decode the eight words that make a sentence. This sentence relates to the main idea discussed in this chapter.

9 6 8 7

8 4 6 3,

3 6 3 7 4 9,

2 6 3

6 6 6 3 9

2 7 3

2 2 7 4 2

7 3 7 6 8 7 2 3 7

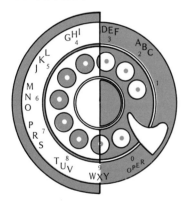

Write a story about a society where there are no clocks or time pieces. How do people manage their time? How did people in ancient civilizations tell time?

Write and present miniskits showing why it is often necessary for a homemaker to allow for flexibility in a time schedule.

A typical school system may have Kim as one of its students. Kim may have two well-known, but very busy, parents. They may or may not be living together, and their income is very large. From their income, Kim may have any amount of money asked for. While Kim may buy almost anything desired, it would be useless to ask for Kim's parents' time or energy. These resources are used mainly for making more money or pursuing their own interests.

Lyn may attend the same school. Lyn, several brothers and sisters, and their mother may live on welfare payments and the small amount of time and physical energy left over from their struggle for survival.

Perhaps a worse situation must be faced by Tony. He has a working father who chooses not to support his family. Perhaps this family's money is supplied only through part-time jobs Tony and his mother can find.

These are the extremes. Some teenagers' families provide money for their every want and need, but Kim's parents are unwilling to contribute their own time or energy toward their child's mental, social, and emotional development. Lyn and Tony have little time, energy, or money at their disposal because these basic resources are used for survival.

Fortunately, many school systems provide help for students whose basic resources are not sup-

In many schools, students with different values and backgrounds study, learn, and work together.
St. Louis District Dairy Council

plied at home. Teachers, counselors, and school friends can spend some of their own time and energy helping a student like Kim. Among friends there are some who will give of their time and energy so that Kim's life will have more meaning. Lyn and Tony can also find help. School lunches, dental and medical care, and help with transportation and school clothes are frequently available for students who need them. The ears of school nurses, principals, and understanding teachers are especially tuned for such needs. Even though your problems may seem too big to discuss, other students have problems of equal importance. Pride need

Wise planning before a party allows you to spend time with your guests when they arrive.
Farley Manning Associates, Inc.

not get in the way of a successful solution.

Most teenagers fit somewhere between the two extremes represented by Kim on the one hand and Lyn and Tony on the other. Although they may feel that they are short of one resource or another, most of them have some money. They are allowed to use some of their family's time and energy as well as their own. In other words, they have a range of resources to use. Their success lies in their ability to recognize time, physical energy, and money as real resources and to combine them for successful living.

DEVELOPING ATTITUDES ABOUT TIME

You have probably noticed that people have many different attitudes about time. Some treat time with respect, knowing it is a valuable resource. Others abuse it. Some people cherish every minute, while others can't seem to wait for the hours to pass. Even the same person feels differently about time in different situations. You may feel that time flies as you try to fit many activities in one day's schedule. On the other hand, you may feel that time drags while you wait for a special telephone call. These different feelings about time are based on your goals and interests.

Some people always seem to be cool and composed while they

Make a daily time schedule using the suggestions below. Follow the schedule a few weeks and then evaluate it for effectiveness.

1 Keep a record of the things you now do and the time required to do each. Keep records for several school days and a few weekend days. If you are planning a schedule for doing a particular thing, keep records of your work on two or three typical occasions.
2 Make a list of additional activities you feel you need to carry on within your available time. Estimate the time necessary for each activity.
3 Take a critical look at your activity list to see what other worthwhile things you can and want to do. Try planning to substitute them for current activities you consider less important.
4 Leave some unscheduled time.
5 Evaluate your schedule after trying it. If needed, make changes to improve it.

Give examples to show how the ways people may *need* to spend their time can differ from how they *want* to spend their time.

Discuss the advantages and disadvantages of making a time schedule. Make a schedule for a time when you will have an unusually large number of responsibilities. Use the plan to schedule all these activities. Did you find the time schedule was helpful? Why, or why not?

Make a time schedule for preparing the following meal for your family:

Hamburgers
Buttered Carrots
Mashed Potatoes
Lettuce and Tomato Salad
Lime Gelatin
Milk

Indicate the time when you will begin each major step, including preparing and cooking the various foods, setting the table, and cleaning up.

Use convenience foods and do some of the tasks the previous day if you wish, but include these tasks in your schedule. If possible, prepare and serve this meal as planned, or plan and use another menu and time schedule. Evaluate your schedule. If necessary, make recommendations for improving it for use another time.

accomplish a lot. Other people appear to be busy and rushed most of the time, but despite all the flurry of activity they actually accomplish very little.

There are many pressures for speed in modern life. There is also the need for slow, careful activity. How you feel about time at a particular moment is not as important as how you use the twenty-four hours you have each day. How do you use time as a valuable resource? How do you waste time as a resource?

Managing Your Time

Time is something that can't be seen, tasted, heard, or felt. Yet it is real. Like other resources, it can be spent wisely or wasted. Time, like money, requires careful management. People who realize this have taken an important first step toward making wise use of their time.

Management of time does require more than just understanding its value. You need to plan the use of your time. Your plan must be realistic. It should provide for needs before it can be concerned with wants. In making such a plan, you also need to recognize your limitations. You should understand that any plan will fail unless you are willing and able to follow it. The wise use of your time depends in part on the amount of self-discipline you are willing to exercise. It also depends on the habits you develop as you follow your plans.

Good students usually give priority to time for study. *St. Louis District Dairy Council*

Planning a Time Schedule

Busy people usually want to spend their time wisely. Many find that the best way to do this is to work by schedules. A schedule helps you to be sure that you will have enough time for each important activity each day. A plan may be quite general, or it may be worked out in detail.

Listing your activities

Everyone must decide which type of activity plan will work for him or her. Perhaps all you have to do is to note your major activities in a notebook or on a calendar. Other people may prefer to list all their activities, large and small.

Before making a time plan, you must determine your activities. List *all* activities for the day. Then double check your list. Don't forget to include time for personal grooming and care of clothes. Activities involving family and home responsibilities also need to be considered. Time for classwork and for study should be included. You also need to list your other school-connected activities. Perhaps you have a part-time job which must be included on the list. Social activities and any special uses of your leisure time need to be noted. For example, if you are planning to paint a bookcase for your room, you must remember to list this activity.

Next to each activity on your list, write the amount of time it will probably take. If you leave for school at eight each morning and get home at four each afternoon, you can list these exact times next to *School.* You will need to estimate the time for many of your activities. For example, you may be preparing a special school project at home. Next to this activity on your list, you can note that you expect to spend about one hour, from seven to eight o'clock, on this project.

A carefully planned time schedule should still be flexible. No one can tell ahead of time that heavy traffic or a rainstorm will cause a daily trip to take longer than usual.

But a time schedule *can* allow extra time each day for the unexpected. Then, too, some activities will take longer than you expected. You can't stop washing dishes halfway through the job because your schedule says it's time to stop. If you schedule your time wisely, you will be able to adjust your plan to take care of occasional poor time estimates.

Considering your priorities

Look over your list. It may seem that you have scheduled more activities than there is time for. This often happens to people who are learning to plan their time. One way people spend their time unwisely is simply by trying to do too much.

Go back over your list. Separate the activities which you *need* to include from those which you *want* to include. As you become more skillful in managing your time, you will find that you have more leisure time. You will have learned to take care of your needs effectively. In the meantime, you can place your unscheduled wants on a standby list. Then work these wants into your schedule as time and energy allow.

High on your list of needed activities will be those which affect your health and those which affect your important goals. You will also want to give priority to promises you have made and to activities which concern the people you care about.

Use the following suggestions to improve your personal study habits:

1 Look over the entire assignment to get an idea of its length and difficulty.

2 Glance over all the assigned pages quickly. Do not try to read them carefully at this point.

3 Read the pages of the assignment carefully, studying charts, maps, and the captions under the pictures. Be sure you understand what you read.

4 Summarize the lesson in your own words. Determine the main points of the lesson.

5 Go over the parts that need to be remembered accurately. Be sure you can recall names, dates, and special points.

6 Make notes on cards or in a notebook if you are using a textbook which belongs to the school. If the book belongs to you, you may want to underline parts of the text or write important points in the margin.

Keep a time record of your activities for several days to determine whether you are getting enough sleep, rest, and exercise. If the record shows that you should increase the time spent for one of these activities, suggest ways of using your time to allow for this change.

Act out a situation in which a person may be hurt or offended because another person is unwilling or unable to change a time schedule to . . .
Talk at length on the phone
Sit and visit
Go somewhere unexpectedly
  Discuss whether the second person's annoyance was justified. Could the situation have been handled better? How?

Bulletin board IDEA
Title: *Balance Your Day*
Directions: Use a silhouette of a balance scale. On one side write *sleep*, *exercise*, and *nutrition*. On the other side write *study*, *recreation*, and *work*.

Physical energy can be conserved through the use of labor-saving equipment.   *Westinghouse Electric Corporation*

Considering your limitations and strengths
No one has more than twenty-four hours to spend on any day's activities. This absolute limit on available time is the reason for giving a priority rating to each of your activities. But there are other limitations which must be considered as you plan your time.

There are limits which come from outside your schedule. Perhaps it would be more convenient for you if school would start at noon on one day or if the bus came five minutes later each morning. However, picture the troubles that would develop if schedules were changed to suit the individual wishes of each student or each bus rider.

As you go over your list of activities, make a note of those which must fit specific time schedules. List these activities in the order in which they happen throughout the day. Then you can plan your other activities around these fixed schedules.

The needs of other people in your family can limit the ways you schedule your time. If someone in the family goes to work at 8 P.M., the evening meal will often be served early enough to allow this person time to enjoy eating with the family. You might prefer to eat at a later hour. Yet, as a responsible family member, you will plan your time schedule to fit the family needs.

Your body makeup also limits how you spend your time. People have different periods throughout the day when they can work more efficiently than at other times. At first it may seem that outside schedules will not allow you to make good use of these periods of high efficiency. But you can learn to take advantage of them as you learn to adjust your total plan to include other limitations.

For example, you may find that you must struggle through your afternoon study period to finish a math assignment. You may be able to do the same assignment in fifteen minutes at home after the evening meal. You can't change your school program. However, you can plan to spend your total study time wisely. Study the math at home when you can efficiently concentrate on it.

Use the school study period for other subjects which require less of your concentration.

Even when outside schedules are not involved, it is wise to plan your activities to match your periods of high efficiency. You might find that you spend thirty minutes straightening out your room in the evening when you are tired. Perhaps you can do a better job in ten minutes in the morning when you are fresh. By scheduling this task for the morning, you can save twenty minutes.

Evaluating your schedule

Once you have made a time schedule and followed it for several days, evaluate it. How could it be improved? In what ways does it need to be more flexible? What important activities did you forget to include? Each time you improve your plan, you will learn how to make time schedules which are more satisfactory to your needs.

Disciplining Your Use of Time

Perhaps your time schedule was a wise one but you failed to follow it effectively. Maybe you are willing to interrupt your schedule for almost any reason. Perhaps each interruption seems important at the moment. Yet at the end of the day you find that many of your scheduled activities were never completed. Think of your time schedule as a tool to help you reach your goals. Then you will be able to judge whether it is wise to change it

 Develop the following work habits to get the most from your courses of study:

At School
Have the necessary tools.
Concentrate on the lesson.
Contribute to discussions.
Take notes accurately.
Ask questions when you don't understand.
Write down the assignments.
Use the school library.
Make up assignments you miss.

At Home
Set definite times to study.
Have a quiet place and the right tools for studying.
Set goals for accomplishing something definite in the time allotted for your study.
Rest for a few minutes every half hour or hour when studying.

For Tests
Start reviewing several days beforehand.
Get your regular amount of sleep the night before the test.
Eat a good breakfast on the morning of the test.

Follow these guidelines for the most efficient use of your study time.

Begin your studies before you are too tired to concentrate.

Select a quiet place.

Dress comfortably.

Choose a comfortable chair and a good light.

Alternate your favorite subjects with those you do not like as well. Be sure to allow time for each assignment.

Concentrate on what you are doing.

Take a short rest period after studying about an hour. Do something entirely different from what you have been doing. Resume studying with renewed energy.

Evaluate study habits shown in pantomime. Include some of the following:

1 Writing while slouched in a lounge chair
2 Reading an assignment while the TV is on
3 Studying notes late at night when very tired
4 Being distracted with any excuse not to study
5 Having poor light in which to read or write

A person who plans and completes necessary tasks before enjoying leisure activities prevents the fatigue often caused by last minute rushing. *Jell-O Gelatin*

for other things. A flexible time schedule can be adjusted to include worthwhile interruptions.

Developing Habits about Using Time

By the time people reach school age, they have formed a great many habits. As they grow older, new habits are learned and old habits become stronger. In one way, all such habits save time. Think of the time you would spend if you had to go through the problem-solving process each time you brushed your teeth, took a bath, or made your bed. But these habits can also cause you to waste time. Maybe you

learned to make your bed when you were very young and much shorter than you are now. Perhaps you are still making the bed the same way. How can you take advantage of your added height now to save time?

It is wise to evaluate your habits as you evaluate your time schedule. You may find you have some time-consuming habits which contribute little to your well-being. You may find that you are doing some tasks inefficiently.

At first, a new way of doing something may take longer than the old. This is because time must be spent to break the old habit and develop the new one. But if the new habit is a useful one, the time taken to learn it is time well spent.

Valuing the Time of Others

Time is a resource which is often shared. To waste other peoples' time is to misuse resources which are not your own. People may be justified in becoming annoyed when their time is wasted waiting for a scheduled appointment. In a sense, students who create disturbances which interfere with classwork are stealing the time of others. So are people who talk unnecessarily at meetings.

You probably know people who seem to have very few responsibilities. Such people sometimes make things difficult for their friends who are expected to use their time wisely. They may interrupt your work without being aware of it.

Possibly their goals and those of their families are different from yours. If you wish to achieve your goals, you must let others know your time is valuable. If you treat time as a valuable resource, your friends will respect your attitude. Whether or not time is important to them, they will recognize its importance to you.

If you have made a professional appointment or a social engagement, be sure to be there on time. Remember to leave promptly when the time is up. A visit may be spoiled if a guest does not know when to go home. Leaving a professional appointment promptly may be even more important, since other people may be waiting.

If you ever need to break an appointment, do so as far in advance as possible. This will give the other person the opportunity to make new plans for the time which was scheduled for you.

Using Leisure Time

Many young people think of leisure time as free time, time when there is nothing to do. But leisure time includes more than that. It is time free from assigned duties. A good manager often plans leisure time so that it is balanced between *individual* and *group* activities.

Conduct a survey to find out which leisure activities are enjoyed most often by students in your school. Point out which activities are usually enjoyed in families, with friends, and alone. Discuss the advantages of having a balance of leisure-time activities, that is, some enjoyed with family and friends and some enjoyed as an individual.

Discuss how individuals and families of the past spent their leisure time. In what ways did their leisure-time activities differ from those of today? Explain these differences.

Tell about an experience when it took you or a member of your family a very long time to do something because of being tired or being preoccupied with some other problem.

Bulletin board IDEA
Title: *Be Fresh as a Daisy*
Directions: On large cutouts of petals write leisure-time activities enjoyed and suggested by class members. These might include reading, watching TV, playing tennis, and going to a ball game. Use the petals to form a large daisy. Underneath write *Enjoying Leisure Time Is Not Being Lazy.*

A professional ball player may choose to spend leisure time helping others. *Converse Rubber Company*

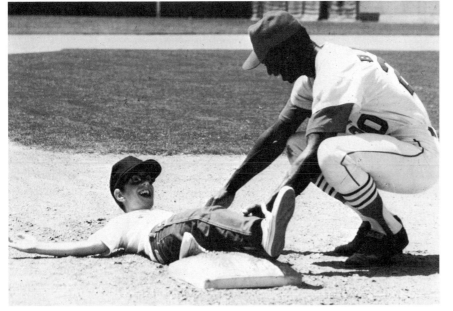

Define *dovetailing* as it applies to homemaking tasks. Give examples to show how a homemaker may dovetail several jobs to save time, energy, or money. For example, show how one task can be begun before another is finished, such as vacuuming a carpet while the mopped floor in another room is drying. Show how several tasks requiring the use of the oven could be dovetailed to save resources. Give examples to show how trips in the family car can be planned to save energy.

Identify factors having an obvious effect on your personal energy and production level.

Give examples to show how mental-emotional fatigue can affect a person's level of efficiency.

Tell about some of the techniques used by coaches to get a team *up* for a game. Why are these tactics very often effective? Discuss the psychological advantages of playing on the home court or field. Why is the underdog team sometimes able to greatly outscore the seemingly better team? Discuss the effects of a losing season, from the first game to the last.

Some leisure time should be free, or unplanned. This time can be used for relaxation. It is a time for unwinding when the pressure is off. Students with no free time in their schedules may be trying to achieve more than their abilities will permit.

Most people find that they do not want very much free time. The problem for them is to find enjoyable ways to use their leisure time. A part of this time can be used for self-improvement. There are many creative projects which can enrich your life. Examples are drawing, writing, cooking, sewing, building things, taking photographs, and joining a musical group. Creative activities such as these give individuals a chance to express their inner selves. Whatever leisure activities you choose, be sure they relax you and you enjoy them. When the desire for perfection exceeds the desire to have fun, leisure ceases.

Most people spend some of their leisure time in social activities. It is good to be with other people. Those who work with an athletic team or join a group such as the Scouts are using some of their leisure time to meet their social needs. Many people enjoy using some leisure time for serving others. This may be done through community organizations.

There are also opportunities to serve others on an individual basis. In most neighborhoods there are people who are cut off from others through old age or ill health. A phone call, a gift of home cooking, or simply an offer to run errands for such people can be a very effective way to use leisure time. You gain from the joy of helping others. They gain when their basic needs are met.

DEVELOPING ATTITUDES ABOUT ENERGY

Perhaps you have friends who appear to have an unlimited supply of physical energy. To such people, no activity seems too much. You may have other friends who are constantly tired. What causes this difference in people?

There appear to be real differences in the amount of energy available to different people. Some people are able to do more work than others. Not only do some people have more energy, but also each person shows a wide variation in his energy supply from time to time. As a person uses up his energy, he begins to experience *fatigue*, or tiredness. Fatigue levels, like energy levels, differ from person to person and from time to time.

The energy-fatigue pattern is affected by many things. There are physical factors and mental-emotional factors. Some of these are under a person's control, and others are not. For example, most people can more or less determine that they will get eight hours of rest each night. But some people may have many family responsibilities as well as school and work activities. They may not be able to change these responsibilities. Yet they can plan to do each activity at a time when it is easiest for them.

Understanding Your Physical Energy Pattern

Energy patterns are affected by physical makeup. Inherited patterns will determine, to a degree, whether you have a naturally high- or low-energy level. The size and shape of your body can further affect your total need for energy. More energy is needed to move a heavy body than a light one. Your physical makeup also determines the number of high-energy level periods you have each day.

Many people who have inherited low-energy levels have learned to use their energy effectively. They actually accomplish more each day than some of their friends who have a more abundant supply of energy. People who have a natural pattern of late-afternoon energy peaks can learn to use these peaks effectively even though they must start work earlier in the day. The type of energy pattern you have is partly inherited. How to use inherited energy patterns skillfully becomes an individual decision.

There is a definite relationship between peoples' eating habits and their supplies of physical energy. Sometimes a person with poor eating habits may have more energy

than someone who does eat wisely. Even so, most people who make poor food selections can increase their energy supplies by improving their eating patterns. Regular amounts of sleep and rest and regular physical exercise can also affect energy levels. A good general health program, suited to individual needs, will help maintain energy at its most productive level.

Understanding Your Mental and Emotional Patterns

Maybe you have had the experience of telling yourself you were too tired to enjoy a party simply because you were worrying about something else. Another time you may have felt exhausted just thinking about a special school assignment. This lack of energy is real. It is not imagined. Your mental-emotional state affects your energy level. Negative attitudes seem to drain your energy, while positive attitudes seem to bring forth an additional supply.

Physical energy and mental-emotional energy may seem very much the same. Either can make you enthusiastic. Either can carry you successfully through a period of activity which requires energy. However, there are important differences between these two types of energy. People who mistake mental-emotional energy for physical energy can cause permanent damage to their health. For example, a person with little energy

Act out humorous situations in which one person wakes up full of zest and raring to go in the morning while other family members act as if they are walking in their sleep. Reverse the situation to show how some people seem to wake up at night, when for others it is definitely time to go to bed. Discuss the ways these two types of energy patterns could be used to advantage within the same family.

Use cartoons, pictures, or pantomime to show how body position and posture can increase fatigue.

Give a demonstration to show how with practice and experience you have learned to do some task quickly and efficiently. The task might be something like cleaning a room, sewing on a button, changing a plug on an electrical cord, or preparing a certain food.

Present a humorous diary in monologue form entitled: *My Day as a Muscle in _____'s Right (or Left) Arm.*

Save time, energy, and money by using the following set of guidelines to care for your possessions.

Decide where each article can be best kept when not in use, and make a practice of putting the article away in that special place.
Inspect the things you wear and use frequently. Repair them if necessary.
Find ways to mark your belongings so they will not be confused with similar items belonging to other family members and your friends.

Write and present a skit about Terror Tizzy and Tidy Terry as they get ready to go out. Use props to make the situation seem real. Tizzy cannot find anything because the bedroom is a mess, clothes have been thrown around, and dresser drawers are unorganized. Terry has clothes ready to wear and a room that is orderly. Compare the time it takes Tizzy and Terry to get ready.

Bulletin board IDEA
Title: *Use YOUR Resources Wisely*
Directions: Mount silhouettes of three owls. Label one *time*, one *energy*, and one *money*.

because of a recent illness may use emotional energy to play in an important ball game. It is possible to mistake one type of energy for the other at times. Skillful managers learn to recognize and develop both types of energy to their fullest. They use both mental-emotional and physical energy together to reach their important goals.

Managing Your Energy Resources

No two people have exactly the same energy pattern. Therefore, your plans for managing your energy must be very personal. What may work for you may not work for your best friend. This does not mean that you must work alone as

you learn to manage your energy. Perhaps one of your friends or relatives can help you improve your management skills.

Consider the energy required for each of your planned activities. Then schedule high-energy tasks for periods in the day when you experience energy peaks. You can save energy for other uses by tackling required tasks early in the day. Mental-emotional fatigue can build up as you postpone necessary activities. Students who convince themselves they can study most effectively after 2 A.M. are probably fooling no one but themselves. The young mother who dreads bathing the baby would wisely schedule this

The arrangement of storage shelves and work tables often relates to the amount of energy necessary for completing a given task. *Farley Manning Associates, Inc.*

activity for early morning. Such a plan would prevent the loss of energy caused by practicing put-it-off tactics.

Plan to use your energy for needs before you spend it for wants. As you develop skill in managing your energy resources, you will find that wise management allows energy supplies for both your needs and your wants.

You can replenish both physical and mental-emotional energy by alternating strenuous activities with more relaxed activities. For example, you might choose to organize your notebook after you have washed the car. On the other hand, a fast game of catch might build up your energy after heavy mental activity at school. When you undertake a long, difficult project, you may find that you have worked until you can no longer think clearly. Take a short break. Spend ten or fifteen minutes in a completely different activity. If you choose the activity wisely, you will return from your break with a clear mind.

Check your activities to see if you are using your energy efficiently. Perhaps you can develop a dishwashing system that is better than the one you have been using. Compare the ways you use both time and energy. You can plan activities to make the best use of each resource. You may need to spend physical energy to save time at some point each day. You can balance this with a period in which you spend time to save energy. Sometimes you may need to spend available money to save both time and energy. Energy is wisely managed when it is combined with available time and money to reach the greatest number of priority goals.

DEVELOPING ATTITUDES ABOUT MONEY

Most teenagers have worried about money from time to time. For many people, money is the biggest source of trouble in life. Perhaps you have friends who borrow money regularly. Others will do without true necessities to save money. Some seem to spend their money as soon as they get it, with no thought for future needs.

Why do some people seem to have all the money they need while others with larger supplies of money are always broke? Like time and energy, money is a basic resource which can be used poorly or well. It is valuable because it can buy goods or services.

Individual goals affect people's attitudes toward money. The ease with which money can be obtained is also a factor in each person's attitude. For example, money may be spent freely when jobs are plentiful. But a business change which makes jobs hard to find may change a family's spending habits. In the same way, young people who have grown up in families which easily supply money for most of their

 Identify factors to be considered when choosing clothes for traveling. Add to the following list:

Select clothes that are light in weight.

Take shirts, pants, and other garments that can be laundered quickly and easily, dry fast, and need little if any pressing or ironing.

Pack clothes that do not wrinkle easily.

Select clothes that will be suitable for the anticipated activities.

Plan so clothes are interchangeable — such as slacks that go with several other garments and clothes that can be worn in a variety of ways with a change of accessories.

Keep a record of the amount of money spent over a period of time for dry-cleaning clothes. Add this amount to the original cost of the garments to determine the total cost. Did some garments prove to be more expensive purchases than others? How will your findings affect your future clothing purchases?

Take a survey to determine sources of students' spending money. Summarize the findings. From what sources do the largest number of students get spending money?

List possible sources of family income other than that obtained as wages and salary.

Discuss the reasons why the proportion of income spent for different items varies greatly from one family to another.

List the desirable features of any good spending plan or budget.

Keep a written record of your personal expenditures for two or three weeks. At the end of that time, combine the expenditures into such groups as lunches, bus fares, clothes, magazines, grooming items, and recreation. On the basis of your record, decide whether you need to improve your spending habits. If so, make a plan for improvement, follow it, and evaluate the results.

Discuss factors which determine whether a person should make or buy certain garments.

List sources in your area for buying usable secondhand clothing and household items.

Spending money for needs before wants is a sound consumer practice. *Celanese Fibers Marketing Company*

wishes may feel that money is not important. On the other hand, those who must struggle to provide money for basic needs may value money highly. People who think of money in relation to the time and energy they must spend to earn it will probably have a different attitude than people who think only of the things money can buy.

Managing Your Money

At some time in their lives, most people must consider two basic questions about money: "How can I get the money I need?" "How can I manage it to reach my goals?"

Considering sources of money

People work to earn money. That is, they spend time and energy to furnish goods or services other people will buy. For their efforts they receive money. Most families depend on the money they earn on the job for their basic income.

People who have developed a good savings program can use their savings to earn extra money. For example, interest on savings accounts or government bonds can add money to a family's total income. Rent from property or dividends from business investments may also add to a family's income.

Teenagers may have special sources of income to consider as they plan to use their personal money resources. Perhaps they are given money from the family income when they ask for it. They may earn extra money for special jobs or receive it as a gift. Although this money is not part of a regular income, it is unwise to spend it wastefully.

Many teenagers operate on an *allowance,* a definite amount of money received on a regular schedule, such as once a week or once a month. Many parents feel that an allowance gives a teenager a chance to learn basic responsibilities that go along with money management.

The size of an allowance and the goods and services it is expected to provide depend on the individual situation. The number of people in the family and the total family income need to be considered in determining each allowance. The age of a family member and individual needs usually affect the size of an allowance. Family needs and goals will help determine the items each allowance is to cover. Individual experiences in handling money will also affect the size and purpose of each allowance. School expenses and other activities may affect the amount of money each person needs. For instance, the cost of transportation or lunches bought at school, as well as some personal spending, must be considered if allowances are to be workable.

Making a Spending Plan

Some people seem to be afraid of the idea of planning how to spend money. Perhaps such people fear that a plan will prevent them from using their money as they wish. A spending plan is a way of using available money to reach your goals. It is known as a budget. In the long run a spending plan will provide money for more of your goals than will unplanned spending.

Considering your resources

A realistic spending plan for managing your money will begin with a list of your available resources. Your list should include the sources of your income, the amount of money from each source, and the times when each amount can be expected. You will also want to note which amounts can be depended upon and which are estimates.

You may be certain you will receive a definite amount of money regularly. This will probably be true if you have a steady part-time job or receive a definite allowance. Plan your spending to match this regular basic income. You can add any extra income to your total whenever you receive it. It is easy to adjust a spending plan to take advantage of extra money. It is not so easy to make adjustments for expected income you do not receive.

Perhaps you do not have a regular income. You may be asked to baby-sit three times in one week

Prepare oral reports on the care needed for athletic equipment such as skis, tennis rackets, bicycles, and bathing suits. Discuss the relationship between money management and care of belongings.

Bulletin board IDEA
Title: *Who's Boss? You or Your Money?*
Directions: Mount pictures of items for which teenagers often spend their money. Include items such as snack foods, grooming aids, records and tapes, magazines, and fad clothes.

Your career
Accountant

You would study the financial dealings of private businesses and government agencies and report on your findings. You might specialize in such areas as taxes, budgets, or reviews of the financial records of businesses. You might be self-employed or work for an accounting firm, a large corporation, or the government.

Keep a record of your income and expenses for a given period of time. You may use the form below or develop one of your own.

Sample Expense Record

I: Income
Allowance
Earnings
Gifts, loans, others
   Total income

II: Fixed Expenses
Lunch
Transportation
School supplies
Clothes
Contributions

III: Flexible Expenses
Recreation
Snacks
Personal grooming items
Bicycle repairs
Gifts
Club dues
Sporting goods
Others
   Total expenses

IV: Savings

but get no jobs the following week. In this situation you need to estimate your basic income. You can figure out your average weekly income over a fairly long period, perhaps the last six months or all of the last year. There may be some weeks when you earned nothing and other weeks when you earned ten or twelve dollars. Perhaps your average income was six dollars a week. Since it is relatively easy to adjust a spending plan upward, you may prefer to plan for a basic income of five dollars a week. This estimate allows a small safety margin for times when your earnings are lower than usual.

Considering your expenses
What items need to be covered by your basic income? Begin making your spending plan by listing all your expenses. Some of these expenses are for true needs. Others are for items and activities you want. Some of your expenses are fixed, and you cannot control their cost. Others are flexible. Have you forgotten any expenses that should be listed? Do you owe money? Did you include savings?

Maybe your list of expenses exceeds your basic income. If you listed *all* your wants, it probably did. Your next step is to adjust your list so that your spending plan agrees with your actual income. Your priority spending will be for those items which are true needs. Perhaps this includes money for lunch at

school and money for bus fare to school or to work. Money for savings, money you owe, and contributions you have promised must also be included. If you and your parents have agreed that you are responsible for buying some of your basic clothing, your priority list will include these items.

Some items on your priority list will be fixed expenses. You cannot pay less than the regularly charged bus fare or buy food at school for less than the school charges. Sometimes it is possible to change the amount of these fixed expenses by spending some of your time and energy. For example, consider the possibility of walking to school. Consider taking lunch from home instead of buying it. Before you decide to make such substitutions, however, be certain they will provide true savings. The lunch you can buy at school may be more nutritious than the lunch you can prepare at home for the same cost. If so, you are wasting some of your resources by preparing your lunch at home.

The other expenses on your priority list are usually more flexible. Perhaps they can be lowered through careful buying. Wash-and-wear pants may cost more than a similar dry-cleanable pair. But the cost of dry cleaning may mean that the wash-and-wear pants save money in the long run. Try to decide whether you buy too many items of the same type. For example, how

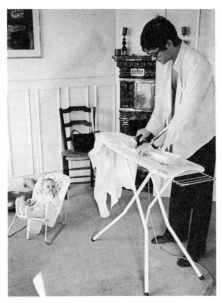
Cooperation in performing household tasks can help a family to stretch its available money. Why do you think this is so? *Richard Frieman/Photo Researchers*

many different colored pairs of shoes do you really need?

Once again, compare your total expenses with your basic income. When your total planned expenses become lower than your basic income, your plan becomes workable. You may then select items from your list of wants to be included in your spending plan. Your personal goals and values will determine which of your wants are most important to you. The most important of these can be added to your spending plan as soon as your resources permit. Your standby list will be helpful whenever you find you have extra income.

What can you do if you find that your priority expenses are greater than your basic income? Perhaps you have mistaken some of your wants for true needs. Maybe you have overlooked some of your resources. Look again at your resource list and your list of expenses. Perhaps you overlooked a source of income. Maybe you can spend time and energy to save money. You may have skills you can use to earn money or to save your basic resources. Perhaps all the expenses on your priority list are not absolutely necessary at this time. Most people can't afford to buy everything they want. As you grow more experienced in using your resources, you will probably begin to have money available for your most important wants.

Considering your savings

Perhaps you are wondering why savings are included in your list of priority expenses.

First, savings can help you meet emergency situations. For example, an accident in the family could increase your necessary expenses and at the same time decrease your basic income.

It is also wise to have money available for emergency wants such as ball-game tickets or costumes for special plays or parties.

You need to decide on the amount of money to be saved each week. Some people decide that they will save a certain part of their

Divide into small groups to discuss some of the following issues:

Teenagers should account to their parents for every cent of their allowances.

Teenagers should give their earnings to their parents.

Teenagers should be punished by having their allowances cut.

Teenagers should be able to spend money they earn for anything they want.

Teenagers' allowances should be cut when their families have financial emergencies.

Teenagers should save some of their allowances every week.

Teenagers should be required to spend within their allowances and earnings.

Bulletin board IDEA
Title: *Happiness Is . . .*
Directions: Use a happy-looking cartoon character. Around it mount pictures of teenagers enjoying leisure-time activities that involve some expense. You might include enjoying a ride at a fair, skating, or going to a movie. Underneath write *Having Money for Things You Like to Do.*

Recall stories from newspaper articles or fiction about people who hoarded their money by hiding it in unusual places. What happened to the money?

List possible ways and places to keep your savings. Give advantages and disadvantages for each of the following:

1 Giving it to your parents to keep for you
2 Having a bank in your room that cannot be opened easily
3 Putting it in a savings account
4 Buying government bonds

Your career
Budget consultant

You would help families plan the spending and saving of their income. You might advise them on the most economical way to satisfy their needs so there is extra money available for their wants. You would find employment with banks and loan companies.

total income, perhaps as little as one cent out of every dollar. Others begin by adding up their fixed expenses. They then decide how much of the rest of their income could be saved. This amount becomes a fixed expense. Good management involves a savings plan. As you grow in savings experience, you will be able to select the right amount for your purposes.

Once you have planned your savings program, you need to decide where to keep the money. Money kept in your home is available when you want it. This could be an advantage in case of true emergencies. On the other hand, savings which are so readily available are easily misplaced or spent for wants which are not emergencies. And it is unwise to have too much extra money around the house. If you place your savings in a bank account or buy government bonds, your savings will earn interest. This will increase your total savings fund. Since this type of saving is harder to spend, you will be less likely to spend it unwisely. On the other hand, you may find it difficult to make such money available in case of a true emergency.

Perhaps you can compromise. Many people keep a small emergency fund on hand. Money being saved for a special purpose in the near future is also kept at home. But the major part of their savings is placed in an account where it will earn interest. Such a savings plan is

usually flexible enough to meet changing situations.

Evaluating your spending plan

After you have used your spending plan for a short time, evaluate it. Maybe necessary expenses were forgotten. Perhaps you underestimated some of your expenses or overestimated some of your income. Mistakes such as these are common. Perhaps you think you are spending according to your plan, but find you don't know exactly where your money goes.

Try keeping a record of your actual spending. Records are especially helpful when you plan for your flexible expenses. Perhaps you are actually spending some of your clothing money for after-school snacks. Perhaps you neglected to include some extra bus fare in your original plan. A record of your spending will help you adjust your spending to meet your *real* needs. Some people struggle with an unrealistic spending plan for a month or two, then give up the whole idea of budgeting. They say a spending plan won't work for them. In reality, such people are refusing to learn to manage a basic resource.

As you examine your records, you may find that you have spent money for items or activities which conflict with your important goals. Successful managers have learned to measure the cost of each purchase in terms of their personal values. They ask, "Will this expense

Professional financial counseling often adds to the security of a family. *New York Life Insurance Company*

Discuss the following situations. What positive and negative effects might each of these actions have on all the people involved?

1 Jo, age six, and Fran, age thirteen, receive the same allowance. Their parents feel they want to be very fair to both children by treating them equally.
2 Chris started delivering newspapers every morning and Jerry started delivering papers in the evening. Their mother feels they should not receive allowances any more.
3 Lou and Manny's father punished them by refusing to give them their weekly allowances.
4 Lupe and Toby do not receive allowances. However, they do get paid for doing homemaking tasks such as making their beds, washing dishes, and mowing the lawn.

Bulletin board IDEA
Title: *What Controls YOUR Spending?*
Directions: Hang cords from the top of the board as if they were puppet strings. From each set of strings hang a card. On the first card write *Values,* on the second write *Goals,* and on the third write *Standards.*

help me reach my goals? Will I be spending extra money, or money which I had planned to use for another, more important and worthwhile purpose?''

Once you have developed a realistic spending plan, you may be tempted to follow it without further checking. It is true that a good plan can continue to serve you well. But your situation is likely to change from time to time. Your income may change. Needs can change quickly. Goals may change more slowly, but they do change from year to year. Even your *values* change as you mature.

Wise managers check their plans and their actual spending regularly. They decide whether their spending plans continue to meet their needs. You can evaluate your actual purchases in terms of their value to you and their relation to your goals. You can compare your use of money with your planned and actual uses of time and energy. Only in this way can you be sure you are using all your basic resources for successful living.

Number from 1 to 31. Beside each number indicate if the corresponding statement is true or false. *Do not* write in this book.

1 People's wants are affected by their values and goals.
2 To be efficient you must be rushed and busy.
3 The first step in planning a time schedule is to list all your personal weaknesses.
4 A time schedule should allow for some flexibility.
5 To be an efficient manager all old habits should be changed.
6 Leisure time is free of assigned responsibilities.
7 Students who disturb classes are using other people's time.
8 Spending time for wants before needs may cause frustration.
9 A time schedule should be followed several months before it is evaluated.
10 Time and physical energy may be spent to save money.
11 Physical energy is a basic resource all people have in equal amounts.
12 Your mental outlook can affect your physical energy.
13 Lack of enough sleep may cause fatigue.
14 There are individual differences in physical energy patterns.
15 Emotional factors may affect your efficiency.
16 People use their physical energy to help them reach their goals.
17 People's values affect their attitudes toward money.
18 Expenses which change and vary are called fixed expenses.
19 Priority spending should be for wants.
20 Another name for a spending plan is a budget.
21 It is impossible to make a spending plan when income is irregular.
22 In making a spending plan you need to list your current expenses.
23 Records of previous expenditures are needed to make a spending plan.
24 A good basic spending plan can be used for many years.
25 All children the same age should receive the same allowance.
26 The main purpose in saving is to have money for fixed expenses.
27 A savings program requires that 10 per cent of your income be set aside each week.
28 Money kept in a savings account earns income in the form of dividends.
29 Large sums of cash should not be saved at home.
30 Resources can be used to help people reach realistic goals.
31 Needs change more quickly than wants.

Fill in the blank in each sentence with the best word or words to complete the statement. *Do not* write in this book.

1 Money is spent for goods or (1) .
2 Living in a particular neighborhood, owning a certain make of car, or buying special brands may be important to people seeking social position or (2) .
3 An advertisement suggesting that you will be more popular or good-looking after using a certain product appeals to your (3) .
4 Federal law requires that most garments have (4) labels sewn in them.
5 Nutrition labels on food products provide nutrition information for one (5) .
6 Shelf labeling that helps consumers compare prices easily and quickly is called (6) pricing.
7 The two kinds of warranties are full and (7) warranties.
8 A canceled check or a(an) (8) is your record of payment.
9 The Federal agency that handles most consumer complaints made by individual consumers is (9) .
10 Many stores have sales after an important (10) .
11 Goods with flaws, or imperfections, are called (11) .
12 Emergency buying allows little time to check or (12) prices and quality.

Chapter 12

Making Satisfying Consumer Decisions

After reading this chapter, you should be able to:

1 Define *status symbol*.
2 Explain factual and emotionalized advertising.
3 Summarize your responsibilities as a consumer.
4 Describe permanent care clothing labels and nutrition food labels.
5 Show how unit pricing and dating of food products can be used by consumers.
6 Determine the value of different warranties.
7 Point out how government agencies and legislation help protect consumers.
8 Analyze situations to determine if purchases were bargains.
9 Point out factors to consider in choosing a marketplace.
10 Weigh the advantages and disadvantages of using credit.
11 Compare different kinds of credit available to consumers.

A consumer is one who uses goods. Because the use of goods is on the increase, the consumer is big business and big news. When people produced or made the things they needed and wanted at home, they knew the content and quality of a product. This is no longer true. Seeing goods on display in a store is not enough for today's buyers. They need some background information to make wise buying decisions. Informed consumers need to know about how long a product can be expected to last and what it is made of. They also need to know if a product will serve the intended purposes.

Learning how to produce needed or wanted goods has been, and will continue to be, an important part of the learning process. However, most people *buy* most of their material possessions as well as many services. The emphasis has changed from producing to buying. People need

Unscramble the words below, one letter to each square. Arrange the circled letters to find the secret word. Tell how each of the unscrambled words relates to the secret word.

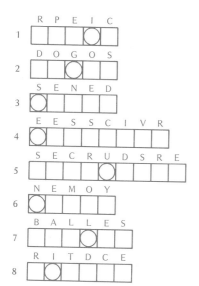

1. R P E I C
2. D O G O S
3. S E N E D
4. E E S S C I V R
5. S E C R U D S R E
6. N E M O Y
7. B A L L E S
8. R I T D C E

Bulletin board IDEA
Title: *Seeds Worth Sowing*
Directions: Outline the bulletin board with packages of plant seeds. In the center write the following:
Staying Informed
Reading Tags and Labels
Determining Quantity and
    Quality
Keeping Records
Handling Merchandise Carefully
Paying Promptly

to learn how to get the most for their money.

SPENDING MONEY

Money is worthwhile only in terms of what it buys. The reason for learning how to spend it wisely is to make your life more satisfying.

It has been said that it is just as important to know how to *spend* money as it is to know how to *earn* it. Some people can earn a great deal of money without knowing how to spend it for real satisfaction.

Fulfilling Needs and Wants

You understand that *needs,* from a consumer viewpoint, are materials necessary to sustain life. *Wants* are those goods or services which add pleasure and meaning to your life. Many consumers seem to face problems when they try to distinguish between needs and wants. As a result, wants are sometimes fulfilled while needs are neglected.

A need for one person may be a want for another. Ski instructors need skis to give lessons. Other

It is a wise consumer practice to select clothing that fulfills both needs and wants. *Bob Smith/Photo Researchers*

people may want skis because they enjoy the sport. Sometimes an item used to meet a need can also be used to satisfy a want. For example, ski instructors who use skis in their work can also use their skis for recreation when not working.

A problem close to the lives of all teenagers is selecting food for needs and wants. Do you have friends who drink only a soft drink for breakfast or who eat only a bag of potato chips for lunch? Anyone who understands the body's nutritional needs would assume that such practices are for the fulfilling of wants rather than needs. Your body needs certain foods if you are to enjoy good health and have plenty of energy. Meat, milk, fruits, vegetables, and cereal are food needs. Soft drinks and potato chips are more correctly classified as wants. However, some foods can be used to meet both needs and wants. A glass of orange juice will meet your need for vitamin C. It may also meet a want by satisfying your desire for a cold drink.

Choosing Goods and Services

Money is spent in two major areas: goods and services. Demands for both continue to rise. Many teenagers have become accustomed to buying both goods and services. When buying ready-made clothes, you practice buying goods. When eating in restaurants or having your hair professionally styled, you are buying services. The problem-solving process will help you plan to include priority items when selecting goods and services.

In choosing between goods and services, a teenager might have a hard time deciding between buying a new record and going to the movies. Someone else might need to decide between new shoes and a new hair style. Whether to buy a new car or to invest money in expensive repairs for an old one might be another problem. Perhaps a family would struggle with a decision between buying a new TV set and having their home painted. Goals and values usually influence such decisions. Some people seem to value material possessions, while others prefer to spend their money on services. It is possible for either to provide immediate satisfaction or lasting value. The success of any purchase is determined by the goals of the buyer.

Understanding Status Symbols

When were you last tempted to buy a record, a tape, or an article of clothing because a friend had the same thing? You probably know adults who want to keep up with neighbors by buying things similar to those the neighbors have. Many wants are created by the possessions of others.

There are many ways in which people show status, or social position. For example, they might choose to live in a certain neighborhood, own a certain kind of car,

Use a flannel board to show the relationship of the family life cycle to finances. Represent each stage with a different color pie-shaped wedge. Discuss how each stage relates to the financial needs of the family. Show that everyone is a consumer from birth to death and that consumer demands differ from one stage in the life cycle to another. As you discuss each stage, put the wedges together to make a circle or the whole cycle.

Your career
Consumer service representative

You would test products, write bulletins, and make an effort to keep consumers informed about new items on the market. You might do this through radio or TV programs, columns in newspapers or magazines, or by giving talks to special interest groups. You might work for a local, city, state, or Federal government agency.

Explain the meaning of the statement: *It is just as important to know how to spend money as it is to know how to earn it.*

Describe the buy of a lifetime which you have just found. Discuss whether or not others would buy it. Why, or why not?

Plan and give a sales talk to *sell* your classmates a particular household item. Ask the class members to analyze the *sales pitch*. Ask them what was said and done to influence them to buy the product. What may have influenced them *not* to buy the item?

Analyze and discuss advertising slogans that appeal to various personality types and age groups.

Pretend that you are an advertising consultant for station KXYZ. Create advertisements that try to persuade different types of people to buy a product. Work up ads especially for groups such as:
Teenagers
Boys or men
Girls or women
Parents
Grandparents
Students in your school

You may need to buy a service from someone who has the knowledge and skill to perform a specific job.   *Bob Cook*

or shop in a particular store. Students sometimes feel that one school has higher status than another. Other teenage symbols of status may include athletic jackets, club pins, sports equipment, labels in clothes, and the brand or amount of makeup a girl carries in her purse.

The search for status sometimes reveals a weak self-concept. People who do not think well of themselves may go out of their way to present an image which looks successful. These people feel that things, rather than their actions, show other people what they are. To buy status symbols, they may use money which would better be spent on needs.

Understanding Advertising

Your life is affected in many ways by advertising. You may look at the ads for movies before deciding which one to see. You probably have gone to stores to look at items you saw advertised on TV or in newspapers. Much space in your favorite magazine is taken up by the ads. Your parents may check the grocery ads before doing the shopping. Or, they may study advertisements for tires before going to buy.

Advertising has contributed to the American way of life. Other countries have produced goods similar in quality to those of the United States without attaining the same standard of living. Why? Probably advertising, which provides knowledge and creates wants, contributes more than any other single factor to your desire for specific consumer goods. The nation's business people know how to *sell* through advertising. You can reap the rewards of advertising when you learn how to use it wisely.

Advertising can be very useful. It can make people aware of the many new products available on the market. It can show people how to tackle problems in new and creative ways. Some advertising provides facts to use in comparing products. These facts might refer to such things as color, size, price, or materials contained in the product. The kind of advertising that gives helpful facts and information about a product is called *factual* advertising.

On the other hand, some advertising can be misleading. Can you tell by reading ads carefully just what a certain company is trying to sell? It isn't always a product. Often it is the idea that you'll be more attractive, desirable, or popular when using certain goods. Such advertising is sometimes called *emotionalized* advertising.

Young consumers can learn to evaluate advertising. They can learn to weigh advertising carefully by checking claims against reality. They can use factual information as they make decisions. They can learn to understand the difference between *factual* and *emotionalized* advertising.

List sources of consumer information available in your area. Name organizations concerned with protecting or informing consumers. List publications and specific newspaper and magazine columns designed to help consumers.

Prepare oral or written reports about the following organizations:
Better Business Bureau
Credit Bureau
Chamber of Commerce
Consumers Union

Make a consumers' guide for various items frequently purchased by teenagers. Examples might include jeans, shirts, shoes, bathing suits, and grooming items.

Make a display of care labels and informative tags. Discuss how such labels and tags can be of value to you as a consumer.

Bulletin board IDEA
Title: *You Be the Judge*
Directions: Fasten a cutout of a gavel near the title. Mount advertisements which appeal to consumers' emotions rather than providing valuable information about products.

Unscramble the letters below, one letter to each blank, to form twelve words. Another word will appear in the vertical column. Explain how each of the twelve unscrambled words can contribute to the feeling expressed in the vertical word.

1. SEROTS
2. GATS
3. DETBUG
4. REANINGS
5. LASES
6. FASETY
7. TENMAYPS
8. SOCT
9. LIQATUY
10. VATINGSDIER
11. TONCTRAC
12. CONESDS

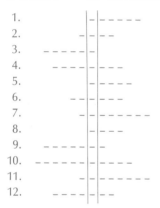

1. _ - _ - _ - _ - _
2. _ - _ - _
3. _ - _ - _ - _ - _
4. _ - _ - _ - _ - _ - _
5. _ - _ - _ - _
6. _ - _ - _ - _ - _
7. _ - _ - _ - _ - _ - _ - _
8. _ - _ - _ - _
9. _ - _ - _ - _ - _ - _
10. _ - _ - _ - _ - _ - _ - _ - _ - _
11. _ - _ - _ - _ - _ - _ - _ - _
12. _ - _ - _ - _ - _ - _

Discuss advertisements that could be misleading. Describe how the ads could mislead an uninformed consumer. What can the government do about misleading advertising?

An attractive window display is one effective method of advertising. However, a product, in many cases, sells itself if there is a demand for it. *Joel Gordon/McGraw-Hill Photography*

ASSUMING RESPONSIBILITIES AS A CONSUMER

Much is written and said about the ways certain businesses and industries take advantage of consumers. Informed consumers are their own best protection against such practices. Staying informed on current consumer affairs, making comparisons, reading tags and labels, handling goods carefully, returning faulty merchandise, keeping records, and paying promptly are all part of your consumer responsibility. When consumers take their reponsibilities seriously, all businesses will be forced to conform to the high standards most businesses expect of themselves.

Staying Informed

Being an informed consumer is a continuous process. As products change, you must re-educate yourself. Although you may gain a basic understanding of consumer problems in school, there is a steady flow of new consumer information available. This information might be considered required reading for the person who wants to be well informed on the subject.

Does your family receive a daily newspaper? If not, there are probably several in your library. They offer education for consumers of various ages. Some of the best authorities in finance and consumer affairs write for the press and are quoted in the newspapers. Read what they have to say. Discuss such articles with your parents, friends, and teachers. Television and radio coverage also provide consumer information. Many news reports include regular consumer education spots.

Magazines and journals are another excellent source of current information. Many have regular features concerning management of money and other resources. In addition, their articles on buying and caring for food, clothes, homes, and home furnishings are helpful.

A number of government and commercial publications are useful. They are particularly timely in terms of the specific products discussed. Such references may be found in public libraries. They can be consulted as a resource when you are trying to arrive at a consumer decision.

Mail-order catalogs are found in many homes. They are excellent sources of information on general prices and current styles of merchandise. They also answer questions you might have about trends in future clothing styles and new household items. Some catalogs feature a consumer information section which describes various aspects of catalog items. This section answers many of the shopper's questions in regard to the merchandise advertised.

Reading Tags and Labels

Federal and state laws require that certain information appear on tags and labels of various products. Regulations apply to food, clothing, and many other items. Tags and labels give information

Examine tags and labels to identify information that is of value to you as a consumer. Give examples to show how each kind of information can be helpful.

Determine why some garments are not covered by the Federal Trade Commission rule for permanent care labels. Discuss why care labels do *not* have to be permanently attached to hosiery, headwear, handwear, footwear, and disposable items. A manufacturer may seek permission not to attach permanent care labels to furs, leather goods, household items, and see-through garments. Why might these items be exempt from the care label ruling?

Locate the following information on food labels:
1 The name of the product
2 The manufacturer's name and address
3 The quantity of the contents in net weight or volume
4 The common or usual names of the ingredients, listed in order of their amounts
5 The variety and style of the product, when applicable
List on the board all the other information provided on food labels. How can each of these kinds of information be used by consumers?

Choosing to see a particular movie might be one of the first consumer decisions a child will make. *Mimi Forsyth/Monkmeyer*

Supply rhyming words to complete the Careless Consumer poem. Then make suggestions to help CC manage money better.

- CC thinks it's one big bore
  To compare prices from store to __?__.
- Though CC likes gimmicks and gags,
  CC seldom stops to read the __?__.
- CC needs help, he does indeed,
  In order to tell a want from a __?__.
- 'Cause CC spends almost every penny,
  They'll soon be gone and he won't have __?__.
- CC could make money behave
  If only CC could learn to __?__.
- Things wouldn't look quite so bleak
  If CC put some aside each __?__.
- If CC used resources with more care,
  His pockets wouldn't be quite so __?__.
- But every cent CC earns,
  Will soon be gone unless he __?__.
- Please help CC and suggest a few
  Things that CC could begin to __?__.

Care labels are attached to garments for quick and easy reference by the consumer.

concerning content, fibers and finishes, amount, quality, additives, nutrients, and special instructions for using a product. Tags and labels may also advise you as to the care of the product and some of its possible uses.

Clothing tags and labels

Tags on garments give you much useful information. Tags usually give the price and size of a garment as well as the brand or manufacturer's name. Tags also provide information about fabric finishes. For example, a tag will tell you if an item is colorfast, water-repellent, or spot-resistant. It often tells you if a garment might shrink and how much shrinkage may be expected.

Hangtags tell the fiber content of fabrics. With few exceptions, it is required by law to give the percentage of each fiber in a blended fabric.

Permanent care labels must be attached to most garments. These care labels must be made so they are readable for the life of the garment. Most care labels are sewn in garments. Permanent care labels must state fully the *regular* care a garment needs, but they do not have to provide information about spot removal. Regular care refers to hand washing, machine washing, or dry cleaning. Any garment labeled *washable* can be dry-cleaned unless the care label states otherwise. If a garment is washable, the tag tells if hot, warm, or cold water would

be best. A wash cycle is recommended. Suggestions for drying garments and ironing temperatures are given. Permanent care labels also give advice about using bleach. Because care labels give you so much valuable information, they should not be removed from your clothes.

The Federal Trade Commission advises you to compare care labels when you shop for clothes. The care labels will help you determine which items will be easier to care for and cost less over the life of the garment. Care labels must be easy to find on a garment. For packaged items, care labels must be easy to see through the wrapping or care instructions must be easy to read on the package itself.

When you shop for fabrics, ask the salesperson for the proper care label for each garment you plan to make. Sew care labels in garments as you make them.

Food labels

There are several government agencies concerned with regulations on buying, selling, and labeling food products. The Food and Drug Administration requires nutrition information on labels of all foods to which a nutrient is added and all foods for which a nutrition claim is made. Many other foods also have nutrition labeling.

Nutrition information is given for one serving. The label gives the size of a serving and tells how many

Discuss reasons why some consumers do not use unit price food labels. Visit a store that uses unit price labels. Copy several labels. Show the class how they can be used to compare prices. Give examples of times when you might not want to buy the least expensive item.

Discuss the true value of special offers such as trading stamps, gift china, or glasses intended to attract consumers to buy at a particular marketplace.

Give examples of food products for which date labels are especially helpful. Why are date labels important on these products? Give examples of foods for which date labels are of less importance. Why are date labels less important for these products?

Display some possible choices when buying hand lotion, deodorant, detergent, soap, thread, and other consumer products. Have examples of different brands, various sizes, and different types. Explain which would be the best choices under certain situations. When would a small size be more economical than a large size?

239

Consumer Care Guide for Apparel

This guide is made available to help you understand and follow the brief care instructions found on permanent labels on garments. Be sure to read all care instructions completely!

WHEN LABEL READS:	IT MEANS:
Machine Washable	
Machine wash	Wash, bleach, dry, and press by any customary method, including commercial laundering and dry cleaning
Home launder only	Same as above but do not use commercial laundering
No chlorine bleach	Do not use chlorine bleach. Oxygen bleach may be used
No bleach	Do not use any type of bleach
Cold wash / Cold rinse	Use cold water from tap or cold washing machine setting
Warm wash / Warm rinse	Use warm water or warm washing machine setting
Hot wash	Use hot water or hot washing machine setting
No spin	Remove wash load before final machine spin cycle
Delicate cycle / Gentle cycle	Use appropriate machine setting; otherwise wash by hand
Durable press cycle / Permanent press cycle	Use appropriate machine setting; otherwise use warm wash, cold rinse, and short spin cycle
Wash separately	Wash alone or with like colors

The American Apparel Manufacturers Association, Inc.

WHEN LABEL READS:	IT MEANS:
Non-Machine Washing	
Hand wash	Launder only by hand in luke-warm (hand comfortable) water. May be bleached. May be dry-cleaned
Hand wash only	Same as above, but do not dry-clean
Hand wash separately	Hand wash alone or with like colors
No bleach	Do not use bleach
Damp wipe	Surface clean with damp cloth or sponge
Home Drying	
Tumble dry	Dry in tumble dryer at specified setting—high, medium, low, or no heat
Tumble dry Remove promptly	Same as above, but in absence of cool-down cycle, remove at once when tumbling stops
Drip dry	Hang wet and allow to dry with hand shaping only
Line dry	Hang damp and allow to dry
No wring No twist	Hang dry, drip dry, or dry flat only. Handle to prevent wrinkles and distortion
Dry flat	Lay garment on flat surface
Block to dry	Maintain original size and shape while drying
Ironing or Pressing	
Cool iron	Set iron at lowest setting
Warm iron	Set iron at medium setting
Hot iron	Set iron at hot setting
Do not iron	Do not iron or press with heat
Steam iron	Iron or press with steam
Iron damp	Dampen garment before ironing
Miscellaneous	
Dry-clean only	Garment should be dry-cleaned only, including self-service
Professionally dry clean only	Do not use self-service dry cleaning
No dry-clean	Use recommended care instructions. No dry-cleaning materials to be used

servings are in the container. Nutrition information for a serving is given in this order:

Calories
Protein
Carbohydrate
Fat
Vitamin A
Vitamin C
Thiamin
Riboflavin
Niacin
Calcium
Iron

Always having nutrients listed in the same order and in the same place on a food label makes it easy for you to compare foods for nutritive value. Nutrition labels list the U.S. Recommended Daily Allowances (USRDA) by percentage. To be sure you get enough of the nutrients listed, the percentages from the foods you eat should add up to at least 100 percent each day.

Nutrition labels show amounts in grams rather than ounces. Grams are smaller units of measurement than ounces. Because some nutrients are present in certain foods in small amounts, it is easier to read nutrition labels in grams than it would be in ounces. The following is a guide to help you read nutrition labels:

1 pound = 454 grams (g)
1 ounce = 28 grams (g)
1 gram = 1000 milligrams (mg)
1 milligram = 1000 micrograms (mcg)

You can use nutrition labels for the following:
To plan more nutritious meals
To get more nutrition for your money by comparing the nutritive values of different foods and brands
To select foods for special diets recommended by doctors
To count calories

Determining Quality and Quantity

Your needs and available money should be your guides when deciding on the quality and quantity of an item to be purchased. For example, in regard to clothing, would you rather have only a few high-quality garments, or would you rather have more inexpensive things? In regard to housing, would your dream home fit better in a small apartment or a large house? Such concerns involve choices between quality and quantity.

In regard to food, there are many times when you may wish to buy a lower quality because of the way you plan to use the particular item. For example, fancy peach halves would not be the best buy if you were going to cut them up for a gelatin fruit salad. Overripe bananas might be fine for making banana bread but would be unappetizing served on cereal. If you have the storage space, it might be wise to buy in quantity when prices are low. If the item is perishable, decide whether you could use it before it spoils. A bargain is not a

Present skits showing desirable and undesirable shopping practices. Include situations that show shopping with and without a list, using good and poor manners, returning merchandise, and seeking information about goods in order to make a wise selection. Discuss the characteristics of a salesperson from whom you enjoy buying. Discuss the reasons why a responsible consumer has many of these same qualities.

Observe consumers who act irresponsibly. What are some of the things shoppers do that show a lack of consideration for others? What effects do their actions have on businesses and on other consumers?

Write a *Code of Ethics for Consumers.*

Write and present miniskits showing how intelligent consumers shop for specific items such as fabrics, small tools, appliances, winter coats, or sports equipment.

Debate the following topic: *Honorable businesspeople like to sell to informed consumers.*

Select one of the following government agencies and find out how it is involved in consumer protection. Present your findings in an oral or written report.
Office of Consumer Affairs
Consumer Product Safety Commission
United States Department of Agriculture
Department of Health, Education and Welfare
Food and Drug Administration
Department of Justice
Environmental Protection Agency
Federal Trade Commission
National Bureau of Standards
Public Health Service

Your career
Technical writer

You would give consumers information to help them to best utilize their resources. You might write how-to newspaper columns, articles in special interest publications, or directions in equipment manuals. You would find employment with publications and companies that produce items that need instructions in order to be used correctly.

bargain if you neither need nor want it.

Unit pricing is being adopted in many stores to help consumers compare prices quickly. Unit pricing has been used for many years to show the cost of meat, dairy products, and fresh produce. Shelf labeling is now being used to give unit prices for canned and packaged goods. Unit pricing gives the price for a single unit of weight, measure, or count of a product. Unit prices tell you at a glance which brand or item costs less per gram, ounce, pound, or piece. The sample below shows how unit pricing can help you as a consumer.

A	Store brand peanut butter	
B	5.2¢ per ounce	Price you pay 93¢ D
C	06572 43	18 ounces (510 g) E

A Brand name and common name of the product
B Price for a standard and specified measure
C Store code number
D Actual price you pay
E Actual weight, measure, or count of this purchase size

Of course you may not always want to buy the least expensive brand. You may not like it. You may have to buy it in a size too large for your needs. Sometimes the freshness of a product may be more important to you than the price. Many products are now dated for one of the following:

1 *Package date*—tells when the item was packaged. Fresh meats wrapped in the store usually have a package date.
2 *Expiration date*—tells the last day the product should be used. Expiration dates may be found on canned biscuits, yeast, and photographic film.
3 *Pull date*—tells store clerks when to remove a product from the shelf. This kind of dating is often used on dairy products.

Dating gives some indication of freshness, but it does not guarantee it. The original quality of the product and the way it is handled and stored may affect freshness as much as when it was packaged, processed, or purchased.

Sometimes the apparent size of a package can fool you. One package may look larger than another package but contain less. The shape and color of a package may make it look larger than it is. A bottle may appear to hold more than it does because of the shape of the bottom. Many products come in packages labeled *small*, *medium*, and *large*. Although the large size usually costs less per gram, ounce, or pound, this is not necessarily true. Consider your storage space and how much or how often a product is used. Develop the habit of using unit price labels. If they are unavailable, compare package labels to find the actual weight or measure.

Understanding Warranties

The Federal Trade Commission considers a warranty similar to a guarantee. There are no laws requiring manufacturers to offer warranties. However, if a warranty is provided, certain standards must be followed. These rules cover only *written* warranties for products costing more than five dollars.

It is very important to read a warranty before making a purchase. For a product costing over ten dollars, there may be either a *full warranty* or a *limited warranty*. The type of warranty must appear on the main display panel of the product container and on the product itself in the form of a tag or sticker. A limited warranty must state what items and services will and will not be paid for or provided. A warranty also may be limited by protecting only the original owner of a product. Other limitations may be set by state laws.

Some of the information which must appear in a warranty follows:

the name and address of the company offering the warranty

steps to take and whom to contact for warranty service, including name, address, and telephone number

what the warranty includes and excludes

when and under what circumstances the warranty coverage begins and ends

what will be done in case of defect or failure (repair, replace, or refund if a full warranty)

anything the buyer must do to get warranty protection, such as paying any expenses

if words like *life* or *lifetime* are used, the life referred to must be disclosed

Some warranty coverage depends on returning an owner registration card. The warranty will state this condition. Failure to mail this card can make a warranty useless. It is your responsibility as a consumer to see that the warranty company gets the card filled out accurately and promptly.

Keeping Records

You probably have seen adults refer to their financial records to determine when a certain item was bought or when they paid for it. Keeping accurate records is time-consuming. Yet it is necessary in a complicated consumer economy. For example, records can tell your family whether a large appliance is still covered by a warranty.

By keeping records of the names of manufacturers and of the stores where purchases are made, you will have this information if goods need to be serviced or returned. Some stores require the sales slip when exchanging or returning any type of merchandise.

When you pay for something at school, your receipt is your record

Find out how one of the following legislative acts or amendments gives you protection as a consumer. Share your findings with the class. Discover what other students found concerning additional legislation.

Federal Meat Inspection Act
Wool Products Labeling Act
Textile Fiber Products
 Identification Act
Food and Drug Administration
 Amendments
Flammable Fabrics Act
 Amendment
Interstate Land Sales Full
 Disclosure Act
Radiation Control for Health
 and Safety Act
Truth-in-Lending Act
 Amendment
Federal Boat Safety Act

Collect and discuss newspaper and magazine articles about new legislation affecting consumers.

Your career
Home service representative

You would demonstrate the use and care of various kinds of home equipment to groups who visit company facilities or to individuals in their own homes. You would work for utility or equipment companies.

Match the *provisions of consumer legislation* given in List A with the *Federal acts* given in List B. Use an act in List B only once. Do *not* write in this book.

List A: Provisions of consumer legislation

A Requires manufacturers to state exactly what a package contains, who made it, and how much it contains

B Sets safety standards for clothing and household items

C Bans sale of dangerous toys and articles intended for children

D Requires full information about terms and conditions of finance charges in credit contracts

E Sets standards for child-resistant packaging of dangerous products

List B: Federal acts

1 *Child Protection Act*
2 *Consumer Credit Protection Act*
3 *Fair Packaging and Labeling Act*
4 *Flammable Fabrics Act*
5 *Poison Prevention Packaging Act*

to share with anyone who may question your payment. If you get a medical prescription filled, the receipt is a record for tax purposes. It may be important when your parents or guardians account for deductions from their income taxes. Keep receipts of payment for school yearbooks, tapes or records, club pins, and other items you may have ordered. You would not want to pay twice for the same article because you kept careless records.

Handling Merchandise Carefully

What do you notice when you look at things piled on a counter during a clearance sale? You may find rips, heel marks, lipstick smudges, broken zippers, missing buttons, or other signs of damage. Who pays for such carelessness and destruction? You and other consumers. Such damage is considered when prices are marked on goods throughout the store.

In self-service stores it is important for shoppers to handle goods carefully, because items usually receive little care from salespeople. If you step into a garment, first remove your shoes. If you are wearing lipstick, place a cleansing tissue over your lips before putting on or removing a garment over your head. When trying on a knitted garment, make sure your nails have no rough edges which could snag the fabric. If clothing is obviously too tight, avoid breaking the zipper.

Do not force it closed. If a button comes off, give it to a salesclerk or drop it into a pocket of the garment. These are ways consumers show consideration when handling store merchandise.

In what ways have you seen grocery shoppers show their lack of concern for others? Perhaps you have seen someone take the lid off a jar to sniff the contents. There are those who squeeze the fruits and vegetables. People knock articles on the floor, ignore them, and go on. Sometimes a shopper may decide against keeping a carton of ice cream and leave it to melt among the canned goods. You and other consumers pay for the cost of these practices in the total price you pay for food items. Only when all consumers learn to accept their responsibility in handling goods will the general public be relieved of such costs.

UNDERSTANDING CONSUMER PROTECTION

As consumer problems increase, the need for consumer protection also increases. Many laws have been passed to protect consumers. For example, you feel that it is safe to eat packaged meat bearing a government stamp. Consumer protection extends from local rulings to international laws. You as a consumer should know what you are buying and be reasonably certain it is what you want before you buy it.

If you find a product or service unsatisfactory, explain your problem to the seller. Most of the time, an honest complaint is well received by conscientious businesspeople. They will usually refund the cost or replace faulty merchandise. Sometimes the retailer may advise you to write directly to the manufacturer.

In most states there is more than one agency for advising and protecting consumers. Nearly all states have laws concerning consumer rights and responsibilities. State agencies also provide materials explaining the laws to its citizens.

There are many agencies in the Federal government concerned with consumer problems. Those agencies with the largest budgets are the United States Department of Agriculture, the Food and Drug Administration, the Federal Trade Commission, and the Office of Consumer Affairs. The responsibilities of the Office of Consumer Affairs are as follows:

to advise the President on consumer affairs

to coordinate all Federal consumer activities

to work with industries to find areas of consumer concerns

to help state and local governments in promoting and protecting consumer interests

to conduct research and investigations on consumer problems

to handle consumer complaints

There are many government agencies involved in consumer protection. It is often difficult to know which agency to contact with a specific complaint. Therefore, you should take the following steps before writing to a Federal agency:

1 Compare before you buy.
2 Bring your complaint first to the seller.
3 Report false advertising to the media carrying it.
4 Report deception to local organizations concerned with business standards, such as the Better Business Bureau.

If these methods fail to bring answers to consumer problems, there are additional possibilities. You may wish to consult a family lawyer. You may seek advice from an organization such as a Legal Aid Society. In many areas, local businesses police their own ranks.

If you fail to get help at the local level, write to the Office of Consumer Affairs in the Executive Office of the White House. If this agency is unable to handle your complaint, you will be advised of what else to do.

Some Federal consumer protection laws have been in effect a long time; others are new. Still more are in the process of being enacted. A few examples of existing laws determining the rights of consumers are the *Traffic Safety Act*, the *Wholesome Meat Act*, the *Whole-Poultry Product Act*, the *Public Health Cigarette Smoking Act*, the *Clean Air Amendment*, the *Lead-Based Paint*

Identify the time of year when the following kinds of merchandise are most likely to be sale priced:

Christmas cards
Ice skates
Camping equipment
Winter jackets
Bathing suits
Summer sandals
Air conditioners
Bicycles
Water skis
Blankets
Fishing equipment
School supplies
Gardening tools
Toys
New cars

Explain what *seconds* in merchandise are. Give an example of a second you may have bought that turned out to be a real bargain. Give an example to show when a second might not be a good buy.

Explain the meaning of the term *white elephant*. Describe a white elephant you have bought. Tell why you consider the purchase a poor buy.

Discuss how the cost of services such as delivery, credit, personal shopping, and merchandise returns must be absorbed by a business. How are the costs of these services passed on to consumers?

Distinguish among different types of stores and compare their goods and services. What are the advantages and disadvantages of shopping in each of the types of stores? Although stores sell similar kinds of goods, why do *you* prefer to buy some types of merchandise in one store rather than another?

Find newspaper or magazine articles about the concerns of city businesses which are losing trade to stores in suburban shopping centers and malls. What are downtown businesses doing to regain some of the lost trade? Suggest other steps that might be taken by merchants to encourage more downtown shopping. Send your suggestions to the appropriate Chamber of Commerce, Downtown Merchants Association, or local newspaper.

Develop a survey sheet which store managers could use to find out what shoppers like and dislike about a particular store.

Elimination Act, and the *Product Safety Act.*

Usually where there is a sincere consumer complaint, there is a way to solve the problem. It may take time and it may take patience. However, time, patience, money, and energy are resources well spent if they are directed toward improving this consumer-oriented world.

BUYING

There are a number of types of buying. In addition to general buying, there are *bargain buying* and *emergency buying.* Most everyone will find it necessary to take part in all these types of buying from time to time. The person who plans ahead and knows how to handle a given situation usually comes out best — both in the quality of goods and in the cost.

Most people buy something every day or at least several times a week. Buying know-how can be applied to any given situation. Buying can be profitable when a person learns to distingush wants from needs and to use advertising to advantage. Knowing *when* to buy can

When items are being purchased to suit the particular needs of a person, a second opinion is sometimes of great value. *Owen Franken/Stock, Boston*

also improve a consumer's buying skills.

At Christmas time, some people would like to have a gaily wrapped gift under the tree while others would prefer to have money to spend at sales after the holiday. Clothes usually cost less at preseason and postseason sales than during the height of a certain season. Some stores have more specials early in the week than on the weekend. Foods cost less and are more nutritious when they are in-season than when they are out-of-season. Many products are less seasonal now than they once were. Year-round production, refrigeration, and other modern technology make more products available more of the time. However, the season of the year still affects the price you pay for many items.

With experience, you will begin to notice when special sales are held. If you look forward to sales, you can save money and make your income go further. However, you need to judge value. Some sales are not real sales at all. Instead, they are actually another means of advertising.

Shopping for Bargains

It has been said that the whole world loves a bargain. Shopkeepers understand this reaction on the part of customers. Often they try to make all sorts of merchandise look like a bargain. Did your family ever buy a car or rent an apartment because they were warned that the price would soon go up? Did you ever buy a jacket at a summer sale, only to find that it didn't fit when winter came? Did you ever buy a twelve-dollar garment on sale for ten dollars and find one exactly like it selling in another store for a regular price of nine dollars?

A bargain is only a bargain when you and the storekeeper are satisfied. Consider this list as possible bargain situations:

1 *Seconds*, imperfect merchandise bought at low cost from a factory, may be sold at greatly reduced prices in a local store. If flaws can be mended or do not matter, seconds are real bargains.

2 Summer clothing is often reduced so it can be moved out to make room for fall clothing. Winter clothing is also reduced in early spring. Cars, refrigerators, TV sets, and other appliances are sometimes reduced when a new model is on the way. When you are more interested in performance than style, any of these items can be a bargain.

3 Sometimes a store will buy out a warehouse at reduced prices. These savings can be passed along to customers. When you find such items marked below the price you would usually pay, the purchases can be good buys.

When shopping for bargains, remember that there are real bargains and imitation ones. When tempted to take advantage of a bargain,

 Tell the class about an incident in which a person lost credit cards or had them stolen. In such cases, what should the credit card owner do?

Conduct a survey of lending agencies from which small loans may be obtained. Compare interest rates, repayment terms, security required, and the amounts available to borrowers. Summarize your findings in chart form. Share your findings with the class.

Visit a local bank. Find out how to start a savings account and how to fill out deposit and withdrawal slips. Practice filling out the slips.

Select a motorcycle, electric guitar, color TV set, second-hand car, or some other item of your choice. Find the various ways a person might pay for it. Give the advantages and disadvantages of buying the item by each of the following methods:

1 Paying cash
2 Buying on an installment plan
3 Borrowing money from a bank to pay
4 Borrowing money from a finance company
5 Borrowing money from a credit union

247

Find forty words in the scrambled letters below. The words are in straight lines —across, down, or diagonally. For example, *credit terms* begins in the top left corner and goes across to the right. Some words are printed backwards. Define the hidden words. Tell how they relate to being a consumer.

```
C R E D I T T E R M S T E G D U B
A A T D N P S B A N K S W S C P A
P Q S M S T A T A G S T D F R N R
A G C H T D L Z S E C O N D E M G
C K C R A V E T Q B O R J C D E A
I N A O L G N E X G U E Y O I C I
T L O I L E N U R N S A N T A N
Y L B T M K M O N E Y I W T O L F
N A D Y E P Y V I D Q M A R R P R
A M A N N S A V I N G S Y A F T E
L P R D T P O H S E U A A C J E T
P A W N S H O P T L Y T L T C K C
Q Y D R Q C E R N M U P I H K R A
C C A P I T A L A T B Q A D C A R
S L E B A L R E W O R R O B E M A
M O R T G A G E W N G Y C G H R H
E S I D N A H C R E M R X A C B C
```

Bulletin board IDEA

Title: *There's More to Credit Than Signing Your Name*

Directions: Write the word *credit* in green or red letters, using the opposite color for the other words. Use a picture or cutout of a cash register and a picture of a person who appears to be signing an agreement. If such a picture cannot be found, use actual contract agreements. Around these mount mock paper bills which look as if they are flying away.

make sure you understand all aspects of the situation.

Buying for Emergencies

Maybe you have had people drop in unexpectedly for an evening visit. You may have had to rush out to buy refreshments at the last minute. Perhaps you have had the happy feeling of being chosen to represent your school or club at an area meeting, only to find you had nothing suitable to wear. You may have made wise emergency purchases, but it is easy to make mistakes when you buy in a hurry. Being rushed can cause you to overspend. It can even make you buy items you would otherwise not choose.

Emergency buying usually does not give you time to compare prices. You may even settle for inferior quality because you don't have time to look further. Because your time is valuable and your money is probably limited, you need to find ways to lower the cost of emergency shopping.

DECIDING WHERE TO BUY

Places where people come together to exchange goods and services are called *marketplaces*. People can discuss the exchange of goods by telephone and goods may be sent through the mail. Yet most sales are made on a person-to-person basis. The choice of where to buy depends on who sells the goods or services you need and who sells the quality which suits your purposes.

Considering Types of Marketplaces

The American marketplace has undergone sweeping changes. In populated areas the general store has become a department store, and the grocery store has been replaced by the supermarket. The pharmacy is now a drugstore, where medicines and prescriptions account for only a part of the sales each day. Other marketplaces include service stations, convenience stores, trading-stamp stores, utility companies, discount stores, bookstores, and countless other stores of both general and special natures. Your home becomes a marketplace when a door-to-door salesman calls on you.

The concept of going to town to shop is being rapidly replaced. Malls and shopping centers scattered conveniently near housing areas tend to be on the increase as downtown shopping declines. Available public transportation and free parking are strong attractions for the shopping center. Laundry and cleaning may be done by one member of the family in a laundromat, while other family members shop in an adjoining shopping center.

Choosing the Marketplace

There are a number of factors to consider when choosing a marketplace. Most people are interested

Craft fairs often appeal to bargain hunters. They offer the opportunity for purchasing unusual, one-of-a-kind items for yourself and for others. *Charles Harbutt/Magnum*

Your career
Home extension aide

You would work with community groups for adults or teenagers and individual homemakers to help them improve their food buying, food preparation, housekeeping, and money management skills. You would also assist professionals in their work. You would find employment with various government agencies or extension agencies affiliated with colleges and universities.

Hidden Words
(for puzzle on previous page)

ads	loan
banks	mall
bargain	marketplace
borrower	merchandise
budget	money
buy	mortgage
capacity	needs
capital	note
cash	pawnshop
character	pay
charge	payments
check	plan
contract	record
creditor	sale
credit union	savings
goods	second
installments	shop
labels	stores
layaway	tags
lender	wants

Copy and complete the crossword puzzle using a separate sheet of paper. *Do not* write in this book.

In many areas, the local fruit and vegetable stand is slowly being replaced by the large supermarket. For the shopper in a rush or looking for unusual produce, the stands are still a welcome convenience. *Gwenn Mayers*

in using their time, energy, and money wisely. All three may be accomplished if the best marketplace is chosen.

Suppose you want to buy a popular record or tape. You know they are sold in department stores, discount stores, drugstores, music stores, and gift shops. If you have information about the kind of record or tape you want, you may save time by telephoning the various stores for prices. You could also read the various ads for the stores in newspapers to see if the record or tape is on sale. These are ways you can make price comparisons without going from store to store.

Sometimes you may shop in stores because of convenience. Other times you may choose a store for its efficiency or for the services it offers.

There are some supermarkets that have begun to use a new electronic checkout system for greater efficiency. Items in the stores have special computer codes on the labels. At the checkout counter, the clerk passes these items over a scanner which sends detailed information to a central in-store computer. This information includes the name of each product, its price, the tax, if any, the date, time, and checkstand number. The final sales slip gives the consumer a complete and itemized record of the bill. This system not only gives the consumer detailed sales slips but also pro-

vides fast service. The information in the computer can be used by the store to check the inventory. The records can help a store to keep fresh items on the shelves without running out. A possible disadvantage of this system for consumers is that products are seldom price-stamped individually. Prices usually are given only on the store shelf.

It is always important to buy from a store you know to be reliable. There may be a variety of reliable stores. You might consider a store

ACROSS

2 A penny is a small ____.

4 Instant credit is available with a bank credit ____.

5 Nutritious food is a(an) ____ for everyone.

8 The things you have to help you reach your goals are your ____.

11 Read the ____ of any contract.

13 In establishing priorities, you consider your needs and ____.

14 If you once got credit from a bank, the bank ____ you money.

near your home or where transportation is convenient. If you're in a hurry, you may prefer a store with trained salespeople rather than a self-service market. The best selection of a store combines all the good aspects of shopping. You have made a wise choice of marketplaces when, with the least amount of time, energy, and money, you can buy needed goods.

CONSIDERING HOW TO PAY

Credit cards and checks have largely replaced currency in marketplaces. An interbank charge card is a form of credit which can be used for buying goods or services in a wide variety of marketplaces across the country. Transportation systems and vending-machine owners in some large cities have developed plans for accepting tokens in exchange for services. The tokens may be bought at banks and various marketplaces.

Even with the increase in credit buying, cash buying accounts for millions of dollars worth of trading done each year. In many situations only cash is accepted for the goods or services purchased.

Paying Cash

You may know people who pay cash for everything. Often they seem proud to say that if they can't pay cash for something, they don't buy it. Such people may be very successful shoppers. Debt-free families are usually happier than debt-ridden families. While they often have fewer material goods, many say their freedom from concern over debts offsets their lack of possessions.

While there are many advantages to cash buying, there are some disadvantages. People who pay cash, but keep few records, may not remember exactly how their money was spent. This makes it very difficult to evaluate spending habits. Also, credit ratings are developed through payment habits. Cash-only buyers actually have no credit rating. The lack of a credit rating may be a problem if such a family wants to buy a home, car, or home appliance on credit.

Using Credit

Recent studies show that people who use credit have more material goods than families of equal income who don't. However, serious family problems can be traced to the overuse of credit.

From the time you first use credit, you are establishing a credit rating. Any time people use credit in a community, they establish a credit-risk record. People known for their steady payment of debts have established good credit ratings. A credit rating may be a real asset if a family decides to make a large credit purchase. The record may be kept by a profit-making credit bureau, or it may be operated by a group of businesses. A good

15 It is difficult to have a credit rating if you pay ____ for everything.
17 What you still have to pay is what you ____ .
18 You settle a debt when you ____ your bill.
19 Some states have both income and sales ____ .
23 In some families your allowance depends on your ____ .
25 Air and water are ____ resources.
26 One of your basic resources is ____ .
27 Currency is a form of ____ .
28 Merchandise and products for sale are sometimes called ____ .

DOWN
1 An advertisement is sometimes called a(an) ____ .
2 Currency is used less than in the past because of the more frequent use of credit cards and ____ .
3 Consumers buy and ____ goods and services.
4 Your payment habits determine your ____ rating.
6 The amount of money spent for food is *not* a fixed ____ .
7 A self-service store with lower prices may be a(an) ____ store.
9 A bank is one place to keep ____ .

10 Fatigue can be caused by
____ .

12 The foods you eat affect your
____ .

15 The price of an item is the
same as the ____ to the
consumer.

16 The largest expenditure
many families ever make is
for a(an) ____ .

18 A budget is a(an) ____ for
spending and saving.

20 Winter clothes may be
placed on ____ in the early
spring.

21 Intelligence and creativity are
____ resources.

22 If you do not read the fine
print in a contract you may
be very ____ .

24 Interest is the money you
____ on a savings account.

26 Information about fiber
content is found on a(an)

____ .

Your career
Tester and developer

You would help to develop and
test new household products.
Prepackaged foods, cleaning
products, and small household
equipment are just a sample of
the types of items you might
test. You would work for testing
laboratories and research
departments of various
industrial companies.

credit rating shows that you pay
your bills on time. Stores, banks,
and insurance companies with
whom you do business, and even
prospective employers, may be interested in your credit rating.

Understanding the cost of credit
Understanding the costs of various
kinds of credit helps you to understand when each can best be used
to reach certain goals. Perhaps you
buy a pair of shoes, charge them
to your parents' account in the
store, and your parents pay for
them less than a month later.
Thirty-day credit is considered to be
cash payment. Usually no charges
are made for this kind of credit.
The cost of this service is absorbed
by the store, which in turn pays
for it by selling at higher prices.
Your family might decide to buy a
car and finance it through a bank,
automobile-finance corporation, or
credit union and pay for it within
a two- or three-year period. You
may have relatives who buy a
house, finance it through a savings
and loan association, and agree to
pay for it over a period of twenty-
five or thirty years. Different situations call for different kinds of
credit, each available at a different
interest rate.

In general, the length of time
goods remain resalable determines
the cost of interest on money borrowed to pay for them. For example, the cost of credit for buying
clothing and household goods is

very high. Once used, such items
have very little resale value. Cars,
which have a longer resale value
than clothes, can be bought on
cheaper credit terms. Real estate,
which can be sold and resold year
after year, can generally be bought
on credit at lower interest rates
than other purchases.

Some people do not handle
credit wisely. They buy more than
they can afford, or they do not
make their payments as agreed.
Such people do not have good
credit ratings. When they must
buy on credit, they are forced to
go to lending agencies which
charge very high interest for the use
of money. Often a person pays
twice as much for the use of money
borrowed from such agencies. It
may become necessary to buy expensive credit from time to time. If
you have any doubts about the real
cost of credit in a given situation,
ask for help. If you are being
rushed to sign a contract, you will
be wise to obtain the help of a
trusted and reliable financial adviser or consultant.

Using credit cards
An amendment to the *Truth-in-
Lending Act* prohibits businesses
from sending credit cards to consumers unless a card is requested.
Consumers who have good credit
ratings can obtain several different
types of credit cards. Some are
issued by local stores and can be
used only in that one store or its

Wise consumers are satisfied with their shopping decisions and are responsible when it is time to pay for them. *Montgomery Ward*

Give examples of specific credit cards available to consumers with good credit ratings. Name a credit card that can be used in each of these situations:

1 In only one place of business in your local area
2 Across the country, but only in branches of the same nationally organized business establishment
3 Nationwide in many types of business establishments.

Explain the following terms in your own words:
Consumer
Credit
Credit card
Fixed expenses
Flexible expenses
Goods
Interest
Installment contract
Services

branches in the local or regional area. Credit cards can also be obtained from nationwide chain stores. These cards can be used at any of the store's outlets in any state. The cards can also be used for catalog purchases made through that chain. Credit cards issued by oil companies are widely used for local and out-of-town purchases made at service stations. Many motels, department stores, and oil companies issuing their own credit cards often, but not always, also accept bank credit cards.

Bank credit cards offer instant credit and can even be used for cash advances. Bank credit cards can be used in a wide variety of marketplaces. Grocery stores, hair styling shops, restaurants, travel agencies, auto repair shops, and specialty stores are only a few examples. Some doctors and lawyers accept credit cards and many states accept them for buying auto license plates.

After a bank credit card owner uses the card, the business sends the charge slip to the bank. The bank subtracts a handling fee, 3 to 5 percent, from the amount showing on the charge slip. The bank deposits the rest to the account of the business. The bank then bills the credit card owner for the amount of goods and services charged.

Clip newspaper and magazine advertisements from different types of businesses. Categorize each business as one of the following:

Department store, chain or privately owned
Specialty store, chain or privately owned
Mail-order establishment
Discount store
Convenience store

Compare the cost and quality of national and private or store brands of food items, grooming aids, or appliances.

Find examples of emotional advertising in newspapers and magazines and on billboards, radio, or television. What does each advertisement imply to you as a consumer? Find factual advertisements that provide information which is helpful to you as a consumer. Locate advertisements that both appeal to your emotions *and* provide valuable consumer information.

As with other forms of credit, businesses which accept bank credit cards must absorb the cost of the service. This cost is passed on to customers in the form of increased prices. There is usually no interest charge if the entire bill is paid within a specified number of days after it is mailed to the credit card owner. If the balance is not paid monthly, a finance charge is added. This is usually 1.5 percent per month or 18 percent per year on the unpaid balance.

Prompt payment is a consumer's obligation. In some places teenagers may have credit extended to them. Responsibility is a vital part of a successful credit operation. If you fail to pay your bills, you will have a poor credit rating. This can be held against you later when you try to enter into new, and often more important, business transactions.

If you have a good reason for not paying a bill when it comes due, explain your problem to the person you owe. Most businesses will give you a chance to arrange for future payments. However, businesses can continue to operate only when they are paid bills due them. Prompt payment should be made except in cases of real emergency.

Advantages and disadvantages of credit cards are subjects of frequent discussion. Actually most credit card problems involve the users

Credit cards allow consumers to purchase items when cash is not on hand. Because of this, overspending can be a problem to many. *Cary Wolinsky/Stock, Boston*

rather than the actual credit cards. With the easy credit a card provides, some people overspend. However, many people feel the advantages of credit cards greatly offset the disadvantages.

There are many times when it is unsafe to carry large sums of money. With credit cards, people can carry small sums and still obtain the goods and services they need and want. Credit cards also offer security to persons away from home in the event of an emergency.

Many people like to have written records of all expenditures. Such people may find credit card services quite convenient. There are times when people wish to buy something but will not have the money until payday. Rather than risk having someone else buy the item, they simply use a credit card. When using credit cards, avoid charging more than you have planned to spend, whether your money is in your pocket, in the bank, or in the form of unpaid wages.

Lost credit cards may be more serious than lost money. The finder of a lost credit card could possibly charge things to the owner's account. The credit card owner is legally obligated to pay charged bills up to a total of fifty dollars. In case of loss, the credit card owner should immediately notify the company that issued the card, informing them by telephone *and* by letter. This will enable the company to stop charging goods or services to

the old card number and to issue a new card. A card user is not obligated to pay for goods or services charged to a lost card number after the issuing company has been informed of the loss.

Buying on installment contracts

Such items as TV sets, furniture, and appliances are frequently bought on an installment plan. The buyer pays a certain amount of cash as a down payment and then signs a contract agreeing to pay the remainder, so much per month, during a stated period of time. In addition to the cost of the item, the buyer also pays carrying charges. These charges include interest, credit charges, and perhaps insurance. Carrying charges add appreciable amounts to the real cost of installment purchases. Contracts for installment plans usually provide for *default*. That is, if the buyer fails to make payments, the merchandise can be repossessed by the seller.

Anyone using installment credit should read and understand the fine print in the contract. Consult a financial expert if you don't understand the conditions of the contract. Installment payments to be paid over an exceedingly long period of time are generally to be avoided. Carrying charges paid over the years can amount to more than the price marked on an item. Some companies have ninety-day installment contracts available for large

Bulletin board IDEA
Title: *A Penny Saved Is a Penny Earned*
Directions: Tack up a large poster board cutout of a piggy bank. Around it mount pictures of teenagers doing things that save money, such as cleaning up the yard, washing a car, painting the house, and sewing clothes.

Determine which of these items in an advertisement for a bar of soap would be of real value to the consumer.

Endorsement by a famous person

Ingredients

Color

Size of the bar

Approval of physicians

Net weight

Price

How much it lathers in different kinds of water

What it can do for your social life

Kind of wrapper

Special features, such as for dry or oily skin

Compare the actual cost of one hundred dollars worth of merchandise financed by the following methods:

1 Paying by check

2 Charging goods to your account and paying the full amount within thirty days

3 Charging goods to your account and making equal installment payments for eighteen months

4 Borrowing the cash from a finance company and repaying the loan in equal installments for eighteen months

A bank can offer many services which may enable you to pay for purchases by either cash, check, or credit card.   *James H. Karales/Peter Arnold Photo Archives*

purchases. On some ninety-day accounts there is no interest charge if the entire bill is paid in only three installments. Usually one-third of the total purchase price is due on each payment date.

SUPPORTING BUSINESS-CONSUMER ACTIVITIES

Perhaps after watching the operations of certain businesses and the misuse of their consumer rights on the part of some people, you wonder how businesses can survive. Many consumers seem to buy without knowing, use without reading instructions, give very little thought to quality, avoid paying promptly, keep no record of when articles are bought, and misuse merchandise.

You may have wondered if consumer protection is needed or deserved. You may have asked how many business people deal unfairly with consumers.

Most consumers are honorable. Most businesses are run by honorable people. Laws have been enacted to protect the vast consuming public against a few businesses that might deceive them. All consumers and businesses should be equally interested in reforming the relatively small number of consumers who practice poor consumer activities. Only when businesses and consumers work together will both prosper. At that time, businesses can be profitable, and consumers can get a dollar's worth of goods for each dollar spent.

Number from 1 to 38. Beside each number indicate if the corresponding statement is true or false. *Do not write in this book.*

1 Consumers are people who help make or produce goods.

2 A want for one person may be a need for another.

3 When people have their hair styled they are buying a service.

4 Spending money for status symbols may be a means of seeking acceptance and security.

5 The purposes of advertising are to sell goods and services, to provide information, and to create wants.

6 Advertising may be planned to appeal to buyers' emotions rather than to their common sense.

7 Advertising that provides accurate information about a product is called *factual advertising.*

8 Informed and alert consumers can be their own best protection against business concerns that try to take advantage of them.

9 Garment tags may provide valuable information about fiber content and fabric finishes.

10 Permanent care labels give information about the regular care garments need.

11 Any clothing item labeled washable can be dry-cleaned unless the care label states otherwise.

12 All food labels provide nutrition information.

13 Nutrition labels are helpful to people on special diets.

14 Unit prices are stamped on canned food items.

15 The date stamped on fresh meat containers is a *pull date.*

16 *Package dates* on food items tell the last date the product should be used.

17 A food package may appear to hold more than it does.

18 Manufacturers of small electric appliances must provide warranties.

19 All warranties cover the cost of parts and service in repairing merchandise.

20 A cancelled check can serve as a receipt for payment of goods.

21 If consumers have purchased faulty merchandise, the first thing they should do is make a complaint to the Office of Consumer Affairs.

22 Many stores have sales after Easter.

23 The time of year when winter clothes are least expensive is in September, about the time school starts.

24 Seconds are usually sold at higher prices than other merchandise.

25 It is a good consumer practice to compare the price and quality of goods before buying.

26 *Scanning* is an electronic checkout system used by stores to prevent shoplifting.

27 The best way to establish a good credit rating is to pay for everything with cash.

28 Families using credit may have more material possessions than families not using credit.

29 A thirty-day credit account may be considered cash payment.

30 The cost of credit when buying a home is usually less than the cost of credit when buying clothing.

31 Consumers with good credit ratings are sent credit cards automatically when a new store opens in the area.

32 Bank credit cards can be used in many types of marketplaces.

33 One of the disadvantages of using credit cards is the possibility of overspending.

34 One disadvantage of paying cash for all purchases is the necessity of keeping written records.

35 Carrying charges paid over a long period of time add to the total cost of goods financed through installment contracts.

36 A monthly finance charge of 1.5 percent is the same rate as a yearly finance charge of 18 percent on the unpaid balance.

37 A ninety-day installment contract may *not* involve interest charges if payments are made promptly.

38 Businesses providing you with goods and services have the major responsibility for protecting you as a consumer.

Unit 4

Your Clothes

Fill in the blank in each sentence with the *best* word to complete the statement. *Do not* write in this book.

1 The secondary colors are violet, green, and (1) .
2 All colors can be made by mixing the (2) colors.
3 Colors appearing next to each other on the color wheel and sharing a common hue are called (3) .
4 Opposite colors make each other look (4) .
5 White added to a color makes a(an) (5) of the color.
6 Blue and orange are (6) colors.
7 The brightness or dullness of a color refers to its (7) .
8 If you want to appear smaller, choose dull, cool, and (8) colors.
9 Colors that seem to advance are (9) colors.
10 The main thing to consider in selecting a color to flatter you is the color of your (10) .
11 The roughness or smoothness of a fabric is called its (11) .
12 A line of buttons down the front of a garment creates a(an) (12) line.

13 A pair of dark blue slacks worn with a dark blue shirt will make you look taller and (13) than when worn with a white shirt.
14 Stripes going around your body make your look heavier and (14) than stripes going up and down.
15 A wide, contrasting color belt will cut your height, making you look (15) .
16 Large, splashy designs in a garment make you look (16) .
17 A round face looks longer when a (17) neckline is worn.
18 The term *silhouette* refers to the (18) of the body or garment.
19 A thick, fluffy fabric makes you look (19) than a smooth fabric.
20 Contrasting belts, yokes, and cuffs create (20) lines.
21 Because they are cooler to wear, summer clothes are often (21) in color.
22 A smooth, shiny fabric like satin makes you look larger because it (22) light.
23 Figure faults can be hidden by wearing (23) -fitting clothes.

24 The lightness or darkness of skin is determined by the amount of (24) it contains.
25 Accent colors are used to call attention to your (25) features.

Match the *colors* given in List A with the *color schemes* given in List B. Use a color scheme in List B only once. *Do not* write in this book.

List A: Colors
A Yellow and violet
B Navy blue and baby blue
C Red, yellow, and blue
D Gray and bright red
E Yellow, yellow-green, and green
F Red-orange, blue, and green

List B: Color Schemes
1 Accented neutral
2 Analogous
3 Complementary
4 Monochromatic
5 Split-complementary
6 Triad

Chapter 13

Choosing Clothes for You and Your Activities

Clothes have long been a favorite topic of interest and conversation in the female world. In recent years the male population has rediscovered a similar interest. History is repeating itself. Once again both sexes are interested in bright colors and clothing fashion.

This interest in clothes is easy to understand. Consider the importance of your appearance to your feeling of worth. The nineteenth-century poet Ralph Waldo Emerson once said that being well dressed gives a person the feeling of inward tranquillity which all other forces are powerless to bestow. This is doubtless an overstatement. Nevertheless, if your appearance can bring a feeling of peaceful satisfaction and self-respect, doesn't it seem wise to draw upon every available tool to achieve that feeling?

On the surface it sounds a little shallow to say clothes make the person. When you think about

261

Determine your wardrobe needs considering items in this list.

1 Your clothing left from other years.
2 Colors already in your wardrobe.
3 Kinds of clothes you feel comfortable wearing.
4 Colors and lines best on you.
5 What to make and what to buy.
6 Points to consider before shopping.
7 Your outfit as a whole, including accessories.
8 Fabrics and finishes, how they wear, and what care they need.
9 Combining quality and style to suit your figure type.
10 Your needs in relation to those of your family.
11 Your posture, the way you carry yourself.

Choose three of your garments you feel make you look your best. Decide why these garments are so becoming to you. Is it the color, the lines, the texture? Is it a combination of all of these? Make a list of the reasons you like these garments particularly. Consider these reasons in the future in selecting new clothes.

it, though, maybe clothes are more important than some people realize. If your suit or dress sags, your shirt or blouse is rumpled or soiled, or your shoes need polishing, isn't it natural for people to think you may be careless about other details?

DEVELOP A PLAN

If you are a person who looks *just right* most of the time, you probably already know that you must spend a certain amount of time in careful planning. Such planning involves figuring out the kinds of activities you like and the kinds of clothes you need for those activities. It also involves choosing colors, styles, and fabrics that look well on you and that go with the clothes and accessories you already have.

If you want to look your best and use your money wisely, perhaps you need to spend more time planning and less time buying. Start today and try following these suggestions:

1 List the places you go and the things you do.
2 Check the clothes you have. List the number and kinds of clothing according to color and style.
3 Mark the clothes that will need altering to fit properly. Use some other kind of mark for clothes needing remodeling to be in style. Discard those which cannot be used.
4 Think again about the places you go and the clothes you would

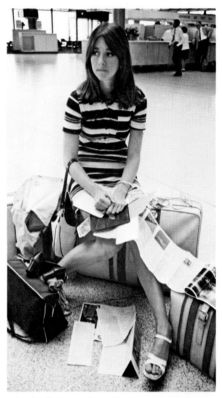

A good clothing plan allows a person to have suitable clothes for many occasions, whether traveling or staying at home. *Iberia International Airlines of Spain*

like to wear. This will help you decide exactly what clothes you need to buy or make. Write down a list of these clothes.
5 Decide how much money you will be able to spend on each new item. Put the major part of your clothing dollars into the clothing you expect to wear the most.
6 Shop in a number of stores and check ads before you buy. This will

help you know which styles are up-to-date and the price range you can expect to find.

7 Buy only the clothing that fits into your plan. Spur-of-the-moment shopping should be avoided. It can prove to be disappointing and expensive.

8 Learn how to select clothing and accessories best suited to your figure, coloring, and personality. A study of color, design, and texture of clothes will help.

Choosing clothes to complement your physical features can give you confidence in knowing you look your best. *Simplicity Pattern Co., Inc.*

CHOOSE CLOTHES FOR ATTRACTIVENESS

Wise decision making in buying requires several things. You want your clothes to be right for your activities and to be in line with the current fashions. However, your greatest concern is how attractive they are on you. Consider, too, how your clothes make you feel.

You already know that when you wear certain clothes you feel much happier and more self-confident than when you wear others. The clothes you enjoy the most usually are the ones you find the most becoming to you. They make you look more attractive and feel more comfortable when you wear them.

Color

Color brings pleasure to your life. It affects your feelings and it affects your looks. The colors you choose can make you feel and look happy or attractive, or they can make you feel and look droopy and tired.

The colors you associate with the sun, fire, and warmth are called *warm* colors. These colors include reds, yellows, and oranges. They make you feel warm, cheerful, and peppy. The colors you associate with trees, sky, grass, water, and shadows are the *cool,* or restful, colors. The blues and greens fall into this class. Violet can be either a warm or cool color, depending on how much red or blue it contains. It is often considered neutral.

Discuss how your choice of clothing can contribute to some of the following feelings. What other feelings can result from your choice of clothing?

Attractiveness
Confidence
Comfort
Creativity
Friendliness
Individuality
Poise
Popularity
Satisfaction
Security

Determine if your skin tones are warm or cool. Put a white towel around your shoulders. Pull your hair back so as much of your face is exposed as possible. Hold pieces of various colored fabrics up under your chin. Observe the effect each color has on your skin tones. Can you see yellow, red, or bluish tones in your skin? What does this tell you about your skin coloring?

Brainstorm to name well-known sayings associated with color, such as *green with envy, blue Monday, yellow streak, red with rage,* or *in the pink.* What are the psychological effects of these sayings?

Make a color wheel using the figure 1 for each of the primary colors and the figure 2 for each of the secondary colors. Use the figure 3 for the intermediate colors. Attach a dial with three moveable hands that can be rotated to determine different color schemes.

Name items such as fire engines, school buses, and caution flags that attract attention because of their colors. What might go unnoticed because of its color?

Bulletin board IDEA
Title: *Hues Take Their Cues from Flowers*
Directions: Collect pictures of garments illustrating different color schemes. Mount the pictures along with paper flowers in colors to match the color scheme of each garment.

As you glance around the room, what things catch your eye first? Doesn't the bright red shirt catch your eye before the pale blue shirt nearby? Do you see the bright orange books on the shelf before you notice the green ones? Do the warm-colored objects seem to be closer and larger than the cool-colored objects? What does this tell you about the effect colors give when you wear them? The warm colors will cause you to be noticed. They will help you to feel cheerful, and they may make you appear larger than you are. The cool colors will cause you to blend into a group. They will help you to feel calm and will make you appear smaller than you really are.

Look at the color wheel on page 265. Pick out the *primary* colors of red, yellow, and blue. Colors made by combining two primary colors in equal amounts are called *secondary* colors. Orange, green, and violet are secondary colors. Each one appears on the color wheel between the two primary colors it is made from. All other colors are made from combinations of the primary and secondary colors. As you look at the wheel, you can see how red shades into red-violet, violet, and blue-violet as it moves toward blue. On the other side, red moves into red-orange and orange as it moves toward yellow.

Any three colors that are equally distant from each other on the color wheel form a triad. Red, yellow, and blue make up a triad, so do green, orange, and violet. What are some others?

A color scheme built around one color and its various values and intensities is called *monochromatic*. For example, the red-blue colors combined as plum, lilac, and pink can be worn together for a rich monochromatic effect.

Colors appearing next to each other on the color wheel and sharing a common hue are called *analogous,* or related, colors. Such colors as yellow, yellow-green, and green are analogous and can be combined to make an interesting color scheme.

Those colors directly opposite each other on the color wheel are called *complementary* colors. This means that if these color pigments are mixed together, they will produce gray, or will neutralize each other. They are opposites, or complements. When placed next to each other, each makes the other look brighter. Thus, green and red look much brighter when they appear together than when each color is used separately. Worn together in full strength, they can be too bright and distracting. However, when used in *tints* (lighter values of a color) and *shades* (darker values of a color), they can be pleasing.

Determining your skin tone
While colors are important for the effect they have on your apparent size and your emotions, their most

COLOR WHEEL

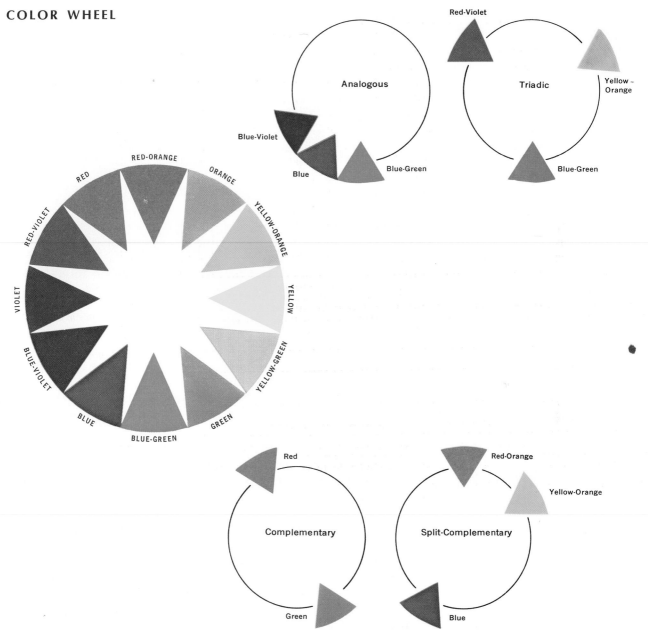

The color wheel can be referred to as a guide for choosing colors that make pleasing color combinations.

Find pictures of clothes in magazines, catalogs, or old pattern books to illustrate the following color schemes. Label and explain why each is an example of one color scheme.

1 Monochromatic: A single color with variations of value and intensity.

2 Analogous: Two or three colors appearing next to each other on the color wheel, all with one color in common.

3 Accented neutral: Large areas of neutral color with one or more small areas of bright or intense color.

4 Complementary: Two colors located opposite each other on the color wheel.

5 Split-complementary: A color used with hues from both sides of its complementary color.

6 Triad: Any three colors spaced an equal distance from one another on the color wheel.

Use colored paper to make small streamers or banners of the school colors for each school in your area. Analyze why these colors may have been chosen for each school. Pretend you have been selected to choose colors for a new school. Defend your selection.

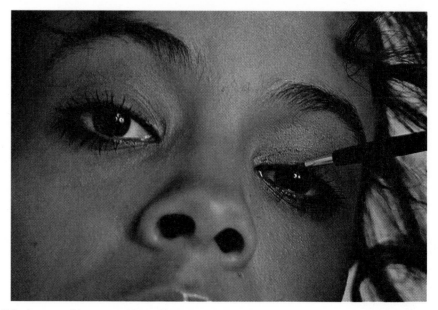
Whether your skin tone and hair coloring are dark or light, makeup is available in colors which will blend with your coloring. *Avon Products, Inc.*

important use is their effect on your appearance. Colors can clash with or compliment your personal coloring. Your skin tone can be flattered or dulled by colors worn nearest your face. To determine the total effect a color will have on your appearance, you should also consider the color of your hair and eyes. Your most becoming clothing colors will flatter all three: your skin, hair, and eyes. However, as a general guide for choosing colors, your first concern should be skin coloring.

When buying clothing, keep your skin color in mind. With the wide selection of colors available, each person can choose colors which are personally flattering.

There appear to be five basic skin colors: black, brown, red, white, and yellow. Actually, however, the colors found in all skins are tints or shades of red, yellow, or blue, or combinations of them. The amount of pigment in the skin causes the degree of lightness or darkness. The more pigment the skin contains, the darker it will be. In reverse, if skin contains very little pigment, it will be very light.

When choosing becoming colors, it is far more important to consider undertones than the amount of pigment in your skin. Undertones are caused by the amount of red or yellow pigment present. Since all skins are colored by a mixture of red and yellow, the skin color of any one person is likely to lean toward either the yellow or the red side of orange. These red or yellow undertones divide people into two special groups. Their skin is either *warm* or *cool* in appearance. Orange and red-orange tones produce a warm effect. Red-violet and yellow tones produce the cool effect.

The color of clothing can be chosen to either emphasize or minimize warm or cool skin tones. You may need help in deciding whether your skin tone tends toward yellow or red. Once this is known, you will be able to select colors which look good on you.

Choosing your best colors

The safest and easiest way to know what a certain color will do for you is to hold it close to your face. Do this in a good light and look at yourself closely. It is rare that any one color is always becoming to an individual. Colors vary so much in lightness and darkness. You can usually find some tint or shade which looks well on you. But there will be other tints or shades of the same color which are not becoming. You may be able to wear a tint of orange. Yet a deep shade of orange may bring out unflattering undertones.

When you are checking a color to see how it looks on you, be sure to use the kind of light under which

Use two male and two female fashion dolls, paper cutouts, or sketches to compare the effects of clothing lines. Dress one pair of figures according to List A and the other pair according to List B. Discuss the effects.

List A
1 Vertical lines
2 All one-color outfits
3 Belts which match the outfits
4 Contrasting color at neckline
5 Dark colors
6 Dull intensities of colors
7 Smooth-textured fabrics
8 Small designs in fabrics
9 Loose-fitting styles

List B
1 Crosswise or horizontal contrasting color lines
2 Contrasting pants and shirts
3 Contrasting color belts
4 Contrasting band or trim at the hip line
5 Bright colors
6 Light colors
7 Bulky-textured fabrics
8 Large designs
9 Flaring skirts, pants legs, or sleeves

Design a package for any product you choose. Select a color scheme appropriate to the product. Explain your choice of colors.

A small accent of color may be all that is needed to highlight your own coloring. *The Savings and Loan Foundation, Inc.*

Study each of the sets of lines shown below. What comes to mind as you look at each set? Describe any special feeling or mood you think each set could create.

Vertical

Horizontal

Curved

Diagonal

Your career
Buyer for teenage clothing

You would buy clothing and accessory items from manufacturers to suit the needs and wants of your customers. You might plan seasonal, quarterly, and special purchase sales, and might also help train sales personnel. You would work for a large department store or specialty shop.

you expect to wear it. For example, if the garment will always be worn at night under artificial light, check it under artificial light. If the garment will usually be worn during the daytime, look at it under both artificial and natural light.

When shopping, it is sometimes inconvenient to hold every garment or piece of cloth up to your face to see what it does for you. If you know your skin tone, you can determine the effect basic colors will have on it. This will help you to shop more selectively. Then only your final selections will need to be checked against the color of your skin.

As you look at the color wheel, you see that the opposite of yellow is violet. Remember, complementary colors intensify each other. Therefore, people with yellowish skin will find violet clothes tend to make their skin look even more yellow. Likewise, the greens and blue-greens emphasize the pink tones in the skin.

Colors may be emphasized in other ways. One way is by repeating the color in large amounts and in a deeper shade. Thus, pink in the skin will be emphasized by wearing a red dress, sweater, or shirt.

Colors are also emphasized by repeating a small amount of the same color in a brighter intensity. Thus, a bright yellow collar will make yellow skin or hair look more yellow. A bright pink collar will bring out the pink in the skin.

Colors may be made to appear less obvious by overpowering them with very bright colors or by combining them with a dull color of about the same *value* (no lighter or darker) and a slightly different *hue* (color). For instance, a person who has sallow, yellow skin might overcome the problem by wearing an outfit of bright orange or red. A person with a reddish skin can overcome the problem by choosing a garment of medium-dull orchid or plum or perhaps by choosing pastel pink, which dulls the skin while highlighting the eyes. You may find that certain colors you like do not go well with your skin. You can still wear these colors by using white or another more becoming color at the neck of your outfit.

Using color effectively
Many people find their wardrobes more flexible if outfits for various occasions are chosen in one basic color or in neutrals such as brown, beige, gray, black, or white. By highlighting them with different colored accessories, such clothes can be appropriate for a large range of activities. Colors vary in *intensity* (the brightness or dullness of a color). A bright spot of color in an accessory can balance the larger area of dull color in a basic outfit.

Color plays tricks on your eyes. If used well, it can help cover up figure faults and attract attention to your good features. You can use colors to make you look larger or smaller. Color can also be used to make you look shorter or taller. For example, white and pastels reflect light and make you appear larger. Dark, dull, or grayed colors absorb light and make you appear smaller. A one-color outfit will add height, while contrasting tops with pants and skirts will reduce your apparent height.

Black emphasizes your *silhouette* (outline of your body). It usually looks best with a contrasting color accent. You can wear black well when your figure is in good proportion. On the other hand, black calls attention to a figure of poor proportion. A figure with large hips, short legs, or short waist attracts less attention when it is dressed in a dull or grayed color instead of black.

Accent colors attract more attention than the basic, or background, colors. You can use them to call attention to your best features.

A hat of an accent color adds height. Select the size and shape of hat most becoming to you. Look at yourself in a full-length mirror before buying a hat. Pocketbooks, shoulder bags, and knapsacks of accent colors carry the eye to the part of the body they touch. A person with a slender figure may wish to carry a bag of contrasting color, while someone larger might well choose a bag to match an outfit. Select the size and shape of your bag in proportion to your size.

A spotty look can be caused by using too many accent colors. Spots

Color and combinations of color make our wardrobes interesting. *Butterick Fashion Mktg. Co./A Div. of American Can Co.*

of a single color can have the same effect. When shoes, bag, gloves, tie, or scarf vary greatly in color or are identical, the eye jumps from one spot of color to the next. Try for a blend. There are two good ways to achieve a blend. Choose one accessory which matches either the basic outfit or blends with both the outfit and the other accessories. For example, if you are wearing a red hat and scarf, your mittens or gloves and boots should be more subdued in color.

Look through a magazine or mail-order catalog. Find several pictures of the same model in different outfits. Cut the pictures out and mount them for a flannel board or poster. Compare the effects of the different styles on the model's:

Facial shape   Weight
Leg length   Coloring
Height   Proportions

Cut out and mount magazine or catalog pictures of faces showing different skin colorings and types. Using fabric or paper in several colors, cut out matching T-shirts for each face. Discuss how different colors look with each of the various skin colors. Prepare a series of neckline accessories such as collars, scarves, ties, and necklaces in a variety of colors. Try the accessories on each skin type and note the effect.

Find pictures of garments such as coats, jackets, sweaters, and socks showing a variety of textures. Determine ways in which texture may affect the apparent size of the figure, call attention to certain features, or create a formal or informal appearance. Select from fabric swatches of different textures those that would make a person look slimmer or heavier.

Notice in the drawings below what happens as vertical lines are spaced farther and farther apart. What does this tell you about the spacing of vertical lines in clothes?

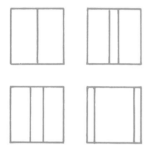

Point out garments with vertical lines that make the figure look taller and slimmer. Show vertical lines in a garment that actually make the figure look shorter and heavier.

Suggest ways in which the lines shown below are used in clothing. Explain the effects of horizontal lines on the apparent size of the figure.

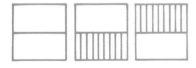

Find pictures of garments illustrating horizontal lines that make the figure appear shorter and heavier.

Use placement of color to advantage. You can add to or cut your apparent height by the arrangement of color on your body. Short, stout figures appear taller when dressed in one color. To add further height, use an accent color at the neck, on the head, or down the center of the figure. Two-piece outfits of different colors cut the apparent height. These may be worn if you are tall and slender or if you look slender. A belt of contrasting color is also good for the tall, slender figure. Certain placement of contrasting colors adds width to the figure. For example light-colored gloves or mittens worn with a dark outfit or coat add inches to the hips, because the eye jumps from one white hand to the other. Also, a contrasting belt or trim draws the eye and emphasizes the size of the area it covers.

Texture

The *texture* (roughness or smoothness) of a fabric surface affects its apparent color and the size of your figure. Rough surfaces reflect light in tiny spots and in different directions. This causes little shadows that dull the intensity of the color. If a piece of rough fabric and a piece of smooth fabric were dipped into the same dye bath, the rough fabric would appear to be duller in color. In other words, the rough texture of the fabric *softens* the color of the fabric.

A smooth fabric such as chino, used in pants, adds less bulk to the figure than a rough fabric like corduroy. Chino makes you look smaller when wearing it than does corduroy. But a smooth, shiny fabric such as satin will make you look larger. On the other hand, a rough, nubby texture, even though its color is dull, will make you look heavier because of its bulk.

Fabric Designs

The design, or pattern, of a fabric affects the apparent size of the person wearing it. When you look at large, splashy designs you usually move your eyes from one spot of pattern to the next. Such patterns give the impression of increased size. On the other hand, small designs are more restful to look at and blend into an all-over effect. This makes the figure appear smaller. Thus, a garment made from a large-print or plaid fabric will make a person look heavier than will one with a small design.

Design is a question of relationships. Fragile, dainty designs may look out of place on a large individual, while large designs can be overpowering to a small person.

In planning your outfits, try to determine which fabric designs relate best to your figure. You may choose large or small designs in some part of your costume if you work toward a unified effect.

Lines in Clothes

Do you remember having noticed at some time or other that a certain

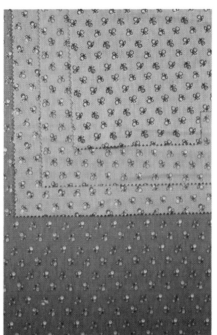

The design of fabric, such as a bold plaid or a dainty print, often determines the end result of the garment. What type garments would be made with these fabric designs? *Cotton Incorporated*

Use copies of the figures below to show how shoulders, waist, and hips can be emphasized by clothing lines and color. Sketch belts, yokes, pockets, buttons, collars, and structural lines. Determine if you have made the figure look taller, shorter, heavier, or thinner. Color some of your sketches to create additional effects.

outfit made you look taller and thinner than you thought you were? This might have happened when you were trying on clothes in a store or when you were dressing at home. You may have tried on a garment that belonged to a friend and found that it didn't look as well on you as expected. Why do you think these things are true?

The becomingness of a garment depends upon where the seams fall, as well as on the color, texture, and design of the fabric. The style, or way the garment is put together, creates lines that catch the eye. The most important line is the outline (silhouette) of your figure. When people look at you from a distance or when the light is behind you, your silhouette is most apparent.

As people look at you from close range, the details of the construction of your clothes become more noticeable. The direction of its fashion lines determines the impression a garment gives. As you examine the lines of a garment, you will see that some of the lines go up and down the figure vertically. Some

271

Pretend you must plan a bus trip to attend a wedding and visit a friend in a nearby town. You will be there three days. Your friend has also planned for you to go to a baseball game, a rodeo, a home party, and a cookout. Decide what clothes you will need to take to be ready for the fun. Plan to use only one small weekend suitcase. List everything you plan to take. Describe, including color, everything on your list. If possible, sketch your weekend wardrobe. Compare your plan with those of your classmates. Who will need the fewest separate pieces to be ready for everything?

Select pictures of clothes you like and would like to own. Are there any that your parents would not like? Try to analyze their objections from their point of view.

Pretend you own a pair of white slacks and a matching jacket. You will have to wear this outfit to attend a summer concert in the park, a party at a friend's home, and a graduation ceremony. Describe accessory items you would like to have to make the outfit appropriate for each occasion.

lines travel across the figure horizontally. Since vertical lines carry the eye up and down, it is natural that they make the person wearing them look taller and more slender. When the eye travels from one side to the other, the person naturally appears wider.

Other lines are formed where the different parts of the garment are put together. For example, the waistline, the neckline, and the lines made where sleeves are sewn into a garment all form fashion lines in an outfit. The hemline, the edges of the sleeves, and the collar and cuffs form other lines. Such things as pleats, rows of buttons, yokes, pockets, and lines of trimming also create lines for the eye to follow.

The other fashion lines you find in clothes are more or less variations of the vertical or horizontal lines. Diagonal lines run from one side to the other on a slant. The more nearly vertical the line, the more slenderizing it is. V-shaped lines may be slenderizing or not depending upon how broad the V is. Curved lines add graceful width and softness to clothes.

Dominant, or outstanding, lines influence clothing appearance. Since the eye follows these dominant lines, choose designs to add height or width in the body areas where it is needed. Be sure these lines emphasize your best features and hide your faults.

If you have a round face and full neck, a round neckline will make your face look rounder and your neck fuller. In reverse, a narrow V-neckline will carry the observer's eye down away from your face and make your face appear longer. A wide belt will carry the eye around your figure at the waistline and make that part of your body look larger. If you have a small waistline or hips you may want to call attention to them with a brightly colored belt.

One of the most interesting ways to create lines is through the use of color. Stripes and plaids in fabrics create definite color lines for the eye to follow. The way a garment is cut from such fabrics will determine whether the lines add height or width to your figure. A tall or thin person might choose horizontal lines, while vertical ones would be better for a short or heavy person.

CHOOSE CLOTHES FOR APPROPRIATENESS

Knowing what to wear for each occasion is a skill developed through planning and practice. People who put forth the effort to dress appropriately show through their actions that how they look is important. They are showing their awareness of the pleasure a well-chosen outfit brings, not just to themselves, but mainly to others.

For the Individual

Your personality, along with your body build, will determine what

When purchasing clothes for another person, consider the age, size, personality, and the activities of the individual. *Mimi Forsyth/ Monkmeyer*

type of clothes you will look best in and enjoy wearing. Some people look and feel best when they are wearing classic, tailored clothes. Others look and feel better in the latest trend-setting clothes.

One way to help you decide on the type of clothes best for you is to think about the clothes you now have. Which clothes make you feel the best? Which bring you the most compliments? You will probably discover that these clothes are best suited to your personality as well as

to your coloring and your figure type or body build.

In the past girls and boys were dressed from early childhood, according to very rigid rules. Both everyday and dress occasions saw girls in pastel colors, ruffles, and bows. Even their play clothes had these characteristics. Boys, too, were allowed only a limited selection of colors and styles of clothing.

Through the decades some dress codes have remained the same; others have changed drastically. Women and girls still wear skirts and dresses, but their wardrobes are not restricted to these alone. At one time, pants were only acceptable for women to wear for certain sports, such as horseback riding; girls could only wear pants out to play. Now, for many women and girls, pants are a basic part of their wardrobes for any and all occasions.

Significant changes in men's and boys' clothing have come about more slowly. While their garments are basically the same, they are more casual and colorful than in generations past. Men and boys, too, have become more open to fashion change. With increased leisure time, men are now responding to fashion change much like women have for quite some time.

For Your Age

Today's teenagers can find clothes they like. They are not expected to wear styles that are either too childish or too mature-looking for them.

Look through magazines and catalogs to find garments with distinctive design lines. Analyze the effects of the lines on the model's figure. Imagine how the garments would look on you.

Make or find two sketches of similar garments — one showing structural lines and one showing decorative design. Label your illustrations accordingly.

Study examples of optical illusions created by clothing lines. Sketch a garment with lines that would flatter your own body shape.

Create a design for a fabric. See what different effects you can achieve by using the same design but varying the colors.

Your career
Fashion designer

You would create new types and styles of clothing or accessories. You might sketch your ideas and select the color and type of material to be used. You might work within the garment or accessory industry, for a manufacturer of paper patterns, or you might free-lance your designs to manufacturers.

Clothing that was traditionally for men or women is now being worn by both sexes. *Simplicity Pattern Co., Inc.*

Consider your activities when you select a wardrobe. Special items that are needed for a sport can also be used as basic garments. *Clyde H. Smith/Peter Arnold Photo Archives*

Nor are they expected to wear clothes which fail to fit their activities. As a matter of fact, it seems the clothing world is, to a degree, teen-oriented, since so many styles are keyed to the figures, personalities, and activities of teenagers.

Fashion designers often seem to emphasize the older teenager. This sometimes creates problems for younger people. Have you ever bought something because you thought it would make you look grown-up? When you got home, did your choice turn out to be a disappointment? Perhaps your parents were also unhappy with your purchase.

For the Occasion

Different kinds of activities require different kinds of clothes. Some of these differences are due to the kind of activity itself, and some are due to social customs. Casual clothing is becoming more and more popular in today's informal way of living. It is no longer customary for women and girls to wear hats and gloves or men and boys to wear suits and ties for a shopping trip. In fact, many communities no longer demand that dressy clothes be worn to church services.

Unfortunately, some people have misinterpreted the word *informal*. They feel that informal means sloppy. As a result, they seldom dress carefully for any occasion. People who think and dress in this manner often forget that careless dress implies to others they are generally careless people.

The value you place on your personal appearance is a part of the value you place on your own importance. People who have faith in their own worth will be able to accomplish more than those who do not. Wearing clothing that is right for the occasion will give you a feeling of confidence in your appearance and in yourself.

CHOOSE CLOTHES FOR WEARABILITY

One of the greatest advantages of the new fibers and finishes used in clothing is wearability. Most synthetic fibers are more durable than natural fibers. They hold their shape better and resist wrinkles. Yet natural fibers also have some important advantages. (See pages 288–289.) Careful selection of the fabrics from which your clothes are made is as important as color and style. Fabrics that wrinkle easily, stretch out of shape, shrink, or do not wear well can spoil your enjoyment of the garment. The way a garment is made, its fiber content and fabric finish, and the care it needs are all a part of wearability and contribute to its being enjoyed.

CHOOSE CLOTHES FOR ENJOYMENT

Sometimes you need to buy clothes just for fun. You may be surprised to read such a statement because you have heard so much about buying for wear, buying for care, buying for color, buying for many other good reasons.

Care in buying can't be overemphasized. Timing, also, must fit into the family situation. Nevertheless everyone needs to feel special once in a while.

There is no need to overdo it, but occasionally buy something simply because you want to. Can you recall the feeling of buying something not because you needed it but because you wanted it badly? Such clothes add spice to your wardrobe and extra pleasure to everyday living.

Your career
Textile designer

You would create designs for fabric, specifying weave, pattern, color, and thread to meet fashion trends. You might develop new ideas for combining natural and synthetic fibers, different colors, and weaves to make fabrics that are in demand. You would work for a textile mill, chemical textile company, art studio, or you might free-lance your designs to manufacturers.

Having a good time often depends on your being dressed comfortably and appropriately for the outing.   *Simplicity Pattern Co., Inc.*

Number from 1 to 25. Beside each number indicate whether the corresponding statement is true or false. *Do not* write in this book.

1 A bright color will call attention to the area it covers.
2 A centered vertical line will make you look taller and slimmer.
3 Dark green slacks will make you look heavier than bright red slacks.
4 Colors opposite each other on a color wheel are called complementary colors.
5 Analogous colors intensify each other.
6 A purple sweater can make a yellowish skin look more yellow than it really is.
7 A turtleneck sweater or shirt will look better on a person with a short neck and round face than on one with a long face and neck.
8 Any personality type or any figure size can look equally well in any style just as long as it is in fashion.
9 A smooth, shiny fabric like satin reflects light and makes the wearer look larger.
10 Dull or grayed colors absorb light and make the wearer look slimmer.
11 An outfit of one color is more slenderizing than one made of two contrasting colors.
12 Having plenty of money to spend for clothing assures you of being well dressed.
13 Lines in clothes are created by the design of the garment as well as the pattern of the fabric.
14 The main thing to consider when buying clothing is how it looks in the store.
15 A red sweater will make a pink skin look whiter.
16 A blue-green shirt will bring out the yellow in your skin.
17 A thick waistline will look smaller in a wide white belt.
18 Dominant lines in clothes can be created by color contrasts.
19 If a garment is flattering to you, it will be a good buy.
20 Two people in the same outfits will be equally well dressed.
21 A tight black garment is the best choice for hiding wide hips.
22 The lightness and darkness of skin is determined by the amount of pigment it contains.
23 A rough, nubby, thick fabric will make you look smaller because it hides the size of your figure.
24 If you want to appear larger, choose bright, warm colors.
25 The clothes you choose should suit your personality, figure type, coloring, and activities.

Fill in the blank in each sentence with the *best* word or words to complete the statement. *Do not* write in this book.

1 Styles are popular for longer periods than fads and (1) .
2 Laws passed to protect buyers are called (2) laws.
3 The two main classes of fibers are synthetic and (3) .
4 When two or more fibers are combined to make a fabric, the result is a(an) (4) .
5 The best source of information about fiber content is the hang-tag or (5) attached to the garment.
6 How a fabric wears can be changed by the addition of a (an) (6) .
7 All natural and synthetic fibers are divided into generic groups according to their (7) composition.
8 Orlon, Dacron, Fortrel, Dynel, and Acrilan are (8) names for synthetic fibers.
9 A fabric which has been treated so it requires little or no ironing, will stay smooth, and keep sharp pleats will be labeled (9) .
10 A fabric that does not catch fire when touched by a match is called (10) .
11 Before buying, consider appearance, price, and the way the garment is (11) .

Chapter 14

Buying Clothes for Use and Fashion

After reading this chapter, you should be able to:

1 Name current *fads* in clothing.
2 Define *fashion*.
3 Describe how *styles* are different from fads and fashions.
4 Give examples of ways consumer laws protect you as a consumer.
5 Make a chart giving the names of natural and synthetic fibers, their chief uses, characteristics, and recommendations for care.
6 Point out the advantages of blending various fibers to make a fabric.
7 Tell why various finishes are applied to certain fabrics.
8 Develop checklists for judging the quality of different garments.
9 Judge the quality of various garments.

The fashion industry is a big business. One of its jobs is to persuade people that they need new clothes. The more successfully this is done, the more people buy and the more the industry grows. When you understand how the fashion industry uses advertising techniques to create clothing wants, you can avoid being misled by them. Then you can buy clothes that will fit your *needs* rather than fit the *wants* advertising has helped to develop.

There are three terms to keep in mind in referring to clothing: *fads*, *fashions*, and *styles*. Fads come and go rapidly, usually lasting no more than a season. They are often very extreme. Fashions are slower to be accepted but stay popular for a longer period of time. Styles last for many years in different fashionable versions.

Research books on the history of clothing since 1900. Find styles that reappear from time to time.

Look through pattern books and select the current fashion versions of classic styles such as shirtwaists, shifts, and T-shirts. How have they changed?

Analyze your own wardrobe to see which items are classic styles, current fashions, and passing fad items.

Bring one out-of-fashion but wearable item to class. Suggest ways it could be recycled into the current fashion picture by making minor changes. Some suggestions might be:
Cut slacks or jeans to make shorts.
Reshape the legs of pants which are too flared to make them straighter.
Shorten a dress to make a top for pants or skirts.
Cut long sleeves to make a short-sleeved shirt or jacket.
Cut a T-shirt or pullover sweater down the front. Bind the edges and add buttons and buttonholes or ribbons to make a collarless cardigan.

Plan a minidebate on the topic: *Comfort and fashion do not go together.*

Much of what people consider to be fashion is really *fad*. Many people become slaves to fads. They constantly buy articles of clothing because they want the newest look. Fads frequently are poor buys. These highly popular items are usually quite expensive both in original cost and in cost per wearing. They usually fade in popularity long before they are worn out.

The term *fashion* refers to the accepted, popular style at any given time. Such things as width of shoulder or lapels, length of skirts, width of pants legs, and loosely belted, tightly belted, or beltless styles are all parts of the current fashion picture in a given season.

The *style* of a garment may refer to such things as shirtwaist dress, princess dress, trench coat, kimono sleeve, and button-down collar. A style may go out of fashion, only to return at a later date.

The wise buyer learns which styles are personally becoming and then buys the fashionable adaptations of those styles. Though fad items can be fun to own and can add spice to some of your outfits, they will soon be out of fashion and no longer popular. Buy only those you can afford to discard soon.

Well-made, comfortable outfits are often fashionable for many seasons. *Butterick Fashion Mktg. Co./A Div. of American Can Co.*

LAWS PROTECTING CONSUMERS

Over the years several attempts have been made by the government to provide protection for the buyer by means of *consumer laws*. There are laws and regulations controlling the labeling of wool products, silk products, fur products, and flammable goods.

As the synthetic fibers, such as nylon and the acrylics, came into the clothing picture, it became increasingly difficult for a consumer to distinguish the content of a fabric. The Textile Fiber Products Identification Act, put into effect in 1960, was a real help to consumers. It provided that all garments and piece goods be labeled, stating the percentage of each fiber contained in the fabric. This act, however, controls only one aspect of clothing — the fiber. Fiber content *is* important in the performance of a garment. However, so are the construction of the yarn and the fabric, the type of dye used, and the finishes applied to the fabric. Certainly, too, the way a garment is made affects how it looks and wears.

According to the Textile Act, all fibers of similar chemical composition are classified into basic groups called *generic* groups. The natural fibers of wool, cotton, silk, and linen are such generic groups. Other fibers are known as polyesters, nylons, rayons, etc. When the law was passed, there were only sixteen different generic fiber groups. Since then, more groups have been developed and the number keeps growing. (See the chart on pages 288–289.)

Perhaps you are thinking that you know the names of some generic groups and have in mind Orlon, Acrilan, Creslan, and Zefran. These names do *not* refer to generic groups. Rather they are trade names adopted by certain companies for single generic fibers. Thus, Orlon, Acrilan, Creslan, and Zefran are all trade names for individual members of one generic group, the acrylic fibers.

On a label you might read that a garment is made of 60 percent acrylic and 40 percent wool. The manufacturer may also use the trade name, Orlon. The law requires that the generic term *acrylic*, be used. However, the use of trade names is optional. The charts in this chapter will provide you with a better understanding of the characteristics and care of the individual generic fibers.

In 1972 a new Federal Trade Commission ruling went into effect. This ruling regulates permanent care labeling. It requires that instructions for the proper care of a garment or home-sewing fabric be provided. In ready-made clothing, this information must be permanently attached to the garment in the form of a label. In fabric stores, the care labels must be available for fabrics purchased. The home sewer can attach them to the garments at home.

Bring to class examples of as many different kinds of care labels as possible. Analyze the garments to determine why each label was used.

Examine your wardrobe and decide which garments need to be restyled to be wearable again. Find pictures of accessory items you could use to make an old outfit fashionable. Select outdated fad items and brainstorm ways to update them.

Bulletin board IDEA
Title: *It Pays to be Snoopy*
Directions: Use a cutout of a magnifying glass placed as if it is helping the viewer read a hang tag or care label.

Your Career
Alterationist

You would adjust ready-made garments to fit an individual. You might also change the hem length on garments or replace zippers. You would work for a department store or specialty shop.

Act out a situation where a person has washed a jacket with a care label which stated *Dry-clean only*. The person tries to return the jacket for a refund at the store where it was purchased.

Discuss why you would still want to know the fiber content of a garment even if you knew how to care for it. Refer to the charts on pages 288–289 for your reasons.

Bring two wash-and-wear garments to class, or try this experiment at home. Wash one garment according to the instructions on the care label. Wash the other one in hot water using the regular wash cycle. Dry both in the same dryer. Explain what you learn from the results.

Bulletin board IDEA
Title: *Swing into Fashion*
Directions: Draw a swing. Around it mount pictures of fashionable garments that are popular with teenagers.

Having proper instructions for the laundering or dry cleaning of a garment makes it much easier to keep your clothing looking its best. Read these care labels before buying any clothing item. If an outfit must be dry-cleaned, can you afford the extra expense? Will the garment be unused for long periods of time because of the expense or inconvenience of having to give it special care?

Many manufacturers go beyond the requirements of law to help the buyer of their products. They are providing much more information voluntarily. Calling attention to such qualities as shrinkage control and spot-resistant or durable-press finishes makes their goods seem more desirable. It is also to their advantage, as well as to yours, that you care for the garment properly. Therefore, many labels or hang tags now give you information such as:

1 Fiber content
2 Size
3 Brand name
4 Shrinkage expectancy
5 Special finishes
6 Care suggestions
7 Price

This information is a real asset to those who use it. Learn to understand what a label tells you. Then follow through with proper care. If the label tells you to dry-clean or hand-wash a jacket, and you wash it in the washing machine with a load of machine-washable clothes, the label will be of no help to you. You will not be justified in returning such a garment to a store or manufacturer for a refund. On the other hand, you might hand-wash the jacket as the label suggests. If at this point you find the jacket zipper has shrunk so much that the jacket is short in front and puckers, it should be returned. A reputable store wants to know when its goods are not up to standard. The store will return the item to the manufacturer. This kind of cooperation between buyer, store, and manufacturer will help produce better and more satisfying goods.

MAKING QUALITY JUDGMENTS

Quality is one of the key factors to consider when buying clothing. Occasionally poor quality may be acceptable. For instance, the quality of fabric in a fad accessory is usually not very important. On the other hand, it is quite important that clothes which will be worn many times for a number of years be made of high-quality fabric. It is also important that the garment be attractive and carefully made. The fabric should be easy to care for and the fiber content suitable for the garment.

Appearance

Whether you are buying pajamas, a winter coat, or a pair of slacks, appearance should be your first consideration. Money spent on

Appearance is the key consideration in choosing clothing successfully. *Simplicity Pattern Co., Inc.*

unbecoming clothing is usually wasted money. Style, color, line, and fabric design are to be considered in relation to your skin color and figure type. (See pages 263 through 272.) When you find the correct blend of fashion characteristics, a garment will look well on you. If such a garment is also well made, it will be a good buy.

Some people can almost be correctly labeled *lucky*. They seem to have precisely the physical build and personal coloring the fashion designer had in mind when their clothing was designed and con-

structed. However, very few people have this ideal combination of body build and coloring. It is best to make the most of the assets you have, including looks and personality.

If your body shape is not quite model-perfect and your skin color out of tune with this year's fashion colors, use the problem-solving approach. Think through your problem carefully. Choose garments which flatter you most from among the currently fashionable styles.

You might be surprised to learn that someone else would gladly exchange problems with you. People with yellow skin tones may think reddish skin is far more attractive than theirs, and vice versa. Some people want to be shorter and others want to be taller. Your own physical problems always seem biggest to you.

Fibers and Fabrics

Teenagers buy a large share of the clothing sold in the United States. Most young people need to buy outer wear, undergarments, and accessories sometime during the year. For each item you have to buy, there are specific details to be considered before actual purchase. Yet there are general fiber and fabric details which apply to most clothing items. Good questions to ask yourself before buying a garment include:

1 Are the fabric fibers suitable for the garment?

Answer these questions that relate to your own wardrobe.

1 What kind of climate do you live in (cold, moderate, warm) and what clothes do you need because of it?

2 What types of clothes are popular and appropriate in your community?

3 Who are the "best dressed" among your friends?

4 What are your main activities? How do they affect your clothing needs?

5 What season of the year are you planning for?

6 Do you have a clothing allowance? What is it for?

7 Do you keep a record of how much you spend on clothing each year?

8 Approximately how much do you spend on clothing each year? Are you satisfied with this amount? Do you feel you need more? Could you get by on less?

9 About what percentage of your wardrobe is:
 a Purchased ready-made?
 b Made at home?
 c "Handed down" to you or traded?

10 In what way are you responsible for the care of your own clothes?
 a Washing and ironing?
 b Removing spots and stains?
 c Mending and patching?

Rate your shopping IQ by answering the following questions to see how you stand as an informed shopper.

1 Do you compare quality as well as price?

2 Do you rely on well-known manufacturers who stand behind what they make?

3 Do you check the fiber content of the fabric?

4 Do you look carefully at the fabric, rejecting any garment made off-grain?

5 Do you know what information to look for on labels and hang tags?

6 Do you read labels before you buy?

7 Do you think ahead about care and know how to choose clothes that don't require too much care?

8 Do you ask yourself these two questions about the color of the garment:
a Will it combine well with other clothes in my wardrobe?
b Is it becoming?

9 Do you study the lines of a garment to see if they flatter your face and body shape?

10 Do you insist on good fit?

11 Do you look for signs of quality construction?

2 Is the fabric suitable for the garment?

3 Will the fabric performance be in keeping with that expected of the garment?

4 Are the fabric finishes desirable for the type of garment?

Suitable fibers

The fibers from which clothes are made fall into two main classifications — natural and synthetics. The natural fibers come from plant or animal sources. The animal fibers most often used are silk and wool. The common plant fibers are cotton and linen.

Before the twentieth century, all known fabrics were made from either plant or animal fibers. The natural fibers have both good and poor wearing qualities. For example, cotton is relatively inexpensive, cool to wear, and easy to launder. On the other hand, it wrinkles easily, soils readily, and doesn't stretch well with the movements of your body. Wool is warm, wrinkle-resistant, and can be tailored beautifully. However, it shrinks easily, it usually needs to be dry-cleaned, and it is attacked by moths. Similar kinds of advantages and disadvantages can be listed for all the natural fibers.

Just before the beginning of the twentieth century, scientists discovered that fibers could be made in the laboratory. Since the first of these fibers, rayon, was developed, the synthetic-fiber industry has

changed the whole world of textiles. The first manufactured fibers were made from natural products like cotton and wood and are called *semisynthetic* fibers. Now, many fibers are made entirely from chemicals and are called *synthetics*.

Most of the synthetic fibers have very desirable qualities. However, they, too, have certain poor wearing qualities. So far, no fiber has been produced that is perfect for every use.

Suitable fabrics

Does this sound like something that has happened to you? You bought a jacket that looked wonderful in the store. The color looked well on you. The lines were becoming to you. The texture of the fabric was just what you wanted. Then, the first time you wore it, it wrinkled. Worse still, perhaps the first time you washed it, it faded and stretched out of shape or shrank. Maybe it held its shape fairly well, but when you wore it, you found it was uncomfortably hot or it scratched. Perhaps you have had other problems similar to these.

Fabric performance

The fiber content will give you a good indication of the wear and performance you can expect from a fabric. Cloth made from a blend of two or more fibers performs more like the fiber which makes up the greater part of the fabric. Thus, a shirt made of 65 percent polyester

The fabric's fiber content, construction, and finish are vital considerations when you purchase a garment. Such information is found on hangtags attached to ready-made garments and to bolts of fabric.   *Cotton Incorporated (above); Celanese Fibers Mktg. Co. (below)*

Find the names of twenty-one terms related to fibers or fabrics in the puzzle below. The words are in straight lines—across, down, and diagonally. *Do not* write in this book.

```
S A R A N A V U D D V L E Q P O C U
Y I Z D A C R O N Y E G H Z O B K N
N D L I N E N Z C N R S K E L P A Y
T A W K X T B N T E E Y Q F Y U C L
H R V I C A R A S L L C K R E P R O
E V A V R T A C R I L A N A S D Y N
T A C Y A E L C R E S L A N T D L D
I N L O O O R L O N V E Y O E U I I
C O T T O N A T U R A L N E R E C D
```

Adapted puzzle used by courtesy of Wilkie and Trapnell, *Fun Things for Learning in Home Economics.*)

Hidden words in puzzle:

ACETATE	ORLON
ACRILAN	POLYESTER
ACRYLIC	RAYON
COTTON	SARAN
CRESLAN	SERGE
DACRON	SILK
DARVAN	SYNTHETIC
DYNEL	VEREL
LINEN	VICARA
NATURAL	ZEFRAN
NYLON	

and 35 percent cotton will have the wrinkle resistance and strength of polyester and be cool and absorbent because of the cotton. However, you can expect this fabric to attract oil because of its polyester content.

If you have a sweater made of wool and acrylic fibers, you can expect it to have the warmth of wool but to hold its shape and be less apt to shrink than pure wool because of the acrylic fibers.

Each fiber performs in its own way. Fabrics made of a given fiber can be judged before they are bought. If you have found garments made of a certain generic fiber, or

Copy and complete the crossword puzzle below, using a separate sheet of paper. *Do not* write in this book.

ACROSS

1 Yarns, or the direction of yarns, in a fabric
5 Fashions that pass quickly
7 Cannot be made longer in permanent-press garments
9 A color with white added to it
11 Stitch
12 A term used with fabrics like corduroy
14 A long sleeve should reach this bone
15 A stocking hazard
16 Head covering
18 One of the jobs an alterationist does
20 Should be even and invisible
22 Any pastel color (same as 9 Across)

---

fiber blend, to give desired wear, you will know what to expect from similar garments.

Fabric finishes

To overcome some of the natural disadvantages found in a given fabric, manufacturers have developed many finishes that are applied to the fabric or to the completed garment. A finish may prevent garments from wrinkling, staining, shrinking, or flaming. By reading garment labels, you can usually tell which finishes have been applied and whether such a garment will perform in a way that is useful for you.

Durable-press and permanent-press are terms frequently appearing on garment labels. Both refer to a shape-setting process which makes it possible for entire garments, if cared for properly, to be washed and worn many times with little or no ironing. This process can be applied to many types of fabrics and can be used on a wide range of fiber blends. The finish helps a fabric to stay smooth, and it helps pleats and creases to keep their sharpness. However, it can have disadvantages. The chemicals used to produce the finish may weaken the fabric so the garment will not wear as well. The durable-press finishes are cured, or baked onto a fabric. Any wrinkles or construction creases in the fabric when the cloth is cured will probably remain in the fabric for life. This can make it

---

difficult to alter durable-press garments to fit. Therefore you should be sure the length and size are both correct when you buy them. Too, the color of durable-press fabrics sometimes fades during laundering. Grease stains may be difficult or even impossible to remove.

In spite of what seems to be a long list of possible disadvantages, most people are buying durable-press fabrics. They feel that the no-iron feature outweighs the problems the finish causes. In fact, much of the clothing sold today has some form of durable-press finish.

Soil releasants were developed to overcome the tendency of some fabrics to hold on to oily soil. Such nonabsorbent fabrics as the polyesters and permanent-press fabrics have this tendency. A soil-releasant finish may be a film, or coating which protects the fibers so oil- or water-borne stains wash out easily. It may be a chemical which reacts with the fiber so that the nonabsorbent surface becomes absorbent. Fabrics treated with soil-releasant finishes should be laundered like no-iron fabrics. Oily spots can be pretreated with full-strength detergent or a prewash spray before laundering. A fabric softener can be used in the final rinse or in the dryer to help reduce static electricity.

Water repellents are applied to rainwear to keep the water out. Some of them react chemically with the fiber and will last through either dry cleaning or laundering. Another type will withstand several launderings. Then the fabric requires another treatment to restore the water repellency.

Soil and oil repellents protect wearing apparel and home furnishings from spills and stains. The fibers are coated with a finish which makes it difficult for stains to soak into the fibers. Any spill should be carefully blotted as soon as it is noticed, however. If rubbed in or neglected, a stain tends to be more difficult to remove. Scotchgard and Zepel are two common brands of soil- and oil-repellent finishes. A fabric may be made water-, soil-, and oil-repellent by spraying it.

Antistatic finishes prevent the tendency of many of the synthetic fibers, such as nylon and the acrylics, to collect static electricity. While harmless, this electricity buildup is irritating in that it can cause you to feel a shock after walking across a rug or cause a skirt or pants to cling to you.

Some fabrics are permanently treated with chemicals so that they do not collect this static electricity. Garments which do not have antistatic finishes will cling less if a liquid fabric-softener is added to the rinse water or non-woven cloth sheets containing fabric softening agents are used in the dryer. These softeners coat the fibers and thus keep them from collecting static electricity.

Flame-retardant finishes are applied to fabrics to slow their ability to burn or flame up when exposed to a source of heat. Textile companies have spent millions of dollars on research to find the best ways to do this. The earliest chemical finishes proved unsatisfactory as they washed out after a few launderings. Too, they tended to make fabrics harsh and stiff.

Children's sleepwear was the first clothing required by law to be treated for flame resistance. However, before the end of the 1970's, many more clothing and textile items will come under Federal regulations requiring this safety feature.

The best answer to the problem seems to be in the development of new fibers and combinations of fibers with a built-in flame resistance.

Construction Details

The way a garment is put together not only affects its looks when it is new, but also gives an indication of the wear you can expect. Learn to check each construction detail in a garment you are considering. Buy garments which are carefully constructed and finished. Your clothes will look better and you will feel better when wearing them.

Good questions for you to consider before actually buying a garment include:

1 Has each piece of the garment been cut straight, or on the grain of the fabric?
2 Do plaids, stripes, or prints in the fabric match at the seam lines?

24 Difficult stains to remove from permanent-press finishes
25 Extra room in a garment to allow for comfort and fit
26 A plain- or neutral-color garment
28 Decoration added to a garment
29 Fabrics that stretch with your movements

DOWN

1 Some of the neutral colors
2 Term used with seam to mean width
3 Common synthetic fiber that is very strong
4 A part of a pair of slacks
6 Changes made in clothes to make them fit better
8 Color that makes underwear invisible under light-colored garments
10 A look you achieve when you add accessories
13 Folds in fabrics that give fullness
17 Neckwear
19 Popular garment worn by men and women
21 Where pieces of fabric are sewn together
23 Pocket flap
27 Principles used in clothing design

Pull the fibers from a cotton puff ball. Twist them together to form a yarn. Make a tightly twisted or loosely twisted yarn. How do they differ in strength, smoothness, and crinkle?

Rub samples of polyester, nylon, and acrylic fabrics. Which ones resist pilling best? Which ones show the most wear? List garments you would like made from each fabric. Why?

Bring a pair of slacks or a skirt with a permanent-press finish to class. Take out the hem and try to remove the hem crease. What does this experience tell you about buying garments treated with such a finish?

Bulletin board IDEA
Title: *It's Raining New Fabrics*
Directions: Mount a construction-paper silhouette of an umbrella on the board. Place fabric swatches cut in the shape of raindrops around it.

3   Has the stitching been carefully done?
4   Are the seams well made and correctly finished?
5   Are the buttons of good quality and are the buttonholes well made?
6   Are closures, such as zippers, of good quality, well attached, and inconspicuous?
7   Are the hems of an even width and invisible?
8   Are the trimmings fashionable yet serviceable enough to last the lifetime of the garment?
9   If the garment is washable, are the linings, paddings, and interfac-

Check garments before purchase to assure yourself that they are cut on the straight of the fabric, that fabric designs match, and that seams are sturdy. *Adam Woolfitt/Woodfin Camp and Assoc.*

ings made of washable fabrics? If the garment is to be dry-cleaned, are these items made of dry-cleanable fabrics? Are they well attached to the garment?

Grain
The direction in which the yarns, or threads, of a fabric run is called *grain*. When the vertical and horizontal yarns are at right angles to each other, fabric is *on-grain*. The center of each garment piece should be lined up with the grain of the fabric. If the yarns in a finished garment slant to one side or curve upward or downward across the body, the garment will generally hang unevenly. It has been cut *off-grain*. You should avoid buying improperly cut garments.

Matching pattern
In a garment made of patterned fabric, the designs should match at the waistline, center, and side seams. Pockets, sleeves, and collars should match each other. All parts should look well in relation to the body of the garment. If plaids or stripes meet at the side seams, the lines in a well-made outfit are carefully matched. Be sure the appearance is satisfactory before you buy.

Hand or machine stitches
For a garment to wear well, stitches should be small, even in length, neat, continuous, straight, and securely fastened at the end of seams. For the sake of appearance,

thread used for stitching needs to be matched to the color of the garment.

Seams
Strong seams are important to the wear of a garment. Check to see that they are uniform in width and have been pressed as the garment was constructed. Wide seams are a mark of quality garments. They lie smoothly, wear well, and allow for alterations. Changes to make a garment larger are often impossible in garments with narrow seams. If the fabric ravels easily, the raw edges should be finished in some suitable manner which will prevent raveling. Many knit garments are made with very narrow seams that have been overcast. That is, the cut edges are covered with stitching. This is called *serging*. It makes a neat finish and allows the seams to stretch without breaking. On the other hand, it makes alterations very difficult.

Buttons and buttonholes
The main purpose of buttons is to hold a garment together. However, buttons can also add decoration to a garment. Buttons on washable clothes must be able to withstand the water movement and heat of washing and drying. In dry-cleanable clothes, avoid buttons which must be removed before cleaning. Leather-covered buttons or those with jeweled insets may be poor selections because they would be injured in the cleaning pro-

cess. Many inexpensive or bargain clothes may be improved by simply replacing the buttons. New buttons can add a new look to a garment.

Buttonholes should be neither too long nor too short to fit over the buttons easily. Check to see they are made on the grain of the fabric. Check also to see they are evenly and firmly stitched or bound and have well-reinforced ends.

Closures
Check zippers and other types of fasteners to see that the placket opening is long enough to permit getting into and out of the garment without strain. Look for a placket which lies flat and is unnoticeable. You can learn to tell by the appearance and movement of a zipper whether it will last under continued use. Since a garment is unwearable until a broken zipper is replaced, avoid garments which contain poorly made zippers. Hooks and eyes, snaps, and buttons should also be securely fastened.

Hems
Hems which are flat and even in width generally look well and hang well. The stitching is usually invisible on the right side of the garment hem. Deep hems permit lengthening, unless the garment is made of a durable-press fabric.

Trimmings
Check all forms of trimming to see that they are securely attached. Be

Have a Dye Day. Bring to school undergarments that have become discolored from improper laundering or wear. Dye some tan, dye others in colors you like. Hold the dyed underwear under a white top. Hold white underwear under the same top. Which colors show the most? Why? What does this tell you about selecting undergarments to wear with white clothing?

Dye a knit T-shirt or tank top to freshen the color. Add an applique, patch, textile paint design, or embroidery to give interest and a new look.

Dry a polyester or cotton garment in a dryer to see how it collects static electricity. Put the garment on to see how it clings to the body. Rinse the same garment in water with fabric softener added and redry, or dry with commercial fabric softening spray or nonwoven cloth sheets in the dryer.

Explain the difference in the amount of static electricity present.

Show actual garments or pictures of garments which depend on trimming, such as buttons, for the major interest. Imagine each garment without the interesting trim. Discuss the differences.

Textile Fibers

Natural fibers

Fiber	Chief uses (home and apparel)	Characteristics	Care
Cotton	Lightweight apparel—general Household fabrics—general	Is versatile and durable Endures frequent laundering Can be easily ironed at high temperatures when damp	Limited only by finish, dye, and construction of item Avoid risk of mildew
Linen	Dresses, blouses, and slacks Summer suiting Table linens and other household fabrics	Endures frequent laundering Does not shed lint Wrinkles easily unless treated Resists dye-type stains Is more expensive than cotton	Limited only by finish, dye, and construction of item Iron at high temperatures Avoid pressing in sharp creases Avoid risk of mildew
Silk	Light- and medium-weight clothing Accessories Some expensive upholstery and drapery fabrics	Is strong, with natural luster Is moderately resilient Resists wrinkling Is more expensive than synthetic (filament) silky yarns	Dry cleaning usually preferred May be hand laundered in mild suds Avoid overexposure to light Protect against insect attack
Wool	Outerwear Medium-weight clothing Blankets Upholstery Carpets	Springs back into shape Requires little pressing Has great versatility in fabrics Has insulating capacity which increases with fabric thickness	Dry cleaning usually preferred Will shrink and felt in presence of moisture, heat, and agitation, as in laundry Protect against insect attack

Synthetic fibers

Fiber	Chief uses (home and apparel)	Characteristics	Care
Acetate Acele[1] Estron[1] Triacetate Arnel[1]	Light- and medium-weight clothing Drapery and upholstery fabrics Fiberfill	Drapes well Dries quickly Is subject to fume-fading Is inexpensive Triacetate is wrinkle-resistant	Iron at low temperatures only Dry cleaning preferred Triacetate is washable
*Acrylic Acrilan[1] Creslan[1] Orlon[1] Zefran[1] Zefkrome[1]	Tailored outerwear Knitted wear Pile fabrics Blankets Carpets	Resists wrinkling Has high bulking power Can have wool-like texture, if desired Is very resistant to effects of sunlight	Remove oily stains before washing Waterborn stains easily removed Washable or dry-cleanable Iron at medium temperatures only
Aramid Kevlar[1] Nomex[1]	Protective clothing Sailcloth Marine and sporting equipment	Has no melting point Is very strong Has low flammability	Fiber is still being tested
*Modacrylic Dynel[1] Verel[1]	Deep-pile and fleece fabrics Carpets (in combination with acrylic)	Is soft and resilient Resists wrinkling Is nonflammable	Iron at extremely low temperatures only Hand washable

Fiber	Chief uses (home and apparel)	Characteristics	Care
Novoloid Kynol[1]	Flame-protective products— fire-fighter garments, work clothes, blankets, and coveralls for race-car drivers and pit crews	Is flame-resistant Has no melting point	Fiber is still being tested
*Nylon Antron[1] Cantrece[1] Enka[1]	Hosiery Lingerie Sweaters Wind jackets Dress fabrics Carpets	Has exceptional strength Has excellent elasticity Retains shape Woven fabrics are often uncomfortable in contact with skin; textured yarns are less so	Remove oily stains before washing Wash with care to maintain whiteness; washes easily Press at low temperatures May be dry-cleaned
*Olefin Herculon[1] Marvess[1]	Seat covers for automobiles and outdoor furniture Carpets—indoor and outdoor	Does not absorb water Has low melting temperature Is strong and abrasion-resistant	Shampoo with mild detergent and lukewarm water
*Polyester Dacron[1] Fortrel[1] Kodel[1] Trevira[1]	Wash-and-wear clothing—often in combination with other fibers, especially cotton Curtains Carpets Fiberfill	Has sharp pleat and crease retention Some are spill-resistant Has exceptional wrinkle resistance Reinforces cotton in durable press fabrics	Remove oily stains before washing Wash with care to maintain whiteness; washes easily Needs little ironing or pressing Use steam iron at warm setting
Rayon Avril[1] Bemberg[1] Coloray[1] Nupron[1] Zantrel[1]	Light- and medium-weight clothing Drapery and upholstery fabrics Some blankets, throw rugs, and table coverings	Is absorbent Lacks resilience; wrinkles easily Is flammable in brushed or napped fabric Is inexpensive	Dry-clean if required Can be laundered Tends to shrink and stretch unless proper chemical finish is applied Washable
*Saran Rovana[1] Saran[1]	Seat covers Screening and awnings Luggage	Resists soil, stains, and weathering Is flame-resistant	Blot stains; rinse with clear water Avoid heat; heat sensitive
Spandex Clospan[1] Lycra[1] Vyrene[1]	Foundation garments Swimwear Surgical hose Ski pants and other sportswear	Has high stretch and recovery rate Resists abrasion and body oils Discolors	Machine launder with warm water Dry on lowest heat, shortest cycle
*Vinyon	Mixed with other fibers for heat bonding	Is resistant to chemicals and light Is nonflammable Has low melting temperature	Choose care practices suitable for fabrics which have been bonded with Vinyon

General characteristics of the * fibers:
Have moderate to high strength and resilience
Are abrasion, moth, and mildew resistant
Are sensitive to heat in ironing
Resist stretching and shrinking
Are completely washable

Tend to accumulate static electricity
Are nonabsorbent; easy to wash; quick drying
Resist nonoily stains, but body oils penetrate the fiber and are hard to remove
Hold pleats because of thermoplastic qualities
[1]Trademark name

Adapted from the Textile Handbook/American Home Economics Association

Match the *fibers* given in List A with the *generic terms* given in List B. Use each generic term in List B only once. *Do not* write in this book.

List A: Fibers

A Lycra and Vyrene
B Dacron, Fortrel, Kodel, and Trevira
C Dynel and Verel
D Herculon and Marvess
E Orlon, Creslan, and Zefran

List B: Generic Terms

1 Acrylic
2 Modacrylic
3 Olefin
4 Polyester
5 Spandex

Check your answers in the chart on pages 288–289. Look for these terms on clothing labels and hangtags.

Divide into discussion groups. Each group select a clothing item such as shoes, coat, sweater, bathing suit, ski wear, undergarments, or gloves. Discuss how to judge quality and fit for that type of clothing item. Report your findings to the class.

sure they require the same care as the rest of the garment. Sometimes washable garments are trimmed with materials that must be dry-cleaned or that have been glued to the garments. Some dry-cleanable garments are trimmed with materials that must be washed. Such trimmings can result in a total loss once the garment is soiled.

Linings, paddings, and interfacings

Any materials used to give a garment shape should be made of fabric which requires cleaning care identical to that needed by the rest of the garment. If you are in doubt about the cleaning care necessary for a jacket lining, interfacings, or shoulder pads, for example, check the care label. The information on the care label will tell you what you need to know. Frequently, because of the linings in a garment, an otherwise washable garment requires dry cleaning. This additional cleaning cost should be considered when purchasing such a garment.

BUYING OUTERWEAR

Outerwear garments include blouses and shirts, pants and skirts, sweaters, coats and jackets, and dresses and suits.

In general, outer garments can be a good buy if they are made of a suitable fabric and the construction details are well done. A garment weak in several construction details might still be a good buy, however.

For example, poorly attached buttons or snaps can be quite easily fixed. Hems can be straightened, if necessary, and rehemmed with invisible stitches. On the other hand, if the fabric, style, or cut of the garment is poor, these defects can't be remedied. Try to avoid buying garments which have such built-in weaknesses.

Always try on clothes before you buy them. If possible, model them for someone whose judgment you trust. Such a person will be able to point out features you cannot see for yourself. Your main concerns are to feel comfortable and look attractive in the clothes you buy.

Coats, Jackets, and Suits

This group of clothes requires a combination of all your fashion know-how and buying skills. Each garment is a relatively expensive item. It will be worn many times; and when it is worn, everyone who sees you looks at it. There is no way to cover up a poor buy.

Most coats and jackets require dry cleaning. Knowing this, consider becoming colors which do not show soil easily. Wrinkle qualities of fabrics are also important. Since soil- and wrinkle-resistance are important, it follows that all-wool or wool–synthetic fiber combinations are fabrics to be considered.

Tailoring in coats and jackets is also important. This is, in a sense, unfortunate, because you may still need to learn a good deal about

Many large stores have several departments with a great selection of all types of garments. *Montgomery Ward*

tailoring but need to buy these items now. When shopping, look between a coat and its lining. By doing so, you can tell whether a garment has been carefully made or poorly stitched together. To improve your knowledge of tailoring, go to a high-quality store during a slow buying time. Ask the salesperson to show you the work in a coat or jacket which represents good tailoring detail. If you go alone or with an older person and show a polite interest in learning, a good salesperson will be flattered if you ask for help. With the quality guidelines you are shown, you can wisely choose coats and jackets in the price range you can afford.

Suits are the basis of many well-planned wardrobes. They may consist of matching jackets and pants or skirts or have contrasting tops and bottoms. Many growing teens find the best choice for them to be jackets and contrasting slacks that can be replaced as growth continues. Suits are usually one of the most expensive items in a wardrobe. Many other articles may be purchased to be used with a basic suit. It is important that suits be selected with variety, wearability, and appropriateness in mind.

Garments must fit well to look and wear their best. People vary greatly in size and shape. That is why manufacturers make such a wide variety

Match the *characteristics of fibers* given in List A with the *names of the fibers* given in List B. Use a fiber given in List B only once. *Do not* write in this book.

List A: Characteristics

A Wrinkles easily unless treated, luster remains through frequent launderings at high temperatures, very absorbent, may retain lint

B Natural luster, more expensive than synthetic fibers with similar appearance, fairly resistant to wrinkles

C Wrinkle-resistant, sharp crease- and pleat-retention

D Low melting temperature, no water absorption

E Wrinkles easily, only moderately durable, inexpensive

List B: Fibers

1 Linen
2 Olefin
3 Polyester
4 Rayon
5 Silk

Check your answers in the chart on pages 288–289. How might these fiber characteristics affect your clothing choices?

Analyze yourself in relation to the following questions. How can your answers help you to make wise clothing decisions?

1 What is your face shape?
2 Is your neck long or short?
3 What hair styles are most becoming to you?
4 What necklines are most becoming to you?
5 What are your nicest features — ones you want to emphasize?
6 What are your poorer features — ones you want to deemphasize?
7 What clothing lines are most flattering to you?
8 What textures do you especially like?
9 What textures are most becoming to you in terms of your size, personality, and weight?
10 What are your favorite colors? Least favorite?
11 What colors are most flattering on you, considering your coloring, size, personality?
12 What types of clothes do you prefer — sporty, plain, tailored, high-fashion, flashy, classic styles, others?

of sizes and styles. They are trying to fit as many types as possible. However, sizes are not always the same from one maker to another. Therefore, it is always best to try on any garment before buying to check fit and appearance.

When you try on a suit or jacket, check the following:

Does the coat fit smoothly through the chest and lapel area with no pulling or gaping?

Does the coat hang from the shoulders to the hem with no wrinkles or bulges?

Is the coat smooth across the back, shoulder, and neck area?

Does the collar fit smoothly with about ½ inch (1.3 centimeters) of shirt showing in the back?

Do the armholes follow the natural arm line? Are they cut deep enough to prevent binding?

Is the coat the proper length? For boys, it should be long enough to just cover the trouser seat. For girls, tailored suit jackets may be the same length or may vary according to the specific design of the garment.

Is the lining smooth and easily fitted without wrinkles? Does it allow easy movement?

If the jacket is unlined, are the seams finished neatly to prevent raveling?

Is the coat comfortable when reaching, stretching, or folding the arms?

Are the pockets flat, smooth, and well matched, with the corners

reinforced? Are the pocket linings firm and smooth?

Are the sleeves full enough for comfort and long enough to come to the wrist bone?

Pants and Skirts

Pants and skirts may be part of a suit or may be bought separately. Either way they make up a large part of most wardrobes. They are usually sized according to the waist measurement.

When selecting pants, ask yourself:

Is there a wide enough back seam to allow for alterations in the waist if necessary?

Is the seat full enough for comfort when sitting, walking, and bending, without sagging?

Is the crotch nonbinding and wrinkle-free?

Do the legs fit comfortably over thighs and calves?

Do they hang straight from the waist to the hem with the creases along the lengthwise grain of the fabric?

Are the slacks the right length? Styles in pants lengths change but usually they should just touch the top of the shoe at the instep.

When selecting skirts, check the following:

Does the skirt fall smoothly over the hips with enough ease to prevent pulling under the hips? If there are wrinkles across the front or under the waist in back, the skirt is too tight in the hips.

Do pleats hang straight and closed when you are standing?

Is the waistband loose enough to be comfortable but tight enough to hold the skirt in place?

Does the hem hang straight and even? Is the stitching nearly invisible? Can it be lengthened if necessary?

The necessary care and wrinkle-resistance of pants and skirts weigh heavily in determining whether they are good buys. Check, too, to see that seams and hems are sturdy, that zippers are strong and neatly sewn, and that the fabric looks well and will wear well.

Fads hit even the skirt and pants industry. Just about everyone oc-casionally buys one of these fad garments. Sometimes a fad grows into a fashion trend. Try to think through some of the new looks when they first appear in the stores.

A new skirt length is suddenly seven inches longer than current fashion. Could you adjust the skirt if the new length later seems too long? On the other hand, if you buy a skirt several inches longer than current fashion, is all lost if your skirt turns out to be a fad? Can you shorten it and continue to wear it? The same kind of judgment can be made with pants. Wide or flared legs can be tapered if styles change. Long pants can be made into shorter ones. Wise decisions on

Match the *characteristics of the fibers* given in List A with the *names of the fibers* given in List B. Use each fiber given in List B only once. *Do not* write in this book.

List A: Characteristics

A Withstands frequent laundering, durable, relatively inexpensive

B Absorbs moisture, slow to dry, warm, resilient

C Resists effects of sunlight and wrinkling, high bulking power

D Absorbs little water, hot to wear in warm weather, very strong, excellent wrinkle recovery

E Dries quickly, excellent drapability, may fade due to fumes in the air

List B: Fibers

1 Acetate
2 Acrylic
3 Cotton
4 Nylon
5 Wool

Check your answers in the chart on pages 288–289. Explain why it is important to know the characteristics of fibers in the clothes you choose.

Some smaller stores specialize in a certain type of clothing or cater to a special type of person.
Montgomery Ward

Match the *chief use of the fibers* given in List A with the *name of the fibers* given in List B. Use each fiber given in List B only once. *Do not* write in this book.

List A: Chief Uses

A Handkerchiefs and tablecloths
B Scarves and ties
C Blankets and winter coats
D Hose and lingerie
E Seat covers for outdoor furniture
F Double knit blended fabrics
G Foundation garments

List B: Fibers

1 Linen
2 Nylon
3 Polyester
4 Saran
5 Silk
6 Spandex
7 Wool

Check your answers in the chart on pages 288–289. Describe the characteristics of the fibers to explain why each is used for these items.

your part can allow you to be part of the current fashion scene while preventing extreme waste through poor buying practices.

Dresses

Guidelines for buying dresses are difficult to establish. This is due to a large number of varying conditions. For one thing, there are many fabrics available. The list of activities to which a dress may be worn is also varied. Too, the body build and coloring of an individual should be considered when a dress is bought.

For the most part, dresses for home and school should be washable. Party dresses may or may not be made of washable fabrics. In all types of dresses, check to see that seams and hems are firm and well made. Choose dresses you can wear for a variety of occasions. Very few people have enough money to buy a dress for each special occasion. The girl who thinks ahead to the kinds of activities she may be attending can own a few dresses which serve many occasions.

Blouses and Shirts

Blouses or shirts make up an important part of most wardrobes. The key considerations in buying these popular garments are *fabric* and *fashion*.

Blouses and shirts can be a joy to wear and care for if they are made of carefully selected fibers. Usually blends of the synthetic and natural

fibers are wise selections. For example, a polyester-cotton blend is usually very successful. The polyester gives strength to a fabric and the absorbent qualities of the cotton make the fabric comfortable to wear. If the blend has been given a durable-press finish, the garment may be an even better buy.

Fads come and go in blouses and shirts just as in all areas of the clothing industry. Try to buy *fashion*. If the collar, sleeves, and general body cut of a shirt or blouse are in current fashion, you can expect the garment to remain smart-looking during the years ahead.

Look, too, for sturdy, well-made seams, full cut through the shoul-

Besides choosing a particular color or style of a shirt or blouse, select one that will be easy to launder and will match a number of outfits.
Robert J. Capece

der area, sufficient length, well-made buttonholes, and buttons which will last through many washings. Blouses and shirts are worn often. It is rarely necessary to buy the most expensive garment available. Yet you should buy garments of a quality that will give you reasonable wear. Often the decision to spend an extra dollar or so on this type of garment is a very wise decision.

When trying on blouses and shirts, ask yourself:

Is the garment smooth-fitting at the neck without binding or pinching? Does the collar stay in place?

Is there enough room through the shoulders, back, and chest area to allow for comfort and freedom of movement?

Do the shoulder seams come to the edge of the shoulder bone? Are the armholes cut full enough to prevent binding?

Do long sleeves come to the wrist bone when the arms are bent? Are the sleeves full enough to allow for comfortable movement? Will the sleeve placket open smooth and flat for easy ironing if necessary?

Are the pockets well located, attached firmly and reinforced at the corners?

Sweaters

Sweaters almost seem to be made for teenagers, since they fit a wide range of teenage activities. Their knit texture provides *give* qualities which adjust to the needs of active people.

Fiber content is a key consideration when buying sweaters. Read the label before buying. Today's sweaters are commonly made of treated and untreated wools, synthetic fibers, and blends of these fibers. The cost of care makes the fiber selection important. Some wools are machine washable. Most of the synthetic-fiber sweaters can also be washed at home. Be careful, however, in considering sweaters which must be dry-cleaned. They may be beautiful, and they may be worth the price. Simply understand the total price before you buy. For example, can you afford a white wool sweater which requires a professional cleaning after one or two wearings? If so, fine. If not, by thinking ahead you might decide to buy an acrylic machine-washable sweater. Such planning might provide you with a clean sweater any day it is needed, instead of one which lies in your drawer a good deal of the time for lack of cleaning funds.

Another consideration in buying sweaters is the knit of the fabric itself. If the knit is extremely loose, it tends to stretch. Loose threads may hang and pull when you wear the sweater. Check to see that the sweater is big enough to allow for easy movement, especially across the chest and back areas. The seams of a good sweater are sturdy and

Bring to class a wide variety of accessories. Divide into groups and select accessories suitable for the tall, slim figure; the tall, full figure; the short, slim figure; and the short, full figure. Use the following guidelines in making choices. Defend your selections.

Tall and slim

Large accessories of contrasting colors
Bold, dramatic jewelry
Wide, contrasting belts
Full garments with bulky textures

Tall and full

Large accessories matching garments in color
Plain but unusual jewelry
Clothes with moderate flare, not tight- or close-fitting

Short and slim

Small accessories matching garments in color
Small jewelry
Narrow belts

Short and full

Narrow belts matching garments
Simple accessories
Accessories with vertical lines
Shoes matching garments in color

Present a display of do-it-yourself accessories. Include easy-to-make items such as scarves, macramé belts, and jewelry.

Play the game *Accessory Items to Ring Your Number.* Some of the most common ways to have fun with fad accessories are given below. Use the telephone dial to decode the seven accessory items given. Remember, each number identifies three different letters. For example, a "2" could be "A", "B", or "C". Number a sheet of paper from 1 to 7. Decode the following numbers. *Do not* write in this book.

5 3 9 3 5 7 9
7 2 2 7 8 3 7
8 3 7 8 7
2 3 5 8 7
7 4 6 4 7
7 6 2 5 7
7 8 7 7 3 7

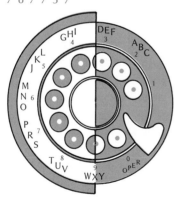

finished to prevent raveling. Buttonholes are well finished, and buttons are carefully attached.

BUYING UNDERGARMENTS

Selecting the proper undergarments can have a definite effect on both your comfort and the appearance of your outer garments. Since cleanliness is so important in undergarments, select fabrics which will hold their shape and appearance through many washings. Also, undergarments must have the ability to absorb perspiration. Otherwise, they will be uncomfortable, particularly during hot weather.

The comfort and fit of undergarments is due largely to their cut, the fabric, and how they are made. When buying underwear, look for smooth fabrics. Most underwear is usually available in knit or woven fabrics made of cotton, rayon, nylon, polyester, spandex, or a blend of these fibers. Rayon is generally inexpensive and, like cotton, is absorbent; nylon and polyester wear well; spandex is elastic. Knowing the strong feature of each fabric, you can choose underwear which best suits your needs.

When choosing underwear, also look for how it is made. Finished seams will prevent irritation as they lie next to the body. Points of strain should be reinforced.

Proper fit of undergarments is important. Underwear should be large enough to allow for easy movement and to prevent binding and discomfort, yet it should be snug enough to provide support and not bunch under your clothing. You are in a period of rapid growth. As your body changes and develops, you will find your underwear size changing, too.

The cut, fullness or slimness, and style of underwear will also affect how it fits on the body. Therefore it is usually wise to check underwear labels and compare your body measurements for correct fit. It is also advisable to try on some types of underwear, such as bras and slips, in order to help determine the correct size.

BUYING ACCESSORIES

Accessories such as shoes, hose, handbags, scarves, ties and jewelry, can change almost any outfit into something special. The knack for using accessories effectively takes a sense of adventure tempered by taste. Too many or poorly chosen accessories can overpower an outfit. Carefully selected, they can make you look fashionable and well dressed.

The wise shopper buys accessories after major clothing needs have been met. This practice prevents overspending on less important items. It also helps you choose accessories which go well with your clothes. When selecting accessories, keep your eyes open for ideas in store displays and in fashion

Consider comfort, style, and your activities when you select footwear. *Montgomery Ward*

Point out fashion changes in shoes, socks, stockings, and footwear within the last few years. Why have these changes taken place? Decide which styles make the foot look longer, shorter, wider, and narrower.

Use pictures of shoes from catalogs and magazines, or have classmates bring in various kinds of shoes. Determine the type of outfit each pair of shoes would complement. Tell when and for what occasions you would wear each pair of shoes.

Bulletin board IDEA
Title: *If the Shoe Fits*
Directions: Use a large silhouette of a shoe. Around it write briefly points to consider when buying shoes.

Your Career
Shoe Repairer

You would restore worn or torn shoes and other leather or leatherlike goods to a usable condition. You would learn the skills and gain experience in the trade with on-the-job training. You might be self-employed or work for a chain of shoe-repair shops.

magazines. Before buying an accessory, ask yourself these questions:

1 Which outfit will it go with especially well?
2 Does it go with other outfits I own?
3 Does it suit my personality?

Shoes

Because it is a necessity, footwear is the best place to begin your collection of accessories. *Shoes* is the term used most often in reference to footwear, including the different types of boots, sandals, sneakers, and slippers as well as regular shoes. They can be expensive, so try to select shoes for practical use as well as for fashion. Buy shoes of the best quality you can afford. It is smart to choose a neutral color that will harmonize with most of your clothes. Select shoes made of leather or other material which will be easy to keep neat and clean.

Select a style that flatters your feet. Simple styles in dark colors will make your feet look small. Chunky, heavy styles and light colors will increase your apparent foot size. Small-boned persons can look loaded down by footwear that makes their feet look bigger. Choose shoes for a general pleasing effect. When trying on shoes, study your total appearance in a mirror before making a decision.

Accessories add color and variety to a basic wardrobe.   *Montgomery Ward*

Since fit and comfort are of utmost importance in shoes, these features should be checked with particular care. Shop for shoes after walking awhile to allow for normal foot expansion. Have both feet measured each time you buy new shoes. Shoes should be fitted to your larger foot. Try on both shoes and walk around. Stand with your weight on both feet to judge the shoe length and width. Then check the following points:

1   Is the shoe flexible enough for comfort when you walk?
2   Does the shape of the shoe conform to the shape of your foot, with the big toe pointing straight forward and the toe cap standing above, rather than pressing on, your toes?
3   Does the widest part of your foot correspond to the widest part of the shoe?
4   Is the shoe ½ to ¾ inch (1.3 to 1.9 centimeters) longer than your longest toe when you are standing?
5   Is the fit from the ball of the foot to the heel smooth and firm without pressure or gaping?
6   Does the heel section provide firm fit and comfortable support for your foot?

Decide what style, heel height, material, and color in footwear will best suit your purpose. Before buying, be sure that both the style and materials used are appropriate for your wardrobe and that the shoes are becoming and comfortable.

Hosiery

Your choice of socks and hose will depend upon your taste, wardrobe, and activities. It is often a good idea to buy at least two identical pairs so that if one sock or stocking is lost or worn, its mate can be used as a spare.

Correct size is a major point in getting good wear from hose. It is important to know both the width and length of your foot as well as the length and fullness of your leg. If your foot is wide or narrow, you may take a half size larger or smaller accordingly. If your leg is full, you might require a longer stocking length. Many stocking packages suggest the proper size for you according to your shoe size. Wearing hose that are too short in the foot area can be as harmful to your feet as wearing improperly fitted shoes. Hose too short for you in the leg are unsightly and uncomfortable.

Handbags

Handbags, or purses, are more useful when chosen to look right with a variety of clothes — shoes, a coat in winter, and suits, slacks, skirts, or dresses during all seasons of the year. A neutral color is usually a wise selection. When buying handbags, try to choose them in relation to the size of the body and the length of the garments they will be worn with. The items to be carried will also affect the size of the bag. In general, huge bags may look wrong with short garments and small people, just as tiny bags may look wrong with large people.

Regardless of size, try to find a handbag designed to hold a variety of articles. A medium-size bag with several compartments or expandable sides will generally hold everything really needed. Such a bag is more effective than a bottomless-pit type in which things are jumbled together and lost.

Gloves

Keep glove colors simple. A pair or two chosen for their neutral colors usually provide enough variety. Gloves or mittens may also be keyed to the color of your coat or other accessories.

Ties, Scarves, Belts, and Jewelry

Accessory items can be chosen which are interesting to look at as well as becoming to you. Ties, scarves, belts, and jewelry are available in a wide variety of choices. Styles change almost from season to season. In this clothing area, the latest fads and ideas can frequently be enjoyed without the danger of wrecking your clothing budget, because each piece can be relatively inexpensive.

Accessories offer dozens of ways to give clothing a new look. You can look casual or dressed up, dramatic or conservative. Different effects can be achieved by the ways you select and use accessories with your outfits.

Your Career
Tailor

You would make garments such as suits, topcoats, overcoats, and formal clothes. You might construct garments yourself or supervise others in the designing, measuring, cutting, padding, sewing, fitting, and finishing. You might also make alterations on garments or restyle them to suit the customer's preference or fashion trends. You would find employment in a garment factory or tailoring shop, or you might be self-employed.

Bulletin board IDEA
Title: *Put Your Best Foot Forward*
Directions: Mount pictures of shoes on construction paper cutouts of shoes. Show well-kept, attractive, and fashionable shoes. Pictures could also be used of shoes which are inappropriate with the garments with which they are shown.

14 Chapter Posttest

Number from 1 to 25. Beside each number indicate whether the corresponding statement is true or false. *Do not* write in this book.

1 Two or more fibers may be blended to obtain the desirable qualities of each.
2 Fibers of similar chemical composition are classified together into generic groups.
3 The Fiber Identification Act requires that the fiber content of all fabrics be stated on a label or hang tag attached to the garment.
4 The proper way to care for a garment must be listed on the hang tag.
5 Cotton fibers are blended with polyester fibers to make a fabric more wrinkle-resistant.
6 A wool and acrylic blend will shrink less than an all-wool fabric.
7 Fashions are popular for longer periods than fads.
8 Styles stay popular for years in different fashionable versions.
9 Durable-press finishes will last as long as permanent-press finishes.
10 Kodel, Fortrel, and Dacron are all trade names for polyester.
11 Permanent-press creases are baked into cloth and cannot be pressed out.
12 Handbags and purses should be selected in relation to the size of the person using them.
13 Light-colored shoes make feet look larger than dark-colored shoes.
14 Once you find the size that fits you, it is not necessary to try on garments to know they will fit.
15 The need to iron ready-to-wear garments can be eliminated if you choose appropriate fabrics.
16 If the garment fits you and your spending plan and is well made, the fiber used in the fabric is unimportant.
17 It does *not* matter if the fabric grain of a garment is out of line.
18 Everyone should buy clothes styled in the latest fashion since fashion is the most important consideration in appearance.
19 It is usually more important to consider quality of construction in a winter coat than in a formal outfit.
20 Accessories are not important fashion items.
21 Shoes can be selected for practicality as well as for fashion.
22 Cotton fibers are wrinkle-resistant.
23 Polyester fibers are absorbent, elastic, and wrinkle-resistant.
24 Wool fibers are absorbent, wrinkle-resistant, and easily tailored.
25 There are consumer protection laws concerning fiber content, care of garment, flame retardance, and finishes.

15 Chapter Pretest

Fill each blank with the best word or words to complete each statement. *Do not* write in this book.

1 The cleanliness and neatness of people's clothes reflect their sense of responsibility and (1).
2 It is desirable to press most fabrics from the (2) side.
3 Many garments labeled handwashable may be washed successfully by machine if agitated slowly, washed in warm water, and rinsed in (3) water.
4 Fabric softeners help prevent the build-up of static electricity on (4) fibers.
5 Spots and stains should not be allowed to (5) before removing.
6 Liquid chemical solvents are used for (6).
7 Two laundry agents that should *not* be used together are soaps and (7).
8 A product that weakens fabrics if used too frequently or in concentrated form is (8).
9 If laundered correctly, minimum-care fabrics need little or no (9).
10 Moth repellents should be used when storing (10) fabrics.
11 Snaps, hooks and eyes, and buttons are usually sewn on a garment with a (11) thickness of thread.
12 Remodeling last year's wardrobe can help you save (12).

Chapter 15

Keeping Your Clothes Attractive

After reading this chapter, you should be able to:
1 Name tasks in the daily care of clothing.
2 List steps in machine-laundering clothes.
3 Give reasons for each step in the machine-laundering process.
4 Explain how to line-dry and machine-dry clothes correctly.
5 Describe how to launder and dry minimum-care fabrics.
6 Explain the differences between laundering and dry cleaning, ironing and pressing.
7 Demonstrate the correct way to wash clothes by hand.
8 Develop a plan for taking care of your clothes at the end of each season.
9 Propose ways to recycle old clothes so they are fashionable.

The difference between a well-dressed person and a poorly dressed person often lies in the care each gives his or her clothes. You may have many becoming outfits hanging in your closet. However, you cannot use and enjoy them if they are not in wearable condition. A rip in a seam, a missing button, a soiled neckline, or a spot can give a poor impression. Wearing messy or ripped clothes can make you look like a careless person. Clothes more or less show those who look at you, "I care" or "I don't care what you think of me."

Taking good care of your clothes is one of the ways you can show your family that you are growing up and accepting responsibility. Being responsible at home may even help to persuade others that you are mature enough to hold a job or to go on dates.

Complete the lines in this poem by *saying* what rhymes. *Do not* write in this book.

Since you want to be the
well-groomed kind,
Here are suggestions to keep in
  (?) .

No matter if one sews or buys,
It's important that clothes be
the right (?) .
When you stand and when you
sit,
You really want your clothes to
  (?) .

Whether your clothes are
fashion or fad,
There's no need ever to look
  (?) .
Care for your clothes the right
way
To look your best every (?) .

Carefully mend all tears and
breaks,
A little time is all it (?) .
If your clothes have been hung
with care
When in a rush you'll have
something to (?) .

For a place a button once was in
It may seem easy to use a (?) .
But take care of repairs one by
one
And before you know it, they're
all (?) .

DAILY CARE

Many teenagers feel that weekly washing and ironing is the only care their clothes need. The laundry is frequently someone else's responsibility. Unfortunately, these young people don't stop to think that daily care can make weekly clothes care easier. Brush your clothes and carefully return them to their proper places after each wearing. Treat spots and stains, and repair rips, tears, and other damage as soon as possible. Then you will find your clothes are generally in good condition and will look neat and attractive when you want to wear them.

Brushing, Hanging, and Sorting

As you hang each garment on the hanger, brush away any lint or dust that has accumulated. Place clothes straight on hangers, and button or zip them so they won't slip off. It usually takes less than a full minute to find a hanger, fit a garment on it properly, and hang up the garment to air. This is a good time to check to see if there are any loose buttons, split seams, or spots resulting from the day's wear.

Some loosely knitted fabrics stretch if hung on hangers. It is better to air such knits and then fold them neatly in a drawer. If you wish to hang tightly knitted or double-knitted garments, use padded hangers. Be sure the shoulders are placed properly on the hanger so the fabric is not poked out of shape.

If garments are hung to air after each wearing or are occasionally sprayed with a bacteria-killing deodorant, they may be worn a number of times before cleaning is necessary. *Lysol Home Service Bureau*

Wire hangers can be padded with plastic foam or strips of old towel wrapped around the upper curve of the wire.

Clothes which require washing before further wear can go directly into the clothes hamper or laundry bag. Clothes left on the floor or carelessly thrown on a chair are likely to wrinkle and soil.

Some people wash their personal things, such as underwear or hose, each evening as part of getting

302

ready for bed. Such regular washing will ensure a clean supply of these items when they are needed.

Spots and Stains

The longer a spot or stain is allowed to remain in clothes, the more difficult it is to remove. Such stains as perspiration, soft drinks, and tea or coffee can become permanently set in the fabric. Insect damage can be encouraged by certain food stains. The insects eat the fabric as well as the food. There are spot removers available in spray form, liquid, cream, and powder. Enzyme detergents and presoaks can also be used to remove spots. Most spots can be easily and quickly removed if they are treated soon after a fabric is stained. If the fabric must be dry-cleaned, take the garment to a dry-cleaner. Show the cleaner the stain, and if possible explain what type of stain it is.

Sometimes a stain is not visible immediately but will become noticeable if it is allowed to remain in the garment. This is particularly true of perspiration and sugar stains. To avoid permanent damage, wash or dry-clean your clothes often.

Mending

When brushing and hanging clothes, you may find they need minor repairs, such as replacing a button, snap, hook, or thread loop. Everyone should be able to do this type of mending. (See the illustrations on pages 304–305.) If a seam has started to rip, a few stitches on the sewing machine can repair it. If you do not have a sewing machine at home, you can use small back-stitches made with matching thread and an ordinary sewing needle.

Patches may be used to repair tears, holes, and worn spots in clothing. They can be sewn or ironed on to most fabrics. A patch can be applied from the inside of a garment so it will not be so noticeable. Patches can also be used to add decorative color and design to the outside of a garment.

WEEKLY CARE

When you get home each day, you may usually change from your school clothes into other clothes. You may not have time to do much more than brush, remove spots, and hang up your school clothes before another activity requires your attention. Sometime during the week, however, you need to set aside a certain amount of time for the care of your clothes. This care includes machine- and hand-laundering, taking items to the dry-cleaner, mending and ironing, and pressing.

Machine-Laundering and Drying

Many families prefer to own an automatic washer and a dryer or a combination washer-dryer. A source of an additional water supply, perhaps a sink, is also desirable near the washing machine. Some

A stitch in a hem should be nearly blind
And certainly very hard to (?) .
A stitch in time can save you nine
And keep your clothes just looking (?) .

If about washing you're in doubt
The care label will help you (?) .
It's a very useful guide
To help you keep your clothes with (?) .

It really doesn't take much brains
To remove most common household (?) .
A little effort, not really a lot,
Can help you get rid of most any (?) .

When you see the need to repair and mend
You may feel sorry for your (?) .
But on wardrobe care you shouldn't get burned
If this chapter you have (?) .

Knowing exactly what you should do
Keeps you from making errors (?) .
If in your clothes you take great pride
There'll be no reason for you to (?) .

STEPS IN SEWING ON HOOKS AND EYES

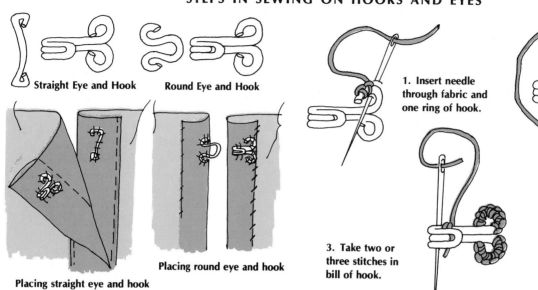

Straight Eye and Hook

Round Eye and Hook

Placing straight eye and hook

Placing round eye and hook

1. Insert needle through fabric and one ring of hook.

3. Take two or three stitches in bill of hook.

2. Bring thread under point of needle. Loop the thread in the same direction for each stitch, and pull tight.

STEPS IN SEWING ON SNAPS

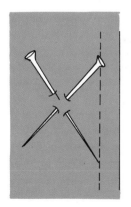

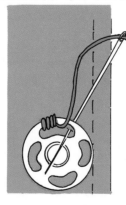

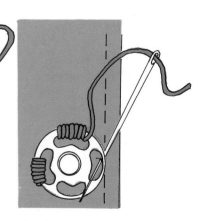

1. Mark location of snap, using two pins.

2. Take small stitch in position to be covered by snap.

3. Placing stitches close together, go over the edge of the snap and into the fabric several times. Be careful that stitches do not show on right side of garment.

4. Insert the needle under the snap and into the next hole, and continue stitching. Fasten thread on wrong side under snap when finished.

STEPS IN SEWING ON BUTTONS

1. Using double thread, take one or two small stitches at the point where the button will be attached.

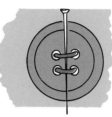

2. Hold a pin across the top of the button and take a stitch over it.

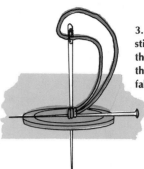

3. Take several stitches over the pin and through the fabric.

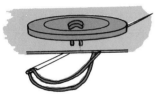

4. Remove the pin, and bring the needle and thread through the fabric.

5. Wind the thread around under the button several times to make a thread shank. Fasten the thread on the underside of the fabric.

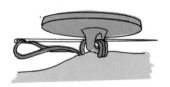

6. For a button with a shank, take several stitches over the shank and through the fabric. Fasten.

families wash their clothes at home and dry them on lines. Other families find that coin-operated washers and dryers fit their needs. Most families do have use for a steam-and-dry iron. Storage space for laundry supplies, such as detergents, stain removers, and bleaches, can be provided near the home laundry area. A hamper or cabinet for soiled clothes, a flat surface for sorting them, an ironing

and pressing board, and a clothes rack for freshly ironed garments are all useful laundry equipment.

Laundry aids

At most large stores you can choose from a large assortment of laundry aids. For general laundry purposes, you will want to keep on hand both mild and all-purpose detergents, some kind of bleach, and perhaps an enzyme presoak powder or

Bulletin board IDEA
Title: *Try Your Hand with Tricks and Trims*
Directions: Mount pictures of garments showing embroidery, appliqués, decorative patches, and sew-on tapes. Place the pictures on poster board or heavy paper cut in the shape of playing cards with rounded corners. Arrange in fan shape, as a person holds playing cards.

Observe the way television actors and actresses dress to establish the character they are playing. Make notes on the kind of clothing and grooming habits shown for the confident, happy characters, the ignorant characters, the losers, the winners, and any others you see. Draw conclusions about the importance of dress on the impression you make on others.

Discuss occasions when your appearance does *not* make any difference in the way people react to you. Do you feel people as a whole make too much or too little of the way people dress? Defend your answer.

Inventory your clothes to find those needing repair, mending, alterations, and dry cleaning. Make a schedule for doing these tasks. Report your progress.

Bulletin board IDEA
Title: *Tender Care Means Longer Wear*
Directions: Mount pictures or real items to illustrate each of these subcaptions:
1 Read care labels.
2 Follow care instructions.
3 Remove spots and stains.
4 Repair immediately.
5 Store properly.

spray spot remover. Some people, particularly those living in hard-water areas, also use water softeners and fabric softeners in their laundry.

Detergents include a wide range of cleaning agents which mix with water to help remove dirt from fabrics. There are two main classes: soaps and synthetic detergents.

Both soaps and detergents will help water as it acts to clean fabrics. However, the kind selected and the amount used does affect the cleaning process. The label on the package will give information as to when to use the product and how much of it to use. Soap and synthetic detergents cannot be used successfully in the same wash load. They work differently. When combined, they tend to react with each other instead of the soil and dirt in garments.

Bleaches are used to help remove stains from fabrics. They are effective on many kinds of stains. Yet they can be hard on or weaken fibers. Weekly bleaching is seldom necessary if fabrics are washed frequently and correctly.

Enzyme stain removers contain enzymes which act to break up stains that cannot be removed by detergents alone. Since their natural action is slow, they should be given time to work. Some people simply add the presoak powder to the laundry water. Others feel they get best results by soaking heavily stained items for several hours.

Water softeners are compounds used for softening water in areas of the country where the water supply is *hard*. Hard water contains minerals that combine with soap to make a scum, or curd, on the surface of the water. The scum clings to the fabric, and clothes cannot be washed clean. Water softeners combine with the water minerals to prevent the formation of this curd.

Fabric softeners are laundry compounds sometimes used in the final rinse water or in the dryer. As their name implies, they make the fabric soft and fluffy. They do so by covering the fabric yarns with an oily coating. This also helps prevent the collection of static electricity in synthetic fabrics.

Steps in the machine-laundry process
Whether you have your own washing machine and dryer at home or use commercial laundry equipment, there are some things to remember in getting the clothes ready for laundering.
1 Separate items into piles according to their color, the degree of water temperature to be used, and the amount of soil. White fabrics are kept separate from colored ones. Sheets, towels, and other items that need to be washed in hot water are separated from shirts, dresses, lingerie, or fabrics that require warm water. Dark clothes, especially those that might lose some color during washing, are washed separately.

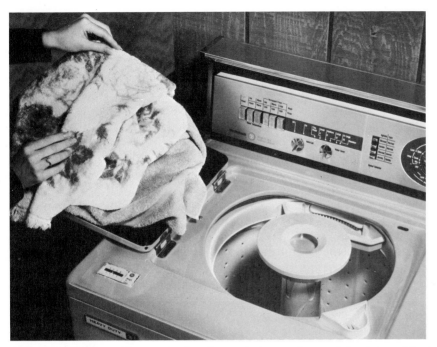

Whether laundry is done at home or in a laundromat, for best results sort clothes into wash loads of similar fabrics and colors. *Westinghouse Electric Corporation*

Experiment with different methods and products for removing spots and stains from a variety of scrap fabrics. For example, use different water temperatures — cold, lukewarm, and hot, various soaps and detergents, presoak and prewash sprays, and dry-cleaning solvents. Compare results. Draw conclusions about how to remove various spots and stains.

Your career
Clothing repair specialist

You would mend broken seams and replace buttons, zippers, worn-out pockets, and linings. You might also sew on hooks and eyes, thread loops and belt carriers, and rework buttonholes. You might work in laundries and dry-cleaning shops, or you might be self-employed.

2   Check for spots, stains, and excessive soil. Most of these can be treated successfully by using either an enzyme presoak, a prewash spray cleaner, or a full-strength detergent. Stains such as grass, perspiration, blood, and food can be removed with enzyme presoak. Oily spots and stains, which are frequently found around collars and cuffs, respond well when treated with concentrated liquid detergent rubbed directly into the soiled area.

3   Use the proper water temperature for each type of fabric. Hot water and all-purpose detergent will give good results on most white and light-colored cotton fabrics. Dark and brightly colored fabrics are best washed in cold water. Delicate fabrics, synthetic fibers, and durable-press finishes respond best to warm water and mild detergents. Cold water rinses work well on all types of fabrics and are energy-conserving as well.

4   Load the washing machine according to the manufacturer's directions. *Avoid overloading,* but do keep fuel consumption to a minimum by washing a *full* machine load each time.

Write skits or act out situations showing how conflicts may arise when family members do not take care of their clothing. The following may give you ideas to develop your drama:

Grandmother bought Lani a new dress for her birthday. Grandmother comes to visit and finds the new dress in a heap on the floor.

Jack dripped catsup on his new tie the last time he wore it. He is rushing to get dressed for a special occasion. The stained tie is the only one that goes well with the clothes he planned to wear.

Joe is going to hear a concert in the park. His favorite jeans have just split in the back seam. Mother has company and it is inconvenient to stop and repair the jeans just then.

Suggest ways in which the problem situations might have been handled to avoid unpleasantness.

Suggest methods for hanging clothes in a room without a closet. Examples might include:
Back-of-the-door racks
Portable closets
Movers' hanging wardrobe cases
A broom or mop handle fastened securely across a corner
A laundry rack

Care for clothes as you wear them

1   Avoid carrying bulky or heavy objects in your pockets.
2   Keep your hands out of your pockets.
3   Lift a tightly fitted skirt or pants slightly before sitting down.
4   Protect your clothing from food stains or spots by wearing an apron when cooking, by using a napkin during meals, and by sitting up straight at the table. Before sitting down in a place where food is served, look at the chair seat to be sure that no food has been spilled on it.
5   Unfasten a fitted jacket when you are seated. To avoid wrinkling your outfit, adjust or straighten your skirt or pants and the back of your jacket as you are seated.
6   Before lying down for a rest or nap in your room, take off any clothes that may wrinkle.

5   Use the correct amount of detergent for the size of the laundry load. Too much detergent may cause suds to bubble out of the washing machine. Nonsudsing detergents are frequently recommended for automatic washing machines because they help avoid this sudsing problem. Use the amount suggested on the detergent box. Add more later if needed.

6   When using a clothes dryer, dry clothes at the correct temperature. Untreated cotton can withstand high temperatures. Synthetic fibers require low drying temperatures. A hot dryer will set wrinkles in a durable-press garment, while a warm one will remove wrinkles caused by wear or washing. When fabrics are overdried, they tend to lose their softness. Remove clothes from the dryer as soon as the drying cycle is finished. Fold flat items and hang other clothes on hangers while they are still warm.

Hand Laundering

With today's up-to-date laundry equipment, practically all clothing referred to as *hand-washable* could be washed by machine without injury. That is to say that fancy lace-trimmed blouses, underwear, hosiery, and handkerchiefs can often be machine-washed effectively. There are, however, several *ifs* which make a knowledge of hand-laundering techniques essential for most people.

Many home-owned automatic washers as well as many of those found in laundromats have only one agitation speed. They are set to wash work clothes and such cottons as sheets and towels. This heavy agitation is hard on delicate fabrics. Many automatics are set for a hot-water wash and a warm-water rinse. Your delicate clothing will look better and last longer if it is washed in warm water and carefully rinsed in cool water. Also, it is a real temptation to mix fabrics and colors when you have only two or three delicate garments to wash. White synthetic fabrics may pick up dye from the colored fabrics and become gray or yellow.

Laundering Minimum-Care Fabrics

Whether washed by hand or machine, minimum-care fabrics require special laundry attention. If handled correctly, these fabrics require little or no ironing.

Besides knit and seersucker fabrics, there are two other kinds of fabrics that should have minimum-care treatment:

1 Fabrics made entirely of synthetic fibers or of blends of synthetic and natural fibers.
2 Fabrics treated with special resin, or durable-press, finishes.

Minimum-care garments require small washer and dryer loads to prevent wrinkling. Additional precautions include washing in warm — not hot — water and rinsing in cool water. Slow, gentle agitation during the washing period and a slow spin during the drying time are advised. If hung on a hanger to dry or if dried gently in an automatic dryer, these garments may require no ironing or perhaps just a touch-up with a warm iron.

Dry Cleaning

If your clothing budget is limited, you will be wise to consider the cost of upkeep when selecting your clothing. The expense of dry cleaning can add greatly to your total clothing costs. Some expensive clothes, garments made of delicate fabrics such as silk, and noncolorfast items should be trusted only to a commercial dry-cleaner.

Quality dry-cleaners are up-to-date on the latest developments in fabrics. They know the proper way to care for them. They can remove most spots and stains if they know what the stains are made of. If a fabric loses body and becomes limp during the cleaning process, your dry-cleaner can usually restore the original finish.

Many homemakers find they can save money and also get good results from coin-operated dry-cleaning machines. To use them successfully, be sure to follow the posted instructions carefully. Avoid overloading the machine. It is a good idea to put the light-colored clothes in a nylon mesh bag separate from the dark clothes. Do not include noncolorfast items. Spots and stains should be pretreated before garments are placed in the machine. To prevent wrinkling of the freshly cleaned garments, be ready to remove them and hang them up to air immediately after the machine stops operating.

Ironing and Pressing

With the many synthetic fibers and special finishes used in today's wardrobes, there is little need for

 Hand-wash delicate items such as underwear, a sweater, a special shirt, a tie, or hose using the following steps:

1 Squeeze gently in warm sudsy water.
2 Rub soiled areas lightly.
3 Rinse thoroughly so all soap is removed.
4 Roll in a towel to remove excess moisture.
5 Hang carefully over a line or smooth towel rack, or place on a sweater rack. Attach so the garment will not pull out of shape or snag.

Care for neckties correctly:
1 Remove spots and stains as quickly as possible.
2 Press lightly from the wrong side with a steam iron or with a damp cloth and a dry iron.
3 Hang ties on a rack or wooden hanger so they do not wrinkle.

Demonstrate ways of hanging various items on a clothesline to prevent stretching and puckering and to eliminate as much pressing as possible. Use items such as underwear, slacks, and shirts. Try to include woven and knit fabrics as well as permanent-press and regular fabrics.

Compare the unit cost of various washing powders, detergents, and bleaches. Plan and carry out experiments to compare their effectiveness. Make some conclusions about how to buy laundry aids effectively.

Dry two minimum-care garments. Dry one in an automatic dryer and the other by hanger drying. Compare the results.

Find out how to clean a steam iron inside and out. You might check use and care manuals for various makes of steam irons. You might also ask a small-appliance dealer or repair person for information. Demonstrate your findings for the class.

Show how to use a fusible bonding material to form a new hem. Make a display of commercial products for lengthening hems. Include narrow and wide bias hem facing, stretch laces, and other tapes. When might each be used most suitably? What are the advantages and disadvantages of each?

Demonstrate hand stitches suitable for mending broken seams.

Dry-cleanable clothes may be cleaned economically at a coin-operated dry-cleaner or sent to a dry-cleaning establishment. Choose either type of dry-cleaning system on the basis of time, cost, and the results desired. *Westinghouse Electric Corporation (above); Neighborhood Cleaners Assoc. (below)*

long hours spent on weekly ironing chores. However, since some ironing and pressing are necessary, the well-dressed person still needs to develop ironing and pressing skills. *Ironing* is the back-and-forth motion of the iron on fabric to remove wrinkles and improve its appearance. *Pressing*, on the other hand, involves the use of steam with an up-and-down motion of the iron to smooth and shape a garment. General hints and skills for both include:

1 Sprinkle untreated linen or cotton clothing with warm water. Fold such clothes away in a plastic container, where they should remain for an hour or so before ironing.

2 Use a steam-and-dry iron to touch up or press durable-press clothing. Fill the iron with the type of water recommended by the manufacturer.

3 Use a well-padded board or table with a clean, heat-resistant cover.

4 Set the iron at the proper setting for the fabric you are ironing or pressing. (See page 240.)

5 Remember it is the heat and the steam that remove wrinkles, *not* the amount of pressure you apply.

6 If a starch or silicon finish is desired, apply it before ironing.

7 Press with the grain of the fabric (along the straight yarns) to avoid stretching the garment out of shape.

8 Press on the wrong side of the garment whenever possible. This will help to prevent shine or scorch marks.

9 If the fabric becomes shiny when touched with the iron, use a press cloth between the iron and the fabric.

SEASONAL CARE

Most people like to dress in harmony with the seasons as much as possible. Perhaps this desire is due to an inborn feeling. Perhaps it is due to training. But when the seasons change, almost everyone wants a change of clothing. A crisp, cool autumn day may bring a desire for warm clothes in the fall colors of red, orange, gold, and brown. On the other hand, a sunny springlike day in February or March may make winter clothes seem dull and drab. You are ready for spring clothes in clear, bright shades of pink, green, and yellow.

This seasonal change is a signal that it is time to give your clothing a special kind of care. It is time to carefully clean and store the clothes from the season just ending. It is also time to prepare your clothes for the season ahead.

Storing

Because so many buildings are climate-controlled, a number of your clothes can be worn all year long. These can be kept in wearing condition all year round. However, many summer clothes should be washed or cleaned and folded away

Find a garment labeled *dry-clean only*. Determine why this garment should not be washed. Is it because of the lining, interlining, lack of colorfastness, or fiber content? What other reasons could there be? About how much would it cost to dry-clean this garment?

Compare costs, advantages, and disadvantages between dry-cleaning various garments in a coin-operated machine and sending them to a professional dry-cleaner. Why might you prefer to dry-clean one type of garment in a coin-operated machine and send another to a professional?

Your career
Professional dry-cleaner

You would clean garments and household items in solvents other than water, identify stains and remove them without damaging fibers, and finish items with special steam-and air-pressing equipment. You might specialize in one or all of these dry-cleaning procedures. You would be self-employed or work for a dry-cleaning establishment.

Copy and complete the crossword puzzle below, using a separate sheet of paper. *Do not* write in this book.

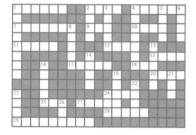

ACROSS

1 Should be removed before storing garments
2 Caused by soap in hard water
4 What a person does to fabrics at a laundromat
7 Do this to remove heavy soil
9 To place items flat to dry
10 To remove wrinkles
11 Used in measuring a hem
12 Area where soil leaves a ring
15 What a garment does when threads break
17 To put away out-of-season clothing
18 To look over someone's appearance
20 Made by detergents
24 Appearance of well cared for clothes

Hanging up your clothes or storing them neatly will protect your garments and increase their wearability.

in a drawer or box. Be sure all stains have been removed before packing the clothes. Such stains may be almost impossible to remove if allowed to remain for a six-month storage period.

There will be less chance of discoloration if clothes are simply washed and dried before storage. Both starch and heat from ironing can discolor clothes over a long storage period. Also, starch-eating pests, such as silverfish, may eat holes in starched garments left in storage for several months.

When preparing to store your cold-weather clothes, be sure they, too, are absolutely clean. Moths can eat fibers during the storage season. Garments containing wool should be protected with moth preventives of some kind. Some people prefer to use sprays, while others like to use crystal or cake types of moth repellents. Any one of these can be effective. Be sure all clothes are carefully brushed and wrapped in tissue paper or plastic. This will lessen the chance of staining or fading during storage and will help keep insects away from fabrics.

Remodeling

Upon removing your clothes from storage for the new season, you may find some of them need only pressing to be ready for wear. Others may not be in wearable condition. Perhaps hemlines need to be lengthened or shortened. A dress may have a good skirt, while its bodice is too tight. The jacket of a suit may be too tight or the wrong length for current trends in fashion.

Imagination and *ingenuity* are the keys to successful wardrobe rebuilding. Can this skirt be combined with a different sweater or jacket? Could the jacket be made into a vest? How about cutting the dress to a new length to be worn over several different skirts or pants? These are the kinds of questions you can ask yourself as you try on clothes left from last year's wardrobe. Remodeling can be a creative challenge. Building a wardrobe around last year's holdovers is less expensive and allows more variety than buying all new clothes each season.

25 Water temperature for linen
27 What careful clothing selection does to figure faults
28 Color that should be washed separately
29 A synthetic cleansing agent

DOWN

1 To sort laundry
2 Water temperature for bright colors
3 Fiber that needs special care in laundering
4 To crease by improper laundering
5 A way to wash very delicate fabrics
6 A cleaning agent that may be flakes
8 Soft, stretchable fabrics
13 To complete a hem alteration
14 Characteristic of cotton
16 To remove lint and dust
19 To hand-wash fine fabrics
21 To freshen faded colors or add new color
22 How you look when your clothes look nice
23 What clothes may do if left damp too long.
24 A garment just made or bought
26 Attached to clothes by manufacturer

Number from 1 to 26. Beside each number indicate if the corresponding statement is true or false. *Do not* write in this book.

1 The way you take care of your own clothes tells your family how mature you are.

2 The way you and your friends dress is no one else's business.

3 It is efficient to drop or place your clothes on a chair and hang them up at the end of the day rather than take time to hang them as you take them off.

4 Many out-of-fashion garments can easily be remodeled or restyled to become current again.

5 Loosely knitted garments should be stored folded or hung on padded hangers.

6 Any garment should be cleaned or laundered after each wearing.

7 Mending should be done before, rather than after, laundering.

8 Buttons are sewn on a garment with a double thickness of thread.

9 Drip-dry fabrics will *not* wrinkle no matter how you care for them.

10 Pretreatment with a liquid detergent or prewash spray will remove most oily stains from synthetic fabrics.

11 Sorting clothes by color before laundering is unnecessary.

12 Bleach should be used every time white clothes are washed.

13 Detergents may combine with minerals to form a scum or curd on the surface of hard water.

14 Stained clothes should be soaked in hot water before laundering.

15 All kinds and colors of synthetic fabrics can safely be washed together if cold water is used.

16 The most efficient way to wash clothes is to have a full load for your size washer.

17 Durable- or permanent-press garments have to be laundered carefully to avoid wrinkling.

18 All stains can be removed from fabrics with soap and hot water.

19 Clothes should remain in the dryer to cool after they are dry.

20 Spots should be pretreated before placing garments in coin-operated dry-cleaning machines.

21 All stains are removed by dry-cleaners with the same spot remover.

22 Some stains cannot be seen until a garment has been cleaned.

23 Cotton fabrics can be ironed at higher temperatures than can cotton-polyester blends.

24 Fabrics should be pressed with the grain.

25 Silverfish may eat holes in starched garments.

26 Clothes should be clean before they are stored.

Fill in the blank in each sentence with the *best* word or words to complete the statement. *Do not* write in this book.

1 The lengthwise yarns of fabric are called (1) .

2 When pressing the curved parts of a garment, it is desirable to use a pressing (2) .

3 For machine sewing, number (3) thread is most often used.

4 The lower thread for machine stitching is wound on the (4) .

5 The metal plate directly under the sewing machine needle is the (5) .

6 The device used to regulate the looseness or tightness of the top thread on a sewing machine is called the upper (6) .

7 Always thread any sewing machine needle from the (7) side.

8 A thimble is worn on the (8) finger of the hand used for sewing.

9 When the lengthwise and crosswise yarns of a fabric are *not* exactly perpendicular to each other, the fabric is (9) .

10 The greatest single aid to sewing with a pattern is the (10) .

11 In transferring construction markings from a paper pattern to fabrics, it is often possible to use a (an) (11) wheel.

12 More fabric may be needed when making a garment from fabrics with large or one-way designs, napped surfaces, stripes, or (12) .

Chapter 16

Planning Projects to Match Your Ability

After reading this chapter, you should be able to:

1 Name large equipment items needed for sewing.
2 List small equipment items needed in sewing.
3 Give the purposes of various sewing equipment items.
4 Describe what to look for when buying small sewing equipment items.
5 Describe the function of different parts of the sewing machine.
6 Cooperate with class members in using the clothing laboratory, as shown by your help in keeping it orderly and your willingness to share equipment.
7 Choose appropriate fabric and notions for your sewing project.
8 Straighten your fabric so it is grain-perfect.
9 Improve your work habits in using the sewing machine.

The variety in ready-to-wear garments available at popular prices continues to grow. Thus, it may seem strange there is also a growing trend toward home sewing. You might think families would no longer find a need to sew. Yet the reverse seems to be true. The sale of fabrics, patterns, and sewing machines has grown at an even greater rate than has our population. What are the reasons for this interest in home sewing?

Perhaps you think of home sewing as an economy. It is that. For the same amount of money, a person who has the time and ability to sew can have many more clothes than if buying similar ready-made clothing. Also, one who sews can cut garments to fit particular figure problems. What are some other reasons for the growing trend in home sewing?

SEWING LABORATORY EQUIPMENT

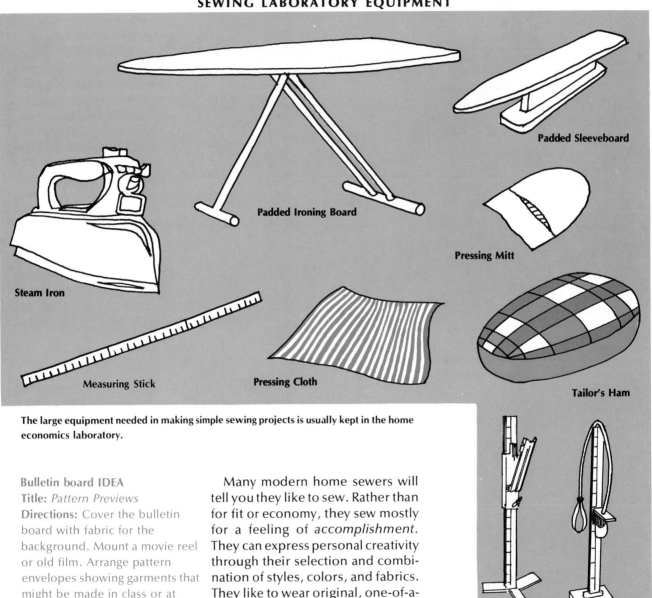

Steam Iron

Padded Ironing Board

Padded Sleeveboard

Pressing Mitt

Measuring Stick

Pressing Cloth

Tailor's Ham

Hem Markers

The large equipment needed in making simple sewing projects is usually kept in the home economics laboratory.

Bulletin board IDEA
Title: *Pattern Previews*
Directions: Cover the bulletin board with fabric for the background. Mount a movie reel or old film. Arrange pattern envelopes showing garments that might be made in class or at home.

Many modern home sewers will tell you they like to sew. Rather than for fit or economy, they sew mostly for a feeling of *accomplishment*. They can express personal creativity through their selection and combination of styles, colors, and fabrics. They like to wear original, one-of-a-kind garments. Even if they never say it to anyone else, to themselves they can say, "I made it myself."

Sewing is a skill which can be enjoyed by both males and females. In addition to home sewing, there are many career opportunities in the fields of clothing and textiles. The well-known jobs of designers, tailors, dressmakers, and alterationists are only a beginning. There are also jobs in textile research, design, and production, in pattern companies, in ready-to-wear factories, and in retail stores, not to mention a wide range of jobs in the field of sewing equipment. Anyone who senses an interest in this type of work can begin to use a sewing machine and handle fabric by making a school banner, stuffed toy, tote bag, apron, vest, or some other simple item. Even if you have no interest in sewing as a vocation, the skills you learn can be put to good use. Knowing how to sew helps you to know what to look for when buying ready-made clothes, too.

SHARING THE CLOTHING CONSTRUCTION CENTER

Just as a carpenter or a mechanic uses tools of the trade, the home sewer needs tools for sewing. Part of learning to use tools, whether at home or at school, is learning to share the responsibility for keeping the tools in place and in good repair. For instance, if a school sewing machine fails to stitch, it becomes your responsibility to report the problem to an assigned student or the teacher. Too, it is necessary for

you to put away equipment you have used. Friendly cooperation between class members will help make the laboratory serve all students more efficiently.

Most school clothing laboratories furnish the large pieces of equipment. These include sewing machines, irons and pressing aids, measuring aids such as hem markers, and other similar equipment. School money is limited and comes from your families' taxes. It is your responsibility to avoid damaging any of this equipment. Time is also important. Sometimes several people may be waiting to use one set of ironing equipment. In such difficult situations, consider the time of other students as important as your own.

SELECTING SEWING EQUIPMENT

When buying sewing equipment you will want to consider each type of equipment carefully. You may be considering a sewing machine and pressing equipment as well as the smaller sewing tools. Compare several brands of each piece of equipment before making a decision.

Large Equipment

The sewing machine is the most expensive piece of sewing equipment. Machines can be bought in portable-case models as well as built-in desk or table models. Many may be used either way. Other equipment, sometimes called large

Discuss how much money can be saved by making a garment at home. Ask people who sew what items save them the most money. Compare the amount of savings with the cost of sewing equipment. How long would it take to pay for a machine and other sewing equipment with the money saved?

Take a survey to find reasons why people do home sewing. Summarize your findings. What reasons were given most frequently?

Make a list of jobs for which some sewing knowledge and skills are needed. Describe ways you could start to earn money with your sewing skills.

Select a garment you would like to buy from a store. Note the price. Then find a similar pattern in a pattern book. Select fabric and notions and make a list of the costs. Total up how much it would cost to make the garment at home. Compare the cost of the two garments.

Under what conditions is it economical to make your own clothes? Under what conditions would it be inadvisable for a person to decide to make clothes at home?

Demonstrate the use of battery-operated, plug-in electric scissors and serrated, scalloping, and pinking shears. Give the advantages and disadvantages of each. When might each be used?

Use a pair of sharp, high-quality shears to cut and snip several slashes in different scraps of fabric. Repeat with shears that are dull or have a broken point. What did this experiment tell you about keeping cutting equipment in good working order?

Relate an experience when a person should have, but did not, use a thimble. What have you seen people do to push or pull a hand needle through heavy fabric? Why are these methods undesirable?

equipment because it won't fit into a sewing box, includes an ironing board, a steam-and-dry iron, pressing equipment, a measuring stick, a hem marker, and a padded sleeve board. In clothing laboratories where advanced classes are taught, still other equipment may be used as students work on special fabrics and more involved projects.

The sewing machine

You may find the sewing machines in your school are all alike or of

Before purchasing a sewing machine, try it out in the store to be sure you are comfortable with it. The sales person should be able to answer your questions concerning the machine. Montgomery Ward

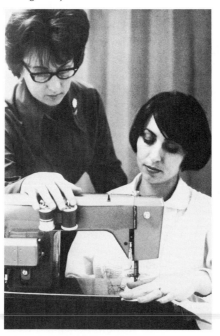

various brands and models. All brands of machines operate very much alike. Once you have learned to thread and operate one kind, you can generally, by reading the instructions, operate any machine. If you are thinking of buying a machine for home use, you will want to consider these points:

1 Buy from a dealer known for reliable service.
2 Choose a machine for the kinds of sewing you intend to do. Lightweight machines, usually less expensive than heavy ones, are easy to handle and are good for most ordinary sewing. Heavy machines should be considered if you are making slipcovers and heavy coats.
3 Be sure you need and will really use fancy stitches and gadgets before choosing a machine with such features.
4 Compare desirable features of various brands in relation to prices.

The ironing board

An ironing board is almost as important to successful sewing as the sewing machine itself. An adjustable metal ironing board or table with a clean, well-fitted, heat-resistant cover and pad will provide the necessary place for pressing large, flat areas of garments as they are being made.

The steam iron

Since moisture is necessary for effective construction pressing, a steam iron is also an essential part of your sewing equipment. A steam-and-dry-iron, which can be used for general ironing as well as pressing, is a good selection.

The press cloth

Many fabrics develop an undesirable shine when they are touched by even a warm iron. For this reason, a press cloth (usually made of a fabric similar to the garment) is used. It is placed between the garment and the iron when pressing is done during construction. For example, when a garment is pressed after the zipper is put in, the zipper area is covered by the press cloth.

The pressing mitt

Rounded or hard-to-reach areas of a garment can be pressed with the aid of a pressing mitt. The mitt can be placed over your hand or over a sleeve board. The garment is slipped over the mitt and covered with the pressing cloth. Then it can be steam-pressed into the desired shape.

The tailor's ham

A well-made garment is *blocked*, or steam-shaped, to fit your body. By using the tailor's, or pressing, ham you can shape a garment to fit the curves of your body. A tailor's ham is used with the ironing board and steam iron. Darts create the curves in the garment and should always be pressed over a pressing ham rather than flat.

The measuring stick

A measuring stick is used for drawing long, straight lines. It is used to check grain lines and to mark hems during the construction of projects. Measuring sticks are also called yardsticks or metersticks depending on the units of measure marked on them.

The hem marker

An adjustable hem marker consists of a measuring stick placed upright on a base of some kind. It may require the use of pins or chalk to mark a desired length from the floor. The pin marker is more accurate but must be used by a helper. You can use the chalk marker by yourself. Be careful, however, that the chalk marks are not dusted away as you pin the hem into the garment.

The padded sleeve board

The sleeve board can be used for much steam pressing during the construction of a project. A sleeve can be slipped over it wrong side out, and the seam easily pressed open. If the board is well padded, it can also be used when sleeve caps and other small circular garment areas are steamed into shape.

Your Small Equipment

Having your own sewing tools handy when you need them contributes to the success of early sewing experiences. Such tools include a supply of needles, pins, and

 Copy and complete the puzzle below, using a separate sheet of paper. Find the proper places in the spiral for the names of the small sewing equipment items in the list given. Some of the letters have been filled in for you. *Do not* write in this book.

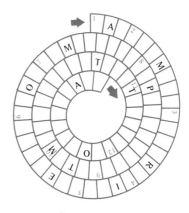

Sewing Equipment

Ironing board	Mitt
Ham	Thimble
Iron	Pins
Hem marker	Thread
Shears	Needle
Measuring stick	Tape measure

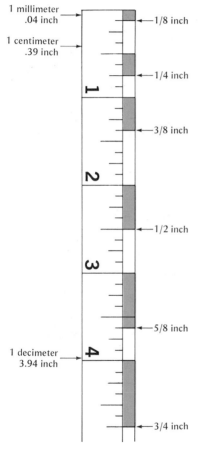

1 millimeter .04 inch → | ←1/8 inch

1 centimeter .39 inch → | ←1/4 inch

1 | ←3/8 inch

2 |

| ←1/2 inch

3 |

| ←5/8 inch

1 decimeter 3.94 inch → 4 |

| ←3/4 inch

thread, as well as scissors or shears, a thimble, a tape measure, and a small ruler or hem gauge. Mark each item with your name and class section. Misplaced items can then be returned to you.

Scissors and shears

Scissors and shears differ in their sizes and uses. For cutting your garment from fabric, select shears with bent handles. Such shears make it easier to cut the fabric while it is flat on the table. Small sewing scissors are good for most small cutting jobs necessary while the garment is being made. Pinking shears are only used to finish seams after the garment is fitted and stitched.

Both scissors and shears will keep their cutting edges well if they are made of good steel. Be sure they are sharp. They will stay sharp if they are used only for cutting fabrics, not for cutting paper or other things around the house and school. Keep them in a dry place and avoid dropping them. At home, keep them out of reach of small children.

Tape measure

A tape measure is useful and necessary in accurate clothing construction. Select one made either of plastic or of a strong fabric that will not stretch when it is used. The tape should have metal tips on each end to protect it and to help in accurate measurements. For convenience in use, select a tape measure that is 60 inches (153 centimeters) long and clearly numbered in opposite directions on the two sides.

Pins

Dressmaker's pins are thin and sharp. Because they are made of brass or stainless steel, they are rustproof. Size 17 is a good choice. Dressmaker's pins may have either metal or plastic heads. They may have sharp or ball points. They are available in paper packages or in 1/4- and 1/2-pound (113.5- and 227-gram) boxes.

Pincushion

Pincushions may be purchased in many sizes and shapes. They are also fairly easy to make. You may find that a small cushion that fits over your wrist with either a plastic or elastic bracelet will keep your pins handy at all times.

Tracing wheel

Tracing wheels are used to transfer the construction markings from patterns onto fabrics. They are very useful sewing tools, and many students want to buy one of their own. Marks made by a tracing wheel help you know how to put a garment together. Tracing wheels are available with very sharp teeth or smooth, round discs. However, most beginners find a wheel with rather blunt teeth works best for marking regular lightweight to medium-weight fabrics.

SMALL SEWING EQUIPMENT

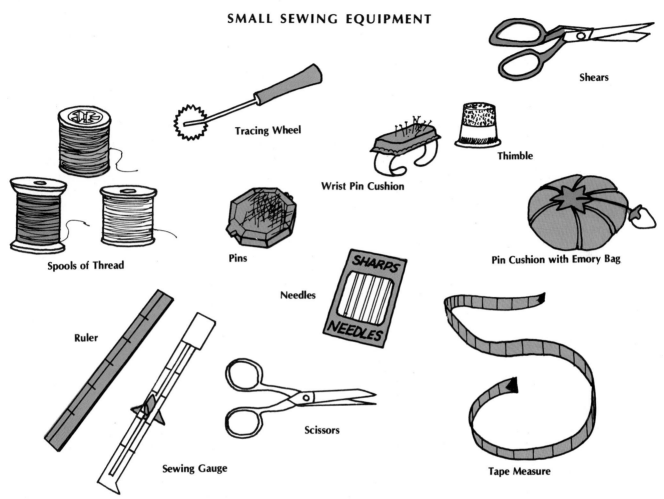

Tracing Wheel

Shears

Thimble

Wrist Pin Cushion

Spools of Thread

Pins

Pin Cushion with Emory Bag

Needles

Ruler

Scissors

Sewing Gauge

Tape Measure

The small equipment needed in making simple clothing projects is usually owned by individual students and kept in boxes or tote trays provided by the school.

Needles

Needles are sold in variety packages or in regular packages of twelve and twenty-four. They vary in size from 1 to 12. The smaller the number, the larger the needle. For ordinary sewing, size 7 or 8 needles are a good choice. Be sure they are sharp and rust free. To keep your needles sharp, you can use a small emery bag. These bags are filled with finely ground metal. Needles can be sharpened by slipping them into and out of the bag.

Bulletin board IDEA
Title: *Don't Forget*
Directions: Mount a cutout of an elephant. List or illustrate clothing construction supplies students are expected to bring to class.

321

Identify the information found on the spool labels shown below. What would be helpful to you as a consumer? Why do you need this information?

Silk

Synthetic

Mercerized Cotton

Heavy Duty

Thread

Thread is made of different fibers and in a variety of sizes and colors. Mercerized cotton thread was the strongest and most popular for many years. It is still a good choice for many fabrics. It is sized by numbers from 8 to 100. The larger the number, the finer the thread. For ordinary machine sewing, number 50 is most frequently used. Number 40, or heavy-duty thread, is suitable for slipcovers and other heavy sewing. Numbers 80 to 100 are used only for very sheer fabrics.

In addition to cotton thread, there are other kinds available. The list includes linen, silk, monofilament nylon, polyester, and cotton-covered polyester. Synthetic-fiber threads are strong and stretchable. As threads become stronger, there is a trend toward producing them in only one size. Cotton-covered polyester threads sew like all-cotton but have the strength of polyester. They do not cut into fabrics the way some all-synthetic threads do.

In selecting thread for a specific project, choose synthetic thread for synthetic fabrics, silk thread for animal-fiber fabrics, and mercerized cotton for cotton fabrics. As nearly as possible, match the thread color to the predominant color in the fabric. In keying thread to fabrics, choose thread which, on the spool, appears slightly darker than the fabric itself. Thread looks lighter after you have stitched it into the fabric.

Thimble

A thimble is used to protect your finger from the needle when you are hand sewing. Some beginning sewers think a thimble is more of a nuisance than a help. In a way, a thimble is a little like a pair of glasses. It may be hard to get used to, but after you have learned to use it, you wonder how you ever got along without it.

In selecting a thimble, try several different sizes on the middle finger of the hand with which you sew. A thimble should fit comfortably. It should be tight enough to stay on your finger when you shake your hand, but loose enough not to pinch the end of your finger.

Sewing gauge

A sewing gauge is useful for measuring and marking hems, buttonholes, pockets, and seams. It may be made of metal or plastic and should have a sliding marker.

CHOOSING A PROJECT

Try to choose a first project which will give you plenty of opportunity to practice using the sewing machine. Be realistic as you search for a project. Choose something you are fairly sure you will be successful in making. Also, your choice should be something you'd like to own.

Sometimes students become discouraged about sewing and give up after their first attempt. It is unreasonable to expect perfection on

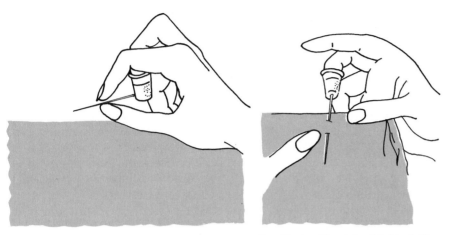

To use the thimble while hand sewing, push the needle with the side of the thimble (left) or with the end of the thimble (right). Practice with an unthreaded needle.

Make a tailor's ham following the directions below.
Discuss why the use of such equipment will improve the appearance of a garment you might make.

Make the ham with a wool cover on one side and a heavy cotton cover on the other side.

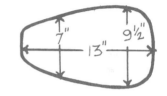

your first project. Don't be upset over mistakes. There is seldom one that can't be corrected.

The first thing you attempt to make should be simple enough to complete in a few class periods or a relatively short time. Such a project can help you build self-confidence as well as skill.

If you elect to make something such as a sewing or barbecue apron that does not require a pattern, but can be made by cutting the pieces into the proper shapes, you will save money, time, and effort. You can learn to handle the sewing machine before struggling with other problems, such as using patterns, marking fabrics, and fitting garments.

Projects Requiring Patterns

If you decide to use a pattern for your first project, try to find a very simple one. Perhaps your teacher will suggest one or two patterns that will be suitable for you to work on.

You are more likely to be successful with your first project if you choose something simple. Consider making a beach poncho, a toy animal, a vest, or a shirt which has no more than two or three basic pattern pieces. The pattern you select should be marked with such words as *easy to make*.

SELECTING FABRIC

Beginning projects require sturdy, easy-to-handle fabrics. In your rush to make something you may want to buy a shiny, slippery fabric for a special effect. This could be a serious mistake. Just one failure at the beginning could cause you to lose interest in sewing altogether.

Cut two pieces of fabric according to the dimensions shown above. Sew the pieces together, right sides together, with a ⅜-inch seam. Leave a 2-inch opening at the large end. Press the seam and turn the cover right side out.

Stuff the ham as tightly as possible with clean builder's sand, pitch-free sawdust, or wool scraps. Hand-sew the opening together. The ham is correctly about 5 inches thick when finished.

Make fabric grain-perfect before cutting the pieces of a garment. When a fabric is off-grain, it cannot be folded straight. Either the torn edges will be uneven (a), or the selvages will be uneven (b). By pulling the fabric on the bias or by machine-stitching and steam-pressing, most woven fabrics, except durable pressed ones, can be straightened (c).

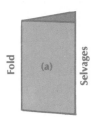

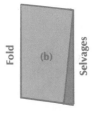

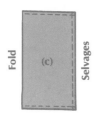

Your first project is for learning to use the sewing machine. You may need to rip some stitches. You may need to press creases which will stay in the cloth. Take all of these things into consideration. Try to choose fabric which will encourage success.

Choose Sturdy Fabric

Don't be surprised if your family feels you should buy inexpensive fabric for your first project. They may feel you will become tired of your project and discard it after it is finished. Too, they may feel such fabric is fine to practice on. They may be right. On the other hand, low-quality fabric may not last long enough for you to complete your project. It could lose its shape while you are working on it. It might fade, stretch, or shrink the first time it is washed.

Since much of the fun and satisfaction of sewing is being able to wear or use something you make yourself, try to buy an attractive and sturdy piece of fabric. It can be discouraging if all your work in learning to sew is for practice only.

Choose Preshrunk Fabric

Some synthetic fabrics do not seem to shrink to any great degree when they are washed. But cotton, linen, and wool, the washable natural fibers, as well as rayon, have always given a certain amount of shrinkage trouble to both manufacturers and home sewers. If you are consider-

ing one of these fabrics, or a blend of them, check very carefully for shrinkage-control guarantees before buying the fabric.

Most of today's fabrics are preshrunk. They have been treated in such a way so they will not shrink enough to make a garment unwearable after washing. However, it is wise to check the label before buying any fabric. Imported fabrics may or may not be labeled.

Sanforized is a trademarked shrinking process. It guarantees that the fabric will shrink no more than 1 percent. If a fabric is simply marked *preshrunk*, you need to know how much additional shrinkage to expect. Some preshrunk materials may still shrink enough to make them unwearable, while others are within the bounds of safety. If a label says a fabric will shrink no more than 2 percent, you can buy with assurance. Such a fabric will not need home shrinking.

Avoid fabrics which are not preshrunk. Home-shrinking methods are bothersome, messy, and time consuming. By buying only clearly labeled, preshrunk materials, you, as a consumer, are encouraging manufacturers to shrink fabrics effectively before putting them on the market for purchase.

Choose Easy-to-Handle Fabrics

Fabrics vary considerably in the ease with which they may be handled. Before you buy, try to determine whether your fabric will be

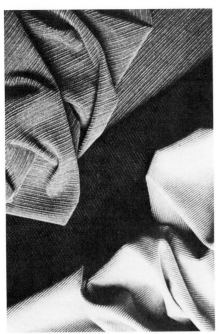

For beginning sewers, fabrics that are neither too stiff nor too bulky are easier to work with. *Cotton, Inc.*

easy to handle. This means easy to cut, easy to stitch, and easy to press.

Some fabrics made of nylon, acetate, and polyester slip and slide around on the sewing machine and are difficult to stitch straight. Some very bulky fabrics are difficult to cut. Some knit fabrics stretch while you are working on them and pucker at the seams. Some fabrics are so firmly woven that pin and needle marks show. If you rip out and replace stitches, the first needle holes continue to show. Other fabrics tear when you are ripping out unwanted stitches. Still others are

very loosely woven or have loops that catch on the presser foot of the machine while you are stitching.

In general, cotton or cotton-synthetic blends with a firm weave and dull finish are easy to work on. Try to find one of these materials for your beginning project.

Effects of fabric design on sewing projects

From year to year the kinds of designs in fabrics change with the current fashions. Sometimes large, splashy prints are popular. Sometimes plaids and stripes are big fashion news. Sometimes small all-over prints are very popular. Solid colors, however, are usually fashionable. Your choice of fabric will depend to some extent upon what is popular and available in the stores. In making your choice, consider how fabric designs may affect the difficulty of a project.

1 Large designs must be placed carefully so the finished garment will appear balanced. If there is a huge flower on one sleeve, the shirt will look one-sided if the other sleeve is rather plain. A large design generally is more pleasing if centered in the garment or balanced in its distribution. Large designs are difficult to work with, and extra fabric may be required because of the waste involved in balancing the design.

2 Stripes, plaids, and large checks are difficult designs for

View the sketches below to see how the placement of dominant lines in a striped fabric call attention to certain parts of the body.

What does this tell you about the placement of dominant lines to emphasize your good features? What does it tell you about the placement of dominant lines if you do *not* want to call attention to certain parts of your figure? What conclusions can be made relating to the placement of dominant parts of a patterned fabric?

Observe in the garments below the effects of mismatched and matched plaids.

Why is the matched plaid more pleasing to the eye? What special problems are there when making a garment from a striped or plaid fabric?

Your career
Fabric coordinator

You would study fabric, fashion, and color trends to select suitable fabrics for garments each season. You might specialize in selecting fabrics for one line of clothing such as sportswear, or be responsible for assembling fabrics for display garments and fashion show collections. You would find employment with garment manufacturers, pattern companies, and fabric stores.

a beginner. They should be cut and stitched to match at the center front, center back, and side seams. It is best to wait until you have mastered many of the other sewing skills before you attempt this matching problem.

3   Plain fabrics might seem to be the best choice as there is no problem relating to matching designs. However, the loss of one problem creates another one. On plain fabric, all top stitching is very noticeable. This means that stitching must be straight. If you need to rip out stitches during your work, the marks of the old stitches may be hard to remove.

4   Small all-over designs are usually the easiest to work with. They do not require matching or balancing in a garment. Also, stitches or the marks of ripped-out stitches blend with the fabric.

Effect of fabric grain on sewing projects

Grain refers to the yarns with which the fabric is woven or knitted. In woven fabrics, the yarns that run parallel to the selvage or woven edges are called the *warp*, or lengthwise grain. The yarns that interlace with the warp yarns are called *filling*, or crosswise grain. These yarns should be absolutely perpendicular to each other. If so, they are said to be *grain-perfect*.

With new fabric construction methods and special finishes becoming so common, the grain may

not affect the way a garment hangs. However, grain is still important to both the way the fabric will handle and the looks of the finished product.

If something has happened in the manufacturing process to make the warp and filling yarns run untrue, or not perpendicular, the fabric is said to be *off-grain*. Fabrics go through so many processes while the designs, colors, and finishes are applied that it is easy for them to become off-grain. If this has happened to a fabric you are considering, check the label to see whether a durable-press finish has been ap-

Fabric which is properly prepared for cutting is grain-perfect. As such, lengthwise yarns are absolutely perpendicular to crosswise yarns. *Coats & Clark Inc.*

For fabrics

To convert fabric widths and yardages from inches and yards to centimeters and meters, compare what is listed in each yardage block to the chart below.

Fabric widths	in	cm	in	cm	in	cm	in	cm	in	cm	in	cm	in	cm	in	cm
	25	65	27	70	35	90	39	100	42	107	45	115	54	140	60	150

Yardage	yd	m	yd	m	yd	m	yd	m	yd	m	yd	m	yd	m	yd	m
	⅛	0.15	¼	0.25	⅜	0.35	½	0.50	⅝	0.60	¾	0.70	⅞	0.80	1	0.95
	1⅛	1.05	1¼	1.15	1⅜	1.30	1½	1.40	1⅝	1.50	1¾	1.60	1⅞	1.75	2	1.85
	2⅛	1.95	2¼	2.10	2⅜	2.20	2½	2.30	2⅝	2.40	2¾	2.55	2⅞	2.65	3	2.75
	3⅛	2.90	3¼	3.00	3⅜	3.10	3½	3.20	3⅝	3.35	3¾	3.45	3⅞	3.55	4	3.70
	4⅛	3.80	4¼	3.90	4⅜	4.00	4½	4.15	4⅝	4.25	4¾	4.35	4⅞	4.50	5	4.60
	5⅛	4.70	5¼	4.80	5⅜	4.95	5½	5.05	5⅝	5.15	5¾	5.30	5⅞	5.40	6	5.50
	6⅛	5.60	6¼	5.75	6⅜	5.85	6½	5.95	6⅝	6.10	6¾	6.20	6⅞	6.30	7	6.40

Reprinted from THE VOGUE SEWING BOOK, Revised Edition, with permission of Butterick Publishing

plied over the fabric. If so, the threads will be permanently held in the off-grain position and cannot be straightened. If it does not have a durable-press finish, it can probably be made grain-perfect with heat, moisture, or tension.

Sometimes the designs are printed crooked or off-grain. Check the *selvage* (woven edge) of the fabric to see that the design is straight along the edge and doesn't run off the cloth. Check the torn or cut end of the fabric for the same thing. If the design is printed off-grain, buy from another bolt of fabric.

Key Points in Buying Fabric

A fabric is a good buy if you can answer yes to the following:

1 Ease of handling: Will fabric stay in place on the sewing machine or table and be easy to hold?

2 Sturdiness: Will fabric hold its shape without stretching easily when worked on?

3 Strength: Will the fabric remain intact when ripping is necessary?

4 Shrinkage: Is the fabric guaranteed to shrink no more than 2 percent when it is laundered or dry-cleaned?

5 Design: Will it be easy or unnecessary to match designs in putting the garment together? Can mistakes be hidden by the design itself?

6 Grain: Are the lengthwise and crosswise threads at right angles to each other, allowing the fabric to hang straight?

Your career
Textile tester

You would work in a laboratory testing the properties of fibers, fabrics, and finishes, then reporting on your findings. Testing might be done to discover a fabric's strength, flame-resistant or absorption qualities. You would work for textile manufacturers or private testing laboratories.

Imagine how a garment would look if it were cut from a fabric with a directional pattern and some of the pieces were cut incorrectly. Observe the sketch below.

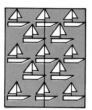

Preparing the Fabric

If fabric was carefully checked in the store before purchase, pressing may be all that is necessary before you begin your project. However, there may be reasons why you wish to use fabric which is less than grain-perfect. A bargain buy or a gift fabric may have become stretched on the bolt. There are ways to correct such imperfect fabrics, but they take time and energy.

Straightening the grain

Before cutting into any fabric, check to see that it is grain-perfect. To do so, fold the fabric down the center with the selvages straight along the edge of the table. Smooth out the wrinkles. If the fabric is straight, the torn or cut edges will fit together perfectly and the fabric will lie flat. If the fabric is stretched out of shape, one layer will be longer on the corner than the other. If the ends have been cut unevenly, you will need to straighten them by cutting along a pulled yarn. If the edges were torn but do not fit together, do not cut off the excess. Fabric tears along the straight thread. Uneven ends mean one side has stretched more than the other. Sometimes this stretching can be corrected by hand. To do so, grasp the fabric by the shorter end and pull it carefully.

Pin together the cut edge, if it follows one thread, or the edges which have been torn at each end of the fabric, and pin the selvages. If the fabric does not lie flat with all of the edges pinned together, you will need to *block* it. Blocking is done with a steam iron. Gently lower the steaming iron to the fabric. Then lift, lower, lift, lower, until all the fullness and wrinkles have disappeared and the fabric is straight and flat.

USING THE SEWING MACHINE

Sewing machines come in many price ranges and styles. Having a variety of machines in school gives the student an opportunity to become acquainted with more than one type. However, having all one kind of machine makes it possible

Many modern sewing machines offer such features as self-winding bobbins, built-in buttonhole makers, dial-a-stitch mechanisms, special stretch stitches for knit fabrics, and the chain stitch for basting. *Viking Sewing Machine Co.*

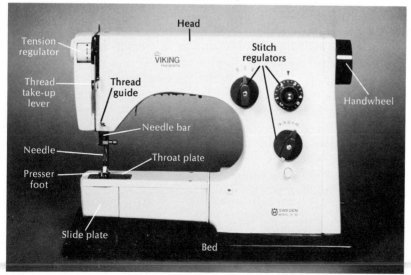

Parts of a sewing machine

1 *Head:* Portion of the machine which contains most of the sewing parts.
2 *Bed:* Flat base of the head which rests in the cabinet.
3 *Handwheel* or *balance wheel:* Wheel at the right of the upright section of the head, used in starting and stopping the machine.
4 *Bobbin:* Spool which holds the lower thread in stitching. It fits into a *bobbin* case, or *shuttle.*
5 *Slide plate* (or *bed slide*): Metal plate covering the bobbin case, or shuttle, which carries the lower, or bobbin, thread.
6 *Spool pin* and *thread guides:* Pieces which hold and guide the upper thread in stitching.
7 *Needle bar:* Piece that holds the needle and carries the upper thread down to the needle.
8 *Needle:* Thin metal shaft with an eye and a point at one end. It is inserted into the needle bar and held in position with a clamp. It carries the thread through the fabric.
9 *Presser foot:* Piece which holds the fabric in place as you stitch. It is raised and lowered by means of a lever called a *presser-bar lifter,* found on the back of the machine. For stitching, the presser foot is lowered gently, with the fabric in place. It is then raised when the fabric is removed after the stitching is finished.
10 *Throat plate:* Metal plate directly under the needle.
11 *Throat-plate positioning lever:* Lever on the front of the bed of some sewing machines. It regulates the up-and-down position of the throat plate for general sewing, darning, embroidering, or button sewing, and it unlocks the throat plate for removal.
12 *Feed* or *feed dog:* Toothlike part located under the pressure foot. It projects upward through the throat plate. This part keeps the material moving along toward the back of the machine as it is being stitched.
13 *Stitch regulator:* Device usually located on the right portion of the head for lengthening or shortening the stitch.
14 *Thread take-up lever:* Lever through which the upper thread passes and which moves up and down as the machine is operated.
15 *Upper tension:* Device which regulates looseness and tightness of the stitch by controlling the pull on the thread as it comes from the needle. There is a similar tension on the bobbin thread.

Find the numbers of the pattern pieces placed incorrectly for a napped or directionally designed fabric.

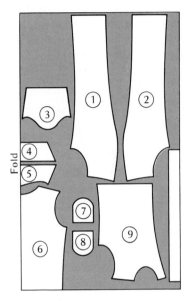

Your career
Converter

You would purchase large bulks of loomed or knitted fabric from mills to do the necessary finishing to make attractive, serviceable, fashionable, and salable fabrics. You would give instructions for special bleaches, dyes, prints, and finishes to be applied to the fabric. You would work for a textile manufacturer or be self-employed.

Observe stitches made on various sewing machines. Determine if the tensions are adjusted correctly. Beginners can usually adjust the upper tension. Correction of the bobbin tension requires the attention of an expert.

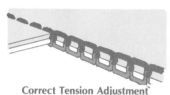

Correct Tension Adjustment

When both tensions are in adjustment, the needle and bobbin threads are locked in the center of the fabric.

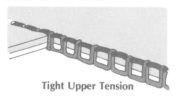

Tight Upper Tension

When the tension on the needle thread is too tight, the needle thread will lie straight along the upper surface of the fabric.

Loose Upper Tension

When the tension on the needle thread is too loose, the bobbin thread will lie straight along the under side of the fabric.

to interchange bobbins and other small parts. You can use different machines on different days without the need for winding a new bobbin.

You will find it is easier to understand your teacher's directions if you take the time to learn the correct names of the various parts of the machines you will use. (See pages 328 and 329.)

Threading the Sewing Machine

Before threading the machine you plan to use, study the instruction booklet. Perhaps your teacher has a large chart for you to follow. Every model of sewing machine is threaded in its own particular way. However, there is a general procedure which is similar for threading most machines. It follows this order:

1 Raise the presser foot to the *up* position with the presser-bar lifter. With the handwheel, raise the take-up lever to its highest position.
2 Put the thread on the spool pin. Keep one hand on the spool to hold the thread firm as you thread.
3 Pull the thread through the top thread guide or guides.
4 Continue pulling it through the tension discs.
5 Find the next thread guide and secure the thread in it.
6 Feed the thread through the take-up lever.
7 Continue pulling the thread through any other thread guides you find.

8 Thread the needle from the same side as the last thread guide. There will be a long groove running down the side of the needle on this side.
9 Pull the thread through the needle for 4 or 5 inches (10 or 12.5 centimeters).

Types of Bobbins

In general, there are two kinds of sewing machine bobbins. One is called the *conventional* bobbin because it has been used in various brands of machines for many years. The other is called the *self-winding* bobbin. As the name implies, this bobbin almost fills itself.

Filling the conventional bobbin

Most bobbins are filled on a special spindle on the surface of the machine head. The filled bobbin is then inserted into the lower part of the machine. It supplies a second thread so the machine can make a durable locked stitch. To fill the conventional bobbin, follow these steps:

1 Unscrew the smaller knob in the center of the balance wheel to disengage the wheel.
2 Place the bobbin on the bobbin winder, and snap it into position. (Check the instruction booklet for your machine.)
3 Place the spool of thread on the bobbin thread pin, and pull the thread through the thread guide, which holds it firm. Then thread it through one of the small

holes from the inside of the bobbin to the outside. Hold this thread with your left hand.

4   Apply pressure to the knee or foot lever and watch the thread wind evenly and smoothly. If it does not, recheck each step.

5   When the bobbin is full, it will snap out of the winding position automatically. Tighten the balance wheel.

6   Open the slide plate and place the bobbin in the bobbin case or shuttle according to the instructions in the sewing machine booklet. Grasp the end of the top thread in your left hand. With your right hand, turn the balance wheel, or handwheel, one complete turn. As the needle is lowered and raised, the top thread loops around the bobbin thread and pulls it back through the needle hole in the throat plate.

7   Pull the bobbin thread up and pull both threads to the back under the presser foot for about 4 or 5 inches (10 or 12.5 centimeters).

8   Close the slide plate. You are ready to sew.

The self-winding bobbin

For certain sewing machines, the bobbin can be filled while it is fastened securely in the bobbin case. In most of these machines the bobbin is located in the lower part of the machine. Thread is supplied to the bobbin from the spool on top of the threaded machine. To fill the self-winding bobbin, follow carefully the instructions in the machine manual. If you forget a step or make a mistake, the machine may become jammed.

Caring for the Machine

Every machine will operate better if you take good care of it. Keep the working parts of the machine free of loose threads and lint. Use a small brush rather than a pointed object to do this. Oil the machine regularly, depending upon how much it is used. If the machine becomes noisy or stiff, it probably needs oil. Some machines may have a small dot of color, such as red, on the spots to be oiled. Or you may need to refer to the machine manual for directions. One drop of oil at each place shown is usually enough. It is unwise to use more than one drop. The machine may then become gummy from too much oil. Or oil may leak onto the fabric as you sew. After you oil the machine, it is a good idea to sew on a scrap of fabric before sewing on garment pieces.

Adjusting the tension

The tension on the top and bobbin threads should be adjusted to each other so that the two threads meet and interlock evenly between the two layers of fabric being stitched. Test the stitch on a scrap of fabric before sewing to be sure it is threaded correctly and the tension is right. If the top thread lies straight

 Earn a SEWING MACHINE OPERATOR'S LICENSE. Obtain your operator's license before beginning to construct your clothing project. Use the following idea as a guide for the license to be issued in your class.

SEWING MACHINE
OPERATOR'S LICENSE
DATE   SCHOOL
NAME
ADDRESS
GRADE
      HOME ROOM
      TEACHER
THE STUDENT NAMED ABOVE
HAS MET REQUIREMENTS
FOR OPERATING THE
SEWING MACHINE
NONTRANSFERABLE

REQUIREMENTS
SATISFACTORY SKILLS
IN THE FOLLOWING:
1. THREADING THE MACHINE
2. THREADING THE BOBBIN
3. STITCHING A STRAIGHT
LINE
4. NAMING IMPORTANT
PARTS
5. BRINGING UP THE
BOBBIN THREAD
SAFELY

Use the tables below to complete the work sheet that follows them. *Do not* write in this book.

Common Units of Metric Length

1 inch = 2.54 centimeters
1 foot = 30.48 centimeters
1 yard = 0.94 meters

1 millimeter = 0.04 inches
1 centimeter = 0.39 inches
1 decimeter = 3.94 inches
1 meter = 39.37 inches

Conversion Figures

Multiply by
25.4 for inches to millimeters
30 for feet to centimeters
0.9 for yards to meters
0.04 for millimeters to inches
0.4 for centimeters to inches
1.1 for meters to yards

Work Sheet

3 yards	= (?) meters
36 inches	= (?) centimeters
2 feet	= (?) millimeters
5 inches	= (?) decimeters
4 meters	= (?) yards
3 feet	= (?) centimeters
100 millimeters	= (?) inches

Your waist measurement in centimeters is (?) .
Your height in meters is (?) .
Your head size in millimeters is (?) .

along the top of the fabric, the top tension is probably too tight. Loosen it by moving the tension regulator to a lower number. If the bobbin thread lies straight along the bottom of the fabric, the top tension is probably too loose. Adjust it by tightening the tension regulator. The bobbin tension rarely needs to be changed. Most adjusting can and should be done with the top tension regulator. The bobbin tension is adjusted by a tiny screw in the bobbin case. This screw can be tightened or loosened with a tiny screw driver, when absolutely necessary. Your teacher may not want you to make any

Good posture at the machine is important. If you are too short, a phone book or pillow might raise you to sew in a more comfortable position. *National Education Association*

attempt to adjust the bobbin tension in the school machines. If you cannot adjust the tension properly with the tension regulator, tell your teacher and ask for help.

Replacing the needle

Needles may need to be changed frequently. Some fabrics require a smaller needle than others. The needle may become blunted by hitting a pin or from sewing heavy fabrics. Sometimes a needle will break.

To replace the needle, loosen the clamp (screw) on the needle bar until the needle can be pulled out. Insert the new needle as far up into the hole in the needle bar as it will go. Check to see that you have placed the needle so the long grooved side is turned in the direction of the last thread guide on the machine. Tighten the clamp screw. If the needle is inserted backwards, the thread will break after every few stitches as you are trying to sew. If you find you are having this trouble with a machine you are using, check to be sure the needle has been placed correctly.

Work Habits at the Sewing Machine

In learning to make straight stitches on the sewing machine, give attention to control of the speed. It is easier to learn to handle fabric as it moves through the machine when you stitch at a slow, even rate. At first you may want to practice stitching on lined paper.

Keep the bulk of the fabric to the left of the needle as you sew. Learn to watch the right edge of the fabric rather than the needle. Guide the edge of the fabric along the seam guide lines marked on the throat plate of the machine. If your machine does not have lines on it, a piece of masking tape stuck on the throat plate may be used as a guide. There is also a machine attachment called a seam guide, which can be fastened to the machine to help you sew straight, even seams.

Posture

When machine-sewing, sit squarely and erectly in front of the machine with your feet flat on the floor. Choose a chair or stool which allows you to place your arms comfortably and easily on the bed of the machine. This will ensure free movement of both hands in the needle area of the machine and enable you to reach the handwheel easily with your right hand. Check to see that you are also able to reach the knee or foot lever (speed control) comfortably.

Lighting

Good lighting is necessary for accurate sewing results. While the small light on the machine helps by shining directly on the stitching area, it is not sufficient to prevent eyestrain. If possible, sew in a well-lighted room. Position the sewing machine so that light is projected over your left shoulder.

 Use the chart on page 327 to complete the following statements. *Do not* write in this book.

1 Linda is going to make a long dress. Her fabric is 54 inches wide. It is (?) centimeters wide.

2 Bill was given 2½ yards of shirting fabric. It is 45 inches wide. This is the same as 112 centimeters of fabric in width and (?) centimeters in length.

3 Beth has a blouse pattern requiring 1⅜ yards of 54-inch fabric. She would need (?) centimeters of fabric the same width.

4 Tom wants to make spreads for his bunk beds. He has two pieces of fabric. Each is 2⅞ yards long and 58 inches wide. In the two pieces of fabric he has (?) centimeters of length.

5 Jon is going to design a beach towel. His fabric is 113 centimeters wide and 160 centimeters long. That means it is (?) inches wide and (?) yards long.

6 Mary has a large piece of fabric to hem for a tablecloth. The fabric is 150 centimeters in width and 252 centimeters in length. Therefore, it measures (?) inches in width and (?) yards in length.

Match the *functions* in List A with *machine parts* in List B. Use a machine part from List B only once. *Do not* write in this book.

List A: Function

A Holds fabric in place when you sew.

B Regulates looseness and tightness of thread coming off spool.

C Lengthens or shortens size of stitch.

D Moves the top thread up and down.

E Moves fabric forward or backward.

List B: Machine Part

1 Feed dog
2 Presser foot
3 Stitch regulator
4 Take-up lever
5 Upper tension

Fill in the blank in each sentence with the *best* word or words to complete the statement. *Do not* use a word that already appears in the sentence. *Do not* write in this book.

1 Making your own clothes can help you express personal _(?)_ .

2 A trademarked finishing process guaranteeing a fabric will shrink no more than 1 percent is called _(?)_ .

3 When the lengthwise and crosswise threads of a fabric are exactly at right angles the fabric is _(?)_ .

4 The crosswise threads of the fabric are called _(?)_ .

5 It is easier not to buy off-grain fabric than to _(?)_ it later.

6 To keep your shears in top condition and to avoid frustration, never cut anything but _(?)_ with them.

7 Pinking shears are only used to trim seams _(?)_ they are stitched.

8 Small cutting tasks such as snipping threads are done with _(?)_ .

9 The easiest fabric designs to work with are _(?)_ .

10 Curved areas of a garment should be pressed over a pressing _(?)_ .

11 A sewing machine should be cleaned and _(?)_ regularly.

12 The most expensive item of sewing equipment at school or at home is the _(?)_ .

13 In machine stitching, the part holding the lower thread is called the _(?)_ .

14 Always be sure the needle is placed in the machine so the grooved side is facing the last _(?)_ .

15 Correct machine tension allows the top and bottom threads to lock together smoothly _(?)_ the layers of cloth.

16 If the top thread lies straight along the stitching line, it means the top tension is too _(?)_ .

17 Most tension adjustment can be made with the _(?)_ tension regulator.

Fill in the blank in each sentence with the best word or words to complete the statement. *Do not* write in this book.

1 In buying a pattern for slacks, select the size by your _(?)_ measurement.

2 The extra room needed in your clothes so you can move comfortably is called _(?)_ .

3 Garments made from woven fabrics require more room for movement than garments made from _(?)_ .

4 You find information on size, amount of fabric needed, and notions required on the pattern _(?)_ .

5 The diagram for placing the pattern on the fabric is the _(?)_ .

6 The cutting line on a pattern is indicated by the _(?)_ line.

7 Cutting with the grain of the fabric is called _(?)_ cutting.

8 Patterns usually allow 1.5-cm, or _(?)_ -inch, seam allowance on all visible seams.

9 To find out which pattern pieces fit together, match the _(?)_ .

10 The true diagonal of a square of fabric is the _(?)_ .

11 The fabric placed between the garment and facing to add body is the _(?)_ .

12 A facing cut to the same shape as the area it is to cover is a (an) _(?)_ facing.

Chapter 17

Creating Clothes to Wear and Enjoy

After reading this chapter, you should be able to:
1. List the steps in taking measurements to determine pattern size.
2. Identify specific information found on pattern envelopes.
3. Give examples of the information provided on pattern instruction sheets.
4. Explain the purposes of various pattern markings and symbols.
5. Adjust your pattern to fit.
6. Choose fabric that suits your pattern.
7. Lay your pattern on the fabric correctly.
8. Cut out your pattern correctly.
9. Transfer the pattern markings to your fabric correctly.
10. Construct your project using acceptable sewing techniques.
11. Demonstrate correct pressing techniques in making your project.

The first sewing was probably done by primitive people trying to put the skins of animals together. They needed the warmth and protection of clothing. Animal skins were the only materials available. The first needle was probably a shaped and sharpened piece of bone used to punch holes in the skins. The first thread was probably a strip of untreated animal skin, or rawhide. As people became more civilized, learned new methods, and found new tools and materials, sewing became more sophisticated.

Today people sew with a wide variety of tools, fabrics, patterns, and techniques. They still make clothes for warmth and protection. However, the main reason so many people sew their own clothes is probably because they enjoy creating them.

Everyone who sews well had to learn how. You can too. The success of your first sewing project depends somewhat on how careful and patient

List the sewing techniques you would like to learn in your first school sewing project. Decide what type of garment would give you these experiences. Look through pattern books to find a pattern for your project. Determine if the style will be flattering to you. How will it fit in your wardrobe? Are there any details that may be too difficult? What else should you consider?

Look through catalogs for patterns which include more than one garment; for example, a coordinated shirt, vest, and pair of pants. Discuss the advantages and disadvantages of choosing such a pattern for a beginning project.

Bulletin board IDEA
Title:

Super Swift Sewing

Directions: Mount pattern envelopes showing garments that are easy to make and contain few pieces. Display fabrics appropriate for beginners.

you are as you learn. Remember you are just beginning. Even if you have some sewing experience, patient practice is necessary to become an expert.

Just as in other activities, some days everything seems to go wrong in sewing. Other days everything will fall into its proper place. If your project is moving slowly, instead of hurrying, try taking only a step at a time. The use of sewing aids will also make your work move faster. Successful first projects are important because early successes contribute to your enjoyment of sewing.

SELECTING A PATTERN

There are several brands of commercial patterns on the market. These patterns offer a wide choice of up-to-date styles. Best of all, they are carefully drafted for accuracy, and they fit together with a minimum of trouble. The directions that come with the pattern tell you every step to take in putting a garment together. It is to your advantage to learn to understand the instructions and to follow them carefully.

Commercial patterns have been developed for many different figure types. You may find there are several students in your class who wear a size 13 pattern. Yet, if they all stood side by side, you would see how much they vary in height, weight, and body development. Some students mature more rapidly

than others and are larger in the shoulders and hips than their friends of the same age. Some grow tall before they mature in other ways. Naturally, it would be difficult for the same pattern to fit all of these figures the same way. So pattern companies, taking into consideration the many ways figures develop, have made patterns to fit many figure types.

Patterns for Girls

To accommodate all the different ways girls develop, the pattern companies have worked out series of sizes for the various figure types. According to her development, a girl might choose a pattern from any of these series: Girls, Young Junior/Teen, Junior Petite, Junior, Miss Petite, Misses, Half-Size, and Women. Commercial pattern books have charts explaining all of these pattern types and sizes, usually in the back of the book.

As you study these charts, you will notice how to determine which type will best fit you. *Girls* patterns are for short girls who have not started to mature physically. They require few darts for figure contours. *Young Junior/Teen* patterns are for tall girls who are just beginning to develop in the bust and hips. *Junior Petite* patterns are for girls who are short but well developed. *Junior* patterns are for girls who are well developed but are too short for a Misses size. *Miss Petite* patterns are for girls who are well developed but shorter than average from the shoulder to the waistline. *Misses* patterns are for medium-tall to tall, well-proportioned figures. *Half-sizes* are made for fully developed shortwaisted figures who are larger than average in the waist and hip areas. *Women's* sizes are designed for larger figures.

Each pattern type is made in a range of sizes, such as 10, 12, 14, and 16. To distinguish Junior from other patterns, their sizes are marked in odd numbers, such as 7, 9, 11, and 13. Young Junior/Teen sizes are marked 5/6, 7/8, 9/10, etc. Each pattern size is scaled for a definite measurement in the bust, waist, hip area, and the back waist length.

After you have determined which figure type you have, you need to decide which size will be best for you. Remember your figure size or type will probably change as you mature. The girl who wore a Young Junior/Teen size 9/10 last year may this year require a Misses size 8. Take your body measurements before buying the fabric and pattern for each new project. Very few people can buy a pattern that fits them exactly, but you can find one that requires few alterations.

Patterns list the measurements for bust, hip, waist, and back waist length for the different sizes. You will need to know the measurement of your corresponding body areas. You may find they are almost identical to one particular figure type and size. If you do not fit any size

exactly, choose the size nearest to your bust measurement. The waist and hip sections of a pattern are much easier to adjust than the shoulder and bust areas. Of course, if the project you have chosen is a skirt, shorts, or slacks, your concern should be for the hip and waist measurements. Since the waist section of a pattern can be altered more easily than the hip section, buy such patterns to fit your hips.

Steps in taking measurements

To get accurate measurements, take them over well-fitting undergarments. Remove bulky dresses, sweaters, skirts, or pants. If the garment you are wearing fits you well and is not bulky, you may be able to measure over it. Be sure to stand straight and look straight ahead while your measurements are being taken. If you look down, you tend to bend your body and the measurements may not be accurate.

It is preferable to have a partner take your measurements for you so you can stand still and erect.

The bust measurement is taken by placing the tape measure around the fullest part of the bust. Be sure to keep the tape straight across the back shoulder area. The tape should be tight enough to stay in place but loose enough for you to place one finger underneath it.

The high-chest measurement is taken by placing the tape around the body, up high under the arms. Check to see that the tape is straight

Discuss the following common fitting problems and the causes. Explain why the suggested solutions will help improve the fit of garments.

Skirt or pants side seams slant to the front—a flat posterior or a prominent tummy
 Take up the waistline in the back.
Skirt or pants side seams slant to the back—a prominent posterior
 Take up the waistline in the front.
Hemline tilts—hips have different shapes
 Take up waistline on one side
Skirt or pants ride up at waistline—garment is too narrow across hips
 Raise from the waistline.
Fitted dress or shirt bulges across the back—garment is too long-waisted
 Relocate waistline or waistline darts or reshape back seams.
Back zipper or center back seam stands out from neck—garment is too wide across the back
 Take in seam.
Scoop neck gaps—garment is too large in front
 Take in neckline slack at shoulder seams.

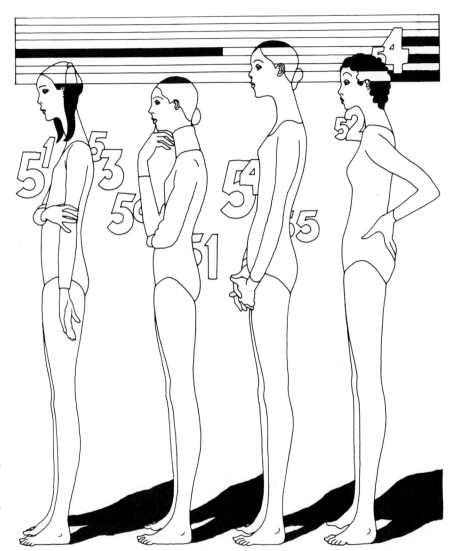

Young Junior/Teen designates the developing teen and pre-teen figure which has a very small, high bust with a waist larger in proportion to the bust.

Junior Petite is a short, well-developed figure with small body structure and a shorter waist length than any other type.

Junior is a well-developed figure slightly shorter than a Miss in waist length and in overall height.

Miss Petite is a shorter figure than a Miss with a shorter waist length than the comparable Miss size, but longer than the corresponding Junior Petite.

Young Junior/Teen	Junior Petite	Junior	Miss Petite
5'1" to 5'3" (1.55 to 1.60 m)	5' to 5'1" (1.53 to 1.55 m)	5'5" (1.63 to 1.65 m)	5'2" to 5'4" (1.58 to 1.63 m)

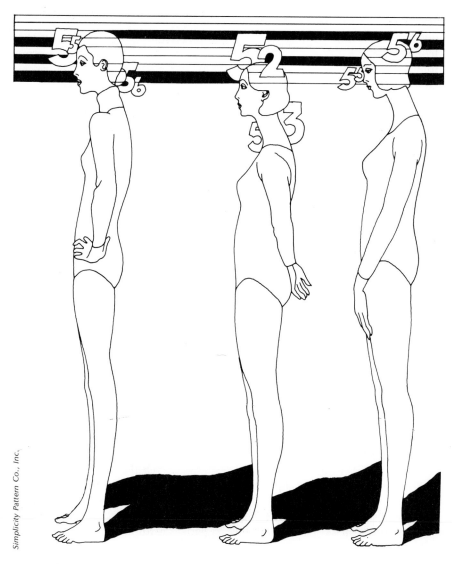

Simplicity Pattern Co., Inc.

Misses
5′5″ to 5′6″ (1.65 to 1.68 m)

Half-Size
5′2″ to 5′3″ (1.58 to 1.60 m)

Women's
5′5″ to 5′6″ (1.65 to 1.68 m)

Your career
Pattern maker

You would make the master pattern, following the design and details of a sample garment or sketch. You might also be a tailor or the one who made the sample garment. A background of design and clothing construction is necessary. You would find employment with clothing manufacturers and home-sewing pattern companies.

Misses is well-proportioned in all body areas and is the tallest of all figure types. This type can be called the "average" figure.

Half-Size is a fully developed shorter figure with narrower shoulders than in the Miss. The waist is larger in proportion to the bust than in the other mature figure types.

Women's is a larger more mature figure about the same height as a Miss. The back waist length is longer because the back is fuller, and all measurements are larger proportionally.

Check your measurements carefully according to instructions in the text. Tie a tape or string around your natural waistline to make it easier to find. Stand straight while being measured.

Some measurements are used to select the correct pattern type and size. Others are used for alterations. List them all for reference.

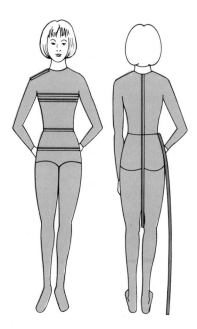

For girls and women: Your height, bust, waist, hip, and back waist length measurements are needed to select your correct pattern type and size.

and firm but not too tight. Some people are full-busted but narrow through the shoulders. By using their high-chest measurement in place of the bust measurement, they can select patterns that fit them more accurately. If there is doubt about whether to use the bust or high-chest measurement, ask your teacher's advice.

The waist is measured by placing the tape around the natural waistline, and holding it snug but not tight enough to squeeze the body. The natural waistline is located well above the hip bone in the narrowest part of the body.

The hip measurement should be taken around the largest part of the hips. This may be anywhere from 6 to 10 inches (15 to 25 centimeters) below the natural waistline, depending on your figure.

The waist length is measured from the bone you can feel at the back of your neck down to the natural waistline. Stand erect when this measurement is taken. Tie a string or piece of tape around your waist so your partner will know the exact location of your waistline.

The skirt or pants length is determined by measuring from the center back of your natural waistline to the floor. From this number, subtract the number of inches you like to wear your skirts above the floor. If the garment you wore to school is the length you like, you may find it easier to measure it than to establish a new length. Be sure to add at least 2 inches (5 centimeters) for a hem allowance. Length for pants is determined in the same way, except that the measurement is taken along the side of the body.

Patterns for Boys

As boys develop, they, too, fall into several different figure types. Some boys grow taller than others. Some have sloping shoulders while others have square shoulders. Some are broader through the shoulders than others. Some develop a larger chest. Some have longer arms.

Boy's clothing does not require the use of darts, and the fitting differs from girl's clothing. The size ranges offered are Boys, Teen-Boys, and Men, according to the height and chest or waist measurement. For each of these sizes, a range of measurements for chest, neck, finished length of garment, and the finished length of the sleeves is given. Shorts and slacks are sized according to the waist measurement. Men's patterns may also be sized as Small, Medium, and Large, according to the chest and waist measurements.

Most clothing for men and boys requires careful tailoring. Such garments as jackets, slacks, and dress shirts are better left to more experienced sewers. However, sports shirts, T-shirts and pullovers, and boxer-type shorts, pants, or swim trunks can make successful beginning projects for the new sewer.

For boys and men: Your height, chest, waist, hip, and neck measurements are needed to select your correct pattern type and size.

Simplicity Pattern Co., Inc.

Teen-Boys' 5'1" to 5'8" (1.55 to 1.73 m) Teen Boys' patterns fit young men whose sizes fall between Boys' and Men's sizes. Comparable to Young Junior/Teen sizes.

Men's 5'10" (1.78 m) Men's patterns are sized for men of average build about 5'10" (1.78 m) tall without shoes.

Write on a separate sheet of paper the underlined letters in the words below. Rearrange the letters to form a secret word. See the drawing for a clue to the word.

M E A <u>S</u> U R E

F I <u>T</u>

L A Y <u>O</u> <u>U</u> T

<u>C</u> U T

M <u>A</u> R K

S T I <u>T</u> C H

P R E S <u>S</u>

F <u>I</u> N I S H

W E <u>A</u> R

☐☐☐☐☐☐☐☐☐☐☐

I made it myself

Your career
Cutter

You would cut out garment pieces from several layers of fabric. Special tools would be used to cut through up to 9 inches (22.5 cm) of fabric. You might also mark the pieces and prepare them for construction. You would find employment with clothing manufacturers.

Steps in taking measurements

To get accurate measurements, remove bulky sweaters, jackets, or shirts. Stand straight and look straight ahead while your measurements are being taken. If you look down, your body may bend slightly and change the measurements.

It is preferable to have a partner take your measurements for you so you can stand still and erect.

The chest measurement is taken by placing a tape measure around the fullest part of the chest. Keep it straight across the shoulder blades in back. Inhale slightly to expand your chest and allow for an easy fit.

The waist is measured by placing the tape around the natural waistline. Hold it snug but loose enough to place one finger underneath it. If you have difficulty finding your natural waistline, bend your body slightly to one side or the other. The point at which the body bends is the natural waistline. Measure over your shirt but under the top of your trousers.

The sleeve length is measured from the base of the neck, across the shoulder down to the bent elbow, and then to the wrist bone.

The shoulders are measured across the back of the shoulders from the prominent bone on your shoulder to the same bone on the other shoulder.

The neck measurement is taken around the middle of the neck. Allow ease of ½ inch (1.3 centimeters) for comfort.

The length for a shirt or vest is determined by measuring from the prominent bone at the base of the neck to the length you want the shirt to cover. Bend your head forward slightly to find the bone.

To measure the length for shorts, start at the natural waistline and measure down the outside of the leg *(outseam)* to the length you like. Add at least 1 inch (2.5 centimeters) for a hem. For long pants, measure from the waistline to the top of the shoe and add the extra length needed for a hem or a cuff.

The hip measurement is taken around the fullest part of the hips.

Judging Pattern Difficulty

As a general rule, the smaller the number of pieces in your pattern, the easier the garment will be for you to make. Styles requiring careful fitting are more difficult than loosely fitting styles. Designs featuring scallops, points, tucks, gussets, and bound buttonholes require more skill and patience than beginners generally possess.

Many simple patterns are difficult because they do not fit correctly. Once you know your own body measurements, you can determine the type and size pattern to buy for your figure. Many classrooms have large charts posted on which you can locate the figure type and pattern size to buy for good fit. After you have decided on the size you think you need, check with your teacher to be sure you are right.

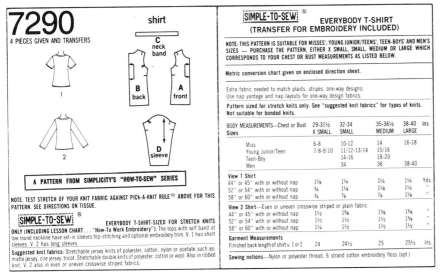

7290

4 PIECES GIVEN AND TRANSFERS

shirt
C
neck
band
B
back
A
front
1
2
D
sleeve

A PATTERN FROM SIMPLICITY'S "HOW-TO-SEW" SERIES

NOTE: TEST STRETCH OF YOUR KNIT FABRIC AGAINST PICK-A-KNIT RULE™ ABOVE FOR THIS PATTERN. SEE DIRECTIONS ON TISSUE.

SIMPLE-TO-SEW® EVERYBODY T-SHIRT-SIZED FOR STRETCH KNITS ONLY (INCLUDING LESSON CHART . . . "How-To Work Embroidery"): The tops with self band at low round neckline have set-in sleeves top-stitching and optional embroidery trim. V. 1 has short sleeves. V. 2 has long sleeves.

Suggested knit fabrics: Stretchable jersey knits of polyester, cotton, nylon or acetate such as: matte jersey, cire jersey, tricot. Stretchable double knits of polyester, cotton or wool. Also in ribbed knit. V. 2 also in even or uneven crosswise striped fabrics.

SIMPLE-TO-SEW® EVERYBODY T-SHIRT (TRANSFER FOR EMBROIDERY INCLUDED)

NOTE: THIS PATTERN IS SUITABLE FOR MISSES', YOUNG JUNIOR/TEENS', TEEN-BOYS' AND MEN'S SIZES — PURCHASE THE PATTERN, EITHER X SMALL, SMALL, MEDIUM OR LARGE WHICH CORRESPONDS TO YOUR CHEST OR BUST MEASUREMENTS AS LISTED BELOW.

Metric conversion chart given on enclosed direction sheet.

Extra fabric needed to match plaids, stripes, one-way designs.
Use nap yardage and nap layouts for one-way design fabrics.

Pattern sized for stretch knits only. See "suggested knit fabrics" for types of knits. Not suitable for bonded knits.

BODY MEASUREMENTS—Chest or Bust **Sizes**	29-31½ X SMALL	32-34 SMALL	35-36½ MEDIUM	38-40 LARGE	Ins.
Miss	6-8	10-12	14	16-18	
Young Junior/Teen	7/8-9/10	11/12-13/14	15/16		
Teen-Boy		14-16	18-20		
Men		34	36	38-40	
View 1 Shirt					
44" or 45" with or without nap	1⅛	1¼	1¼	1¼	Yds.
52" or 54" with or without nap	¾	1⅛	1⅛	1¼	"
58" or 60" with or without nap	¾	⅞	⅞	1⅛	"
View 2 Shirt—Even or uneven crosswise striped or plain fabric					
44" or 45" with or without nap	1½	1⅝	1⅝	1⅝	"
52" or 54" with or without nap	1½	1½	1½	1⅝	"
58" or 60" with or without nap	1¼	1½	1½	1½	"
Garment Measurements					
Finished back length of shirt v. 1 or 2	24	24½	25	25½	Ins.

Sewing notions—Nylon or polyester thread, 6 strand cotton embroidery floss (opt.)

For a beginning project, choose a simple pattern with only a few pattern pieces. To determine the amount of fabric to buy, draw a line *across* from your fabric width and a line *down* from your pattern size. Where the two lines cross, you will find the number of yards to buy. *Simplicity Pattern Co., Inc.*

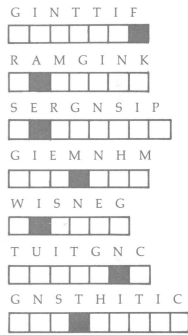

Unscramble the seven words below, allowing one letter to each square. The unscrambled words describe essential steps in clothing construction. *Do not* write in this book.

G I N T T I F

R A M G I N K

S E R G N S I P

G I E M N H M

W I S N E G

T U I T G N C

G N S T H I T I C

Now arrange the shaded letters to form the surprise word which describes the product of clothing construction efforts.

Judging Becomingness of Pattern Designs

People are frequently disappointed with a finished garment because the style is not becoming to them. To avoid this disappointment, choose patterns with flattering lines. The lines in the pattern should be becoming to your figure as well as to the fabrics you choose. It might be helpful to review the section on lines in clothes in Chapter 13. (See pages 270–272.)

Understanding the Pattern Envelope

The pattern envelope provides useful information. Study it carefully before beginning a project. It provides basic information to help in buying fabric and notions for your project. The following is given on all brands of pattern envelopes:

1 The brand name of the pattern and the pattern number.
2 The size of the pattern in the envelope.
3 The number and shape of the pattern pieces. (The number of pieces to be used generally indicates the amount of difficulty you can expect in assembling a garment.)
4 Pictures of the way the garment will look when it is completed and the different versions of it you can make from the one pattern.

Copy the puzzles on a piece of paper. Write the words that complete the clothing ladder. Some words are written backwards. *Do not* write in this book.

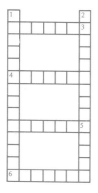

1 Stitching under the folded edge of a facing so the raw edges are hidden.
2 Stitching through the facing and seam allowances to make the facing lie flat.
3 A group of fibers including cotton.
4 Separate pieces used to hide raw edges.
5 A hem stitch barely does this.
6 Trimming the inside seam allowance to a narrower width than the outside seam allowance.

5 Back views of the garments.
6 A list of fabrics from which the garment can be made successfully.
7 A chart indicating the amount of fabric required to make the garment in each size.
8 A list of notions — such as buttons, zippers, tape, and trimming — you will need.

CHOOSING FABRIC TO SUIT THE PATTERN

Certain fabrics are much more suitable to some patterns than others. Your pattern envelope will list several kinds of fabrics that are satisfactory to use for that particular garment design. If you do not recognize the fabrics suggested, ask the salesclerk to help you. A trained person should be able to help you decide whether the fabric you are considering will make a satisfactory garment.

Heavy, bulky fabrics do not do well in gathered, full, or tucked designs. Firmly woven fabrics work better for tucks and pleats. Soft fabrics gather and drape better than stiff ones. Printed fabrics do not show off seams and stitching details to their best advantage. Choosing suitable material for your design could mean the difference between satisfaction and unhappiness. Buy easy-to-handle fabric which will look well when made into your chosen design.

Be sure the fabric you buy has been finished *on-grain*. It is far better to make a change in fabric selection than to try to correct fabric grain after it has been pulled out of shape in the manufacturing process. (See pages 323–328.)

PREPARATION FOR SEWING

As you prepare to lay your pattern on the fabric, follow these steps:

1 Study the instruction sheet to find the suggested layout for the size and version of the pattern you have selected and for your fabric width.
2 Draw a circle around the cutting layout you have selected so you will see it immediately each time you want to refer to it for help.
3 Separate the pattern pieces you will need, returning any unneeded ones to the pattern envelope.
4 Put your name on the body of each pattern piece, on your instruction sheet, and on the envelope.
5 If the pattern pieces are wrinkled, press them with a slightly warm iron. Avoid pressing tiny wrinkles into the pattern pieces.

Understanding the Pattern Instruction Sheet

The instruction sheet inside the pattern envelope is your guide to easy sewing. You should refer to it often throughout the construction of the garment. It is poor management to spend time trying to figure out how to put two pieces together when the directions on the instruction sheet explain every step.

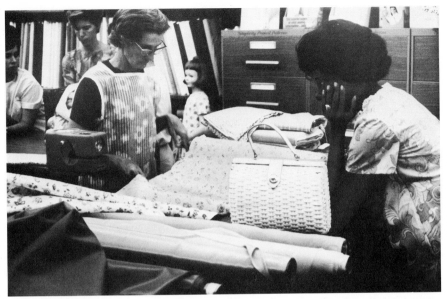

When you select fabric for a sewing project, consider the pattern's design and consult the pattern envelope for suggestions. *Talon Consumer Education*

In addition to step-by-step construction directions, you will also find directions for laying and pinning the pattern on various widths of fabric. Instructions for straightening fabric, transferring the pattern markings to the fabric, and general sewing directions are provided on most instruction sheets.

Understanding Pattern Markings

The pattern pieces themselves are marked with lines, dots, and notches to show you where to alter, how to place the pattern on the fabric, where to cut, where to match pieces together, and where to sew. Darts, pockets, centers, fold lines, buttonholes, pleats, and tucks are all marked on the pattern. (See the illustration on page 347.)

Adjusting Patterns for Fit

Since few people have measurements exactly the same as any one pattern size, each person may find a need to change the size of a pattern in some area. However, if you have selected your pattern carefully according to your measurements, you should not find it necessary to make many changes.

Because people vary widely in size and shape, you will want to check your pattern to see if it will fit *you*. If any part of the pattern is too long, too short, too large, or too small, adjust it to fit. It is much

Pinning

1 Grain arrow not pinned first, no pins in corners, too few or too many pins, pins across cutting lines
2 Grain arrow pinned first for most pieces, pins in most corners, few pins across cutting lines
3 Grain arrow pinned first for all pieces, pins in all corners, pins 6–8 inches (15–20 cm) apart, no pins across cutting lines

CUTTING

Direction
1 Cut against grain
2 Cut most edges with grain
3 Cut with grain

Tools
1 Used pinking shears or scissors
2 Used shears but they were dull or blunt
3 Used sharp, clean shears

Accuracy
1 Used short strokes resulting in uneven, choppy, and jagged edges
2 Used long strokes but cut to ends of blades, fairly even edges
3 Used long, even strokes stopping about 1 inch (2.5 cm) from end of blades, straight edges

Remove from the pattern envelope all the pattern pieces you will need for your project. The guide sheet has a list for you to check.   *Simplicity Pattern Co., Inc.*

easier to make the necessary changes in the paper pattern than to change the pieces after they have been cut from cloth. Since your first project will be made with a pattern containing only a few pieces, you will probably find the changes easy to make.

Measuring pattern pieces

Use a tape measure to check your pattern for correct fit. Measure from *seam* line to *seam* line rather than from edge to edge in determining the length or width of a pattern. Since many pieces are cut double, they are measured from the fold line to the seam line. The number of inches or centimeters is then doubled to determine the width of a pattern piece. By adding together the width of the back and front of a pattern, you have a good idea of the size of a garment made by it.

Ease allowance

Don't be surprised if you find the dress or shirt pattern you bought for a 32-inch (80-centimeter) bust line or chest to be 36 inches (90 centimeters) when you measure it with a tape. You need this extra room in your clothes to allow for the movement of your body. If your clothes measured the same as your body, you wouldn't be able to get them on. Even if you could, they would be uncomfortable to wear.

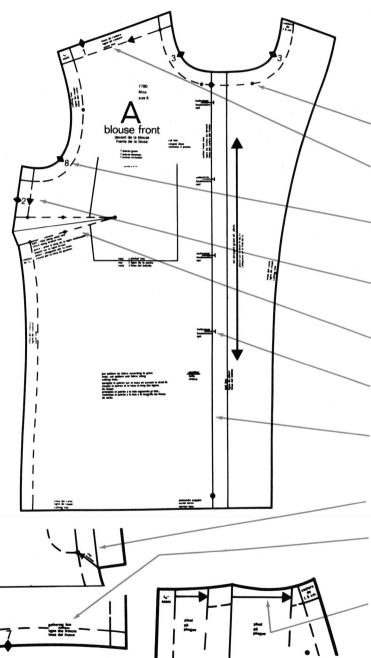

Construction Markings

Construction markings are the guide posts for putting together and sewing your garment. Some patterns have many of these markings, others have only a few, depending on the design details of the style.

Dots are aids for matching seams and other construction details.

The seam line (stitching line) is indicated by a broken line. It is usually ⅝″ (1.5 cm) from the cutting line, but it can vary in certain areas.

Notches are V-shaped symbols along the cutting line which aid in joining pattern pieces. Two or more notches may be grouped together to form a block for easier cutting.

Arrows on the seam line indicate the direction in which the pieces should be stitched so as not to distort the fabric grain.

Darts are indicated by two broken lines for stitching and a solid line at center for folding.

Buttonholes are indicated by a solid line having a short line at right angles to one end when horizontal or at both ends when vertical.

Solid lines are used also to indicate center fold lines, some hemlines, placement for pockets and trimmings that go on the outside of the garment.

"Clip" with a short arrow indicates where to clip into the seam allowance to release it.

Gathering or **easing** is indicated by a broken line similar to a seam line, but labeled "gathering line" or "ease." Usually, you gather or ease between two points on the pattern.

Pleats are usually indicated by an alternating solid and broken line. Arrows show the direction of the pleating with the instruction "fold along solid line; bring fold to broken line."

347

Notches

1 Uncut or cut into seam line
2 Most cut out
3 All cut out

Fold lines

1 Pieces to be placed on fold
were cut along fold line, too
few or too many pieces cut
2 A piece placed on fold was
cut a short distance on fold
line, extra piece had to be
cut or too many were cut
3 Pieces placed on fold were
cut on only three sides, right
number of pieces cut

STAYSTITCHING

Direction

1 Not stitched with grain
2 Some stitching with grain
3 All stitching with grain

Placement

1 Done on only a few curved
and bias lines, done on
straight edges where not
needed
2 Done on most curved and
bias edges, may be done a
few places where unneeded
3 Done on all curved and bias
edges, not done where
unneeded

STEPS IN ALTERING A PATTERN

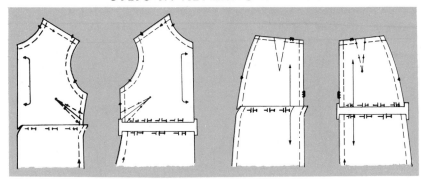

Simple alterations in patterns can be made by pinning tucks in the pattern pieces to make them smaller or by inserting strips of paper to make them larger.

The amount of extra room you need in your clothes in order to move freely is called *ease allowance*. It is logical that you need plenty of room through the chest and bust area so you can move your arms without tearing out your sleeves. For nonstretchable woven fabrics, most people find an extra 3 or 4 inches (7.5 or 10 centimeters) in this area is a good amount for comfort. Thus, if you measure 32 inches (80 centimeters) around the fullest part of the bust or chest, you will want your dress or shirt to measure 36 inches (90 centimeters) in this area. Since knitted fabrics stretch as you do, the ease allowance required in knitted garments is much less.

The next greatest need for ease allowance occurs in the hip area, where ample width must be provided for sitting down. Here you need a minimum of 2 extra inches (5 centimeters) in the width of a garment. The waistline comes next with a requirement of 1 extra inch (2.5 centimeters).

Do you notice that each ease requirement is exactly half the amount of the one before it? Thus, if you can remember that the bust or chest area requires 4 inches (10 centimeters) for ease, it will not be difficult for you to remember the ease requirements for the hips and waist.

Altering, Laying, and Pinning the Pattern

After you have selected and prepared the pattern pieces you will use, you are ready to prepare for cutting. Be sure to check the pattern measurements with yours. Make any necessary changes before pinning the pattern pieces to your fabric. As you proceed, follow these steps:

1   Measure from the center front to the side seam and from the center back to the side seam. Add these two measurements together. Since most pattern pieces are for one side of a garment only, the measurement must be doubled to get the total measurement around the garment. If a pattern piece is to be placed on the fold of the fabric, measure from the fold line to the side seam. For a bodice or shirt, measure at the widest part of the bust or chest area. For skirts, shorts, or slacks, measure the hip area. Check to see that the fullest part of your body corresponds to the fullest part on the pattern. For example, if your widest part is 8 inches (20 centimeters) from your waistline, you will measure the pattern 8 inches (20 centimeters) down from the waistline. Check the back waist length and the skirt, slacks, or shorts length. Make any alterations needed to make your pattern fit your body measurements. Remember to allow for ease in woven fabrics.

2   Fold the fabric as suggested in the cutting layout, making sure the right sides of the fabric are together on the inside. Match the selvages perfectly, and be sure the fabric lies smoothly on a flat surface.

3   Place the pattern pieces on the fabric in the positions shown on the cutting guide to make sure they will all fit.

4   Make sure the grain lines on the pattern are placed on the grain

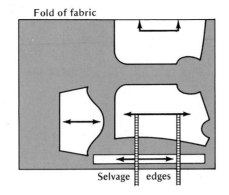

Fold of fabric

Selvage edges

When you place the pattern pieces on the fabric, check the instruction sheet to be sure you are doing it correctly and are not wasting fabric unnecessarily.

line of the fabric. The arrows on the pattern pieces are the grain-line markings. In most cases, they should be parallel to the straight edges of the fabric.

5   Pin the pattern to the fabric at the point of each arrow shown on pattern pieces. To be sure your arrows are on the straight grain, put a pin in one point of the arrow. Measure from this point to the edge of the fabric. Move the pattern so the other point of the arrow is the same distance from the edge. Pin the second point.

6   Smooth the pattern, and put a pin in each corner. Be sure the pins are inside the cutting line. Place enough pins around the edge to hold the pattern securely. Avoid using too many pins. One pin placed every 6 to 8 inches (15 to 20 centimeters) should be sufficient.

Stitching

1   More or less than ½ inch (1.3 cm) from cutting line, not straight, stitch too long or too short, continued around corners

2   Most stitching ½ inch (1.3 cm) from edge, fairly straight, stitch about right length, usually sewn to edge of fabric

3   All stitching ½ inch (1.3 cm) from edge, straight, 10 to 12 stitches per inch, always sewn to edge of fabric

Thread

1   Color does not match fabric, threads left hanging

2   Color a little too dark or light for fabric, some threads clipped

3·Color matches fabric, all threads clipped

Your career
Quality control inspector

You would check garments after they had been made to ensure quality construction. You would mark any defects, such as loose or skipped stitches, and might make minor repairs. You would work for manufacturers.

Practice using the points of small scissors for ripping. Hold the scissors near the points of the blade rather than by the handles. About every inch cut through a stitch. Slip the small point of the scissors under one of the threads in the center of the cut section and pull out the thread. Continue in this manner to the end of the section to be ripped. Pull away the long thread on the underneath side.

Follow these safety practices:

1 Avoid using razor blades for ripping. Handle stitch rippers with care to keep from jabbing yourself or cutting the fabric.
2 Pass sharp objects, such as scissors and shears, to others with the handle first.
3 Store scissors and other sharp objects in holders or in other secure places.
4 Keep blades of shears and scissors closed when they are not in use.

PINNING PATTERN TO FABRIC   CUTTING GARMENT PIECES

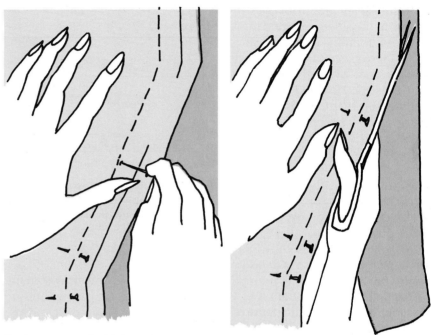

Pin the pattern to the fabric, and cut the pieces as they remain flat on a cutting table or cutting board. This will insure you of the correct size and shape of the pieces.

7 Recheck your complete pattern layout against the cutting layout on the instruction sheet. When you are sure all pieces are placed accurately and on the straight of the fabric, check with your teacher before cutting.

Cutting Pattern Pieces

The word *directional* is used over and over in the study of clothing construction. This sewing term means *moving with the grain*. In cutting garment pieces from fabric, look at the pattern piece. You will find that by cutting from the wide to the narrow part of a piece, you cut with less pull on the grain of the fabric. This is called *directional cutting*.

Use sharp shears to cut the fabric. Cut carefully along the cutting line shown on the pattern. Use long, even strokes. Stop each stroke about 1 inch (2.5 centimeters) from the end of the blades of the shears. If you close the blades with each stroke, the resulting edge will be choppy and uneven. As you come to the *notches* (diamond-shaped marks) on the cutting line, cut around them away from the pattern.

Transferring Pattern Symbols

The markings on the pattern are there to guide you in putting the garment together. Carefully transfer these markings to your fabric pieces so they will be visible when you need them.

Tailor's tacks, marks which are made of thread, have been used for many years. They are the best type of marks to use on white, sheer, or heavily napped fabrics.

Tailor's chalk and pins are used mainly for temporary markings. The chalk rubs off, but it is useful in places where stitches can be made

immediately. Pins may drop out, but if they are inserted carefully and the sewing is done immediately, they can be used to mark locations of seams, darts, or buttonholes. You may find pins a satisfactory form of marking at home, but they are usually not permanent enough for use in a school class.

The tracing wheel can be used for all fabrics except light-colored, sheer, heavily napped, or loosely woven fabrics. To use a tracing wheel, place the special tracing paper face down between the wrong side of the fabric and the pattern itself. Then place another piece of tracing paper face up under the wrong side of the fabric. With the

Play the word clue game described below. Number off in 1's and 2's to form team pairs. One person in each pair begins by writing a secret word on paper. The partner cannot see the word. This word should be related to clothing construction. A one-word clue is given to help the partner figure out the secret word. Nonverbal hints may not be given. If the secret word is guessed the first time, the team scores 1 point. If three clue words are needed before the secret word is named, the team scores 3 points. After five clue words have been given, give the team 5 points but start again on a new word. Each person in a pair has a chance to write a secret word for the partner to guess. The team with the lowest score wins. Examples:

Pat has written *sew* as the secret word. Pat says needle, and Dan answers stitch; Pat says machine, and Dan answers *sew*. Their team scores 2 points.

The secret word is *selvage*. Sue says lengthwise, and Marion answers warp; Sue says pin, and Marion says arrow; Sue says edge, and Marion answers *selvage*. Their team scores 3 points.

To use the tracing wheel and tracing paper, place one layer of paper, colored side down, between the pattern and the fabric. Place another layer of paper, colored side up, below the garment piece. Using the tracing wheel and a straight edge for a guide, trace marks onto the *wrong* side of the garment pieces.   *Scovill*

Study the diagram below to help you remember the right direction in which to staystitch. Note that each time the stitching is started on a bodice piece, it starts at the edge that will lie on the body closest to the ear lobes. On a skirt or pants piece, the stitching goes from the wider to the narrower part.

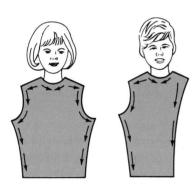

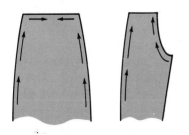

pattern in the proper place, hold a ruler along the line to be marked and run the tracing wheel along the line at the ruler's edge. The prongs of the tracing wheel will transfer bits of color from the paper onto the fabric.

Since the prongs on the tracing wheel might dig through the fabric into the table surface, be sure some form of protection, such as an old magazine or heavy cardboard, lies between fabric and table. Tracing marks can be very permanent. *Be careful to avoid marking on the right side of the fabric.*

Mark the center front, darts, fold lines, buttonholes, and any other construction marks shown on the pattern. Usually you will find it unnecessary to mark the seam lines. They can be stitched straight by using the seam guide on the machine.

ASSEMBLING A GARMENT

After you have completed the markings, you are ready to put the garment together. It is wise for beginners to leave each pattern piece pinned to the fabric until the piece is needed. Something which looks to you like an armhole facing may turn out to be a neck facing. The pattern will help you identify it. Also, the pattern helps to keep the fabric from wrinkling when stored.

Unit Method of Construction

The method of construction in most common use today is called the *unit*

method of construction. This method will help you to attain professional-looking results in a minimum of time.

In the unit method, all possible construction is completed on each section of the garment before putting the pieces together. For example, in making a dress, the staystitching, darts, tucks, pleats, and seams are put in the bodice front, back, sleeves, collars, and skirt pieces. All pieces are pressed carefully before they are joined together. Every seam and dart must be pressed before it is crossed with another seam.

Construction details

Only a few construction details are needed to complete simple garments. These details can be practiced over and over as you make simple tops and blouses, shirts, skirts, slacks, vests, dresses, and many other garments worn by teenagers. As your ability increases, you may want to learn still other skills for tailoring a coat or suit. However, when you have mastered the following skills, you can make most garments worn by today's teenagers.

Staystitching is a line of stitching that keeps the edges of garment pieces from stretching out of shape while you are working on them. It is particularly important on bias and curved edges. It is done by machine stitching a single row of regular-size stitches ½ inch (1.3 centimeters)

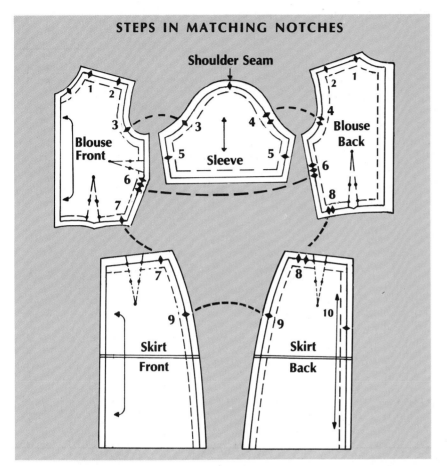

STEPS IN MATCHING NOTCHES

Shoulder Seam

Blouse Front

Sleeve

Blouse Back

Skirt Front

Skirt Back

Look for numbered notches or groups of notches. By matching them, you fit the pieces of a garment together correctly.

 Pin and stitch samples of single-pointed and double-pointed darts. Steam press them into shape, using a tailor's ham.

SINGLE-POINTED DART

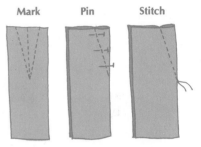

Mark · Pin · Stitch

DOUBLE-POINTED DART

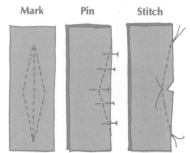

Mark · Pin · Stitch

from the cut edge. Staystitching is done through a single thickness of the fabric before seams are stitched together. Since the purpose of staystitching is to hold the yarns of the fabric in place so they will not stretch out of shape, the stitching must be done in the proper direction to achieve this.

Darts and tucks are folds stitched into a garment to control fullness. While tucks have various shapes, a dart is stitched to a sharp point at one or both ends where fullness is needed. It is wide where fullness is to be removed. Darts point toward but do not extend over the fullest curves of the figure. Dress and

Backstitch 3 or 4 stitches at the widest part and then stitch forward in a straight line gradually tapering to a very smooth point with the last 2 or 3 stitches right on the fold of the fabric. Leave about 1 inch (2.5 cm) of thread at the end of the dart. There is no need to backstitch or tie the ends.

STEPS IN THE UNIT CONSTRUCTION METHOD

1. Complete front blouse unit.

2. Complete back blouse unit.

3. Complete sleeves.

4. Complete neck facing and press.

5. Make shoulder seams and press.

6. Attach neck facing and press.

7. Make underarm seams and press.

8. Attach sleeves and press.

9. Join seams in front and back skirt unit.

10. Press skirt seams.

11. Join blouse and skirt.

12. Attach zipper to garment.

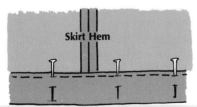

13. Measure, trim, and cleanfinish hem. Pin in place and attach to garment with invisible stitches.

blouse patterns frequently have darts at the waistline and at the shoulder and underarm seams to provide for fullness through the shoulder and bust area. Waistline darts provide for fullness in the hip area of skirts or pants. Darts are indicated on the patterns by lines which can be carefully transferred to the garment pieces. (See pages 351–352.)

Darts are pressed on the underside of the garment. Underarm darts are turned down toward the waistline as they are pressed. Shoulder and waistline darts are turned with the fold toward the center of the garment. Block darts carefully into shape by using a pressing ham and a steam iron.

Directional stitching of seams is a method for joining two pieces of fabric. When two pieces of fabric are sewn together with any kind of stitching, the resulting line of stitches is called a *seam*. Seams should be smooth and flat. While there are many kinds of seams, probably most of the articles you make at this time will require only plain seams.

Seams should be stitched with the grain of the fabric. This *directional stitching* helps to prevent them from stretching or puckering. For example, in directional stitching, the side seams of a skirt are stitched from the wider bottom to narrower top. The stitching direction is determined by the grain of the fabric edge. Most patterns show

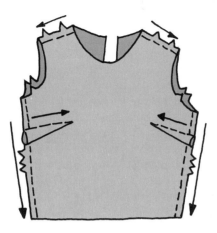

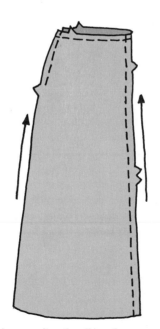

Stitch seams directionally as the arrows on the pattern suggest so that your garment will hang correctly when completed.

 Follow these guidelines in construction pressing. Add other points you have found to be useful.

1 Try the iron on a sample of the fabric to check the effect of the temperature and moisture on the fabric.
2 Press with the grain, usually lengthwise.
3 Press by lifting and lowering the iron to avoid stretching the fabric.
4 Press on the wrong side whenever possible.
5 Plan construction procedures so that each difficult pressing task can be done on as small a section of the garment as is possible.
6 Press shaped parts over a tailor's ham and flat parts on a flat surface.
7 Remove shiny surfaces and basting thread imprints by steaming and then brushing.
8 Avoid pressing in seam lines by slipping strips of brown paper between the garment and the seam allowance.

Grade invisible facing seams so there is as little bulk as possible. After seams are sewn, but before clipping or notching seam allowances, trim the seam allowance on the garment side to ⅜ inch (.9 cm). Trim the facing side to about ¼ inch (.6 cm). Clip or notch as needed. Understitch.

GRADING

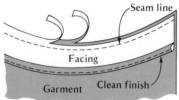

Seam line
Facing
Garment
Clean finish

UNDERSTITCHING

Seam allowances turned toward facing
Clean finish
Garment
Facing

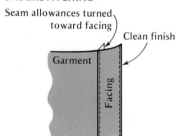

you in which direction to stitch. However, if you are in doubt, stitch from the wide toward the narrow area.

Facings and interfacings are garment reinforcements. A *facing* is an extra piece of fabric added to an edge, such as the edge of a neck or sleeve. It is used to reinforce and cover the raw edges. Facings that are shaped the same as the edges they are used to cover are called *fitted facings*. Another common kind is called a *bias facing*. This type of facing is made by cutting a strip of fabric from the true diagonal area of a square of fabric. Bias-cut fabric is very stretchy and can be shaped to fit curved edges.

Interfacings are extra pieces of fabric, usually the same shape as a fitted facing. They are used between the body of the garment and the facing. Their purpose is to add firmness, thus helping the garment hold its shape during wear. Interfacings can be made of firmly woven or matted fabrics which are stitched into the garment. Some interfacing can be bonded onto a garment with the heat of an iron. Then the facing is *fused* (stuck) to the garment with heat.

Clean finishing is a commonly used method of finishing the edges of sleeves, hems, and facings. By this method, the edge to be finished is first staystitched ¼ inch (.6 centimeter) from the edge. Then, with the right side of the garment piece face up, the edge of the fab-

ric is folded under along the staystitching line. Stitching is made along the fold as close to the edge as possible. The bed of the machine holds the fold in place as the stitching is done. Excess fabric may be trimmed away when the stitching is completed.

Understitching is an extra line of stitching applied to the top side of any facing to make it fold under, lie perfectly flat, and remain unseen. It is used on neck facings, collar seams, and cuff seams. To understitch a seam, separate the facing and the garment part it joins. Turn both edges of the seam toward the facing. From the right or outside of the garment, stitch through the facing and both seam edges. Keep your stitching as close to the original seam as possible. Before understitching, trim and clip the seam if necessary to make it lie flat.

Pressing

The importance of careful step-by-step pressing during the construction of a garment cannot be over-emphasized. Often people think it is too expensive or too much bother to heat the iron to press every seam. They are tempted to wait until they have completed a garment before they press. This is a false savings of time and money. Such people find their garments never look as well as if they had pressed during the construction process.

Actually, the unit method of construction requires only three or four

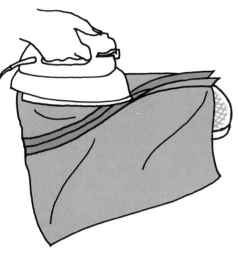

Press curved seams over a tailor's ham to mold them to fit your body. Press each group of seams before they are crossed by other stitching.

pressing sessions. Carefully press each section of the garment after the units have been completed. Press again after the shoulder seams, underarm seams, and side seams are stitched. Press again after the garment is stitched together and during the construction of the hem. Your trips to the pressing board are frequent enough if you press each line of stitching, or seam, before crossing it with another seam line. For example, darts must be pressed before side and shoulder seams are stitched. Side seams must be pressed before a skirt and bodice are joined.

Most of the fabrics used in beginning projects require only simple pressing on the wrong side. First,

press the line of stitching flat. Then, pull the garment over the board and open the seam with the fingers of your free hand. Lay the steaming iron gently on the flattened seam. Lift, move forward one iron length, and lower the iron again. Continue this process for the entire length of the seam. It is the steam and heat that do the work, not the amount of pressure you apply. Remember to press rather than to iron.

Special Construction Skills

Almost anyone who can operate a sewing machine can stitch darts and straight seams. It is the care given to the finishing details that will make a garment look homemade or give it a custom-made look. With a little extra care, you can learn to make clothes you will be proud to wear.

Trimming and clipping seams

Pattern companies usually have a full ⅝-inch (1.5-centimeter) seam allowance on all pattern pieces, even though they know you may have to trim some of the fabric away. In this way you have enough fabric to handle so that you can get a smooth stitching line. Also, it is easy to remember that all seams are stitched ⅝ inch (1.5 centimeters) from the edge and then trimmed where necessary.

It would be difficult to remember that side seams and seams that give the garment its style and shape are always at least ⅝ inch (1.5 centimeters) and that collar, facing, and

Clip or notch curved seams to help them lie flat and remove bulk.

On an outward curved seam, the raw edge is a larger arc than the stitching line arc. Cut tiny triangle-shaped pieces out of the trimmed seam allowance. This will remove excess fabric so the turned seam will be flat. Be careful *not* to cut into the stitching line. Use on the outside edges of rounded collars.

On an inward curved seam, the raw edge is a smaller arc than the stitching line. The raw edge must be clipped close to the stitching line at ½-inch (1.3 cm) intervals. This will allow the raw edge to spread to the same size as the stitching line. It will then be flat when the seam is turned. Use on collars at the neck edge.

Rate your finished garment, considering the construction features below. Assign points according to the scale. Add all points together to get your total score. If an item does not apply to your garment, place an "X" in the last column. Consider your previous sewing experience in making your ratings.

CONSTRUCTION	Excellent	Very good	Good	Fair	Poor	Not needed
Fabric preparation						
Preshrunk						
Grain-Perfect						
Layout						
Guide sheet followed						
Fabric flat, right sides together						
Pattern pinned correctly						
Cutting						
With grain						
Accurate						
Sharp shears used						
Notches cut out						
Staystitching						
With grain						
½ inch (1.3 cm) from edge						
10 to 12 stitches per inch (2.5 cm)						
Marking						
On inside of fabric						
Appropriate type						
Appropriate color						
Accurate						
All necessary markings made						
Darts						
Accurate stitching						
Smooth point						
Pressed in right direction						

belt seams might be narrower. When trying to decide whether to trim a seam, turn a similar garment wrong side out. Any seam which shows is left untrimmed. Those covered by facings and hems are trimmed to remove bulk. Visible seams are the strain-bearing seams and need the width for strength. Hidden seams, such as those inside a collar or some pockets do not bear much strain and can be trimmed to give a garment a finished look.

Curved seams require clipping in order to have an attractive appearance. There are two kinds of curved seams: One curves in, while the other curves out. An inward curved seam, such as a neck edge, requires only simple clips in enough places to allow the edge to spread so the seam will lie flat. Outward curved seams on the outer edges of collars may require wedge-shaped pieces clipped from the seam to remove excess fabric without making the seam weak.

Making collars

Well-made and well-attached collars lie smooth and wrinkle-free. The underneath layer is not visible. Collars vary in shape and size. Regardless of the type of collar you are making, the underneath layer should not show. The under collar, the one that will be next to the garment, can be understitched. This will prevent the under collar from showing from the top side and will help the outside seam lie flat.

To make a professional-looking collar, trim away excess fabric after the collar seam is stitched. Then follow the clipping directions given.

When preparing to join a collar to the neck edge, pin it accurately into place. To do this, pin one end of the collar to one end of the neck edge. Then pin the other end of the collar to the other end of the neck edge. Find the center of the collar. Depending on the type of garment, pin the collar center to either the center-front or the center-back neckline edges of the garment. Match the notches. Find the marks on the collar neck edge that show where it is to join the neck at the shoulder seams. Pin the collar and neck edge together at both shoulder seams. Ease and pin the collar and neck edges together between the points already pinned.

If the collar is smaller than the neckline, clip the seam allowance of the collar at ¾- to 1-inch (2- to 2.5-centimeters) intervals down to the line of staystitching. If the collar is larger than the neck edge, clip the neck the same way. If you have been careful to make ⅝-inch (1.5-centimeter) seams throughout, you will find that the collar, neck edge, and facing will fit together accurately. If you have been careless about the width of seams, you may find that your pieces will not fit together as they should.

When pinning together two parts of a garment, first pin the ends together. Then pin the centers together. Then ease the rest of the seam area into place before pinning it together. In pinning any seam together, if you begin at one end of the seam and work toward the other end, one side may stretch more and become longer than the other. Avoid this problem by pinning the ends together, then the centers, and finally the areas between these points.

Types of closures

Almost everybody looks and feels better in well-fitted clothes. Did it ever occur to you just how difficult it would be to have well-fitting clothes without fasteners and closures? Of course, there are some stretch garments, such as underwear and knit wear, that can be slipped over the body. They are made without closings. Many clothes, however, look better for a longer time if they have been made to include closures and fasteners, such as zippers, buttons, and snaps.

Zippers are the most common kind of closure used in clothing. There are two types of zippers on the market today. They include the traditional zipper, with visible teeth, and the invisible zipper, so called because the teeth are hidden behind a fold in the zipper tape. Either type of zipper can be purchased in several lengths and weights. Those with metal teeth are stronger and are used with firmly woven or heavy fabrics. The syn-

thetic zippers are lighter and more flexible. They are made for use with lightweight fabrics and most knits. Each can be considered satisfactory if the finished closing keeps the zipper invisible and the stitching is straight. Since there is such a wide variety of acceptable zipper application methods, follow the one on your zipper package. You will probably find that it gives you very satisfactory results.

Attractive, simple garments made by beginners can give confidence for sewing more complicated projects. When using plaid fabric, choose a pattern with few seams. *Butterick Fashion Mktg. Co./A Div. of American Can Co.*

Seams						
Stitching straight ____						
Correct width ____						
Pressed open and flat ____						
Zipper						
Straight stitching ____						
Flat ____						
Hidden ____						
Lap in right direction ____						
Facings						
Clean-finished ____						
Trimmed and clipped ____						
Understitching close to seam line, both seam allowances caught ____						
Seams match those of garment ____						
Hand work and hemming						
Not visible from right side ____						
Suitable stitch and thread ____						
Fullness eased ____						
Even width ____						
Pressing						
Unit principles followed ____						
With grain ____						
Steam used ____						
No shine or seam or dart imprints ____						
Fit						
Ease for comfort and movement ____						
No wrinkles or strain ____						
Darts appropriately placed ____						
Seams in proper place ____						

Bulletin board IDEA

Title: *Busy as Bees*
Directions: Mount large cutouts of bees to look as if they are flying around a hive. On each bee, write words appropriate for the construction techniques students are expected to be using that week.

Determine the cause of wrinkles in an ill-fitting garment. Make needed alterations to eliminate them.

Vertical or near-vertical wrinkles mean a garment piece is too wide. Alter by taking a tuck, increasing the size of the seam, or by adding an additional seam.

Horizontal or near-horizontal wrinkles indicate that the garment piece is too tight horizontally or too long.

a If tight, alter by letting out the vertical seams.

b If long, alter by recutting or by taking a wide horizontal seam.

Diagonal wrinkles are due to strain or excess length at one edge. If you trace the wrinkle to the point, or points, of origin, you will locate the trouble.

a If due to strain, alter by letting out nearest seam to allow more fabric.

b If due to excess length at one side, alter by taking up nearest horizontal seam, increasing size of a dart, or adding an additional dart.

c If due to dart too small for size of bulge, alter by making dart bigger. Obtain needed length or width by letting out seam.

Buttonholes are of three kinds: machine-made buttonholes, hand-worked buttonholes, and bound buttonholes. The type you decide to make might depend on your fabric, as well as on the equipment you have available.

In clothing for women and girls, buttonholes are placed so that the right side of the garment laps over the left. In men's clothing, the reverse is true. All buttonholes are made through two or more thicknesses of fabric. Most buttonholes wear better and hold their shape longer if some type of interfacing is used between the facing and the garment piece.

The size of the button used determines the size of the buttonhole. The buttonhole should be just large enough for the button to pass through easily.

When making buttonholes by any method, follow the markings on the pattern which indicate where the buttonholes are to be made. Use machine basting stitches to transfer marks from the wrong to the right side of the fabric.

When making machine-made buttonholes, follow the directions given by the manufacturer for using the machine or its special attachments. When the buttonhole has been made, cut it open between the two lines of zigzag stitching.

When making hand-worked buttonholes, cut the marked buttonhole, and use the buttonhole stitch. This knot-type stitch keeps the cut edge of the buttonhole from raveling when a garment is worn or laundered.

A bound buttonhole can be made by a variety of acceptable methods. Since these buttonholes are usually used only in tailored garments, most beginners do not make them. If you are particularly interested in learning this sewing process, perhaps your teacher will give you directions for making a sample bound buttonhole.

Making and setting sleeves

Many students select sleeveless garments for beginning projects. These projects do not require set-in sleeves. However, since there are sleeves in so many of the garments teenagers like to wear, most students decide to learn how to put sleeves in garments while they have help from a sewing instructor. Sleeves are really quite easy to set into garments if the sleeves are attached before either the underarm seam of the sleeve or bodice is sewn. Follow this easy step-by-step process:

1 Leave the sleeve flat with the underarm seam open.

2 Staystitch the top of the sleeve on the seam line. Use regular stitches from the sleeve edge to the first notch. Change the stitch length to a basting stitch, and continue stitching over the cap of the sleeve to the next notch. Return to the regular stitch length, and continue

 Make a list of sewing techniques not included in your project such as making buttonholes, attaching zippers, or sewing special seams. Make another list of ways to keep the clothing lab in order such as organizing supplies, catalogs, and magazines, dusting and straightening shelves, watering plants. Keep your lists in a folder. When you have spare time (as you wait for help or your turn at a machine), do one of the items on your lists. Place a memo or sample in your folder. Share your folder with your teacher for evaluation.

 Your career
Dressmaker

You would make garments for the individual customer and fit them accordingly. You would provide the fabric for the garments, or the customers might supply their own. Skills in sewing techniques and fitting accurately are important. You might work in a dressmaking shop, be self-employed, or free-lance your services to pattern companies.

Often, just one sewing project will introduce you to many of the *special construction skills.*
Butterick Fashion Mktg./A Div. of American Can Co.

Match the clothing construction *procedures* in List A with the *terms* in List B. Use a term from List B only once.

List A: Procedures

A Done on folded edge of facing so raw edge is hidden

B Done through facing and seam allowance so facing will lie flat

C Done so garment pieces will not stretch out of shape

D Done to eliminate bulk on facing seam allowances

E Done on outward, curved seams

F Done on inward, curved seams

List B: Terms

1 Clean finishing

2 Clipping

3 Grading

4 Notching

5 Staystitching

6 Understitching

stitching to the other edge of the sleeve.

3   If the lower edge of the sleeve is to be finished with a hem, stay-stitch it ¼ inch (.6 centimeter) from the edge, and clean-finish it. (See page 356.)

4   With the right side of the sleeve to the right side of the bodice, match the notch at the top of the sleeve to the shoulder seam or notch at the shoulder of the garment. Match the front notches and the back notches of sleeve and garment. Pin the ends of the sleeves to the ends of the armholes.

5   Adjust the sleeve to fit the armhole by pulling the machine basting slightly.

6   Sew the sleeve to the garment with a ⅝-inch (1.5 centimeters) seam. Sew from the sleeve side with the garment side on the underneath. Avoid stitching puckers into the seam line if the sleeve has a smooth cap.

7   Stitch the underarm seam of the garment and sleeve all in one seam, being careful to match the underarm seams together.

Hems

The bottom edge of skirts, blouses, sleeves, and other parts of garments must be finished in some way to keep the raw edges from showing. The most common finish used is a hem formed by folding the fabric up and sewing it in place with invisible hand stitches that barely catch the outside fabric. Hems vary in width depending upon the fabric and style of the garment. There are many suitable hemming stitches that may be used, but none should be noticeable on the right side. Many garments can be hemmed easily and successfully with a fusible bonding material which sticks the fabric together.

A good hem is the same width all the way around, hangs evenly, and contains hemming stitches which are invisible from the top side of the garment.

Number from 1 to 25. Beside each number indicate if the corresponding statement is true or false. *Do not* write in this book.

1 Patterns are purchased in the same size as ready-to-wear clothing.
2 To get accurate measurements, remove heavy outer clothing before measuring your body.
3 Successful pattern selection involves understanding what the lines of a garment will do for you.
4 Ease-allowance patterns are quick to make.
5 The pattern envelope shows the number of pieces included.
6 A pattern envelope shows how to lay out your fabric.
7 A guide sheet tells how much fabric to buy.
8 *Unit method of construction* means the pattern has one main piece.
9 Buy a pants pattern to fit your waist measurement.
10 The waist length is measured from the bone at the back of your neck to the natural waistline.
11 To find the hip measurement, place the tape measure around the fullest part of the hips.
12 In making a particular garment, use of a fabric which is 60 inches (150 cm) wide may require less yardage than a fabric which is 45 inches (115 cm) wide.

13 Pins should be placed 2 inches (5 cm) apart when pinning pattern pieces to fabrics.
14 The sewing line on a pattern is indicated by a broken line.
15 In transferring pattern markings to fabric, the shiny side of the tracing paper is placed against the wrong side of the fabric.
16 Staystitching is done ¼ inch (.6 cm) from the cut edge of a pattern piece.
17 Stitching done on the right side of the fabric is *directional stitching*.
18 Stitching lines show more on plain than on printed fabric.
19 Pressing as you sew is as important as stitching.
20 V-shaped symbols that aid in matching pattern pieces are *darts*.
21 *Directional cutting* is done to prevent raveling of raw edges.
22 Interfacing is used for body.
23 Patterns should be adjusted to your measurements before they are cut.
24 A fitted facing is made from a piece of bias fabric cut 1 inch (2.5 cm) wide.
25 Understitching is done ⅝ inch (1.5 cm) from the seam line.

Number from 1 to 6 on a piece of paper. Beside each number write the letter corresponding to the *incorrect* response for that item. *Do not* write in this book.

1 Male pattern sizes do *not* come in:
A Boys
B Teen Boys
C Mens
D Talls
2 Female pattern sizes do *not* come in:
A Junior Petite
B Junior Miss
C Misses
D Half-size
3 Information *not* found on a pattern envelope is:
A Side view
B Yardage required
C Suggested fabrics
D Number of pattern pieces
4 Information *not* found on an instruction sheet is:
A Layout
B Directions for alterations
C Suggested fabrics
D Directions for staystitching
5 Pressing is *not* done:
A With grain
B So visible seams are open and flat
C From the outside of garment
D With steam

364

Unit 5

Your Foods

Copy and complete the crisscross word puzzle below, using a separate sheet of paper. Write the answers to correspond to the ACROSS and DOWN items. *Do not* write in this book.

ACROSS

1 A butter substitute with vitamin A added
6 The calories you need depend in part on this
8 High-calorie source of energy
9 Found in sugars and starches
10 Richest source of vitamin C
12 Classification for chicken
14 Ingredient in many high-calorie foods
16 Best source of calcium
18 As important as food
20 Measurement of heat
21 A food containing vitamin A, protein, and iron
25 Good source of vitamin C
26 Helps skin manufacture vitamin D
27 Food product made from skim or whole milk
28 Vitamin A helps you see better then

DOWN

1 Calcium, phosphorus, iron, iodine
2 Good sources of the B vitamins
3 Dried fruit source of iron and energy
4 Vitamin B_3
5 Protein food from young sheep
6 Vitamin necessary for healthy skin and eyes
7 Help regulate body processes
11 Good way to eat fruits and vegetables
12 Nutrient needed for growth and repair
13 Vitamin B_1
15 Excellent source of vitamin A
17 Excellent source of protein
19 A low-calorie source of protein
22 High-calorie foods with no nutritive value
23 Mineral that prevents goiter
24 Provided by calories

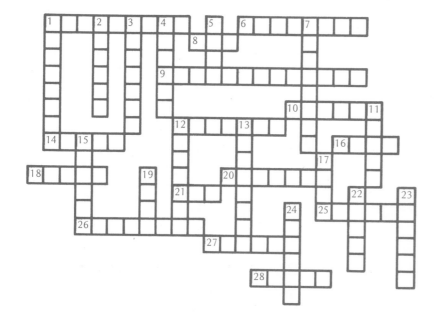

Match the *body functions* in List A with the *nutrients* which encourage them in List B. Use a nutrient from List B only once. *Do not* write in this book.

List A: Body Functions

A Helps prevents colds, sore gums, and easy bruising
B Helps prevent dry skin
C Helps in formation of strong bones and teeth
D Promotes tissue growth and repair
E Helps body utilize calcium

List B: Nutrients

1 Calcium
2 Protein
3 Vitamin A
4 Vitamin C
5 Vitamin D

Chapter 18

Choosing Food for Your Appearance and Health

After reading this chapter, you should be able to:

1 Name the four food groups that make up the *Daily Food Guide*.
2 State the number of servings recommended daily for each of the four food groups.
3 Give examples of various foods in each of the four food groups.
4 Describe how good nutrition can affect you both now and in the future.
5 Explain what a calorie is.
6 Summarize what affects how many calories a person needs.
7 Point out how various nutrients affect the growth and maintenance of your body.
8 Determine how a lack of various nutrients can affect your body.
9 Point out why your body needs specific vitamins and minerals.
10 Analyze menus for nutritive value.

Food serves several purposes in our lives. It not only keeps us alive but fulfills social and psychological needs. You have probably heard the old saying that some people eat to live and other people live to eat. Some people eat because their friends are eating or because it gives them something to do. Many people eat more than they need just because they enjoy food so much. Some people eat when they are bored, nervous, or unhappy. People who are both healthy and attractive have learned that certain foods, eaten in proper amounts, give them the materials their bodies need for growth, repair of body tissues, and energy. This is what nutrition is all about.

THE IMPORTANCE OF GOOD NUTRITION

Just as an engine will not run without fuel, so your body will not operate very long without food. An

Write the alphabet on a sheet of paper. Number each letter in order. Decode the names of the following food service career jobs.

3 15 15 11

3 8 5 6

2 1 11 5 18

23 1 9 20 5 18

3 1 20 5 18 5 18

4 9 19 8 23 1 19 8 5 18

19 1 12 1 4 / 13 1 11 5 18

4 9 5 20 9 20 9 1 14

18 5 19 20 1 21 18 1 14 20 /
   13 1 14 1 7 5 18

3 1 11 5 / 4 5 3 15 18 1 20 5 18

6 15 15 4 / 16 18 15 4 21 3 20 19 /
   20 5 19 20 5 18

6 15 15 4 / 3 8 5 13 9 19 20

19 8 15 18 20 / 15 18 4 5 18 /
   3 15 15 11

6 15 15 4 / 16 18 15 4 21 3 5 18

3 15 21 14 20 5 18 /
   23 15 18 11 5 18

4 9 5 20 9 20 9 1 14 19 / 1 9 4 5

6 15 15 4 / 19 5 18 22 9 3 5 /
   13 1 14 1 7 5 18

22 5 7 5 20 1 2 12 5 / 3 15 15 11

16 1 19 20 18 25 / 3 8 5 6

6 15 15 4 / 18 5 19 5 1 18 3 8 5 18

6 15 15 4 / 2 21 25 5 18

13 5 14 21 / 16 12 1 14 14 5 18

3 8 5 6 19 / 8 5 12 16 5 18

3 1 18 8 15 16

13 5 1 20 / 3 21 20 20 5 18

19 20 15 18 5 / 13 1 14 1 7 5 18

engine may run along for a while on low-quality fuel. However, it will run better and longer if provided with the type and amount of fuel it was built to run on. In much the same way, your body can operate longer and more efficiently when you provide it with the kind and amount of food it needs.

In recent years some alarming facts have been discovered about the importance of good nutrition for young children. Studies have proven the slow physical and mental development of children who received poor nutrition during the first months of life. Such children are never really able to recover fully. Mothers who eat poorly prior to, and during, their pregnancies are unable to provide proper nutrition for their babies, let alone themselves. This is true in areas where the people suffer from famine. But surprisingly, it is also true in areas where people have plenty of food but are uninformed or careless about what they do eat.

When you are in your teen years, the nutritional needs of your body are higher than at almost any other period of your life. You are usually growing rapidly, burning up massive amounts of energy, and going through many changes in physical development. The need for a balanced diet coincides with the time when you have more freedom to select your food without the control of adults. Most teens enjoy this freedom. Yet many also make un-

wise food choices that deprive them of the food they need to look and feel their best.

Remember, the food you eat greatly influences the health of your skin, eyes, fingernails, bones, teeth, and body proportions. Eating the right foods every day can do more for your looks than any other single thing you can do. No matter how carefully you select your clothes, put on makeup, or groom your hair, poor nutrition can spoil it all.

Being able to select a balanced diet requires some understanding of nutrients. The truth is that the food you eat during these teen years will have far-reaching effects on how you look and feel now and in the future.

WHAT ARE NUTRIENTS?

Your body needs several kinds of materials to make it work properly. These materials are called *nutrients* because they nourish the body. The nutrients include proteins, carbohydrates, fats, vitamins, and minerals.

Proteins

Protein is necessary for body growth and repair. Without protein, your body is unable to grow or to repair its own bruises, cuts, broken bones, or injured muscles.

High-quality protein is found mostly in foods from animal sources. Therefore, meat, poultry, fish, cheese, milk, and eggs are considered the best protein sources. Because these animal products contain all of the necessary building blocks, they are called *complete proteins*. Most vegetable protein contains only some of the building blocks. Such protein is called *incomplete protein*.

Carbohydrates

Plant foods which contain large amounts of starch or sugar are called *carbohydrates*. Your body can easily change both starch and sugar into a form usable as energy. Cereals, fruits, and vegetables are examples of carbohydrate foods. They come from plants, contain a large amount of starch or sugar, and are rich in energy.

Many foods containing starch and sugar are good food choices because they are also rich in other important nutrients. On the other hand, some foods are almost pure carbohydrate with very few other nutrients. Since it is easy for your body to change carbohydrate into fat and to store the fat in your tissues, these can be poor food choices.

To keep your weight in proportion to your height and body build, you need to select carbohydrate foods wisely. For example, even though potatoes, corn, and fruit contain large amounts of carbohydrate, their minerals and vitamins are important to your health. Carbohydrate-rich snacks such as candy and soft drinks contain very few valuable nutrients. Since they have little real food value except energy, calories in such foods are often called *empty calories*.

Fats

Fats are high-energy nutrients found in both animals and plants. Cup for cup, they contain more than twice as many calories as pure sugar. The amount of fat you eat each day should be limited if you are to have a trim, attractive figure and a smooth, clear complexion. However, since fat is rich in certain vitamins and in energy, it is important to the diet of most teenagers.

Recent studies indicate that certain fats, particularly animal fats, tend to damage the blood vessels of older people. Research also indicates that such damage begins early in life. If research continues to show danger connected with eating animal fat, perhaps you will want to limit the amount you eat. However, you will still want to include some butter or margarine in your daily diet.

Vitamins

Vitamins help to regulate body processes. Without them, your body cannot function properly or use the nutrients in the food you eat. Although required in very small amounts, they are essential to life and health. For hundreds of years, scientists suspected that foods contained unknown life-supporting

 Explain the term *balanced diet*. Give reasons why a balanced diet is essential for attractive appearance and good health. Relate experiences that show how the foods people eat or do not eat may affect their dispositions.

Answer these questions:
1 What observations have you made about the way people eat to supply their emotional as well as their physical needs?
2 What effect may this habit have on a person's appearance and health?
3 What emotional needs may be satisfied by food?

Show your understanding of nutrition by defending these statements:
1 Food is needed to live, to grow, to be attractive and healthy, to keep well, and to give you energy.
2 A variety of foods is needed to have a well-balanced diet.
3 All nutrients needed by the body can be obtained by eating a well-balanced diet.
4 No one food has all the nutrients your body needs.
5 Nutrients have specific functions in the body.
6 Some nutrients must work with others to be effective.

Pretend one of your friends wants to go on a diet to lose weight. Your friend has asked for your advice about which diet to follow. What advice would you give? What shortcomings should you point out about each of these diets?

1 Eat 6 bananas a day, one every 2½ hours. At the evening meal also have an apple, orange, and 1 cup (240 ml) of cottage cheese. Drink at least 12 glasses of water throughout the day. Continue diet for a month.

2 Eat twelve small meals a day. Eat only one food at each meal. For the first meal have only dry toast. For the second, have a peach. For the third, an egg. For succeeding meals eat just one of these foods and in this exact order: 2 ounces (57 g) tuna, 1 glass skim milk, 1 raw carrot, 3 large lettuce leaves, a 3-by-6-inch (7.5-by-15 cm) wedge of watermelon, 1 slice American cheese, 1 cup (240 ml) cooked beets, 3 crackers, and 2 bran muffins.

Growing young people burn up several thousand calories per day as they engage in many activities. *Sears, Roebuck and Co.*

elements. The actual discovery of vitamins, however, did not occur until the twentieth century.

During the Golden Age of Greece, fifth century B.C., physicians began to suspect that certain foods contained hidden particles necessary for good health. Various of the food-connected diseases were described during that time and soon after. Early scientists learned that some diseases could be prevented by eating certain foods. However, they could never

find exactly what it was in the food that made the difference.

Early in this century, with the aid of improved research techniques, scientists finally discovered the vitamins which had been only partially understood for so long. As each vitamin was discovered, it was given a letter name. Thus the letters A, B, C, and D simply denote the order in which research work developed. As the complicated vitamin B was examined, it was found to consist of several similar vitamins. The different vitamins were then named B_1, B_2, B_3, and so on, and called the *B complex*.

Finally, vitamins were isolated and their exact contents were determined. As scientists came to understand the content of each one, they were able to make that vitamin in the laboratory. Thus the vitamins used today are frequently laboratory products, made as a result of centuries of research.

During early research, some people thought there were only two vitamins: one that dissolved in fat and one that dissolved in water. Then it became clear that there are several *fat-soluble* and several *water-soluble* vitamins. Because the vitamins within each of these groups have much in common, they can be studied as a large group. By studying vitamins according to how they dissolve rather than according to letter order, you will be able to understand better where to find and how to care for each one.

The fat-soluble vitamins

The fat-soluble vitamins, A, D, E, and K, dissolve in fat. As you might expect, they are found in the fatty parts of plants and animals. The fat-soluble vitamins your body needs are taken directly from the foods you eat. Extra vitamins are stored in your body.

Since they do not dissolve in water, the body does not throw away vitamins A, D, E, and K in the food waste. It is therefore possible to get more of these vitamins than your body can use. An overdose of vitamins is very unlikely from simply eating vitamin-rich foods. However, it is possible to get a bad vitamin reaction or vitamin poisoning if you take large doses of pills containing vitamins which your body does not need.

Vitamin A helps to keep your skin in good condition. It also affects your eyesight. Without vitamin A, your eyes cannot adjust well to bright light or semidarkness. For example, if you have trouble adjusting to the dim light of a movie theater when coming in from the light outdoors, you may need more vitamin A. If your skin is dry and rough, or if the linings of your nose, mouth, and throat are easily irritated, you may need more vitamin A.

Vitamin A is found in the fatty parts of animal products. Cream, butter, cheese, and egg yolks are good sources of vitamin A. Animal liver is extremely rich in vitamin A because the unneeded vitamin an animal has eaten is stored in its liver.

Many bright-colored vegetables are good sources of vitamin A. Does this statement seem surprising when you know vegetables contain very little fat and vitamin A is found in fatty foods? It can be explained this way: Bright-colored vegetables contain a material called *carotene*. Your body can change carotene into vitamin A. Therefore, when

Number off from 1 to 4. Form groups according to like numbers. Select a nutrient and write a skit about it. Research to find the following information to include in the skits:

1 History of its discovery
2 Functions in the body
3 Deficiency symptoms
4 Food sources

Use the following information to help get you started:

Vitamin A
Early Greeks with night blindness were told to eat liver dipped in honey. Later, fishermen blinded by the glaring sun on water ate the livers of codfish and sea gulls to improve their vision. The vitamin A eaten by the Greeks and fishermen not only improved their vision but contributed to their overall health.
Deficiency symptoms: night blindness, flaky and dry skin.
Riboflavin
Scientists discovered test animals lacking in other nutrients continued to grow if fed whole grains. The fact that people are taller today than before enrichment programs can be seen in the size of medieval suits of armor.
Deficiency symptoms: cracked lips in corners, sore mouth, shiny and purple-colored tongue.

Vitamin C

In 1591, on the first English expedition to the East Indies, crews on three of the four ships were so disabled by scurvy they could barely sail. On the fourth ship, the daily ration included citrus juice, usually lime. That is why British sailors became known as *limeys*.

Deficiency symptoms: sore and bleeding gums, frequent colds, easy bruising, loss of appetite, and slow-to-heal cuts.

Vitamin D

Rickets was first recognized about the time the Pilgrims landed at Plymouth. About 150 years later it was found that oil from the liver of codfish prevented this bone-weakening disease. This fact was discovered too late for George Washington, who suffered from rickets and also lost his teeth in early adulthood.

Deficiency symptoms: weak bone structure, slow blood clotting, poorly formed teeth.

Bulletin board IDEA

Title: *The Shape of Things to Come*

Directions: Pin up a silhouette of a slender and an overweight figure. Around the slim figure place pictures of nutritious, low-calorie foods. Around the heavy figure put pictures of high-calorie, empty-calorie foods.

Vitamins, A, D, E, and K are fat soluble vitamins. They are stored in your body for use when needed. *St. Louis District Dairy Council*

you eat bright green or bright yellow or orange vegetables and fruits, your body can make its own vitamin A. Cantaloupes, carrots, broccoli, and spinach are rich sources.

Vitamin D is called the *sunshine vitamin*. It was given this name after it was discovered that the human body, when exposed to the direct rays of the sun, can make its own supply of vitamin D.

Vitamin D is essential to bone growth. Without it, the human body cannot use the minerals needed to build strong bones. Since a young child's bones grow at a rapid rate, it is vital that children receive vitamin D either in the diet or by exposure to sunlight.

Vitamin D is stored in the livers of many animals. The best-known form of this vitamin is found in fish-liver oil. In times past, children were fed cod-liver oil when they were young. Since scientists have discovered how to make this essential vitamin in the laboratory, it is now being fed to children either in drop form or as part of their milk supply.

Other fat-soluble vitamins include vitamins E and K. Vitamin E seems to provide protection for vitamin A, preserving it from destruction until your body can use it. It is definitely known that vitamin K helps the blood to clot when your body is injured. Both vitamins have many other uses, some of which have not been discovered.

Vitamins E and K seem to be found in many of the foods generally eaten for good health. Green leafy vegetables, fruits, and liver contain both vitamins. When enough of the foods are eaten to provide for general good health, a plentiful amount of vitamins E and K is included.

The water-soluble vitamins

The water-soluble vitamin group is made up of the vitamin B complex and vitamin C. Since these vitamins dissolve in water, they remain in liquid solution within your body. Thus, unneeded vitamins are discarded daily along with body waste. The body does not store them.

The vitamin B family was found to be a complex group of vitamins. Some scientists feel there may be fifteen or more vitamins in the B group. As each numbered vitamin was chemically understood, it was given a name related to its content. Among the group for which names have been established are *thiamine* (B_1), *riboflavin* (B_2), and *niacin* (B_3). It is not known whether every B vitamin is essential to human growth and health. These three, however, are very important.

The B vitamins help keep your appetite and digestion normal, your nervous system healthy, and your skin smooth. They are found in many foods. If you are careful to eat meat, milk, fruits and vege-tables, and grain products, most of the B vitamins will be provided.

Because the B vitamins are water soluble, they are not stored in your body but are discarded daily. This can be a problem, because you must eat vitamin B-rich foods daily.

Vitamin C, like the B complex vitamins, is water soluble. The amount of vitamin C supplied by one serving of citrus fruit or other food rich in this vitamin is not stored in the body. Therefore, one serving of a vitamin C-rich food is recommended every day.

Vitamin C is also easily oxidized. In other words, it easily combines with oxygen and thus is no longer vitamin C. If a vitamin C-rich food comes in contact with a sodalike compound, or is left in the open air, much of the vitamin C is oxidized, or lost.

Vitamin C is a very essential vitamin found mostly in such fresh fruits and vegetables as oranges, grapefruit, lemons, strawberries, tomatoes, and broccoli. People who fail to get enough vitamin C over an extended period of time may notice that they bruise easily and have frequent colds. Their gums may bleed easily, their teeth may loosen, and their joints may become sore. Although death from lack of vitamin C is not common in the United States today, many people suffer vitamin C shortage. To prevent this shortage, include at least one vitamin C-rich fruit or vegetable in your food each day.

Use the telephone dial below to decode the following names of vitamin C-rich foods. Each food mentioned will supply your daily requirement from one serving.

6 7 2 6 4 3 7
5 3 6 6 6 7
4 7 2 7 3 3 7 8 4 8
5 4 6 3 7
7 8 7 2 9 2 3 7 7 4 3 7
2 7 6 2 2 6 5 4
2 6 5 5 2 7 3 7
7 3 3 / 7 3 7 7 3 7
8 8 7 6 4 7 / 4 7 3 3 6 7

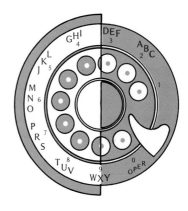

Bulletin board IDEA
Title: *Health Is More Than Luck*
Directions: Use a cutout of a four-leaf clover. On each leaf write the name of one of the food groups and/or use pictures of foods in that group.

Divide into groups. Select one nutrient. Write some TV commercials to sell this nutrient. Present your commercials in class. What made the ads appealing? How might they be changed to influence consumers more positively?

Choose a nutrient. Pretend it is running for public office. Write a short campaign speech telling about the good qualities of this nutrient. If you could vote for only one nutrient on the basis of these speeches, which would it be? Why?

Act out an interview for a job application. Have one class member do the interviewing. Have each of the others represent a food nutrient. During the interview each nutrient must explain why it is the best applicant for a job with the Appearance Company.

Bulletin board IDEA
Title: *Bull's Eye to Good Health*
Directions: Draw circles to look like an archery target. On three cutouts of arrows pointing toward the bull's eye, write *balanced diet, exercise,* and *sleep.*

Vitamins B and C dissolve in water. Since they are not stored in your body to any extent, it is important each day to eat foods containing these vitamins. *St. Louis District Dairy Council*

It is not a good health practice to take very large quantities of vitamin C over a long period of time. When the intake of vitamin C is then reduced to the recommended daily serving, such as a glass of orange juice, it takes time for the body to readjust. In the meantime, vitamin C deficiencies often appear. Your body can become dependent upon excessive quantities of vitamin C.

Minerals

You know minerals in the form of rocks and salts. Your body needs tiny amounts of certain of these minerals to function properly. Among the minerals you need every day are calcium, phosphorus, iron, and iodine. You also need tiny amounts of a long list of minerals called *trace elements.* They include copper, sodium, potassium, magnesium, cobalt, chlorine, sulfur, and zinc.

Scientists are still searching to find exactly what the trace elements do for you. Although they have not yet determined exactly how much you need, they know that the person who eats plenty of the foods containing calcium, phosphorus, iron, and iodine seems to get enough of the trace elements for good health.

Calcium and phosphorus

The minerals calcium and phosphorus seem to work together as a team. The bones and teeth contain most of the calcium and phosphorus found in the entire human body. Milk and milk foods are extremely rich sources of calcium. Calcium and phosphorus are found together in similar amounts in many other foods. But your body needs more calcium than phosphorus. When bones and teeth are being formed, it is especially important to drink milk. During the teen years, your daily diet should include four cups of milk daily in some form.

Vitamin D fits into the bone-making process. Without vitamin D, your body can't use the calcium and phosphorus you take in. Only when you have vitamin D, calcium, and phosphorus present in proper proportion are you able to build strong bones and teeth. (See page 372 for discussion of vitamin D.)

Iron

Iron, found in your red blood cells, combines with the oxygen you take into your lungs and is carried to all parts of your body. Without this iron-oxygen combination, you could not change the food you eat into the energy you need.

A lack of iron in the blood causes a disease called *anemia*. Whenever blood is lost, iron is lost, too.

Your body can store iron in the liver as well as in the blood. Therefore, you need not eat great quantities of iron-rich foods daily. If you eat meats, eggs, leafy vegetables, whole-grain cereals, and dried fruits and vegetables, you probably get enough iron for your needs.

Iodine

Your body uses iodine to help the thyroid gland produce the thyroid hormone. The thyroid hormone affects growth and weight. A lack of iodine in the body can affect the metabolism and slow the normal growth of children. In adults, it usually causes a lack of energy and a general tired feeling. The slowing down of body movement can cause a person to gain unwanted weight. If you do not get enough iodine, the thyroid will enlarge in an effort to produce its hormone. This produces a condition called *goiter*. Goiter causes an unsightly swelling at the front of the neck. Today goiter hardly exists as a disease in this country. Most people avoid iodine shortage by using *iodized* salt.

Fish and seafood are among the best natural sources of iodine. If you frequently eat a variety of seafoods or use iodized salt, you probably get all the iodine you need. Your body loses a little iodine every day, however, so you must constantly replace it with a new supply.

Your career
Dietitian

You would plan diets and menus for one person or a large group of people. You might supervise food preparation and service, and manage food service activities. You might also teach dietetics and nutrition, counsel clients regarding proper nutrition, or do dietary research. You would find employment with hospitals, schools, the armed forces, large restaurants and cafeterias, and colleges and universities.

Your career
Nutritionist

You would research and study the composition of foods, and determine how each nutrient is utilized by the body. You would also determine how each nonnutritive component in food affects the body. You might plan menus and food guides to insure proper nutrient intake. You would work for food companies, test kitchens, government agencies, or specialized clinics and health centers.

Food appears to be more appetizing when the colors are bright and varied than when they are dull and similar. *Green Giant Company*

Foods seem tastier when they are varied and chosen to complement each other than when they have similar flavors. *Green Giant Company*

Foods are more interesting when their shapes vary than when there is a sameness in their shapes.
Green Giant Company

Foods are more palatable when their textures vary from soft to chewy to crisp than when they are prepared to have similar textures. *Green Giant Company*

List food fallacies and tell old wives' tales about food selection and preparation. Judge the merits of the following beliefs and related facts.

Fallacies

1 All disease is caused by poor nutrition.
2 Crops have less nutritive value than in the past because the soil has lost its vitamins and minerals.
3 Chemical fertilizers poison soil.
4 Foods grown with organic fertilizers are better for you than those grown with chemical fertilizers.
5 Modern processing removes most of the nutrients in foods.
6 Drinking milk and eating fish in the same meal will make you sick.
7 Protein is the only nutrient that meat contributes to the diet.
8 Meat should not be eaten in the summer because it increases body temperature.

Facts

1. Some diseases such as rickets, scurvy, and beriberi are caused by dietary deficiencies, but these are rare in the United States. Some diseases are hereditary; others are caused by viruses.

WATER IN THE DIET

Water is not a nutrient, but it is essential to life and good health. Your body uses liquids to carry food materials used by the body. Water is needed to help your body digest the foods you eat. The body also gets rid of waste matter in the water it eliminates. Liquids help to keep you cool as perspiration evaporates from the skin. A person can live for a much longer period of time without food than without water.

Your body cannot function without water. Foods such as fruit juices and milk contain a large proportion of water. These foods help you meet the requirement for six to eight glasses of liquid every day.

WHAT ARE CALORIES?

You have probably read and heard the word *calorie* many times. Do you know what a calorie really is? It is not something you can touch or see at all. It is not a food nutrient. Rather, it is a measure of the heat given off by food when it is burned. Your body can turn food into heat, or energy. The ability to produce heat determines whether a food is high or low in calories. For example, a spoonful of burning fat gives off a large amount of heat, while a spoonful of burning green vegetables gives off very little. This is the reason fat is called a high-calorie food, while green vegetables are low in calories.

Your body needs food enough to provide a certain number of calories each day for energy and heat to keep you warm. If the food you eat contains more calories than you need, your body changes the food to fat, stores it, and you gain weight. If you eat fewer calories than your body needs, your body uses the excess stored fat, causing you to lose weight.

How many calories do you need? That depends on your sex, age, size, weight, and activities. There is one other factor, sometimes called *metabolism*, which affects your need for calories. Metabolism refers to the rate at which your body uses the food you eat to maintain your vital processes. These processes are your heart beat, breathing, blood circulation, elimination of waste, and production of new cells.

Do you know someone who seems to eat anything and everything without gaining weight? Do you know other people who seem to eat much less but gain weight easily? How can this difference be explained? Differing rates of metabolism are often the answer. Because people with high rates of metabolism tend to burn up calories, they usually remain thin. On the other hand, because of low rates of metabolism, other people can remain warm and active on far fewer calories. This type of person burns few calories and tends to store extra calories as fat. Such people must be careful of their food choices to remain trim and attractive.

A GUIDE TO NUTRITION

As you study nutrition, it may seem to be a difficult science. Indeed it is. Years and years of research went into the discovery of each of the nutritional facts today's students learn in their early school years.

During this long process of research and discovery, each nutrient had to be fitted into the total health picture. To put all the information together into a workable eating plan probably seemed like a giant jigsaw puzzle.

People who study the content of foods are called *nutrition experts*. Through studies and experiments they have learned which foods contain materials for energy, growth, and body repair. To help you make wise daily food choices, nutrition experts have divided the foods you need into four groups. By choosing daily from these four groups, you choose foods for good nutrition. Eating a wide variety of foods within each of the four groups will help you to be sure that you are getting enough of each nutrient. (See page 380.)

Food Groups

The four food groups include meat, milk, fruits and vegetables, and cereal products. Together these four groups make up the foods included in the *Daily Food Guide*.

Nutrition experts have found that healthy people who eat a certain amount from each of these four groups each day continue to be well fed. In other words, they have plenty of nutrients for energy, growth, and body repair. To round out meals and to satisfy appetites, they use some other foods.

By calling this plan *the 2-4-4-4 Food Guide*, you can easily remember your own food needs. Your body needs two servings of meat, four cups of milk, four servings of fruits and vegetables, and four servings of bread or other cereal products for good daily nutrition. A growing teenager may want more food, but this guide is the place to start. Eat these foods for good health. Add others if you need them for growth and energy.

The meat group

Beef, pork, lamb, fish, poultry, cheese, and eggs are included in the meat group because they are excellent sources of body-building protein. At least two 3-ounce servings of these foods are needed daily. (See page 380.) They contain the building blocks necessary for body growth and repair. Milk, another animal product, is a valuable source of protein. But, because of its high bone-building value, it has been placed in its own separate food group.

Other foods, for example, dry beans, dry peas, lentils, and gelatin, contain protein. However, these

2 Fertilizers are used to restore depleted soil.

3 Chemical fertilizers are needed to grow enough food for all the people in the world.

4 There is no scientific proof to defend this statement. No fertilizers are absorbed directly by plants. However, organic fertilizers may contribute to the spread of some infectious diseases.

5 Modern processing retains nutrients so that canned, frozen, and dried foods are almost as good for you as fresh foods.

6 Any foods that can be eaten separately can be eaten together.

7 Meat not only provides protein but also B vitamins, iron, minerals, and fat.

8 Meat is needed for good nutrition throughout the year. It was once believed that a high-protein diet increased the heat produced by the body. However, recent studies have shown the effect of protein on body temperature is very slight.

Pretend a friend has just made a comment showing belief in a food fallacy. You know the statement is untrue. Why would you want to change your friend's mind? What could you say to change your friend's thinking? How would you say it?

Meat Group

Milk Group

Fruit-Vegetable Group

Bread-Cereal Group

Following the 2–4–4–4 Food Guide enables you to have a nutritious, varied daily diet.
National Dairy Council

foods do not contain all the essential protein building blocks. When several of these foods are eaten together, or when they are eaten in combination with meat or milk, your body can take from each of the different foods the materials needed for growth. Because these foods are substitute sources of the building blocks found in meat, they are sometimes called *meat alternates*. When the alternates are eaten, a smaller amount of meat is necessary for good nutrition. Many people use only alternates and eat no meat at all.

The milk group

Milk and milk foods, such as cheese and ice cream, make up the milk group. Without milk in some form, it is almost impossible to get the minerals necessary for building strong teeth and bones. Teenagers need at least four cups of milk each day served in drinks or in milk-rich foods. Milk and milk products are also important growth and repair foods.

The fruit-vegetable group

The fruit-vegetable group furnishes several vitamins. These vitamins are necessary if your body is to use the foods you eat. In addition to helping your body use foods for growth and repair, the vitamins act as body regulators. They also help prevent diseases. Various vitamins are found in almost all foods, but fruits and vegetables are among the richest vitamin sources.

The fruits and vegetables also provide various minerals, sugar for energy, and the roughage needed for good digestion and elimination. Teenagers need to eat four servings of fruits and vegetables each day. You may choose among raw, cooked, and liquid forms of these foods.

The bread-cereal group

Cereal foods provide energy. They also contain some proteins as well as valuable vitamins. Include four servings of bread or cereal foods among your daily food choices.

Hope of the Future

Scientists have shown us which foods to eat and how to produce food for all the world's peoples. They continue their research in an effort to keep the food production rate ahead of food needs. Can this goal be attained? Yesterday's scientists determined the foods you need. Tomorrow's scientists will be faced with producing these foods through methods not yet discovered.

Prepare a display of foods, food models, and/or pictures showing approximate 100-calorie portions. The list below may give you some ideas:

5 small pretzels
1 small bottle cola
1-in. (2.5 cm) piece pecan pie
9 oz. skim milk (270 ml)
2 T. sugar (30 ml)
1 medium baked potato
7 French-fried potato pieces
1 large banana
1 large cantaloupe
1 T. margarine (15 ml)
2 c. fresh strawberries (480 ml)
1 T. salad dressing (15 ml)
¾ oz. caramels or fudge (21 g)
1 compact head lettuce

Use a table of food values to analyze the foods above for nutritive values other than calories. Which are empty-calorie foods? Which are the best sources of specific vitamins and other nutrients? Which foods should an overweight person choose? Why? Which foods should an underweight person choose? Why?

Bulletin board IDEA
Title: *Please DO Eat the Daisies*
Directions: Use large petals cut from construction paper and mount them to form four daisies. Label the petals with the four food groups.

Match the *functions* in List A with the *nutrients* in List B. Use a nutrient from List B only once. Not all the nutrients in List B are used.

List A: Functions

A Helps prevent colds and other infections

B Helps keep eyes healthy

C Affects blood count

D Helps form healthy bones and teeth

E Helps blood to clot

F Promotes growth and repair of tissue

G Helps prevent goiter

H Affects nervous system

I Helps body use calcium

List B: Nutrients

1 Calcium

2 Iodine

3 Iron

4 Niacin

5 Phosphorus

6 Protein

7 Riboflavin

8 Thiamine

9 Vitamin A

10 Vitamin C

11 Vitamin D

12 Vitamin K

Number from 1 to 7 on a piece of paper. Beside each number write the letter of the *best* answer for that question.

1 Which are good sources of vitamin A?

A Citrus fruits and tomatoes

B Breads and cereals

C Leafy green and bright yellow vegetables

D Dry beans and dry peas

2 Which are good sources of vitamin D?

A Fortified milk and sunshine

B Rice, noodles, and macaroni

C Meat, fish, and poultry

D Bananas, corn, and potatoes

3 Which are good sources of thiamine?

A Oranges, grapefruit, limes

B Cheese, ice cream, and ice milk

C Carrots, spinach, and greens

D Enriched bread and cereal products

4 Which are minerals needed for good health?

A Riboflavin and niacin

B Phosphorus, iron, and iodine

C Starch and sugar

D Ascorbic acid and thiamine

5 For which food group are two daily servings recommended?

A Fruit-vegetable

B Bread-cereal

C Meat

D Milk

6 Which are *all* fat-soluble?

A Vitamins A, B, and C

B Vitamins B, D, and E

C Vitamins C, D, E, and K

D Vitamins A, D, E, and K

Fill in the blank in each sentence with the *best* word to complete the statement. *Do not* write in this book.

1 The amount of money a family spends for food is affected by its size, nutritional needs, food likes and dislikes, and (1) .

2 All food labels are required to give the name and address of the producer, the name of the product, and the net contents of the container in liquid measure or in (2) .

3 Nutrition labeling must be used on all foods for which a nutrition claim is made and all foods which are (3) .

4 Shopping without a list and seeing foods attractively displayed may result in (4) buying.

5 All meat that has passed inspection by the Federal government has a round stamp that is (5) in color.

6 Even distribution of fat throughout meat is called (6) .

7 An egg that is not fresh will have a thin, watery white and a(an) (7) yolk.

8 When milk has been heated to kill harmful bacteria, it has been (8) .

9 Margarine has vitamin (9) added to it.

10 Four forms in which foods may be purchased are fresh, frozen, canned, and (10) .

Chapter 19

Buying Food

Good nutrition is not determined entirely by the amount of money spent for food. Many families who spend a great deal of money are poorly fed without realizing it. Other families who plan carefully and spend less are well nourished. In most cases, the lower a family's cash income, the higher the percentage of income spent on food. Food spending is also related to a family's size, its stage in the family life cycle, and its special health needs and food preferences.

How does a family know how much money to spend on food? The first consideration, of course, is the amount of available money. The second consideration is resources other than money a family may use to place food on the table. For instance, families who have gardens or farms that produce food usually spend less money than families who must buy all of their food. Government assistance

Give examples of foods characteristic of various parts of the country. Some examples might be pinto beans in Texas, macadamia nuts in Hawaii, and pralines in Louisiana.

Explain why food is more expensive in states like Hawaii and Alaska than in mainland states. Which foods are less expensive in your area than in the other parts of the country? Tell why this is true.

Make a calendar and show the fresh fruits and vegetables available each month in your area. Indicate the months when market supply is best.

Make a list of your family's favorite foods. Try to determine why these foods are especially well liked.

Explain ways a family's life-style affects the selection of foods it uses most often. Some examples are:

The homemaker who works may use more convenience and partially prepared foods.

The family with a garden may use more fresh vegetables than canned or frozen.

A large family may buy food in large quantities.

in the form of food stamps or other such plans or meals provided at school or by an employer are also a part of a family's food resources.

The amount of money spent on food also may reflect the amount of time and energy available for food preparation. Families whose members all work or attend school may buy many partially prepared or ready-to-serve items. This tends to increase the total cost of food. Busy families are also tempted to serve snack foods. Unless special attention is given to wise choices, a sacrifice is made in good nutrition.

Families have different customs with respect to food. No matter how families differ in cultural backgrounds, however, they all share the need for good nutrition. The people responsible for planning meals and buying food for the family become responsible, to a large degree, for family health.

WHY FOOD COSTS DIFFER

From day to day and from week to week, food costs change. This change is due to a number of factors. Supply and demand, the cost of producing food, and the cost of shipping and storing it until it is sold all affect food costs. Because of rapid transportation and modern preservation and packaging methods, a wide variety of foods is usually available the year round. Still, the cost of a single item of food may vary greatly from one time of the

year to another. Watch food prices. Compare them when you shop. You will gain a better idea of how much food costs change. You will be better able to recognize good buys and to take advantage of them.

The Source

Food produced and sold locally has little or no shipping costs. It is usually lower in cost than food coming from far away. Thus, if you buy fruits or vegetables grown in your own community, they will probably cost less than those shipped in from another state.

The Season

When there is an abundance of locally produced food on the market, it is usually inexpensive. If the food has been specially handled, stored, or shipped from another part of the country, it is usually expensive. Fresh strawberries and tomatoes, for example, are costly in the North during January and February. They are less expensive in Southern localities where they are in season at that time.

As facilities for storing foods are improved, more and more foods are available in markets all over the country at all seasons of the year. However, the total price paid for a food is affected by storage costs.

The Packaging and Advertising

Each time food is handled, the price goes up. Prewashed, trimmed, and

Preparation of certain foods may be influenced by different cultural backgrounds. However, people of all cultures require good nutrition.
Michal Heron/McGraw-Hill

 Make a list of foods which vary considerably in price from one season to another. Beside the name of each food, write the time of year when it is least expensive in your area. At what time of year is this food most flavorful?

List several foods, such as peas and potatoes, which can be purchased in four forms: fresh, frozen, canned, and dried. What is the price per serving of each? Is the nutritive value the same for each at the time of purchase? What could cause changes in the food value after purchase?

Bulletin board IDEA
Title: *Know the Facts*
Directions: Make a cartoon drawing of a talking can and grade stamp.

Below the cartoon list several facts required by law to be listed on can labels. Also list requirements for a U.S. grade stamp.

packaged fruits and vegetables cost more than those you buy in bulk and clean yourself. For example, cabbage by the head costs much less than shredded cabbage in a package or cole slaw in a plastic container. Buying in large amounts or in bulk form is usually a saving. One large box of cereal costs less, for example, than the same amount of cereal packaged in ten individual boxes. Most supermarkets now display the *unit cost*—price per ounce or gram—on the shelf where the item is displayed. Check these unit prices to know how to get the most for your money. Foods sold in fancy display packages usually cost

Suggest information, other than that required for nutrition labeling, which may be helpful to the consumer when buying canned foods. Include items such as number of servings, recipes, and serving suggestions.

Compare the cost and food value of foods of similar calorie content. Some examples are orange juice and cola, bread and crackers, whole grain bread and enriched white bread, peanut butter and jelly. Which foods give the best nutrition for the money?

Bulletin Board IDEA
Title: *It's in the Bag*
Directions: Pin up a large paper bag. Mount empty food containers to look as though they are coming out of the bag. Tack from the inside to create a three-dimensional effect. Use cereal or rice boxes, egg and milk cartons, frozen vegetable packages, and other empty cartons to represent foods in the *Daily Food Guide*. Underneath write *Using Your Money Wisely*.

Food costs in general are determined by the amount of handling, processing, and packaging necessary to supply a given food in the form in which you wish to buy it.   *Kaiser Aluminum*

more than the same product sold in bulk form. National name brand foods that are highly advertised in magazines and on TV are often sold for more than similar, unadvertised foods or store brand products of the same quality. This possible difference in price may pay for the cost of advertising. On the other hand, advertising may increase the total sales to the point where no increase in price is necessary, or perhaps the price is lowered.

CONSUMER INFORMATION AND PROTECTION

Consumer legislation has been passed to protect the buyer from misleading pricing and packaging. Many foods are also graded according to quality. Try to learn about regulations and laws governing the production, grading, labeling, and marketing of each food item. If you know the laws, you will be a better food buyer. (See pages 236–246.)

All foods moved over state lines are subject to regulation by the United States Food and Drug Administration. Food packagers are required to provide labels telling the name of the product inside, the name and address of the company producing it, and the net contents of the container, by weight or liquid measure.

Since 1975, all fortified foods and all foods for which a nutrition claim is made must contain nutrition information on the labels. In addition to the usual information, the new label tells you the nutritional value of the food. This information must appear in a standard format. It should always be to the right of the main panel of the label so you can find it easily. The following nutrients should be listed per serving: calories, protein, carbohydrate, fat, vitamin A, vitamin C, thiamine, riboflavin, niacin, calcium, and iron.

Some labels also tell you the variety, style, and type of pack. For instance, a label might tell you that you are buying Blue Lake variety of green beans, cream style corn, or pear halves. Another label might tell you that you are buying peaches packed in water or in light or heavy syrup.

If there are additives such as preservatives, fillers, or seasonings, they must also be listed. If you are buying wieners, you can expect the label to tell whether they are all beef, all meat, or contain cereal.

Labels usually contain a picture showing how the product inside looks. Thus, if you are selecting pineapple for a salad, the pictures will show you whether a can contains slices, chunks, or crushed fruit. If you are buying peaches, you might want halves for a salad or ragged pieces for a pie. A label illustration will usually help you identify the form of the product.

Since you cannot see inside cans or packages, brand names are very important as you decide which package or can to buy. As you practice buying and using foods, you will learn which companies produce foods of the quality you desire. You will also learn which *store*, or *house*, *brands* offer good value for money spent. A store, or house, brand is sold in only one chain of stores. The prices of these brands are usually lower than those of national brands of similar products sold in the same store. A dollar or so spent now and then on trial brand products is usually money well spent.

Becoming an informed shopper requires careful observation, reading, and practice. If at all possible, try to shop with the food shopper in your family. This will allow you to practice using consumer information under guidance.

SHOPPING FOR FOOD

The wise shopper knows the types of food necessary for good health.

List food products commercially available in the following forms:
Mixes
Uncooked or unbaked and frozen
Fully cooked or baked and frozen
Chilled and ready-to-eat
Room temperature and ready-to-eat
Compare different forms of the same food for cost, flavor, texture, ease of preparation, and time for preparation. Describe situations when it would be most suitable to use each of the forms mentioned.

Your career
Food products tester

You would develop new food products, or new recipes for items already on the market. You might do kitchen supervision, research, experimental cooking, or promotion work. You might be expected to travel widely to introduce products with demonstration meals and programs for selected audiences. You would work for large food companies.

Select convenience foods from an imaginary emergency shelf and plan menus using them in the following situations:

1 On the spur of the moment, your friends decide to go on a picnic. Everyone begins to tell what they can bring. You do not speak up right away. Only a dessert is still needed.

2 The electric power in your home has gone off. You cannot use the electric range or any appliances. Your family has waited, hoping the power would come back on, but it has not. It's way past your usual dinner hour and everyone is very hungry.

3 A high school friend of your father calls from the service station. He was traveling through your town with his daughter when their car developed engine trouble. It will take three hours to get a needed part and make repairs. It is dinner time and your mother would like to invite them to your home, but there is only enough food prepared for your family.

(See pages 379–381.) If you shop for food needs, rather than whims, your food dollars will go farther. In choosing a food market, consider convenience. If you must walk several blocks with heavy bags of food, it might be wise to pay a little more in a store nearer your home. The kind of cooking your family does may also influence your choice of a market place. The family with more time to spend on cooking may buy large quantities of flour, sugar, shortening, and other staples. They may also keep a large supply of frozen meats and vegetables at home. On the other hand, working families who must prepare the evening meal in a few minutes may form the habit of buying freshly cooked foods as they return home from the day's work. Other quick foods may be a part of their daily menu. All of these factors can in-

Large food processing companies produce, process, and package a broad range of products. The foods are produced to fit company standards and to comply with laws which are made and enforced by government agencies. *Swift & Company*

fluence the family's choice of a marketing place.

Planning the Shopping Trip

Try to plan your food shopping trip before leaving home. Then carry out your plans while shopping. Plans can be altered, if necessary, in the food store. However, a pre-planned trip is usually a more rewarding one. Before leaving home, make the following decisions:

1 Decide which foods are to be served in the meals ahead, and check to see what supplies are already on hand.
2 Decide on the supplies needed, and make a market list.
3 Choose the market carefully. Consider location, service, and advertised prices. Find out when the store gets its supply of fresh produce. Try to shop when food is fresh.

Selecting the Food

Regardless of your family's eating habits, decide what you will buy before entering the store. Plans will help you to avoid picking up something because it looks good rather than because you need it. *Impulse buying* increases the amount of money spent on food, often without improving nutrition.

Before choosing a food, determine whether it is a wise choice.

1 Check labels on packages. Look for information about number of servings, ways to prepare the food, and ways to store it. Compare brands for cost per unit and quality.
2 Keep in mind the way the food is to be used. Select the quality and quantity best for the purpose you have in mind.
3 Check to determine whether in-season locally produced foods are available at a good price.
4 Consider the amount you can use or store easily. If you shop for a small family or if storage space is inadequate, small purchases may be more economical for you than large ones.
5 Consider whether it is wiser to buy fruits and vegetables by weight or by number.
6 Watch for new foods on the market. Decide whether new preparations can add pleasing dishes to the family menu at a saving in cost or time.

BUYING FOOD FOR GOOD NUTRITION

There are a number of ways the nutritional value of a certain food can vary. The way the food is grown, stored, shipped, or prepared may affect its nutritional value. You want to be sure you are buying foods rich in nutrition. You will need to know how to judge the quality of the food you choose.

The protein, carbohydrate, fat, vitamin, or mineral content can vary from one sample of food to another. For instance, one tomato can have more nutrients than another

 Explain in your own words the meaning of the following terms which are used in the U.S.D.A. grading of meat.

USDA Prime: Has liberal quantities of fat marbled within the lean portion and is juicy and tender.
USDA Choice: Contains less fat than does the prime grade but is of high quality.
USDA Good: Contains little fat, but the meat is relatively tender.
USDA Standard: Has very thin covering of fat, but is tender if properly prepared. The flavor is bland and the meat lacks juiciness.
USDA Commercial: Is from slightly older animals. The meat requires long, slow cooking with moist heat to make it tender and juicy.
USDA Utility: Is from old animals. The meat lacks tenderness and must be chopped, ground, or prepared by pot roasting, stewing, or braising.

Classify popular saltwater fish into two categories: finfish and shellfish. Add to the following list.

Finfish	Shellfish
Bass	Clams
Flounder	Crabs
Halibut	Lobsters
Red Snapper	Mussels
Salmon	Oysters
Swordfish	Scallops
Tuna	Shrimp

Explain the differences and similarities between freshwater fish and saltwater fish. Name several examples of both types of fish.

Name edible fish which can be caught in your area. Plan a menu in which one of these fish is served as the main dish. Include a recipe for the fish.

Explain in your own words the following ways that fish are marketed.
Whole (as caught)
Drawn (with entrails removed)
Dressed (with scales, entrails, head, tail, and fins removed)
Steaks (cross-section slices)
Fillets (sides of the fish)

Suggest different methods of cooking and serving various types of fish. Prepare some locally caught fish in a way other than frying.

NUTRITION INFORMATION
(PER SERVING)
SERVING SIZE = 1 OZ.
SERVINGS PER CONTAINER = 12

CALORIES	110
PROTEIN	2 GRAMS
CARBOHYDRATE	24 GRAMS
FAT	0 GRAM

PERCENTAGE OF U.S. RECOMMENDED DAILY ALLOWANCES (U.S.RDA)*

PROTEIN	2
THIAMINE	8
NIACIN	2

*Contains less than 2 percent of U.S. RDA for Vitamin A, Vitamin C, Riboflavin, Calcium, and Iron.

This is the minimum information that must appear on a nutrition label.

of about the same size. The kind of seed planted, the climate and soil in which the plant grew, and the time of year it ripened, whether spring or fall, all affect its nutritional value.

After a plant is harvested, the way it is handled between the field and the market can also affect its food value. Some nutrients are easily destroyed by exposure to air and light. Some nutrients are destroyed by heat but preserved by cold. Sometimes cold temperatures or moisture will make foods such as bananas and citrus fruits spoil quickly. Some foods, such as potatoes and apples, can be held in

NUTRITION INFORMATION
(PER SERVING)
SERVING SIZE = 8 OZ.
SERVINGS PER CONTAINER = 1

CALORIES	560
PROTEIN	23 G
CARBOHYDRATE	43 G
FAT (PERCENT OF CALORIES 53%)	33 G
POLYUNSATURATED*	2 G
SATURATED	9 G
CHOLESTEROL* (20 MG/100 G)	40 G
SODIUM (365 MG/ 100 G)	830 M

PERCENTAGE OF U.S. RECOMMENDED DAILY ALLOWANCES (U.S. RDA)

PROTEIN	35
VITAMIN A	35
VITAMIN C (ASCORBIC ACID)	10
THIAMINE (VITAMIN B₁)	15
RIBOFLAVIN	15
NIACIN	25
CALCIUM	2
IRON	25

*Information on fat and cholesterol content is provided for individuals who, on the advice of a physician, are modifying their total dietary intake of fat and cholesterol.

A label may include optional listings for cholesterol, fats, and sodium.

From among thousands of food items found in local markets, consumers should select foods which fill their family's nutritional needs at a price they can afford to pay.   *Progressive Grocer*

 Decide on ways to use each of the following grades of poultry and eggs.

Poultry Grades

The grading considers *fat covering of the bird, shape, pin feathers, cuts,* and *discoloration.*

U.S. Grade A: Poultry for table use.

U.S. Grade B: Poultry for table use but graded lower on the items listed.

U.S. Grade C: Poultry graded still lower on the items listed.

Egg Grades

U.S. Grades AA and A: Eggs for table use, especially for cooking in the shell, poaching, or frying. They are top quality eggs.

U.S. Grade B: Eggs for table use, baking, and other cooking.

U.S. Grade C: Eggs for baking and other cooking.

Grade B and Grade C eggs are useful for many cooking purposes where appearance and flavor are not important.

Sizes

Extra large: Must weigh 30 ounces (850 g) per dozen.

Large: Must weigh 24 ounces (680 g) per dozen.

Medium: Must weigh 21 ounces (595 g) per dozen.

Small: Must weigh 18 ounces (510 g) per dozen.

cold storage for long periods of time without damage. Other foods lose nutrients if they are held in storage.

Even after food is delivered to the store, nutrients may be lost. This happens when frozen foods are allowed to thaw, when fresh fruits and vegetables get warm, and when eggs, meat, milk and other dairy products are not kept refrigerated. Knowing this, try to buy food at stores with up-to-date storage and refrigeration equipment. Try, also, to buy from a store with a rapid turnover of perishable goods. Many

foods lose quality rapidly. Such foods have dates marked on the package to show when they should no longer be used. Check these dates before you buy.

Buying Meat

The word *meat* to most people means beef, pork, or lamb. Each can be bought more wisely if you have a general knowledge of meat. For example, all fresh meat is moist and of even color.

Meat bearing a round purple stamp shows that it has passed Federal government inspection. This

Buy perishable foods in limited quantities since they spoil rapidly and lose food value. Use the following guidelines for judging the amount to buy.

ITEM	SAFE STORAGE TIME
Meat, Poultry, and Fish	
Meat, fresh	3 to 5 days
Meat, ground	1 to 2 days
Variety meats	1 to 2 days
Poultry, fresh	1 to 2 days
Fish, fresh	24 hours
Shellfish, fresh	24 hours

(All fresh meat, fish, and poultry require loose wrapping. Store in the coldest part of the refrigerator.)

Eggs	
Fresh in shell	2 to 4 weeks
Fresh yolks	2 to 4 days
Fresh whites	2 to 4 days

Milk	
Fresh	5 days
Evaporated, can opened	3 to 5 days

Cheeses	
Cottage cheese	3 to 5 days
Other soft cheese	1 to 2 weeks
Hard cheeses	3 to 6 months

Cooked Milk Foods	
Custards, cream-filled cakes and pies	1 to 2 days in coldest part of refrigerator

When buying beef, veal, pork, or lamb, check it for firmness of texture, brightness of color, and good distribution of fat.   *National Live Stock and Meat Board*

stamp is required on all meat shipped across state lines. The stamp means that the meat was wholesome at the time it was inspected. Meat sold in the same state where it was processed is not required to pass the Federal inspection laws. However, it must be wholesome. If meat does not bear a government stamp, you have only the butcher's reputation and your own ability to recognize quality meats to use as buying guides.

In addition to the Federal inspection stamp, meat also bears a grade stamp. Most meats are labeled *prime, choice, good,* or *standard.* Pork is graded simply *U.S. No. 1,*

IDENTIFY BONES IN RETAIL CUTS

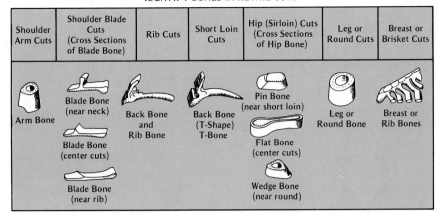

Shoulder Arm Cuts	Shoulder Blade Cuts (Cross Sections of Blade Bone)	Rib Cuts	Short Loin Cuts	Hip (Sirloin) Cuts (Cross Sections of Hip Bone)	Leg or Round Cuts	Breast or Brisket Cuts
Arm Bone	Blade Bone (near neck) / Back Bone and Rib Bone / Blade Bone (center cuts) / Blade Bone (near rib)	Back Bone (T-Shape) T-Bone	Pin Bone (near short loin) / Flat Bone (center cuts) / Wedge Bone (near round)		Leg or Round Bone	Breast or Rib Bones

No. 2, No. 3, or *medium*. The terms *prime* and *U.S. No. 1* indicate highest quality. High grades of meat, except for that from young animals, have a thick outside layer of fat. They also have an even distribution of fat or marbling, throughout. High quality beef is bright red, while pork is pink. The fat is nearly white, dry, and flaky. If the meat is dark and the fat is yellow and oily, the meat is probably from an old animal and therefore of poorer quality. If you plan to use meat for stew or barbeque, low grades will usually serve the purpose at a lower cost than high grades. If you plan to serve a tender oven roast or broiled steak, however, you will want to buy a higher grade of meat.

Because most *prime* (highest quality) meat is reserved for fine hotels and restaurants, the highest quality of meat available to the general public is labeled *U.S. choice*.

Chapter 21 contains information about cooking methods for meats.

Lamb comes from young sheep. Veal comes from young beef. These meats do not have the fat covering and marbling found in older beef and pork. High-quality pork has a heavy fat covering that may or may not be trimmed away by the butcher. If pork is not light pink, or if it is watery and soft, the quality and flavor are usually poor.

When buying special meats, such as wieners, hamburger patties, or prebreaded meat cuts, check the label carefully. Find out how much meat and what kinds of meat are included. A large amount of fat will result in excessive shrinkage during cooking. High cereal content may indicate a poor buy.

Buying Poultry

Poultry, as offered on the market, includes chickens, ducks, geese,

Prepare a display of a canned food, such as green beans or peaches. Use several national and store brands and different grades. Rank them from the most expensive to least expensive as judged by appearance, texture, and flavor. Compare your rankings with the actual prices. Why were some products more expensive than others? How would the way the food is to be used influence a consumer's choice? Give examples of ways in which lower grades of canned goods might be used just as well as higher grades.

Use the following information when buying and preparing canned foods. Discuss in class how this information might help you.

A rusty can is safe to use unless the rust has caused a leak in the can.

If the ends of the can are bulged and swollen, the food is spoiled and should not be eaten.

The contents of a dented can are safe unless the can is leaking.

Canned vegetables are safe to eat without further cooking.

It is safe to keep nonacid food in opened cans in the refrigerator.

Save and use the liquid in which fruits and vegetables are canned. It contains valuable nutrients.

and turkeys. In some markets you will also find Rock Cornish hens, guinea hens, and young pigeons, called squabs.

Like meat, plucked and cleaned, or *dressed,* poultry is graded by Federal and Federal-state programs. A label bearing the grade tells the quality of the poultry you are considering.

In buying whole dressed poultry, look for a pliable breast bone, a good covering of fat, and a Federal or state grade label. In buying cut-up poultry, check the color and size of the individual pieces and the difference in price you are paying for this convenience.

Generally, any poultry available in fresh form can also be found in frozen form. If you have freezer space available, frozen poultry can be an economy buy.

Buying Fish

To choose fish for freshness, look for firm, elastic flesh, bright clear eyes, reddish-pink gills, and a light, pleasant odor.

A large variety of frozen fish is also available. It may be used just as fresh fish is used. Take care to keep fish frozen until shortly before cooking time. Do not refreeze frozen fish after it thaws.

Shellfish includes shrimp, clams, crabs, oysters, lobsters, and scallops. Choose those that have clean shells, good color, and a fresh, light odor. In some parts of the country, shellfish are sold alive in the shell.

In other areas they have the shells removed and are packed in containers for sale by liquid measure or by weight. Shellfish are sometimes sold cooked.

Heat-and-serve frozen fish dishes are also available. Since fish cooks quickly, the choice of these foods saves preparation time rather than cooking time.

Fish spoils easily. Keep all fresh or frozen fish ice cold until cooking time. Buy only well-refrigerated fresh fish or frozen fish which is solidly frozen. Avoid refreezing any kind of uncooked fish.

Buying Eggs

The Federal government sets the standards for grading eggs. Grade AA eggs are the highest quality available on the market. Grade A eggs are also considered to be of high quality. Both grades have a large amount of thick white that stands up well around a firm, high yolk. Eggs with a thin, watery white and a flat yolk are not fresh. They are graded either B or C. Their flavor may be stronger and less pleasant than that of high-grade eggs. (See pictures on pages 395 and 396.)

Eggs are also graded by size and weight per dozen, from *jumbo,* at least 30 ounces (850.5 grams) per dozen, to *small,* at least 18 ounces (510.3 grams) per dozen. The label on the egg carton tells you the grade, or quality, of the contents. When buying eggs, look for the letters *U.S.,* the grade letter, and the

Fresh, high-quality eggs have round, firm yolks that are centered in the whites. *USDA*

Determine what influences a consumer to shop at one store rather than another. Interview several people to find out their reasons. Compile a class list. Which reasons are given most often?

Select four common food items such as bread, cheese, milk, and canned peaches. Compare the cost of the same size package of each in a large supermarket, a small convenience store, and an independent neighborhood food market. Discuss the reasons for the differences in the costs at each type of store. When is shopping for specials a good idea? When may it not be?

Check the prices of selected food items in stores which give trading stamps, have delivery service and charge accounts, and are open long hours. Do the food items cost more in these stores? Why or why not? Under what circumstances might it be necessary to shop in stores with higher prices?

Check food ads in newspapers for special-item sales. Calculate the cost of driving from one store to the other to buy the specials. Would you save money to shop this way? How much extra time would it take?

size. If the prices of the various sizes of eggs vary only a few cents, it is a better choice to buy the larger size.

Shell color has no bearing on egg quality or flavor. There may be a regional preference for either white- or brown-shelled eggs. This can affect the cost and availability of eggs in that region. Flavor and freshness, rather than shell color, determine quality. Buy refrigerated eggs, since eggs retain their freshness best when kept in well-refrigerated storage areas.

Buying Milk and Milk Products

Milk and milk products, such as ice cream, cheese, cottage cheese, and yogurt, are sold and used widely. Milk can be bought in many forms. They include homogenized milk, chocolate milk, skim milk, half-and-half, buttermilk, evaporated milk, and dried milk. The form of milk to choose depends partly on whether you plan to drink the milk or cook with it. (See pages 434–439.)

Milk spoils easily. Spoilage is caused by the growth of bacteria. Useful bacteria causes milk to sour, making the production of all kinds of cheese possible. However, harmful bacteria can also be easily carried by milk. Such diseases as tuberculosis and undulant fever can be contracted by drinking milk contaminated with disease-bearing

Your career
Food chemist

You would conduct chemical experiments to discover the composition of foods. You would experiment with natural and synthetic materials or by-products to develop new foods, preservatives, anti-adulteration agents, and similar products. You might also test food samples to ensure compliance with government food and health laws, and to determine that products meet standards of quality and purity. You would find employment with government agencies and food companies.

Discuss how planning meals by the week can shorten shopping time and expense.

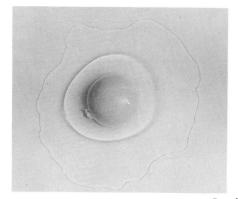
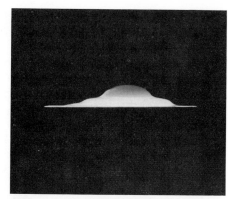

Grade AA

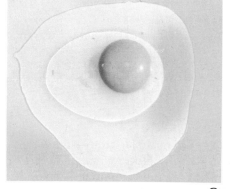
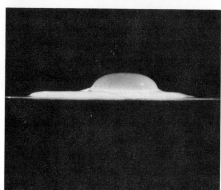

Grade A

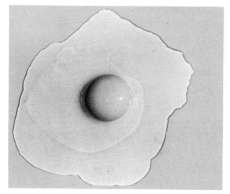

Grade B

The quality of an egg may be determined by the amount the white spreads when the egg is cracked and by the profile of the yellow held suspended within the egg white.   *USDA*

bacteria. For this reason, the quality of any milk supply must be carefully controlled. State, municipal, and county regulations and laws cover the production and handling of milk and milk products. Federal, state, and city inspections of cows, dairies, and dairy foods help to insure a safe milk supply and to protect the consumer.

Most communities require that milk be pasteurized. Pasteurization protects consumers from the diseases that may be carried by raw milk. In pasteurization, milk is heated to 143 degrees Fahrenheit (71 degrees Celsius) for 30 minutes, or to 161 degrees Fahrenheit (80 degress Celsius) for 15 seconds, and then cooled rapidly. This process kills harmful bacteria.

Grade standards for raw and pasteurized milk have been established by the United States Public Health Service. These standards are based on the bacterial counts. Grade A pasteurized milk has a low bacterial count, which makes it safe to drink.

Today many nondairy foods are used as substitutes for real milk products. You are probably familiar with nondairy forms of whipped toppings, coffee cream, sour cream, and milk. Many of these products are less expensive and keep longer than real dairy products. They are vegetable products that have many of the same nutrients as the milk foods. They may make acceptable milk substitutes in many cases. Read their labels carefully to compare their food value with that of milk.

Buying frozen milk products

Many frozen milk products are available. They include ice cream, ice milk, sherbet, ice-cream cakes, frozen cream pies, and individual desserts. Products labeled ice cream must contain a given amount of fat. Other frozen desserts, such as ice milk and sherbet, contain lower amounts of fat. Frozen milk desserts are generally eaten for enjoyment rather than nutrition. Therefore, a certain amount of trial and error is necessary in order to get the best product for the amount of money you wish to spend.

Since the quality of a frozen milk product is harmed by melting, ask the grocery packer to place such items in insulated bags. Place frozen items in a freezer as soon as possible after buying them.

Buying cheese

Cheese is a milk food that is sold under several hundred different names. Although typed differently by different experts, all cheese may be grouped into five large classifications. They include *very hard* (Parmesan), *hard* (Swiss and cheddar), *semisoft* (blue and brick), *soft* (cottage and cream), and *processed* (a blend of cheeses which is pasteurized, mild, and soft).

Most cheese produced today is marketed in foil, wax cartons,

Your career
Produce manager

You would select, order, and purchase large bulks of fresh fruit and vegetables to be sold to consumers in grocery stores and supermarkets. You might work for a single store, a chain of food stores, or be self-employed.

Experiment to determine the effects of different storage techniques on foods. Examples:
When fresh eggs are frozen, the yolk becomes gummy.
When cheese is not wrapped tightly it may develop mold or dry out.
When salad greens are not kept in airtight packages, they lose moisture and become limp.

Make a market list for your family following these guidelines.

1 Plan meals, check recipes you will use, and list groceries needed. If possible, plan menus around items currently featured as bargains in local grocery stores.
2 Check supplies on hand.
3 Group together the foods that are alike or that will be found in the same location in the store.
4 Place perishable items like frozen foods at the end of the list, so you pick them up last.
5 Write the amount or size of the can or package you expect to buy.

Make a list of practices of inconsiderate shoppers that add to the cost of food for everyone. For example, leaving foods that require refrigeration on a shelf with the canned goods or leaving a shopping cart in the store parking lot where it can be damaged or stolen.

Discuss this question: How may food shopping when you are hungry influence your choices?

Learn to recognize cheese according to its type and to buy according to how it is to be used. *National Dairy Council*

plastic wrapping, or glass jars. When buying cheese in any container, read the label to check the weight and description. Buy cheese according to texture or flavor or for the recipe in which it is to be used. Most cheese is a good buy because of its protein content.

Buying Fruits and Vegetables

High-quality fresh produce is firm and heavy for its size but must be developed to a stage where ripening is assured. Fruits and vegetables that were picked too soon have a tendency to shrivel and fade before becoming edible. The color of high-quality fruits and vegetables is bright, and the skins are unmarred. Some fruits, such as bananas, peaches, pears, and other tree fruits, will continue to ripen after they are picked. Other fruits, such as melons, have better flavor if they are vine-ripened. Choose leafy vegetables which are crisp.

Canned and frozen fruits and vegetables can be produced under a U.S. government grading system.

Producers can also market these products under their own grading systems. Government grades in canned goods include grades A (fancy), B (extra standard), and C (standard). Frozen goods are simply labeled A or B.

Color, weight, texture, and size should be considered when you purchase fresh fruit.
USDA

The American public has never considered the grading of fruits and vegetables to be as important as the grading of milk, meat, and eggs. The reason for this is probably that few serious diseases are carried by processed fruits and vegetables. Too, many varieties and qualities are marketed under *brand* names. When you become acquainted with a certain brand and quality of tomatoes, for instance, your experience can tell you more than can government grading about the effectiveness of this food in the recipes you use.

399

Use the diagram below of a store to make a market list. Plan the list so you can begin at the entrance and go up and down each aisle only once. What part of the store would you visit just before checking out? Why?

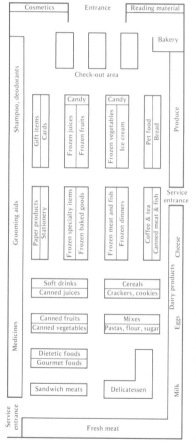

Bright color and crisp texture guarantee freshness in vegetables. *The McIlhenny Co.*

Buying Cereal and Grain Products

Breads and cereals are foods that most families buy frequently. They are offered for sale in a wide range of varieties for many uses. Among the most popular cereal foods are all kinds of breakfast cereals, breads, biscuits, rolls, crackers, flours, grits, corn meal, and macaroni products.

Some people, concerned about the high starch or *carbohydrate* content of cereal foods, avoid buying them. In doing so, they overlook one of the richest sources of the B vitamins. Cereals also contain protein and iron.

Select only well-packaged or well-wrapped breads, breakfast cereals, and mixes. Good packaging offers protection against germs and moisture. Because the labels on most cereal products give information you should use in making a selection, take time to read them.

Most American families keep ordinary bakery bread on hand at all times. Heat-and-serve rolls and breads and ready-to-cook biscuits, rolls, and bread are additional timesavers in busy homes. Various kinds

400

of mixes are also available. The consumer will need to study nutritive value, number of portions, taste appeal, and time involved to decide which ready-to-serve or partially prepared products are good buys.

Breakfast cereals are sold in three forms:

1 Cereals which must be cooked before eating. You are probably familiar with oatmeal, which makes a hearty breakfast dish.

2 Cereals of the *instant* variety, which can be prepared merely by adding hot water or hot milk.

3 Cereals which have been precooked and are ready to eat just as they come from the package. Such cereals are usually more expensive than the uncooked cereals. They often supply less nutrition per dollar spent, too.

New cereal products appear on the market regularly. For example, a new grain called *Triticale*, resulting from a cross between wheat and rye, has recently been developed. It has a protein content similar to soy concentrate and can be used the same as other grains. It is also possible to buy noodles, macaroni, and rice packaged with special seasonings and sauces. By following the directions on the package, the be-ginning cook can add variety to many cereal dishes.

Buying Fats and Oils

Fats and oils include butter, margarine, shortenings, and oils. Butter is made from cream and is a valuable source of vitamin A. Margarine is made from vegetable or animal fats other than butterfat. During the manufacturing process, margarine is fortified by the addition of vitamin A to make it equal to butter in vitamin content. Margarine has the advantage of economy, while being as nutritious as butter and having the same number of calories. Buy only refrigerated packages of butter or margarine. Both, but especially butter, are likely to melt and to develop strong, unpleasant odors and flavors if stored at room temperature.

Many families keep both solid shortening and liquid vegetable oil on hand. Each can be used in various recipes. The type of fat used may affect the quality of a given product. Solid and liquid shortenings are similar in price and calorie content. Food research shows, however, that vegetable oils produce fewer harmful health effects than either solid vegetable fat or animal fats.

 Use the jumbled market list below. Use the store layout on page 400 and determine the steps it would take to pick up the items as listed.

Bananas	Frozen lemonade
Hamburger	Cake mix
Buns	Milk
Aspirin	Eggs
Magazine	Crackers
Ice cream	Bologna
Cereal	TV dinners
Crackers	Noodles
Paper towels	Lipstick
Tuna fish	Lettuce
Potatoes	

Rearrange the list, grouping similar items together. How many fewer steps and how much less time would it take to pick up the items now?

Number from 1 to 30. Beside each number indicate if the statement is true or false. *Do not* write in this book.

1 Shopping in the corner store every day costs less than going to a supermarket several times a month.
2 Food prices may vary from week to week.
3 Good nutrition depends on the amount of money spent for food.
4 Unit pricing can be used to determine which brand is least expensive.
5 The amount of money spent by a family for food may reflect the time available for food preparation.
6 When deciding whether to use a convenience food or basic ingredients, the amount of money available needs to be considered.
7 All foods which cross state lines are subject to regulation by the United States Department of Agriculture.
8 The Food and Drug Administration requires that food labels contain a picture of the product.
9 Unplanned purchases may be the result of impulse buying.
10 Available storage space influences the size of purchases.
11 The way in which foods are stored affects their nutritive value.
12 Quick freezing is an effective way of preserving all foods.

13 The way a food will be prepared influences the quality purchased.
14 The labels on foods advertised as good for you must list amounts of specified nutrients in each serving.
15 Yellow fat on beef cuts means the animal was corn fed and will have better flavor.
16 The four beef grades are standard, good, very good, and *prime*.
17 High-quality beef is dull in color.
18 Lamb comes from young sheep.
19 High-quality pork is grayish.
20 Cornish hen and duck are classified as poultry.
21 Fish should be kept on ice or refrigerated until cooking time.
22 Shrimp are finfish.
23 The shell color of eggs has no influence on the nutritive value.
24 The best eggs are Grade A.
25 If a dozen large eggs cost 77¢ and a dozen medium eggs cost 74¢, the larger eggs are a better buy.
26 Diseases such as undulant fever and tuberculosis can be contracted by drinking raw milk.
27 Cheese is high in protein.
28 Breads and cereals should be included in the diet every day because of their vitamin A content.
29 Cereal products to which thiamine, riboflavin, niacin, and iron have been added are *enriched*.
30 Butter and fortified margarine contain the same food value.

Fill in the blank in each sentence with the *best* word to complete the statement. *Do not* write in this book.

1 An efficiently arranged kitchen will save you time and __(1)__ .
2 The most efficiently arranged kitchen is the __(2)__ shape.
3 A piece of kitchen equipment that reduces the size of garbage by crushing it is a garbage __(3)__ .
4 An electronic oven cooks foods by __(4)__ .
5 A meal of pear and cottage cheese salad, cream of chicken soup, bread and butter, milk, and custard is poorly planned because of its __(5)__ .
6 When writing a menu correctly, the item written last is the __(6)__ .
7 Flour should be __(7)__ before being measured.
8 Brown sugar should be __(8)__ into a measuring utensil for an accurate measurement.
9 One tablespoon measures the same as __(9)__ teaspoons.
10 In the metric system, liquid measurements are based on __(10)__ .
11 In the metric system, temperature is measured in __(11)__ .
12 A metric cup is equal to __(12)__ milliliters.
13 Measuring dry ingredients by weight requires less handling and __(13)__ than using standard measuring cups.

Chapter 20

Managing Meals

After reading this chapter, you should be able to:
1. State the advantages and disadvantages of different kitchen arrangements.
2. List guidelines for planning interesting meals.
3. Use established guidelines for planning interesting meals.
4. Cooperate in the foods laboratory by distributing jobs fairly, scheduling time carefully, and accepting responsibility for assigned tasks.
5. Dress suitably for laboratory work.
6. Follow recipes accurately.
7. Measure foods correctly.
8. Practice safety rules when working in the foods laboratory.
9. Demonstrate time- and energy-saving work habits in the foods laboratory.

In the rush of daily living, the skill of putting a nourishing, appetizing meal on the table in minutes instead of hours is a real asset. Family health and happiness depend heavily on the quality of meals and mealtime atmosphere.

There are few people who do not look forward to a well-prepared meal. Your ability to cook can help give you and your family nourishing food you can enjoy together. Nutritious, appetizing, and attractive meals show that you care about the well-being and happiness of your family.

If you help with meal preparation, you can understand the importance of time- and energy-saving methods at mealtime. If you know how to plan carefully and prepare food well, entertaining can also be easy for you and enjoyable for your

Make a list of everything you can think of that goes on in your kitchen.

Include activities such as:
Washing dishes
Cooking meals
Mixing cakes
Cleaning vegetables
Storing foods
Organize your list so all the jobs using one kind of equipment are arranged together. How many special areas or centers would you need? Give each center a name indicating its use, such as *cleaning center.*

List all the jobs you can think of that need to be done to prepare, serve, and clean up after the following meal.

Broiled Fish
Fresh Broccoli
Boiled New Potatoes
Tossed Salad   Muffins
Custard Pudding
Coffee   Milk

Decide where in the kitchen each job would be performed. How would you use each of the work centers?

guests. Good planning leads to successful meals and is even more important than the amount of time or money you spend on food. When you make a careful plan, you will have the right food on hand and the right equipment to use. You will also have a tested recipe to follow. Working with others in a school foods class helps you further appreciate the importance of planning.

Whether at home or at school, there are several aspects of successful meal management. They include knowledge of the use of equipment, planning, and cooking skills.

GETTING ACQUAINTED WITH THE KITCHEN

It has been said that the kitchen is the heart of the home, and this may also be true of a home economics department. A well-arranged kitchen, either at home or at school, makes meal preparation easy and enjoyable.

Ideally the kitchen is arranged so the sink is placed between the range and the refrigerator with a work surface on each side. Usually, however, the home economics department has only one or two refrigerators placed so they are convenient to several kitchens. In your department you may find electric and gas ranges and refrigerators in different models. It is desirable for each pupil to have the opportunity of working with more than one kind of fuel in the kitchens at school.

Types of Unit Kitchens

Your home economics department will probably have more than one unit kitchen. These unit kitchens may be planned in several different ways, with different arrangements of the equipment.

The U-shaped kitchen
The U-shaped kitchen is generally the most efficiently arranged one. The equipment and cabinets are grouped on three sides of the kitchen with the sink in the center of the U. This arrangement has the advantages of grouping equipment conveniently and of eliminating the need for others to pass through the kitchen while work is in progress.

The L-shaped kitchen
The L-shaped kitchen usually ranks second in efficiency. The equipment and cabinets are placed on two adjacent sides. This arrangement saves steps and, consequently, saves time and energy. When possible, the sink and the range are placed at right angles to one another.

The island kitchen
The island kitchen is a variation of the U- and L-shaped kitchens. It is planned to add extra working area. Usually the sink or range or a work and eating counter is placed in the open area of the kitchen. For this arrangement to work well, the room should be fairly large. The

 Act out a situation in which a mother and daughter are making a meal together. Assume they do not work well together. Suggest solutions to their problems.

Given the plans of U-shaped, L-shaped, one-wall, and two-wall kitchens, locate and label the work centers in each. List the advantages and disadvantages of each type of kitchen. In which type of kitchen would you prefer to work? Why?

Make the same single dish or simple meal in a U-shaped, L-shaped, and one-wall kitchen (or whatever types of kitchens are in your school laboratory). Trace your steps on a scaled sketch of the kitchen. Measure the total length of the lines drawn. In which type of kitchen did you walk the least? Does that make it the best type of kitchen? Why or why not? Other than the kitchen shape, what influenced how much you walked? What conclusions can you draw from this time-and-motion study?

Planning and preparing meals that are nutritious, appetizing, and attractive can be a creative challenge. *Idaho Potato Commission*

Use two identical sketches of one of the unit kitchens in your laboratory. Select two students to prepare the same simple food, like a tuna fish sandwich or cookies from a mix. Have the first student prepare the food when the kitchen equipment and utensils are *not* arranged in logical centers. Trace the student's movements on one of your sketches.

Make a plan of the cabinets and drawers in the kitchen. Decide on the most convenient place to store each type of dish, pan, and utensil. Label each area with the items to be placed there. Reorganize the kitchen according to the new plan.

Have the second student prepare the same food as the first student, but using the rearranged kitchen. Trace this student's movements on the second sketch. Compare the lines drawn. What conclusions can you draw from this activity?

The one-wall kitchen is the most efficient usage of limited space, such as in small apartments. *Window Shade Mfrs. Assn.*

island kitchen is intended to be an efficient, useful design, but it could prove to be inconvenient if it crowds the room, breaks the work triangle, or interrupts the smooth flow of traffic through the kitchen.

The two-wall kitchen

The two-wall, or double-wall, kitchen is economical to plan. The equipment is placed along two parallel partitions, or walls, separated by a passage which may be fairly narrow. Remodeled kitchens may be of this type because of space limitations. Meal preparation often requires more walking and, therefore, more time and energy in the two-wall kitchen than in the more efficiently arranged U-shaped and L-shaped types.

The one-wall kitchen

The one-wall kitchen is simplest of all kitchens to plan. All equipment is placed along one wall. The person using this type of kitchen must take many steps and must retrace steps in preparing and serving a meal.

The aisle kitchen

The aisle-type laboratory is an innovation in some schools. U-shaped kitchens are placed in long rows, one after the other, with a narrow aisle between the rows of kitchens. The purpose of this type of plan is to give the teacher an opportunity to observe and help students in six or eight kitchens during the class period. One disadvantage of this type of arrangement is little or no overhead storage space for dishes. Too, students must take many extra steps in carrying food and dishes back and forth, as tables are located in a different part of the room.

Large Kitchen Equipment

When you prepare meals or clean up afterward, you will work sometimes at the sink and sometimes at the range, the refrigerator, or the cabinets. In each of these work centers, you will need to have space to work and a place for storing things temporarily. You will store food, prepare it, serve it, and clean up at the end of the meal. As you work, you will use some of the large pieces of kitchen equipment.

The refrigerator

The refrigerator is designed to preserve nutrients in foods and to keep food cold. A properly operating refrigerator keeps foods at a temperature of 38 degrees to 42 degrees Fahrenheit (4 degrees to 6 degrees Celsius). Many refrigerators have special sections for storing eggs, raw fruits and vegetables, meats, and dairy products.

Most refrigerators have a separate freezer compartment for ice and for storage of a few days' supply of frozen food. Some refrigerators have large freezer sections with separate doors located either beside, on top of, or below the refrigeration area. Such freezers hold large quantities of food at a temperature low enough for safety for a few weeks or months.

The freezer

The freezer is a piece of equipment used for storing frozen foods for a long period of time. Most foods remain safe from spoilage for six months to a year if kept at a temperature below 0 degrees Fahrenheit (−20 degrees Celsius). It is important that foods be wrapped or packaged in airtight containers before storing.

The range

The range is usually a gas or electric model. Gas ranges heat by actual exposure of the cooking pan to the gas flame. Electric ranges have surface units which are heated as the electric current passes through them. Another development in electric ranges features a surface area of ceramic material. This cooking surface appears to be a part of the counter top. Heating units are located beneath the tile surfaces. While the flat surface has the advantage of making it easier to wipe up

Make a first aid kit for your kitchen at home. The kit could be given as a gift which would be both useful and practical. Discuss how accidents in the kitchen might be avoided.

Make a file of low-cost recipes. It might also be useful to include definitions of cooking terms. Cover and decorate a cardboard box or accordian file to be used as a container for recipes. This might be given as a gift or used for recipes collected in class.

Draw a clock to show the amount of time that can be used for each part of a laboratory lesson. For example, if you have 55 minutes:

Allow at least 3 minutes at the end of each laboratory lesson for your teacher to check your kitchen.

Your career
Kitchen designer

You would plan layouts for kitchens to utilize time, energy, and space most efficiently. You would consider work and eating areas, equipment, and storage needs. A background in architecture and drafting is important, as well as an understanding of kitchen activities. You might find employment with a home and apartment architectural firm, a restaurant chain, or be self-employed.

Bulletin board IDEA

Title: *Don't Let Your Nutrients*
Go
D
o
w
n
t
h
e
D
r
a
i
n

Directions: Sketch a pan tilted as if liquid is being poured from it. Use a sketch of an uncovered pan made to look as if steam is rising from it. Use the subtitle:

e
k
o
m
S
n
i
U p

Ranges with ceramic-covered cooking units add extra counter space for use whenever the range top is completely cool.   *Corning Glass Works*

spills and splashes, such units require specially made flat-bottomed pans to conduct the heat to the food.

The electronic range is another rather recent development in cooking equipment. It cooks the food by microwaves. The microwaves enter the food in the range oven and cause the molecules in the food to rotate so rapidly that they generate their own heat. The food cooks while the oven remains cool. However, since the food is cooked without heating, special browning units are added to some electronic ovens. Roasts, pies, and other foods can be browned to look appe-

tizing. Because electronic cooking is very fast and uses less energy than other methods, it may become the main cooking method of the future.

The sink

The sink is used for washing food during its preparation, for washing dishes, and for general cleaning. Some sinks have single and some have double compartments, with drainboards on one or both sides. Sinks are generally made of iron coated with porcelain or stainless steel.

A garbage-disposal unit may be a part of the sink. The unit is electrically operated and cuts the garbage into tiny pieces that can be washed through the drain and into the sewer.

Small Kitchen Equipment

Any worker needs the proper equipment to do a good job. Cooks are no exception. In the kitchen, small equipment is as important to cooking success as are such major appliances as the range and refrigerator. You will learn to know and use the small equipment available in your school kitchen. As you learn that a certain piece of equipment works well for a given job, you may be able to choose a similar one for use at home.

Choosing small kitchen equipment

Stop to think of all the jobs involved in preparing and serving meals. You will see how many kinds of equipment you need. You will see, too, the advantages of selecting multi-purpose tools. A tool that can do more than one job saves space. Resist buying special-purpose gadgets that take up space and are rarely used. Discard or give away gadgets you do not use.

In selecting small kitchen equipment, ask the following questions:

1 How much use will a tool get? If it is an often-used item, such as a paring knife, buy the best quality you can afford. You want it to last even with frequent use.

2 Will the tool be used in more than one place in the kitchen? If the item is not too expensive, consider buying one for each place it might be used. You often need mixing spoons and paring knives in more than one place in the kitchen.

3 Is it well-made of suitable material? The quality of construction and of material affects the usefulness of any tool. Look for rustproof, unbreakable materials.

4 Did a label or any other information come with the tool when it was purchased? Study the information. Keep it for later reference in caring for the tool.

5 Is there a guarantee? If so, keep it to be sure the materials and construction are of the promised quality.

Caring for small equipment

With proper care, good-quality equipment will give good service.

Try to arrange space so tools are easy to find and easy to put away. Drawer dividers and space-saving shelves and racks can help you organize equipment.

Kitchen work often requires sharp knives or knives with serrated edges. Serrated knives do not need sharpening. Sharpen other knives as often as necessary to keep them easy to use. It is safer and easier to cut with a sharp knife, and less pressure is needed than with a dull one. To avoid injury, set aside a special place for sharp knives. To keep the knives sharp, store them with the cutting edge protected. Plastic foam can be used for knife-edge protection. You can make a storage bed by cutting a piece of plastic foam to the desired size. Then cut slits in the foam so that the knife blades can be set into them.

Wash knives and forks carefully so sharp edges and points are not dulled or nicked. Avoid soaking them in dishwater. Serious cuts can be caused by hitting a knife which was forgotten and left in the dishwater. Dry all knives and forks thoroughly. Pay special attention to those that are not made of rustproof materials, since dampness causes rust.

It is especially important to return small equipment to its proper place. Much time and energy can be wasted looking for misplaced tools. For example, keep measuring cups and spoons in their assigned places so they will be easy to find.

 Play Food Bingo. Write the names of various small equipment items arranged in the form of a Bingo card. Use items such as a paring knife, corer, tomato slicer, tongs, ricer, meat tenderizer, vegetable peeler, nut cracker, grapefruit spoon, whisk, egg beater, pepper grinder, pizza cutter, colander, baster, pastry brush, cake decorator, and mixing spoon. Include other items you can think of.

Each bingo card should have 25 items. There should be several different cards, which can be duplicated so each student has one. As objects are held up, cross out the square with that item on your sheet. The *winners* are those students who have the most squares crossed out at the end of the game.

Hold each item up a second time. Discuss its use and practicality. Name possible uses other than those for which it is intended.

Make a list of tools and equipment that should be located in each of the work centers. Be practical and economical. Are there any small articles which could be duplicated at more than one center for convenient arrangement? If so, which ones?

Take a tour of the kitchen in your school lunchroom. Note the equipment used for preparing foods in large quantities. Observe the methods used to keep the food clean and safe to eat. Note the techniques used by the lunchroom personnel to ensure personal cleanliness when working with food.

List different safety rules on slips of paper. Choose slips and explain, act out, or give examples of the use of that rule to the rest of the class.

Write jingles for safety slogans, such as:

"A holder for a pot
Keeps your hand from getting hot."

"Everybody can afford
To do cutting on a board."

"In the dishwater you cannot see
A knife that might cut you and me."

PLANNING INTERESTING MEALS

Colorful meals are more appetizing than dull ones. Most foods start out looking bright and colorful. You can keep them that way if you follow several general rules in meal preparation. Use the principles taught later in this unit to keep food nutritious, appetizing, and colorful. (See Chapters 21–25.) Use these eight principles to add interest to the meals you are preparing. Also study the color photographs on pages 376 and 377.

1　Choose foods that make attractive color combinations. If the food itself has little color, plan to add a garnish such as parsley, lemon, or spiced apple slices.

2　Avoid repetition of flavors in a meal. For example, try to avoid serving tomatoes as a soup, salad, and

An interesting meal will be attractive and flavorful, with a variety of shapes and textures.
Tuna Research Foundation

sauce all in the same meal or apples in the form of a beverage, salad, and pie in a single meal.

3   Select flavors that blend. Some favorite go-togethers are roast pork and apples, turkey and cranberries, and lamb and mint jelly. Serve mild, or bland, foods with highly seasoned or strong-flavored foods. For example, bland spaghetti goes well with a highly seasoned sauce.

4   Avoid repetition of shapes in the foods served in a meal. For instance, meat balls, boiled potatoes, and whole buttered beets are all ball-shaped. Meat balls, mashed potatoes, and buttered shoestring beets provide varied shapes and more interest in the same meal.

5   Contrast the texture of foods served together. A meal is more interesting if some foods are soft and others are crunchy. For example, crisp cookies are a favorite with ice cream. On a vegetable plate, a raw vegetable might be served as contrast in texture to soft, cooked vegetables.

6   Use more than one preparation method for each meal. For instance, add a crisp, fresh salad to an oven meal made up of meat loaf, baked potatoes, scalloped tomatoes, and apple pie. Avoid serving a meal in which all the foods have been fried or all have been creamed.

7   Provide variety in the temperatures of the foods served. The hot oven meal would be improved in this respect by the addition of cold salad and ice cream on the pie. Ex-

cept in very hot weather, an all-cold meal has more appeal when served with a hot beverage such as cocoa, coffee, or hot soup.

8   In planning meals for guests, avoid foods or food combinations with strong, unusual flavors. Unless you know your guests' preferences, it is best to serve foods that are liked by most people.

MEAL PREPARATION

Whether at school or at home, learning to cook takes practice. It takes patience, too. Successful cooking requires precision movements and timing. Skills come easily with a good plan, good equipment, and enough practice. Expect some failures. You don't have to be ashamed if the first things you make are not perfect. Every good cook learns from mistakes. You will too.

Working Together in the School Kitchen

In your school foods laboratory you will probably be working in groups of two or more. The number of workers in the group will depend on the size of your class and the way the work is organized. Successful results require cooperation in these areas:

1   The group needs a plan they have worked out together for the food preparation lesson. All should understand the reason for the work plan.

 Write menus to include the points below so you can visualize the meal as it will appear.

1 Write the menu so dishes appear in the order in which they are to be served.
2 Begin the names of dishes with capital letters. Do not capitalize prepositions and conjunctions.
3 Put the main dish first unless there is an appetizer.
4 Write two dishes served together on the same line.
5 Write breads to the left and butter or margarine to the right when they are served together.
6 Write the dessert next to last.
7 Write the beverage last.

Conduct this experiment:
1 Sift flour directly into a cup, or sift it into a bowl or onto waxed paper and then pour it gently into the cup.
2 Put flour into a cup without sifting.
3 Spoon flour into a cup without sifting and tap the cup to pack the flour down. Weigh each cup of flour and note the differences. As a result of this experiment, establish a procedure to follow when measuring flour.

Suggest ways to improve the following menus. Use the meal planning guidelines on page 410.

Roast Pork
Whole Potatoes
Boiled Onions
Pear and Cottage Cheese Salad
Angel Food Cake
Milk

Hamburger Patty
with Cream Gravy
Corn on the Cob   Rice
Yeast Rolls   Butter
Bread Pudding with Raisin Sauce
Milk

Creamed Tuna on Noodles
Mashed Hubbard Squash
Stewed Tomatoes
Applesauce
Milk

Peanut Butter and Jelly Sandwich
Chocolate Pudding
Pineapple Milkshake

Pan-Fried Liver
Black-Eyed Peas   Baked Potato
Chocolate Ice Cream on Brownie
Coffee

Fruit Cocktail
Pancakes with Syrup
Coffee Cake
Cocoa

Fried Perch
String Beans   Peas
Raw Spinach Salad
Lime Gelatin
Milk

Laboratory experiences are usually successful when students follow well-planned schedules and cooperate in their work.   *Miriam Reinhart/Photo Researchers*

2   The group needs an easy-to-follow schedule that distributes jobs fairly among the workers.

3   Each worker should accept responsibility for doing his or her job.

4   Each worker should understand the total plan. Then all workers will be able to help out in any emergency.

5   Each worker should understand what the other workers are doing. In this way, all the workers will be able to repeat the complete activity at home or in the school unit kitchen.

Scheduling Time

At school, certain tasks must be finished during a class period. Therefore, the schedule you make for work at school will not be the same as the one you would make to prepare the same meal at home, where you would not be subject to the same time restrictions. In each case, you will need to consider:

1   The time available.

2   The number of people in the work group.

3   The equipment available.

4 The time needed to prepare and cook the food to be served.

5 The time needed to eat and to clean up the dining and kitchen area.

Dressing Suitably

On days you plan to work in the foods laboratory, wear clean, washable, comfortable clothes. Avoid clothes that absorb odors easily or require dry cleaning. As a safety measure, avoid fuzzy or long-sleeved garments, or any other clothing that might catch fire easily. Remember, dangling necklaces or bracelets can catch handles of pots and pans.

A clean apron or smock is desirable, especially if you are wearing nonwashable clothing. If you have a short, neat hair style, you probably won't need to do anything special to your hair. Long hair should be held back with a band, ribbon, or cap. Never comb or brush your hair in the kitchen or foods laboratory. Loose hairs carry germs and are unpleasant when found in food. They can be avoided by these simple, thoughtful efforts.

Once washed, your hands should be kept away from your hair, mouth, and face. They can carry germs from your body to the food you are preparing. Keep the dish towel off your shoulder where it may touch your hair.

Using Recipes

You need good recipes to prepare good meals. If you learn to read recipes and to know what the terms mean, you can learn to prepare almost any food.

As you can see by the chart on page 414, standard measuring cups and spoons for metric measuring will be slightly larger than the ones you may have been using. However, if you use all metric measuring cups and spoons, you can still use recipes giving the ingredients in the old type measurements. The end product will be somewhat larger than it would have been before. Yet the proportions will still be correct in relation to each other. It is *not* possible, however, to successfully convert old recipes to metric measures if you use a mixture of old and new measuring cups and spoons.

A good recipe lists the kinds and amounts of ingredients needed in the order they will be used. It also gives step-by-step directions for combining ingredients. As a beginner, follow recipes carefully. Use the exact amount called for in the recipe, no more and no less. Accurate measuring is essential to success.

To follow directions, you must understand the words used in a recipe. You should know the meaning of such words as *cream*, *stir*, *beat*, *fold*, and *roll*. *Bake*, *fry*, *broil*, and *boil* are cooking methods you'll soon learn to recognize. (For definitions of these terms see pages 503–505.)

Some techniques in food preparation are not explained in most

 Use the thermometer below to determine how long and at what temperature to store foods:

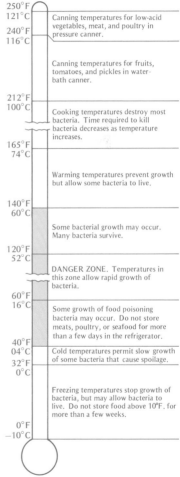

Temperature of food for control of bacteria

250°F / 121°C	
240°F / 116°C	Canning temperatures for low-acid vegetables, meat, and poultry in pressure canner.
	Canning temperatures for fruits, tomatoes, and pickles in water-bath canner.
212°F / 100°C	
	Cooking temperatures destroy most bacteria. Time required to kill bacteria decreases as temperature increases.
165°F / 74°C	
	Warming temperatures prevent growth but allow some bacteria to live.
140°F / 60°C	
	Some bacterial growth may occur. Many bacteria survive.
120°F / 52°C	
	DANGER ZONE. Temperatures in this zone allow rapid growth of bacteria.
60°F / 16°C	
	Some growth of food poisoning bacteria may occur. Do not store meats, poultry, or seafood for more than a few days in the refrigerator.
40°F / 04°C	Cold temperatures permit slow growth of some bacteria that cause spoilage.
32°F / 0°C	
	Freezing temperatures stop growth of bacteria, but may allow bacteria to live. Do not store food above 10°F. for more than a few weeks.
0°F / −10°C	

Cooperative Extension Service, Monroe County, N.Y.

Answer the following questions after one of your food and nutrition laboratory experiences.

1 Did your group work well together? Why or why not?
2 Did your work plan help?
3 What caused you the most trouble? the least? Why?
4 What changes would you make if you were to have this lesson again?
5 What did you learn from this experience?

Check how well your group cleaned up after a food and nutrition laboratory lesson. Use a plus for good and a minus for poor. *Do not* write in this book.

1 Dishes scraped, rinsed, stacked, and washed in logical order
2 Dishes stored in proper places
3 Cooking utensils left in proper places
4 Counter and table tops left clean
5 Range left clean
6 Sink left clean and free of garbage
7 Leftover foods stored properly
8 Dish towels put in washer
9 Waste can emptied and clean
10 Floor checked for spills
11 Apron neatly folded and put away

Metrication in the kitchen

The most common prefixes for metric measurements are:

mega-(M) meaning million   centi- (c) meaning hundredth
kilo- (k) meaning thousand   milli- (m) meaning thousandth
deci- (d) meaning tenth

Volume, or capacity, measurements are based on the cubic meter. (A meter corresponds to the yard—1 yard = 0.9 meters.) A *cubic decimeter* (called a liter) is the common unit for measuring liquids in the home. A *milliliter* (ml) is a thousandth of a liter.

Customary measuring units	Metric translation	Proposed metric measures
¼ teaspoon	1.2 ml	1 ml
½ teaspoon	2.5 ml	2 ml
1 teaspoon	5.0 ml	5 ml
1 tablespoon	15.0 ml	15 ml
¼ cup	59.0 ml	50 ml
½ cup	118.0 ml	125 ml
1 cup	237.0 ml	250 ml
1 pint	474.0 ml	500 ml
1 quart	948.0 ml	1000 ml = 1 liter

Mass, or weight, measurements are based on the gram. The *gram* is equal in weight to one cubic centimeter of water. The *kilogram*—1000 grams—replaces the pound as a unit of weight. A kilogram is equal to approximately 2.2 pounds. Consumer goods sold by the pound convert to half a kilogram or 500 grams.

Temperature, or degrees of heat or cold, is expressed in *Celsius (° C)* rather than *Fahrenheit (° F)*. The Celsius scale is based on zero degrees as the point at which water will freeze and 100 degrees as the boiling point of water.

Oven temperature equivalents:

Very cool	250° F	120° C
Cool	300° F	150° C
Moderately cool	320° F	160° C
Moderate	360° F	180° C
Moderately hot	375° F	190° C
Hot	400–430° F	200–220° C
Very hot	450–500° F	230–260° C

recipes because they are so basic. You should know them before you start to cook. For example, you should know how to sift flour, separate and beat eggs, pare vegetables, and wash leafy vegetables.

Measuring Accurately

If you think measuring ingredients is a waste of time, you may never have had a real cooking disaster caused by failure to measure. Some people can't understand why others cook without stopping to measure. Actually, experienced cooks *do* measure. Many have learned to estimate measurements correctly by *eye* or by *feel*. They also know which preparations require exact measures. That is, they can judge by looking at or handling a mixture whether it is the right texture, or consistency. This skill takes many hours, or perhaps years, of practice. With daily practice you, too, can learn shortcut measuring techniques with certain recipes. However, you will always need to

Evaluate your group's management skills when working in the food and nutrition laboratory by answering the following:

1 Was the food ready to be served at the appointed time?
2 Was there enough to eat? Was there too much?
3 Did we forget any of the food when shopping or planning?
4 Did we forget anything that should have been on the table?
5 Did we stay within the money alloted to us?
6 Could we have prepared the food in less time?
7 Did we use more utensils and dishes than needed?
8 Did we keep our table and counter neat and clean as we worked?
9 Did we keep ourselves neat and clean as we worked?
10 Did we wash the cooking utensils as we worked?
11 Did the members of our group work well together?
12 Did all members of our group do their share of the work?
13 Did we throw away any food that could have been used?
14 Did we leave the laboratory in good order?

Compared to our customary measuring cups, the new metric measures are slightly larger.
Pedro A. Noa

15 Did we put leftovers away properly?

16 Did we keep the dish towels off our shoulders and away from anything dirty?

17 Did we leave any dishes unwashed or any work unfinished?

18 Did we hand in our written plans and evaluations on time?

Figure the cost of foods prepared in the laboratory using the following format:

1 Food item
2 Usual purchase size
3 Cost of usual purchase size
4 Exact amount needed for class use
5 Cost of actual amount used in class
6 Total item number 5 for all the food items used in one laboratory lesson

Allow time at the end of each laboratory lesson for the teacher to check your kitchen. Leave cabinet doors and drawers open so the teacher can easily see that certain pieces of equipment are in their correct places. After each lesson, different pieces of equipment may be checked, so be prepared.

measure ingredients for some foods.

A beginner is wise to measure ingredients carefully both in class and at home to ensure successful cooking results. By changing the proportions of ingredients by as little as a teaspoon or a gram, the end product can be altered. So minor a change sometimes explains why a dough meant for cake turns out to taste like muffins or why a frosting is so thin it runs off the cake.

Measuring tools

To get good results, you need to use standard measuring cups, spoons, and scales. Dry ingredients weigh differing amounts for the same volume. Such ingredients may be measured by weight or by volume. It is easy to see why professional cooks and others who cook and bake in large quantities prefer to weigh ingredients rather than use measuring cups. Sifting or packing ingredients to be sure of a standard measurement by cup can be eliminated if scales are used. The correct amount of flour will weigh the same whether it is packed down or fluffed up. Weighing is also faster and involves less equipment to handle and wash.

In the not-too-distant future, metric measurement will become an everyday part of American life. In light of this and because the American homemaker is accustomed to measuring dry ingredients by volume, the American Home Economics Association Metric Committee is proposing metric measures that are similar to the customary measuring cups and spoons for use in the home. For example, the customary measuring cup equals approximately 237 milliliters. The metric measuring unit, however, will be 250 milliliters, which is an easier number to work with for dividing and multiplying recipes.

Cups and teaspoons used at the dining table come in various sizes. They are not standardized and so are not accurate. They are not used to measure ingredients by either metric or nonmetric measures.

Measuring dry ingredients

Measuring cups for dry ingredients come in nested sets made of either plastic or metal. The correct measurement is even with the top of the cup. Finely ground foods such as flour or powdered sugar may settle or pack down during storage. To ensure the same measurement each time, these foods need to be sifted before they are measured so they will be uniformly fluffy. To measure flour, sugar, baking soda, or baking powder, fill the cup or spoon to overflowing. Run a straight edge, such as the edge of a spatula, across the top to level the measure. Since brown sugar is sticky and cannot be sifted successfully, it should be tightly packed into the cup. This will insure that all air spaces have been filled and you will have the correct amount.

Measuring liquids

To measure liquids, set the measuring cup on a level surface. Have your eyes level with the line on the cup. Pour in the liquid until the desired line of measurement is reached.

To measure spoonfuls of a liquid, dip the spoon into the liquid. If you pour the liquid into the spoon, hold the spoon above a cup or bowl to catch spills.

Measuring fats

A ¼-pound (113 g) stick of butter or margarine is equal to ½ cup (118 ml) of fat. Some wrappers on sticks of butter and margarine are marked off into tablespoon divisions. When metric packages of butter—500 grams—replace the pound packages, half of the package will still be equal to one metric cup. If you are using unmarked butter or other fat, measure the soft fat by pressing it into a nest-type measuring cup or spoon. Level it off as you would for dry ingredients. Be sure all air bubbles have been eliminated by pressing the fat firmly into the cup until you cannot add any more.

Observing Safety Rules

In your unit kitchen or home kitchen, you must work with sharp knives, hot pans and dishes, boiling liquids, gas or electric ranges, and equipment with moving parts. Accidents happen easily. If there are young children or elderly people living in your home, kitchen safety rules become especially important. (See pages 166–167.)

Saving Time and Energy

One of the first lessons you learn in a foods class is to make every minute count. Most class periods are short. If a schedule is to mean anything, it must be followed to the minute. To make your schedule work, keep in mind these seven time- and energy-saving work habits.

1   As the class begins, go straight to your assigned place. Keep talk and confusion to a minimum.

2   Keep each needed recipe card and the work schedule where you can see them as you work. A rack or clip attached to a partition or cabinet makes a convenient spot. Copy recipes from books onto cards. Store all textbooks in a safe place away from the food preparation area so they won't get soiled.

3   Gather all the utensils and supplies you will need before beginning to work. Make as few trips out of your work area as possible. Use a tray and carry several items at one time to save steps.

4   Use utensils correctly. Use the proper utensil for the purpose. Use only the equipment you need.

5   Be aware of the time and your schedule as you work.

6   Do your own work, and expect others to do theirs.

7   If things go wrong, check the plan. Offer your assistance in an emergency.

Rope off a foods laboratory kitchen and have a "hunt" to locate unsafe practices which have been "planted" in that kitchen. Hunt for items such as these:
pot holder near a burner
pot handle turned toward the front of the range
electric cord extending over the edge of the counter
unlabeled bottles of potentially dangerous chemicals stored under the sink
knives left on the counter top
bottom drawer left open

See who can list the greatest number of safety hazards in a set length of time.

Make a poster pointing out guidelines for safety and cleanliness in the kitchen.

Bulletin board IDEA
Title: *Do You-Hoo Use Your Time Wisely?*
Directions: Use a picture of an owl wearing glasses. On a piece of paper which the owl is supposed to be reading write Plan ahead as if there were not enough space for the writing on the page. Mount suggestions for wise meal planning.

In the diagrams below S means *sink,* C means *cooking range,* and R means *refrigerator.* Use the diagrams to answer questions 1 to 5. On a separate piece of paper, next to the number of each question write the letter corresponding to the diagram that *best* answers that question. *Do not* write in this book.

A.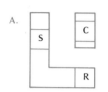

B.

C.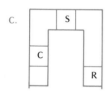

D.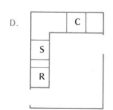

E.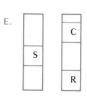

1 Which is a two-wall kitchen?
2 Which is an island kitchen?
3 Which kitchen is most efficient?
4 In which kitchen would you have to retrace the most steps?
5 In which kitchen is the cook *least* likely to be disturbed by other people walking through?

Fill in the blank in each sentence with the *best* word or words to complete the statement. *Do not* write in this book.

1 In organizing a kitchen, equipment is arranged into three main __(1)__ centers.
2 A well-organized kitchen will save you energy and __(2)__ .
3 The most efficiently arranged kitchens are the U-shaped and the __(3)__ -shaped.
4 A menu of diced carrots, milk, fruit cocktail, and stewed beef with cubed potatoes is poorly planned because of its __(4)__ .
5 Dry measurements should be __(5)__ with the top of the measuring utensil.
6 A ¼-pound stick of margarine equals __(6)__ cup(s).
7 To get good results when using a recipe, it is necessary to use __(7)__ measuring utensils.
8 In the metric system, the boiling point of water is __(8)__ degrees.
9 In the metric system, weight measurements are based on __(9)__ .
10 In writing a menu correctly, put the __(10)__ first unless there is an appetizer.

Fill in the blank in each sentence with the *best* word or words to complete the statement. *Do not* write in this book.

1 Examples of plant foods that can be used as alternates for meat are dried peas, lentils, peanuts, and dried __(1)__ .
2 Stewing, braising, and pot-roasting are examples of __(2)__ -heat cookery.
3 Spaghetti with meat sauce, beef stew, and meat loaf are examples of meat- __(3)__ dishes.
4 The bone shape found in the most tender cuts of meat is shaped like a(an) __(4)__ .
5 Meat is a good source of protein, the B vitamins, phosphorus, and __(5)__ .
6 The richest known source of natural iodine is __(6)__ .
7 The most important consideration in egg cookery is __(7)__ .

Copy the following list of protein-rich foods on a sheet of paper. Put the letter D beside those foods generally cooked by dry-heat methods. Place an M by those foods usually cooked by moist-heat methods. *Do not* write in this book.

Pork Roast   Tongue
Spareribs   Round Steak
Veal   Perch
Sirloin Steak   Meat Loaf

Chapter 21

Preparing Protein Foods

After reading this chapter, you should be able to:

1   List principles of protein cookery.
2   Identify *dry-heat* and *moist-heat* methods of cooking.
3   Select the correct method of cooking for different protein-rich foods.
4   Give examples of meat-extender dishes.
5   Explain the differences between *tender* and *less tender* cuts of meat.
6   Give examples of *variety* meats.
7   Determine if certain protein-rich foods should be cooked by dry-heat or moist-heat methods.
8   Point out the nutritional contributions of meat, fish, poultry, and eggs to your diet.
9   Determine if eggs are a binding, coating, leavening, or thickening agent in given food products.

Do you enjoy adventure stories about people who lived in prehistoric times? Meat was very important to such people. These primal tribes created animal pictures on their cave walls. They thought these pictures would help the hunters find enough meat to feed the tribe. There were people who lived in lake regions where they could catch fish and birds for their food. Other groups kept herds and flocks so they could provide food for their tribes. These early people probably ate eggs whenever they found nesting birds. Milk and meat were easily available for those who tended flocks.

Since animal foods are *complete proteins* (see page 368), they continue to be important foods. Meat, poultry, fish, shellfish, and eggs furnish a large percentage of the protein eaten in the United

Make a list of variety meats. Suggest ways of preparing and serving them.

List foods that can be eaten in place of meat as a source of complete protein. Compare the nutritional value of an egg, peanut butter, various cheeses, and textured vegetable protein.

Collect recipes for dishes using dry beans, dry peas, and lentils. Try some of the recipes and report how well you and your family liked them.

Compare the nutritional value of equal servings of roast beef, sirloin steak, lean ground beef, and ground beef-soy concentrate mixtures. What conclusions can you draw about the price and food value per ounce of various cuts of beef?

Your career
Animal Husbandry Specialist

You would study domestic farm animals to ensure their health and productive yield. You might conduct research in the animal's environment, breeding and feeding habits, or on possible disease development. You might work on large farms, or for government agencies.

States. Milk and milk products also provide animal protein.

It takes about ten times as much land to produce the animal protein to feed one person as it takes to raise enough cereal to keep one person alive. For this reason, animal foods are expensive. In many countries where land is scarce, farmers must use the land to grow cereal and vegetable crops so the people can survive. Worldwide food shortages have emphasized the necessity to utilize land and crops more efficiently for human needs. Even in countries with enough farm land for both plants and animals, the animal proteins tend to cost more than other foods.

Recently a new product called *textured vegetable protein* has appeared on the market. This product consists mostly of protein from the soybean. Soy protein contains all eight of the amino acids necessary for human nutrition. The textured vegetable protein is made even more nutritious by the addition of protein from other sources, such as wheat, corn, milk, and egg white. When combined together, these vegetable proteins have the same protein value as meat products. This type of vegetable protein can be used as a meat extender with animal protein. Or it can be flavored and textured to be used as a meat substitute. Flavored vegetable protein is available in forms which taste much like chicken, ham, bacon, sausage, and ground beef.

PRINCIPLES OF PROTEIN COOKERY

What do you suppose causes some hamburger patties to be tender and juicy while others are tough and dry? Why does the cheese in one sandwich seem to be like stringy rubber bands while the cheese in another sandwich is creamy smooth?

Low cooking temperatures are the key to successful protein cookery. Protein-rich foods lose their juices and fats in high heat. They also shrink if overcooked. This makes them dry and tough. Since the juices and fats hold many of the vitamins and minerals present in protein-rich foods, high temperatures can also destroy these valuable nutrients. To help seal in the juices in meat during the cooking process, sear or brown all surfaces of the meat first with high heat. Then lower the temperature for the rest of the cooking period.

Some people cannot get enough meat for an adequate supply of protein. Others prefer not to eat animal foods. These people can eat dried beans, lentils, dried peas, peanuts, nuts, and textured vegetable protein in place of meat protein. Most vegetable protein foods, except for peanuts and textured vegetable protein, do not contain the complete protein needed for growth. People who eat vegetables in place of meat must eat different ones every day to get enough proteins to remain healthy. Milk, a complete

Beans are a valuable source of protein and make up meals that are not only nutritional but economical as well. *S & W Fine Foods, Inc.*

protein food, can also replace meat protein in the diet.

Vegetable proteins, such as dry beans and dry peas, also require low cooking temperatures. To keep them tender and help them retain their shape, simmer rather than boil them, or bake them slowly at a moderate or low oven temperature.

Selecting the Cooking Method

The tenderness and taste appeal of protein-rich foods are affected by other factors, too. For example, additional fat may improve such protein dishes as baked beans. In a high-fat food such as sausage, removal of some fat improves the

Give reasons for the following guidelines for storing and cooking meat:

Do not leave meat at temperatures of 45° to 120° F (7° to 49° C) for more than four hours. Remember this when you do your grocery shopping, let frozen meat thaw, or put it in the oven before roasting starts.

Do not leave cooked meat at room temperature after it has reached 110° F (44° C). Cover it loosely and put in the refrigerator.

Cook tender cuts of beef, most lamb, and most pork by dry-heat methods such as roasting, panfrying, broiling, panbroiling, deep-fat frying, stir-frying, and cooking on a rotisserie. Veal usually does not contain enough fat to be cooked by dry-heat methods.

Cook less-tender cuts of beef and veal by moist-heat methods such as braising, stewing, pressure cooking, barbecuing, and cooking in a crock pot.

Cook pork by this guide:

Cook until well done for taste and safety. Cooking to an internal temperature of 170° F (77° C) will help to ensure the destruction of any trichinae larvae that might be present. Well-done pork may still have some natural pink color. This color is not harmful and does not mean that the meat is underdone.

Copy and complete the crossword puzzle below, using a separate sheet of paper. *Do not* write in this book.

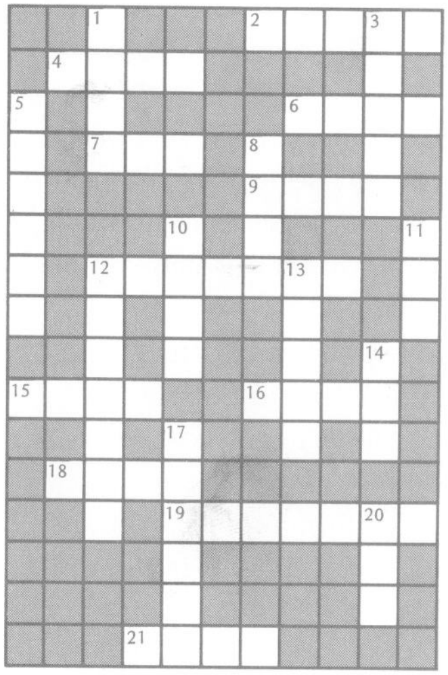

[Crossword puzzle grid with numbered squares 1-21]

ACROSS

2 In cleaning fish a sharp __(2)__ is needed.

4 Food from mature hogs is called __(4)__ .

6 Foods in the meat group help you __(6)__ .

7 Broiling is __(7)__ -heat cooking.

9 Foods used to thicken, bind, and act as leaveners are __(9)__ .

12 Chicken and turkey are examples of __(12)__ .

15 Bacon, salmon, and egg yolks are rich in __(15)__ .

Textured vegetable protein is a popular ingredient in sausages and other breakfast meats. *Morning Star Farms*

food. The presence or absence of moisture during the cooking process is also important. Meat, fish, and poultry products are often divided into those which are cooked by *dry-heat* methods and those which are cooked by *moist-heat* methods.

Dry-heat cookery

Dry-heat cooking methods are used with the more tender cuts of meat, fish, and poultry. These methods include broiling, roasting, cooking on a rotisserie, and frying.

Broiling is cooking by direct heat over coals or under an open flame or electric unit. *Panbroiling* is cooking food uncovered on a griddle or in a skillet on top of the range.

Broiling is probably the most popular form of dry-heat meat cookery. It is effective because it seals in the meat juices by quickly searing the surface of the meat. Because broiling is usually done at higher temperatures than other types of meat cookery, special care must be taken to avoid overcooking, toughening, or burning the meat. You do this by controlling the distance between the heat source and the meat. Thick cuts of meat are placed farther from the heat than thin cuts. In this way each cut of meat can be cooked to the desired degree of doneness without toughening the meat or burning the surface. When panbroiling, avoid overcooking by watching the time since you cannot control the distance from the heat.

Roasting is cooking uncovered food by dry heat, usually in an oven. Tender beef, pork, lamb, fish, and poultry may be roasted successfully in an ordinary oven. Use a shallow pan with the meat placed fat side up on a rack, and a low cooking temperature, for best results.

Poultry and ribs are frequently cooked on a rotisserie, which roasts the food by turning it on a spit over or before direct heat. Many meats can be *panfried* in a shallow layer of fat, or they can be *deep-fat fried*. Frying is a dry-heat method of cooking because water is not added and it is done in an uncovered pot or pan.

Dry-heat cookery, such as roasting, is suitable for many types of meat, poultry, and fish.
Turkey Information Service

16 The government agency responsible for grading meat is the (16) . (Abbreviation)
18 Perch, bass, and flounder are kinds of (18) .
19 Delicacies served on the half shell are (19) .
21 Ground meat with very little fat is called (21) .

DOWN

1 The third lowest grade of meat is (1) .
3 Clams, crabs, and shrimp are sea (3) .
5 T-bone steak is a(an) (5) cut.
8 Beef, veal, and lamb are types of (8) .
10 A game bird hunted for food is a(an) (10) .
11 A popular way to cook hamburgers is to (11) them.
12 The nutrient which helps your body grow is (12) .
13 To cook food uncovered in dry heat in the oven is to (13) .
14 One kind of cured meat is (14) .
17 The high-quality grade of meat that contains less marbled fat than Prime is (17) .
20 An example of finfish is (20) snapper.

Moist-heat cookery

Moist-heat methods are used to cook the less tender cuts of meat and poultry. These methods include braising, barbecuing, pot-roasting, poaching, and stewing. In moist-heat cookery the meat is simmered in liquids until the tough connective tissues are broken down and the meat is tenderized. Sometimes the liquid used is somewhat acid, as in barbecue or tomato spaghetti sauces. This acid helps to tenderize the meat. The liquid used can also add flavor to the food being cooked. Vegetables, noodles, dumplings, or biscuits added to a stew or pot roast near the end of the cooking time may add nutrients and absorb any extra liquid in the pot.

Fish and eggs, although tender, may also be cooked by some moist-heat methods.

Extenders

Cereals and sauces are used in certain meat dishes as meat or protein extenders. They include such things as noodles, spaghetti, rice, bread, soybean meal, white sauce, and soups. Extenders spread the flavor through the entire dish, causing the protein to be extended, or to go further. Crustless bread cubes soaked in mayonnaise for an hour

Complete the following with the first foods that come to mind:

Bacon and . . .
Macaroni and . . .
Peanut butter and . . .
Ham hocks and . . .
Sauerkraut and . . .
Why did you name the foods you did? What other combinations would be equally pleasing?

Gather recipes of main dishes using meat extenders or meat alternates. Name ethnic foods that can be used as extenders or alternates. Prepare a meal including one of these foods. What is the main advantage of using meat extenders and alternates?

Plan and prepare a low-cost dinner. Explain how to use lower grades and less expensive cuts of meat and still have nutritious meals. Describe how to cook these meats so they are tender and appetizing.

To help tenderize less-tender cuts of meat, brown them before liquid is added during moist-heat cooking. *National Live Stock and Meat Board*

may be used to extend tuna, shrimp, crab, and other seafood salads. Meat and protein extenders also serve in other ways. For example, bread crumbs mixed with ground meat to form a meat loaf help the meat to hold its shape during the cooking process. The crumbs raise the nutritional value of the dish as well. You will find that many casserole dishes, stews, and ground-meat dishes include extenders.

MEAT

To most Americans, the word *meat* means beef, veal, pork, or lamb. When the cost allows, meat is widely used for the main course in most meals. In addition to its pleasing taste and texture and its high

protein content, meat is also a good source of iron, phosphorus, and the B vitamins.

Meats contain muscle, connective tissue, and fat. Toughness or tenderness depends on the amount and the strength of the muscle tissue. Breeding, age, exercise, and feeding of the animal all affect the tenderness or toughness of muscles. Meat from young animals, such as veal and lamb, is more likely to be tender than meat from older animals. Aging (handling and storage) of the meat in the packing plant or injecting the animal with an enzyme helps to tenderize the meat.

Meat Cuts

The part of the animal from which the meat is cut affects both the flavor and the texture of the meat. The *retail cuts*, or individual pieces of meat, sold by the butcher have been given special names. These names can help you tell the tenderness of meat cuts you are considering.

Meat can be divided into *tender* and *less tender* cuts. The less tender cuts come from the legs, shoulders, and neck and contain the muscles used most by the animal. These cuts are made up of strong muscle tissue held together by connective tissue. This meat can be tenderized before cooking by grinding, pounding, or adding chemicals to break down connective tissues. Less tender cuts can also be tenderized by cooking with moisture or with acid foods, such as tomatoes.

Both tender and less tender cuts of meat can be equally good for you. If you choose a suitable cooking method, both types can be made into pleasing dishes. If you are able to determine whether a meat is a tender or less tender cut, you can choose a proper cooking method.

One way to determine the tenderness of a meat cut is to look at the shape of its bone. Most animals have the same bone structure.

Though cows, pigs, and sheep are of different sizes, their bones are much the same shape. Five general bone shapes are found in most meat cuts. One is *T*-shaped, one is *wedge*-shaped, one is *round*, one is a rather thin *blade*, and the fifth bone is the *rib*.

The *T-bone* is part of the backbone and is found in the most tender cuts. The *wedge* is a part of the hip bone of an animal. It, too, is found in tender meat cuts. The *rib* cuts are also tender. The *round bone*, which comes from the leg,

Match the *animals* given in List A with the *food in the meat group* in List B. Use a meat in List B only once. *Do not* write in this book.

List A: Animals
A Duck
B Fish
C Young pig
D Young sheep
E Calf less than three months old

List B: Foods in meat group
1 Chitterlings
2 Lamb
3 Poultry
4 Salmon
5 Veal

Use the Table of Food Values beginning on page 506 to compare equal weights of the following for nutritive value:
Bacon
Ground round beef
Beef liver
Roast pork
Fish sticks
Fried chicken
Broiled chicken
Which has the most fat? Which is the best source of thiamine, iron, iodine, vitamin A, and other specific nutrients? How does the cooking method used affect food value and calorie count?

Meats of various cuts and shapes require different cooking methods. Can you select the ones that would require a dry-heat method of cooking and those that would need a moist-heat method?
National Live Stock and Meat Board

Demonstrate how to clean fish and prepare it for cooking. Follow these guidelines:

1 Place the fish on a large piece of paper which can be disposed of afterward.
2 Use a sharp knife to rub off the scales from the tail toward the head.
3 Skin the fish, if desired, by cutting through the skin of the back and abdomen, loosening it at the tail, and pulling it off.
4 Cut off the head.
5 Open the abdomen and remove the entrails.
6 Bone the fish, if desired, by slitting the flesh down the back, separating the flesh from the side bones, and pulling out the spine and other bones.
7 Wash the fish.
8 Wash the fish knife.
9 Wash your hands in cold salt water to remove the fish odor.
10 Store the fish at a very cold temperature for a short time only.

NOTE: Usually fish may be purchased at a lower price per pound if bought fresh but not dressed.

and the *blade bone,* which comes from the shoulder, are both found in less tender cuts. If the bone was removed before the meat was put on display, the name of the cut should be on the package, or the butcher will be able to tell you what shape of bone was removed.

Very bony cuts of meat, such as the neck, are less tender. Since these pieces are generally for grinding or stewing, the tenderness of the cut is less important than in large pieces used for broiling or frying.

Beef and Veal

Beef, the meat of cattle over one year old, is a favorite meat throughout North and South America. *Veal* comes from cattle butchered before they are three months old. *Baby beef* is meat from animals three months to one year old.

Although veal and baby beef are tender meats, they have a large amount of connective tissues in proportion to the amount of muscle tissue. Both veal and baby beef generally require cooking by moist-heat methods in order to break down these tissues. Veal has a pale color and a mild flavor. Herbs and spices are often used to add flavor. Baby beef is a deeper pink, contains more fat, and generally has more flavor than similar cuts of veal.

Pork

Pork comes from mature hogs. For this reason you might think the meat would be tough. However, hogs are usually fat animals raised in small pens. They do not move about to find food. This fact explains why most domestic pork is tender and can be cooked by dry heat.

Hogs carry a parasite called *trichina* which is harmful to humans. So pork is always served well done. Authorities recommend cooking pork to an internal temperature of 170 degrees Fahrenheit (77 degrees Celsius) to be sure it is safe to eat. While trichina is seldom found in pork sold in markets, most people know safety is worth the extra time it takes to cook all pork thoroughly.

Cured pork products such as ham and bacon are very popular. Originally pork was cured as a means of preserving the meat. While curing is not an important preservation process today, the flavor of cured pork appeals to many people. It is as important to thoroughly cook bacon, fresh ham, sausages, and most other pork products as it is to thoroughly cook fresh pork in the form of chops or roasts. Some pork products, such as canned or boiled ham, are cooked before you buy them, and further cooking before you eat them is not necessary. Read the package label or check with the butcher to be sure.

Lamb

Most of the meat from sheep used in the United States comes from young lambs. Most lamb is tender and can be cooked by dry heat. The meat from older sheep, called *mutton*, is nutritious but strongly flavored. It is not as popular in the United States, as in other parts of the world.

Variety Meats

Many internal organs of animals are also served as food. These products are called *variety meats*. They provide protein and are excellent sources of iron, phosphorus, vitamin A, thiamine, riboflavin, and niacin.

Variety meats include *liver, heart, kidney, brains,* and *tongue. Sweetbreads,* a gland from young animals, *tripe,* the stomach wall from beef, and *chitterlings,* the intestine from young pigs, are also included in the variety meats. When properly prepared, variety meats can provide lower cost dishes with high protein value.

Liver, kidney, brains, and sweetbreads are so tender they need little cooking. These cuts can be broiled, fried, or roasted. Tongue, heart, and tripe have a texture somewhat like the less tender meat cuts. They require longer cooking with moist heat.

FISH

Fish and shellfish are good sources of protein. Once people who lived near rivers, lakes, and oceans could depend on having fish or shellfish to provide the protein in their diets.

Today water pollution has cut down the fish supply. Some types of fish cannot live in polluted waters. Other fish can survive in polluted water, but they are not safe to eat. Fish commercially transported across state lines is carefully checked for safety. Precaution must be taken in eating fish, clams, oysters, etc., which come from polluted waters.

Fish contains complete protein. It is as good a source of protein as any meat. Fish is the richest known source of natural iodine, a mineral necessary for health. (See page 375.) It is also a source of the bone-building minerals, calcium and phosphorus.

Fish such as salmon, mackerel, and tuna contain some fat. Fish oil is chemically different from animal fat. It does not seem to damage human blood vessels. The unusual combination of protein and minerals along with vitamin-rich oils makes seafood worthy of consideration in meal planning.

Fish is a tender form of protein. It requires a short cooking period at a low temperature. Fish is ready to eat when a fork can easily pierce it and separate the flakes of flesh from the bone.

The amount of fat in a fish is an indication of the preferred cooking method. Moist-heat cooking methods keep lean fish from getting dry while it cooks. Lean fish such as cod, trout, bass, flounder, perch, and shellfish are frequently cooked

Tell how the expression *a good egg*, which describes someone who is honest, good natured, and dependable, can be related to the nutritional qualities of an egg.

Hard boil one egg and *hard cook* another. Run cold water over both. Shell and cut in half. Note differences, such as the grayish-purple ring between the yolk and white in the boiled egg. Note any difference in odor. Mash both with a fork. How do they differ in texture? Give reasons why hard-cooked eggs are more desirable than hard-boiled eggs.

Your career
Chef

You would prepare or supervise the preparation of foods served in restaurants and other large eating establishments. You might specialize in a certain cuisine, use various cooking styles, or concentrate on one food area. This would depend on the type and size of the establishment where you worked. You would find employment with restaurants, hotels, and other places where prepared meals are served to customers.

Demonstrate separating an egg white from the yolk, and beating egg whites.

1 Break the egg.
2 As the shell divides into halves, let the egg yolk remain in one half while the white runs out into a bowl.
3 Transfer the yolk to the other shell half so that the white runs out.
4 If more than one egg is to be used, separate each white into a second bowl before adding it to the other whites. This avoids getting yolk in the bowl of egg whites. (Egg white will not beat stiff if there is even a trace of yolk or other fat on beaters, bowl, or spatula.)
5 As an alternate method, an egg separator may be used.
6 For greater volume in beating egg whites, use them at room temperature.
7 Beat egg whites until soft peaks form when the beater is raised. If sugar is used, add it very gradually throughout the beating process.

Show how to use small equipment associated with egg cookery. If possible, include a slicer, poacher, separator, whisk, electric mixer, and rotary beater.

For a quality end product, cook fish for a short time at a low temperature. *USDA*

by steaming or poaching. To poach fish, wrap it in cheesecloth and lower it into simmering water for a short time. The cheesecloth helps preserve the shape of the fish while it is cooking.

Fat fish such as salmon, catfish, and red snapper are tastier when prepared with one of the dry-heat cooking methods. Such fish are usually baked, broiled, or fried. To fry them, brush small fish or small pieces of large fish with beaten egg or milk. Then roll the moistened fish in cracker crumbs, cornmeal, or bread crumbs. This coating will help to hold the fish together while it fries. Since the coating will also absorb some of the cooking fat, fried fish is richer in fat and higher in calorie content.

POULTRY

The term *poultry* refers to the meat from various birds. The most popular poultry are chicken, turkey, duck, and goose. The lesser known kinds are Rock Cornish hens, guinea hens, and squabs or pigeons.

Poultry is an important food because it contains complete protein, iron, and the B vitamins. Poultry

Conduct an experiment frying eggs at high and low heat. Use the following method first:

1 Melt a tablespoon (15 milliliters) of fat in frying pan over *low* heat.
2 Break eggs, one at a time, into saucer.
3 Slip eggs from saucer into frying pan.
4 Cook eggs over *low* heat about three minutes, or to desired doneness.
5 Sprinkle with salt and pepper to taste.

Repeat procedure using *high* heat. Observe difference in texture and appearance. Which is more appealing? Why? How does the taste compare?

Cook an egg using the first procedure above, adding a tablespoon of water to the fat. Cover the pan while the egg is cooking. Why would this be a good way to cook eggs?

Name ways to serve eggs for breakfast, in sandwiches, in salads, and as main dishes. With what foods from other groups in the *Daily Food Guide* can eggs be combined?

Roasting a turkey at a low oven temperature keeps it juicy and tender. Added garnishes make it appealing for a festive meal. *Turkey Information Service*

429

Prepare bacon for minimum shrinkage following these directions:

Panfried

1 Place unseparated slices of bacon in a cold pan.
2 Use medium-low heat.
3 Separate pieces gently with a fork as they begin to heat.
4 Turn bacon only once while it is cooking.
5 Pour off excess fat into an empty can or nonplastic container and save it for other cooking. *Do not* pour fat down the drain.
6 Drain on absorbent paper before serving.

Broiled

1 Place bacon slices close together on a broiling pan. *Do not* place them near the edge, as they may splatter.
2 Put broiler pan in the oven about 3 inches (7.5 cm) from the broiler unit. Turn on broiler.
3 Broil for about 2 minutes on each side, turning once.
4 Drain on absorbent paper.

Bulletin board IDEA

Title: *Learn the Egg-sentials*
Directions: Use illustrations of egg dishes such as omelets, soufflés, and custards. To the side write: *Cook Slowly with Low Heat.*

Egg dishes, such as soufflés, can be tasty and tender if baked at low oven temperatures. *United Dairy Industry Assoc.*

generally costs less than other meats and contains fewer calories. It can be cooked in a variety of tasty ways.

Like other protein foods, poultry stays juicy and tender if cooked at low temperatures. Young birds are tender and can be fried, broiled, cooked on a rotisserie, and oven-roasted. Older birds are sometimes lower in cost than young ones, but they are tougher and require longer cooking by a moist-heat method. When used in soup, pot pies, fricassees, or stews, older birds become tender and their flavor improves.

EGGS

Eggs of many kinds are a favorite food all over the world. They may be served at any meal. Eggs are generally a low-cost, easy-to-cook form of protein. They also contain phosphorus, iron, vitamin A, riboflavin, and fat. Most eggs sold in this country are produced by domestic chickens.

Eggs can be fried, scrambled, poached, baked, or cooked in the shells. They are often combined with other ingredients to form egg dishes such as omelets, soufflés, and custards. Like other protein foods, eggs should be cooked at low temperatures.

People refer to some shell-cooked eggs as *hard-boiled* eggs. These eggs are correctly called *hard-cooked* eggs. Eggs should be cooked in water below the boiling point (212 degrees Fahrenheit or 100 degrees Celsius). Boiling eggs makes them tough, with a rubbery texture. The outside of the yolk darkens and the flavor is strong and unpleasant.

When cooking eggs in the shell, place them in cold water. Bring the water to the boiling point. Turn the heat down. Cover and simmer to cook. Soft-cooked eggs require about three minutes of simmering time; hard-cooked eggs, about twenty-five minutes. When the eggs are cooked to your liking, pour off the hot water and add cold water at once. Fast cooling makes eggs easier to peel and helps prevent overcooking.

Frying, scrambling, baking, and poaching eggs should also be done at low temperatures. Poach eggs in simmering rather than boiling water. They will hold their shape and remain tender. Fry eggs over low heat. Try adding 1 tablespoon (15 milliliters) of water and then covering the skillet for faster cooking with tender results.

Uses in Cooking

Eggs are used in many ways in cooking. They thicken mixtures such as custards. They help to bind together mixtures like meat loaves. They are often used to add flavor and nutritive value to such foods as pudding. They act as leaveners in dishes such as chiffon cake and soufflés. In such dishes, it is the air beaten into the eggs that makes the product light and fluffy. Since egg protein hardens quickly with heat, it forms a kind of structure, something like plastic foam, that holds other parts of a mixture in place.

When you mix beaten eggs and a hot mixture, as in making sauces, the hot mixture *must* be added slowly to the eggs with constant stirring. Thus the temperature of the eggs is raised slowly so they cook evenly. Pouring eggs into a hot mixture cooks them immediately. Hard lumps of cooked egg form in the process. Adding the hot mixture to the eggs while stirring assures a smooth blend, free from particles of cooked egg.

 Make a flannel board jigsaw puzzle for the tender and less tender cuts of beef. Use two colors of construction paper backed with flannel, or use two colors of felt, flannel, or any other napped fabric. (They will adhere directly to the flannel board.) Fit the pieces together in the shape of a steer. Point out the location of the tender and less tender cuts. Discuss why cuts are tender or less tender.

Use the idea above to make a puzzle showing various cuts of meat from a hog.

Bulletin board IDEA
Title:

Directions: Use pictures of meats and other protein foods with the subtitle *Grow with Proteins*. Use pictures of fruits and vegetables and the subtitle *Glow with Vitamins and Minerals*. Add pictures of sugars and starches with the slogan *Go with Carbohydrates*.

Fill in the blank in each sentence with the *best* word or words to complete the statement. *Do not* write in this book.

1 Many ground-meat and casserole dishes are classified as meat (1) .
2 Meat cuts are classified as tender and (2) .
3 In moist-heat cookery, meat is cooked in liquid in order to break down the (3) .
4 The five general bone shapes in most meat cuts found in retail meat markets are T, round, blade, rib, and (4) .
5 Kidney, tongue, brains, and heart are classed as (5) meats.
6 The meat from cattle butchered before they are a year old is baby beef or (6) .
7 Meat can be tenderized before cooking by adding chemicals, grinding, or (7) .
8 Pork should be cooked thoroughly, *not* served (8) .
9 For best results, fat fish such as catfish, salmon, and red snapper are baked, broiled, or (9) .
10 Fish is a source of the bone-building minerals phosphorus and (10).
11 Rock Cornish hen, squab, and duck are examples of (11) .
12 Eggs are a good source of protein, fat, phosphorus, iron, riboflavin, and vitamin (12) .

Copy the following list of cooking methods on a separate paper. Put the letter D beside those methods that are dry-heat cookery. Place an M by those methods that are moist-heat cookery. *Do not* write in this book.

1 Broiling
2 Roasting
3 Barbecuing
4 Stewing
5 Panfrying
6 Poaching
7 Cooking on a rotisserie
8 Braising
9 Baking
10 Pot-roasting
11 Steaming

Copy the following list of food products on a sheet of paper. Next to each food indicate the main use of eggs in that product. Use the following abbreviations.

B for binding
C for coating
L for leavening
T for thickening

1 Custard sauce
2 Meat loaf
3 Chiffon cake
4 Salmon loaf
5 Soufflé
6 Fried perch
7 Pie filling
8 Sponge cake

Fill in the blank in each sentence with the *best* word to complete the statement. *Do not* write in this book.

1 Milk is an excellent source of the minerals phosphorus and (1) .
2 Milk is often fortified with vitamin A and (2) .
3 A sauce made from milk thickened with starch is called (3) sauce.
4 Milk is a basic ingredient in (4) soups.
5 If cheese is cooked at a high temperature, it may become dry, tough, and (5) .

Match the *definitions* in List A with the *forms of milk* in List B. Use each form of milk only once. *Do not* write in this book.

List A: Definitions
A Milk from which about half the water has been removed and to which sugar has been added
B Milk that has been heated to kill disease-causing bacteria
C Artificially fermented milk
D Milk containing as much calcium but less fat than whole milk
E Whole milk that has been processed so the butterfat does not rise to the top

List B: Forms of Milk
1 Buttermilk   4 Homogenized
2 Condensed   5 Skim
3 Pasteurized

Chapter 22

Preparing Milk and Milk-Rich Foods

After reading this chapter, you should be able to:

1 Name the nutritional contributions of milk to the diet.
2 State the rule for cooking all milk products.
3 Explain different methods for making white sauce.
4 Describe what happens if milk-rich foods are cooked at too high a temperature.
5 Show how milk can be included in the diet by using a variety of milk-rich products.
6 Point out why milk is considered a food rather than a beverage.
7 Distinguish between curd and whey.
8 Plan menus including milk-rich foods.
9 Make milk-rich food products with confidence.

Milk has been an important food since people first kept flocks and herds. In many countries babies are quickly transferred from mother's milk or special formula directly to some form of cow's milk. In other countries milk is supplied by goats, water buffalo, and reindeer, as well as by milk cows. Some researchers have even suggested that great sea mammals may become important suppliers of milk. This new milk source might be used as people's need for milk outgrows the supply available from land mammals.

Milk is an excellent source of calcium and phosphorus. If vitamin D is added at the dairy, milk contains all three nutritive elements needed for

Plan a menu for one day without milk. Using a chart of food nutrients, check the calcium content of your menus. Would you get enough for the day? Change the menus until you do get enough calcium without using milk. How successful were you? Why would it be easier and better for you to drink milk?

Discuss the meaning of the following statement: *Milk is nature's most nearly perfect food.* Does milk contain all the known nutrients? In what nutrients is milk especially rich? Does this vary according to the type of milk?

Compare the nutritive value of a glass of milk with a glass of soft drink. How are they alike? How are they different? Compare the prices of one quart of milk sold in different forms. (Evaporated, condensed, and dried milk are not usually sold by the quart. Figure the costs of the amount of each necessary to make a quart of liquid milk.)

Compare the price of fluid whole milk sold by the half-pint, the pint, the quart, the half gallon, the gallon, and in multiple-gallon containers. Suggest situations when each would be the best buy.

bone-building. Milk also provides riboflavin and thiamine, two of the important vitamins of the B complex, and some vitamin A. Milk is a good and inexpensive source of complete protein. In fact, a quart of milk contains about half the protein a person needs for one day.

Since milk is such a good source of necessary nutrients, most people include it in their daily diet. Adults and teenagers sometimes think it is not important to drink milk since their bodies have almost reached full size. But growth is only part of the story. Bone and muscle cells continually wear out and die. They can be replaced only if your body

continues to get the nutrients it needs. Since milk is one of the best sources of such nutrients, there is a great deal of truth in the expression *You never outgrow your need for milk.*

MILK IN THE MENU

Milk can be served in many ways. In addition to its popularity as a drink, it is used as the basis for many cooked dishes. It can be used in sauces, gravies, custards, sherbets, and ice cream. Milk is often used as a binder to hold food mixtures together. Cheese, a milk food, can be used in meals to sup-

Drink milk as a snack food as well as with meals, in order to meet your daily requirements for calcium and protein. *Poinciana, Florida*

Milk can be used as a major ingredient in many different recipes, such as this creamy clam chowder.   *United Dairy Industry Assoc.*

 Use the recipes below and on the next page for less expensive substitutes for commercial products.

Cottage Cheese Sour Cream
1 T. lemon juice (15 ml)
1 c. creamed cottage cheese (240 ml)
Put ingredients in a blender. Cover and process at high speed until smooth and creamy. High in protein, lower in calories than sour cream. Use for dips, on baked potatoes, or any other way you would use sour cream.

Sweetened Condensed Milk
1 c. dry milk solids (240 ml)
⅞ c. sugar (210 ml)
2 T. melted butter (30 ml)
½ c. warm water (120 ml)
Combine milk solids and sugar. Add melted butter. Gradually add water and mix until smooth. Use in recipes calling for condensed milk.

Bulletin board IDEA
Title: *Milk Isn't for the Birds*
Directions: Use a caricature of a bird and an empty milk carton. Place a straw so it looks as if the bird is sipping milk from the carton. Around the board, list the benefits of drinking milk.

ply many of the same nutrients contained in meat.

Milk as a Drink

Most teenagers often like to drink plain milk with their meals and with between-meal snacks. Flavored milk, buttermilk, and milk shakes are also popular. Whole milk contains butterfat. When chocolate is added, the fat content is further increased. The addition of flavorings such as chocolate and sugar also adds calories to the drink.

For those fortunate people who are not troubled with overweight or with oily skins, any form of milk is acceptable. People who are bothered by weight or complexion problems should choose the form of milk they drink with care. Fat is high in calories. For this reason, low-fat milks, such as skim milk, dried skim milk, and buttermilk are good choices. Vitamins A and D are usually added when these milks are processed. If so, low-fat milk is just as rich as other milks in the vitamins, protein, and minerals necessary for body growth and repair.

The *Daily Food Guide* suggests that teenagers need a quart (0.95

Buttermilk

Mix 1⅔ cups (400 ml) dry milk solids with 3¾ cup (900 ml) water. Add ½ cup (120 ml) fresh buttermilk. Stir until smooth. Leave at room temperature overnight. Refrigerate. Use in recipes calling for buttermilk.

Whipped Topping

Chill bowl and beater. Whip ½ cup (120 ml) of dry milk solids with ½ cup (120 ml) ice water or ice-cold fruit juice. Beat until soft peaks form (3 to 4 minutes). Add 2 tablespoons (30 ml) lemon juice (if made with water) and beat until stiff. Fold in ¼ cup (60 ml) sugar. Serve at once.

Your career
Dietitian's aide

You would help professional dietitians in carrying out their duties. You might work under the supervision of a registered dietitian or under the guidance of a supervisor who consults with dietitians. You would find employment in hospitals, nursing homes, schools, and camps.

liters) of milk every day. You can be sure you are drinking plenty of milk if you drink a glass with each meal. The rest of the milk supply can be furnished by milk foods such as cheese and by milk-rich foods such as custards, gravies, and cream soups. Even bread, cake, and cookies often contain small amounts of milk.

PRINCIPLES OF MILK COOKERY

However you plan to include milk in your menus, treat milk and cheese as protein foods. Like *all* proteins, they require low heat in cooking. Whether you are making cream soup, cocoa, cheese sauce, custard, or any other milk-rich food, use low cooking temperatures.

Many ranges can be adjusted to temperatures low enough for successful milk cookery. However, one of the best ways to be sure the temperature remains low is to cook milk over steam, as in a double boiler. Cooking dishes containing baked custards and soufflés can be placed in a pan containing hot water, then set in the oven to bake. In this way the outside of the container holding the milk mixture will not get any hotter than the water surrounding it.

Milk and cheese mixtures scorch easily during cooking. To prevent the scorching of foods cooked on top of the range, stir the mixture constantly during the cooking pro-

cess. Cook baked milk dishes at a low oven temperature to prevent scorching. Some milk dishes, such as custard, are cooked at a high temperature for a few minutes to start the cooking process. However, if the heat is not lowered rather quickly, the custard will separate into tough protein clots surrounded by watery fluid.

Basic White Sauce

White sauce is a sauce made from milk thickened with a starch, usually flour. Various spices and fats may be added for flavor. White sauces in various forms are used as the basis for cream soups, gravies, croquettes, and many other mixtures. If you can make a good white sauce, you can make a great variety of dishes just by adding other foods to it. Many cooks today use canned soups to replace white sauce in food mixtures. This is a good practice as long as you happen to have the right kind of soup on hand. However, if you know how to make your own white sauce, you will always be prepared for a wide assortment of recipes.

The thickness of the finished sauce depends upon the amount of flour or cornstarch used in proportion to the amount of milk. There are four different thicknesses of white sauce: *thin*, used in cream soups; *medium*, used in creamed dishes and gravies; *thick*, used in soufflés; and *very thick*, used as a binder in making croquettes. A

In any form, products made from milk and cheese supply needed nutrients. *United Dairy Industry Assoc.*

Look through cookbooks for two different methods of preparing white sauce. Make a white sauce following the directions for each method. Compare the results as to smoothness, flavor, and ease of preparation. Which recipe did you like best? Why?

Find recipes for cream soups and creamed dishes. Find recipes for main dishes made with soups or white sauce. Suggest variations for serving these, such as in toast cups or poured over biscuits or corn bread.

Follow these suggestions for using 2 cups (480 ml) of thick white sauce:
To ½ cup (120 ml) add ¼ cup (60 ml) grated cheese for sauce.
To ½ cup (120 ml) add canned tuna, cooked noodles, and seasoning for a casserole.
To ½ cup (120 ml) add leftover chopped vegetables for soup. Add milk to make the desired consistency.
To ½ cup (120 ml) add ground cooked meat, seasonings, and beaten egg white to make a soufflé.

Prepare a milk dessert for a young child. Think of ways it might be garnished to make it a suitable adult party dessert.

Copy and complete the crossword puzzle below, using a separate sheet of paper. *Do not* write in this book.

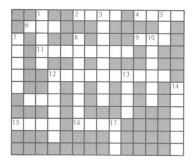

ACROSS

2 Milk with most of the butterfat removed is __(2)__ milk.

4 A homogenized mixture of equal parts of milk and cream is half-and-__(4)__ .

6 Milk with all the fat and water removed is instant nonfat __(6)__ milk.

9 The milk you buy usually comes from a(an) __(9)__ .

11 Cheeseburgers are often made with __(11)__ cheese.

12 One type of fermented milk is __(12)__ .

15 A substitute for Roquefort cheese is __(15)__ cheese.

16 If liquid milk is left in a warm place it may __(16)__ .

DOWN

1 Milk butterfat is sold as __(1)__ .

3 A frozen milk dessert is __(3)__ .

5 Skim milk is __(5)__ in calories.

Custards, chowders, cheese omelets, and cream sauces are only a few examples of milk cookery.
United Dairy Industry Assoc.

medium white sauce is made with 2 tablespoons (30 milliliters) of flour to a cup of milk. (See White Sauce recipe, page 516.)

You can prepare a basic cheese sauce by adding grated cheese to melt in a hot, thickened white sauce mixture.

Milk Puddings and Custards

Milk puddings are made in much the same way as white sauce. The flour or cornstarch is mixed with the sugar, and the cold milk is added slowly before the mixture is heated. Then the entire mixture is cooked, sometimes in the top of a double boiler, while being stirred. Eggs are added to some puddings for texture and flavor. (See page 431 for adding eggs to a hot mixture.) The addition of chocolate, brown sugar, or other ingredients determines the final flavor of the pudding. Milk pudding can be used to fill cream puffs, éclairs, or pie shells. It can be combined with fruits such as peaches, bananas, or berries to make a pie filling or a pudding.

Fewer steps are involved in making puddings from commercial mixes than from basic ingredients. In these mixes the starch, sugar, and flavoring are usually in the package. You add the milk before cooking. Some of the instant pudding mixes contain an enzyme, rather than starch, which thickens the mixture without cooking.

A milk dessert that is thickened with egg is called a *custard*. Egg-milk mixtures that are cooked on top of the range are called *soft-custard* or *custard sauce*. They may be drunk from a cup or used as a sauce over cakes, fruits, or meringues. If the egg-milk mixture is cooked in the oven until it thickens, it is called a *baked custard*. Baked custard may be varied by the addition of different kinds of flavorings, spices, sauces or toppings. It may be served hot or cold. Since custards contain many valuable nutrients and are easy to digest, they are especially recommended and are favorite foods for small children, elderly people, and persons on special diets.

Low cooking temperatures are necessary if dairy dishes are to be tender in texture and mild in flavor.

7 Milk thickened with starch is the basis of a white (7) .

8 Meat, fish, eggs, cheese, and milk are excellent sources of (8) .

10 An egg dish which often contains cheese is a(an) (10) .

12 Cream is churned into (12) .

13 The name of *Nature's most nearly perfect food* is (13) .

14 Cheddar, cottage, and Swiss are kinds of (15) .

17 Unpasteurized milk is (17) milk.

Your career
Dairying

You would feed and care for cows to ensure their greatest productivity. You would milk the cows twice each day with special equipment. Caring for the milking machines and utensils would be another farming responsibility. You might work on a dairy farm, or own one yourself.

Bulletin board IDEA
Title: *Count Your Calories by the Friends They Keep*
Directions: Use pictures of nutritious snack foods. Label the pictures with the nutrients each food contains.

Discuss the following terms describing various milk products. Determine which products are available in stores in your area.

Raw milk: Fresh, whole milk which has not been pasteurized.

Pasteurized milk: Milk which has been heated to kill harmful bacteria and then chilled immediately.

Homogenized milk: Whole milk in which the butterfat has been broken into tiny particles that will not rise.

Vitamin D milk: Whole milk which has vitamin D added.

Certified milk: High-quality whole milk which has very low bacterial count used mostly for special infant and invalid diets.

Skim milk: Milk from which most of the butterfat has been removed. Because skim milk is usually fortified with vitamin A, it is just as nutritious as whole milk and is sometimes cheaper. In fact, the calcium content of skim milk is slightly higher than that of whole milk. Low-fat milk may contain 1 to 2% fat and is labeled accordingly.

Flavored milk: Milk to which chocolate or other flavors have been added. Chocolate milk is usually made from skim milk with cocoa added.

Cheese casseroles can be varied in flavor and texture by the addition of chips.   *Frito-Lay, Inc./A Div. of PepsiCo, Inc.*

CHEESE

Cheese is made from milk by the thickening, or coagulation, of milk protein. The *curd*, the solid part of the milk, is separated from the *whey*, or liquid part. This is done either by allowing the milk to sour, as in the case of cottage cheese, or by adding an enzyme to the milk, as in the making of hard, semihard, or processed cheeses.

Cheese Cookery

Care must be taken in cooking foods containing cheese. If too high a temperature is reached, the cheese becomes tough and stringy. As with all protein foods, a tem-

1	Swiss	7	Blue	13	Teleme	21 Cream Cheese
2	Cheddar	8	Baby Gouda	14	Monterey Jack	22 Cream Cheese
3	Edam	9	Sliced	15	Queso Blanco	23 Monterey Jack
4	Processed		Natural Brick	16	Camembert	24 Cream Cheese
	American	10	Sliced	17	Breakfast	25 Mozzarella
5	Processed		Natural Cheddar	18	Schloss	26 Mozzarella Twist
	Pimiento	11	Ricotta	19	Brie	27 Salame Provolone
6	Gouda	12	Cottage Cheese	20	Pimiento Cream	28 Boccini Balls

Flavor, texture, and shape often determine how the different cheeses will be used. *National Dairy Council*

perature of 300 degrees to 325 degrees Fahrenheit (150 degrees to 177 degrees Celsius) is best for baking cheese mixtures.

Macaroni with cheese is a favorite main dish; lasagna is another.

Cheese is also combined with eggs, another protein food, to make cheese soufflé or omelets. A melted cheese fondue is a party favorite. (See recipe for Baked Cheese Fondue on page 517.)

Buttermilk: The liquid of milk or cream that remains after butter is churned. Cultured buttermilk is the "soured" product.

Evaporated milk: Canned milk from which approximately one-half of the water has been removed before canning. Evaporated milk is available as both whole milk and skim milk.

Sweetened condensed milk: Milk from which approximately one-half of the water has been removed and to which sugar has been added before canning.

Dried milk: Milk from which the water has been removed. It is available as both whole milk and skim milk. Nonfat dried milk is more common.

Half-and-half: A mixture of equal parts of milk and cream, usually homogenized.

Cream: A portion of whole milk with a high butterfat content. Kinds are light, medium, heavy, and whipping, grouped according to the fat content.

Sour cream: Cream that contains about 18% fat. It has been homogenized and then soured by the action of lactic acid bacteria.

Yogurt: A cultured milk product made by fermenting whole or partially skimmed milk. Nonfat milk solids, fruits, and flavorings may be added.

On a separate paper, number from 1 to 22. Beside each number indicate if the corresponding statement is true or false. *Do not* write in this book.

1 Milk has been nicknamed *nature's most nearly perfect food* because it is rich in every nutrient.
2 As you grow older, you do not need to have milk daily.
3 Curd is the solid part of milk.
4 Condensed milk tastes sweet.
5 A glass of whole milk contains more calcium than the same size glass of skim milk.
6 Pasteurized milk will *not* sour.
7 Milk products should be cooked at high temperatures.
8 Milk is one of the best sources of complete protein.
9 Milk is fortified with vitamin C.
10 White sauce is made with milk that is thickened with flour or cornstarch.
11 Custard is a milk dessert thickened with eggs.
12 For equal amounts, cottage cheese contains fewer calories than cheddar cheese.
13 American cheese is a good source of vitamin A.
14 A temperature of 400° F (205° C) to 425° F (218° C) is best for cooking cheese dishes.
15 The whipping quality of cream is related to its butterfat content.
16 Most large markets sell raw milk.
17 Certified milk is used for special infant and invalid diets.
18 Cheese supplies many of the same nutrients that meats do.
19 The *Daily Food Guide* recommends a pint of milk for teens.
20 Yogurt is a nondairy product.
21 The key to successful cheese cookery is low heat.
22 Whole milk usually costs more than skim milk.

Match the *definitions* in List A with the *forms of milk* in List B. Use a form of milk from List B only once. *Do not* write in this book.

List A: Definitions

A Fresh milk that has not been processed in any way
B Whole milk in which the butterfat has been broken into tiny particles that will not separate
C Usually the least expensive form in which either whole or skim milk can be bought
D Milk from which about half of the water has been removed
E Milk with fewer calories but as much calcium as whole milk

List B: Forms of milk

1 Dried
2 Evaporated
3 Homogenized
4 Low-fat
5 Raw

Match the *vegetables* in List A with the *parts of plants* in List B. Use each item in List B only once. *Do not* write in this book.

List A: Vegetables

A Asparagus
B Broccoli
C Carrot
D Corn
E Onion
F Spinach

List B: Parts of plants

1 Bulb
2 Flower
3 Leaf
4 Root
5 Seed
6 Stem

Fill in the blank in each sentence with the *best* word to complete the statement. *Do not* write in this book.

1 Some fruits and vegetables can be bought fresh, frozen, canned, and (1) .
2 Citrus fruits are the best source of vitamin (2) .
3 Apricots, peaches, and cantaloupes are excellent sources of vitamin (3) .
4 Minerals, the B vitamins, and vitamin (4) dissolve in water.
5 To help preserve the shape of fruit during cooking, add (5) to the cooking water.

Chapter 23

Preparing Fruits and Vegetables

Historians do not know very much about the early use of fruits and vegetables. Along with hunting stories, there are some legends about farming. However, most of these stories are concerned with the growing of grains. Perhaps it was so natural to eat the plant life around them that people did not think it important to record anything about it.

Can you imagine hunters watching birds pecking at the berries in the thicket where they were hiding? Perhaps they nibbled a few of the berries and discovered that the juicy fruit satisfied both thirst and hunger. The berries were not only good to eat but also easy to harvest.

Today many people still take fruits and vegetables for granted. Most cooks and menu planners

Play Vegetable Bingo. Make bingo cards with five squares going each way. Fill the twenty-five spaces with the words: stem, flower, root, seed, leaf, and fruit. Change the order in which they are used for each card. Cross out the appropriate square as a vegetable is named. To win you need to cross out five squares in a straight line—across, up, down, or diagonally.

Vegetables

asparagus	lettuce
artichoke	mushrooms
beans	mustard
beets	greens
broccoli	okra
Brussels sprouts	onions
cabbage	parsley
carrots	parsnips
cauliflower	peas
celery	peppers
chard	potatoes
collards	pumpkin
corn	radishes
cucumbers	spinach
dandelion	squash
greens	sweet potato
endive	tomato
kale	turnips

do not pay as much attention to fruits and vegetables as they do to protein foods. Yet fruits and vegetables are a very important part of a well-planned diet. They add a wide range of flavors, colors, shapes, and textures to menus. They are rich in vitamins A, B, and C. Many also contain important minerals. Fruits and vegetables are the main source of the fiber and acid which help with the elimination of wastes and so help keep your body regulated.

AVAILABLE FORMS OF FRUITS AND VEGETABLES

You can buy fruits and vegetables in many forms. They may be bought fresh, frozen, canned, and dried. Some are best served raw. As such, they are particularly popular as between-meal snacks. Some seem to taste better cooked, while others are delicious either way.

Fresh fruits and vegetables may lose part of their vitamin content when exposed to heat or air. For this reason they contain more food value when they are garden-fresh than at any other time. When fresh fruits and vegetables are shipped over great distances or are stored for a long time, valuable nutrients may be lost. Knowing vitamins are easily lost, food processors often build their plants near the fruit and vegetable growing areas. The ripe foods are picked and taken immediately to the plant. When foods are picked, prepared, and canned

or frozen at a nearby plant, they often contain more nutrients than they would if sold as fresh produce in the market.

Fruits and vegetables may also be dried for future use. Many dried foods have distinctive flavors which make them more suitable for certain dishes than other forms of the same food. Dried apricots, prunes, and raisins are popular in desserts. You find dried vegetables in soup mixes and sauce mixes. Instant potato is another form of a dried vegetable. Dried beans have long been popular for protein-rich main dishes.

Vegetables

There are several recognized ways of classifying vegetables. Perhaps one of the most useful ways is to group vegetables according to the part of the plant used.

Leafy vegetables

You probably know many of the leafy vegetables. Among them are spinach, collards, turnip greens, mustard greens, beet greens, kale, and chard. Salad greens such as lettuce, cabbage, curly endive, parsley, watercress, romaine, and escarole are also leafy vegetables. Many leafy vegetables are eaten raw. Others may be served raw or cooked.

The leafy vegetables contain varying amounts of vitamins A and C. In general, the deeper green the color, the richer the vitamin

Fruits and vegetables are popular in cold salads and in hot dishes. Many fruits and vegetables may be enjoyed raw or cooked, depending on personal preference.   *United Fresh Fruit and Vegetable Assoc.*

Make one list of vegetables you like, one list of vegetables you don't like, and one list of vegetables you have never tasted. Which list is longest? Do any of the vegetables appear on more than one list? How many times have you eaten those on the "don't like" list? Have they been cooked more than one way? Try to find a recipe for cooking one of your "don't like" vegetables in a way you think you might like.

Plan and prepare a vegetable-plate luncheon menu. Choose four vegetables with interesting color contrasts. Select one frozen, one fresh, one canned, and one dried vegetable. Cook each by a different method.

Plan and prepare a vegetable-tasting party. Select a different vegetable and recipe for each guest to prepare and bring. Everyone should taste each dish. Which were liked best? Least? Why?

Plan the vegetables to be served at family meals for a week. Choose at least two different vegetables for each day. Plan the 14 meals without using the same vegetable more than once, and use different methods of cooking.

445

Sit in a large circle to play the Fruit and Vegetable Game. Begin by choosing one student to name a fruit or vegetable beginning with the letter A, such as apricot or apple. The next player gives a name beginning with B, like broccoli. Continue moving around the circle until someone misses. The next person then has a chance to name a fruit or vegetable beginning with the missed letter. The ones who miss drop out of the circle. The players continue as long as they can name appropriate foods. The alphabet may be covered several times. Continue until only a few players remain.

Prepare different forms of the same vegetable—frozen, canned, and fresh. Figure the price per serving of each. Compare for flavor, cost, appearance, and the time and effort involved in the preparation of each.

Brainstorm to find a large number of ways to prepare potatoes. Suggest various ways to fix instant potatoes.

Vegetables are as varied as the plants they come from. For example, scallions are the root of a plant; broccoli, the buds.   *The McIlhenny Co.*

content, particularly the vitamin A content. For example, broccoli provides more vitamins than lettuce.

Root vegetables
Some of the more common root vegetables are carrots, turnips, beets, radishes, parsnips, potatoes, sweet potatoes, and onions. Potatoes are sometimes classed separately as *tubers*, meaning they are only the thickened section of the plant root. Onions, which also grow underground, are further classed as *bulbs*. The underground vegetables are formed to help supply the plant

with food. They are the plant's storage bin.

Since root vegetables grow under the ground and do not contain green color, you might not expect them to be good sources of vitamin A or C. However, if you look at a chart showing all the nutrients in the different foods, you will see that carrots and sweet potatoes contain a great deal of vitamin A. Like any other bright yellow or orange fruit or vegetable, carrots and sweet potatoes are rich in vitamin A. In fact, it is fairly safe to say that the deeper green or yellow the color of a fruit or vegetable, the higher its vitamin A content. The paler the color, the poorer the source of vitamin A. Thus, sweet potatoes and carrots are good sources of vitamin A, while white potatoes and onions contain only a trace.

A study of the nutrients in vegetables might further surprise you. While white root vegetables, such as potatoes, parsnips, and turnips, contain very little vitamin A, they are relatively rich in vitamin C. If cooked correctly, a serving of one of these vegetables can provide up to one-fourth of your daily requirement for this vitamin.

Stem vegetables

The stem is eaten along with the leaf of many vegetables, such as spinach, chard, and turnip greens. Yet there is another group of vegetables used primarily for their stems. This group includes aspara-
gus and celery. Many people are willing to pay more for blanched, or whitened, asparagus and celery than for a bright green vegetable. This is not a nutritionally wise practice, since green stem vegetables contain more nutrients than the white ones. Again, the deeper the green, the richer the vitamin content in practically any green vegetable.

Flower vegetables

Broccoli and cauliflower are two familiar plants eaten in the flower, or bud, stage. Broccoli, a deep green vegetable, is much richer in vitamins A and C than the white cauliflower. Actually, the leaves of cauliflower have more food value than the white buds. Unfortunately, people have not developed a taste for the leaves and usually throw them away.

Seed vegetables

The seeds and seed pods of plants are probably the largest single group of vegetables. Beans, peas, and corn are plant seeds. Okra, cucumbers, squash, pumpkins, tomatoes, sweet peppers, and green beans contain plant seeds, although these vegetables are eaten more for their covering than for the seed itself. The nutritional values of seed vegetables vary greatly. While seeds tend to be rich in the B vitamins, many of the seed vegetables are also rich in vitamins A and C.

 Find the names of twenty-nine fruits and vegetables in these scrambled letters. The names are in straight lines—across, down, or diagonally. Some of the names are printed backwards. Fruits and vegetables may be listed more than once.

```
S E O T A T O P E
S Q U A S H B G L
Z P L U M Y A K E
M U L P R B J C M
L I M E B A R K O
D P L A P C O R N
F E C R P A Y I E
C P O N G R L F C
H P C A R R O T U
A E A E Q O A O T
R R B E E T C P T
D W A C O U H M E
A L N M Y R N G L
R N A E B N P P Q
K T N W T I F E U
O K A L E P E A R
```

Hidden words in puzzle:

banana	lettuce
bean	lime
beet	okra
berry	pea
cabbage	pear
carrot	pepper
celery	plum
chard	potatoes
corn	squash
grape	tomato
kale	turnip
lemon	

Read the statements below. Research to find facts to prove each statement true or false.

1 Frozen orange juice is not as good for you as fresh orange juice.
2 Vegetables should always be eaten raw because they lose their nutritive value when cooked.
3 The juices from vegetables have special health-giving qualities.
4 Cucumbers, radishes, cabbage, and onions cannot be digested.
5 Worn-out body tissue is destroyed by sweet, ripe cherries.

Your career
Vegetable cook

You would direct the ordering, cleaning, preparing, and cooking of vegetables and fruits used with regular meals. You might also prepare salads or supervise the salad-making procedures. You would work in large restaurants, institutional dining rooms, and large school cafeterias.

Fruits

Almost everyone enjoys fruit of some kind. A wide selection of fresh fruits is available during most seasons of the year. Fresh fruits probably vary in price more than any other type of food. Like vegetables, fruits add a variety of color, flavor, and texture to meals. They are valuable sources of vitamins and minerals. Dark yellow fruits, such as apricots, peaches, cantaloupes, mangoes, and persimmons, are

For adding variety to meals and vitamins to the diet, a broad range of fruits are available during the year. *United Fresh Fruit and Vegetable Assoc.*

good sources of vitamin A. Fruits such as the citrus fruits, cantaloupes, and strawberries are rich sources of vitamin C. So valuable are these C-rich fruits that the *Daily Food Guide* encourages each person to eat some of them daily. (See pages 379–381.)

Fruits, like vegetables, can be classified in a number of ways. Sometimes they are classified according to food value, and other times according to the texture or shape of the fruit. Probably the most common classification, however, is according to the plants which bear them. Many, many fruits grow on trees. These include apples, pears, cherries, peaches, oranges, grapefruit, lemons, dates, limes, mangoes, figs, persimmons, plums, and tangerines. Fruits which grow on vines include melons, grapes, and some kinds of berries. Other fruits grow on bushes. Most bush fruits are berries, like blueberries, cranberries, and raspberries. Pineapples and strawberries grow on plants which remain rather close to the ground. Papayas and bananas grow on short-lived tree-like bushes. These bushes grow rapidly but have a short life span.

PRINCIPLES FOR COOKING FRUITS AND VEGETABLES

Of all the food groups, fruits and vegetables are the most susceptible to vitamin loss, as well as to changes in flavor, texture, color, and shape.

Knowing this, you should select and prepare fruits and vegetables with three main goals in mind: to preserve nutritive values, to preserve or enhance food flavors and textures, and to retain attractive colors and shapes.

Vegetables

Vegetables may be cooked by many different methods. The most common methods are boiling, baking, and frying. Often vegetables are combined with other foods in casseroles. No matter what method you use to prepare them, there are basic facts to remember when cooking vegetables:

1 The B vitamins, vitamin C, and minerals dissolve easily in water. Therefore, the less water used in vegetable cookery, the more vitamins and minerals saved.

2 The B vitamins and vitamin C are easily destroyed by exposure to heat and air. By cooking vegetables containing these vitamins in a closed container, more of the vitamins are kept.

3 Vitamins B and C are destroyed by exposure to oxygen. Boil the cooking water a few minutes before adding the raw vegetables. This will allow excess oxygen to escape from the cooking water and prevent some vitamin loss during cooking.

4 Vitamins A, D, and E dissolve in fats. They are drawn out into the cooking liquid when fats such as bacon drippings or butter are

 Follow these quick and easy steps to prepare broiled grapefruit:

1 Wash and dry fruit.
2 Cut in half crosswise.
3 Loosen pulp from membrane in each segment, using a small sharp knife. *Do not* cut the membrane.
4 Sprinkle each half with 1 T. (15 ml) brown sugar and dot with 1 t. (5 ml) butter or margarine. Honey may be used in place of the sugar.
5 Place on rack in broiler pan and position in oven so top of fruit is 3 inches (7.5 cm) from broiling unit.
6 Broil for 5 to 10 minutes, or until sugar melts and top of grapefruit is lightly browned.
7 Top with maraschino cherry, raisins, or chopped nuts, if desired.
8 Serve hot as an appetizer or dessert.

Plan menus for a day, without using citrus fruits or tomatoes. How will you include an adequate supply of vitamin C for the day? Consult the Food Composition Charts beginning on page 506 for various foods that might help to meet the daily requirements for vitamin C. Compare your menus with those submitted by others in the class. What is the most practical way to include vitamin C in your diet?

Check cookbooks, magazines, newspapers, and other sources for recipes using citrus fruits and juices. Experiment with some of the recipes to include citrus in the diet as appetizers, salads, garnishes, and desserts.

Follow these steps in sectioning a grapefruit or orange for fruit cup or salad:

1 Pare the skin away, cutting just deep enough to remove the white outer membrane as well as the outside skin.

2 Insert a sharp paring knife along the membrane of one section of the fruit and twist to lift out the segment.

3 Continue around the fruit until all the segments are free of the membrane.

4 Remove seeds.

5 Mix with other fruits, if desired, for fruit cup. Arrange sections on lettuce leaf or other salad greens. Alternate with unpeeled apple slices or avocado slices. What other combinations are possible?

Fruits and vegetables lend themselves to various methods of preparation. With this in mind, choose a method that will preserve nutritive value while enhancing flavor and appearance. *Florida Dept. of Citrus*

added to vegetables during cooking.

5 The more inner surface of the vegetable exposed to water and air, the greater will be the nutrient loss in cooking. Cook vegetables whole or in large pieces.

6 Many of the nutrients are near the surface of the vegetable. If the skin must be removed, cut as little of the vegetable as possible with the peeling. Peeling vegetables after cooking saves the most nutrients of all.

7 Many vegetables, such as cabbage and spinach, contain acid which will destroy the color during the cooking process. To prevent this color loss, cook these vegetables as rapidly as possible and leave the pan uncovered so the acid may pass off in the steam.

8 Baking soda will destroy some vitamins. It should not be added to

vegetables, even though it will shorten the necessary cooking time.

9 To preserve food value and flavor, cook vegetables only until they are tender.

10 Overcooking of vegetables such as cabbage and onions will cause the flavor to become strong and unpleasing.

The above facts provide information about vegetables. The following set of rules for cooking vegetables is based on these important facts. Follow them to get the best flavor and nutrition from your cooked vegetables.

1 Leave vegetables whole when cooking them, or cut them into large pieces only.

When vitamin A-rich vegetables, such as carrots and broccoli, are cooked in soups or casseroles, their vitamins remain in usable form. *American Home Foods*

2 Do not soak vegetables, especially after peeling.

3 Cook vegetables in a small amount of water and watch them to prevent burning.

4 Cover the pan as the vegetables cook, except for strong-flavored vegetables.

5 Start vegetables in rapidly boiling water, and cook them as quickly and briefly as possible.

6 Avoid adding baking soda or fat to vegetables during the cooking period.

7 Serve the cooking liquid with the vegetable, or save it to use in sauces or soups.

Fruits

Many of the principles for vegetable cookery also apply to fruits. Fruits, like vegetables, are commonly cooked by boiling, baking, or frying. The following rules apply directly to preparing fruits.

1 Cook the fruit as quickly as possible after peeling, since vitamins are easily lost by exposure to heat and air.

2 Dip peeled fruits, such as apples, bananas, and peaches, into a slightly acid liquid, such as citrus juice, pineapple juice, or a salad dressing to prevent browning. Since the protective coating may dissolve some of the nutrients, plan to serve the coating with the fruit. A commercial preparation which prevents discoloration may be sprinkled over a cut fruit to protect

 Follow these quick and easy steps to prepare orange slices:

1 Wash and dry fruit, then chill.

2 Set fruit to be peeled on cutting board. With a sharp knife, cut down the fruit from top to bottom in sections to remove the skin and white membrane.

3 Slice crosswise.

4 Use in salads, with desserts, or as garnishes. When used for garnish, the peeling may be left on. For extra interest, cut evenly spaced grooves all around the fruit from stem end to the other end. Slice crosswise for fluted slices.

Bulletin board IDEA
Title: *Don't Poke Along—Speed Up for Good Health*
Directions: Use a picture of a turtle in the center. Mount pictures of bright yellow fruits and vegetables and leafy green vegetables. Under these write *Vitamin A.* Use pictures of citrus fruits and write underneath *Vitamin C.* Mount pictures of bread and cereal products and underneath write *B Vitamins.* Use a picture of milk and write *Vitamin D* and *Calcium.*

Prepare and serve a fruit or vegetable gelatin salad that fits into a color scheme appropriate for a special occasion. For instance, use a red salad made with cherry gelatin and red fruit for Valentine's Day. Use red and green gelatin layers with appropriate fruits or vegetables for Christmas. Be sure each layer is thoroughly set before adding the next, which should have begun to thicken.

Investigate the different methods of preserving fruits and vegetables. What are the most important reasons for doing each? Choose to either freeze, can, or jelly your favorite fruit or vegetable. How would you go about doing it?

 Your career
Horticulturist

You would work with plants. You might specialize in those that bear fruits and vegetables. You might develop new or improved plant varieties, or research better methods of growing, harvesting, storing, and transporting crops. You might work for large orchards or farms, or with government agencies as a consultant to farmers.

Fruits can be served separately or combined with pudding, pastry, or other fruits in a wide variety of dessert and salad combinations. *Good Seasons Salad Dressing Mix*

its appearance during freezing, serving, and eating.

3   Cook fruits to prevent spoilage, to make them easy to digest, to change the flavor, to add variety to the menu, or to combine them with other foods.

4   Adding sugar to the cooking water helps preserve the shape of a fruit. If you are cooking fruit to use in a salad or as a garnish, add the sugar early in the cooking process. If you are making applesauce, add the sugar after the fruit has cooked to a softened state.

5   Peel fruits before cooking only when necessary.

PRINCIPLES FOR PRESERVING FRUITS AND VEGETABLES

Although fruits and vegetables may be purchased on the market in a wide variety of forms, people sometimes take special pleasure in the home preservation of fruits or vegetables. In all forms of food preservation, the bacterial growth is slowed or stopped so the food may be kept for an indefinite period of time. When there is an oversupply of a given food produced at home or an especially good buy at the marketplace, home preservation of foods can help stretch the family food money. If you are planning to preserve foods at home, be sure to get accurate directions and follow them carefully. Poorly preserved foods can cause dangerous food poisoning.

Most preservation is done by freezing and canning. However, many families have treasured recipes for pickles, relishes, jellies, or fruit preserves. They enjoy making these items to serve as their own specialty.

Vegetables may be preserved in the following ways:

1　Fresh vegetables may be frozen after cleaning and *blanching* (heating in water).

2　Fresh vegetables may be canned either by following the hot-water-bath method or by cooking them under pressure in sealed jars or cans.

3　Vegetables may be preserved with the addition of salt, vinegar, sugar, or a combination of these ingredients.

4　Vegetables may be dried.

Fruits may be preserved in several ways:

1　Fresh fruits may be frozen, with or without sugar.

2　Fruits may be canned in sealed jars or cans by either the hot-water-bath method or by cooking them under pressure.

 Look at the picture on page 487. Practice making the vegetable garnishes shown in the picture. Find pictures of other garnishes and practice making them.

Study the produce counter in a large supermarket. What are the salad greens you can identify? Do you recognize romaine, escarole, Bibb lettuce, leaf lettuce, watercress, and raw spinach?

Remove the core from a head of lettuce by banging the head down sharply with the core side down. The core should loosen so you can lift it out easily.

Wash and drain salad greens thoroughly. Store in a tightly closed plastic bag or covered bowl to retain crispness. To use in salad, tear rather than cut. Add dressing at the last possible moment to prevent wilting.

Suggest salads which may be served as appetizers, accompaniments, main dishes, and desserts. Tell why each was selected for that category.

Many families have favorite recipes for jellies, jams, or relishes, and they take pride in making and serving them on special occasions.　*Certo Fruit Pectin*

Select a fruit grown in or near your part of the country. Develop ways to garnish foods using that fruit. Some examples might be:

Oranges — slices, sections, baskets

Apples — spiced, sauced

Peaches — broiled halves, stuffed, sliced

Pears — filled with jelly

Grapes — small clusters dipped in egg white and then sugar

Prunes — stuffed with cream cheese or nuts

Prepare two fruit salads which are identical except for colored garnishes such as cherries or mint. Which has more eye appeal? Why?

 Your career
Food service manager

You would be responsible for hiring, training, and supervising the employees in restaurants, cafeterias, and other food service places. You would select food and equipment; keep accounts and records; plan or approve menus; enforce sanitation regulations; and deal with the customers. You would find employment in restaurants, cafeterias, drive-ins, schools, or wherever meals are planned and prepared.

Small pieces of fruits and vegetables can be combined in a gelatin mold to provide colorful additions to otherwise bland or colorless meals. *Cling Peach Advisory Board*

3 Fruits may be prepared, packed in suitable jars or cans, sealed, and processed in a pressure cooker.

4 Fruits and fruit juices may be cooked with a large proportion of sugar to make preserves, jams, and jellies.

5 Fruits may be dried.

6 Fruits may be candied. Candied fruits and fruit peel are often used as garnishes or in baking.

PRINCIPLES FOR SERVING RAW FRUITS AND VEGETABLES

Many of the vitamins and minerals supplied by fruits and vegetables are lost during the cooking process. Thus, a daily serving of raw fruits or vegetables is an important contribution to good health. Fruit and vegetable juices can also add valuable nutrients to the daily diet. Raw fruits and vegetables may be added to a cooked food as a garnish. These garnishes tend to make the dish pleasing to the eye. They also add interesting texture contrasts which make the food appetizing.

Making Salads

Salads are high on the list of food favorites of many people. They may be made of fruits or vegetables or a combination of both. Almost any type of food may be used as an ingredient in a salad. In addition to fruits and vegetables, meat, fish, poultry, cheese, or bread cubes are often used. Salad ingredients may be cooked, fresh, frozen, or canned, but most salads contain some raw fruits or vegetables.

Small pieces of fruits and vegetables may be served in molded gelatin salads. Carrots, cabbage, and celery, as well as many canned fruits and vegetables, are favorites in gelatin molds. Such salads may stretch a small amount of food to make satisfying servings for everyone. Relatively inexpensive molded salads can add flavor and color to any meal. (See the recipe for Gelatin Mold, page 518.)

Salad making is a form of art. With practice, you can combine various shapes and colors of foods in interesting arrangements. A few simple principles will help you to prepare colorful, tasty, and nutritious salads.

A well-planned salad, hot or cold, is pleasing within itself and complements other foods with which it is served. *Cling Peach Advisory Board*

1 Plan flavor, color, and texture combinations to be pleasing in themselves and to complement the other foods in the meal.

2 Select cold, clean, crisp, fresh fruits or vegetables.

3 Pare or scrape fruits and vegetables only if necessary. Then remove only a thin outer coating to avoid loss of nutrients.

4 Cut fruits and vegetables as close to the time you expect to serve them as possible.

5 Keep prepared fruits and vegetables in tightly covered containers until serving time.

6 To cut down on loss of nutrients, avoid soaking salad ingredients in water.

7 In general, use fruits and vegetables dry or thoroughly drained.

8 Arrange the base, or salad greens, to prevent their hanging over the edge of the salad plate.

9 Tear, rather than cut, salad greens into bite-size pieces to avoid bruising them with a knife.

10 In general, add the seasonings and salad dressing at the last possible moment. This will prevent wilting and keep the salad crisp and fresh looking.

 Consult the Food Composition Charts beginning on page 506. Compare and contrast the nutrients and calories in vegetables such as broccoli, beets, corn, okra, potatoes, and squash. Compare and contrast the nutrients and calories in such fruits as oranges, strawberries, bananas, pineapple, peaches, and watermelon. When would some fruits and vegetables be recommended over the others? Why?

Classify various fruits and vegetables according to the part of the plant from which they come:

Stem   Seed
Leaf   Flower
Root   Fruit

Compare the groups for nutritive values. What seems to be a major difference between fruits and vegetables?

Bulletin board IDEA
Title: *Toss Up an Appetite*
Directions: Below the title attach a mock salad bowl or platter with salad greens coming out of it. Cut fruit, vegetable, and salad pictures from magazines or store ads and arrange them around the bowl or platter.

Number from 1 to 13 on a piece of paper. Beside each number write the letter corresponding to the *best* answer to each question. *Do not* write in this book.

1 Which is a *leafy* vegetable?
  a Asparagus
  b Cauliflower
  c Lettuce
  d Parsnips
2 Which is a *seed* vegetable?
  a Beet
  b Cabbage
  c Celery
  d Pea
3 Which is a *root* vegetable?
  a Carrot
  b Celery
  c Spinach
  d Squash
4 Which grows on a vine?
  a Blueberry
  b Peach
  c Pineapple
  d Watermelon
5 Which is a fruit?
  a Chard
  b Endive
  c Mango
  d Pumpkin
6 Which is a vegetable?
  a Cranberry
  b Fig
  c Okra
  d Papaya
7 Which has the most vitamin C?
  a Carrots

  b Dried beans
  c Oranges
  d Spinach
8 Which is the best source of vitamin A?
  a Broccoli
  b Grapefruit
  c Lettuce
  d White potato
9 Which vitamin dissolves in water?
  a A
  b C
  c D
  d E
10 Which nutrient is fat-soluble?
  a B vitamins
  b Calcium
  c Iron
  d Vitamin A
11 Which should *not* be done when cooking vegetables?
  a Bring water to a boil before adding raw vegetables.
  b Cook in a small amount of water.
  c Cook only until tender.
  d Cut in small pieces.
12 Which *cannot* be bought fresh, frozen, canned, *and* dried?
  a Apricots
  b Corn
  c Peas
  d Tomatoes
13 Which is *not* a preserved food?
  a Carrot sticks
  b Jam
  c Raisins
  d Relish

Fill in the blank in each sentence with the *best* word to complete the statement. *Do not* write in this book.

1 When the bran and germ are removed from grains during milling, the resulting product is called white or __(1)__ flour.
2 Breads made without yeast as the leavening agent are classified as __(2)__ breads.
3 Hot breakfast cereals can be bought in regular, quick-cooking, and __(3)__ varieties.
4 The main reason for heating cereal is to thoroughly cook the __(4)__ to make it easy to digest.
5 Pancakes, waffles, and popovers are made from pour __(5)__ .
6 When flour is mixed with water, the protein in flour forms __(6)__ .
7 When salt and leavening are added to all-purpose flour, it is labeled __(7)__ flour.
8 When substituting all-purpose flour for cake flour in a recipe, use __(8)__ tablespoon(s) less per cup (240 ml).
9 The three types of leaveners are carbon dioxide, air, and __(9)__ .
10 Carbon dioxide is produced by three leavening agents: baking soda, baking powder, and __(10)__ .
11 Any type of fat used in a flour mixture is called __(11)__ .
12 The bran and germ of grains contain most of the roughage, B vitamins, and __(12)__ in cereals.

Chapter 24

Preparing Cereal Products

After reading this chapter, you should be able to:

1 Define the term *enriched flour*.
2 Identify ways cereal products can be included in the diet.
3 State how flour mixtures are classified.
4 Explain how the development of gluten affects the texture of different products made with flour.
5 Explain how various bread and flour products are leavened.
6 Tell in your own words how various types of shortenings differ.
7 Give the reasons for using sugar in different flour products.
8 Practice making a variety of products using a biscuit master mix.
9 Demonstrate the principles of cereal cookery.

Since the dawn of civilization, cereals have been cultivated and their seeds harvested to use as food. In early days, cereal grains were pounded or ground, mixed with liquid, and cooked as little cakes or crackers. Modern breads such as *tortillas* from Mexico, *chapati* from India, and *brods* from Sweden are still made in this primitive manner.

At first whole grains were used in bread-making, just as they sometimes are today. But there are two problems involved in making breads from whole-grain flours. While whole-grain flours make delicious, nutritious breads, the breads are somewhat dark and coarse in texture. Also, whole-grain cereal products are apt to spoil rather quickly because of the relatively high fat content of the germ, or life-giving portion of the seed.

Look through cookbooks to find recipes with cereals as a basic ingredient. Pick out those you think your family could use. See Oatmeal Cookie Mix recipe on page 522.

Find out how many kinds of flour are available in the grocery store where your family shops. How do the flours differ? Which kind of flour seems to be stocked in greatest quantities? Why?

Bulletin board IDEA
Title: *Stop Draggin'*
Directions: Use a picture of a dragon made to look as if it is breathing fire. In red write: *Fire Up with a Good Breakfast.*

Your career
Farm mechanic

You would study farm equipment and develop the skills to keep the machines working in their best condition. You might specialize in field equipment or dairy machinery. You would find employment on large farms, farming equipment companies, or be self-employed in farm areas where you could be of service to several farmers.

As the manufacturing process continued to develop, ways were found to remove the *bran*, which is the hard outer coating of cereal grains. Milling techniques were also developed to remove the germ. These milling techniques leave the soft, whitish grain center which can be ground into very fine particles. The finely ground product is then called white flour, or *refined flour*. Since the germ of grain contains fat, and therefore spoils rather quickly, refined flours keep better than whole-grain flours. They also produce breads with a much finer texture than those made with whole-grain flours.

The bran and germ contain most of the B-complex vitamins, iron, and roughage in cereals. Most of this food value is removed during the milling of refined flours. Therefore, it is necessary to return these nutrients to food products if they are to be nourishing. When the iron and vitamins of the bran and germ are restored to the flour, this treated flour is called *enriched flour*. Except for roughage, enriched flour contains all of the food value of a whole-grain product. The Federal government has set standards for this enrichment, and manufacturers who use the word *enriched* must follow these standards. Because of the high food value of the wheat germ, it is packaged and sold separately. People buy it to sprinkle on cereals or fruits or to add to home-baked products.

TYPES OF CEREAL FOODS

We often think of cereal as a breakfast food only, but it is hard to plan a meal which does not include some cereal product. Rice, macaroni products, and all breads are cereal foods. Sauces and gravies are often thickened with cereals.

Breads

Breads are the most frequently eaten cereal products. Modern breads come ready-prepared, partially prepared, or in the form of mixes. These breads save time, have uniform quality, and add variety to meals. However, many cooks have one or two favorite bread recipes. These homemade breads are easy to make if you understand the basic principles involved. Cookbooks separate breads into *yeast breads* and *quick breads,* or those which do not use yeast for leavening.

Breakfast Cereals

Many people in the United States feel that breakfast must include cereal in order to be complete. The cereal foods customarily served for breakfast have therefore come to be known as *breakfast cereals.* While these cereals are good energy foods for the start of the day, their use need not be limited to breakfast.

Some of the breakfast cereals on the market have already been cooked. These are called *ready-to-eat* cereals. When you buy ready-to-

 Make toast cups as a substitute for patty shells, noodles, or biscuits to use when serving a creamed mixture, such as creamed tuna.

1 Trim the crusts from slices of soft white bread.
2 Brush one side with melted butter.
3 Press the buttered side of the bread down into muffin pans.
4 Bake in very hot (450° F or 232° C) oven for 10 to 12 minutes or until golden brown.
5 Remove from pan and place on serving plate. Fill with creamed mixture.

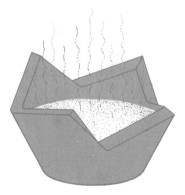

Bread products, rich in the B vitamins, are frequently made from enriched white flour.
Sugar Information, Inc.

Make gluten balls to understand how much of flour is starch and how much is protein.

1 In a small bowl mix 2 to 3 tablespoons (30 to 45 ml) of water with ¼ cup (60 ml) unsifted, all-purpose flour.
2 Beat hard with a spoon about 10 minutes or until gluten develops. Mixture will become stringy and follow the spoon 6 to 8 inches (15 to 20 cm) above the bowl.
3 Wet your hands.
4 Pour the mixture into your hands and hold it under running water until the water becomes clear, showing all starch has been removed. The remaining gluten should look and feel like a soft rubber ball.

What did you learn about:
1 The proportion of protein to starch in flour?
2 The way beating causes the gluten to develop?

Compare how equal amounts of cornstarch and flour thicken liquids. Use the information in checking recipes for gravies, sauces, and puddings.

Cereal foods such as noodles, spaghetti, and macaroni are often combined with protein foods as the main dish in a meal.   *Aluminum Association*

eat cereals, you pay extra for the precooking and for the convenience of serving them without extra preparation. These cereals provide a quick way to have breakfast or a snack.

Oatmeal and various wheat and rice cereals are common forms of the *hot breakfast* cereals. These cereals are cooked in water or other liquids. Many of the hot cereals have been processed to cook in a very few minutes. When buying such cereals, notice whether the package is labeled *regular, quick-cooking,* or *instant.*

Other Cereal Foods

Macaroni, spaghetti, and noodles are cereal products. They are frequently used in the main dish served at lunch or supper. Rice and other cereal grains such as buckwheat and barley are used in similar dishes. Like the macaroni products, these cereals are used in many casserole dishes.

460

PRINCIPLES OF CEREAL COOKERY

The main purpose of cereal cookery is to cook the starch content for easy digestion. Correct cooking procedures will help you achieve the desired texture and appearance for a given product.

Breads

Breads are made from a mixture of cereal products and liquid. Other ingredients commonly used in bread are leaveners, shortening, eggs, sugars, and other flavoring ingredients. If you understand the functions of these different ingredients, you can expect good results in your baking.

Flour mixtures are usually classified by the amount of flour they contain in proportion to the amount of liquid. Mixtures thin enough to be stirred by a spoon are called *batters*. Batters may be thin enough to be poured or thick enough to be spooned out in a soft mass. Griddle cakes, popovers, and waffles are examples of quick breads made from pour batters. Muffins, drop cookies, and drop biscuits are popular baked products made from thick batters.

Mixtures containing a high proportion of flour are called *doughs*. Doughs are too thick to be mixed entirely with a spoon. The final mixing must be done by hand. Yeast breads, rolled cookies, and regular baking-powder biscuits are among the familiar baked products made from doughs.

Give the reasons for the following procedures used in making quick breads:

1 Sifting the flour before it is measured
2 Measuring the ingredients accurately, using standard measuring cups and spoons
3 Sifting the dry ingredients together
4 Mixing only until the ingredients are well moistened, unless it is a sweetened mixture
5 Using the size of baking pan called for in the recipe

Your career
Agricultural engineer

You would develop new and improved farm machines and equipment. You might research farm problems such as irrigating crops and fertilizing soil to determine how these could be done most efficiently and economically. You might also study new methods of harvesting, transporting, storing, and processing farm products. You would find employment with government agencies and farm research firms, as well as with agricultural colleges and universities.

Pancakes are made by pouring a thin batter onto a heated grill or skillet. The pancakes are turned and browned on both sides. *Aluminum Association*

Conduct an experiment to observe the effect of sugar on gluten development.

1 Beat one egg thoroughly.
2 Put one cup (240 ml) of All-Purpose Master Mix (see page 520) into each of two bowls.
3 To one bowl add 1 tablespoon (15 ml) sugar, ⅓ cup (80 ml) water, and ½ egg. Mix lightly until dry ingredients are moistened but still slightly lumpy—about 20 strokes.
4 Fill four greased muffin cups two-thirds full.
5 Beat the rest of the muffin batter until well mixed.
6 Fill the other two muffin cups with the well-beaten batter.
7 To the other bowl add 3 tablespoons (45 ml) sugar, ¼ cup (60 ml) water, and ½ egg.
8 Beat until well blended.
9 Pour into a greased 8-inch (20.5-cm) cake pan.
10 Mix 1 tablespoon (15 ml) brown sugar with ½ teaspoon (2.5 ml) cinnamon. Sprinkle this mixture over the batter.
11 Place both the muffins and the coffee cake in a 400° F (205° C) oven. The muffins will bake in about 15 minutes and the coffee cake, in about 20 minutes.

Flour

Flour is the basic ingredient of yeast breads, quick breads, cakes, pastries, and cookies. While flour can be made from many grains, the most commonly used flours are made from wheat, rye, or barley. Flour can be coarse, as in whole-wheat flour, or very fine, as in pastry flour.

Since the kind of flour used has a decided effect on the finished product, you need to understand something about the differences in flours. Wheat flour contains a protein known as *gluten*. The hardening of this protein during the cooking process gives shape to the finished product. Have you ever looked closely at a slice of yeast bread and noticed the small bubbles, or cells? The walls of these bubbles are formed by the gluten. Cake slices contain cells, too, but they are not as easy to see as those in bread. Since most people want soft, fine-textured cakes, they choose a different type of flour for cake than for bread making.

The flour bakers use for bread is made from hard wheat. This flour has a high gluten content and is commonly called bread flour. The flour bakers use for cakes is made from soft wheat. This flour has a low gluten content and is commonly called cake, or pastry, flour. Most homemakers use *all-purpose flour*, a combination of the hard and soft wheat flours. Self-rising flour, all-purpose flour to which salt and

Muffins are cereal products made by dropping a thick batter into muffin tins. Muffins are baked in a hot oven.   *Kellogg Company*

leavening have been added, is also used in many homes. Cake made from all-purpose or self-rising flour will not be as fine as cake made from cake flour, but the product will be acceptable. In bread making also, results with all-purpose flour are not as good as if bread flour had been used. However, bread made from all-purpose flour is acceptable.

The real difference between all-purpose and bread and cake flours is the amount and type of gluten they contain. When a recipe calls for cake flour, you can substitute all-purpose flour by using a smaller amount. You will be cutting down on the gluten and making a more tender cake. And by adding more all-purpose flour than the amount of bread flour called for in a bread recipe, you can increase the gluten and improve the quality of the bread product.

A good general rule to remember is to remove 2 tablespoons (30 milliliters) of flour from each cup when substituting all-purpose flour for cake flour. Add 2 extra tablespoons (30 milliliters) per cup of all-purpose flour when substituting it for bread flour. Your results may not be exactly the same as those you could obtain from using the kind of flour called for in the recipe, but they will be acceptable. Most modern recipes are planned for all-purpose flour, so you will not need to change the amount of flour unless bread or cake flour is specified in the recipe. If you use self-rising flour in place of all-purpose flour, you do not add the salt and baking powder called for in the recipe.

Liquids

Water and milk are the liquids most commonly used in flour mixtures, but vinegar, sour milk, fruit juices, and even soups are sometimes used. The liquid helps bind the mixture together. It releases the carbon dioxide from certain leaveners, produces steam when heated, and adds flavor.

Leaveners

If you have ever made a cake or muffins and forgotten to include the baking powder, you already know what a leavening agent does. It causes a flour mixture to rise. There are three types of leaveners: carbon dioxide, air, and steam. They inflate baked products and make them light and fluffy.

The leavener used in the greatest number of foods is *carbon dioxide*. Baking powder, baking soda, and yeast can all produce carbon dioxide. Carbon dioxide may be formed in two ways. When liquid is mixed with baking powder or baking soda, carbon dioxide gas is released. Baking powder reacts with any liquid, but baking soda needs an acid-type liquid for this chemical reaction. As yeast plants grow and multiply, they give off carbon dioxide. When either the chemical or plant is present in a warm flour-liquid mixture, released carbon dioxide causes the mixture to rise.

Double-acting baking powder acts once when moistened and again when heated. This double action makes it easy to have success in preparing breads and cake products. The longer yeast plants are allowed to grow, the more carbon dioxide they will produce. In fact, if a yeast dough is left too long, the carbon dioxide will stretch the gluten until it breaks. At that point, a yeast bread falls.

Air is put into a mixture by means of beating or whipping. Large amounts of air can also be folded into a mixture by adding beaten egg whites. Angel food and sponge cakes are leavened with the air in beaten egg whites.

12 When baked, cool slightly and break both the lightly mixed and the beaten muffins in half. Compare their textures.
13 Cut the coffee cake and examine its texture.

Answer these questions:
Why does one muffin have tunnels and the other a smooth texture?
Why is the coffee cake free of tunnels even though it was beaten?
What conclusions can you draw about the role sugar plays in tenderizing gluten?
Remember, all the ingredients were exactly the same except for the amounts.

Bulletin board IDEA
Title: *Get Up Chirping*
Directions: Use pictures of cheerful-looking birds chirping about the pictures of attractive breakfast foods placed around them.

Compare three of the same type of products (muffins, biscuits, or pancakes), one made from a commercial mix, one made from a master mix, and one made from a conventional recipe. Compare and contrast them for flavor, texture, appearance, keeping quality, cost, time required in preparation, and ease of preparation.

Use a cookbook and list a variety of quick breads. What do they all have in common?

Prepare quick breads for a class project. Have students in one unit kitchen following the recipe accurately. Let students in other unit kitchens make the same recipe, leaving out one ingredient, over- or under-mixing the dough, or baking the mixture at the wrong temperature. Compare the results and keep a record of your findings. How can such information be useful?

Prepare a basic quick bread recipe adding various ingredients to create interest and variety.

The texture of cake is more tender than that of bread because cake is made from flour that has either weaker gluten or a smaller amount of gluten. *Kraft Kitchens*

Steam is used as a leavener in such baked products as popovers and cream-puff shells. A hot oven is used during the first minutes of baking so that the liquid in these batters is quickly turned to steam. The steam makes the batter puff up. The heat then sets and cooks the gluten and the egg proteins, causing the walls to harden. After the protein has set, the heat in the oven is reduced for the remainder of the baking period so the protein will remain tender.

Shortening

Any type of fat used in a flour mixture is called shortening. Commonly used shortenings are oil, margarine, lard, and hydrogenated vegetable fats. Shortening is added to a flour mixture to improve the flavor, to aid in browning, and to increase the tenderness. Thus, there is a much higher proportion of fat to flour in a tender product such as pie crust than in a firmer product such as yeast bread.

Sugars and other flavoring ingredients

While sugar adds a sweet flavor to a product, it also serves other purposes. Sugar helps to tenderize the gluten in the flour and gives yeast food to grow on. For example, since coffee cake has a softer texture than bread, it re-

Cream puffs rise in a hot oven as the liquid in the batter forms steam that causes the soft dough to puff. *Jell-o Gelatin*

Compare the costs of the same size loaf of fresh bread, day-old bread, and frozen bread you bake yourself. Which costs the least, the most? What things might you consider in addition to price? When would day-old bread be as satisfactory as fresh bread? When might it be better? What products can be made from frozen bread dough?

Make a list of common baking failures, such as tunnels, peaks in top, and fallen center. Next to each failure, write the usual cause of that failure such as overmixing, oven too hot, and extreme change in temperature.

Your career
Agronomist

You would research and develop methods for improving the growth and yield of field crops, such as cereals and grains. You would find employment with government agencies, colleges or universities that have special programs to help farmers, or with farm consultant firms.

quires a larger proportion of sugar. Actually, the main use of sugar in yeast breads is not for either tenderness or flavor. Rather, sugar provides the energy needed by the yeast plants as they grow to produce the carbon dioxide for leavening.

Ingredients such as spices and flavoring extracts are added only for flavor. They have little effect on the texture of the finished product.

Eggs

Eggs are added to many flour mixtures. The egg proteins harden during the baking process, adding to the structure of the final prod-uct. Air beaten into the eggs helps make many baked products lighter. And eggs give additional flavor and nutrition to baked products.

Using a Biscuit Master Mix

In your foods class or at home, you might like to experiment with using a master mix. A master mix is a basic recipe that can be varied to make several products. (See the recipe on page 520).

Make a half recipe of the master mix in your school kitchen or at home. This will give you an op-portunity to practice careful and accurate measurements. It will also give you a chance to practice

Follow one recipe
using each of
the following
leavening agents:
Air—angel food cake, soufflé
Steam — popovers, cream-puff
   shells
Carbon dioxide — muffins,
   cakes, and breads

What are other examples of air-
and steam-leavened products?

Experiment with kitchen
chemicals used to produce
carbon dioxide to leaven flour
mixtures.
   Dissolve 1 teaspoon (5 ml)
of baking soda in bottles
containing:
½ c. (120 ml) water
½ c. (120 ml) water and 3 T.
   (45 ml) vinegar
½ c. (120 ml) water and 2 t.
   (10 ml) cream of tartar
Immediately top the bottles with
balloons. Compare the sizes
of the balloons. What
conclusions can you make
about leavening agents and
the chemical reactions that take
place with each?

Repeat the above experiment
using baking powder.

List products which are made
from pour batters, thick batters,
and doughs.

The Biscuit Master Mix, like many quick breads, is made by cutting together flour and shortening. Liquid is added afterwards. *Wheat Flour Institute*

cutting a recipe in half. If you follow directions and make the master mix correctly, your products will be successful.

You might try making biscuits from the master mix to practice handling, rolling, and cutting dough. Later you may decide to make muffins or a coffee cake. These two products use exactly the same ingredients but in different proportions. These experiments should help you see that accurate measurements are important. Too, they will help you understand the actual functions of the various ingredients in bread products.

Breakfast Cereals

Hot breakfast cereals are cooked in boiling water or other liquid.

Breakfast cereals are usually cooked by gradually adding the cereal product to boiling water and by stirring constantly until the cereal starch is well cooked. *Household Finance Corporation*

Cereal products, in one form or another, have traditionally been a basic part of many meals. Breads in various shapes and textures add interest to the menu. *Kitchens of Sara Lee*

Read nutrition labels on several cereal boxes. Determine which brands give the most nutritive value for the money. Compare the cost of one serving of the same brand of ready-to-eat cereal when it is purchased in small, large, and individual packages. Is the larger size always a better buy? Why or why not?

Compare instant, quick-cooking, and regular varieties of a particular cereal. Consider each type of cereal from the viewpoint of cost, flavor, ease of preparation, and the time involved in preparation. When is one type better than another?

Bulletin board IDEA
Title: *Start Your Day with a Song*
Directions: Cut out a bass and a treble clef from construction paper. Use pictures of attractive breakfast foods arranged like notes on lines representing the staff.

After a certain amount of cooking, the cereal starch softens and swells as it absorbs the liquid. This is the reason cornstarch pudding, white sauce, oatmeal, and other cereal mixtures thicken when they are cooked.

Softened starch granules may stick together, making a lumpy mixture. The softened starch also tends to stick to the sides and bottom of the cooking pan, where it will scorch unless constantly stirred back into the mixture.

The lumping of cereal can be prevented easily. The cereal can be added slowly to boiling liquid while being stirred vigorously. It can be mixed with cold liquid to make a smooth paste before being combined with boiling liquid.

To cut down on stirring, cook cereal mixtures over steam, as in a double boiler.

Other Cereal Foods

Macaroni products and cereal foods such as rice and barley are cooked in the same way as hot breakfast cereals. They are added to boiling salted water and cooked until tender. As they cook, they absorb water and swell to greater bulk. Use the exact amount of water given in recipes for preparing each of these foods. As in cooking breakfast cereals, it is important to prevent these foods from sticking to the pan and scorching. However, overstirring can produce an undesirable texture in them.

Number from 1 to 10 on a piece of paper. Beside each number indicate if the following foods are made from a dough, a pour batter, or a thick batter. Use these abbreviations:

D for dough
P for pour batter
T for thick batter

1 Bread
2 Pancakes
3 Drop biscuits
4 Waffles
5 Muffins
6 Pie crust
7 Popovers
8 Rolled cookies
9 Waffles
10 Yeast rolls

Fill in the blank in each sentence with the best word or words to complete the statement. *Do not* write in this book.

1 The basic ingredient used in all breads, pastries, cakes, and cookies is __(1)__ .
2 The hard outer coating of cereal grains is called the __(2)__ .
3 The life-giving center of cereal grain seeds is called the __(3)__ .
4 When the B vitamins and iron are restored to flour after milling, it is called __(4)__ flour.
5 The type of flour that spoils most easily is __(5)__ .
6 In cereal cookery, the starch content is cooked for easy __(6)__ .

7 Cornstarch and flour are products of cereals and are used to __(7)__ gravies and sauces.
8 Self-rising flour is an all-purpose flour to which leavening and __(8)__ have been added.
9 Cake or pastry flour has a low __(9)__ content.
10 Breads are classified as either quick breads or __(10)__ breads.
11 The three leaveners are air, steam, and __(11)__ .
12 Two chemical leavening agents are baking powder and __(12)__ .
13 Yeast is actually a(an) __(13)__ that grows and multiplies in a mixture of warm liquid and flour.
14 Angel food cake and sponge cake are leavened with __(14)__ .
15 Popovers and cream puffs are leavened with __(15)__ .
16 Shortening is added to flour mixtures for flavor, browning, and __(16)__ .
17 Spices and extracts are added to baked products for __(17)__ .
18 A name for a homemade quantity mix that can be used to make a variety of baked products is the __(18)__ .
19 The *Daily Food Guide* recommends __(19)__ servings from the bread and cereal group every day.
20 Cereal grains include breakfast cereals as well as all bread foods, macaroni products, and __(20)__ .

Fill in the blank in each sentence with the *best* word or words to complete the statement. *Do not* write in this book.

1 Energy foods are in three main groups: flour, sugar, and __(1)__ .
2 Sugars and starches are classified as __(2)__ .
3 Liquid shortening may be olive, cottonseed, corn, or peanut __(3)__ .
4 Frying in a small amount of fat is called pan frying or __(4)__ .
5 The texture of piecrust should be tender and __(5)__ .
6 Coarse frosting or candy contains large __(6)__ of sugar.
7 Cake batter contains more liquid, egg, and __(7)__ than bread dough.
8 The two methods for mixing cakes from basic ingredients are the conventional method and the __(8)__ method.
9 In the conventional method for mixing a cake, the first step is to cream the shortening with the __(9)__ .
10 Brownies are an example of __(10)__ cookies.
11 Chocolate chip cookies are an example of __(11)__ cookies.
12 Cookies cut into shapes with a cutter are an example of __(12)__ cookies.
13 Pastry for pies is made by mixing flour and fat together before adding the __(13)__ .

Chapter 25

Preparing Energy Foods

After reading this chapter, you should be able to:

1. List advantages and disadvantages of using commercial baking mixes.
2. Name the groups of high-energy foods.
3. Identify specific foods high in carbohydrates.
4. Identify ways fats are included in the diet.
5. Describe the desired texture of cooked candies and frostings.
6. Describe the procedures for making creamy sugar products.
7. Make a cake using the conventional *or* one-bowl method of mixing.
8. Make different types of cookies.
9. Make pie crust using one of the methods described in the text.
10. Demonstrate safety precautions when frying foods.
11. Serve snack foods so they are attractive and appetizing.

Perhaps you have been wondering about the place of sugars and fats in the daily diet. Do you need fats and sugars at all? Many delicious foods such as cakes, candies, and doughnuts seem to be missing from the *Daily Food Guide*. What place do they have in your total eating program? Actually sugars and fats serve two purposes: they provide energy, and they are enjoyable to eat.

Gram for gram, fats contain over twice as many calories as carbohydrates. A gram of fat contains 9 calories; a gram of carbohydrate, 4 calories.

There are two important points to remember as you plan to include these foods in your menus. First, make selections from the *Daily Food Guide* for your basic nutritional needs. Then, knowing your body can store excess energy foods as fat, eat them with a certain amount of caution. Eat energy foods for needed energy. Avoid them

Check the snacks you eat with the activity it takes to burn that many calories in one hour.

Ride a bicycle 175
   17 potato chips or
   1 2-oz. (56 g) frankfurter
Run.......................490
   2-in. (5-cm) piece layer cake
   or 1 c. (240 ml) dried raisins
Wash dishes.................70
   ½ cake-type doughnut or
   ½ c. (120 ml) whole milk
Lie still (awake) 7
   1½ small pretzel sticks
   or 1 large stalk celery
Machine sew 28
   1 T. (15 ml) sour cream
   or ⅓ 5-in. (12.5 cm)
   cantaloupe
Swim (2 mph or 3.2 km/h) ...533
   ⅔ c. (160 ml) peanuts or 10
   slices cracked-wheat bread
Vacuum floor...............189
   ½ c. (120 ml) ½-inch (1.3-cm)
   avocado cubes or 2 medium
   grapefruits
Type rapidly 70
   ¾ c. (180 ml) corn flakes or
   1 c. (240 ml) skim milk
Walk (3 mph or 4.8 km/h) ...140
   1 cola and 4 potato chips or
   ½ c. (120 ml) meat balls,
   spaghetti, and tomato sauce
Write 28
   1½ saltines or ½ c. (120 ml)
   strawberries
Climb steps (50 pm) 84
   8 olives or 1 hard-cooked egg

when they cause you to gain unwanted weight.

So many packaged energy-food mixes are available on the market today that it really isn't necessary any more for a cook to spend long hours in the kitchen. These commercial mixes have several advantages:

1 They may be kept for an indefinite period ready for use when needed.

2 They save time and effort.

3 They make it unnecessary to keep on hand the separate ingredients included in conventional recipes.

4 Good results are assured if the directions on the package are followed carefully.

5 They make it very easy for the homemaker to add variety to family menus.

Some of the commercial mixes do not have the homemade flavor families have learned to like in their quick breads, cakes, and cookies. Also, they may be more expensive than food made from basic ingredients. For these reasons many homemakers make their own mixes. With an all-purpose mix as a base, and with the addition of other ingredients, many kinds of energy foods can be prepared quickly. (See the recipe for the All-Purpose Master Mix and the chart "How to Use the Master Mix" on pages 520 and 521, and the Oatmeal Cookie Master Mix on page 522.)

TYPES OF FOODS

Energy food falls into three main groups: flour, sugar, and fat. These groups tend to overlap. For example, pastry is made of fat and flour, while cake is a combination of all three. The energy foods have been grouped here simply so they can be studied one at a time. Flour is considered a cereal food and is discussed in Chapter 24.

Fruits, too, are energy foods because they contain natural sugars along with vitamins. They are discussed in Chapter 23.

Sugars and Other Sweet Foods

Sugar, as sold at the grocery store, is pure carbohydrate. It furnishes energy to the body, but nothing else. Honey, table syrups, jams and jellies, and other sweet spreads are also largely carbohydrate. Candy, cakes, cookies, puddings, ice cream, and similar desserts are all high-carbohydrate foods. Although some contain useful nutrients, their chief function in the diet is to provide energy.

Sweet dishes are usually served at the end of a meal. A small amount of sweet food may be served along with the main dish as a contrast to other flavors. For example, jelly on a hot biscuit may enhance the flavor of roast beef. Generally, though, it is a good idea to save sweet foods for last, because if eaten before the end of a meal, they tend to destroy the appetite.

Foods That Contain Fats

The fats used most often in pre-paring meals are butter, margarine, lard, and hydrogenated vegetable shortening. Corn, cottonseed, olive, safflower, and peanut oils are commonly used liquid shortenings. These fats and oils are used in such foods as pies, breads, and salad dressings. They add flavor to many foods, such as bread and cooked vegetables.

Fats are also used in frying foods. Meats, eggs, and some fruits and vegetables are sometimes pan-fried, or sautéed. This type of frying requires a small amount of fat. Most types of food can be fried in deep fat. Foods fried by either the pan-fry or deep-fry method contain more fat and calories than if prepared another way.

Snack Foods

The snacks that most people serve are chiefly energy foods. Corn puffs, pretzels, and crackers are largely carbohydrate. Potato chips, salted nuts, and spreads and dips, because of their high fat content, are also high-calorie foods. Raw vegetables and fruits are good snacks. Their carbohydrate content makes them good sources of energy. Fruits also provide nutrients that other snack foods lack.

PRINCIPLES OF COOKERY

Cakes of fine texture and delicate flavor are more popular than coarse, strong-flavored products. Creamy candies and frostings are more appetizing than coarse, grainy ones. Tender, flaky pie crust is preferred over a tough, chewy one, as are crisply fried foods over soggy, heavy ones. Through study and experience you can gain an understanding of the functions of fats and sugars in food mixtures. This will help you to achieve satisfactory cooking results.

Sugars and Other Sweet Foods

Cakes and cookies are called sweet foods because they contain a large amount of sugar. However, their sugar content is far less than that of candies and frostings. Sometimes candy and frostings are termed simply *sugar cookery.*

Candies and frostings

Granulated sugar, used in most cooked frostings and candy, consists of large grainy crystals which dissolve in liquids such as water and milk. When a sugar solution is cooked and then cooled, as in making frosting or candy, the syrupy mixture hardens to a crystalline form. If the crystals are small, the frosting or candy is creamy. If the crystals are large, the frosting or candy is coarse and grainy. The aim of sugar cookery is to obtain a creamy product.

Four general procedures will help you make creamy products:

1 Add corn syrup, egg whites,

 Check the common sweet foods listed below for calorie content. Discuss using these foods as between-meal snacks.

Food	Calories
Jelly 1 T. (15 ml)	49
Jam 1 T. (15 ml)	55
Chocolate syrup 1 T. (15 ml)	93
Sugar 1 T. (15 ml)	42
Candy 1 oz. (28 g)	
Sweet chocolate	147
Fudge	115
Caramel	120
Plain cake 2-in. (5-cm) piece	180
Plain cake with icing	
2-in. (5-cm) piece	320
Honey 1 T. (15 ml)	60
Cola drink 1 c. (240 ml)	96
Sugar cookie 3-in. (7.5-cm)	
diam.	89

Write mathematical equations using high- and low-calorie foods. For example:

1 c. (360 ml) grapes
= 1 c. (240 ml) cola drink
2 c. (40 ml) fresh strawberries
= 2 T. (30 ml) jam
1 watermelon wedge 4 × 8 in. (10 × 20 cm)
= 1 oz. (28·g) caramel candy
1 c. (240 ml) skim milk
= 1½ T. (22 ml) honey
4½ apples
= 1 piece of plain cake with icing, 2-in. (5-cm) wedge

Compare several brands of commercial cake mixes for cost, flavor, and keeping quality. Are there any other advantages one commercial cake mix might have over the others? What are they?

Make two cakes — one from a commercial mix and one from a conventional recipe. Compare the cakes from the standpoint of flavor, appearance, time and effort required in preparation, total cost, and keeping quality. List the advantages and disadvantages of the commercial mix and the cake made from "scratch."

Wrap or seal in airtight containers several pieces of cake and freeze them. Every two weeks, thaw one piece of cake. Note the quality and flavor of the defrosted cake. Were there any differences after several weeks of storage?

Make a personalized cake for someone's birthday or a special season of the year. The cake may be made in a special shape such as an animal, bells, or baseball mitt. Think of something suitable for the occasion and decorate the cake appropriately.

Candy making is sometimes a holiday-time experience. Many people make special treats to use for family entertaining or to give as gifts. *Peter Pan Kitchens*

marshmallows, or cream of tartar to the mixture before cooking.

2 Cover the pan to help prevent the formation of crystals on the sides of the pan during cooking. Before and after cooking, wipe away any sugar crystals which are left sticking to the sides of the pan.

3 Cook the syrup to exactly the right stage, or temperature. This means following the directions of the recipe exactly.

4 Cool the syrup slowly. Do not stir the mixture until it has cooled.

Cakes

Cakes are very popular as desserts for family meals, as between-meal snacks, and as refreshments for social occasions. Cakes are usually divided into two groups: those containing some form of shortening and those containing no shortening. Most cakes are leavened with baking soda and baking powder. However, chiffon and angel cakes are leavened mainly by air beaten into egg whites.

Many good cake mixes are available in the market. You may enjoy using them because they save time and energy. Many cooks prefer to make cakes from basic ingredients. Since cakes are a leavened flour mixture, many of the principles which apply to bread making also apply to cakes. However, cake mixtures usually contain more sugar and eggs than bread doughs. These ingredients call for different methods of preparation than those used for most breads.

Cakes with shortening may be made with a solid shortening, such as butter, margarine, lard, or hydrogenated vegetable shortening. They also may be made with a liquid shortening. There are two methods for mixing cakes made with solid shortening: the *conventional* method and the *one-bowl* method. Chiffon cakes are mixed by a third

Chiffon, sponge, or angel cakes (center) are leavened mainly by the air which is beaten into egg whites. The other cakes are made from mixes or conventional recipes that are usually leavened with baking powder.
Aluminum Association

method because they are made with liquid shortening.

In the conventional method, the shortening is creamed with the sugar, and then the eggs are added. Next the liquid and mixed dry ingredients are added alternately. The egg whites, if beaten separately from the yolks, are added last.

In the one-bowl method, the ingredients are combined in one bowl and stirred until mixed. This is the method called for in commercial cake mixes.

Chiffon cakes are made by combining the oil, egg yolks, and flavorings; adding the dry ingredients; and folding in the beaten egg whites.

Cakes without shortening, such as angel food and sponge cakes, are leavened mainly by the air beaten into the mixture. The egg whites are beaten thoroughly, and then the remaining ingredients are folded in gently to prevent the escape of air from the egg-white mixture.

Cookies

Cookies are popular throughout the world. Each country may have its national favorites. These versatile sweets may be served as lunchbox or picnic desserts. They are popular as between-meal snacks and as party refreshments. Boxes of fancy cookies are frequently given as gifts for special holidays. Cookies may be a useful source of nutrients or simply an energy food, depending upon the ingredients used.

Keep cookies in suitable containers to retain freshness. Follow these directions for the best results:

Store crisp cookies and soft cookies in separate containers. They will keep for as long as a week, and longer if stored in the refrigerator.

Freeze cookies in air-tight containers or wrappers.

If the cookies become soft on storing, place them on an ungreased baking sheet in a slow oven for a few minutes to restore crispness.

Your career
Cake decorator

You would decorate cakes, cookies, and sandwiches with icing or cheese mixtures for special occasions. You would work for catering services, bakeries, hotels, restaurants, or you might be self-employed.

Discuss what you think the expression *That takes the cake* means. How do you think the saying may have started?

473

Discuss the differences between frostings and icings. How are frostings and icings alike and how are they different?

Frostings

Frostings are used on cakes only. They are thicker than icings and may be cooked or uncooked.

Butter frostings are uncooked and are made of butter or margarine, confectioners' sugar, liquids, and flavorings.

Cooked frostings are mixtures of sugar and liquid, cooked like candy. Examples are brown-sugar frosting and chocolate fudge frosting.

Icings

Icings are used on cakes, breads, coffee cakes, and sweet rolls. They are thinner than frostings.

Fluffy icings are cooked mixtures of sugar, corn syrup, or other syrup, water, and unbeaten raw egg whites.

Thin icings are uncooked mixtures of confectioners' sugar and liquid, of a consistency that spreads easily.

Bulletin board IDEA

Title: *Snack Facts That Figure*
Directions: Use a picture of an attractive teenager. Around the figure place pictures of nutritious snack foods such as a peanut butter sandwich, crackers and cheese, and fruit.

A cookie recipe may be much like a cake recipe, with some changes in the proportions of the ingredients. Cookies are sometimes separated into seven types, according to content and the way the dough is shaped for baking. (See recipes for All-Purpose Master Mix, Refrigerator Cookies, and Oatmeal Cookies on pages 521 and 522.)

Drop cookies have a soft consistency. They are dropped from a spoon onto a baking sheet, about 2 inches (5 centimeters) apart. They spread and flatten as they bake.

Pressed cookies are made from a dough soft enough to pass through the openings in a cookie press and drop onto a baking sheet in fancy shapes.

Refrigerator cookies are made from a soft dough rich in shortening and sugar. The dough is shaped into rolls or blocks, which are chilled in the refrigerator for several hours. Slices are then cut from the roll and placed on a baking sheet for baking.

Cookies of a wide variety of shapes, flavors, and ingredients are used at many types of social get-togethers throughout the year. *Baker's Chocolate*

Bar cookies are baked as a sheet in a shallow pan, cooled, and cut into squares or bars.

Molded cookies are made by forming the dough into small balls and flattening with a fork or other utensil to form designs on top.

Rolled cookies are made from a stiff dough. The dough is rolled on a lightly floured board, cut into circles, squares, or fancy shapes, and baked. The cookies may be decorated before or after baking.

Rolled cookies may be cut into interesting shapes such as hearts, stars, bells, trees, turkeys, and bunnies, according to the season. When frosted with white or colored icing, the plain rolled cookie can carry out the theme of a party.

Pinwheel cookies are especially attractive. They are made by placing a portion of thinly rolled cookie dough on top of another portion of cookie dough of a contrasting color —for example, chocolate dough on top of plain white dough. The two portions of dough are rolled together and placed in the refrigerator to chill. Later the roll is cut into thin slices and baked.

Filled cookies are layer cookies. Each cookie is made from two pieces of thinly rolled cookie dough. Jelly, jam, cooked fruit, or other filling is placed between the two pieces of dough. Then the edges of the dough are pressed, or sealed, together. Cookies made with fruit fillings add valuable nutrients to snacks.

Foods That Contain Fats

Fats are added to foods to improve the flavor or to control the texture. Satisfactory results can depend on the type of fat used and the way in which the food is prepared. Be sure the fat is fresh. Fats, especially butter, become *rancid* or spoiled with age. No matter how carefully the food is prepared, rancid fat will give it a disagreeable flavor.

The texture of many baked foods depends in part on when the shortening is added and how it is mixed in. For example, pie crust has a tender texture because shortening is mixed with flour *before* a liquid is added. Pancakes have quite a different texture because shortening is added *after* the flour and liquid have been combined. Recipes state the method which will give the desired result for a product.

Making pie crust

Pies have worldwide appeal. They taste good and satisfy hunger. They can add valuable nutrients to the meal, depending upon the pie filling. Most of the popular dessert pies have either fruit fillings or fillings made of some form of egg and milk mixture. Pastry crusts are also used with meat, egg, or cheese mixtures to make main-dish casseroles.

Pastry for pies is made by mixing flour and fat together before adding liquid. The fat helps prevent the formation of gluten when liquid is stirred into the flour mixture. Thus,

 Suggest reasons, other than hunger, why people eat snacks.

List all the kinds of foods you eat between meals for snacks. Separate your list into two shorter lists — empty- or high-calorie snacks and low-calorie, nutritious snacks. Which of your lists is longer? Why? How might you improve your selections of snacks?

Prepare a low-calorie dip to be served with pieces of fresh fruits and vegetables, such as carrot sticks, cauliflower or broccoli flowerets, celery sticks, strawberries, apples, and strips of bell pepper. Try the same dip with crackers, pretzels, potato chips, or taco chips. Compare nutritive value, calorie intake, and eye and taste appeal. Which group wins? Defend your choice.

Bulletin board IDEA
Title: *U Are What U Eat*
Directions: Arrange pictures of foods in the *Daily Food Guide* so they form the shape of a human figure. For example, use an apple for the body, two carrots for the legs, and an egg for the head. The arms could be weiners, celery stalks, or any similarly shaped food.

Make a list of main dishes and appetizers or party foods made with a pastry crust.

Name as many kinds of dessert pies or tarts as you can. Check the calorie content of a 4-inch (10-cm) piece of various pies. Which kinds give you the most nutrition for the number of calories?

Find recipes calling for cake mixes in making cookies, fruit cobblers, or other dessert. Make one of the recipes for your class or family to try.

Your career
All-around baker

You would bake breads, rolls, hot breads, and muffins. You might also supervise different helpers who would be responsible for regulating oven temperatures, setting and kneading the dough, or placing and timing the products in the ovens. You would work in bakeries, restaurants, or catering businesses.

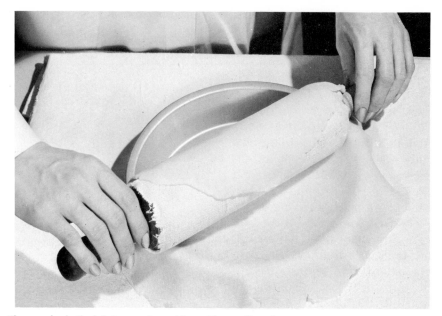

Pies can be both delicious and nutritious. The quality of a pie is usually determined by the tenderness of its crust. *Armour and Company*

a tender pie crust can be produced. Packaged mixes and prepared pastry dough are widely available. Frozen pastry shells are also available. They may be more expensive or less desirable than homemade products but you can depend on the quality.

There are several good ways to make pastry. The *conventional* method, or *cold-water* method, produces a very flaky crust. However, dough made in this manner is sometimes hard to handle. The *hot-water* method, the *paste* method, and the *oil* method may be easier to master. All of these methods produce satisfactory pies and pastries.

You might want to try each method and compare the results.

Using fats and oils in frying

Well-fried foods are crisp but not hard. Some fats, particularly butter, burn easily. These burned, or decomposed, fats give an unpleasant flavor to foods fried in them. If the frying fat is too hot, the outer portion of the food may overcook or burn, while the inner portion is undercooked. If the fat is not hot enough, the food tends to soak up the fat, making it soggy, greasy, and generally unappetizing.

Panfrying requires a heavy, flat-bottomed skillet, or frying pan.

Choose a pan large enough to hold the pieces of food without crowding them. The fat used should not smoke or brown at low temperatures. (See recipe for Strawberry Blintz Sandwiches, page 520.)

Deep-fat frying is a popular method for preparing French-fried potatoes, doughnuts, fritters, and croquettes. This method of frying is quick and easy. However, accidents can occur unless care is taken during the cooking process. The following precautions will help avoid spills, burns, and kitchen fires:

1 Fill the pan to no more than one-third of its capacity.

2 To prevent spattering, dry the food thoroughly before putting it into the fat.

3 Use kitchen tongs to turn food or to remove it from the hot fat.

4 Watch carefully to prevent the fat from overheating or catching fire.

Doughnuts are made mostly of flour but are considered fat-rich foods because they absorb fat during the deep-fat–frying process. *Swift & Co./A Martha Logan Release*

Discuss the advantages and disadvantages of displaying the desserts first, as is done in many cafeterias. How is it a good idea from the standpoint of selling food? What about from the standpoint of buying food? Why did you answer the questions as you did?

Write on the chalkboard the names of snacks which are suitable for different occasions. Consider snacks for TV time, after a game, after school, or when friends drop by. Discuss why the snacks you choose are appropriate for each occasion.

Your career
Bakery driver

You would deliver baked foods to grocery stores or homes along your route. You would also try to enlarge your route by increasing customer sales and the number of customers. You might also collect payment for products delivered. You would work for wholesale or home service bakeries.

Check various popular foods for fat content. Remember, fat adds more calories per ounce than any other single food. Deep-fat frying, panfrying, and adding fat to vegetables for seasoning increase the calorie count by the amount of fat used. How might knowing the fat content of these foods change your attitude toward them?

The number of calories in 1 T. (15 ml) of some common fats are as follows:

Fats	Calories
Vegetable oil (cooking)	125
Oil (salad)	125
Butter and margarine	100
Mayonnaise	110
Lard (bacon fat)	125

Experiment by placing on a sheet of notebook paper mashed, hard-cooked egg yolk; a strip of cooked bacon; a piece of french-fried potato or a potato chip; and a piece of fried chicken. Warm slightly over a light bulb or by placing in the sun. Remove the foods and hold the paper up to the light. Any food containing fat will leave a grease spot on the paper. What did you see? What conclusion can you make from this experiment?

5   If a kitchen ventilation fan is available, use it.

Serving Snack Foods

Snack foods are easy to serve, but they are more attractive and appetizing when served on colorful plates, in baskets, or in bowls than when served directly from packages. Foods like potato chips and pretzels are intended to be crisp and crunchy. The contents of fresh packages is usually acceptable. Occasionally, on opening a package, you may find its contents wilted and soggy. If this happens, spread the food in a shallow pan and place it in a warm oven for a few minutes. Usually this will freshen any type of pretzel or chip, even those which have been left in an open package.

Bananas dipped into melted peanut butter, honey, and chocolate, then rolled in chopped nuts make nutritious, flavorful snacks.
Peter Pan Kitchens

Tortilla-wrapped weiners and chili can be combined for a hot party snack after a ball game or a winter skating party.   *Rice Council*

The attractive appearance and taste of spreads and dips depend on their temperature and consistency. Most of these mixtures are served cold, so you may wish to keep them in the refrigerator until time to serve them. Spreads should be firm but soft enough to spread easily. Dips are much softer than spreads. Avoid making dips so thin that they drip from chips or vegetables.

Many spreads and dips can be bought in ready-to-serve form. If you make your own, you may be able to serve special flavor combinations which are different from commercial varieties. Be sure that spreads and dips are carefully mixed, so their consistency and flavor are the same throughout the mixture. Prepare them ahead of serving time so the flavors have time to blend.

Recipes for spreads and dips are very similar. By adding a liquid to a favorite spread, you can often turn it into an appetizing dip. Or by adding more cheese, peanut butter, or meat to a dip, you may develop a new, appetizing spread.

 Compare the following foods served plain and with fat-rich flavorings.

Food	Calories
1 c. (240 ml) mashed potato, plain	126
Add 1 T. (15 ml) butter	226
1 baked potato (5 oz. [142 g]), plain	132
Add 2 T. (30 ml) sour cream	182
Add 2 T. (30 ml) cottage cheese-sour cream (see page 435)	162
Baking potato, French-fried (10 pieces)	116
1 c. (240 ml) mixed green salad	20
Add 1 T. (15 ml) oil dressing	145
Add 1 T. (15 ml) mayonnaise	130
Add 1 T. (15 ml) lemon juice	24

From these examples do you see an easy way to add or subtract calories from the diet? What might this mean for the athlete who needs a high-calorie intake for extra energy? What about a person who is dieting?

Bulletin board IDEA
Title: *Seconds Count When Dieting*
Directions: Use a large cartoon figure holding a plate in each hand labeled to show first and second helpings.

For an after-school snack or party treat, make your own pizza. Slices can be garnished to each person's liking with cheese and onion and pepper rings. *American Home Foods*

Number from 1 to 30 on a piece of paper. Beside each number indicate if the corresponding statement is true or false. *Do not* write in this book.

1 The *Daily Food Guide* recommends two servings of high-energy foods every day.
2 Mixes need to be used within three weeks of purchase for satisfactory results.
3 Using mixes saves time.
4 Sugar is a carbohydrate.
5 Pure sugar contains some vitamins and minerals.
6 Sweet foods decrease the appetite.
7 Granulated sugar is fine and powdery.
8 Frostings should be creamy.
9 In sugar cookery, cover the pan.
10 Sugar syrups should be stirred as they cool.
11 Bread dough contains less liquid, egg, and sugar than cake batter.
12 Steam leavens angel food cake.
13 Sponge cake contains shortening.
14 In the *conventional* method of making a cake, the liquid and dry ingredients are added alternately to the mixture of shortening, sugar, and egg.
15 Commercial cake mixes call for the *one-bowl* method of mixing.
16 Cutting fat into flour helps prevent the formation of gluten.
17 Butter has a lower burning temperature than vegetable oil.
18 The amount of fat absorbed by a fried food is related to the temperature of the cooking fat.
19 When deep-fat frying, the pan should be only ⅓ full.
20 Food should be dry before it is put into hot fat for frying.
21 Commercially made slice-and-bake cookie dough is a type of refrigerator cookie.
22 *Molded* cookies are cut into shapes with cookie cutters.
23 Chocolate chip cookies are a *filled* cookie.
24 *Bar* cookies are cut after baking.
25 Balls of cookie dough that are flattened with a floured fork or glass are *pressed* cookies.
26 The nutritional value of cookies depends on the ingredients used.
27 Potato chips, salted nuts, and doughnuts are high-fat, high-calorie snack foods.
28 If corn chips lose their crispness, they should be thrown out.
29 Spreads are thinner than dips.
30 Spreads and dips should be prepared just before serving.

Fill in the blank in each sentence with the *best* word or words to complete the statement. *Do not* write in this book.

1 Tablecloths, place mats, napkins, glassware, and serving dishes are classified as __(1)__ .
2 The plates, cups, saucers, bowls, and dishes used at the table are called __(2)__ .
3 Because knives, forks, and spoons are not necessarily made of silver, they are called __(3)__ .
4 Place a bread-and-butter plate at the tip of the __(4)__ .
5 At the end of a meal, place your napkin on the __(5)__ .
6 Bread is buttered, a small piece at a time, with either a knife or a(an) __(6)__ .
7 Potato chips, pretzels, olives, and corn on the cob are __(7)__ foods.
8 When food is placed on a serving table and guests help themselves, it is called __(8)__ service.
9 A reception is more formal than a tea and includes a(an) __(9)__ where guests may greet the host, hostess, and honored guests.
10 When washing dishes by hand, wash glassware and __(10)__ first.
11 When washing dishes by hand, wash the __(11)__ last.
12 When washing dishes in an automatic dishwasher, place dishes so their top surfaces are facing the __(12)__ of the machine.

Chapter 26

Enjoying Food with Others

After reading this chapter, you should be able to:

1 State rules for using table coverings.
2 Define *flatware*.
3 Explain the differences among various kinds of dinnerware.
4 Give examples of different kinds of glassware.
5 Use the guidelines given in the text to set tables for various situations.
6 Practice acceptable table manners in the foods laboratory.
7 Practice using table equipment correctly in the foods laboratory.
8 Serve foods using the different types of meal service.
9 Plan a tea or reception.
10 Make plans for entertaining outdoors.
11 Clean up efficiently after food and nutrition laboratory lessons.

An appetizing, well-prepared meal looks even more inviting when it is attractively served. The way the table is set and the way food is served make a real difference in mealtime atmosphere and enjoyment. Table manners and rules for table setting are intended to make dining relaxing and comfortable. By learning and following a few simple rules, you can enjoy your meals and contribute to the happiness of others.

A table setting provides the background for a meal. You probably have helped to set the family table many times. Simple arrangements of flowers or greenery, either fresh or permanent, provide a special touch to any table. A freshly baked cake in the center of the table can delight the youngest family member as well as the oldest. You can express your own creativity or set the mood for a meal in tasks as simple as table setting.

Distinguish the differences between the various kinds of dinnerware listed:
    Chinaware
    Earthenware
    Pottery
    Plastic
List the advantages and disadvantages of each. Which would you choose for a given situation? Defend your selection.

Distinguish between the following kinds of flatware:
    Stainless steel
    Silver plate
    Sterling silver
List the advantages and disadvantages of each.

Give the advantages and disadvantages of linen, cotton, and plastic tablecloths and place mats. What other types of materials are used? What are their pros and cons?

Choose pictures of flatware, dinnerware, and glassware that look well together. Defend your selections. Suggest a tablecloth or other table covering which would go well with them.

Visit stores that sell flatware, dinnerware, and glassware. Compare varieties of each for cost. What are the reasons for these cost differences?

CHOOSING AND USING TABLEWARE

A table can be attractive whether set with the most expensive or the simplest tableware. The idea that each family must have sterling silver, crystal, and china in order to have a complete home is out of date. Most of today's young families are aware that people are more important than things. The casual living they enjoy allows them to use any tableware they happen to have. Through their choice of colors, shapes, and textures, they produce table settings which show their interest in beauty. Cost becomes relatively unimportant.

Setting the Table

Common practices for table setting and food service have developed because they make sense. A few simple rules for table setting serve as a guide for most occasions. Tableware includes the china, glassware, flatware, table coverings, and table decorations. These are all placed on the table to make the meal easy to serve and easy to eat.

Table coverings

A covering on the dining table not only looks attractive but helps to protect the table surface. It adds color, keeps the table top clean, and adds to the picture you are trying to create.

Coverings are made in a wide variety of materials. Many modern materials used for tablecloths or mats can be wiped clean with a damp cloth. They require no laundering. Other cloths come in permanent press or other fabrics that do not need to be ironed after laundering. Since modern covers are so easy to keep clean, there is really no need to use soiled or spotted table covers.

A place mat is usually about 16 to 18 inches (40 to 45 centimeters) long and about 12 to 14 inches (30 to 35 centimeters) wide. When used on the table, the rectangular mat is placed with one long edge even with the table edge. A round mat can be placed close to the table edge or allowed to hang over just a little. Set the mats an equal distance apart and at the same distance from the table edge. This gives a neat and pleasing look.

A cloth which allows the table edge to show is unsightly and may prove awkward when dishes are moved during a meal. One that hangs down too far gets in the way when people sit at the table. A full-size cloth should hang about 4 to 6 inches (10 to 15 centimeters) over the sides and ends of the table.

Napkins

Napkins are used to keep your hands and face clean while eating and to protect your lap from spilled food. To tuck a napkin under the chin suggests you may not be sure of your dining habits. Napkins are made of different fabrics and in

BASIC STEPS IN TABLE SETTING

Set a table to fit the menu you are serving. Napkins can be placed either at the left of the forks or in the center of the dinner plates.

Location of knife and spoons

Location of napkin and forks

Location of bread-and-butter plate

Location of salad plate

Location of salad plate with bread-and-butter plate

Location of drinking glasses

Location of cup and saucer

Set several covers (complete table service for one person) with different types and patterns of flatware, dinnerware, glassware, and table covers. For example, use dainty flowered dinnerware, modern-looking stainless steel flatware, and glasses decorated with cartoon characters. Arrange them together on a strawlike place mat. Decide why certain choices do and do not go well together. From the items available, set one or more pleasing covers. Prepare guidelines to use in combining table appointments effectively.

Conduct a treasure hunt to locate errors "planted" in several table settings displayed around the room.

Your career
Caterer

You would plan, prepare, and serve special foods for large groups or home entertainment. You would meet with a client to determine the time and place of the affair, the menu desired, the number of guests to be served, and the cost involved. You might work for restaurants, special catering agencies, or be self-employed.

different sizes. They may match or contrast with the table covering. For everyday meals, paper napkins are often used because they can be discarded after the meal.

The size of a napkin can vary with the occasion. Cloth napkins for such occasions as a formal tea party are used only for the lips and finger tips. They are quite small, usually 12 by 12 inches (30 by 30 centimeters). For family breakfasts, lunches, or dinners, larger napkins about 17 by 17 inches (43 by 43 centimeters) give more protection. For formal dinners or banquets, napkins are 24 inches (60 centimeters) square. While napkins of a certain size may be customary for certain occasions, a family does not need a napkin wardrobe to entertain successfully.

In setting a table, the folded cloth or paper napkin is usually placed with the open edge nearest the left side of the fork, 1 inch (2.5 centimeters) from the edge of the table. For formal service the napkin may be placed on the service plate or on the tablecloth where the plate will be set when the meal begins.

Flatware
The knives, forks, spoons, and serving pieces used at the table are known as *flatware*. Flatware can be made of sterling or plated silver and is often called *silverware*. Other metals used for flatware are stainless steel and a mixture of metals that looks like gold. Plastic flatware is popular and practical for outdoor

meals, picnics, and other informal occasions. Families place different values on the importance of flatware. Some invest a good deal of money in it. Others may use an assortment of knives, forks, and spoons rather than trying to keep matched sets, particularly while their children are young and pieces of flatware may be lost or misplaced.

The kind of flatware your family uses is determined by the amount of money they decide to spend, the kinds of meals they serve, and the kinds of dishes they use. So long as it is clean and properly placed, any flatware can add to the attractiveness of the table.

Dinnerware
The plates, cups, saucers, bowls, and dishes used to serve meals are called *dinnerware*. The kind and amount of dinnerware each family owns vary according to personal taste and budget. Family size, family customs, the amount of entertaining to be done, and the amount of money to be spent all affect dinnerware choices.

Earthenware and *pottery* are made of clay. They are rather thick and heavy, but usually colorful and attractive. Earthenware, sometimes called semiporcelain, is slightly more delicate than pottery and usually more expensive. Both kinds of dinnerware are suitable for casual and informal occasions. Some may be used in more formal settings.

An attractive table setting adds to the enjoyment of a meal. *Window Shade Mfrs. Assn.*

Place various pieces of flatware, dinnerware, and glassware in the center of a table. Sit at the table as if you were going to eat. Place the dinner plate in the most convenient location for eating. Put the glass in the place where it is easiest to reach with the least chance of tipping it over. Place the knife where it is most convenient. Continue placing items until all the items most often used by one person at a meal are arranged. How close is this placement to the diagrams on page 483? What does this tell you about the basic rules for setting a table? Repeat this activity using a menu requiring specific pieces of flatware, dinnerware, and glassware. How is the placement of the needed items related to the basic steps in table setting?

Suggest suitable topics for conversation at family meals and meals eaten with friends. What topics should be avoided?

Make up a story of how a carefully prepared meal was ruined because of the table conversation. Discuss the circumstances and what might have been done by others at the table to improve the situation.

Chinaware, or porcelain, is made of very fine white clay. It has been heated to an extremely high temperature in a special oven called a kiln. This process makes it more durable than earthenware. The extra care required to make china explains why it costs more than earthenware.

In addition to earthenware, pottery, and chinaware, *plastic dinnerware* is popular because it is lightweight and practically unbreakable. A good grade of plastic withstands the heat of dishwashing and is resistant to scratches if handled with care. Plastic is available in many styles and colors at different prices. Some families who can afford more than one set of dishes keep china for special occasions and use plastic or pottery for every day.

Attractive combinations of dinnerware add interest to any meal. Whether you select earthenware, chinaware, plastic dinnerware, or some of each, dinnerware can be placed on the table in a way to make the table look attractive.

485

Suggest items that can be used for table decorations or centerpieces. Include several usable items on hand at home or in your school. The list below may give you ideas:

Wild flowers or flowers growing in your yard

Plants

Figurines and porcelain objects

Fruits and vegetables

Shells and driftwood

Dried arrangements

Candles

Seasonal material, including

    Christmas evergreens or ornaments

    Menorah

    Thanksgiving decorations or horns of plenty

    Passover plate

    Easter-egg baskets

Make an appropriate centerpiece as a gift or for a family surprise. Autumn leaves, holiday materials, wild flowers, or fruit may be used.

Make new candles from old candle stubs by melting them and pouring the liquid into waxed cartons. Colored crayons can be melted and mixed with paraffin to make candles. Make a colorful flower or evergreen ring to complete the arrangement.

When selecting dinnerware, try to imagine how it will look with food served on it. Odd colors or highly decorated pieces often fail to harmonize with food colors. The effect may be very unappetizing. Can you picture in your mind steak, spinach, and beets on a dark green plate?

Glassware

The goblets, tumblers, and glass dishes used on the table are referred to as *glassware*. Fine glassware is called crystal. Even inexpensive glassware can add sparkle to a table setting. Attractive break-resistant plastic glasses are made to use with plastic or earthenware dishes.

Glassware is available in many sizes, shapes, and colors. When you choose glassware, consider the flatware and dinnerware with which it will be used. Fine crystal looks well with china and silver, while heavy, casual-looking glassware seems to fit better with pottery or plastic dinnerware.

Accessory items

Among the additional items useful in serving a complete meal are serving dishes, platters, a salt-and-pepper set, a sugar bowl, a cream pitcher, bowls for gravy and other accessory foods, a bread dish or tray, a butter knife, a gravy ladle, a sugar shell, a pickle fork, and serving spoons. Flatware is placed on the table to the right of the dish for which it is intended. Once used,

serving pieces should be left in the appropriate dish or platter.

The centerpiece

One way to add a bright touch of color to the table is by using a *centerpiece*. Although called a centerpiece, it may be placed anywhere on the table.

Fresh flowers, vegetables, fruits, wild flowers, or weeds can be used as a centerpiece. When flowers are too expensive or are not available, artificial flowers of plastic, cloth, or paper can add color and interest to the table. Bowls, vases, and candlesticks in many styles are also popular table decorations.

It is annoying when you must look over or through a centerpiece to see and talk with people on the other side of the table. Therefore, you should keep table centerpieces low enough to see over. Also, some kinds of flowers, such as gardenias or magnolias, have strong odors. Avoid using such flowers at mealtime since their fragrance may interfere with the aroma of food.

Planning and arranging a centerpiece gives you a chance to be creative with a wide variety of materials. Table decorations can be formal or informal. They are successful when they are both attractive and in keeping with the meal.

TABLE MANNERS

Your consideration for other people can be shown by your manners.

A bright relish tray filled with fresh vegetables can serve as an edible centerpiece at a party. *Kraft Kitchens*

 Give reasons for the following guidelines for using candles:
Burn the wicks slightly before displaying the candles.

Place the candles so they do not shine in the eyes of diners.

Use enough candles to light the table sufficiently unless other lights are used.

Use candles after 5 o'clock or when dark enough for them to be seen.

Write the word CENTERPIECE on the chalkboard, arranging the letters in a vertical line. Beside each letter suggest items that might be used for a centerpiece, such as

C Candles
E Easter eggs
N Natural leaves
T
E
R
P
I
E
C
E

Since eating is such a close-range activity, others notice your table manners very quickly. Table manners tell whether or not you are interested in the happiness of others.

To some people, good table manners are to be put on when company comes and removed when they leave. However, good manners should be automatic, and they are more effective if used daily. Slouching at the table, grabbing food, eating while leaning on an elbow, talking loudly, eating noisily, speaking when your mouth is full, quarreling at the table — any of these unattractive actions may be unconsciously performed in the presence of others if they are a part of your day-to-day table manners. Careless habits may spoil dining

Copy and complete the crossword puzzle below, using a separate sheet of paper. *Do not* write in this book.

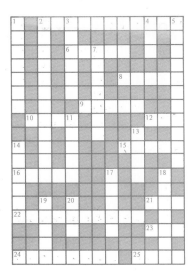

When you place flatware

1 Place each knife, fork, and spoon 1 inch (2.5 centimeters) from the edge of the table.
2 If the meal requires the use of more than one knife, or fork, or spoon per person, arrange the pieces so the piece to be used first is placed farthest from the plate.
3 Place knives and spoons at the right of the plate.
4 Place the knife next to the plate, with the cutting edge toward the plate.
5 Place the forks at the left of the plate, with tines, or prongs turned up.
6 Place the forks or spoons for desserts when that course is brought to the table.
7 Place the fork at the right if it is the only flatware to be used during the meal. If a spoon is also used, place the fork at the left and the spoon at the right of the plate.
8 A cocktail fork may be placed to the right of the spoons or across the cocktail plate. A butter spreader or butter knife is placed across the top of the bread-and-butter plate at right angles to the other flatware with the cutting edge toward the plate. It may also be placed on the rim of the bread-and-butter plate parallel to the other flatware.

When you place dinnerware

1 The plates should be set at the center of each plate, 1 inch (2.5 centimeters) from the edge of the table.
2 Place the cup and saucer at the right of the spoons, with the handle of the cup turned to the right.
3 Place the salad plate at the left of the dinner plate, outside the forks.
4 Place the bread-and-butter plate at the tip of the forks.

When you place glassware

1 Place the water glass at the tip of the dinner knife.
2 Place the milk or juice glass slightly to the right of the water glass.

ACROSS

2 Flowers, candles, and dried arrangements may be used as a(an) (2) .
6 At a picnic, foods are often served on a(an) (6) plate.
8 For a tea or reception, the serving table is usually covered with a table (8) .
9 One of the most popular and inexpensive metals used for flatware is stainless (9) .
10 Table coverings used for informal meals may be place (10) .

pleasure for others, while good habits increase mealtime happiness.

Getting Ready for the Meal

As a matter of courtesy, everyone in the family should be ready a few minutes before a meal is served. This makes it possible for everyone to be seated at once and for food to be served when at its best.

Your appearance can affect the happiness of a meal. When you come to the table, be sure your hands and face are clean and your hair is neat. If you have been doing heavy or dirty work, come to the table in fresh clothes.

Your Place at the Table

Unless you have a regular place, as you probably do at home, pause at the table until the hostess tells you where to sit. Stand behind your chair until each person has been placed and the hostess tells you to sit down. It is proper for a boy to help seat the girl who is at his right. Confusion is prevented if everyone is seated from the left side of the chair. This is especially important if the room is small or crowded or if chairs are close together.

To help with a chair, a boy pulls the chair back, then pushes it forward as the girl sits down. At the end of the meal, he can help her by standing behind her chair and pulling it slowly back as she rises and steps to the side. If no boys or men are present, a girl may help an older woman with her chair.

Your Contribution to Mealtime Conversation

After you are seated, sit quietly in your chair with both feet on the floor. Keep your hands in your lap. If grace is offered, wait courteously until the prayer is over. Begin to eat only after the hostess has started.

During the meal enter into the table conversation. Mealtime should be relaxed. Family arguments or unpleasant subjects can be saved for another time. Unpleasant table talk can ruin a meal and actually upset a person's digestion.

If you can't think of anything pleasant or interesting to say, eat quietly and let others talk. After all, good conversation requires a good listener, too.

Using Table Equipment

A table set with more flatware than you ordinarily use can make you feel awkward. However, the use of table equipment is based on common sense. If you follow your hostess' example, you will know what to do. At home, or at the home of close friends, ask for any directions you may need.

Using the napkin

Since the napkin is folded with the open edge facing the fork, it is easily picked up with your left hand, partially unfolded, and placed on your lap. If the napkin has been left free, with no flatware lying on it, it may easily be picked up without

12 An attractive and edible table decoration might be a bowl of (12) fruit.

15 The dinnerware and flatware placed for one person is a(an) (15) .

16 Many of the finest and most expensive table coverings are made of (16) .

21 A spoon should not be left in the (21) after the beverage is stirred.

22 Cream pitchers, sugar bowls, and gravy boats are called (22) .

23 The guidelines followed when you (23) the table correctly are based on convenience and comfort.

24 Very expensive flatware may be made of (24) silver.

25 The attractiveness of a table setting is *not* related to the (25) of the items used.

DOWN

1 There are times when you may be judged by your table (1) .

2 A pleasant mealtime depends in part upon the (2) .

3 In setting a table informally, the item to the left of the forks is the (3) .

4 An attractively set table is pleasing to the (4) .

5 Dinnerware made from clay and sometimes called semiporcelain is (5) .

7 Unbreakable dinnerware is usually made of (7) .

11 A piece of flatware placed to the right of the knife is a(an) (11) .

13 For salad or dessert, there may be a smaller (13) than the one used for eating the main dish.

14 Carrot sticks, celery stalks, pickles, and tomato slices may be served on a(an) (14) tray.

17 A small plate above the forks may be intended for bread and butter or (17) .

18 Small plates with indentations to hold cups are (18) .

19 In formal table service, the napkin may be placed on the service (19) .

20 A plant may be used to make a table attractive if it is (20) and not too large.

Bulletin board IDEA

Title: *Get Ready, Get Set, Glow*
Directions: Display pictures of candles used as table decorations. Include formal and informal arrangements.

disturbing the other things on the table. Use a patting or blotting motion with the napkin when removing food from your mouth or chin. Great wipes or swabbing motions are awkward and unnecessary.

Passing food

When passing food from one person to another, pass it to your right. The person on your right can then accept the dish with the left hand. The right hand is then free to lift food to the plate. If you are serving from a standing position, offer the food from the person's left so that it can be taken comfortably with the right hand.

Using flatware

You will gain assurance in eating if you know and practice the correct use of a knife, fork, spoon, and other special pieces of flatware.

The knife is used to cut pieces of food on the plate and, if there is no butter spreader, to spread butter, cheese, or jelly on bread. To use the knife for cutting, hold it in your right hand with the handle resting in your palm and with your thumb and last three fingers steadying it. Place your forefinger on the back of the blade as you cut. When the knife is not in use for cutting or spreading, lay it across the back of your plate with the cutting edge toward you. *Used* flatware should not touch the tablecloth. Avoid accidents caused by resting the tip of your knife or fork on the edge of

the plate with the handle on the table.

The fork is used, with tines up, to carry solid food to the mouth. You may use the side of a fork to cut soft food, such as vegetables, cake, or pie.

The fork also holds in place food being cut with a knife. In this case it is held in the left hand with tines down. Brace it with your forefinger near the bottom of the handle. After cutting a bite or two of food and placing the knife across the plate, transfer the fork to the right hand with tines up and use it to carry the food to your mouth. To cut the next bite, change the fork back to the left hand and again pick up the knife with the right hand. In some countries the custom is to keep the fork in the left hand and the knife in the right throughout the meal.

Use a salad fork with the tines up to carry food to the mouth. If the salad requires cutting, try to cut it with the side of the salad fork. If the fork is ineffective, use your table knife as you would to cut food on the dinner plate. If there is no salad fork, a dinner fork is used.

The spoon is used for dipping and carrying soft or liquid food to the mouth. Hold the spoon in your right hand much as you would hold a pencil. Take only as much food onto the spoon as you will put into your mouth in a single bite. Eat from the side of the spoon. Between bites or after the food has been eaten, place the spoon on the

Various fresh fruits and tuna fish make up a colorful and appealing party platter for a nutritious snack. *Tuna Research Foundation*

Give reasons why the following guidelines have developed for serving family and guest meals.

1. Place and remove plates from the left of the person being served. Hold the plate in your left hand. If you are carrying two plates, place first the one in your left hand, then move the other plate to your left hand, and place it before the next person.

2. Place and remove beverages from the right, with your right hand. Avoid filling cups or glasses too full.

3. Refill glasses or cups from the right, leaving them in position on the table.

4. Avoid touching surfaces of plates and rims of glasses. Hold and place silverware by the handles.

5. Offer food to guests from their left, holding it low enough so they can serve themselves with their right hands.

6. Avoid reaching in front of a guest when serving or removing dishes.

7. Remove all dishes used in a course as soon as that course is finished.

8. Avoid stacking dishes which are removed while guests are seated at the table.

saucer or plate that is under the bowl or cup. Leaving the spoon in a bowl or cup may cause it to tip. In eating soup or other liquid foods, dip the spoon into the soup with the spoon bowl tipped *away* from you — not toward you. Touch the spoon on the side of the bowl to remove any drips before moving the spoon to your mouth.

Use your spoon for stirring or for testing beverages. Remove the spoon from the beverage before starting to drink. Place it on the saucer or service plate. This looks better and helps prevent unnecessary accidents.

The butter spreader is used to butter the bread. You may use the butter spreader at your place or your dinner knife to spread butter. The butter knife passed with the butter is not intended for this purpose. It is used to cut off a portion of butter and to place the portion on your plate.

Pantomime or act
out situations
showing what to do
when . . .

a spoon is dropped.
a bone or seed is in your
   mouth.
meat contains gristle and
   cannot be chewed completely.
a food you do not like is passed
   to you.
you want an item that is across
   the table.
food is spilled on your clothing.
you are through with the meal
   and napkin.

Plan and present skits showing
correct and incorrect table
manners and etiquette. Have an
instant replay to improve poor
situations. Give reasons for
manners such as sitting up
straight, not talking with your
mouth full, taking small rather
than large bites of food, and
asking for food to be passed
rather than reaching across the
table for it. While eating, view
yourself in a mirror or on
videotape to judge your table
manners.

Discuss acceptable table
manners for a picnic meal. In
what ways should behavior be
like that used for all other
meals? In what ways may there
be differences? What foods
are especially good for picnics?
Explain your answers.

When you eat bread, break off a moderate-size piece with your fingers. Hold it on the edge of the bread-and-butter plate or the dinner plate, and spread butter on it with the butter spreader. Buttering a slice of bread held in the palm of the hand looks awkward and may soil your hand.

Flatware or fingers?

Particularly when eating away from home, you may find yourself wondering which piece of flatware should be used for a particular food. In general, use a knife to cut and spread. Use a fork for anything that can be picked up with a fork — that is, anything not too liquid. Use a spoon for soft, liquid foods. Use a fork or spoon, never your fingers, when eating foods that are juicy, greasy, or sticky.

Some foods are awkward to eat, and it is a good idea to find out how to eat them correctly. Foods such as fried chicken may be eaten with the fingers if your hostess is eating in this manner. Such foods as corn on the cob, potato chips, crisp bacon, grapes, and whole radishes are definitely finger foods. Use your napkin to clean your fingers after handling these foods.

When the Meal is Finished

When you have finished eating, place the knife and fork across the center of your plate. This lets your hostess know that you have finished eating. It also makes it easier to carry the used tableware away from the table.

At the end of the meal, fold or crumple your napkin, depending upon whether it is to be used for another meal. Place it on the table to the left of your plate. When you use a cloth napkin at home, you may fold it for use at another meal.

TYPES OF MEAL SERVICE

There are several types of meal service. Food can be placed on the table in bowls and served to each person by the host and hostess. It can be placed on a buffet table, where each person helps him- or herself to the food. It can be served directly from the cooking utensils onto plates before they are brought to the table. There are also many variations of these types of service. Choose a type suitable for the particular occasion. If foods are served at the proper temperatures, you can be sure you have chosen an appropriate type of meal service.

Family Service

Families set their own styles in dining. There are several types of service used for regular meals. A family can choose the one it prefers.

In one type of service, the food is placed on the table on platters and in bowls to be passed around the table. Food dishes and serving pieces are placed where they can be easily reached by the person who is to start passing them. The serving dishes are passed to the right, and each person is allowed to help him- or herself. The serving spoon or fork is placed on the table at the right of the dish and is put into the food as serving begins.

In some families the host carves and serves the meat. The hostess may serve the salad and the beverage from the other end of the table. Vegetables may be served to each person with the meat or passed in serving dishes.

Many busy families put the food onto plates in the kitchen and then serve the filled plates to each person at the table. This form of service saves time in table setting and dishwashing. However, it is necessary for someone to carry each plate to the kitchen for refilling if second portions are to be served.

Buffet Service

One good way to serve a large group of people is to provide a buffet service. In this type of service, the food is placed on one large table. Guests are asked to help themselves to the foods they want. Since few people have dining rooms large enough to seat a great many people, the buffet service has become very popular among people who do group entertaining. Many restaurants refer to their buffet service as a *smorgasbord,* the Swedish name for a similar type of meal service. Usually, at a smorgasbord, people are allowed to help

Write the words TABLE SETTING on the chalkboard, arranging the letters in a vertical line. Beside each letter write a word or words describing desirable table settings. For example:

T Tasteful
A Attractive
B Balanced
L Logical
E
S
E
T
T
I
N
G

Food that can easily be eaten with fingers is popular at parties.   *Dr. Pepper*

Bulletin board IDEA
Title: *Setting Pretty*
Directions: Make an attractive three-dimensional place setting by pinning up plastic flatware and a paper placemat, napkin, plate, and cup.

493

Pretend you are going on an automobile trip. Imagine making stops at various kinds of eating places. Include a roadside picnic rest area, a restaurant, and a drive-in. Act out desirable manners at each place.

Bring sample restaurant menus to class. Act out the parts of the restaurant personnel and the ideal customer. Practice ordering, making requests of the waiter or waitress, making a complaint, and tipping.

Demonstrate creative ways of using convenience foods for company meals. Select a convenience food such as a cake mix, canned biscuits, instant pudding, fruit-flavored gelatin, cheese sauce, or canned cream soup, and use it to prepare a product of your own creation. Prepare it in some form, shape, or manner you have never seen before. Share your product with the class.

Bake a dark layer cake using a mix. Use a pudding mix to prepare the filling between the layers. Make a lacy patterned topping by sifting confectioners' sugar through a paper doily placed on the top layer. Remove the doily carefully so the sugar design is not disturbed.

Fresh raw vegetables with a tangy dip are a heathful snack for your next party.   *USDA*

themselves to a wide assortment of meats and fishes, cheeses, salads, and relishes.

When planning a buffet, put the serving table as near the kitchen as housing arrangements will allow. This makes it easy to remove empty dishes and refill empty serving plates and bowls. Place the table to allow for a free flow of guests. Arrange the table so guests may pick up their plates at one end of the table and move in an orderly manner from one dish to another, picking up flatware and napkins last. The meat or main dish is generally placed first. Then come the vegetables, breads, relishes, and salad. The serving piece needed for each dish is placed next to that dish on

the tablecloth. Once used, it is replaced in the serving dish. Guests help themselves to food and move to some other area to eat. Guests are usually expected to help themselves to food as often as they like, without a special invitation from the hostess.

Card tables may be provided where four or more people are asked to sit. Some people provide guests with lap trays or TV trays. Young people can ease the crowded condition of a large party by sitting on the floor or on the stairs.

In planning buffet menus, try to use foods that are easy to serve, give guests a choice, and do not run together on the plate. Since a guest may need to carry a filled plate, flatware, napkin, and sometimes a beverage to the eating area, plan food that can be eaten with a single piece of flatware.

The next time you ask permission to entertain, you might plan a buffet. Planning such a meal in your foods class will give you a chance to practice making up menus for a buffet, arranging a buffet table, organizing a work schedule, working together as a group, and exercising good manners.

Tea or Reception Service

Another way to entertain a large group is by giving a tea or a reception. A tea offers light refreshments in an informal way. A reception is more formal. It includes a *receiving line*, where guests meet the host, hostess, and special guests. They shake hands and exchange brief greetings. Either service may be used for friendly get-togethers at clubs or with friends. If you learn how to plan, prepare, and carry out

Plan a social activity for a home experience project. The party may be for your family or friends. It may be for a birthday, anniversary, or special holiday or event. It might be a shower, tea, or cookout. Make a guest list and decide on a theme and how the guests will be invited. Plan refreshments, sketch the table setting, plan games or entertainment if appropriate, and schedule cleanup. Carry out your plans and report on the success of your activity. What would you do the same if you were having a similar party again? What would you do differently? Why?

Suggest suitable foods for outdoor cooking, such as foil-wrapped potatoes or corn, graham crackers with melted chocolate, hot dogs wrapped in biscuit dough, or hamburgers with cheese sealed in the center. Plan a menu for an outdoor meal.

Plan several inexpensive picnic menus. Divide into family-size groups to prepare and serve picnics. When are picnics appropriate in your area of the country? What arrangement can be made to have fun when weather interferes with picnic plans?

A buffet-type party allows the host or hostess to prepare most of the food before the guests arrive and to enjoy the party with the guests. *The Dow Chemical Company*

Collect recipes for popular foreign dishes. Try some of these recipes at home. Report on your family's reaction to them.

Invite to class someone in the community who has come from another country. Ask this person to tell about the kinds of foods served in that country and to tell how the foods are prepared and served.

Report on food service customs in other countries such as Sweden, Korea, and Japan. Practice eating according to these foreign customs. For example, use chopsticks and sit on the floor on a pillow in front of a low table.

Prepare foreign dishes in groups and combine them for a total buffet meal. For example, one group might make Mexican enchiladas for the main dish, another group a Greek salad, and another French pastry for dessert. Prepare dishes from as many different countries as time and money permit. Use an international theme for the centerpiece.

the service, you will enjoy giving and attending such functions.

A tea is much like a buffet. The food, however, is fancier and lighter. Tea, coffee, or punch may be served. Small decorated cakes, fancy cookies, nuts, candies, and tiny finger sandwiches are considered appropriate for a tea. The table is planned to be as attractive as possible. A tea affords an opportunity to use a beautiful cloth, your prettiest dishes, and your most decorative centerpiece. A bowl of colorful punch surrounded by greenery can be used as a centerpiece. If a tea or reception is held after five o'clock in the afternoon, candles may be used as part of the decorations.

Preparing refreshments for a tea requires careful planning and scheduling. With packaged mixes available, preparation time can be saved. For a school tea or reception, one group can make fancy cakes, one can make cookies, one can make finger sandwiches, and one can make the tea or punch. If guests must stand while eating, plan food that can be eaten from one hand while a small plate with a tea or punch cup is held in the other.

Arrange the table so guests can receive their beverage from the hostess or her helper, serve themselves refreshments, and move away from the table. The plates are placed at one end of the table with the napkins. China and glass cups and plates are considered formal. Paper goods are acceptable and

can be used to carry out a special theme. Paper goods also offer a possible solution where dishwashing is a problem. The trays or plates of food are placed near the front edge of the table center, and the beverage is located at the end. If both a hot and a cold beverage are served, one is placed at each end of the table. The centerpiece is usually placed near the back of the center of the table.

Unless you are planning a small informal tea for just a few people, you will be wise to ask some friends to assist you. Your friends may serve the beverage, remove the used dishes and wash them for a second using, refill the plates of refreshments so they always appear to be attractively filled and inviting, and help you greet and entertain the guests. At a large tea many people may not know each other. Plan to have extra hostesses to introduce the guests to each other and to help them to enjoy the occasion. Try to arrange for enough helpers so each one works only 30 to 45 minutes before being relieved by another friend. That way, you will be giving your helpers a chance to enjoy the party, too.

A tea or reception is a come-and-go party. Guests are expected to arrive between the times given on the written invitation, visit a short time, enjoy the food, and leave to make room for others. They are not expected to stay for the whole time.

Some parties are planned so that snack foods can be prepared and eaten by the guests.
American Home Foods

Discuss the advantages and disadvantages of various types of meal service. Choose a type of meal service for a particular situation and occasion. Defend your selection.

Select from a grab bag by groups the name of one of the types of meal service written on a piece of paper. Pantomime in your group that type of meal service. Practice and then demonstrate for the rest of the class. What are the advantages and disadvantages of each of the different types of meal service? Under what circumstances might each be most desirable?

Plan activities to help class members gain experience in serving as hosts and hostesses. Make arrangements for greeting guests, taking coats, making introductions, serving food, and extending other courtesies.

Bulletin board IDEA
Title: *International Flavor*
Directions: Mount pictures of popular foreign foods. Discuss the chief nutritive value of the dishes shown.

Both receptions and teas are dress-up occasions. Long dresses and suits may be worn in the afternoon as well as in the evening. Gloves are removed before greeting the hostess or before eating. Sport clothes are usually out of place at a tea.

Serving Snacks

Many people like to show hospitality by serving refreshments, or snacks, to guests. Suppose your family has given you permission to entertain a group of friends. What foods would you serve?

When planning foods for a snack party, try to choose things you can prepare earlier in the day. If you do, you will be free to enjoy your own party. Choose foods that can be eaten easily — perhaps finger foods. Teenagers enjoy eating, so you will want to have plenty of food. Consider the cost of different menus when you plan. Check the ads in newspapers for store or seasonal specials. Try to serve foods that are not messy so that clean-up chores will not take you away from the fun of your own party.

Discuss different ways of starting a charcoal fire outdoors, including using liquid chemical starters, electric appliances designed for this purpose, and *do-it-yourself* methods. Which seems to be the quickest, the slowest, the most expensive, the least expensive, and the best all-round selection? Why?

Compare and contrast different types of outdoor grills. For what type of situation is each best suited?

List foods appropriate for gifts, such as cookies, candy, and preserves. Tell why people are especially appreciative of such gifts. Suggest ways in which gift foods can be packaged so they are kept attractive and undamaged. For example, seasonal decals can be used on jars of jellies or jams; a cake may be baked and given in a pan that is also the gift.

Foods for a snack party often include sandwiches, potato chips and dips, cookies, cupcakes, and fresh fruit. Raw vegetable strips to eat with dips are also used. Soft drinks and colorful fruit punches are always welcome.

You might plan a snack party in your class with each kitchen group preparing one item for the class party.

Entertaining Outdoors

Indoor-outdoor living offers many opportunities for next-to-nature entertaining. Outdoor barbecues or picnics can be enjoyed by almost everyone. Everything about this kind of party, even the clothing, can be casual. Outdoor entertainment is especially good when small children are included among the guests.

If you are planning a picnic where food will have to be carried quite a distance, there are several points to keep in mind. Choose foods that do not spoil easily and which can be kept at the proper temperatures. Plan easy-to-serve foods that can be prepared ahead of time and require little attention just before serving. Choose foods requiring very little use of flatware, since you may be eating while sitting on the ground with your plate in your lap. When possible, include easy-to-eat finger foods.

An outdoor barbecue can be a different way to serve a nutritious meal to family or friends. *Rice Council*

Washing dishes by hand

1. Carry the dishes from the dining table to the sink. Using a tray saves time and energy.
2. Scrape and rinse the dishes. Group together those of the same type and size.
3. Stack them on the right side of the sink or on a nearby table. Arrange them for washing from right to left if possible (if right-handed).
4. Half-fill the dishpan with *hot* water. The water can be still hotter if you use a dish mop, gloves, or a dishwashing spray attachment.
5. Use liquid or granular detergent, soap flakes, or soap powder to prepare a suds. Use enough soap or detergent so the suds will last until the dishes are washed.
6. Wash the dishes in the following order: glassware, soft plastic containers, flatware, cups, plates, saucers, small dishes, serving dishes, baking dishes, and pots and pans which have been soaking. Wash sharp-edged tools and fragile articles separately.
7. Use both hands in washing dishes. Reach for the dish with one hand, and hold it while you swab with the other hand. Pass the dish through the rinsing water, and turn it up to drain in the draining rack. Another method is to place dishes in the second sink compartment for rinsing.
8. Rinse with clear, hot water. If you have enough hot water, pass each dish under the hot-water faucet on the way to the draining rack. Otherwise, dip the dishes in the rinsing pan or place them in the drainer and spray them with hot water. When cups and glasses have been rinsed, turn them upside down to drain.
9. Use a clean towel to dry glassware, flatware, pots and pans, and any dishes that are not allowed to dry in the rack.
10. Use a tray to carry the dishes and flatware to their storage places, carrying several pieces each trip.
11. Wash and dry the dishpans, sink, drain board, counter tops, and stove.
12. Wash and dry dishtowels and dishcloths.
13. See that the floor around the sink is free from grease and water.

 Draw your own cartoons to illustrate mold, yeast, and bacteria that can develop when foods that spoil easily are served at an outdoor party.

Mold, yeast, and bacteria are found in water and air and on all surfaces with which they come in contact.

If not destroyed by heat during processing, mold, yeast, and bacteria cause canned foods to spoil.

If the jar is not sealed when stored away, mold, yeast, and bacteria sneak into the jar and cause spoilage.

MOLD

YEAST

BACTERIA

The most common choices for picnics are sandwiches, hamburgers, hot dogs, fried or barbecued chicken, baked beans, potato chips, and roasted corn. Pickles, relishes, fresh fruit, cookies, and cakes add the finishing touches.

Use disposable dishes as much as possible for a picnic. You can make good use of paper goods and of the foil pans saved from ready-to-eat foods. Bowls with plastic covers and covered pans are available in the stores. All are especially good for

Give advantages and disadvantages of drying dishes with a towel and of letting dishes drain. What factors would affect the method generally used by a family? What circumstances might affect the method used on a particular day?

Put a small amount of grease on the inside of two glasses. Wash one by holding it under the faucet, using hot water and no soap. Wash the second in hot water with detergent. Allow both glasses to air dry. Hold each glass to the light. Discuss the effectiveness of the two glass-washing methods.

Compare the use of lint-free and terry-type towels for drying glassware. Demonstrate how to dry and put glassware away without leaving finger marks.

List and discuss points to be considered in buying different types of dishwashing equipment.

Make a checklist for studying the dishwashing practices of groups in your homemaking class. Let each group tell the class about weaknesses they found in their own dishwashing practices.

Washing dishes in an automatic dishwasher
1 Rinse dishes under running water, rub them lightly with a dishcloth, or scrape them with a brush or rubber spatula.
2 Empty glasses and cups. Rinse juice or milk glasses, especially if the dishwasher is not to be run right away.
3 Load the dishwasher according to the manufacturer's suggestions. Usually these recommend placing pots, pans, and bowls on the bottom level to the outside with openings toward the center. If possible, alternate large and small plates for maximum water flow.
4 Load the top level by placing glasses and cups down with openings toward the spray of water.
5 Place flatware, handles down, in the basket made for this purpose. Do not crowd flatware.
6 Use only a detergent especially made for automatic dishwashing. Fill the detergent cup according to the manufacturer's directions. Do not sprinkle detergent directly on any item. Do not use soap or laundry detergent because they make suds which block the washing action.
7 Close the door and turn on the machine according to the directions.
8 Remove the dishes when they have been washed and dried. Some machines can be turned off for the drying cycle so the dishes can air dry. This saves electricity and keeps the kitchen from getting warm.

picnics. Make a check list of everything you will need to carry along for your picnic. Be sure to include salt-and-pepper shakers, drinking cups or glasses, a bottle opener, and any utensils necessary for serving or eating the food.

CLEANING

One of the main responsibilities of a host or hostess is cleaning up after a meal. Whether you are having a party at home or school, cleaning up and putting things away takes organization and care. Your family will be much more willing to let you entertain your friends if you leave your home in good order after the fun is over. In class or in public places, you must leave the facilities ready for the next group to use.

Try to leave things just the way you would want to find them. This means you will wash dishes and put them back where you found them. Put away any other items in their customary place of storage. Wipe up spills, pick up litter, and sweep the floor. (For directions on dishwashing, see charts on pages 499 and 500.)

Number from 1 to 25 on a separate piece of paper. Beside each number indicate if the corresponding statement is true or false. *Do not* write in this book.

1 Stainless steel flatware is as long-lasting as sterling silver.

2 China is more durable than pottery.

3 Tableware consists only of flatware, dinnerware, and accessories.

4 If a fork is the only flatware needed, it may be placed to the right of the dinner plate.

5 When you are through with soup that has been served in a cup, leave your spoon in the cup.

6 A napkin used for a tea is larger than one used for a formal dinner.

7 At the end of a meal, place your napkin on your chair.

8 All the tableware needed by one person for a meal is called a cover.

9 The cutting edge of the knife is placed toward the dinner plate.

10 When having soup, dip the spoon in the bowl away from you.

11 After finishing eating, leave your knife and fork on the table.

12 After a bowl of gravy has been passed around the table, leave the ladle in the bowl.

13 When serving someone from a standing position, offer food from the person's right.

14 A tea is more formal than a reception.

15 At a reception, the guests help themselves to the beverage.

16 Strongly scented flowers make an ideal centerpiece.

17 At a banquet, be seated from the right side of the chair.

18 If in doubt about what flatware to use, observe the piece the hostess is using.

19 Food is passed around the table to the right.

20 A butter spreader remains on the butter dish when it is passed.

21 In buffet service, a butler serves the guests.

22 Candles are an appropriate table decoration for a tea or reception if it is held after five o'clock.

23 When washing dishes by hand, wash the pots and pans last.

24 When washing dishes in an automatic dishwasher, place bowls so their openings are toward the back of the machine.

25 It is efficient to alternate large and small plates when loading an automatic dishwasher.

Number from 1 to 6 on a separate piece of paper. Beside each number, write the letter corresponding to the best answer for that item. *Do not* write in this book.

1 Write the letter of the item in the wrong place.

2 Write the letter of the item in the wrong place.

3 Write the letter of the item in the wrong place.

4 Write the letter showing the correct place for a water glass.

5 Write the letter showing the correct place for a salad plate.

Unit 6

Your Recipes

COOKING TERMS

Bake: To cook in the oven by dry heat.

Baste: To spoon pan drippings, water, or sauce over food while it is roasting.

Beat: To add air to a mixture or to make it smooth by using a quick over-and-over motion with a spoon or fork or by using a rotary beater, electric mixer, or whisk.

Blend: To mix two or more ingredients.

Boil: To cook in boiling water or other liquid that is bubbling and steaming.

Bone: To remove the bones from fish, poultry, or meat.

Braise: To cook in a small amount of water in a covered container.

Broil: To cook directly under or over the source of heat.

Brown: To bake, fry, or toast a food until the surface is brown.

Caramelize: To heat dry granulated sugar to the melting stage.

Chill: To place in the refrigerator until cold.

Chop: To cut into small pieces.

Combine: To mix or blend two or more ingredients.

Cool: To let come to room temperature.

Cream: To make a mixture soft and smooth by rubbing or beating it with a spoon, fork, wooden paddle, rotary beater, or electric mixer.

Crumble: To break into small pieces.

Cube: To cut into small, even-sided pieces.

Cut in: To distribute shortening or table fats in dry ingredients by chopping with a pastry blender or two knives until the fat is in tiny particles.

Dice: To cut into small cubes.

Dilute: To make less concentrated by adding another liquid such as water.

Dissolve: To cause a dry substance, such as sugar or salt, to pass into solution in a liquid.

Dot: To scatter small bits of a substance, usually fat, on top of a food.

Dredge: To coat the surface with flour, meal, or other powdery substance.

Fillet: To bone and slice as with meat or fish.

Fold: To mix ingredients by using two motions, cutting straight down through the mixture and across the bottom of the mixing bowl, turning the mixture over and over.

Fry: To cook in hot fat. The words *pan-fry* and *sauté* mean to cook in just enough fat to cover the bottom of the pan. *Deep-fry* and *french-fry* mean to cook in enough fat to cover food being fried.

Glaze: To coat a food with syrup or jelly and then to heat or chill it.

Grate: To cut food into tiny pieces by rubbing it on a grater.

Julienne: To cut into long thin pieces, as with meat or cheese.

Knead: To press dough by turning and stretching the dough to firm and shape it.

Marinate: To let a food stand in a liquid (usually French dressing or oil and vinegar.)

Melt: To change a solid food to a liquid by heating it.

Mince: To cut into very small pieces.

Mix: To combine ingredients, usually by stirring.

Mold: To place a food in a dish or mold until it gels or hardens.

Panbroil: To cook uncovered in an ungreased or lightly greased frying pan, pouring off the fat as it accumulates.

Parboil: To boil in liquid until partly cooked.

Pare: To cut off the outer covering.

Peel: To remove or strip off the outer covering.

Poach: To cook in hot liquid, usually below the boiling point, taking care to retain shape.

Preheat: To heat an oven to the desired temperature before putting in food.

Purée: To press food through a sieve or ricer to make it smooth.

Roast: To bake (usually meat) in an oven by dry heat.

Roll: To flatten to desired thickness by using a rolling pin.

Sauté: To cook in a small amount of hot fat.

Scald: To heat liquid to a temperature just below boiling point; to heat milk until a *skin* forms; or to pour boiling water over a food.

Score: To make crisscross cuts over food surface.

Sear: To brown quickly with intense heat.

Season: To add salt, pepper, or other substances to make food taste better.

Shred: To cut or slice very fine.

Sift: To put dry substances through a sieve.

Simmer: To cook in liquid that is just at the boiling point.

Slice: To cut into thin, flat pieces.

Sliver: To cut into long flat pieces as with almonds.

Snip: To cut into small pieces with scissors.

Sprinkle: To cover the surface of a food with particles of food or seasonings.
Steep: To let stand in hot liquid to extract flavor.
Stir: To mix with a circular motion.
Toast: To brown by direct heat.
Toss: To mix ingredients lightly without mashing or crushing them.
Unmold: To remove from a mold.
Whip: To beat vigorously to add air.

MEASUREMENTS AND WEIGHTS
(Metric units are rounded equivalents.)

A few grains or a dash	= ⅛ teaspoon or less = 0.6 ml or less
3 teaspoons	= 1 tablespoon = 15 ml
16 tablespoons	= 1 cup = 240 ml
¼ cup	= 4 tablespoons = 60 ml
⅓ cup	= 5 tablespoons + 1 teaspoon = 80 ml
⅜ cup	= 6 tablespoons = 90 ml
½ cup	= 8 tablespoons = 120 ml
1 cup	= 16 tablespoons = 240 ml
2 cups	= 1 pint = 480 ml
2 pints	= 1 quart = 960 ml
4 quarts	= 1 gallon = 3440 ml = 3.4ℓ
1 fluid ounce	= 2 tablespoons = 30 ml
8 fluid ounces	= 1 cup = 240 ml
1 pound (fats and liquids)	= 2 cups = 480 ml
1 cup (240 ml) regular rice	= 2 cups (480 ml) cooked
2 cups (480 ml) macaroni	= 4 cups (960 ml) cooked
8 ounces (225 g) spaghetti	= 4 cups (960 ml) cooked
8 ounces (225 g) egg noodles	= 4 (960 ml) to 5 cups (1200 ml) cooked
1 stick butter or margarine	= ½ cup (120 ml)
¼ pound (114 g) shredded cheese	= 1 cup (240 ml)
1 pound (454 g) brown sugar	= 2¼ cups (540 ml), firmly packed
1 pound (454 g) confectioner's sugar	= 3½ cups (840 ml)

SUBSTITUTIONS

1 cup (240 ml) fresh milk	= ½ cup (120 ml) evaporated milk + ½ cup (120 ml) water
1 cup (240 ml) fresh milk	= ½ cup (120 ml) condensed milk + ½ cup (120 ml) water (reduce sugar in recipe)
1 cup (240 ml) fresh milk	= 4 tablespoons (60 ml) powdered whole milk + ⅞ cup (210 ml) water
1 cup (240 ml) fresh milk	= 4 tablespoons (60 ml) powdered skim milk + 2 tablespoons (30 ml) butter + ⅞ cup (210 ml) water
1 cup (240 ml) sour milk	= 1 tablespoon (15 ml) vinegar or lemon juice + milk to make 1 cup (240 ml)
1 teaspoon (5 ml) baking powder	= ¼ teaspoon (1.25 ml) soda + ½ teaspoon (2.5 ml) cream of tartar
1 tablespoon (15 ml) cornstarch	= 2 tablespoons (30 ml) flour (as thickening)
1 cup (240 ml) cake or pastry flour	= 1 cup (240 ml) all-purpose flour less 2 tablespoons (30 ml)
1 2-ounce (56-g) square chocolate	= 3 tablespoons (45 ml) cocoa + 1 teaspoon (5 ml) to 1 tablespoon (15 ml) shortening (less for Dutch type cocoa)
1 cup (240 ml) corn syrup	= 1 cup (240 ml) sugar + ¼ cup (60 ml) liquid
1 cup (240 ml) dairy sour cream	= 1 tablespoon (15 ml) lemon juice + evaporated milk to make 1 cup (240 ml)

FOOD COMPOSITION CHARTS

*The chart below combines three groups of columns — **Caloric Information**, **Nutritive Values**, and **% U.S. RDA**. (Footnotes: Calories** C, 11–14 and C, 15–18; Protein** C, 15–18, W, 23–50.) Values as read from the rotated table.*

Milk	Calories	% Cal. from protein	% Cal. from carbohydrate	% Cal. from fat	Protein g	Vitamin A IU	Vitamin C mg	Thiamin (B_1) mg	Riboflavin (B_2) mg	Niacin mg	Calcium mg	Iron mg	%RDA Cal. C,11–14	%RDA Cal. C,15–18	%RDA Protein	%RDA Vit. A	%RDA Vit. C	%RDA Thiamin (B_1)	%RDA Riboflavin (B_2)	%RDA Niacin	%RDA Calcium	%RDA Iron
Buttermilk, 1 cup (245 g)	88	55	43	2	8.8	Trace	2	0.10	0.44	0.2	296	Trace	4	4	20	—	3	7	26	1.0	30	—
Cheese, American, 1 ounce (28 g)	104	6	25	69	6.02	236	—	—	0.10	—	172	—	5	5	14	5	—	—	6	—	17	—
Cheese, Cheddar, 1 ounce (28 g)	113	2	26	72	6.9	237	1	0.01	0.1	0.1	202	0.1	5	6	15	5	1.6	0.6	6	0.5	20	0.6
Cheese, Cheddar, 1¼ ounce (35 g)	141	2	26	72	8.7	296	1	0.01	0.13	0.1	252	0.1	6	7	19	6	2	0.8	8	0.5	25	0.8
Cheese, Cottage, ½ cup (113 g)	120	55	11	35	15.4	192	0	0.03	0.28	0.1	106	0.3	5	6	34	4	0	2	16	0.5	11	1.7
Cheese, Swiss, 1 ounce (28 g)	103	2	66	33	8.0	206	—	—	0.09	—	268	—	4	5	18	4	—	—	5	—	27	—
Cocoa, ¾ cup (188 g)	182	34	13	15	7.1	300	2	0.08	0.34	0.4	221	0.8	8	9	16	6	3	5	20	2	22	4
Cream, Sour, 1 tablespoon (12 g)	25	14	8	70	Trace	100	Trace	Trace	0.02	Trace	12	Trace	1.0	1.2	—	2	—	—	1.2	—	1.2	—
Cream, Whipped, 1 tablespoon (8 g)	26	3	3	95	0.2	116	Trace	Trace	0.01	Trace	6	Trace	1.1	1.2	0.4	2	—	—	0.6	—	0.6	—
Half-and-Half, 1 tablespoon (15 g)	20	14	11	79	0.5	72	Trace	0.01	0.02	Trace	16	Trace	0.8	1.0	1.1	1.4	0.7	0.7	1.2	—	1.6	—
Ice Cream, Vanilla, ½ cup, ¼ pint (66 g)	138	8	38	53	2.7	346	1	0.03	0.13	Trace	82	0.1	6	7	6	7	1.7	2	8	0.5	8	0.6
Milk, 1 cup (244 g)	145	22	30	48	7.3	250	4	0.10	0.48	0.2	304	0.1	7	7	16	5	7	7	28	1.2	30	0.7
Milk, ¾ cup (183 g)	109	22	30	48	5.5	188	3	0.08	0.36	0.2	228	0.1	5	5	12	4	5	5	21	0.9	23	0.5
Milk, Chocolate, 1 cup (250 g)	213	17	50	35	8.5	325	3	0.08	0.40	0.3	278	0.5	9	10	19	5	5	5	24	1.5	28	3
Milk, Lowfat (2%), 1 cup (244 g) fortified with vitamin A	118	26	37	37	7.3	500	4	0.10	0.48	0.2	304	0.1	5	6	20	10	7	7	28	1.2	30	0.7
Milk, Skim, 1 cup (244 g) fortified with vitamin A	77	40	57	3	7.3	500	3	0.10	0.48	0.2	304	0.1	3	4	16	10	5	7	28	1.2	30	0.7
Milkshake, Chocolate, 1½ cups (349 g)	391	13	47	21	12.1	688	5	0.11	0.56	0.5	376	0.7	16	19	27	14	8	3	33	3	38	4
Yogurt, Strawberry, 1 cup (227 g)	225	17	72	9	9	90	5	0.07	0.4	0.22	290	0.2	9	11	20	8	5	24	33	1.1	29	1.1

Meat and other protein-rich foods

Food																							
Beans, Refried, ½ cup (150 g)	142	22	75	5	8.85	—	—	—	—	—	4.5	—	6	7	7	14	—	—	—	—	—	0.5	—
Beef, Roast, 3 ounces (85 g)	182	60	0	40	25.5	17	—	0.04	0.20	3.9	11	3.2	8	9	9	57	0.3	—	3	12	20	1.1	18
Beef Liver, 3 ounces (85 g)	195	49	9	42	22.5	45417	23	0.22	3.56	14.0	9	7.5	8	9	10	50	908	38	15	209	70	0.9	42
Bacon, 1³/₅ ounces (15 g)	92	21	2	76	4.6	0	—	0.08	0.05	0.8	2	0.5	4	4	5	10	0	—	5	3	4	0.2	3
Bologna, 1 ounce (28 g)	86	17	1.4	82	3.4	0	—	0.05	0.06	0.7	2	0.5	4	4	4	8	0	—	3	4	4	0.2	3
Chicken, Fried, 3 ounces (85 g)	201	55	3	42	26.0	148	—	0.06	0.38	5.9	12	2.0	8	10	10	58	3	—	4	22	30	1.2	11
Egg, Fried, large (50 g)	108	28	0.7	71	6.9	710	0	0.05	0.15	0.1	30	1.2	5	5	5	15	14	0	3	9	0.5	3	7
Egg, Hard-cooked, large (50 g)	82	35	2	64	6.5	590	0	0.05	0.14	0.1	27	1.2	3	4	4	14	12	0	3	8	0.5	3	7
Egg, Scrambled, large (64 g)	111	28	5	67	7.2	691	0	0.05	0.18	0.1	51	1.1	5	5	6	16	14	0	3	11	0.5	5	6
Frankfurter, 2 ounces (57 g)	172	17	2	81	7.0	—	—	0.09	0.11	1.4	3	0.9	7	8	9	16	—	—	6	6	7	0.3	5
Ham, Baked, 3 ounces (85 g)	179	61	0	39	25.7	0	—	0.56	0.26	4.9	11	3.2	7	9	9	57	0	—	37	15	25	1.1	18
Meat Loaf, 3 ounces (85 g)	230	28	23	48	15.3	106	Trace	0.27	0.24	3.4	68	2.4	10	11	12	34	2	—	18	14	17	7	13
Meat Patty, 3 ounces (85 g)	186	53	0	47	23.3	17	—	0.08	0.20	5.1	10	3.0	8	9	9	52	0.3	—	5	12	26	1.0	17
Peanut Butter, 2 tablespoons (32 g)	186	17	12	71	8.9	—	0	0.04	0.04	5.00	20	0.6	8	9	9	14	—	0	3	2	25	2	3
Peanuts, Salted, ¼ cup (36 g)	211	15	13	71	9.4	—	0	0.12	0.05	6.2	27	0.8	9	10	11	14	—	0	8	3	31	3	4
Peas, Blackeye (immature), ½ cup (124 g)	134	26	68	6	10.0	434	21	0.37	0.14	1.7	30	2.6	6	6	7	15	9	35	25	8	9	3	14
Peas, Blackeye (mature), ½ cup (124 g)	94	23	74	4	6.3	12	—	0.20	0.05	0.5	21	1.6	4	4	5	10	0.2	—	13	3	3	2	9
Perch, Fried, Breaded, 3 ounces (85 g)	193	NA	NA	NA	16.2	—	—	0.09	0.09	1.5	28	1.1	8	9	10	36	—	—	6	5	8	3	6
Pork Chop, 3 ounces (85 g)	308	29	0	71	20.8	0	—	0.82	0.24	4.9	9	2.7	13	15	15	46	0	—	55	14	25	0.9	15
Sausage, 1 ounce (28 g)	270	16	Trace	84	10.3	0	—	0.45	0.19	2.1	4	1.4	11	13	14	23	0	—	30	11	11	0.4	8
T-Bone Steak, 3⅓ ounces (95 g)	212	58	0	42	29.0	19	—	0.08	0.22	5.6	11	3.5	9	10	11	64	0.4	—	5	13	28	1.1	19
Tuna, 3 ounces (85 g)	168	62	0	38	24.5	68	—	0.04	0.10	10.1	7	1.6	7	8	8	54	1.4	—	3	6	51	0.7	9

Vegetables-fruit

Food	Caloric Information					Nutritive Values							% U.S. RDA										
	Calories	% Calories from Protein	% Calories from Carbohydrate	% Calories from Fat	Protein g	Vitamin A IU	Vitamin C mg	Thiamin (B_1) mg	Riboflavin (B_2) mg	Niacin mg	Calcium mg	Iron mg	Calories** G 11-14	Calories** G 15-18	Calories** W 23-50	Protein	Vitamin A	Vitamin C	Thiamin (B_1)	Riboflavin (B_2)	Niacin	Calcium	Iron
Apple, medium (138 g)	80	1.3	90	8	0.3	124	6	0.04	0.03	0.1	10	0.4	3	4	4	0.5	2	10	3	1.8	0.5	1.0	2
Applesauce, ½ cup (128 g)	116	0.9	94	0.7	0.3	51	1	0.03	0.01	Trace	5	0.6	5	6	6	0.5	1	1.7	2	0.6	—	0.5	3
Apricots, Dried, 4 halves (15 g)	39	7	92	2	0.8	1635	2	Trace	0.02	0.5	10	0.8	2	2	2	1.2	33	3	—	1.2	3	1.0	4
Asparagus, 4 spears, ½ cup (60 g)	12	26	65	7	1.3	540	16	0.10	0.11	0.8	13	0.4	0.5	0.6	0.6	2	11	27	7	6	4	1.3	2
Banana, medium (119 g)	101	4	94	1.7	1.3	226	12	0.06	0.07	0.8	10	0.8	4	5	5	2	5	20	4	4	4	1.0	4
Beans, Green, ½ cup (63 g)	16	15	76	5	1.0	338	8	0.04	0.06	0.3	31	0.4	0.7	0.8	0.8	1.5	7	13	3	4	1.5	3	2
Beans, Lima, ½ cup (85 g)	94	24	73	4	6.5	238	14	0.15	0.09	1.1	40	2.1	4	4	5	10	5	23	10	5	6	4	12
Beets, ½ cup (83 g)	31	7	90	3	0.8	17	2	0.01	0.02	0.1	16	0.6	1.3	1.5	1.6	1.2	0.3	3	0.7	1.2	0.5	1.6	3
Broccoli, stalk (78 g)	20	29	62	8	2.4	1938	70	0.07	0.16	0.6	68	0.6	0.8	1.0	1.0	4	39	117	5	9	3	7	3
Cabbage, ⅙ head, ½ cup (73 g)	13	13	80	13	0.7	87	17	0.01	0.01	0.1	30	0.2	0.5	0.6	0.7	1.1	1.7	28	0.7	0.6	0.5	3	1.1
Cantaloupe, ¼ medium (96 g)	29	8	89	3	0.7	3273	32	0.04	0.03	0.6	13	0.4	1.2	1.4	1.5	1.1	65	53	3	1.8	3	1.3	2
Carrot Sticks, 5" carrot (50 g)	21	8	90	4	0.6	5500	4	0.03	0.03	0.3	19	0.4	0.9	1.0	1.1	0.9	110	7	2	1.8	1.5	1.9	2
Cauliflower, ½ cup (60 g)	13	26	69	6	1.4	36	33	0.05	0.05	0.4	13	0.4	0.5	0.6	0.7	2	0.7	55	3	3	2	1.3	2
Celery Sticks, 5" stalk (57 g)	10	12	79	8	0.5	136	5	0.02	0.02	0.2	22	0.2	0.4	0.5	0.5	0.8	3	8	1.3	1.2	1	2	1.1
Coleslaw, ½ cup (57 g)	82	2	12	85	0.7	91	16	0.03	0.03	0.2	25	0.2	3	4	4	1.1	1.8	27	2	1.8	1	2	1.1
Corn, ½ cup (83 g)	70	8	84	8	2.2	291	3	0.02	0.04	0.8	4	0.4	3	3	4	3	6	5	1.3	2	4	0.4	2
Corn, 5" ear (125 g)	114	9	82	10	4.1	500	11	0.15	0.13	1.8	4	0.8	5	5	6	6	10	18	10	8	9	0.4	4
Fruit Salad, ½ cup (170 g)	99	5	90	4	1.5	530	44	0.11	0.08	0.7	45	0.9	4	5	5	2	11	73	7	5	4	5	5
Grapefruit, pink, ½ medium (118 g)	48	4	94	1.7	0.6	94	45	0.05	0.02	0.2	19	0.5	2	2	2	0.9	1.9	75	3	1.2	1	1.9	3
Grapes, ½ cup (71 g)	48	3	92	3	0.4	71	3	0.04	0.02	0.2	9	0.3	2	2	2	0.6	1.4	5	3	1.2	1	0.9	1.7
Greens, ½ cup (78 g)	17	27	61	10	1.9	5306	36	0.08	0.13	0.4	104	1.4	0.7	0.8	0.9	3	106	60	5	8	2	10	8

Food																							
Lettuce, 1/6 head, 1/2 cup (76 g)	10	17	79	8	0.7	250	5	0.05	0.05	0.2	15	0.4	0.4	0.5	0.5	1.1	5	8	3	3	1.0	1.5	2
Lettuce Leaves, 2 large (50 g)	9	19	71	19	0.7	950	9	0.04	0.03	0.2	34	0.7	0.4	0.5	0.4	1.1	19	15	2	2	1.0	3	4
Okra, 4 pods, 1/2 cup (43 g)	12	18	77	7	0.9	208	9	0.08	0.06	0.4	39	0.2	0.5	0.6	0.6	1.4	4	15	5	4	5	4	1.1
Onions, 1/2 cup (105 g)	30	12	87	3	1.3	Trace	7	0.03	0.03	0.2	25	0.4	1.3	1.4	1.5	2	—	12	2	1.8	1.0	3	2
Orange, medium (131 g)	65	7	89	4	1.3	263	66	0.05	0.13	0.5	54	0.5	3	3	3	2	5	110	9	3	3	5	3
Orange Juice, 1/2 cup (125 g)	56	5	93	1.4	0.9	249	56	0.11	0.11	0.4	11	0.1	2	3	3	1.4	5	93	7	0.6	2	1.1	0.6
Peaches, 1/2 cup (50 g)	39	1.7	93	2	0.2	215	2	0.01	0.01	0.3	2	0.2	1.6	1.9	2.0	0.3	4	3	0.7	0.6	1.5	0.2	1.1
Pear, medium (166 g)	101	4	90	6	1.2	33	7	0.07	0.03	0.2	13	0.5	4	5	5	1.9	0.7	12	2	4	1.0	1.3	3
Peas, Blackeye (see meat)																							
Peas, Green, 1/2 cup (80 g)	54	26	71	3	4.1	480	10	0.07	0.22	1.4	15	1.5	2	3	3	6	10	17	15	4	7	1.5	8
Pineapple, large slice (122 g)	90	1.5	95	0.9	0.4	61	9	0.02	0.10	0.2	13	0.4	4	5	5	0.6	1.2	15	7	1.2	1.0	1.3	2
Potato, Baked, medium (142 g)	132	8	91	0.6	3.7	Trace	28	0.06	0.14	2.4	13	1.0	6	7	6	—	47	9	4	12	1.3		6
Potatoes, Boiled, 2 small (122 g)	79	8	90	1.1	2.3	Trace	20	0.04	0.11	1.5	7	0.6	3	4	4	4	—	33	7	2	8	0.7	3
Potatoes, French-Fried, 20 pieces (85 g)	233	4	53	40	3.7	Trace	18	0.07	0.11	2.6	13	1.1	10	11	12	6	—	30	7	4	13	1.3	6
Potatoes, Mashed, 1/2 cup (98 g)	63	10	81	10	2.0	20	10	0.05	0.08	1.0	23	0.4	3	3	3	3	0.4	17	5	3	5	2	2
Potato, Sweet, 1/2 medium (55 g)	78	4	92	3	1.2	4455	12	0.04	0.05	0.4	22	0.5	3	4	4	1.9	89	20	3	2	2	2	3
Prunes, Stewed, 4 medium, 2 tablespoons juice (60 g)	108	2	94	0.8	0.7	456	1	0.04	0.02	0.4	19	0.9	5	5	5	1.1	9	1.7	1.3			1.9	5
Raisins, 4 1/2 tablespoons (43 g)	123	3	96	0.7	1.1	9	Trace	0.03	0.05	0.2	26	1.5	5	6	6	1.7	5	0.2	—	3	1.8	1.0	8
Squash, Summer, 1/2 cup (105 g)	16	17	74	10	1.1	462	12	0.08	0.05	0.8	26	0.4	0.7	0.8	0.8	1.7	9	20	3	5	4	3	2
Squash, Winter, 1/2 cup (103 g)	56	8	92	1.5	1.9	1435	13	0.13	0.05	0.7	40	1.1	2	3	3	3	29	22	8	8	4	4	6
Strawberries, 1/2 cup (75 g)	28	6	81	12	0.5	45	44	0.05	0.02	0.4	16	0.7	1.2	1.3	1.4	0.8	0.9	73	1.3	3	2	1.6	4
Tomato, 1/2 medium (100 g)	22	17	77	8	1.1	900	23	0.04	0.06	0.7	13	0.5	0.9	1.1	1.1	1.7	18	38	4	4	1.3		3
Tossed Salad, 3/4 cup (59 g)	13	14	76	6	0.7	1380	26	0.04	0.03	0.3	26	0.6	0.5	0.6	0.7	1.1	28	43	2	2	1.5		3
Watermelon, 1 cup (200 g)	52	6	89	6	1.0	1180	14	0.06	0.06	0.4	14	1.0	2	2	3	1.5	24	23	4	4	2	1.4	6

Bread-cereal

Food	Calories	% Calories from Protein	% Calories from Carbohydrate	% Calories from Fat	Protein g	Vitamin A IU	Vitamin C mg	Thiamin (B_1) mg	Riboflavin (B_2) mg	Niacin mg	Calcium mg	Iron mg	% U.S. RDA Calories C: 11–14	Calories C: 15–18	Calories W: 23–50	Protein	Vitamin A	Vitamin C	Thiamin (B_1)	Riboflavin (B_2)	Niacin	Calcium	Iron
Bagel (55 g)	165	15	70	10	6	30	Trace	0.14	0.10	1.2	9	1.2	6	8	8	9	0.6	—	9	6	6	0.9	7
Biscuit, Baking Powder, enriched (28 g)	103	8	51	41	2.1	Trace	Trace	0.08	0.08	0.8	34	0.4	4	5	5	3	—	—	5	5	4	3	2
Bread, White, slice, enriched (23 g)	61	13	78	10	2.0	Trace	Trace	0.09	0.06	0.8	19	0.6	2	3	3	3	—	—	6	4	4	1.9	3
Bread, Whole Wheat, slice (23 g)	55	16	74	11	2.4	Trace	Trace	0.06	0.03	0.6	22	0.5	2	3	3	4	—	—	4	1.8	3	2	3
Cornbread, 2½" x 3", enriched (85 g)	191	12	64	24	6.0	264	1	0.14	0.20	0.9	93	1.2	7	9	10	9	5	1.7	9	12	5	9	7
Corn Flakes, ¾ cup (19 g)	72	8	92	1.2	1.5	0	0	0.08	0.02	0.4	3	0.3	3	3	4	2	0	0	5	1.2	2	0.3	1.7
Crackers, Graham, 2 (14 g)	54	7	72	20	1.1	0	0	0.01	0.03	0.2	6	0.2	2	3	3	1.7	0	0	0.7	1.8	1.0	0.6	1.1
Crackers, Saltines, 5 (14 g)	60	8	67	24	1.2	0	Trace	Trace	0.01	0.1	3	0.2	2	3	3	1.9	0	—	—	0.6	0.5	0.3	1.1
Hominy Grits, ½ cup, enriched (123 g)	62	8	91	1.4	1.5	74	0	0.05	0.04	0.5	1	0.4	2	3	3	2	1.5	0	3	2	3	0.1	2
Noodles, Egg, ½ cup, enriched (80 g)	100	13	77	10	3.3	56	0	0.11	0.06	1.0	8	0.7	4	5	5	5	1.1	0	7	4	5	0.8	4
Oatmeal, ½ cup (120 g)	66	13	72	15	2.4	0	0	0.10	0.02	0.1	11	0.7	2	3	3	4	0	0	7	1.2	0.5	1.1	4
Pancake, 4" diameter, enriched (27 g)	61	13	59	29	1.9	68	Trace	0.06	0.08	0.3	58	0.3	2	3	3	3	1.4	—	4	5	1.5	6	1.7
Rice, ½ cup (103 g)	112	7	92	0.7	2.1	0	0	0.11	0.07	1.0	10	0.9	4	5	6	3	0	0	7	4	5	1.0	5
Roll, Frankfurter, enriched (40 g)	119	11	73	15	3.3	Trace	Trace	0.16	0.10	1.3	30	0.8	4	5	6	5	—	—	11	6	7	3	4
Roll, Hamburger, enriched (40 g)	119	11	73	15	3.3	Trace	Trace	0.16	0.10	1.3	30	0.8	4	5	6	5	—	—	11	6	7	3	4
Roll, Hard, enriched (50 g)	156	13	79	9	4.9	Trace	Trace	0.20	0.12	1.7	24	1.2	6	7	8	8	—	—	13	7	9	2	7
Toast, White, slice (20 g)	61	13	78	10	2.0	Trace	Trace	0.09	0.06	0.8	19	0.6	2	3	3	3	—	—	6	4	4	1.9	3
Tortilla, Corn, 6" diameter, enriched (30 g)	63	NA	NA	NA	1.5	6	0	0.04	0.02	0.3	60	0.9	2	3	3	2	0.1	0	3	1.2	1.5	6	5
Waffles, 2, 3½" x 5½", enriched (47 g)	130	13	54	34	4.2	109	Trace	0.09	0.14	0.6	113	0.6	5	6	7	6	2	—	6	8	3	11	3

Combinations

Food																							
Beans, Baked, Pork and Tomato Sauce, ½ cup (128 g)	156	17	63	19	7.8	166	3	0.10	0.04	0.8	69	2.3	7	7	8	12	3	5	7	2	4	7	13
Beef and Vegetable Stew, 1 cup (235 g)	209	29	28	44	15.0	2303	16	0.14	0.16	4.5	28	2.8	9	10	10	23	46	27	9	9	23	3	16
Chili Con Carne with Beans, 1 cup (250 g)	333	22	37	41	18.8	150	—	0.08	0.18	3.3	80	4.3	14	16	17	29	3	—	5	11	17	8	24
Custard, Baked, ½ cup (133 g)	152	20	37	43	7.2	464	Trace	0.05	0.25	0.1	148	0.5	6	7	8	16	9	—	3	15	0.5	15	3
Macaroni and Cheese, ½ cup (100 g)	215	16	38	45	8.4	430	Trace	0.10	0.20	0.9	181	0.9	9	10	11	13	9	—	7	12	5	18	5
Pizza, Cheese, ¼ of 14″ pie, enriched (150 g)	354	20	49	31	18.0	945	12	0.38	0.49	3.8	332	2.7	15	17	18	28	19	20	25	29	19	33	15
Soup, Chicken Noodle, 1 cup (226 g)	59	23	52	27	3.2	45	Trace	0.02	0.02	0.7	9	0.5	2	3	3	5	0.9	—	1.3	1.2	4	0.9	3
Soup, Cream of Tomato, 1 cup (250 g)	173	14	50	36	6.5	1200	15	0.10	0.25	1.3	168	0.8	7	8	9	10	24	25	7	15	7	17	4
Spaghetti, Meat Balls and Tomato Sauce, 1 cup (248 g)	332	22	47	31	18.6	1587	22	0.25	0.30	4.0	124	3.7	14	16	17	29	32	37	17	18	20	12	21
Taco, Beef (108 g)	216	NA	NA	NA	16.9	352	4	0.10	0.19	3.0	174	2.6	9	10	11	38	7	7	7	11	15	17	14

Others

Food																					
Bar, Milk Chocolate, 1 ounce (28 g)	147	6	40	55	2.2	77	Trace	0.02	0.10	0.1	65	0.3	6	7	3	1.5	1.3	6	0.5	7	1.7
Butter, 1 teaspoon (5 g)	36	Trace	Trace	100	Trace	165	0	—	—	—	1	0	—	1.8	—	3	—	—	—	0.1	0
Cake, Devil's Food, 1/16 of 9″ cake (69 g)	234	4	64	32	3.0	104	Trace	0.02	0.06	0.2	41	0.6	10	11	12	5	2	4	1.0	4	3
Cake, Sponge, 1/12 of 10″ cake (66 g)	196	11	72	17	5.0	297	Trace	0.03	0.09	0.1	20	0.8	8	9	10	8	6	2	5	0.5	2	4
Chocolate Syrup, 2 tablespoons (38 g)	93	1.8	91	7	0.9	Trace	0	0.01	0.03	0.15	6	0.6	4	4	5	1.4	—	0.7	1.8	0.8	3
Coffee, Black, ¾ cup (170 g)	2	Trace	Trace	Trace	Trace	0	0	0	Trace	0.5	3	0.2	0.1	0.1	—	0	0	—	3	0.3	1.1
Cookie, Sugar, 3″ diameter, enriched (20 g)	89	6	60	34	1.2	22	Trace	0.04	0.04	0.4	16	0.3	4	4	1.9	0.4	3	2	1.6	1.7
Doughnut, Cake Type, enriched (32 g)	125	5	53	42	1.5	26	Trace	0.07	0.07	0.5	13	0.4	5	6	2	0.5	5	4	3	1.3	2
French Dressing, 1 tablespoon (16 g)	66	0.5	16	83	0.1	—	—	—	—	—	2	0.1	3	3	3	0.2	—	0.2	0.6	0.2	0.6
Gelatin Dessert, ½ cup (120 g)	71	10	90	0	1.8	—	—	—	—	—	—	—	3	3	3	—	—	—	—	—	—

511

Others

Caloric Information / Nutritive Values

Others	Calories	% Calories from protein	% Calories from Fat	% Calories from Carbohydrate	Protein g	Vitamin A IU	Vitamin C mg	Thiamin (B_1) mg	Riboflavin (B_2) mg	Niacin mg	Calcium mg	Iron mg	Calories** C, 11-14	Calories** G, 15-18	Calories** W, 23-50	Protein	Vitamin A	Vitamin C	Thiamin (B_1)	Riboflavin (B_2)	Niacin	Calcium (% U.S. RDA)	Iron (% U.S. RDA)
Jelly, Currant, 1 tablespoon (18 g)	49	0	0	100	0	2	1	Trace	0.01	0	4	0.3	2	2	2	0	—	2	—	0.8	0	0.4	1.7
Mayonnaise, 1 tablespoon (14 g)	101	0.8	98	1.0	0.2	39	—	Trace	0.01	Trace	3	0.1	4	5	5	0.5	1	—	—	0.8	—	0.3	0.6
Pie, Apple, ⅙ of 9" pie, enriched (158 g)	403	3	38	58	3.5	47	2	0.15	0.13	1.7	13	1.1	17	19	20	8	1	4	12	10	11	1.3	6
Popcorn, Plain, 1 cup (6 g)	23	9	11	81	0.8	—	0	—	0.01	0.1	1	0.2	1.0	1.1	1.2	1.8	—	0	—	0.8	0.6	0.1	1.1
Potato Chips, 10 chips (20 g)	114	3	62	35	1.1	Trace	3	0.04	0.01	1.0	8	0.4	5	5	6	2.5	—	7	3	0.8	6	0.8	2
Pudding, Chocolate, ½ cup (130 g)	161	11	21	68	4.4	169	Trace	0.03	0.20	0.1	133	0.4	7	8	8	10	4	—	2	15	0.6	13	2
Roll, Danish Pastry (65 g)	274	7	49	44	4.8	202	Trace	0.05	0.10	0.5	33	0.6	11	13	14	11	5	—	4	8	3	3	3
Sherbet, Orange, ½ cup (97 g)	129	3	8	89	0.9	58	2	0.01	0.03	Trace	15	Trace	5	6	6	2	1	4	0.8	2	—	1.5	—
Soft Drink, Cola, 1 cup (246 g)	96	0	0	99	0	0	0	0	0	0	—	—	4	5	5	0	0	0	0	0	0	—	—
Sugar, 1 teaspoon (4 g)	14	0	0	100	0	0	0	0	0	0	0	Trace	0.6	0.7	0.7	0	0	0	0	0	0	—	—

**There is no U.S. RDA for calories. Thus, percentages are based on caloric allowances for girls, 11-14; girls, 15-18; and women, 23-50, taken from the National Research Council, Food and Nutrition Board, Recommended Daily Dietary Allowances. 8th rev. ed., 1974.

1. Formula for computation of percentages of the National Research Council's Recommended Daily Dietary Allowances (NRC RDA) (See page IX.)

$$\frac{\text{Amount of a nutrient (or calories) in the food}}{\text{NRC RDA for that nutrient}} \times 100 = \underline{\qquad}\%$$

Example:

$$\frac{25.5 \text{ g (protein in beef, roast)}}{44 \text{ g (NRC RDA for protein for girl, 11-14)}} = 0.579 \qquad 0.579 \times 100 = 58\%$$

2. Formula for computation of percentages of the Food and Drug Administration's Recommended Daily Allowances (U.S. RDA) (See page X.)

$$\frac{\text{Amount of a nutrient in the food}}{\text{U.S. RDA for that nutrient}} \times 100 = \underline{\qquad}\%$$

RECOMMENDED DAILY DIETARY ALLOWANCES,[a] revised 1974

Designed for the maintenance of good nutrition of practically all healthy people in the U.S.A.

	Age (years)	Weight (kg)	Weight (lbs)	Height (cm)	Height (in)	Energy (kcal)[b]	Protein (g)	Vitamin A Activity RE (μg)[c]	Vitamin A Activity (IU)	Vitamin D (IU)	Vitamin E Activity[e] (IU)	Ascorbic Acid (mg)	Folacin[f] (μg)	Niacin[g] (mg)	Riboflavin (B_2) (mg)	Thiamin (B_1) (mg)	Vitamin B_6 (mg)	Vitamin B_{12} (μg)	Calcium (mg)	Phosphorus (mg)	Iodine (μg)	Iron (mg)	Magnesium (mg)	Zinc (mg)
Infants	0.0–0.5	6	14	60	24	kg × 117	kg × 2.2	420[d]	1,400	400	4	35	50	5	0.4	0.3	0.3	0.3	360	240	35	10	60	3
	0.5–1.0	9	20	71	28	kg × 108	kg × 2.0	400	2,000	400	5	35	50	8	0.6	0.5	0.4	0.3	540	400	45	15	70	5
Children	1–3	13	28	86	34	1300	23	400	2,000	400	7	40	100	9	0.8	0.7	0.6	1.0	800	800	60	15	150	10
	4–6	20	44	110	44	1800	30	500	2,500	400	9	40	200	12	1.1	0.9	0.9	1.5	800	800	80	10	200	10
	7–10	30	66	135	54	2400	36	700	3,300	400	10	40	300	16	1.2	1.2	1.2	2.0	800	800	110	10	250	10
Males	11–14	44	97	158	63	2800	44	1,000	5,000	400	12	45	400	18	1.5	1.4	1.6	3.0	1200	1200	130	18	350	15
	15–18	61	134	172	69	3000	54	1,000	5,000	400	15	45	400	20	1.8	1.5	2.0	3.0	1200	1200	150	18	400	15
	19–22	67	147	172	69	3000	54	1,000	5,000	400	15	45	400	20	1.8	1.5	2.0	3.0	800	800	140	10	350	15
	23–50	70	154	172	69	2700	56	1,000	5,000		15	45	400	18	1.6	1.4	2.0	3.0	800	800	130	10	350	15
	51+	70	154	172	69	2400	56	1,000	5,000		15	45	400	16	1.5	1.2	2.0	3.0	800	800	110	10	350	15
Females	11–14	44	97	155	62	2400	44	800	4,000	400	12	45	400	16	1.3	1.2	1.6	3.0	1200	1200	115	18	300	15
	15–18	54	119	162	65	2100	48	800	4,000	400	12	45	400	14	1.4	1.1	2.0	3.0	1200	1200	115	18	300	15
	19–22	58	128	162	65	2100	46	800	4,000	400	12	45	400	14	1.4	1.1	2.0	3.0	800	800	100	18	300	15
	23–50	58	128	162	65	2000	46	800	4,000		12	45	400	13	1.2	1.0	2.0	3.0	800	800	100	18	300	15
	51+	58	128	162	65	1800	46	800	4,000		12	45	400	12	1.1	1.0	2.0	3.0	800	800	80	10	300	15
Pregnant						+300	+30	1,000	5,000	400	15	60	800	+2	+0.3	+0.3	2.5	4.0	1200	1200	125	18+[h]	450	20
Lactating						+500	+20	1,200	6,000	400	15	80	600	+4	+0.5	+0.3	2.5	4.0	1200	1200	150	18	450	25

a The allowances are intended to provide for individual variations among most normal persons as they live in the United States under usual environmental stresses. Diets should be based on a variety of common foods in order to provide other nutrients for which human requirements have been less well defined.

b Kilojoules (kJ) = 4.2 × kcal.

c Retinol equivalents.

d Assumed to be all as retinol in milk during the first six months of life. All subsequent intakes are assumed to be half as retinol and half as β-carotene when calculated from international units. As retinol equivalents, three fourths are as retinol and one fourth as β-carotene.

e Total vitamin E activity, estimated to be 80 percent as α-tocopherol and 20 percent other tocopherols.

f The folacin allowances refer to dietary sources as determined by *Lactobacillus casei* assay. Pure forms of folacin may be effective in doses less than one fourth of the recommended dietary allowance.

g Although allowances are expressed as niacin, it is recognized that on the average 1 mg of niacin is derived from each 60 mg of dietary tryptophan.

h This increased requirement cannot be met by ordinary diets; therefore, the use of supplemental iron is recommended.

Food and Nutrition Board, National Academy of Sciences—National Research Council

Protein Foods

THE HAMBURGER MASTER MIX
5 Meals or 1 Meal (4 Servings Each)

5 MEALS	1 MEAL
1 tablespoon butter or margarine [15 ml]	1 teaspoon butter or margarine [5 ml]
5 pounds ground beef [2.25 kg]	1 pound ground beef [454 g]
2½ cups chopped onion [600 ml]	½ cup chopped onion [120 ml]
1 cup chopped green pepper [240 ml]	3 tablespoons chopped green pepper [45 ml]
5 cups chopped celery [1120 ml]	1 cup chopped celery [240 ml]
5 cans tomato soup, undiluted	1 can tomato soup, undiluted
5 15-ounce cans tomato sauce [2.1 kg]	1 15-ounce can tomato sauce [425 g]
5 teaspoons salt [25 ml]	1 teaspoon salt [5 ml]
½ teaspoon black pepper [2.5 ml]	Dash of black pepper

1 Melt butter or margarine over low heat in 8 quart skillet or pot.
2 Crumble beef into skillet, increase heat, and cook until red color disappears.
3 Add onion, green pepper, and celery. Cook until beef is brown and vegetables are tender.
4 Add soup, tomato sauce, salt, and pepper.
5 Cover and simmer for 30 to 45 minutes, stirring occasionally.
6 Cool and divide equally into five freezer containers. Freeze. May be thawed and used for a variety of family dinner meals.

Note: Use a 12-inch (30 cm) skillet when preparing Hamburger Mix for one meal.

EGG FOO YUNG (CHINESE)
5 Servings

2 tablespoons salad oil [30 ml]
3 eggs
1 cup bean sprouts, drained [240 ml]
½ cup chopped cooked pork [120 ml] (almost any other cooked meat or tuna may be substituted)
2 tablespoons chopped onion [30 ml]
1 tablespoon soy sauce [15 ml]
Sauce (recipe below)

1 Heat oil in large skillet or electric frying pan.
2 In separate bowl beat eggs until thick and lemon colored.
3 Stir in bean sprouts, pork, onion, and soy sauce.
4 Pour ¼ cup (60 ml) of mixture at a time into hot skillet. With broad spatula, push cooked egg up over meat to form a patty. When patties are set, turn to brown other side.
5 Serve hot with sauce.

Sauce

1 teaspoon cornstarch [5 ml]
1 teaspoon sugar [5 ml]
1 teaspoon vinegar [5 ml]
½ cup water [120 ml]

1 Combine all ingredients in small saucepan.
2 Cook, stirring constantly, until mixture thickens and boils. Boil and stir for one minute.

How To Use The Hamburger Master Mix			
Product	**Mix**	**Other ingredients**	**Directions**
Beefaroni	1 freezer container	1 8-ounce package elbow macaroni (225 g)	Heat meat mix. Cook macaroni Mix meat and macaroni and serve hot.
Chili	1 freezer container	2 cups drained canned kidney beans (480 ml) 1 teaspoon chili powder (5 ml)	Heat meat mix. Add beans and chili powder. Cover and simmer for 10 minutes.
Pizza	1 freezer container	Biscuit or yeast dough (canned biscuits may be used) 1 teaspoon Italian seasoning (5 ml) Olives, frankfurters, pepperoni, or sliced Italian cheese Parmesan cheese, grated	Add Italian seasoning to meat mix. Simmer meat sauce until it thickens. Line pizza pan with thinly rolled dough. Spread meat sauce over dough and garnish as desired. Sprinkle with Parmesan cheese. Bake in moderate oven (375° F or 190° C) for 15 to 20 minutes. Cut and serve at once.
Spaghetti	1 freezer container	1 8-ounce package spaghetti (225 g) 1 teaspoon Italian seasoning (5 ml) Parmesan cheese, grated	Heat meat sauce. Add Italian seasoning and simmer for 15 minutes. Cook spaghetti according to directions on package and drain. Mix meat and spaghetti and sprinkle with Parmesan cheese.
Spanish Rice	1 freezer container	3 cups cooked rice (720 ml)	Heat meat sauce. Add cooked rice. Cover and simmer 5 to 10 minutes.
Sloppy Joe	1 freezer container	1 package of 8 hamburger buns	Simmer meat sauce for about 1 hour or until thick. Toast buns. Serve meat sauce on hot toasted buns.

Milk-Rich Foods

	White Sauce 1 Cup (240 ml)				
Type	Butter or margarine	Flour	Salt	Pepper	Milk
thin	1 tablespoon (15 ml)	1 tablespoon (15 ml)	½ teaspoon (2.5 ml)	dash	1 cup (240 ml)
medium	2 tablespoons (30 ml)	2 tablespoons (30 ml)	½ teaspoon (2.5 ml)	dash	1 cup (240 ml)
thick	3 tablespoons (45 ml)	3 tablespoons (45 ml)	½ teaspoon (2.5 ml)	dash	1 cup (240 ml)
very thick	4 tablespoons (60 ml)	4 tablespoons (60 ml)	½ teaspoon (2.5 ml)	dash	1 cup (240 ml)

1 Melt butter or margarine in top of double boiler over boiling water in bottom of double boiler.
2 Add flour, salt, and pepper, and stir until smooth.
3 Add milk slowly, stirring constantly.
4 Cook slowly, stirring constantly, until smooth and thickened.

Note: White sauce may also be made in a saucepan over direct heat. Use low heat and stir constantly.

CHEESE SAUCE

Make 1 cup (240 ml) Thin White Sauce. Add 1 cup (240 ml) grated American cheese, and stir until melted.

MUSHROOM SAUCE

Make 1 cup (240 ml) Medium White Sauce. Heat 1½ tablespoons (22.5 ml) butter or margarine in skillet, and add ¾ cup (180 ml) drained canned mushrooms or ½ pound (225 g) sliced fresh mushrooms, and 1 teaspoon (5 ml) chopped onion. Cook until onion is golden brown, stirring 2 or 3 times, and add to white sauce.

EGG SAUCE

Make 1 cup (240 ml) Medium White Sauce. Add 2 hard-cooked eggs, coarsely chopped, and 2 teaspoons (10 ml) chopped pimiento, and stir.

BAKED CHEESE FONDUE
4 Servings

1 cup soft bread crumbs [*240 ml*]
1 cup grated American cheese [*240 ml*]
½ teaspoon salt [*2.5 ml*]
Few grains pepper
1 tablespoon butter or margarine, melted [*15 ml*]
3 eggs, separated
1 cup milk [*240 ml*]

1 Place bread crumbs, cheese, salt, pepper, and melted butter or margarine in mixing bowl, and mix well.
2 Beat egg yolks until thick and lemon-colored, and add milk.
3 Add to bread-crumb-cheese mixture, and stir.
4 Beat egg whites until stiff, and fold into mixture.
5 Pour into greased baking dish.
6 Set in pan containing hot water up to about two-thirds depth of baking dish.
7 Bake in moderate oven (350° F or 177° C) for 30 to 40 minutes, or until firm.
8 Insert tip of knife in center of fondue, and if knife comes out clean, fondue is done.
9 Serve immediately in dish in which it was baked.

Note: This cheese fondue may be made in less time if baked in individual baking cups.

ALMOND VELVET WITH FRUIT (JAPANESE — HAWAIIAN)
8 Servings

2 tablespoons gelatin (2 envelopes) [*30 ml*]
3 cups water [*720 ml*]
1 cup evaporated milk [*240 ml*]
1 cup sugar [*240 ml*]
1 teaspoon almond extract [*5 ml*]
Fruits as desired
Food coloring as desired

1 Soften gelatin in ½ cup (120 ml) of the water.
2 Combine remaining water with milk and sugar; bring to a boil.
3 Add softened gelatin and cook 2 minutes longer.
4 Cool slightly, add extract and pour into a small cake pan or ring mold.
5 Chill several hours or over night.
6 Chill fruits.
7 Cut gelatin mixture into cubes and mix gently with fruit.

Note: You may use sliced peaches, pineapple chunks, mandarin oranges, fruit cocktail, lichees, strawberries, raspberries, mangoes, or any other juicy fruit.

Fruits and Vegetables

TORTILLA CHIP SALAD
8 Servings

1 head lettuce
8 ounces fresh spinach [*225 g*]
1 pound ground beef [*454 g*]
¾ teaspoon seasoned salt [*3.75 ml*]
½ teaspoon each onion powder, garlic powder, chili powder [*2.5 ml*]
⅛ teaspoon cayenne red pepper [*0.6 ml*]
4 drops red pepper sauce
⅔ cup water [*160 ml*]
1 can (14 ounces) kidney beans, drained [*392 g*]
4 tomatoes, cut in eighths
1 package (6 ounces) tortilla chips [*170 g*]
1 cup Cheddar cheese (about 4 ounces) grated [*114 g*]
1 cup chopped onion [*240 ml*]
½ cup mayonnaise or salad dressing [*120 ml*]
1 tablespoon pickle relish [*15 ml*]
2 tablespoons chili sauce [*30 ml*]

1 Wash lettuce and spinach; tear into bite-sized pieces. Chill.
2 Cook and stir ground beef in large skillet until brown; drain. Stir in seasonings, water, and kidney beans; heat to boiling. Reduce heat; simmer uncovered 15 minutes, stirring occasionally. Cool 10 minutes.
3 Combine greens, tortilla chips, cheese, and onion in large salad bowl.
4 Mix mayonnaise, chili sauce, and pickle relish; toss gently with salad mixture.
5 Pour warm ground beef mixture over salad; toss gently. Serve immediately.

GELATIN MOLD
4–6 Servings

1 package fruit-flavored gelatin (lemon, orange, cherry, raspberry, etc.)
1 cup hot water [*240 ml*]
1 cup cold water or fruit juice [*240 ml*]

1 Place gelatin in mixing bowl, add hot water, and stir until gelatin dissolves.
2 Add cold water.
3 Pour into mold, and chill until gelatin sets.
4 Unmold, and serve as a salad or dessert.

VARIATIONS

Fruit: Substitute ¾ cup (180 ml) fruit juice for 1 cup (240 ml) cold water. Add 1 cup (240 ml) grape halves, drained canned pineapple (crushed or diced), cherries, orange sections, sliced bananas, or combinations of fruits, and ¼ cup (60 ml) chopped nuts, if desired. Add fruits when gelatin has partially thickened, and return to refrigerator until gelatin sets.

Vegetable: Use lemon-flavored gelatin, and add 1 cup (240 ml) chopped cabbage, chopped celery, grated carrots, or a combination of vegetables. Add vegetables when gelatin has partially thickened, and return to refrigerator until gelatin sets.

Vegetable-Fruit: Use lemon-flavored gelatin, and add ½ cup (120 ml) grated carrots and ¼ cup (60 ml) drained crushed pineapple, or add ½ cup (120 ml) chopped cabbage and ½ cup (120 ml) chopped apple. Add vegetables and fruits when gelatin has partially thickened, and return to refrigerator until gelatin sets.

Note: To unmold, dip mold to rim in warm water, and shake it slightly. Then cover mold with a plate, turn plate and mold together, and lift off mold.

Timetable For Cooking Green Vegetables[1]

Vegetable	Servings per pound of fresh vegetable[2]	Approximate number of minutes to allow after water returns to boil	
		Fresh	Frozen
Asparagus	4 (4 or 5 whole spears)	10–20	5–10
Beans (Green or String)	6	15–30	12–18
Beans, Lima	2	20–30	6–10
Beet Greens	4	5–15	6–12
Broccoli[3]	3 to 4 (2 or 3 stalks)	10–20	5–8
Brussels Sprouts	5	10–20	4–9
Cabbage	4 to 5 (cooked, shredded)	3–10	—
	4 (cooked, quartered)	10–15	—
Chard	4	10–20	8–10
Collards	4	10–20	—
Dandelion Greens	5	10–20	—
Kale	4 to 5	10–25	8–12
Mustard Greens	4 to 5	20–30	8–15
Okra	4	10–20	—
Peas	2	8–20	5–10
Spinach	2 to 3	3–10	4–6
Turnip Greens	4 to 5	10–30	8–12

[1]Boil green vegetables in lightly salted water. Bring water to a boil, add vegetables, and cover pan. When water boils again, reduce heat, and begin to count cooking time.
[2]Approximate number of ½ cup (120 ml) servings of cooked vegetable.
[3]Heavy stalks should be split.
Adapted from Home and Garden Bulletin No. 41, U.S. Department of Agriculture.

Cereal Foods

ALL-PURPOSE MASTER MIX
13 Cups (3120 ml)

9 cups sifted all-purpose flour [2160 ml]
⅓ cup baking powder [80 ml]
1 tablespoon salt [15 ml]
2 teaspoons cream of tartar [10 ml]
4 tablespoons sugar [60 ml]
1 cup nonfat dry milk [240 ml]
2 cups shortening which does not require refrigeration [480 ml]

1 Sift together 3 times the flour, baking powder, salt, cream of tartar, sugar, and dry milk.
2 Cut in shortening with pastry blender or two knives until mixture looks like coarse cornmeal.
3 Store in covered containers at room temperature.

Note: To measure the Master Mix, pile it lightly into cup and level off with spatula.

STRAWBERRY BLINTZ SANDWICHES
6 Servings

1¼ cup creamed cottage cheese [300 ml]
4 eggs
2 tablespoons white sugar [30 ml]
12 slices white bread
⅓ cup milk [80 ml]
Butter or margarine
2 10-ounce packages frozen halved strawberries (thawed) [280 g]

GERMAN DESSERT PANCAKE
4 Servings

⅓ cup sifted all-purpose flour [80 ml]
¼ teaspoon baking powder [1.25 ml]
⅓ cup milk [80 ml]
2 eggs, slightly beaten
2 tablespoons butter or margarine [30 ml]
1 tablespoon confectioners' sugar [15 ml]
4 lemon wedges

1 Preheat oven to 425 degrees F (218° C).
2 In small bowl, combine flour and baking powder.
3 Beat in milk and eggs, leaving batter a bit lumpy.
4 In a 10-inch (25-cm) skillet with heatproof handle, melt butter or margarine. When butter is very hot, pour batter in all at once.
5 Bake 15 to 18 minutes until pancake is golden.
6 Sprinkle with sugar. Serve hot with lemon wedges to squeeze over pancake.

Note: Strawberries may be served over the pancake instead of the lemon.

1 Beat cottage cheese, one egg, and sugar together in medium bowl until well mixed.
2 Spread about ¼ cup (60 ml) of mixture on six bread slices. Cover with remaining slices.
3 In shallow dish, beat three eggs and milk.
4 Melt butter or margarine in skillet.
5 Quickly dip sandwiches in egg mixture one at a time.
6 Sauté in skillet over medium heat until lightly brown on each side. Keep warm in oven until all six sandwiches are done.
7 Serve with berries poured over the top of each.

How to use the all-purpose master mix							
Product Amount	Mix	Sugar	Water	Eggs	Other Ingredients	Amount of Mixing	Temperature/time
Biscuits (15–20)	3 cups 720 ml		⅔ to 1 cup 160 to 240 ml			Until blended. Knead 10 times.	400° F (205° C) 10 minutes
Muffins (12)	3 cups 720 ml	2 tablespoons 30 ml	1 cup 240 ml	1		Until ingredients are just moistened	400° F (205° C) 20 minutes
Coffee cake	3 cups 720 ml	½ cup 120 ml	⅔ cup 160 ml	1	For topping: ½ cup (120 ml) brown sugar, 3 tablespoons (45 ml) butter, ½ teaspoon (2.5 ml) cinnamon	Until blended	400° F (205° C) 25 minutes
Griddlecakes (18) or Waffles (6)	3 cups 720 ml		1½ cups 360 ml	1		Until blended.	
Oatmeal Cookies (4 dozen)	3 cups 720 ml	1 cup 240 ml	⅓ cup 80 ml	1	1 teaspoon (5 ml) cinnamon; 1 cup (240 ml) quick rolled oats	Until blended.	350° F (177° C) 10–12 minutes
Drop Cookies (4 dozen)	3 cups 720 ml	1 cup 240 ml	⅓ cup 80 ml	1	1 teaspoon (5 ml) vanilla; ½ cup (120 ml) nuts or chocolate bits	Until blended.	350° F (177° C) 10–12 minutes
Yellow Cake	3 cups 720 ml	1¼ cups 300 ml	1 cup 240 ml	2	1 teaspoon (5 ml) vanilla	Add two-thirds liquid, and beat 2 minutes. Add rest of liquid, and beat 2 minutes.	350° F (177° C) 25 minutes

Energy Foods

OATMEAL COOKIE MASTER MIX

    3 cups all-purpose flour [720 ml]
    2½ cups sugar [600 ml]
    1 teaspoon soda [5 ml]
    1 teaspoon baking powder [5 ml]
    2 teaspoons salt [10 ml]
    1 cup shortening [240 ml]
    3 cups rolled oats [720 ml]

1. Sift together flour, sugar, soda, baking powder, and salt.
2. Cut in the shortening.
3. Stir in the rolled oats until well distributed.
4. Store in a tightly closed container.

To Make Cookies
1½ Dozen

    2 cups Cookie Master Mix [480 ml]
    1 egg
    1 tablespoon milk [15 ml]
    1 teaspoon vanilla [5 ml]

1. Add milk, vanilla, and egg to mix.
2. Stir until well blended.
3. Drop by teaspoons on greased cookie sheet.
4. Bake at 375 degrees (190° C) for 10 to 12 minutes.

VARIATIONS

To 2 cups (480 ml) of mix add:

½ cup nuts (120 ml)

½ cup raisins (120 ml)

½ cup chocolate chips (120 ml)

REFRIGERATOR COOKIES
7 Dozen Cookies

    1 cup butter or margarine, softened [240 ml]
    1 cup sugar [240 ml]
    2 eggs
    1½ teaspoon vanilla [7.5 ml]
    3 cups all-purpose flour [720 ml]
    1 teaspoon salt [5 ml]
    ½ cup finely chopped nuts [120 ml]

1. Mix thoroughly butter, sugar, eggs, and vanilla.
2. Stir in flour, salt, and nuts.
3. Divide dough into three equal parts; shape each part into roll, 1½ inches (3.75 cm) in diameter and about 7 inches (17.5 cm) long.
4. Wrap; chill at least 4 hours.
5. Heat oven to 400 degrees F (205° C).
6. Cut rolls into ⅛-inch (3-mm) slices. Place 1 inch (2.5 cm) apart on ungreased baking sheet.
7. Bake 8 to 10 minutes or until light brown. Immediately remove from baking sheet.

VARIATIONS

Substitute brown sugar for white sugar.

Substitute half brown sugar and half white sugar with 3 teaspoons (15 ml) cinnamon for vanilla.

Mix in 1 teaspoon (5 ml) grated orange peel with the butter and ½ cup (120 ml) finely chopped blanched almonds with the flour. Decrease butter to ½ cup (120 ml), and add ½ cup (120 ml) crunchy peanut butter. Substitute 1 cup (240 ml) dark brown sugar for white sugar.

Index